Sharks in the Runway

A Seaplane Pilot's Fifty-Year Journey Through Bahamian Times!

Paul W.J. Harding

Published by Clink Street Publishing 2017

First edition.

ISBNs:
Paperback 978-1-911525-23-3
Hardback 978-1-911525-94-3
Ebook 978-1-911525-24-0

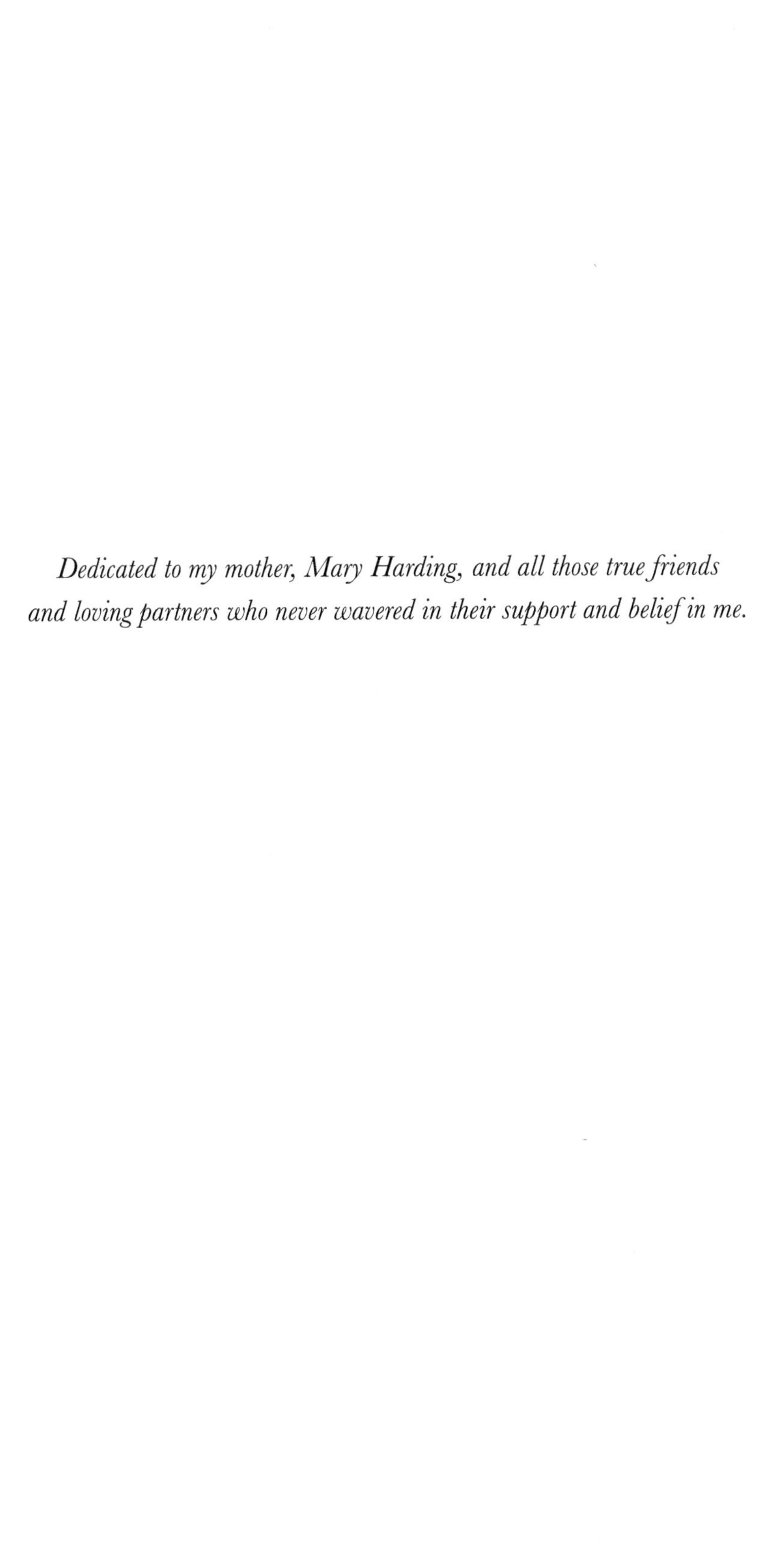

Dedicated to my mother, Mary Harding, and all those true friends and loving partners who never wavered in their support and belief in me.

From *Wings over the Rockies*
Doug Holgate, Aerial Director of Photography:
Narrated by Harrison Ford.

'You ever had a flying dream, I have. One of the first dreams as a kid was a flying dream. What is it that stirs our dreams in flight … what is that turns such dreams into reality?' ~ 'The air is our home, we were meant to fly. The dream of flight never stops. It burns inside longing to be realized; the dream becomes more than simply real, it becomes a way of life!'

'You can find a place in aviation if you look, if you want, a place for your dreams. Aviation is 100 years old and it's brand new. You can help take it into the future. It offers freedom and responsibility, they're not just words. Join us. Flying is like good music it elevates the senses and the very experience of being alive!'

Introduction:

Autobiographers leave us a gift, through pen and ink, a typewriter and now soft touch computer keys. We paint pictures with words spanning decades past, recording thin slivers of history depicting stories of a personal passage through time. My storytelling starts on shaky ground with my parents, and their families before them, rarely sharing their past; a generation locked in silence, denying most of us valuable first-hand history lessons, with a dysfunction to communicate our family tree is comparatively bare of branches.

I was completing some daily paperwork at Odyssey Aviation, my fixed base operation in Nassau one evening after a day's flying, and enquired the date from the lovely young Bahamian lady behind the reception counter.

'November 22nd, Mr. Harding,' she politely replied.

'Now that's a day we will all remember,' I expressed sombrely whilst completing an Arrival Report, her slightly quizzed expression showing no clue what I was referring to. I explained briefly the horrific historical moment in 1963 that our generation had witnessed some forty years past. Her expression still did not register anything; it was something she had maybe read about in a history book having not even been born yet.

This is far from any history book, rather an account of a young boy who landed on Bahamian shores in 1960 and the immense effect a beautiful country and its people had on him, while recalling some extraordinary world events that transpired through this time capsule, such as that awful day in Dallas. Many of the years had noted pages in our history, both tragic and inspirational often flashing past us at lightning speed, sometimes taking the very wind out of us emotionally. I have touched some topics in greater detail, as they were the stories that made a mark on the world and myself. There are important timelines overlooked, too many to record here. Some will remember exactly where you were when events mentioned actually happened, maybe others captivated at some of the additional details I found in researching this project? In fairness, some facts and details are not set in stone for absolute accuracy, although close enough to merit consideration. This writing is for readers who hold an appreciation and love of flying, nature, people, the ocean, and the outrageously adventurous way of life written by a man who ordered a brand-new seaplane having no clue how to even fly.

I describe how things were 'back then' compared to where I stand today, how an English boarding school educational system with the behaviours of its occupants in those early times, not comprehended by our parents yet accepted by society as 'the norm' back then, would today be labelled 'abusive'. One sees the proverbial wheel of life constantly revolving within this story, taking a young English schoolboy's journey of traveling through manhood to the present day, choosing to walk away from the chance of a higher education rather spending seventeen years 'going down' every day for a living, and the last twenty-three 'going up'.

I have asked some of our island friends and legends to sit down and talk with me, feeling a compulsion to record their stories before we lose them. Some mentioned here we have already lost. To those who shared, I express a warm 'thank you' along with those who gave me the occasional nudge to press on recording my personal saga; that of 'starting from scratch' to making a name to be proud.

The journey has been one wild ride after another, yet I often considered some of it as nothing out of the ordinary. I have been labelled impulsive, whereas those who know me well have recognized calculation came first. I visited places never imagined as a boy sharing experiences for the most part only seen on film or in the pages we read. Living in these wonderful islands it all became just a part of life, another day in paradise. They tell me the journey I have travelled is 'far from ordinary' and in fairness, with a few recollections such as jumping out of airplanes, racing ocean powerboats, filming television shows in the Red Sea one week and the mountains of Utah the next, swimming in a three-mile deep ocean with a forty-foot whale and rammed face on by a very large shark to exploring the African bush, makes one reflect, 'they may just be right'...

P.H. May 2009 Nassau, Bahamas.

Chapter 1
'Way back then...'

In the blink of an eye something went horribly wrong with the aircraft. I barely had chance to finish a breath. Time froze in an instant. Racing over the choppy water my new seaplane rose effortlessly into the afternoon air. Take-off and landings are always exhilarating. For seaplane pilots, no two are alike: we incorporate that gifted skill learned and polished over countless hours in the cockpit, forever honing the quest for perfection. Without warning the right wing suddenly dropped perilously toward the water as if sucked downward by some mystical force, the plane instantaneously out of control. With over 10,000 hours of flight experience the next milliseconds would mean the difference in staying alive or not. It had taken fifty years to arrive at this moment.

I was convinced at an early age I had been born in the wrong place. Reflecting back to where my roots lay, my place of birth and family origins in England, everything is foreign to me. Nothing fits. Trying to remember places, old acquaintances, friends and events are somewhere in the fog of early childhood; recollection has not been practised. I endeavour to recreate my early beginnings, bringing to light my Bahamian home while sitting here at a desk in the English countryside where the journey started back in 1960, having no clue the wheel of life would travel full circle. I think it worth recollecting our youth, for it is here where foundations are laid influencing the paths we chose and the decisions made in later life. Bahamian readers and those with similar journeys may well share many of the times I speak of. A friend and fellow writer recently gave a fairly forceful tug at my memory over dinner; suggesting I tell stories of my very early youth, before age twelve she insisted, and asking was I 'a pretty baby?' I laughed in reply, explaining there is so little remembered about the first years hardly deeming it interesting and of course I was pretty! There are minute flashes from very early days as in a dreadful illness from food poisoning after consuming some war rations, food still available to consumers after World War Two. I was just a little fellow when I awoke my mother violently vomiting in the night.

In 1954, fourteen years of rationing in Britain ended, restrictions imposed on food, petrol, clothing and even soap. I was the ripe old age of six.

Scant memories return slowly as I write this English December morning. My partner asking out of the blue today, 'What Christmas's do you remember first?' while we laze in bed sipping the steaming rich morning coffee, watching the bird feeder outside awash in activity. 'Good question, ' I respond, racking my brain to bring the memory out of the misty ethers. I do recall awakening early one morning aware of an unusual weight on the bed covers above my feet. Secretly cracking one eye slightly open, to discover Santa had not left all the packages under the tree, instead a small heap of Christmas presents sprawled over the base of my bed weighing down the blanket. Lots of lovely red wrapping paper tied with ribbon! What toys I received memory has long faded, save a gift from Dad; a fabulous leather cowboy holster set, nicely studded with two matching silver pistols. Playing outside that holiday morning and leaving them hanging on a branch during a lunch break, returning to find the guns stolen. A mortified little boy left only with empty belt and holster. No self-respecting cowboy would walk the streets without guns.

I recall having two friends, sons of my parent's acquaintances, the same age as myself, being wheeled around as babies in those ghastly old fashioned black-hooded prams our mothers had owned with the large spoke wheels pushing us shopping down Camberley High Street with those unsightly scarfs over their hair, and later down our road a cute little girl I liked called June.

The year 1954 holds another recollection, being taken by my father to my first air show at Farnborough watching the introduction of the Britain's first vertical take-off craft, called 'The Flying Bedstead'. A strange metal-framed creation right out of an HG Wells story, that roared off the ground vertically not requiring any runway, gathering data for the upcoming 'Harrier Project'. The machine left little margin for error, none if one of its two engines had failed. Both Bedsteads built did however crash, one fatally, influencing the Harrier jets production to adopt a different lift system altogether.

Our family belonged to a generation all too frugal in sharing family history neither parent sitting us down to tell their stories leading the way to where I entered their lives. I feel cheated from their silence. Where did they go to school, what was life like for them, I knew nothing of their childhood, their families and fun stuff such as 'where they went on holiday?' So many questions; theirs were times of 'stiff upper lip' and 'children being seen, not heard'. Every now and again a small slice of their lives, a morsel of scandal, would surface in conversation, leaving blank pages, void of ink touching paper. Later in life piecing people and information together, I figured out why certain things happened and the influence they had on my life's journey.

This upbringing led me share the guilt having not pursued my family tree as a youngster although quite improper at the time to even inquire. I was a shy young boy not versed in outgoing skills, known unsurprisingly to be more an introvert. My grandparents were the real source of information in the early days having lived with them in Sussex during my years at boarding school. I had made up my mind years ago upon having a child of my own, I would tell the whole story, no more silence.

My father was born December 21 in a small village of Upper Poppleton in the north of England near the ancient and beautiful walled city of York in 1925. His father, Harold was known as 'The Major' from his rank in the British Army; I learned early he was not a well-liked man by most who knew him; an impersonal, arrogant character imposing strict behaviour on all. I saw him only once as a very elderly gentleman, never learning of his personal history other than he was married to my grandmother Edna. That one visit to Yorkshire where my father never formally introduced his son to him or the elder great grandfather seated next to him; simply instructed to seat myself at the far end of the room and be quiet. I refer to Edna as I did my own mother, affectionately calling her 'The Last of the British Empire'. Her speech and mannerisms shaped in perfect English diction and the little finger held aloft correctly while sipping from a teacup. Edna eventually left the likes of the Major, separating to elope with an employee of the British Civil Service, by the name of Jorge Dean. I called him Nanpa as a youngster, a grandfather to love and respect. A fairly small framed man with fringes of white hair bordering his tanned baldness. A neatly trimmed thin matching moustache suited his generous smile perfectly. His quiet and polished nature I admired while he adored the very ground my grandmother stood on. Again, with that silent generation, I never knew anything of Jorge's background or even where in England he was born; nothing of his life and little of his career. I ask how this could possibly have slipped my curiosity as a youngster toward a man that I became close to? A valuable lesson for our children and grandchildren: ask questions to know whence you came?

The Major refused divorce as a totally unacceptable practice in those early English days, Edna eventually changed her name to Jorge's surname by deed poll in the English press. She and her new love lived some of their early life in Madrid, grasping quickly, as an astute chef in her own right, the art of Spanish cooking. They moved back to England and lived outside Camberley in the county of Surrey. Their modest home called, 'White Lodge', lay off the main London Road, a picture-perfect stone cottage backed by open undulating grass land, before reaching a small forest of silver birches and giant oaks where foxes burrowed and our dogs went hunting; Pedro, the grumpy male Alsatian with our soft natured Golden Labrador called Penny; the constant explorer and bad influence to often go astray, sometimes days at a time. When Jorge retired from the Civil Service they moved to the neighbouring county of Sussex, purchasing a lovely old thatched cottage, once the saddle room to a group of farmhouses built over 400 years ago. Here they opened a boarding kennel for dogs as their retirement project, calling it 'Deanwood Kennels'. During half term breaks I stayed with them, some mornings making tea and serving them on a small tray. I would tap gently on their black wooden bedroom door before entering, balancing the tray while lifting the old latch to see them cuddled up to each other in that small double bed. I always admired how they loved each other even in age.

After my schooling, and leaving England for the last time, I learned they finally retired from work and moved back to the warmer climate of Malta to aid their health. She and Jorge loved each other until he died suddenly of heart failure in his garden while his wife prepared afternoon tea. I could easily imagine the scene of her returning to the garden; dropping the tray on the grass to cradle the love of her life as his small body grew cold; a very sad scene to imagine. I had lost track of them in the latter years because of my own family's dysfunction when I was twenty-one. A letter arrived in Nassau one day and I recognised Nana's writing. Slitting open the envelope, a small black and white passport picture of Jorge fell to the floor. I knew the content before reading. I regret to this day not writing to them having left England, never finding out what happened to my grandmother. Careless behaviour quietly haunting me through all my years; reports trickled in time from overseas that my father had placed his mother in a nursing home, where she later must have died.

My mother was also from Yorkshire and lived in the village of Easingwold, born in the same month as her husband, December 5 1920. Her parents James and Faith Hood owned a small a pig farm. James, a big man, always wore the same tattered brown suede hat, thick plastic framed glasses with faded Levi overalls, suspenders, with baggy beige corduroy trousers tucked in the classic dirty green Wellington boots. This family's history has some shady parts, with suggestion of James leaving his wife and marrying his cousin? 'Shame and scandal in the family' became a fun title to a familiar island calypso tune heard later in life after leaving England. James used to take me out back to see the pigs. I loved all animals right from the very first visit and there was nothing wrong in my mind with the way pigs smelled. As we approached the pens, wet concrete floors covered in fresh well-trodden pig poop, I would reach through the cold metal railings and pet the inquisitive pink runny noses that jostled through the openings to see if there was anything to eat. They pushed and shoved each other with their huge pink steaming bodies, the familiar grunting noise growing to a frenzied squealing at feed time climaxed with a deafening crescendo. James's wife, Faith Hood, was the demure, almost speechless lady who drifted quietly around the house like a small silent phantom in her faded pinafore completing her wifely duties. She made the most amazing gravy for the Sunday roast beef and Yorkshire pudding, a recipe that she would never part with. I may have laid eyes on each of my Yorkshire families less than a hand full of times in my life barely understanding the thick north-country accent sounding a different language altogether.

The Hood's daughter Mary grew up to become runner-up in the Miss York Beauty Pageant in her early twenties. She had a brother Cuthbert and another called Peter; a stepbrother, whose freckles and mop of red hair betrayed no resemblance to the rest of the family, a mystery that was taboo to mention. I met Peter maybe a couple of times and remember only a ride on his big motorcycle one night to pick up fresh fish and chips wrapped in newspaper, giving a mouth-watering aroma of salt and vinegar seeping an oily wetness through the print. Mary was considered a really beautiful lady with a wonderful wit. She married John Charles Harding, September 14 1946 when he was just twenty years old, keeping the secret of being the 'older woman' by five years, until the day she died. Mary Hood, much to the disapproval of her father, shared a flat in the cathedral city with her best friend Hilda. The two girls lived quite the life as vivacious singles within the ancient walled city and cobbled streets. I remember faded black and white pictures of my young parents driving a classic old black Daimler car. Father in double breasted pin-striped suit and felt hat with a straight pipe held firmly between his teeth; one foot proudly posing on the running board of the classic car. They never gave me any of the old photos. Their years and experiences together were not ever disclosed to me. I was born on March 5 1948 in the small village of Sawbridgeworth in Hertfordshire, just north of London. I can only put this location being where my father was working at the time training as a flight engineer based at Radlett with Handley Page.

My only contact with this past is my cousin Veronica, who I discovered and stay in touch with thanks to the creation of social media on our computers. Faded black and white photos found in my mother's belongings show we held each other close as small children, only to meet some forty years later on their holiday to Nassau. All I can remember of those early years was living in the south of England, first in Surrey and then Sussex: once a year taken on 'the family visit' by car to the north-country about 200 miles away. Without today's highways it was a dreadful journey through winding country roads, taking hours making me deathly carsick. 'Corner House' in the village of Upper Poppleton was the destination, being my father's family home. It was something out of a Stephen King novel; heavy dark wood furnishings with musty antique Asian carpets and insufficient lighting, rooms with low black-beamed ceilings enough to scare the living daylights out of me. Narrow shafts of sunlight beamed through the small lead framed windows showing a powdered mist of dust in their whiteness. The house was built of flint cobblestones and oak beams as far as I can remember with a beautiful garden of lawns and flowerbeds bearing lupines and roses around the perimeter; the old hand-pushed lawn mower leaving perfectly straight stripes on the manicured grass. Inside I was instructed to be seated in the far rear corner and not make a sound; outside was my escape. The slow and steady dominating tick-tock of the antique grandfather clock standing in one corner breaking the silence of that drab stale room, the chimes suddenly so loud one would nearly jump out of your skin. A polar bear rug centred the room, thick cream-coloured fur and dark lifeless black glass eyes in the massive stuffed head watching every move you dare make. Great-Grandfather Wilson's chair to the right of the fireplace and 'Uncle' Harold seated stiffly to the left sucking deeply on his curved pipe; their crumpled slouching old bodies consumed by the ageing Victorian chairs they sat in. Auntie Phil, a withered frail lady with bent posture topped with swept back wizened grey hair, tied in a knot behind her head looking like the old lady in Hitchcock's *Psycho*, always appearing from nowhere tea tray in hand, the ever-present cigarette hanging from one corner of her mouth. The rising drift of blue smoke giving her wheezing cough that seemed to go on forever as she talked with phlegm filled husky voice. The two old gentlemen sat as if museum pieces, motionless in the blue haze at the end of the room appearing frozen in time. I knew absolutely nothing of who they were or about their life; they barely spoke and never directly looked at me or acknowledged my presence. The scene is imprinted on my mind as an antique faded sepia photograph. Rumour had it that my Great-Grandfather was one of the first paddle wheel Captains to cross the Atlantic; accounting maybe for the ocean in my genes that would come calling to me a few years from now. The news of each of the elderly men's' death would never be announced, they simply slid quietly out of my life as the phantoms they were.

As I write these lines I watch recollections on the CBS Evening News about the 'Lion of the US Senate', the late Edward Kennedy, who died yesterday at the age of seventy-seven of brain cancer. A huge slice of recent history now past with the last of the three brothers leaving us. This American dynasty would weave their way through this story as they did with all of us in my generation. America's equivalent to our 'Royal Family'. Edward Kennedy had a wonderful quote about the sea saying: 'It was truly life's metaphor of which we could always learn its lessons; the sudden storms that arise, the unforeseen disasters, and then the beautiful calm waters that we all enjoy'.

Early life in England was a very lonely childhood with few friends; a childhood without family holidays to leave an imprint of something fun to remember. It is a time that does not leave welcome flavour in my soul. On reflection, I wonder what actual part I played in the lives of my parents? The first grammar school was a nightmare, the beginning of an awful education experience. I hated school from the very first day. Edwardian design red brick buildings with small windows and a bare concrete courtyard fenced all around with black wrought iron gates. Teachers who forced little kids to drink the small bottles of milk during 'break-time'; delivered first thing in the morning nicely chilled, now well warmed in the mid-morning sunshine to sour quickly. I discovered quickly 'herding' did not sit with my psyche well. I rebelled on the spot when someone said I '*had* to do something'. An introverted loner felt a comfortable title to wear. This characteristic plagued me all through my education from the very first school days all through college. In retrospect, I considered it a reward having aided in my self-protection, but the lessons did not come easily. School in those early years was a very cruel world to live in. It was dog eat dog all the time. The aggressive and arrogant came to the forefront of everything. Children for the most part were very mean to each other, especially boys. Small in frame and quiet in nature I did not fare well with those who needed to mark their territory by fist or foul word. Later, way too late, in the last schools I attended, I finally found out how to draw that 'line in the sand'. Those who crossed it from then on would have done well to retreat, for I held nothing back in retaliation. All those years of pent up frustration being the 'lesser being' came bellowing outward. They had come at me incessantly, often beating me to submission, but eventually I learned how to out manoeuvre my foe. Schoolboys I discovered were downright cruel and often belonged in an institution. If only my father had taught me the art of self-defence or explained simply that one strong act of aggression usually stops them in their tracks to rethink what this puny little bastard might do next; bullies are cowards at heart. Father went through this trial as a small boy being sent away at early age to Rugby boarding school: why the hell do parents pass this insane ritual on to their children?

All those years of frustration finally taught me how to stand up to absolutely anything thrown my way. Maybe those early days did bring some value after all? If I did not win the battle, knowing that I was right in principle, I would eventually win the war. This proof came repeatedly in later life dealing first hand with the local justice system. In today's time the headlines in both American and English press show concern about the dramatic effects of bullying; kids these days are dying as a result, either by their tormentors or worse at their own hand, not able to cope with the disastrous pressures placed upon them, not just in England or America, a worldwide dilemma. Bullying can race across the internet instantly; children these days have no escape. Puny kids, considered the geeks and the weaklings, arm themselves with their parents' firearms taking revenge with unimaginable horror. Children and teachers have been slaughtered in the hallways and classrooms of their schools bearing names such as 'Columbine'. While editing this writing in 2014, a fifteen-year old just stabbed his sixty-five-year-old teacher to death in an English classroom. The epidemic is everywhere raising heated debate about America's Second Amendment. After massacres in Australia guns were banned slowing the killings to a trickle. In contrast, it possible to walk into an American gun store on passing background checks to purchase an assault rifle firing 13.3 rounds a second or 800 rounds a minute! I think the Founding Fathers, writing their Constitution during the 1700s, in the days of musket ball weapons, would turn in their graves knowing how modern technology can kill so efficiently; it was after all named an Amendment so those of us on the outside often wonder why it could not be 'amended' into the twenty-first century?

My father, like most of his era, prophesied that boarding school would 'make me a man' as it had been done to him at an even earlier age than he imposed on me. He was right in some sense but at what expense? Before passing this crappy experience to his son in July of 1960, my father worked for Handley Page Aircraft Corporation flying the very secretive high altitude Victor Bomber. I saw a very handsome portrait photo of him in a space suit holding his helmet in his lap, struck immediately with the desire of aviation as a second career choice following veterinarian medicine. The latter proving above my educational ability with high level passes in mathematics required for entry to University; math and my brain did not fare well together. Father was a very meticulous man seeming to have little interest in children. I outgrew him in height eventually but he of better build, gifted technically artistic, enabling the supervision of aircraft hangars at the airport to designing and building his own motorboat in our garden on William Street.

'Love' was not a word ever mentioned between us. During eight years of boarding school he wrote three letters to me, only one ever signed 'Love Dad' the other two signed 'John', a twelve-year-old boy had a difficult time understanding that one. Only my mother religiously wrote weekly, the fold up, light blue paper, pre-stamped air letters on hearing my name 'Harding!' shouted in 'mail call'. Recollections of my father before being sent away to school are scant. I saw him one week each month in between flights to Singapore that consumed the other three. Taking me to see the air shows at Farnborough always were a highlight. Memory retains the tragic crashes of new production fighter jets screaming in front of the crowd; one ploughing with black smoke and flames in to the stands of spectators. The de Havilland 110 losing a section of its tail assembly sending it careening to one side spreading death into a crowd. Air Show regulations changed drastically after this with no major incidents until just last week, August 2015, where a classic Hawker Hunter failed to pull out of a loop, tragically crashing on to the A27 road alongside the Shoreham Air show killing eleven people. The pilot had just flown past me as I walked the South Downs that beautiful afternoon.

Driving close to the Farnborough hangars one day staring out of my car window I asked my father, 'Dad what's that jet was doing?' as it climbed vertically right alongside us.

The canopy suddenly exploded away and the pilot ejected in front of my eyes.

'Holy shit!' Dad exclaimed swerving off the road as the jet fighter reached the end of its thrust to pivot over and fall vertically downward. The pilot had marked his emergency climb perfectly with the airplane exploding in to a fireball impressively between two large occupied hangars as his parachute drifted effortlessly to Earth in a field some hundred yards away. Aviation was making a strong impression on a father's young son.

My grandparents moved to live in the next county south of us. Sussex was a beautiful county with lush green pastures, rolling curves of the South Downs and small country lanes that weaved their way through thick woods and open fields to find the small thatched English village of North Bersted. The Royal Oak Pub, just outside Bognor Regis, lay in the middle of the road intersection. Westward by a few miles, the equally beautiful cathedral city of Chichester, and to the east a small country lane led into the old village itself. Dating back over 400 years, the quaint cluster of thatched-roofed cottages used to make up a complete farm estate. My grandparents purchased 'Grey Thatch' which used to be the saddle room for all the horse tack. The front door caught me about shoulder high having to stoop extremely low to enter, populations four centuries ago were a lot shorter. Constructed from flint, one could not drive a nail into the wall; the black gnarled oak beams acted as main structural supports with each tiny room holding its own special memories.

The only downside I recollect being the nasty smell of boiling tripe that Edna cooked faithfully for all the boarding dogs every morning in a large cast-iron pot on top of the very small gas stove. I became very attached to this property; warm memories of England as the old estate became my escape from the curses of school. I would learn almost every breed of dog during my visits there developing an uncanny bond. Since I can remember I possessed a special communication with all animals from dogs to horses. I relished holding the muzzle of a huge horse to feel their silky muzzle against my face, inhaling their very breath and smiling into those fabulous large eyes. The only animal that curled his lip at me in annoyance was my grandparents Alsatian, Pedro, not warming to little people as did a nasty old potcake, native term for a well-mixed breed, that removed a piece of my earlobe on my offering close affection during early years in Nassau.

In Camberley, Surrey, an epitome of ugly English suburbia, my earliest recollection of a very large block of flats, called 'Dullater' I believe. The complex occupied a sprawling acreage with sweeping lawns that led down to a cluster of silver birch trees in the rear of the property. I recall wonderful moments alone with our Golden Labrador, Penny, lying with me on the smooth lawns under the silver birches watching the wind blow through the branches above us. The main London Road passed to the north, not far away the Army Training College Sandhurst, where one could walk through the grounds and around the lake. Sandhurst offered scenic relief to the rows of red brick semi-detached housing I detested living in. Immaculate black cannons mounted on wheel gun carriages stood elegantly on the manicured lawns guarding the main army buildings. Platoons of brown-clad uniforms and gleaming black boots, the cadets marched in unison on their parade ground to the yelling of a sergeant major, changing direction perfectly like a flock of birds. Our flat was small and memory will not be able to describe accurately. I do remember my father bringing home this tiny box that slowly came alive with a black and white picture he called a 'television'. In 1953 we watched a fuzzy picture, the young Queen Elizabeth's Coronation on a screen about twelve inches in diameter. I am editing today watching the celebrations of Her Majesty's ninetieth birthday! Father designed a modern new home for us to live in, a vast improvement to our small flat, calling it 'Oakwood Rigg', a name my mother and I could not figure out, was short lived in. No sooner becoming acclimated it was moving day again. Father was one of those who did not believe in debt or mortgage; everything was 'bought and paid for'. I imagine he must have been presented an offer unable to be refused, for shortly our new home was gone. He was in a flying career as a Flight Engineer aboard Hermes passenger planes on the routes to East Asia taking over three weeks at a time to complete the long journey round trip. My mother and I were alone for many months a year, with him returning intermittently with small collections from all over the world to be displayed in the ugly semi-detached terraced house on Gordon Avenue being our last home in the UK. The back garden long and skinny quite characterless, neither parent displaying any interest in gardening skills. The railway track adorned the end of the property; British suburbia at its finest instilled a strong distaste to this day. The small villages of Sussex however, another story; their small winding lanes and gorgeous character cottages boasting vast arrays of flowers and trees always enchanted me as a place to comfortably live, little did I know the cost of such real estate! I attended day school while father was away and life clicked by providing little recollection of any noted experiences; days dragged into weeks and months; time was sluggish back then. Up to the age of twelve our family did not take a single holiday together, missing chances that could have exposed me to the stunning vistas of South West England and beautiful beaches of Cornwall. One day while home my father announced surprisingly a recent family decision that would drastically change our lives forever.

Chapter 2
New Horizons.

My father laid a world map on the dining table. His finger travelled away from the United Kingdom across the Atlantic to the east coast of America, downward to the State of Florida and south-eastward to a small group of islands named the Bahamas. My mother's expressions were not of joy. Quietly in anticipation we listened to the story of how my father had been offered a three-year contract as a flight engineer with a small subsidiary of BOAC called Bahamas Airways. Our lives were to take an immense change if he were to accept. In an unusual move, he involved us all in the decision making although in hindsight I knew his decision already made. There was talk of selling or renting the house, giving our dog to my grandparents and the big cruncher of me having to enter an English boarding school. My mother was not a happy lady, her secure little world of home, child, dog and friends all to be traded for life on some foreign island twenty-one miles long and seven wide, a long way from her homeland. The decision was offered to us but stark reality being our duty to follow my father's wishes being breadwinner of the family. He was to leave for Nassau, the capital city, in the spring and find a new home for us to live while launching his new career. My mother was to send me off to boarding school and then pack all of our worldly possessions and join him in the islands.

My grandparents thought the idea was a wonderful opportunity having been world travellers themselves also working abroad, swaying my mother into believing that her son would be well cared for in Sussex during the holidays too short for me to travel to the Bahamas for visits. The dog was more than welcome to live with them at 'Deanwood Kennels' where a Labrador could run through acres of grounds freely at will. Jorge had retired from the Civil Service, his days of commuting up to London every day on the train now over; the umbrella, black bowler hat and pinstriped three-piece suit stored in a closet. The question lay in where was their grandson going to be sent to school? My parents showed me pictures of this towering house on a hill overlooking a body of water in the south of England called the Solent. The house was King James the First School on the Isle of Wight. To get to this place meant a train journey from London to Portsmouth and then a ferry ride across to the Isle. Irony had this island just off the south coast home to the most secure penitentiary in the United Kingdom called Parkhurst Prison, an appropriate analogy that played through my school career.

It must have been after the Easter Term of 1960 my mother escorted me to London's Victoria Railway Station. The huge iron domed ceilings, wide notice boards with revolving letters that changed every few seconds indicating train departures and arrivals. Rows of steam locomotives with carriages as far as the eye could see. Hundreds of people milled around the huge train station, outside red London buses mixed with the black city taxis streaming in and out of the entrance-ways. It was very noisy. Whistles blowing, doors slamming and belches of steam from the locomotives echoed through the massive structure. People milled in different directions like ants, no one made eye contact. Suitcases and clothing trunks having no wheels in those days were dragged across the concrete leaving scratch mark trails. I had never seen a major train station before in my life. Many of the children were boys all dressed in the similar suit that I was now wearing, the uniform of King James the First. This is where the school had told us to meet and congregate. I felt as if being herded as cattle, eyes wide and sense of foreboding. I said nothing while shoved in one direction then another. Feeling utterly bewildered, with my head darting in all directions trying to comprehend the chaos, my mother's hand firmly guiding in the small of my back. The enormous locomotive located at the front of my train, this mass of steel and wheel coated with armour, bellowing white steam from its undersides, as if an impatient steed wanting to bolt from its paddock. Doors were opening and closing as fast as I could comprehend, the latches making a loud bang on closing. A whistle blew very close by with a conductor dressed in black uniform holding his arm upward.

'All aboard,' he yelled, sounding right out of the films I had seen in the cinema. My mother opened one of the doors and asked me to climb up the two steps. The carriages in those days had corridors that one could traverse the length of the train. Obediently in silence I mounted the steps of the carriage finding a window open in the narrow corridor, standing my ground to watch her step backward on the worn dirty platform. She told me 'to be brave' and follow all the other boys after we arrived where transport would be waiting to take us to the school. It then hit me face on; a stark fear I was going to do this alone. Some other boys climbed through the door opening, pushing their way past me chattering loudly to find the best compartment, each having its own door. Well-worn red upholstery covered each bench seat on both sides, one set facing forward, one aft; overhead saggy netting would hold hand baggage. With a huge bellow of steam the locomotive lurched forward nearly causing me to lose balance. I was just tall enough to just reach the sill of the window that was pulled down, enabling me to lean outside as the whistle screamed once more. The train shuddered again as it made its slow motion forward and I watched in disbelief the motionless figure of my mother becoming smaller by the second. There was no smile on her face, just a tentative, barely waving arm held only waist high, while her image faded in size ever so slowly at first and finally to nothing as we cleared the long platform. I stared backwards what seemed forever, hoping to get just one more glance of her figure before the wind became too strong to stay at the window. I often wondered what it must have been like for her to walk away alone. Parted from her young son for the first time. To arrive at her house with no one there but our dog lying quietly on the living room rug. Pieces of soot sent belching from the speeding locomotive were occasionally hitting my face now with small stings. The trees of the countryside came in to view in a blur of green after all the dull city buildings stopped racing past the open window, which I closed by pushing upward on the metal glass frame. I walked the narrow corridor looking for a compartment with available seats. Opening the nearest compartment door, I took a vacant seat in between boys of similar ages. All penetrating eyes were on 'The New Boy', like a young pack of glaring wolves, their bodies swaying in unison of the train's motion. There were no smiles and no greeting. I sat completely silent with my possessions packed in a trunk following me in a rear baggage compartment.

I forget the amount of time the journey took. Riding the train actually became a comfort. A means of travel I always enjoyed even to this day.

The sway of the compartment and clackerty-clack of the wheels on the track were soothing to the soul with blackness of a sudden entry to a tunnel and the explosion of daylight as we exited. The slightly sweet acrid smell of sooty smoke permeating the carriage where it had seeped through the ageing window seams in puffs of light blue. Once free of the monotonous suburbia scenes of Clapham Junction with its unending rows of faded chimney pots, bent television antennas, drab stained brick walls of identical houses, the vistas of a green countryside making travel calming to the very lonesome schoolboy lost in his own thoughts of desertion. Several stops were made as the train made its way southwestward. We finally slowed on the approach to Portsmouth Harbour, a major British Naval station. Various impressive grey hulled frigates, mine sweepers, cruisers and a battleship I recognized lay at their berths, their large deck guns with red capped barrels all pointing directly forward. Each dock lined with huge cranes towering above the grey hulls like skeletal dinosaurs. Not far away was the major Port of Southampton where for the first time I saw some of the great ocean liners of the world suddenly all right there in front of me. The huge navy blue hull and infamous bright red funnels of Cunard Lines' *Queen Elizabeth* and docked close by the royal blue sleekness of the mammoth *France* with her modern shape dark blue funnels; the SS *United States* boasted her sleek lines of navy blue and white hull with bright red funnels capped with white rings and black caps.

A screeching of breaks as the train came to an abrupt halt saw all the doors fly open as if the starting gates of a horse race; everyone bailing out on to the platform behaving if it were some kind of stampede. I followed into the stream of pushing bodies met by teachers and custodians of the school herding us on to buses for the drive to the Ferry Port. The moist air smelt salty and noticeably cool as it blew in one's face. The water was white capping on the surface of an opaque sullen grey brownish colour. We all filed on to the wooden gangplanks to board the ferry being told the luggage would be loaded below and would meet us at the school.

Within a short time, another familiar whistle blasted sending a white plume of steam from the funnel horn while heavy mooring lines cast away to be pulled ashore by the crew on the dock. Engines throbbed from deep inside the hull and the ferry moved with a white flurry of swirling seawater from the stern where seagulls milled, circled and screamed in their chaotic flight waiting for scraps of food thrown aft. We lined up on the boats railings allowing the chill wind to flow over us while securing our school caps lest they be blown into the sea. We all watched in quiet as the mainland slid away from us. The sharp contours of ships and various colour schemes fading to a hazy shade of distance grey blue. This separation played an uneasy feeling of 'no return'. The naval dockyards of Portsmouth grew smaller behind us while the Isle of Wight lay just ahead. We could see small sailboats moored by the hundreds bobbing in rhythm on the grey waters at the entrance of Cowes Harbour neighbouring across from Ryde Ferry Terminal; the mainland now far less define, still visible as a faded grey line only ten miles away.

Strong tides and dangerous coastline made the Isle of Wight a last resting place for hundreds of shipwrecks. A rough diamond in shape, the island was really beautiful in parts. Soft undulating hillside meeting dramatic chalk cliff faces, quiet calm beaches in others. The surrounding waters racing past at three miles an hour became treacherous with the island standing within the flow of the English Channel; no more influenced by the warm clear currents of the Gulf Stream currents, where on the other side of the Atlantic had raced passed the Bahamas and south Florida coastlines, ending on the lovely beaches of Cornwall on the southwest tip of England. The winds off the Solent provided some of best sailing in the South, it is here I would learn the art of capturing the wind in cold capping waters. Underwater has seen recent discovery of an ancient civilization where land was once joined to the mainland. Diving had not yet been introduced to me and after the perfect waters of the Bahamas I could never be tempted to plunge into the English Channel. The ocean however was my escape from the madness of everyday school life and sailing brought much needed peace to a distressed young soul. The weeks and months ahead would be very lonely. This new world my parents had thrust me into was so unwelcome. Watching other boy's race around a wet cold playing field chasing a ball failed to light any spark of enthusiasm; their screams of delight sliding in the chilly mud leaving me to wonder their glee. I could only scratch the days off my calendar impatient to escape these miserable surroundings. My only joy when the small wooden Snipe bit the wind as I pulled on the sheet of the mainsail, a gurgling rush of water from the stern as I raced forward.

A bus met us at the ferry terminal and the drive took us up the sweeping driveway to the front entrance of the school building. The first Junior School of King James was a solitary house standing alone in the countryside called Swainston House near the village of Calbourne. White plastered walls with dark rectangular windows and matching grandiose white columns in the front entrance giving appearance of a once sophisticated country estate. Here I was to spend the first year and memories are faded about how life treated me. The solitary existence from the outside world and insular control of teachers and students left me numb to feelings we left at home in Surrey. Solitude and abandonment killed my memory. I learned to be a quiet individual staying out of confrontation at all costs with an aggressive society of pent up feelings from young boys of similar age and circumstance. We each had different ways with dealing what had been thrust upon us. Our secure private world of parents, home and friends were gone. We had no training or encouragement how a small lad should cope or handle life alone surrounded by strangers in an unknown environment. We had no knowledge of the loneliness that could wash over you at the most unexpected moments; how one would withdraw at times into nagging homesickness with the urge to simply walk outside and run for dear life, but where? Sending young children away to boarding school is a damned crime; sending them unprepared without survival skills worse again. Arriving at the Senior School the next year was another step downward for me. The population here was older and a lot more skilled in their distasteful behaviour of others.

Nubia House was a forbidding sight, something out of the darkest mystery novel of murder and mayhem. One stood on the road, where eyes moving upward from the hedges guarding the old house to the top floors that stared back down at us. Faded stone walls stained with rain soaked algae bearing yards of thick ivy creeping up from the ground, covering nearly all the wall surfaces to reach the dark slate roof with its dormer windows. Ravens circled just above the building calling a mock welcome with an eerie cry set against thick grey overcast English skies as a backdrop to complete the morbid scene. Hitchcock would have done well to use this for a movie set. Our dormitory offered a slightly better view on the other side. Above the tree line we could gaze upon the world's largest ocean liners passing our windows as they came in and out of the Port of Southampton, this northern side of the building had the estate lawn sloping downward to a stand of large trees. I was to find out what secrets they held within very shortly.

Separation became a major issue and influenced behaviour in later life. I had friends who were sent away to boarding school at the age of six, and a fellow writer who told me had been a little girl of just four years old. Here was I twice that age finding the sudden change in life a shock to the system, subjected younger was inconceivable. One minute you were in this sheltered life where a parent would be there to protect and defend and a day later completely alone. There had been no communication from my father as to what I could expect. Here lay the major problem, no hint or lessons on self-defence or valuable insights as to how other boys were going to behave. Being alone later in life became a choice where left alone as a youngster became something of a challenge. The boys who fared well were the team-sport jocks. They had chance to separate themselves in the pecking order, creating an unseen protective barrier around them. They would be near untouchable by the other students. A team sport in those days was the ultimate school priority; educational skills came very much in second place. During my interviews into both schools I entered the very first question asked of me, 'What sport do you play and what position is your specialty?' 'Sir, I have no favourite game or position,' would be my reply; seeing my father's head hang in shame as he had attended his school's national rugby team. I felt a failure in his eyes.

An English boarding school in the 1960s was very similar in experience where ever one ended up in the country. Maybe there are exceptions to the rule but King James the First was one of those considered a bad luck of the draw. My parents had obviously done some research in to schools that were within close proximity of my grandparent's home in Sussex. I was within reach when not enough holiday time allowed the long haul across the Atlantic. Each term, some four, six or eight weeks had breaks in the middle, a 'half-term' as it was called, usually a long weekend or a four-day break. I would travel alone back on the ferry to Southampton and catch the train that arrived closest to Bognor Regis, the nearest major town to 'Grey Thatch'. My grandfather, Jorge Dean, would always be there to meet me at the station. His familiar small frame with balding silver hair and matching groomed thin moustache who spoke in perfect English diction. He was the only man to ever greet me with a kiss on the cheek, a truly amazing human being whom I loved dearly and learned so much from; my fun co-conspirator in later escapades.

In the western schools, it is called 'hazing'. Here in the UK I had no clue what the hell was happening that first day as a group of older students approached me with the look of evil in their eyes and sneers of mischievous intimidation on their faces. The new boy was going to be taught a thing or two. Without explanation I was set-upon by four or five older boys. Strong hands gripping both my arms pulled forcibly by the group out of the main house, down the sloping lawns, my legs unable to keep pace dragging toes in to the uneven grass soiling my new shoes until reaching the tight cluster of huge conifers and deciduous trees. Fighting back would have been futile, being unaccustomed to the art of self-defence. Besides, a scrawny twelve-year-old was no match against stronger senior boys. My heart was thumping with anticipation, adrenaline coursing through my small frame. With good reason, I became afraid, my eyes wide and unblinking, stomach muscles screaming as they clenched tightly with the unknown. I nearly urinated with fear. I had never been assaulted like this in my life. In the dark foliage underneath the tree canopy an opening displayed a homemade swing made from a large log and heavy ropes slung over the giant limbs of the ancient fir. A thick bed of pine needles made the forest floor feel like a carpet with a sweet smell of pine as I was forcefully seated and suddenly blindfolded from behind. Arms outstretched like a crucifixion I was bound to the supporting rope slings. The older boys orally mocked me about where I came from, 'that I was in good old England now'. Those of us 'lucky' enough to live abroad, those of us with brown skins; all might as well have had targets painted on our backs. They started the swing in motion, slowly at first in a sideways motion, taunting me about being 'far away from mummy and daddy so there was no one to protect me anymore'. It was hard to tell which direction I was headed until the limb on which I was sitting unexpectedly struck the main trunk with a shudder. My captors would pull the log backward once again for another harder thrust. If I fell off my seat I would be hanging by my arms. I gripped the rope instinctively tight lest I slip. My heavy log seat suddenly struck the huge fir tree again. I would see later bark from the impact having fallen to the floor below leaving scars on the main trunk of the magnificent fir. What the hell had Mum and Dad got me into? I've done nothing wrong. From a secure quiet suburban English home I had arrived in hell. The impacts went on for quite some time and then everything suddenly fell silent, my tormentor's voices and laughter fading in the distance as they scurried uphill to the main building. All I could hear were the large black crows calling from their circling flight above the tree line and the wind whistling gently through the canopy. 'Someone help me!' I screamed out to the silence hanging there for what seemed a lifetime as the swing slowly came to a standstill in its pendulum motion. Minutes drifted to an hour or more. It seemed eternity. I became aware of suddenly being very cold as the sun lay low on the evening horizon. The thin white shirt, shorts and blazer uniform offering little warmth. I started to uncontrollably shiver as I heard a noise of footsteps in the leaves ahead and snap of a small twig under foot, despairing that something forbidding was coming back? I tried desperately to stop my teeth from chattering so I may hear warning of another threat. Uncontrollable wet tears flowed freely from each eye soaking the cloth blindfold, some seeping down my cheeks to roll off the base of my chin. Why am I crying? Damn, I don't want them to see me like this. Sudden massive waves of relief flooded over me as I realized I was being untied and released by a fellow student who I did not know. I fell on to the soft pine needles as my arms and legs slowly regained use. The blindfold was pulled back in haste allowing me to see my rescuers smile. 'We all went through that crap,' he offered in quiet explanation. The evening light was poor and 'we will be late for dinner roll call if we did not hurry.' My indoctrination over for now but consistent poor treatment through my school experience kept me very withdrawn. I felt the need to rely solely upon myself for survival and not try to engage those around me. Reporting home in letters was not an option. I felt ashamed to give clue about such treatment, believing my parents would not care. Other student's companionship was not to be trusted. The few times I did venture toward another the experience ended in some form of betrayal. Even when I finally was taken away from that first awful school I then attended Seaford College near Petworth, another establishment with similarities shadowing the whole educational experience on a far lesser scale with the advantage of being only a few miles from my grandparents. Only with age did the years slowly give me added height and strength that helped assert in self-defence. I detested school and all those who occupied it, save an American with the same surname as my mother's maiden name, Hood, who new well our favourite Florida radio station, WQAM. Life as it should be started on that last day of school term before leaving England for the first time abroad. Low lying coral islands set in the most gorgeous of seas would breathe new life into my soul, showing me a path to life that I craved to hold on to from here on.

The cruelty of this little closed society was evident on a daily basis, if not from the boys against each other it was endured on rare occasion from the Masters, both physically and physiologically; times when teachers would show their superiority making example of one of the untouchables, much to the horror of the rest of us plebeians. The tactic worked well leaving a lasting impact. One rainy afternoon during a rugby match one of the elite muttered some curse at the referee. Major W. Cook, Housemaster, a very tough character who should not be crossed at all cost. Short in stature, heavy in the chest, thinning swept back black hair held perfectly in place with hair cream, furrowed eyebrows, very tanned skin and strong as an ox. Always dressed in a tweed sport coat, waistcoat with classic teachers' black robe billowing out behind him as if an evil character from a classic comic book. The comment had been overheard and the game came to an abrupt standstill with a shrill scream from his whistle. The master ordered us all in to a giant circle in the middle of the field. The day was cold and grey with a light rain blowing across the grass. Low mist drifted overhead concealing the tops of trees. Conditions were miserable with us standing still in the chill air after running like fools up and down the wet pitch, sweating and covered in spattered mud from head to toe. Standing in the centre of the circle the teacher barked another order for the guilty party take a step forward. There was silence as we stood motionless, cold rain running down our faces and steam rising from our warm soaked shirts as we stood like cattle in the cold. Most of us had not heard the remark and remained speechless. Within seconds a fairly small lad stepped forward. He was one of the definite untouchables amongst us; comparatively small in stature but tough as nails and not to be messed with under any circumstance sporting curly brown hair and pale white skin painted with light orange freckles. From nowhere Cook had a cane in his hand. I too would feel the sting of bamboo more than once, from our Headmaster, Robert

Heron. 'Six of the best' it was called and across one's lowered trousers while bent over his huge office desk, strokes delivered in swift precision faster than you could breathe in. The cane stung so strong that involuntary tears would well up in seconds. 'Pull up your pants laddie, I nay want ta see you here again,' he barked in a thick Scottish brogue, his ruddy complexion from too much alcohol even stronger red after his fit of punishment. The frosted glass windows of his office allowed the next poor sod in line to hear every impact of the wood on our rear end.

This instance the boy was ordered to hold out both hands palms upward, a particularly cruel form of caning. Nothing happened for several moments just the sound of rain droplets hitting our bodies. The outstretched arms never faltered a fraction while the master waiting agonising minutes for the muscles to ache. The Major's cane raised and came down across the bare hands with lightning speed. The harsh sound of impact making all of us wince in unison. The sound cracked across the quiet field, repeated six times, slowly with malice. The flexible piece of bamboo carved its way in to a previous welt sending a splash of rainwater outward, driving home the message to all of us. The culprit never made a sound during each of the blows but salty tears of agony spilled down his cheeks to mix with the fresh rainwater dripping off his chin. His hands now swollen and near bleeding rendered useless for the remainder of the game was 'excused' and sent back to his dormitory. The game resumed.

One would learn in this place how to stand tall and face just about anything thrown at you. The school motto 'Standfast' had been created for good reason. This bony frame with arms so thin I covered them in shame with long sleeves, offered insufficient protection against the bullies. I see now where murderous thoughts could enter those with feeble constitution. Some 'Houses' in the school were better behaved than others. That first institution definitely a place where parents who needed the child out of the house or parents who had moved abroad leaving the child to be educated. A place where children could be left in the custody of others while parents explored the outside world, young children of different creeds from all over the world suddenly subjected to others as mean as venomous snakes in a pit.

The one who 'dogged' me for my days at King James the First was a South African. He was wiry in stature with an olive complexion, a good-looking bastard with curly brown hair and the piercing dark eyes of Charles Manson, a very scary person to deal with on a daily basis. The classic school bully, this psychopath was the one that taught me 'how to draw that line in the sand'. The torment lasted so long that even the most docile amongst us finally reached a breaking point. Cross that line and you face the fury from hell that comes from deep within the meekest of men; where winning didn't even count at this point; just making the shear statement of war was all that mattered. What made a soul wait so very long to react so drastically when the results were so positive to your favour? Why in hell's name did no one teach me how to defend myself as a youngster? Neither this idiot, nor anyone for that matter, would ever behave like that toward me again, whatever their stature in life. A surprise punch to the centre of that smirking face sent his body reeling backward along the wet shower room floor ending in a heap under the heating pipes at the far end of the room. My hand felt great as the blood from his nose dripped on to the green linoleum flooring. The older boys moving aside in respect from the scrawny Bahamian boy who dared to take on their leader so effectively; from here on totally unafraid of any authority figures or any legal system. I respected them but did not fear them. Later in life having to deal with police, lawyers, judges and courtrooms; none offered intimidation. I was the classical non-conformist and thoroughly enjoyed it. As long as I knew within that I was in good standing and in the right, my position remained unmovable. If I screwed up, were quick to admit and always apologise. One was never right all the time and screwing up was a part of the lesson. To me everyone came on even ground, it did not matter what level of society you were placed in, if you behaved properly with respect toward animals, the environment, myself and my loved ones, you had my utmost respect.

Autumn of 1964 another young schoolboy arrived from the Bahamas as a new boy to share the King James experience. Our parents knew each other. We eventually came to save each other from what appeared to be certain demise, a fellow expatriate, who had arrived at the beginning of a new term with his parents also moving to the Bahamas. Graham Lawrence and I became a tag team that would work closely together to find a way out from this madness that our parents had put us in. We both enjoyed chemistry and soon learned how to manufacture explosives from garden fertiliser, icing sugar and other choice ingredients we could buy in town. The small local hardware store displayed innocently the white fertiliser in metal garbage bins that we could purchase by the pound. Terrorism, in those days, was simply the criminals we had to live with at boarding school. A word not used by the general public until decades later. It was common place for the two of us to purchase a couple of pounds of fertiliser in a brown paper bag and fly with it in our hand luggage aboard an airliner across the Atlantic enabling us to continue our 'chemistry studies' during the holidays; how the world has changed since these early days. We survived for several terms before finally deciding each to approach the others parents conspiring 'to get us out of here!'

I vowed if I were to have children, they would under no circumstance be sent away for an education; the infatuation with the 'English educational system being superior to other countries' was utter bunk. The private schools in the Bahamas offered the same teaching curriculum as in the UK with students here taught mostly by expatriate teachers and professors. The examinations were exactly the same as in England. I would have travelled through the same Ordinary Level General Certificate of Education and higher Advanced Levels of GCE had I wanted to. The school terms were similar although favoured the American system with summer holidays longer and shorter in winter than UK schools. It seemed obvious that our parents, or more accurately, one of our parents, just 'wanted rid' of their children for the chance to have more independent time alone in their new tropical outpost. As an individual I think I became, as did many in that system, loners. Boys found different ways of coping with being alone. Those of us with different coloured skin or of privilege would pay a heavier price. One became without choice, a survivalist. I came out of the boarding school system certainly, in part, as my father wanted, 'a man' in most respects and yet sadly lacking in some skills of relationships. Neither our parents nor the educational system that they placed us in, offered any instruction on how to stay emotionally whole, that only came in time with the gorgeous surroundings of island life.

The early years I would make mistakes and lose important connection with those I wanted to be close to, the inability or *want* to stay in touch with my grandparents that had looked after me so well during those difficult years of my life. Once living in the new comfort and beauty of the Bahamas, having left that God forsaken place that was so inhospitable to me, I callously 'let go' of those who remained there and had been so thoughtful. It was the one connection that should have been nurtured. In marriage, there was also failure lacking family education and experience of 'normal' relationships. It took me three tries to finally get close to getting it right and still failed even then. I was however reportedly kind, thoughtful, very loving, generous and polite to my ladies; not wanting to emulate my father's behaviour. On reflection, I must have contributed to failure through 'not paying attention' in some matters with the insatiable thirst to be the competent provider, insipidly enticing me in to becoming the all too familiar 'workaholic'. It becomes an all too easy trap and happens to those of us having to claw our way upward from nothing. In fairness to myself, each of my partners contributed their unique mess to 'rent asunder' what was supposed to be a lifetime union, a discussion for later perhaps as there are always two sides to the coin? Children need to learn from their peers and parents all the values on how to handle the complexity of relationships. It's not an easy course. We can pass down knowledge and experience to the best of our ability and after that it is their path to walk; their passage of learning as we continue on until the end of life.

All through life witnessing the way mankind behaved, was in general, a massive let down for me. Learning from history how the different populations of the planet decimated each other 'in God's holy name' through every existing century and every ethnicity; how incredibly intolerant human beings really are toward each other displaying miserable failure in the ability to learn from the horrors and price of past conflict. Ironically each of the major religions were damned near related; they believed in one God, all believed in a man named Abraham, all had one book as their written word and all had similar philosophies of treating one another the way you would want to be treated. Then entered greed, power, ego, poverty, ignorance and politics to have us watch stunning world events that were a damned shame happening in our lifetime: Jihad or 'Holy War' it was called. History records almost every religion or sect was not guiltless in the madness of aggression. It was as if religion itself was the root of all evil and a way of controlling the masses. From the very British Empire her self and the misery that was cast upon other countries as it conquered and divided nations. A vast empire famous for drawing lines on maps everywhere it went, leaving turmoil, heartbreak, division and death in its wake while arrogantly boasting its introduction of culture, trade, roads and railways. Our Bahama archipelago suffered terribly after Columbus landed in 1492 on San Salvador with subsequent arrival of the Spanish Catholics who decimated the whole Carib Indian civilization of the Bahamas. The Tainos and Arawaks, peaceful light-skinned people of the sea who had hospitably greeted their visitors on to our shores with gifts and fruits, lost every man, woman and child being forcibly taken to mine the gold in Hispaniola. In our century, we learn the insanity of the Great War, the madness and horror of the Second World War. People showing the most astounding cruelty toward each other and the millions of lives lost. Nazi Germany alone exterminating more people than lost in battle in both World Wars. Boarding school for me seemed to lay the foundation for understanding its similarities, where the first seeds of men's aggression germinate. What the hell is it with men, supposedly the 'hunters and gathers' that demonstrate such lust for awful behaviour toward women and each other, in the massive whirlwind of madness called war all, too often in the name of religion? Even our lovely little island nation, floating in its tranquil clear oceans, displays a recent downward turn in society's behaviour. Back in the sixties we could leave cars unlocked, often no keys to hotel rooms. We could swim naked on a moonlit night on Saunders Beach without fear of bodily harm. There was no hint of child abuse. Everyone expressed a polite 'good morning' to each other. There were no guns on the streets, drugs openly for sale, robberies every week, a scandalous murder rate, women assaulted and filthy trash left on pristine beaches.

I witnessed first-hand in my travels different ethnic origins living in perfect harmony alongside each other, eating and laughing together; Palestinians and Jews sitting at street cafes in Jerusalem sharing stories or playing backgammon, until their government policies overflowed and intruded into their lives. Time gave way with brother fighting brother and neighbours who hated each other while building walls or fences to keep them apart. In stark contrast, we are privileged to witness the creativity and brilliance of our species; mankind is truly amazing with its blatant contradictions. Recent history showed us men leaving the ground in crude flying machines and less than a hundred years later walking on the surface of the moon. We witness the slaughter of our whales and dolphins to near extinction by the Japanese; dogs skinned or boiled alive in China, the madness of poaching magnificent elephants and rhino in Africa and India decimated to the loss of complete species in the myth of sexual potency showing mankind a true pestilence upon the planet we inhabit. We listen to music that makes us weep with amazement or feel the hair raise on our arm as our senses are dazzled with the human voice, all contradicted with news footage of human suicide bombers blowing themselves up; hijacking airliners into buildings while others venture across the ice to club baby seals to death by the thousands. Monsters and brilliance seemingly surround us. I sit under a whispering casuarina pine, gazing at the brilliance of turquoise swirls in Shroud Cay Cut, knowing the good fortune of not being sent as young men in to battle during this lifetime and how lucky we Bahamians have it in this world.

Chapter 3
The Bahamas

That first term at King James was the longest of the year for school attendance, about twelve weeks. English schools took their summer break long after the American counterparts already on vacation a month or more earlier. July 1960 saw my first solo transatlantic crossing, labelled 'unaccompanied child', so named in the aviation industry. The last day of school was exhilarating, just the thought of being away from this place enough let alone the unknown experiences about to unfold upon a twelve-year-old.

My grandparents stood waiting on the platform as the train jerked to a halt. Doors flew open and passengers spilled out on to the platform. The stop here would be brief before the whistle blew and the steam gushed taking the engine and carriages forward again. I was to stay a night in Grey Thatch snugged away in the tiny village before driven up to London Airport the next morning.

The ride to London Airport, Terminal Three, seemed to take forever in those days; no highways with cars screaming along at over 70 mph as in the latter years. This was 1960 where winding roads with endless stopping and starting through various towns before arriving to wide open spaces where tails of large aircraft showed above the surrounding perimeter fence lines. My grandfather parked and accompanied me in to the huge terminal building. The echo of announcement speakers constantly boomed as people milled in all directions. The modern building was enormous with high glass ceilings and dozens of escalators moving lines of people both up and down. How on earth would anyone know where to go in this place? Jorge escorted me to a counter and talked to the agent briefly advising them I was an unaccompanied child and 'staff' passenger of an airline employee. I found out in short order that this meant my parents had only to pay ten per cent of the actual ticket price, a real bargain of those days at thirty-two pounds, under $100 from London to Nassau. A downside I was susceptible to being 'bumped' if a full paying passenger was trying to travel with insufficient seats available; a 'staff' traveller either informed at the counter or even to be politely escorted off the aircraft after being seated in some circumstances, the rest of the passengers wondering what this young lad could have possibly done? The baggage in those days remained on board to arrive on schedule. I would be taken to a hotel at the airlines expense to board the next flight, that in 1960 took nineteen hours to cross the Atlantic making an interrupted stay somewhere strange while adding at least a full day or more delay.

My grandfather gave me a hug and wished me well, his grey moustache tickled my cheek as he kissed me goodbye.

'You will really enjoy this adventure and I will see you in a few weeks.'

He was gone, leaving me alone at the airline counter of British Overseas Airways Corporation. I was escorted though passport control and in to the waiting lounge as 'unaccompanied child'. Through the windows I saw the panorama of runways and waiting propeller airliners at their gates. My first transatlantic airliner parked in front of my boarding gate. The cockpit staring at me through the glass allowed me to see the crew in their seats completing paperwork and flipping panels of switches above their heads. The fuselage seemed to stretch forever toward the massive three vertical fins that made up the tail. This was the Super Constellation that would take the better part of a day to cross the Atlantic. The route led across the English Channel to Paris, Madrid in Spain then on to Portugal's capital, Lisbon. The first part of the Atlantic Ocean followed flying to the small islands of the Azores then the long haul into the small island of Bermuda alone in the ocean east of the Carolina coast. After an hour's stop for refuelling, a brief visit inside the airport allowed us to wait in the transit lounge. Next leg of the journey would be my first time stepping ashore in the United States in Miami, Florida. Here I was to change planes and board a Bahamas Airways Handley Page Hermes that my father had come here to fly as a Flight Engineer.

We boarded at Heathrow able to watch through the window seat I had been assigned the four large piston engines come to life with a huge belch of black exhaust smoke from under the wings. In those days, aviation was a glamorous means of transportation where passengers dressed smartly, men in coat and tie, ladies in high heels and latest fashion; attractive uniformed stewardesses served meals in style. The table in front of your seat would be lowered for you and a white table-clothed tray placed in front of you while reading the small menu offered. Our cutlery all stainless steel wrapped elegantly in a starched white cloth napkin. The cockpit door would be left open where leaning into the aisle I could watch the pilots managing the controls confirming what I really wanted for a career. Unlike my father who relished the management of the aircraft systems during flight I wanted to be in that left front seat with my hands on the controls. We taxied to the main departure runway where the engines roared in unison for the take-off. The roll seemed to last forever. Full of fuel, passengers and baggage the Super Connie, as she was affectionately known, finally lumbered upward as I watched the city of London fade below me on my first time airborne and first time abroad. In a short time, the airliner penetrated solid grey skies above the countryside for its long climb to the blue above. I stared outside, as I do to this day, watching the gorgeous white cloud formations fall below us thousands of feet down. In the still air of altitude we settled in to cruise speed toward Paris. There were flights where I was invited to walk up front and stand inside the cockpit behind the captains' seat. Almost every flight in those early days, children and the occasional adult were asked to join the crew for the experience of flying. I often was allowed, with crews I came to know, to sit in the 'jump seat' just behind the pilot in command where I could experience the landing. There was something about being airborne that captured my soul. Walking across an airport ramp to climb the stairway up to the cabin I would breathe in deeply absorbing the aromas of jet fuel and burning kerosene, that unmistakable sweet smell of airplanes. One day, I vowed inwardly, I would fly my own plane.

On that first crossing I made it as far as Bermuda, where on landing informed that indeed I was being 'bumped'. An unaccompanied twelve-year-old now had to leave the airport to stay the night with a total stranger who volunteered to take me home with her. My stewardess host was really pretty. She told me that we could go to the beach and have a swim and that I would re-join the flight that came through the island tomorrow. Things were looking up and this 'bumped thing' turning in to an attractive experience! For the first time, I saw the tropical ocean. Sparkling clear and iridescent blues, the houses all differing colours, everything so clean and bright, the sand noticeably white and the island immaculate. Everything looked so alive! I become instantly drawn to the effects of light in our visual view of life, the contrast so inspiring after the monotonous pastels of England. Policemen guiding traffic dressed in long shorts, knee high socks in immaculate shoes wearing crisply ironed short-sleeved shirts. Standing up to your waist in surprisingly warm water I could see my toes, far different from the English Channel, the warm moist humidity welcome air to breathe. My parents had been informed by the airline that their son had been off-loaded and not able to make Nassau until the following day. My mother must have been really excited about her little one now alone in some 'strange place'. Little did she know how quite content her young schoolboy was, where my father may have smiled at good experience it would be for a young lad?

The following day I watched the island of Bermuda fall behind us on our climb toward Miami: I was met by a Bahamas Airways staff member based in Florida and escorted to the last portion of my journey. The Handley Page Hermes took less than an hour to reach Nassau, just 186 miles away to the southeast of the mainland. Always trying for a window seat, I was fascinated how suddenly the deep indigo turned in to this swirling mass of turquoise below me dotted with small islands and mass of brown coral reefs. You could see right through the water! We passed directly over the islands of Bimini, the ocean much lighter in colour appearing a fabulous painting beneath me. More islands came in to view on the left side of the droning aircraft; I would learn their names as the Berry Islands. The aircraft engines noticeably changed their pitch slowing for the approach in to Nassau some thirty miles ahead.

The northern shoreline came in to view and I could see the entire length of the island. New Providence was only twenty-one miles long and seven miles wide. To my left a couple of cruise ships in the harbour protected to the North by a long narrow island adorned with beaches and trees, void of any buildings save a few set back a gorgeous crescent beach facing the Northwest I would soon frequent as Paradise Beach. The airliner was very low as it skirted the pristine white beaches on its final mile from touchdown on Runway 14. 'Palm trees!' I exclaimed inwardly as we soared over the shoreline. The wheels squealed as they met the hot tarmac. I was home.

In 1960 stairways were wheeled up to the doors of the Hermes where a hot blast of Bahamian summer air rushed in through the main cabin; the atmosphere almost thick with moisture with humidity so high at this time of year. Walking on to the top stair I felt the immediate heat of the summer sun, much warmer than my Bermuda experience of yesterday. Standing below in grey trousers and white short-sleeved uniform shirt was my father looking very tanned. 'Hello son,' shaking my hand briefly. It would be the way I was met from each of my Atlantic crossings three times a year. He had 'ramp clearance' being employed with the nation's airline and my mother first spotted on the balcony above the terminal entrance way. She waved frantically as several male passengers shed jackets uncomfortable in the hot air. The sound of calypso music greeted us as we entered the Customs Hall, a sign by the musicians proclaiming 'Blind Blake'. It was all tropically very surreal. That first family reunion was good one for us all. I was escorted to my fathers' new car, a Morris Minor Shooting-brake, as it was termed in England, a station wagon to the Western world. A cream coloured vehicle complete with wooden varnished framing around all the windows and doors. The local termites would soon find good fodder in this fancy trim work; British car bodies would not fare well in this climate while the engines seemed to last forever. There was no rust prevention for automobiles in those days. The thin sheet metal of vehicles imported to the island soon fell victim to the moist corrosive air and cancerous rusting holes worked their way from the inside panels outward. The 'Interfield Road' wound its way from the airport through Oakes Field and in to town, the Coast Road, known as West Bay Street, followed the northern shoreline through the town of Nassau, roads were rough going. Every few feet there were worn patches of thin tarmac with potholes every few yards washed deeper with each rain. It had been many years since the roads were last resurfaced. The wheels of the Morris shuddered as we hit the large depressions.

Maintaining the 45-mph speed limit was impossible and the ride took quite some time. The coast road offered the most scenic ride to our first home in the centre of Nassau town on Market Street. My father had found the apartment where mother had joined him several weeks later as soon as the English residence had been rented and Labrador dog taken to my grandparents for safekeeping. The shoreline of New Providence was gorgeous with the road running almost along the water's edge in some places.

Vivid turquoise waters lapped quietly on to the white powder. I was spellbound. Lush tall coconut palms lined the road together with seagrape and buttonwood trees. There was little conversation on that ride home as both parents could see their child in awe of his new surroundings. The ocean water held me fascinated in its colour and clarity like the magazines I had gazed through, a long way from suburban England. I cannot fathom the idea of having to ever leave this place. We drove past a beautiful bright pink hotel with surrounding grounds manicured to perfection. Splendid colours of hibiscus bushes, bougainvillea with lush green lawns graced the entrance of the Emerald Beach Hotel. Next door the stately Nassau Beach Hotel and from there mostly private residences; one estate very close where the Canadian gold prospector and millionaire, Sir Harry Oakes, was brutally murdered one night during the Governorship of The Duke of Windsor back in the forties. We passed a tight right hand turn called by the locals Go-Slow-Bend, coming upon a row of black cannons pointing northward in protection of Nassau Harbour. My mother pointed to my right drawing attention to the grey walls of Fort Charlotte up on the hill. Coming in to full view three cruise ships that sailed back and forth to Miami Florida; The Ariadne, The Yarmouth Castle and The Bahama Star. They would appear twice a week most often on Tuesdays and Saturdays, sometimes crossing paths in the night water.

Ahead lay another stately pink hotel, The British Colonial, with tall mature palms, their long bending trunks supporting swaying branches high in the hot July air. Rumour had it that Sir Harry Oakes had an unpleasant experience with the doorman one night being rude to him, so bought the hotel and fired the man. Sir Harry had been born in Maine, December 23 1874 earning a fortune in Canada in the 1930s. He had left medical school before graduating headed for Alaska during the Klondike Gold Rush. Searching for gold for fifteen years from California to Australia finally striking rich in Northern Ontario where some twenty years later his mine was the most productive in the western hemisphere, second largest in the Americas making him Canada's richest individual by 1920. He became a British Citizen and moved to the Bahamas for tax reasons, invited by Sir Harold Christie, a prominent real estate developer. As a major philanthropist, he donated over a million dollars in charities during his residency in the Bahamas and expanded the airfield at Oakes Field.

He owned a house on Cable Beach called Westbourne where at the age of sixty-eight was found battered to death, supposedly with a conch shell, lying on his bed partially burnt and covered with feather stuffing from a pillow? The Duke of Windsor was Governor at the time trying to enforce press censorship that failed. Under normal circumstances he would have been able to acquire the assistance of Scotland Yard but World War Two was raging in Europe forcing the Duke to seek help from two Miami policemen that he was acquainted with proving a disastrous decision with conflict between local authorities. It is suspected the two American policemen were on crime boss Meyer Lansky's payroll being that Sir Harry had openly opposed Lansky's plans to develop casinos in the Bahamas. This theory was dismissed by many putting the crime as a local affair involving local prominent businessmen to stop the millionaire from moving his fortune to Mexico, avoiding currency restrictions during a wartime period. A move that might well have destabilised the Bahamian economy? The mystery includes claim of the Duke of Windsor had hired the two crooked detectives in an attempt to thwart the arrival of the FBI and Scotland Yard who might well have discovered his similar plans for moving money illicitly? Thirty-six hours after the murder they arrested Oakes' son-in-law, Alfred de Marigny, who had eloped with Sir Harry's daughter Nancy two days after her eighteenth birthday speculating he now on bad terms with Oakes. Marigny's trial went on for weeks where a rope for his hanging had been ordered. Fabricated evidence of a fingerprint by the Miami police caused an acquittal for the Count. After the trial the Count and his bride went to stay with friend Ernest Hemingway in Cuba, divorcing in 1949 after he moved to Canada and later Central America where he died in 1998. Nancy died in 2005 survived by two children and two grandchildren from another marriage. The Oakes' murderer was never found.

Traffic flowed from Bay Street toward the hotel as one drove through town.

'Through there is the Straw Market,' my mother pointed out.

I wasn't sure what she meant only to discover later the rows of native stalls with cheerful Bahamian women sitting on stools weaving straw into hats and bags for tourists to buy from nearby cruise ships docked in the port. Horse drawn Surrey carriages trotted by on Bay Street. We turned an immediate right up the hill on to Shirley Street passing yet another beautifully kept pink building that I learned was Government House. A perfectly white statue of Christopher Columbus stood between two black cannons on the summit of stairs leading up to the front entrance from the street. Two smartly uniformed guards stood motionless on duty with shouldered rifles. There was a lot of pink paint in those days. We pulled up in front of an old building with a protruding terrace where my mother pointed upstairs to the second floor.

'Here we are,' she said.

'Your room overlooks the oldest house in Nassau here on Market Street.' The large apartment's décor was straight out of an old Humphrey Bogart movie, the tropical settings and slow turning bamboo ceiling fans with dark stained wooden flooring.

Today our apartment has been replaced by the Central Bank of the Bahamas. The night sky came quickly, much earlier than in the UK. Darkness brought far different sounds with the unmistakable cicada that clung to the nearby limbs of branches. A chorus that seemed to start with one insect then crescendo together by the hundreds; without warning suddenly cease their noise to leave the night in complete silence. I slept well after the hours of air travel. That first morning brought in with the crowing of cockerels from nearby neighbourhoods, even here in town they called out at the approaching dawn. I walked downstairs outside where the air was noticeably cooler than the apartment at this time of day. There was no air-conditioning back then just the gentle hum of the old ceiling fans above you. I walked a few feet across the street and laid my hand against the young coconut palm looking up at the cluster of green nuts sitting in the centre. The sun glinted through the gently moving fronds. I had only seen these beautiful trees in pictures, now I could actually touch one. The palm, much taller now, still stands.

The summer holidays on this first visit were spent mostly with my mother while my father worked at the airport during the week. Weekends would be ours to accept invitations on fellow airline friends' private boats, taking day excursions up to Rose Island about seven miles northeast of Nassau Harbour. My mother had her own car back then. The white Ford Anglia would be our daily escape from town where I was to learn about the island and savour some of its famous recreations. I had learned to swim in that frigid grey water of the Solent while learning to sail Snipe on the weekends.

Here however was something so incredibly different, warm clear inviting water beckoned me at every opportunity. I had followed *Hans and Lotti Haas* on black and white television where their underwater documentaries held my attention every week, and *Sea Hunt* with Lloyd Bridges, who effortlessly threw those double sets of scuba gear over his head to plunge in to the adventures of the underwater world. Never in my imagination thinking I would actually meet the man himself one day, sitting with him for several days to chat one on one; to think that he would ask me to be an 'extra' in one of his movies while working my first job in the outside world. Life in the Bahamas was suiting me well. The islands were magic. The people, the country and the way of life became part of me from that first day.

My mother drove around the coast road as far as the road itself would take us. Past the beautiful Montagu Beach Hotel with its grand entrance to the foyer and an awaiting doorman, one could see the huge glass windows inside a bar downstairs where patrons watched young girls performing water ballet in the swimming pool upstairs. Hotel guests could be seen swimming on the beach accessed across East Bay Street. Lined with young palm trees lay the old Fort Montagu, its quiet stoic cannons having never fired a shot while guarding Montagu Bay from intruders and captured repeatedly by any who ventured conquest. The stick shift Ford would be the car that I learned to drive in the next few years as a teenager. All the way westward we passed the gated community of Lyford Cay hosting many famous names of high society in those days such as E.P. Taylor and author Alex Haley. The road climbed southward and over the hill where a few miles later Clifton Pier came suddenly appeared on the south side of the island. The road was much higher, perched above the cliffs and rugged coastline of the southern shore. Here oil tankers off-loaded their cargo for the generating station of the Bahamas Electricity Corporation. Dark blue waters off the pier told of greater depth immediately below, down to forty feet within yards of the shore. There were no beaches here, just layered strata of limestone proving the islands ancient history had been underwater. The area close by littered with underground caverns and a very narrow precarious staircase cut out of the soft rock face leading steeply downward to the rocky water's edge below, stories this was once where pirates came ashore unnoticed from the city defences on the opposite side of the island. The pier was a large open flat area of concrete where one could drive your car down the side road to the unprotected edge finding several huge iron Sampson posts that held the lines of large ships. It was here that I learned how to first use a hand-line to fish. We bought a hand-sized fresh conch for sixpence from the fishermen and cut pieces for bait. Large yellow grunts and grey snappers gave a good pull when caught. Impressive buoys just off shore bobbed in gentle unison with the ocean swells that came toward the land. Here the worlds tankers secured themselves in position for off-loading of oil, diesel and gasoline taken on by local smaller tankers for Out-Island delivery to marinas and airports. Below the coral reefs ran along the shore and out toward the dark blue line known by divers as 'The Drop-off' a submerged continental shelf mapped as 'The Tongue of the Ocean' coming close to shore as it skirted past the southwestern tip of New Providence: one could imagine the Grand Canyon underwater. The southern tip of the Tongue lay off the South Bight of Andros, the largest of the 700 islands in this country to the south and west of Nassau. Here lay Green Cay teetering on the edge of the underwater precipice, an island unpopulated and not quite circular, hosting only native scrub bushes with a beautiful white sand beach skirting the circumference; here, deserted and pristine, sea turtles could crawl ashore in the darkness to lay their eggs. The shallow coral reefs and surrounding water drop very quickly off the shoreline, the edge found in less than thirty feet of water diving vertically to over 3000 feet below, the underwater canyon in the centre reaching three miles into the darkness.

The Americans had built small AUTEC naval stations, Atlantic Undersea Test and Evaluation Centres, scattered along the east coast of Andros Island. Their submarines, warships and naval aviators out of Navy Jacksonville, Florida, came and practiced their exercises here. The defining edge then runs northward along the coast of Andros boasting the third largest barrier reef on the planet passing New Providence to the east making a narrow passage of twenty-eight miles; beyond Andros the Joulter Cays where the Tongue makes its swing eastward past Chub Cay in the Berry Islands northward to Great Harbour Cay and on toward Grand Bahama. Ocean liners have to find their passage through the deep waters precariously close to shallow rust-coloured coral heads found only inches under the surface; one extreme of depth to another where violent endings to many long voyages across the ocean ventured by the ancient mariners; giving reason why treasure ships were never recovered, blown on to the shallow treacherous corals during vicious tropical storms, shredding the wooden hulls to scatter the cargo along the ocean floor, then huge swells dragging the ruins back over the edge to sink into unrecoverable deep water. The reefs here, along with the Tongue, would provide some fun stories of their own, as my own ventures took me in to the world below during the years to follow.

On weekends, we travelled by speedboat to Rose Island where the shallow waters hosted thousands of coral reefs. As our vessel skimmed across the flat waters I would sit in the bow watching the racing panorama speed underneath. Water so clear that starfish and conch shells could easily be spotted lying on the sand below. We would anchor off a long gorgeous beach known by the locals as MacTaggart's Beach, named after a renowned Canadian family owning property there. Years from now I would maintain a close relationship with flying Sandy MacTaggart in and out of his islands owned within the Exuma Cays; a very tall man of maybe 6 feet 5 inches, slim build and recognisable beard. Sandy and I always maintained a wonderful relationship through the course of my career. A short swim off the beach at any given location would treat a snorkeler to the abundant life of the reefs that lay close to shore. The coral sand stretched for a mile resembling fine talcum powder. Lying to the north were two islands; Green Cay ahead, and westward the famous palm skyline of Sandy Cay belonging to local Bahamian, Ossie Moseley, where, hidden amongst the short coconut palms, were three stone cottages built as weekend hideaways. The centre and eastern end of the Cay supported towering palm trees featured in many magazines and films, earning the title 'most photographed island in the country'. I learned to snorkel here at Rose Island. The warm overly buoyant salty water allowed one to lie effortlessly on the surface for hours simply gazing at the busy life beneath; learning how to seal one's lips around the plastic mouthpiece like a straw; spitting in the mask and wipe the saliva around with a quick rinse to prevent the glass from fogging or using a fistful of turtle grass crushed inside the glass. Letting the legs make slow and deliberate strides allowing the swim fins to propel you through the water, each stroke a slow and graceful motion not disturb the water's surface alarming the life below. Everything underwater moved in slow motion until feeding time. Fish of all size and colours swam in every direction; life down there was so very busy. The vast array of live corals endless and vibrant, the sun's rays dancing off their shapes; hard corals looking as if something out of a biology textbook were indeed called Brain Coral. Soft corals of all shapes and sizes swayed very gently with the currents below. Some corals hosted a tight fist-size matt of tentacles that opened during the night revealing a vast fan of lace called a Basket Starfish; diving at night later in my career discovering the eerie majesty found in the inky darkness. Large purple fans have taken hundreds of years to grow millimetres at a time were firmly attached to the rock faces and shimmered with the filtered sunlight. Some corals when touched felt like satin running through your fingers, thousands of polyps were open along the stems of these gentle feeders. On the bottom were delicate flutes of dark purple, some alone and many in family clusters, these tube worms withdrew suddenly inward for self-protection sensing pressure changes in the surrounding water. Some corals fed during the daylight hours where at night time everything changed, hard corals revealed their secret blossoms while fish snuggle close by in sleep. Over seventeen years, my first career would introduce near 50,000 visitors to the wonders that lay beneath our Bahamian wonderland.

The drive back to town took us along the quiet old south coast road passing through acres of Pine Barrens and the junction down to Adelaide Village. Passing the well-known local watering hole called Hall's Oasis and on to the familiar Coral Harbour roundabout with its classic landscaping, stone towers and native walls. As the policeman stopped traffic flow at Parliament Street we could hear a steel band playing. My mother would park in the grounds of the old Royal Victoria Hotel, hidden in a lush setting of tropical vegetation and towering palm trees. By the main building a huge ageing silk cotton tree that had branched in to several main limbs allowing a tree house platform to be built within the tree itself. The steel band instruments were laid out on the platform and the musicians climbed a wooden ladder to perform above the visiting guests while they dined for lunch and dinner on the patio outside. It was a beautiful setting where time seemed to slip back to the old days. One could easily imagine a Model-T Ford pulling in for valet parking and important political figures coming to stay in the heart of old Nassau.

Chapter 4
A Monster is Born

In late August, thousands of miles away, the summer heat exploded above the African continent. Massive thunderstorms gathered above the hot landscape billowing majestically upward. Gentle offshore winds nudge the swirling mass of weather over the coastline into the warm waters of the tropical Atlantic Ocean. At the surface air pressure was falling and the thunderstorms were generating their own strong winds and heavy rainfall. The winds grow to sustain thirty-nine miles an hour across the ocean's surface; a magic number for it is the season that gives birth to monsters.

Unlike recent decades of climate change, weather was very predictable in those early years during the summer months of the 1960s. Plans could be made months ahead of schedule for Out-Island adventures and fishing charters around New Providence and through the Exuma Cays. With the rains of June subsiding and July entering the scene, days would be steamy, hot and calm, palm fronds lay limp in the stillness and Royal Poinciana trees still boasting brilliant red, recent rains knocking much of their blossom to form a red and orange carpet on the roads below. Afternoon heat built towering cumulous becoming dark and heavy with saturation eventually bursting at their base to drench parts of New Providence, flooding streets when the high tides coincided. Sunshine followed, making the roads steam in the bright light. The ocean would take on an oily characteristic, for days one could not distinguish where the sea melted in to the sky.

Near the Cape Verde Islands off the African coastline the weather was explosive, climatic conditions conspiring to create a beast of nature that is unmatched in strength. A monster able to produce energy equivalent to seventy times the world's total energy consumption, 200 times the world's electrical generating capability or plainly put, a ten mega-ton nuclear bomb! The hot summer sunshine forced the moist air to rise and condense as warm water vapour; a reaction creating incredible heat distributed also in upward direction, the temperature inside this frictional swirling mass now much warmer than surrounding conditions outside. Enter the earth's rotation and pressure gradient to start the mass turning counter clockwise. Nature has successfully manufactured its most deadly engine with the warm ocean waters as its fuel; winds begin to spiral around a tightening circle increasing velocity by the hour. The depression has grown into a tropical storm, the fourth disturbance this season, carrying the ladies name 'Donna'. From the beginning of record keeping storms carried girl's names listed by the National Hurricane Centre in the United States, in later years – from 1979 – they alternated gender. Winds are speeding in greater velocity around the very middle of the system as the spiralling momentum increases, as if some monster is coiling itself to strike. The faster everything moves the more heat generated within, causing massive clouds to blossom dramatically upward thousands of feet above the surface, as high as an airliner flies; condensation gains pace, the natural engine sucking power from the warm saltwater it is racing over, as if an unstoppable massive runaway locomotive.

Donna is observed as a tropical wave off the African coast on August 29 1960 becoming a tropical storm the very next day. On September 1 she became a hurricane. As these storms increase in strength they change category from one through five, this storm developed incredibly fast to gain strength and speed for another five days. When the track courses into higher latitudes cooler oceans slow the evaporation process, the huge weather system losing its fuel begins to die, and if by chance, it passes over a land mass of reasonable size, the oceans fuelling effect completely lost, downgrading it to just another low-pressure weather system. These early days of September see Donna growing to be a phenomenon that will break records of hurricane history as she heads directly toward the Bahamian archipelago.

Bahamas Airways had a policy in the 1960s of evacuating aircraft from a danger zone. As news of the hurricane reached us in Nassau plans were put in to motion. The fleet back then was a mixed bag of aircraft that could handle almost any flight demand for its island nation. A versatile little airline composed of the larger Handley Page Hermes, the ever-popular fleet of DC3s and Vickers Viking to smaller Aero Commanders and amphibious Grumman Goose and Widgeon. Technology was very limited fifty plus years ago; there were no weather satellites in the heavens beaming sophisticated weather images back to Earth. Radio reports from merchant and naval shipping supported the weather forecasters in Florida. Television was intermittent at best, with regular TV antennas perched precariously on Bahamian rooftops, trying to catch the weak signals that would bounce along the atmosphere and Earth's surface from Miami, more often appearing as a snowstorm on our screens. Frustration would rise as black and white pictures faded out when vital information was transmitted. My father would have nothing to do with television so to watch anything involved a short walk to the Pritchard residence in front of us. Local weather reports came from the Bahamas Met Office at the airport and transmitted daily by the one Government run radio station called ZNS, announced by broadcaster Rusty Bethell; his distinctive deep gravel voice reading reports sponsored by his well-known 'OK Flour'. Airline policy in a storm situation allowed the crews who flew to also evacuate their families if they chose to accompany the fleeing aircraft. This year we were heading south to the island of Jamaica allowing the storm to pass safely to our north.

On September 3 1960 in the Leeward Islands the day was started beautifully with high wisps of cirrus clouds decorating the powder blue skies; nature's gentle clue that things are about to change. Birds and animals would become restless possessing the amazing ability to feel within what the horizon held with a worse fate due the following morning. To the east of the islands the outer bands of cloud and heavy rains approach closer by the hour. The whole system has wound itself so symmetrically tight the inner eye wall is a now perfect circle of purple-black cloud surrounding clear blue skies, calm wind and gentle sea, the storms eye. Donna hit the Leewards on the 4th and 5th as a Category 4, just shy of the strongest rating. The airline in Nassau gave the crews just hours to leave. My holiday was to include an excursion to Kingston, Jamaica where Bahamas Airways would hide the fleet letting us enjoy the mountainous region north of Kingston; occupying a small hotel hidden in the thick forest of the Blue Mountains. Here the scenery was quite different from our flat scrub trees and pure white sands. The landscape lush and rich with life through what appeared an impenetrable forest. Breakfast was served on the patio that surrounded the classic colonial building while we watched tropical birds display their gaudy colours floating gracefully through the foliage dripping water from the morning rains.

Donna took a turn slightly north-westward missing Hispaniola and Puerto Rico leaving the islands reeling from near fifteen inches of rain taking 107 lives to flash flooding sweeping away everything in their path. On September 7 she slammed full force with 140 mph sustained winds into one of the most southern islands in the Bahamas named Mayaguana, the island hit with fury where air pressure dropped incredibly low for the record books.

We left Jamaica after the storm had cleared to the North with my father's pilot in command, Captain Phillip Farrington, deciding to detour via the southern Bahamas after hearing of a direct hit. The flight would take us over Mayaguana proving an eye opener for all on board. We made several passes over the flattened terrain. Almost every building was destroyed or severely damaged. Trees twisted off at the stems with millions of pieces of shredded debris scattered all over the island. Not a single piece of vegetation was left alive and all that was green now lay still and black with the saltwater scathing that had thrashed the island. Every living thing had been stripped bare as if burned by a furious fire that did not smoulder; the scene absolutely motionless save an odd person, bedraggled chicken or stray dog walking carefully through the rubble. Everyone on that aircraft fell silent in disbelief at what they could see. This would be my first witness to such destruction, for most veteran Bahamians on board this kind of damage was no stranger from their past history. The start of the so-called 'thirty-year cycle' had begun; some of the worst hurricanes in Bahamian history striking in the late twenties and early thirties with the cycle subsiding each decade until the arrival of the 1960s where it would begin again. Out-Island houses were of simple construction in those earlier days without the modern hurricane-proof windows of today. Crude wooden shutters would have leaked air causing a pushing effect from inside the home. The carnage left most stone buildings destroyed or roofless leaving wooden structures leaning helplessly at a precarious angle, stripped of shingles. The air mass had raced across the ocean and in its wake left the tiny island looking like a nuclear bomb just exploded flattening everything in its path. Atmospheric conditions steer these monsters and Donna would spare New Providence by taking a relieved turn westward, passing the capital to the south, skirting the north shore of Cuba. She drew a direct line for the Florida Keys, presenting the other associated catastrophe known as 'storm surge': strong winds racing across the ocean surface cause a piling effect of water above beyond normal tidal limits, a wall of seawater thirteen feet high over swept the little chain of islands connected altogether with a series of bridges, the umbilical lifeline to Miami and cities up the Florida coast; one little island called Sombrero Key recorded winds of 150 miles an hour. Donna hit the Florida mainland with an atmospheric pressure of 27.46 inches of mercury, making her the fifth strongest storm on record. The day was September 11.

The hurricane raced up the Florida peninsula leaving 114 deaths behind in the Leeward Islands and Bahamas. She exited the landmass as a Category 3 storm and skirted the United States coastline all the way to Canada; her northward journey into cooler waters finally causing the engine to run out of fuel. She was the only hurricane on record to produce hurricane force winds from Florida all the way to New England battering Rhode Island with gusts of 130 mph. Donna had generated an estimated cost in those days of $400 million of destruction.

We left the area with our crew heading northwest toward Nassau. As the next islands came in to view the scene below displayed normal again showing vibrant greens where winds had been less intense and salt damage barely visible. Recent rains had blessed the islands, washing them with welcome fresh water allowing the healing to begin. Within a few weeks it would appear as if spring had arrived for the second time this year, everything still alive sprouting new growth. Nature's cycle thrown out of kilter often left trees to fruit months out of normal sequence and bird life almost extinct for months, leaving our skies ominously quiet of song. The season was still at the peak of activity having two months to go.

The last couple of weeks of that first summer vacation introduced me to the excitement of deep-sea fishing and the big game that swam northward through our clear deep ocean. The waters between the Bahamas and Cuba boasted tales that inspired Hemingway. Monstrous game fish cruised the indigo depths. My parents had established a relationship with legendary charter captain Arthur Moxey who captained the fishing boat *Sea Pie* docked at the Nassau Yacht Haven. It was customary during the Easter Holidays to charter boats like Arthur's and cruise through the Exuma Cays for several days snorkelling, fishing, beaches and exploring all on the itinerary. Some of these early Easter weekends were too short for me to fly the Atlantic leaving my parents and their friends from Bahamas Airways enjoying an annual getaway from Nassau. Their fun stories faithfully told on the air letters received at school from mother. They had cruised out of Nassau Harbour south-eastward to the first stop in at Allan's Cay threading their way through the islands down to Waderick Wells to lay at anchor; several boats in the fleet all meeting in the protected deep water that weaved its way through the renown-haunted island. At night Arthur's crew, along with Captain Milton Pierce's crew aboard 'Blades' would secretly sneak ashore and make their way to the top of 'Boo-Boo Hill'. Dressed in white sheets and candlelight making ghostly noises to scare the hell out of all the first-time cruisers. Captain Pierce and his first mate, Ghost, had an engraved sign above the master cabin bed reading 'Marylyn Monroe slept here!' Year's later Ghost's ashes spread within the shallows of Shroud Cay Cut, a common request from those of us with a passion for Bahamian waters displayed here almost to perfection.

To make up for missing the Easter experience, my first summer holiday would take us on the *Sea Pie* for a day's fishing charter instead. Summertime deep-sea fishing can be slow going. The ocean was too warm. Most of the game fish run through the Bahamas during the spring months where one could get lucky trolling line in the early morning hours and again in the afternoon when fish would rise for feeding in the cooling hours of the day. At twelve years old, sitting in that fighting chair a dream come true. 'Strike!' I was taught to yell the very first time the rod bent over suddenly. The reel screamed as line flew out toward the bubbling wake behind the boat; Arthur's mate Frank came aft showing how to keep the rod upright and hold the tension just right. As the fish slowed its first run I was to crank the reel as I let the rod smoothly down toward the transom, the tackle a little too large for a scrawny twelve-year-old. Once at the bottom of this arc I was to heave the rod firmly upward again to gain ground on the taught line. Repeating this countless times to eventually win the fight or hear the sudden unexpected explosion of snapping monofilament as the prize fish broke free diving into the inky cobalt blue water.

'It's just a Barry,' Arthur called out. Referring to the common predator barracuda that frequented our waters. Within minutes my first fish was gaffed out of the water where Frank slid the fish in to the open fish box in the aft section of the boat. All hell broke loose when the fish was free inside and my father sat on the lid as pandemonium slowly faded with the dying four-foot fish. Frank opened the box and laid the dead fish on the transom and with one motion of a fillet knife slit open the belly taking a white oval slice of meat. I was horrified. What the hell was he doing with 'my' fish? Arthur came back and explained, 'Barry-belly makes real good strip bait 'cause the skin don't tear easy'.

A new line was rigged with a beautiful red and black feather and strong leader wire. A strip of my prize fish threaded on to the hook and dropped overboard in to the foaming wake behind the boat. As if he knew the exact yardage to let out Frank flipped the ratchet on the reel and told me to hang on. They had spotted birds reeling around the ocean surface a hundred yards from the boat. Black and white dots swirling in a circle, some diving vertically into the frothy white turmoil on the surface where schooling fish were furiously feeding. It was just after three thirty in the afternoon east of Booby Rocks at the far end of Rose Island. The dark blue of the ocean had an oily appearance different from the rolling white caps that morning troll had given in the gentle summer breeze. The hiss of a cold beer can opening indicated the adults were all having an afternoon brew and watched eagerly as we approached the birds. The surface was in chaos as small baitfish desperately fled the chase of a racing school of blackfin tuna. Their dark bodies could be seen rolling on the top of the water, swimming faster than our boat was traveling, occasionally hoisting themselves out of the water in desperate pursuit of their prey. I could feel my pulse racing as the excitement grew knowing our trolling feathers would now be racing toward the underwater chaos. We entered the screaming mass of feathers and snapping beaks. Without warning all four rods exploded. Lines screamed in unison and drinks flew all over the boat as three of the grownups scrambled into the other chairs to grasp a bent over rod. I had never seen anything like this before. It was chaos, as if some mad freak show where lines crossed each other causing fishermen to yell at each other as to who went over or under and from left side to right side. Arthur would manoeuvre the boat to keep the lines in view off the stern while Frank leaned against the transom gaff in one hand and glove on the other. As each fisherman conquered his catch Frank would catch the line in his gloved hand while the reel was still being cranked in. With impeccable timing while fish held fast alongside the boat the gaff struck fast scooping the wriggling body in to the boat. Tuna bleed profusely and blood was flying everywhere spattering over boat and bodies. This calamity would be repeated through the schooling fish until it abruptly stopped as if a switch had been turned off. The ocean suddenly lay quiet with birds dissipating in all directions; some just lighting delicately on the ocean surface to take a rest. The meal was finished. Time to head home. Frank rigged one line again for me, this time a yellow and green feather with another piece of barracuda strip bait. He knew that I would rather stay in that chair rather than mingle with the celebrating adults. The ratchet was set and we headed home.

Sea Pie headed west toward Nassau skirting outside the neighbouring cays, the hot summer sun now dipping toward the horizon bathing the boat with a warm golden light. It was customary that lines stay out almost until the very last chance of deep water had passed under us. This afternoon had Booby Channel to our left side and far ahead lay Sandy Cay and Hog Island. I was holding the rod carefully with one hand and daydreaming about the excitement of the day when the big fish hit hard. The rod almost came out of my grip taking a couple seconds to yell 'Strike!' No reaction from either adults or the crew caught up in conversation in the forward section of the boat. The second yell got Arthur's attention and he pulled back on the throttles immediately. The boat slumped forward and my father could be clearly heard exclaiming, 'Holy shit, he has something huge!' The reel screamed much louder than before as line was torn away at amazing speed. Now I had their attention. Everyone gathered in the salon opening just under the bridge to watch young master Paul have the fight of his life! The rod bent far over to rest on the transom, as I was unable to hold the running fish any other way, it was far too strong for these thin scrawny arms to hold; the reel paid out line faster than a racing automobile where it seemingly was going to run all the line off the spool. Not only did it go out but straight down in to the depths.

'That's one big bonito you got there, master Paul,' Arthur said almost casually.

How on earth did he know in an instant what had taken the bait so early, and so far down? Slowly, ever so slowly the fish slowed its acceleration where I could, with a mighty heave, pull the rod slowly upright and then release downward starting to wind the reel to take in foot by precious foot of line. The motion of pulling and lowering the rod had to be smooth lest I jerk the tackle out of my catches' mouth. I was tired from the tuna school hits we had previously brought in. My forearms soon ached beyond belief.

'You got one record fish there, Mr. Paul, and we can't help you if you want to win the tournament.' What tournament was he talking about? The Bahamas Ministry of Tourism recognised any registered and weighed fish during the season this year; awarding medallions and certificates for any trophy catches landed. Half an hour passed and I was getting nowhere. Just as the fish could be seen rolling its light under belly way down in the dark water it would then catch another burst of energy and sound again with as much speed as the first run!

I could not see myself getting this fish to the surface. Cameras clicked pictures of a very tired lad doing his utmost to bring this prize up to the boat. I put all my body weight, not that much at twelve years old, behind each pull and muscles never used like this before screamed at me to stop this madness. Nearing an hour Frank leaned over the side with the line running through the glove. The gaffed slashed through the seawater and came upward quickly sending the spike through the body of the fish under the spine below the dorsal fin. Bonito are a small breed of tuna, averaging about five pounds in weight with their dark blues and define stripes separating them from larger species. Small in size, they run in vast schools to catch their prey of baitfish not known for their food value compared to the other tunas that run through the Bahamas. This fish weighed in at twenty-four pounds and held the Bahamas Record for years after, a record unbroken to this date. Under Arthur's advice, 'He won't see another like that,' my father had the fish frozen in the Pilot House freezer then shipped to Grey's Taxidermists in Florida to be mounted as a trophy, still admired on my patio wall.

Chapter 5
A Decade of Change

Before I could blink eight weeks had passed with arrival of that dreaded day back across the Atlantic to school. The familiar turn off the Interfield Road taking that last turn toward an avenue of Royal Palms became a symbol to me the joy of the islands now over for a while. Nassau International Airport with its stumpy control tower soon comes in to view. Both my mother and I were visibly quiet and no frame for any conversation. I had explained about the poor choice of schools and that Graham had also told his parents of similar experiences of poor treatment to little avail. My father just threw the line 'You'll be all right after another term, just hang in there and let us know.' I wrote letters every week and the only communication from home faithfully came from my mother with no hint of my release.

The hot early September day was near over and I hugged my mother goodbye. We could barely talk with a profound sadness lingering between us. Voice near breaking we managed a whispered 'goodbye'. Leaving all this beauty and excitement behind compared to life in an English boarding school ahead was a huge anti-climax for a young boy. She would make her way upstairs to the open balcony overlooking the runways and gates watching solemnly as my father walked me across the tarmac to the waiting Hermes. He walked me to the bottom of the gangway leading up to the cabin. Stewardesses stood in their uniforms at the top of the stairs. My father shook my hand formally saying, 'See you soon son, do well in school.' I could barely acknowledge with a nod of reply ascending the steps to the top and steal one more gaze toward the terminal building spotting that familiar soul-waving goodbye. I sucked in what seemed the last warm humid breath that I would take for a long while and stepped inside the airliner cabin.

I stared out of the window for what seemed a lifetime as the first of the four giant engines rolled over and coughed to life throwing a belch of exhaust smoke. The airliner taxied out to the main runway and revved all four engines to near maximum. BOAC a year from now would be operating the first of its Boeing 707 direct flights to Heathrow taking ten hours off the flight time. Brakes released she rolled down the runway to climb over Lake Killarney in that familiar left turn over the city, my eyes never leaving the window. The droning sound became unison as the pilots synchronised all four engines. I watched in solemn silence as all the familiar roads and beaches finally slipped from view. I ached inside with the dread of knowing each minute I was being taken further away from my lovely Bahamaland.

Departing Miami the light was failing into darkness; red-hot exhaust could be seen glowing from below the strong engines on each wing. The climb took a long time with the airliner full of fuel and passengers returning to the UK. Reaching cruise altitude, the cabin crew would bring around the menu and take drink orders for the evening meal to be soon served. The stewardess once again would come and lower our tables spreading a white tablecloth for each passenger seat. Welcome aromas of the evening dinner soon wafted through the cabin. I was suddenly quite hungry. Silver cutlery was placed correctly with a clean white cloth napkin held with a ring. Champagne or wine was served in stemmed glassware and the galley sounded busy with activity.

'Would you care for the roast beef or roast pheasant. Mr Harding?'

'May I have both please?' I would try! The lovely lady bent forward to pour me a drink, a wry smile toward a beaming schoolboy; her perfect uniform allowing me the grandest of view; a lad coming of age. The nineteen-hour saga was to take even longer going eastward. First stop would be Bermuda. I learned in a year or two this would be a fun part of the journey with all the Bermudian young ladies attending girls boarding schools in the UK coming on board. For a while at least we could all escape the inevitable gloom of facing yet another term in school while awkwardly polishing our new skills with the opposite sex! The night droned on as we crossed the Atlantic. Crossings later not permitting sleep being so engrossed in the exciting art of passion hidden under a blanket with some lovely schoolgirl just as eager to explore the new game of love. As if on cue the cabin lights would be dimmed and my young traveling companion snuggled next to me eager as I experience the first kiss. On occasion the stewardess would walk the aisle having us feign sleep as she came near and exchanged addresses promising to write often. The letters did arrive to the catcalls of jealous schoolmates as they caught of whiff of perfumed paper and feminine handwriting. We never managed to meet up again during the holiday breaks. One later flight coincidentally had me seated next to my first girlfriend's best friend in Bermuda. One thing led to another and when the lights lowered high above the Atlantic the ritual began anew bringing more letters of young romance thankfully providing greater admiration from schoolmates. The eastern sky lightened as we reached the Azores. On through Lisbon then Madrid and northward toward Paris, where the first return journey ended with the familiar airline jargon, 'bumped'. I was so close to making it in one go. Alas, in France I was to stay the night for some full-paying passenger to have my seat. The ground crew escorted me to the street outside to the ground transportation. Car models I had never seen before sped through the rain soaked streets of Paris. The crew giving the French cabbie an address instructing I am brought back here in the morning for another flight in to London Airport. Again, I was suddenly alone whizzing through the French streets in some strange vehicle by a driver who does not speak to me. The evening of the second day crossing of the Atlantic was already approaching with my grandparents notified that their grandson was staying in a hotel downtown Paris. The taxi entered a side street and the car door was open for me to vacate. 'Merci beaucoup' I tried grandmother's French lessons. The cabbie lifted his arm in acknowledgement.

This hotel was definitely down there in the star value. Two stars on the brochure would have been generous. The front desk said something to me in a very broken English and handed me a key pointing to the staircase. I had to match the number to the amount of floors I went up and navigate various narrow seedy hallways to see which door matched my key. The room was minute, and the mattress so soft one nearly touched the floor with its corroded metal frame creaking with every movement. One bare light bulb suspended from the ceiling swinging from a loose brown lamp cord illuminated the drab peeling wallpapered room. It was raining outside and the streets below were soaked and dark. Neon signs reflected in the wetness. The musty stale smell filled the little hotel room; no Eiffel

Tower to be seen from this view and nothing offered to eat. I could do little else but lay down until the urge for a bathroom visit. No toilet in this single room, no choice but to explore the corridor outside. Turning the loose door handle the old corroded hinges creaked loudly as I ventured down the long poorly lit hallway with the same musty atmosphere of faded paint; finding a door open with what looked like a toilet. It was an elevated rectangular structure of tile with a hole in the centre and wooden seat. Dare I peek in? There was no water; just a decorative tile bottom slightly sloped downward toward a dark gaping hole. A chain hung alongside all the way to the ceiling with what appeared to be a water tank. I had never seen anything like it before. A practice manoeuvre was called for.

'Mon Dieu!' I muttered in practiced French. 'I had heard these Frenchies had a contraption that washed your arse, a bidet I think but alas, none here.' Venturing back to my room I lay there for hours trying to breathe quietly, noting each creak of the floorboards outside in the hallway; frightening, no place for a twelve-year-old on his own.

The antique telephone across the room suddenly made some really strange noise making me jump. I had dozed. Picking up the receiver and said in my best French, 'Ello?' Nothing there. It made another noise and again I answered to silence. I looked at my watch, it's an alarm, idiot! Bolting downstairs, the male receptionist pointed to the taxi waiting outside. I had made it out alive and dear God I was so hungry!

My baggage was re-tagged 'LAP' for London Airport and we flew back to the overcast grey of England. Descending through the endless gloom was really depressing after spending the last eight weeks under power blue skies. Streaks of rainwater crawled diagonally across the airliner window. The Connie broke out of the clouds barely a thousand feet off the ground. It was raining hard. The roads underneath us were soaked and congested with traffic. Even in daylight all the miniature looking cars had their lights on. Everything was very drab and colourless in the English morning.

It was 1953 when young Queen Elizabeth II laid the first ceremonial slab of concrete to build the modern runway at London Airport, also opening the first Terminal Building called 'Europa' known today as Terminal 2. In those early years, it was a busy place catering to some fourteen million passengers a year. Today that figure is closer to sixty-seven million!

British Overseas Airways Corporation or as it was affectionately called by aircrews as 'better on a camel' was founded in November of 1939 and operated several different aircraft of which were Flying Boats, amphibious aircraft that had routes down to the River Nile in North Africa where they would land on the water in transit to East Africa and down to Johannesburg in South Africa. In 1952 they were the first airline to introduce jets to their fleet of airliners with the de Havilland Comet.

Tragedy struck four times with the Comet suffering metal fatigue through constant pressurisation changes, grounded the fleet. In 1956 BOAC ordered fifteen Boeing 707 Jet Airliners, which entered service just after my first Atlantic crossing in a Super Connie. My winter holiday to Nassau was to be in one of these new airliners. Everything about air travel was about to change. Now I could be home within nine hours on a direct flight from London to Nassau with one stop in Bermuda. In the late 60s, BOAC actually was making profit but British Parliament was not having credit given to the American Boeing airliner and pressured to purchase British Vickers VC10, its four engines mounted on the rear section of the fuselage, making the ride I would experience very quiet and comfortable. However, BOAC did not fare so well with this airliner due to operating costs and in 1974 merged with British European Airways becoming the re-known British Airways ironically the largest Boeing customer outside the United States!

I passed through British Immigration where they commented on my tan. Through the cues I could see Jorge Dean who was very glad to see me asking in his frightfully British accent,

'How was my time in Nassow?' his accent so thick at times I wanted to correct him when he mentioned, 'Me-army,' – no sir, that's 'My-am-ee!'

Jorge had spent years of his life working for the British Civil Service in both London, where I believe he had met Edna Harding, living later in Madrid. They were quite the couple and definitely part of the foundation of the British Empire. They did visit the Bahamas once while I was at school in those early days and both fell very much in love with the islands, especially the fresh conch! On one of my early trips back to England I would carry a sealed container of fresh conch salad. By the time it reached Sussex it had marinated perfectly in that lime-juice and bird pepper. I have the old faded photograph of Jorge giving the thumbs up sign at his prize gift!

1960 let me watch young John Kennedy debate Richard Nixon on the first political debate aired on American television, featuring premier shows of *Danger Man* and *The Andy Griffith Show* with that very young boy actor, Ron Howard, who later made quite a name for himself as an actor on *Happy Days* and eventually film director; a field that later on I would have the pleasure of getting some experience in my own smaller way. In England, the first showing of *Coronation Street* on ITV, a program I couldn't tolerate; the damned opening music enough to drive me from the room; returning to England fifty years later I was horrified to hear that dreadful music still on air, although with a new appreciation for the country of my birth, I still feel very foreign here. In the Bahamas, I was obliged on occasion, through my parent's associates and friends, to blend in to what was the 'expatriate circles'. Groups of Brits from different walks of life meeting in regular local hangouts such as Ben Warrys' Pub on Parliament Street where almost every lunchtime they congregated to read their airmail edition of English newspapers, talking consistently about 'this bloody place' and 'we can't wait to go home'. My distaste for expatriate countrymen grew as I witnessed their poor attitude and behaviour abroad; we knew where they all were actually from in the UK and the backgrounds each carried to their oversees posting. History fortunately was to take an interesting turn in the seventies, with me quietly watching from the side-lines, just about all of them *having* to pack their bags and go home: 'good-riddance'. To this day there are the rare stragglers that managed to stay, through good luck, marriage, or a status that was given to them when they were younger called 'Belongers', a kind of Permanent Residency with the right to work but not to vote; a status my father refused to sign us up for because a clause in application stated, 'that you had no intention of living anywhere else'; little did we know he had plans of his own, withheld until ready? Some expats came more recently when Independence was granted in 1973 and with some exceptions, the Brits I have had exposure to, seem to still have the same old ways about them when it comes to 'home'. I feel no connection to whatsoever to the UK; with exception to some good food and a few friendly couples who shared the genuine love of the islands, sticking it out to stay as we did. The real meaningful connections came mostly with the true Bahamians. Colour of skin or walk of life made no scrap of difference. Bahamians were warm and generous people to us. It was the first place on the planet I had been where a total stranger would bid you 'good morning' as they passed you in the street. My mother became close friends with Canadian nurse Ruth Pritchard living in front of our apartment in an old Bahamian wooden house on the corner of William and Bay Street, introducing my mother to other Bahamian ladies that would meet weekly for coffee in the small roomed home. Mrs Dorothy Dupuch would often have her son Peter with her and we got to know each other well. Later in years we smiled one day walking across the ramp at the airport. 'We had no idea back then we would be in the same industry, eh Peter?' I called out. Helen Phillips was a regular visitor and I met Larry, her son slightly older than Brian and myself. His father, Lou Phillips, was in the publishing business and soon Larry was inviting us to join him on his new Donzi given by his Dad, for rides through the canal on Hog Island. Adventures in the next few years of Bahama holidays often were involved with these three boys.

With exposure to different nationalities I developed an international accent similar to my father. Influenced from all those years at school constantly exposed to vastly different cultures and dialects along with the teachings of my grandparents. Americans and Canadians thought I was possibly Australian or South African. My youth had cheated me from appreciating the beautiful side of England. Years later I would learn about my place of birth and enjoy what England had to offer appreciating the privilege of dual citizenship. It would be much warmer in the UK than I remembered. Looking back there were some great lessons from the grandparents, even to the very small things, such as how to lay a set of silverware at the dining table, how to hold your fork correctly, how to sit up straight, and heaven forbid you did something wrong such as shovelling ones' peas off the plate instead of pushing them onto the fork correctly with a knife. One was always firmly corrected at the dinner table. 'The Duke of Edinburgh would never do that!' grandmother would speak sternly.

We had arrived in the islands with a Bahamian surname funnily enough. The Harding's and Deans are known residents of Long Island in the southern Bahamas and their generations go back to the beginnings of island history as many of the established families in the country. Locals joked with me about my being a 'Long Islander without the freckles'. Even the Immigration Department in those early days, who knew us so well with the airline, made light of the fact that we 'shouldn't be applying for Work Permits being already Bahamians from further south!' Long Island actually came back in to my life later both in the eighties and again in the nineties giving me special rewards told later on. Life in the islands is very intertwined, where people and places cross paths all the time. Little wonder in later years the Ministry of Tourism of Stafford Sands era introduced the Out-Islands, 'playground of the western world' now be referred to as the Family Islands. This lasted many years before the old title slipped back in to our comfort zone knowing them yet again as pronounced originally. They liked to be separate from the madness of Nassau and Freeport; they have a lifestyle and time zone all of their own, going back in time fifty years or more suited those of us who visit them.

The 1960s were dramatic times with huge changes all over the world. At the beginning of the decade in January of 1960 the State of Emergency in Kenya was finally lifted ending the 1952 Mau Mau uprising. East Africa and I were to cross paths ten years or more from now and affect my life forever. Kenya's history, even back then, was meaningful seeing the direction in which the nation was heading. Over in this Western world a young US Senator called John Kennedy declared his candidacy for the Democratic Presidency while a fairly well known singer called Elvis Presley returned from Germany after a two-year military duty. In April, the Best Picture was awarded to *Ben Hur* with Charlton Heston starring. The United States launched a rocket with TIROS-1 being the first weather satellite in space. World events so close to the Bahamas were unfolding rapidly during these times. Just ninety miles off the most southern Bahamas lay the beautiful island of Cuba, its young dictator leader, Fidel Castro, had just been excommunicated by the Pope; flying near outer space an American U2 spy plane taking photographs of the secret military activity taking place on the island nation, when the Soviets shot it down and captured pilot Captain Gary Powers on May 1. On this particular day, several major events were also taking place that struck a chord of world history. Russia launched the Sputnik 4 satellite when the USS Triton Submarine completed the worlds' first underwater circumnavigation of the earth. While we were playing in the sunshine on some of the most beautiful beaches on the planet four members of Israel's Mossad abducted, in a brilliant plan, one of the planets worst Nazi war criminals out of Buenos Aires, taking Adolf Eichmann back to Tel Aviv for trial where he was later hanged two years later.

Passing the Bahamas were a flood of Cuban refugees headed for South Florida, estimated near 1000 a week. President Dwight D. Eisenhower authorised a million-dollar relief fund for their aid and settlement. While I was flying out to the Bahamas for the first time in July a British sailor named Francis Chichester sailed solo across the Atlantic in a record forty days and as I returned to school in September a young American boxer called Cassius Clay won the Gold Medal at the Summer Olympics. Toward the end of the year, on November 8, John Kennedy was elected the youngest president of the United States. The year ended with an air disaster over Staten Island, New York, a United Airlines DC-8 colliding with a similar airliner that I had just flown in, a TWA Super Constellation, taking all 128 lives, plus six on the ground.

That first winter term on the Isle of Wight was a tough one. Summertime had allowed us to at least enjoy the outdoors. Swimming was almost acceptable until the first exposure to Bahamian waters! As cold as it was in the English pool, I still became a member of the school swim team. Sailing in the Solent offered good experiences, especially one particular day hearing a strange loud noise coming round the corner from East Cowes. We let the sail of our Snipe luff in the wind to witness something never seen before.

The huge north facing hangar and ramp of Saunders Row was clearly visible from our vantage point. Here, some years earlier, in the late fifties, the large flying boats came for maintenance. They would land in the water and climb up the concrete ramp to the hangar building. This day was something out of a science fiction film. A fairly small contraption roared out of the hangar looking like some homemade flying saucer, the top half consisted of metal tubing and decking, the centre a mounted engine with a wide opening on the top as if a giant fan. The lower half some kind of black skirt around the circumference of what resembled a boat. Dust and debris flew around this weird looking machine and without warning started down the ramp toward the water. Hundreds of people stopped what they were doing and watched the machine enter the water not appearing to sink at all. Huge plumes of white spray flew all around the machine as it moved across the surface of the water towards us. We were watching the world's first hovercraft, the SRN1. We drifted in the Solent allowing the currents take our little sailboat sideways watching spellbound as this new invention flying across the grey waters. Behind the hovercraft a huge Cunard Lines ocean liner, I suspect the *Queen Elizabeth*, sailed in opposite direction entering the approach to Southampton Harbour: a picture to remember. This was the first in a series of Hovercraft that Saunders Row produced where in 1962 they launched the SRN2, displacing twenty-seven tons carrying forty-eight passengers back and forth between the mainland hamlet of Eastney in Portsmouth to Ryde seen from our school. The hovercraft carried over 30,000 passengers before the end of this era and new machines came forth for marine transport use.

Arriving at Grey Thatch gave me chance to acclimatise again. Cooler days and heavier clothing became the norm. The train ride back to Portsmouth was dreary and the English summer was fading very quickly. Brisk winds brought darkening skies signaling winter would be here shortly, a far cry from my Bahamian experience. Low-pressure areas came across the southwest of England bringing chill air to roar up the Solent, bending the huge trees in front of Nubia House. The seas turned angry and white caps raced toward Portsmouth in the west wind that approached. The ferry ride back across to Ryde quite different from two months ago. Isolation seemed even more intense. Days and weeks of school blended as they slipped by ever so more slowly than days spent gliding over warm clear waters and fun in the islands. I was nodding off asleep in class with the boredom of retired Colonel Ilton who taught geography, a heavy pipe smoker often having brown saliva seeping from the corners of his mouth and on to the desk in front of us. We called him 'Slobber' wincing, as his foul breath wafted over those he was closest to, displaying the row of crooked stained teeth and dried cracking lips. Then there was Mathematics. Here I was a lost soul. A huge man wearing black horn-rimmed glasses with thick coke-bottle lenses, our teacher called Mr. Wallace, who sucked air in abnormally loudly with every breath he took, to then expel a torrent of information that was complete nonsense to me. He wrote so fast and hard on the blackboard where many times the chalk splintered into pieces causing us all to snicker with delight. I was dyslexic with numbers and soon had to deal without math, my goal of veterinary college was going to be but a pipe dream. Poor old Wallace finally gave in, after a year or two of mutual torture, allowed me to be the first student in school history to drop out of his class. I smile today at a social media posting exclaiming 'another day I did not use algebra!' Later in life I realised the teaching methods in those days were so set in stone any student who did not have an immediate grasp was to be left behind. Teaching techniques were poor at best, boring and unimaginative. Special tutoring was unheard of, offering no way to catch up with the other students. You were expected to absorb all the presented information then pass final exams at the end of every term.

The end of term report was more often demeaning to one's character or ability. Pass and you moved on, fail and that was the end of the road. I discovered later when something of real interest came along involving mathematics, as with all subjects, comprehension came quite easily. I could calculate any decompression chart in the underwater world along with distance and bearing to stations in the world of flying!

So too was Geography. The Colonel was hopeless. Being a young world traveller the world and its countries fascinated me; so many fabulous academic subjects, yet such incredibly poor presentation. School was a joke. The curriculum so awful reflecting back brings a mere shake of the head. Mr. Victor Flemming, an accomplished violinist, grey bushy unkempt hair, huge overgrown eyebrows and uncontrolled sideburns resembling some acutely mad scientist, taught us music. His passion for the Classical era flowed all over us. We would be seated in his class having to listen to the heaviest of Bach or Beethoven as he sat at the head of the class, waving his imaginary baton, eyes closed in rapture, conducting the scratchy music crawling out of his antique record player whizzing around at 78 rpm. If he ever dropped a record we would hoot with laughter as the LP shattered on the floor. Gramophone records did not bend in those days so well. We were buying the new vinyl 45 rpm records that played the latest rock and roll. He must have known eventually the classics actually would ingrain appreciation. He would be proud at my enjoyment of Ravel's *Bolero* and love of Beethoven's *Ode to Joy*. Music was so diverse in the sixties with rock and roll we played as teenagers had our parents shake their heads in disbelief. They don't make bands like the Rolling Stones or Fleetwood Mac any more, it's hard these days to discover a comparable Cat Stevens or Bob Dylan. Now we are swamped with repetitious 'Rap-Crap' as the old scholars' call it. Later in the seventies I remember listening to my modern stereo system, proudly purchased from my first girlfriend's father; some of the classics that would actually make the hair on your neck stand up. So Flemming did all right in the end. My friend Grahams' year-end report did not reflect well for him back then, reading, 'Has not come to grips with this subject yet!'

1961 saw really interesting world events capture those of us interested in flying. On January 20 we witnessed on television the Inauguration Speech from the newly elected President Kennedy in the United States. The day was clear and very cold in Washington, DC. President Kennedy's breath could be seen with every word he spoke in the frigid air. The speech was riveting and America was looking to their youngest elected leader for a new hope and direction. He had the charm, charisma and a great sense of humour that captivated every audience. He was different from every other recent president. His words echoed through time when he said, 'Ask not what your country can do for you, ask what you can do for your country.' Thousands upon thousands erupted in applause that January day. He spoke of 'Taking a man to the moon and back again.'

Unheard of, as no one had even been in space yet. The president would visit the Bahamas within about a year from now; the Russians had put up Sputnik in the late fifties and various animals later in orbit, a new frontier just around the corner. This year all would change on April 12 with a young Russian Cosmonaut named Yuri Gagarin blasting off the earth's surface in a Vostok 1 rocket to be the first man in space. He was third of four children and parents of very modest means. His Math and Science teachers had flown in the Soviet Air Force planting the seed for him to become an aviator. He joined the local Aero Club and learned to fly where in 1955 entered the Military Flight Academy for fighter training. Standing only five feet two inches high gave him a great advantage fitting into the small cockpits of fighter aircraft. In 1957 he was awarded his Wings from the Air Force flying a MiG-15. Three years later because of his abilities and size he became one of nineteen pilots chosen for the Russian Space Program. On April 12 1961 became the first man in to orbit. In space, he could be heard singing tunes that his mother had taught him. On his safe return to Earth he was an instant hero in the Soviet Union. He became a backup pilot for the Soyuz Program but the Russian Government kept him away from flying best they could, not wanting to lose a national hero. He did however become the backup pilot for the Commander of the first Soyuz flight, which ended in a fatal crash. Colonel Gagarin was protectively banned from space flight but trained and requalified as a fighter pilot. On March 27 1968, along with his flight instructor, on a routine flight aboard a MiG 15 entered an irrecoverable spin where both pilots lost their lives in the ensuing crash. Yuri Gagarin was buried in the walls of the Kremlin.

Living in Sussex part of the year gave me exposure to some unique experiences that would intertwine with my home in the Bahamas. It became commonplace as time travelled by that my life and experiences always rotated back to my 'islands in the sun'. Whether I was in the underwater world, shooting films for television or flying airplanes, the Bahamas became the nucleus. Those early years I was exposed to the exciting world of live auto racing. A short walk through the garden of Grey Thatch, northward toward the orchard, laid a small fishpond full of water lilies and goldfish. The pond shaded by a huge walnut tree and with the wind in a certain northerly direction one could clearly hear the whine of race car engines from the speedway at Goodwood in neighbouring East Sussex. Goodwood was the perimeter track of the old Royal Air Force base becoming famous in the fifties and sixties for its nine-hour endurance races. The races allowed me to see some of the world's finest drivers become legends in their own right, names such as Hawthorn, McLaren, Brabham, Hill and of course Moss.

The Bahamas in this era had a racetrack in Oakes Field, active as a private airfield hosting some of these same celebrities during Annual Speed Week here in Nassau. I was watching these famous drivers in England and later seeing their pictures on the wall inside the bar of 'Sun And…' restaurant in Nassau, years after my parents introduced me to fine dining just off Shirley Street owned by Pete Gardner. It was in this popular courtyard restaurant, once a private house, which all the celebrities from film and auto racing came to dine while staying in the Bahamian capital. Fate took turn for me in 1980 when I purchased a residence from Mr. Emmett Pritchard just around the corner from this landmark in Montague Heights with my workplace a mere block away at the water front marinas.

Goodwood Racetrack was where Sterling Moss ended his international racing career with a near fatal crash of his famous number seven Lotus on St. Mary's Corner. Back in 1960 he crashed at Spa breaking his back and there was no question his career was finished – in a coma and partially paralysed on his left side. To everyone's astonishment he was racing again in seven weeks. He recovered but retired the next year after sixty-six Grand Prix wins. Moss had a loyalty to British cars and quotes, 'Better to lose in a British car than win in a foreign one!'

The early 60s really were an exceptional time. Progress in space travel created rivalries intensifying with the Soviets pushing hard to maintain a lead, the United States beginning to play catch-up very quickly. Project Mercury was launching animals into space and JFK declared within the decade a man would step on the moon and return safely to Earth. On February 20, 1962 astronaut John Glen was picked from the Mercury 7 to climb inside *Friendship 7* and be the first American to orbit the Earth three times. Kennedy would not allow him to fly again quoting he was 'too valuable a hero'. Glen did however return to space on board a Space Shuttle in his 70s to be the oldest man in space. He died aged 95 as I finish this writing in December 2016.

Here in the Bahamas, Sir Stafford Sands who resided across from the Nassau Yacht Club on East Bay Street headed our Ministry of Tourism. His property known as 'Waterloo' would take on a whole new meaning in later years becoming a nightclub. The Bahamas were advertised as 'The Playground of the Western World' and Cable Beach was the place to be, a beach unmatched by any other on New Providence. From one end to the other an uninterrupted shoreline where the calm turquoise water lapped gently on to fine white powder sand. The two hotels, Nassau Beach and Emerald Beach, boasting its bright pink colour scheme, were set back off the high-water line. Elegant pool decks ended with stands of small beautifully shaped gold coconut trees and thatched huts where one could lie in the shade. Smartly dressed Bahamian waiters would serve the visitors exotic rum drinks and the smells of the outdoor bar-b-q cooking would drift down the beach. Guests could venture from one hotel and on to the grounds of the other unimpeded; one could enjoy a fabulous lunch on the deck of the Emerald Beach and then walk next door for cocktails in The Out-Island Bar inside the Nassau Beach lobby. This was the place to be on a weekend evening where the intoxicating pulse of the merengue would seep in to your veins and dancing to the wee hours became ritual.

During the early part of the year school on the Isle of Wight became drudgery and we always counted off the days to take that drive to London Airport. In February this year The Beatles performed for the first time in the Cavern Club, JFK had formed the Peace Corps and by April 17 the Bay of Pigs invasion to topple Castro in Cuba began, only to fail miserably two days later. Alan Shepherd launched into space in May, while on my way back for the second summer in Nassau the Americans lunched Gus Grissom aboard 'Liberty Bell 7' to be the second man in space splashing down, only to survive having his hatch open prematurely and sink the capsule. Grissom tragically died later with his two fellow astronauts in a terrible fire on the ground during the Gemini program in January 1967.

After my first Atlantic crossing in the droning propeller plane, BOAC started flying a fleet of Boeing 707s. Vacation travel would forever change. I would leave London Airport and be in Nassau near nine hours later with the one stop in Bermuda, arriving home drove the coast road through town to a new location on William Street just off East Bay Street near the Pilot House Hotel. The roads were being repaved at last. The apartment my mother had found through her new job with a Bahamian Realty company owned by Basil McKinney and Bill Turtle. The relatively new two-storey building housed a couple downstairs, an eye doctor by the name of Tom Hall and their young son, Randy, while we lived upstairs enjoying a balcony overlooking Nassau Yacht Haven docks. We could also see Potters Cay hosting the Out-Island freight boats tied up to the wharf with Hog Island lying behind to the North. The two-bedroom apartment had a cathedral ceiling belonging to Cyril Lightbourn and his new wife Bessie. While renting this location there would be good years spent here with life taking uncountable turns. Living in William Street would lead me to new destinations and people that would steer my life.

My mother now working downtown each day changed my vacation routine. I was introduced to the neighbours' son Brian, within a year or two in age of me attending St. Andrews School here in Nassau. Brian's father owned a small wholesale grocery in Palmdale and religiously brought home all the paperwork every day to sit with a TV tray in front of the television and work trying to watch Chet Huntley's Channel 7 Miami news on the black and white television. The signal still so poor we could only see through the snow and noise for only a few seconds at a time. Brian would ask me to join him across the street at his grandparents' house to watch *Star Trek* when it first debuted as a TV serial. The double stack antenna grandpa had installed did far better allowing us to actually follow the story becoming devote 'Trekkies'. We became holiday friends and spent many days together exploring the waterfront and local docks learning how to fish with hand lines and spin for shad fish or cast for mullet. Across the road on the waterfront a row of young palm trees so low to the ground we could pick the coconuts when they ripened. Off this shore a single dock ran out in to the water belonging to Eddie Ballard, a Bahamas Airways captain, whose wife 'Buzzy' – from her air force flying career – and daughter Frannie, would intertwine with ours through the history of this story. Buzzy, otherwise known as Lady Lampton, had probably flown every fighter and bomber in the British Airforce and I privileged to have seen the massive collection of logbooks to prove it!

Brian had befriended Dick Slee's son Prescott just a few doors to the east of where we lived. The General Manager of The Pilot House Club said we boys could all use the hotel facilities and pool anytime we wanted opening a whole new world for us. It was here that I would spend some time with other Bahamas Airways crews, looked after by chief stewardess Janet Pyfrom and meet the dive crew that worked across the street with Underwater Tours. The Pilot House Bar in those days a favourite watering hole for this part of the island.

In December of 1962 the Bahamas hosted the British Prime Minister, Harold Macmillan and the young American President Kennedy for four days of talks, ending with an interesting agreement. The United States would provide the United Kingdom with a supply of nuclear capable Polaris Missiles in return for a US Submarine Base in Holy Lock near Glasgow, Scotland. JFK, as he was fondly known, really was a man of the sea since childhood. He loved the Bahamas with its warm sailing waters and great fishing. Bahamians felt a real attachment for the young President and his portrait often seen hanging in many institutions where his presence had been felt.

I had no intention of writing each year's events, just occasional markers that we all will remember, but 1962 broke all the rules. This year saw many world events make a mark on most of us, some not so important maybe but certainly noteworthy! Early in the year the last of the French Foreign Legion left Algiers while the satellite Telstar sent the first television transmission across the Atlantic. It was amazing to comprehend that a picture signal barely able to crawl across 186 miles between Miami and Nassau could now rocket into the heavens and land on the other side of the Atlantic almost instantly. A new rock band called The Rolling Stones made their debut on July 12 in London's Marquee Club, while in South Africa the government arrested Nelson Mandela. Marilyn Monroe died of a drug overdose; her death remaining a mystery full of political intrigue intertwined with the Kennedy's for decades. The Beatles fire their drummer and replace him with a young lad called Ringo Starr, while John Lennon secretly marries Cynthia Powell. In the Caribbean, Jamaica, Trinidad and Tobago gain their Independence from Great Britain while a month later in September the Soviet Union is sending arms to Cuba.

A young Johnny Carson takes host of the *Tonight Show* while *Who's Afraid of Virginia Woolf* opens on Broadway. Nineteen-sixty-two bombarded us with such diverse events it was hard to imagine what possible outcome was to befall us. We watched the United States face off with Castro's Cuba, now holding hands with the Soviet Union. There is talk of an imminent Atomic War where television infomercials of the time demonstrate how children at school should take cover under their school desks! Our cinematic entertainment debuts a new character we will love watching for decades called James Bond. Author Ian Fleming's *Dr No* launches the career of actor Sean Connery who will buy a home on the Lyford Cay Golf Course, after loving his time on location shooting *Thunderball* filmed throughout the Bahamas in 1965.

American underworld figures of eras past are still making headlines, with names such as Meyer Lansky who adorned Bahamian history in earlier decades of the Harry Oakes era. Lucky Luciano dies of a 'heart attack' while in a meeting with Hollywood producers while noticeable gunmen and gangster lieutenants are suddenly disappearing. The Italians have their share of the news and mobsters when Nations Oil Companies' president, Enrico Mattei, dies in a jet plane crash near a small village. He had negotiated concessions in the Middle East and significant trade agreements with Russia. Some Mafia turncoats let out the agreement to their counterparts La Cosa Nostra resulting with some 'foreigner' eliminating

Mattei. Evidence at the crash site was destroyed with flight instruments placed in acid!

In Rome, the Pope excommunicates Fidel Castro while the Mona Lisa makes her first viewing in the United States. Ranger 3 launched earlier to study the moon, missing its target by 22,000 miles. General aviation suffers two loses of Boeing 707s that year with Air France over shooting the runway at Orly, Paris, killing all on board except two flight attendants and an American Airlines is lost on take-off from New York International after losing its rudder.

On October 28 with the real threat of nuclear war close at hand, Nikita Khrushchev announces the removal of missiles from the island of Cuba in reaction to President Kennedy's tenacious opposition. Here in the Bahamas we sighed with relief, located a mere ninety miles away from this strong Soviet influence. After the Russians back down we learn JFK had made a secret deal to remove missiles from Turkey to appease his Russian counterpart. The next month the weapons are dismantled and the quarantine of the island ended. The year was an amazing ride ending with a famous movie having its premier in London with Peter O'Toole starring in *Lawrence of Arabia*, co-starring Omar Sharif who recently died while I edit this in 2015. Some familiar names are born this year putting a fun perspective on this timeline; Sheryl Crow, Jon Bon-Jovi, Matthew Broderick, Tom Cruise, Wesley Snipes, Roger Clemmens, Demi Moore, who I would meet on a Bahama Out-Island later, and Jeff Probst, later to host the popular reality television series *Survivor*; a new wave of television coming to light.

Chapter 6
Pilot House to Powerboats

The Bahamas certainly opened some interesting doors for a young lad fresh out of a sheltered English life. It is an ordinary scene here in the tropics for two boys to sit on a marina dock surrounded by beautiful yachts and glamorous people while throwing a hand line into the crystal-clear water to catch baitfish. This is what we did on holidays during school breaks. While parents were working, we lived our little adventures on a daily basis. The view from our William Street patio displayed a row of evenly spaced young coconut palms on the other side of Bay Street next to the water's edge. As children, we could stand and pick their ripe fruits chopping them open with machetes to eat the soft jelly inside and drink the sweet water. It would be impossible now as the trees tower overhead by more than twenty feet, alas, some succumbed to the destruction of Hurricane Matthew. Beyond lay the grey weathered wooden docks of the Nassau Yacht Haven where I gaze at legendary sailboats *Traveler ll* and the 80-foot ketch *Bahama Alpha.* I became familiar with their masters Capt. Art Crimmins, Capt. Lou Kennedy and fishing fleet Captains Milton Pierce and Arthur Moxey. To the west, anchored in the shallows, a few Bahamian and Haitian sloops protected from the northerly winds by the small island of Potters Cay. After the summer squalls the sloops would hoist their mainsails, hanging limp to dry and steam in the hot summer sun. On the other side of the cay a fast-moving body of water flushed through Nassau Harbour, exiting into the open ocean past the lighthouse built back in 1817 on the western tip of Hog Island. Off the eastern end of Potters Cay protruded a small sharp rock, a marker pole warning its precarious position. The ebbing tides so fierce often lapping in a rage of white caps as the high water beat against the strong easterly winds.

As young boys we walked the edge of the rocky shoreline towards East Bay Shopping Centre passing Toogood's Photography store on the opposing corner of William Street. Stanley Toogood, was a very tall, slim and quiet-spoken man, one of Nassau's well respected photographers along with his two sons Michael and Andrew, often seen in the shop; the former taking the helm of his father's business in years to come. Conch boats floated within a few yards of the road on the spring high tide where on the low water their exposed hulls could be easily worked on; held in place with long anchor lines to the shore and a line tied to the mast tip heeling the boat over on one side. We would sit and talk with the old fishermen who heated black pitch in large tin cans over a wood fire sending soft spirals of light blue smoke out of the coral rock. The fishermen skilfully mixed caulking wool to the steaming hot mixture, tapping lengths with a wooden mallet and old blunt chisel between the worn planking; the mixture drying hard sealing the wood against leakage. The summer sun beat down on their torn faded straw hats; a clay pipe often hung out of the corner of their mouths as the familiar tapping of the mallet could be heard from our apartment. The old men smiled as they watched us walk the shoreline with thin monofilament fishing lines equipped with a wine bottle cork near the end sporting a small barbed hook. They nodded approval when we took a piece of white bread out of our pockets, rolling it into a tight ball, recognising these two boys knew how to catch the shy mullet schooling in the warm shallow water. It took me a few tries before Brian corrected my technique. 'Don't yuck the line so hard when he strikes, let him run a bit first!'

We would venture over to Potters Cay where on the rocky shore facing Hog Island saw a crowd gathering, some pointing with excitement as one could see way out past the lighthouse, a white plume of water racing toward us, then another and another. People were lined on the outer docks of the Yacht Haven with many sitting in boats anchored in the harbour. I had never seen boats move that fast before and within seconds the first came screaming past us, with the name *Moppie* on the side. This was my first Miami to Nassau Powerboat Race, which had first run back in 1956. The crowd applauded and cheered as they streamed past the finish line of the marina and out to Montagu Bay, finally slowing to idle back to the Yacht Haven. Brian and I walked the docks for hours looking at the new race boats; their hatches opened displaying powerful engines while crews, dressed in race suits, being interviewed by television and radio reporters. Cameras clicked the festivity and I was hooked to the sport having no clue I would participate one day!

Powerboat racing was first recognised in 1904 in the southeast of England with a race to Calais in France, while the first race in the United States completed in 1911. When I arrived in the Bahamas, Don Aronow, a successful businessman in the New Jersey construction trade during the late-50s had moved to Miami in 1961 where a year later formed Formula Marine, selling later to be renamed Donzi Marine. By 1966 he started Magnum Marine to start racing the world-famous boats he called 'Cigarettes' in 1970. Aronow received orders for his race boats from all over the world from famous names including The Shah of Iran, Malcolm Forbes, George Bush Senior and fugitive financier Robert Vesco. History tied an interesting knot for a young follower of power-boat racing; not only did I end up working for a man who owned a race boat but actually had the opportunity to crew aboard a race in Nassau fulfilling a boyhood fantasy.

Don Aronow was a name that became synonymous in his field along with Richard Bertram who I watched race *Moppie* across that finish line that beautiful Bahama day, taking exactly eight hours from Miami. Bertram, a competitive sailor, once in Newport for the America's Cup trials, owned a large Miami-based yacht brokerage firm started in 1947 in a one-room office. Four days of winds blowing steadily between fifteen and twenty-five knots churned the water before the 1960 Miami-Nassau race, creating ideal conditions for these hard core competitors and their new 'Deep-V' hull designs. Mr. Aronow designed and built his famous *Blue Thunder*, a 39-foot catamaran for the US Customs Service, trying to combat the drug smuggling boats that were originally designed for racing. Illegal drugs were very big business in those days, as they still are, shipped from Columbia, South America, through the Caribbean, Central America and then Mexico. Trafficking came north through many of the Bahamas into the United States much of the contraband originating from Carlos Lehder's operation on Norman's Cay. The boat of choice for the cocaine runners being Aronow's' Cigarette, and Blue Thunder was the only boat that could catch them. This did not sit well with the cartel, the mystery unravelling on February 3 1987 when a car pulled alongside Aronow's vehicle on the very Miami Street where his boat companies were, and shot him to death. He had won over 350 offshore races in his career as a boat designer and racer.

The world of powerboat racing came to the Bahamas as an annual event with the Miami to Nassau Race. The famous, gruelling Bahamas 500 soon followed where the navigator became as important a position as the driver having to find small checkpoints in the open ocean. I learned my boss Gardner Young was navigating for owner Juan Fernandez while based at the Nassau Yacht Haven. Boats became larger and more powerful where the 1980s introduced the Super Boat Era; boats of 1000-cubic-inch engines designed with two or three power-plants over forty-five feet long with F 16 cockpit canopies for the crew's protection! The roar of immense power could be heard for miles and the crowd draw increased among the local Bahamians. Thousands of people aligned Nassau Harbour and Paradise Island shoreline, from the harbour entrance downtown to the far ends of Montagu Bay lying to the east. Hog Island had been renamed Paradise Island having a bridge constructed in 1965 spanning Potters Cay where spectators lined both sides of the 72-foot span to watch the fast monsters roar underneath. Boats bearing names such as *Nuff Respect* would draw a cry of approval from fans as huge plumes of white spray rocketed outward from its stern. The harbour was strewn with spectators in pleasure craft of all sizes some being local volunteers for emergency services that might be required should something go wrong in the busy waters off New Providence. Helicopters from Florida news stations roared overhead turning suddenly on their own axis to capture the race below. A fire erupted from one of the huge race boats in Montagu Bay nearer to Paradise Island. Flames engulfing the boat putting crew in dire trouble. A local volunteer boat raced to assist fearing a pending explosion from the very volatile fuels on board. The race boat crew abandoned ship into the water seeking refuge while the flaming hull drifted perilously close to the island. Officials from here on decided the sport was becoming too dangerous for the spectators and the growing luxury properties and marinas on Paradise Island. The long-standing tradition of Powerboat Racing in the Bahamas ended that year.

Brian and I were often invited to ride in Larry's 19-foot Donzi water-skiing off Cabbage Beach; two miles of pure white sand with no visible development along the shoreline. In the centre, thick stands of casuarina pine trees lined the slight rise off the beach finding a lone grand house belonging to Huntington Hartford. Born 1911 in New York and heir to the Great Atlantic and Pacific Tea Company, in pre-early seventies the company already worth $2.6 billion. His lineage was successful in their own right with grandfather and uncles owning the A&P Supermarkets supporting over 16,000 stores considered the largest retail business in the world at that time. In 2007 alone, A&P's revenue was $6.9 billion. Mr. Hartford grew up in South Carolina owning properties all over the planet from Palm Beach, Newport, London, New York and the 150-acre farm in New Jersey. Hog Island would weave an interesting tale with all the personalities involved with Huntington Hartford and the Bahamas, people that my life would glance close by as I grew up that my family and friends knew well. Hartford's sister Josephine married Ivar Bryce a good friend of the famous writer Ian Fleming, creator of the James Bond character, choosing the character name from a book he possessed by an ornithologist of the same name! Josephine and her husband resided in Lyford Cay at the western end of New Providence and were the reason for Huntington's first arrival here in 1959. He purchased Hog Island from Axel Wenner-Gren the Swedish entrepreneur who died two years later in 1961, renaming his acquisition Paradise Island. The family threads woven through Bryce's niece marrying David Mountbatten, related to Lord Louis Mountbatten, uncle of Prince Charles, heir to the English throne. Hartford built what is now the original Ocean Club Hotel, later refurbished as The One and Only. Cloisters were transported and reconstructed on the harbour end of his property from unassembled stones of a fourteenth-century French Augustinian monastery that William Randolph Hearst had dismantled in 1920 and stored in a warehouse in Florida. He envisioned Paradise Island becoming the next Monte Carlo having succeeded in obtaining a Gambling License from the Bahamian Government.

In the early years Hartford was also a theatre producer with a work called *Does a Tiger Wear a Necktie* in 1969 starring an unknown actor called Al Pacino. Hartford tried to purchase RKO Pictures from another character whose name would later appear on the Paradise Island history books, Howard Hughes. In 1961 we would water ski along his Paradise Island beach he published in *Show* magazine. Hartford hired Palm Beach architect John Volk to build the Ocean Club, Cafe Martinique, Hurricane Hole Marina and The Golf Club hiring Gary Player as the first island Golf Pro along with Pancho Gonzalez as his Tennis Pro for the Ocean Club courts. I played many a game of tennis here in later years against a young Robin

Brownrigg, son of my mothers' friend Eddie, a real estate appraiser she knew well through business. I could hardly get a point off Robin who could manipulate the ball in to any square inch he wished.

Hartford opened Paradise Island in 1962 covered by both *Time* and *Newsweek* magazines. The original staff of the Ocean Club was taken from Eden Roc at Hotel Du Cap, a fabulous French villa in Antibes on the French Riviera. Opening night was grandiose with a firework display flown in from France. Huntington Hartford had another idea about obtaining oil from rock with interest in western Colorado forming the Oil Shale Corporation now owned by ConocoPhillips worth billions of dollars. In the 1960s Hartford was one of the world's wealthiest men.

In Palm Beach, Hartford met Jim Crosby at the Colony Club inviting him to be an investor of the Bahamian Island having secured a desirable gaming license in place. Crosby had a partner by the name of Jack Davis, a Harvard grad of 1949; the two men forming a company called Resorts International that would assist in the development of Paradise Island's future. Rumours flew wild from casino employees we knew well recommending we should all purchase stock. Profits later parlayed to secure a referendum that was passed in the United States allowing the first gambling institution in Atlantic City. Resorts International shares rocketed from between one and three dollars to $200, profiting $300 million in the first year of operation, becoming the only stock to ever make the front page of the *LA Times*. We all would have been quite wealthy having taken the chance and listened to the two croupiers, Peter Fisher and John Chester living downstairs both coincidentally sharing my birthday in March. We knew Mr. Davis well over the years through close friend and host of Resorts, Alan Hirschorn. Many evenings were spent as their guests on Paradise Island dining at the Cafe Martinique where 'Boy', the very gracious Maître's d, adopted my mother as 'Volkswagen' from the small yellow Golf she always parked illegally in front of the world-famous restaurant. We dined on the Martinique specialties, Caesar salad put artfully together at tableside and decadent Shrimp de Jonghe, recipes that were trade secret to the world with exception to Mary Harding. With her guidance and the culinary skills we honed the recipes to perfection. I inherited the nickname from Boy and his warm embrace and graciousness are still felt entering Luciano's Restaurant on East Bay Street.

The three young lads who water-skied off Cabbage Beach would make their way home by cutting through the ocean-side entrance of the canal that sliced Paradise Island in two. On the North face of the canal lay the dock for the Cafe Martinique restaurant with its large plain glass window overlooking the palm decorated patio and the canal exit way. One could come by boat in the moonlight and tie up to dine there. This small straight waterway ran under a small stone bridge near the harbour exit, a location becoming a well-known movie scene with the James Bond films featured here in the islands. The huge concrete buttresses on the ocean side were designed to throw aloft large rolling ocean swells that bombarded the canal entrance built by Axel Wenner-Gren, the Swede born in 1881 and lived to 1961, a fable amongst local Bahamians that he built the canal to hide German submarines. He was one of the worlds' wealthiest men during the 1930s, working for the Swedish lighting company Electrolux adapting their industrial vacuum cleaner for domestic use. He secured the contract to floodlight the grand opening ceremonies for the Panama Canal. By the early thirties he owned the company making famous its technology in refrigeration. Wenner-Gren owned newspapers, banks, and arms manufactures. He became friends with Herman Göring who was at the time married to a fellow Swede. Gren was convinced that he could avert a world war acting as liaison between the German Göring and both British and American governments; his efforts unsuccessful being considered a nuisance by all parties concerned. He retired to his large estate in the Bahamas befriending the Governor General, the Duke of Windsor who recently abdicated the throne of England; posted to the Colonies keeping him out of the limelight with his controversial American wife. In the early days, rumour of Wenner-Gren's friendship with Goring and suspected German sympathisers the Duke and Duchess of Windsor, led the United States and English governments to blacklist the Swede, enabling them to freeze his assets in Nassau. On the first day of World War Two, Wenner-Gren's yacht, the largest in existence named *The Southern Cross*, would arrive on scene to the sinking of the SS *Athenia* in the Atlantic saving over 300 survivors. The Swedish entrepreneur pursued his interest of monorail train systems trains, designing the first monorail for Disney in 1959 also involving him with designing the railways systems that would reach from California through Canada and Alaska aided with his new machine called a 'computer'.

Exploring the canal on Paradise Island was an adventure for us in those days. Cautiously navigating the winding channels walled on each side. Places where James Bond jumped into the water in the feature film *Thunderball*. We had to manoeuvre carefully not touching bottom with the propeller. On more reckless days with higher tides we would open the throttle of the boat rushing through at full speed, often one of us water skiing precariously close to the stonewalls trying to avoid a later unfortunate accident involving close friend Steve Roberts colliding with the bridge pilings in 1980! Once in the harbour we would race eastward toward the Nassau Yacht Haven and pass the *Tropic Rover*, the dark blue double hulls of the world's largest catamaran tall enough for 007 to race underneath in a small motor boat in 1965.

The casuarina trees leaned over the walls on both sides offering their shade to the water. A small beach offered a place to pull the boat up for a walk through the trees, either to the ocean side or deeper into the woods where tight clusters of palmettos and pines lead us toward Paradise Beach on the Northwest shoreline, the only Bahamian beach where patrons had to pay to enter only accessible by glass-bottom boat from downtown Nassau. In 1960 it was a spectacular place to be. Flat calm waters with a wide expanse of white powder sand stretched westward toward the lighthouse on the point entrance of Nassau Harbour. Small thatched cabanas with short gold and palm coconut trees lined the shoreline providing a perfect setting for film crews. One could swim here peacefully with only a passing fish to be as company. Later years showed the arrival of Club Med constructed half way along the beach providing a fascinating walk for teenage boys to nonchalantly observe the topless European ladies lying in the sand.

Paradise Beach became a local favourite and with new friends of my parents Angela and Eloy Roldan with son, Enrique. We would spend many fun days swimming together off this local hideaway. Eloy worked for Outboard Marine dealing with Evinrude and Johnson outboard boat engines. In later years we saw him on a regular basis across the street having bought and operating the Poop Deck Restaurant with two other partners.

My days were often spent walking a few yards eastward from William Street, passing Bahama Engines where the Ballard's lived upstairs toward the lobby of the Pilot House Hotel. With a pass from our manager friend we could walk through the bar to the small pool deck to flop into the ninety-degree water. Tall palm trees surrounded the pool patios and a Bahamian band would often be playing for the lunchtime crowd. Later in the day the crew of divers from across the street would meet here for a few beers joined by some of the pilots and crews from Bahamas Airways. One day my father joined us after work. Sitting in the Pilot House bar we saw two men enter from the street below, one was huge across the chest with a prominent jet-black goatee beard and crew cut hair whose voice carried easily through the room with his infectious laugh. The older of the two was taller and equally built with close shaven hair and notorious laugh. Both men were very tanned sporting Rolex dive watches and black speedo swimsuits under their white dive-company zipped jackets. Father introduced me as a twelve-year-old to Gardner Young and Charlie Badeau, owners of M/M Underwater Tours diving operation. Telling how his son loved the ocean and always showed fascination in the world underwater, of my watching the *Sea Hunt* series. Gardner interjected that it was he who had worked with Lloyd Bridges on the series shot here in Nassau; locations at Athol Island on the landing craft wreck hard aground submerged at the far end of the cay. He made an offer for me to come and work with them during my holidays. It was hard to contain the excitement with an introduction that would open amazing doors for me later.

'That would be really great Mr. Young, thanks'; dreams were in the making.

My father asked the two gentlemen a very pertinent question in regard to the new Boeing 707 airliners that were flying into Nassau International Airport.

'What if one had a serious problem coming in or out of here and ended up in the ocean? How would we be able to handle a rescue?' The two looked at each other admitting there was no organised body of people here that could be called upon. The only possible rescue could come from one of the visiting British or American Naval vessels in port docked on the opposite side of the island. The only other alternative would be an American ship perhaps working out of the Autec Base in the Tongue of the Ocean. Charlie looked at my father, agreeing that it may just be prudent to get something organised locally. In all appearances, it would have to be on a volunteer basis where local boats and personnel could offer their services. Both men knew iconic boaters such as Ben Astarita who would know what was needed planting the seed of Bahamas Air Sea Rescue that exists through today.

Chapter 7
Good Morning: Underwater!

Arriving on my first winter holiday after meeting with owners of Underwater Tours I was excited to walk across Bay Street to the corner office at the Yacht Haven building. A piece of worn dock piling stood outside with a hard-hat divers helmet perched on top. Charlie Badeau stood outside working on a Dacor Dart single hose regulator, part of the standard equipment he faithfully maintained.

'Good morning young Harding, how are you? Are you swimming with us today?' He smiled, showing that singular bottom tooth remaining in his mouth.

As I entered the office door Gardner was standing in the back of the small room and another very tall man with blonde crew-cut hair and familiar goatee beard. He looked a blonde version of Gardner, by the name of Ray Moore. A certified scuba instructor and ex ambulance driver from Baltimore and the first man hired by Gardner in 1960 after arriving in Nassau on a diving holiday. He sported the familiar Rolex dive-watch while the other wrist a large gold ID bracelet with the initials R.A.M in large letters. The phone had just rung and Ray answered,

'Good Morning, Underwater.'

I thought that was a unique greeting. He acknowledged me with a smile. After hanging up the phone he stood to shake my hand with Gardner introducing. 'Ray, this is young Paul Harding and his Dad works for Bahamas Airways, he will be working with us during his holidays.' Gardner looked at me, 'Make yourself at home here and walk down the dock behind the building all the way to the end and take a left where you will find Captain Ronnie Kemp aboard the *Queen Anne's Revenge*. Tell him who you are and to fit you out with fins, mask and snorkel.' It was 9 am and departure would be in about half an hour.

Gardner Dutton Young was born in Fort Clinton, Ohio, while his father worked the Coast Guard Station. He earned one of the first degrees offered within the United States in Public Relations and Communications from Boston University with a Bachelor of Science offered under the G.I. Bill after leaving the Marines in 1948. In 1954, as a young American lifeguard working at the Lauderdale Beach Hotel in southern Florida, he found a job as mate on board the 56-foot Schooner *Windfall*, owned by renowned charter captain Bill Norton. The vessel made her living in the new and growing business of charter boats that worked up in Newport during warm summer months, sailing south to work the Bahamas during the winters. Bill was acquainted with Bruce Parker, a world-class water skier based in Nassau who ran Bruce Parker Enterprises, a water ski business at the British Colonial, Montagu, Nassau Beach and Emerald Beach hotels. Bruce had actually made a name for himself by water skiing between Miami and Nassau, all 186 miles of it. He was also a pilot with his own small two-seat floatplane. In 1958 after introduction Gardner Young could not resist the job offer allowing him to come back and live in the islands, he had come to love during his sailing days aboard *Windfall*. Parker's business was primarily water skiing, but he also had ventured in to the new tour business of Scuba diving. He needed a qualified dive and swim instructor to work the pool at the British Colonial and teach visitors how they could venture in to the beautiful world underwater.

Also sailing in to Nassau Harbour in the late 50s aboard a Windjammer Cruiser another American, born in New Jersey in 1909, a graduate of Rutgers and now retired Civil Engineer recently divorced and looking for adventure somewhere new. Charlie Badeau, a lover of the ocean soon to meet the dive operator at the British Colonial Hotel. Parker discovered that Charlie's knowledge of air compressors and everything mechanical was an invaluable find in the islands, he would no doubt prove to be the operations genius. Charlie invested in Bruce Parker Enterprises in 1959. Bruce had met a very petite American girl while in the States, also a water skier by profession, who had worked at Cyprus Gardens. Doris had long white blonde hair and tiny frame, often coming over to dazzle audiences at the Nassau Beach, Emerald Beach and Montagu Hotels in the ski shows she and Bruce would stage. She also dazzled Mr. Young, to later become his partner.

After Bruce's unexpected departure from the Bahamas shortly after, Gardner and Charlie partnered with local Bay Street travel agent Michael Maura, a charismatic Bahamian easily recognised wearing a familiar neck scarf with his open pink shirt, casual white slacks and Top-Sider shoes. After meeting Mike, as we all knew him, I often spied his lovely daughter Melissa along the eastern waterfront riding her horse. I would admire her free spirit and generous smile, although a few years younger than I, and often wondered how our different social circles kept us from meeting more closely, a wheel that would take near a decade to come around and an odyssey of living on such a small island. The heavyset ex-marine Gardner Young accompanied by Doris domiciled in the islands with Charlie and Michael, forming a new dive company called M/M Underwater Tours. Between them they had some basic dive equipment and a Hillman Minx used to transport tourists to the glass bottom Bahamian boats located at the Market Range downtown Nassau; the first boats used to take the visitors with their dive masters to the closest coral reefs within reach of Nassau Harbour.

In 1959, Gardner bought a 39-foot yawl named the *Merry Hell* in Fort Lauderdale. Working for Bruce Parker full time, he could not take leave to transport the boat back to Nassau so asked a favour of two friends over in Florida to do the delivery for him. Not particularly seasoned sailors, the two set off for the Bahamas not familiar with the powers of the Gulf Stream, the strong, warm body of water flowing northbound between the Bahamas and Florida on its long track across the Atlantic Ocean at about seven knots to end on the coastline of Cornwall in the UK. They aimed the *Merry Hell* for Gun Cay and found themselves over thirty miles off course quite lost, having to hide in foul weather behind Great Isaac Light, in those days a manned lighthouse. They anchored in the rough water becoming deathly ill with seasickness, forcing them crawl below decks turning all shades of green. The lighthouse-keeper radioed a message to Nassau about the boat lying off his island with no one visible on board. The message eventually reached the dive crew who recognised the boat in question. It was evident that someone needed help. Bruce offered to take Gardner in his small floatplane, explaining he could pay him back for the costs later. At a top speed of eighty miles an hour the light plane, we suspect a Piper Cub, took quite some time to reach the troubled yacht. The seas were rough and spying the boat below the two men shouted to each other that landing was out of the question. Bruce exclaiming back that Gardner should get ready to jump out!

'You have to be fucking joking,' the ex-marine shouted.

'Don't worry I can slow this thing to about 45 mph, we fall off skis faster than that!' Parker hailed back.

Not sensing anything too dangerous Gardner prepared himself for the inevitable plunge. Bruce lined the light aircraft up in to the wind and a course running parallel to the yawl appearing lifeless on board. He eased the throttle, bleeding off airspeed below 50 mph. The floatplane was losing altitude with the ocean looming very close underneath. As the yawl came alongside, Gardner eased up and out of the cockpit with the wind blowing against him. With an inevitable 'Oh shit', let go of the plane to free-fall into the ocean, barely missing the aircraft tail section. He recalls becoming aware on first impact becoming the proverbial stone skipping across the pond water, his rear end and back taking one impact after another until the inertia stopped for him to submerge. Breaking the surface and gulping air he saw the *Merry Hell* at anchor well behind him with the floatplane banking away for its journey back to Nassau. As luck would have it, the tide was flowing toward the boat. Being a strong swimmer Gardner made his path toward the pitching anchor line. Grabbing hold he hoisted his weight up the line and on to the foredeck. Still no crew showed. Making his way back to the cockpit he started growling loudly 'Where the hell is the crew of my damned boat?' Sopping wet he climbed the steps below to find two sorry green souls huddled in the cabin. 'Where the in hell did you come from?' they exclaimed. The *Merry Hell*, aptly named, with master on board, set sail for the capital.

Bruce Parker was considered just another local 'pirate' in those days. The rough and tumble men and women who ventured into the islands seeking new adventure, convinced they could make a living from flying or boating, soon learning the old island ways of survival and the means to become 'creative' in earning a dollar or two! As far back as 1648 'wrecking' was one of the early creative activities in the Bahamas with the arrival of religious dissidents from Bermuda, the Eleutheran Adventurers, establishing a colony on Eleuthera. They became skilled at decoying unwary ships with false beacons and lights, luring the ill-fated vessels to run aground along the coastline. Their regulations of wrecking provided that any salvaged ordnance 'would be held in common for the defence of the colony, and all other salvaged goods would be delivered to designated agents, 'made fit for sale' and then sold, with one-third of the proceeds going to the wreckers'. Most of the adventurers were primarily farmers, but seamen from Bermuda began settling on New Providence also in the 1660s. Many pursued wrecking aggressively, regarding all salvage as their property. They were rumoured to have killed people who had inconveniently survived a shipwreck, driving Spanish salvers away from their own wrecks, even taking goods that the Spanish had already salvaged. Spain regarded the Bahamian wreckers as 'pirates' later retaliating by attacking the wreckers' ships, kidnapping farmers from New Providence, and burning the capital, Charles Town, known today as Nassau. Wrecking was a mainstay of the Bahamian economy through most of the nineteenth century. In 1856 there were 302 ships and 2,679 men out of a total population of 27,000 licensed as wreckers in the Bahamas. In that year alone salvaged wreck cargo brought to Nassau was valued at £96,304.00 more than half of all imports to the Bahamas!

A wooden hull Hawkins powerboat resembling an American PT boat crashed on to the rocks during a storm near Nassau with word soon traveling to Parker's dive operation where Gardner was summoned to assess the salvage prospects. The two divers approached the damaged hull now hard against the rocks, seas pounding her planks lose and swamping her decks. It was impossible to manoeuvre Parkers' shrimp boat *Tabasco* close enough to safely board. It would take one of them a swim in the rough waters while the other kept their boat at safe distance. Donning a pair of fins and mask, Gardner plunged in to the ocean swimming toward the doomed Hawkins. Judging the timing was precarious at best to board the ship and with its moving debris with each crashing wave. Making his way to the cabin entrance Gardner climbed below and noted items worth retrieving, sextants, navigation equipment and radios, nothing of great importance. He climbed back out and dove in to the water again making his way back to Bruce's boat where he sat in idle. They would have to make application to the Wreck Receivers at Prince George Dock to salvage the boat.

The next day they returned and repeated the exercise of trying to salvage anything of value, only this time Gardner came out bewildered that the boat's interior had already been stripped. The two men showed disappointment at being beaten to the spoils. Within a short time, Bahamian Customs arrived at Gardner's workplace knowing he was the likely man to talk with about the wreck. He explained that they had done the first survey and noted some articles worth retrieving but on the second try found the boat to be cleaned out. The officers, dressed in familiar black slacks and crisply starched white short-sleeved shirts complete with gold epaulets found Bruce at home asking for entry and a statement, discovering all of the Hawkins booty in stacked in his garage; he had slyly done a lone trip back diving in the night water to claim the prizes. He was arrested for stealing off the wreck and became guest of Foxhill Prison for three months. After serving time he was escorted to the airport and deported, never returning to the Bahamas, rather ending up in Grand Cayman joined later again by Doris who eventually left Gardner, complaining about the booze. She joined Parker at the Rum Point Club, ironically to die later herself of alcoholism.

Nestled in the Exuma Cays, some thirty-eight miles to the southeast of Nassau lay a private island hosting a popular commercial venture with a small marina offering berths and fuel. Bill and Mary Smith owned Highbourne Cay, he being the owner of an oil company in Pennsylvania. The island manager Don Larson with Skeet Able as his assistant ran a supply boat to and from Nassau to maintain their small store and island provisions. A 38-foot Chesapeake Deadrise of unusual construction with thick keel and diagonal planking to the chine, named the *Highbourne Lady*. The island was, and still very much is, a favourite stopping place for local and visiting sport fishermen. Bill Smith knew Gardner well and one day asked him,

'Why on earth did he not have his own dive boat instead of using the old glass bottomed boats?'

Having acquired a larger boat for his island supply runs named the *Bessie Virginia* Bill offered Gardner the *Highbourne Lady* for sale.

'Do you have any money?'

'I think we could raise £1500?' Gardner replied.

'Would you settle for £1200 right now?' Bill jested back.

'Then she's yours!' Underwater Tours now owned their first dive boat, renamed by Charlie Badeau after his fascination with famous pirates, decided on Blackbeard's boat, *Queen Anne's Revenge.* A young Bahamian Captain by the name Ronnie Kemp was its first Master.

Behind the Yacht Haven building lay two entrances to the main docks, one lay to the east where Bronson and Harriet Hartley berthed a commercial tour boat taking visitors to Athol Island on a half-day trip, where they could descend a ladder off the boats stern sporting a fairly heavy helmet on their shoulders to walk on the sandy bottom viewing the corals in about ten or twelve feet of water. Compressed air was pumped down to each helmet and even non-swimmers could dare the adventure without getting their hair wet. Bronson Hartley had trained a Nassau Grouper to come and feed from their hands allowing petting pictures taken with early plastic housings made for their cameras. The Hartley's were a winter season operation in the Bahamas and left for Bermuda to operate in the summer months.

The dock to the west was home of the larger sailing charter boats that famed this time period such as *Gulliver, Traveller* and *Bahama Alpha.* The wooden docks were well worn and their grey planks starting to rise and twist with years of weathering. The docks centre pathway was a long series of plywood boards laid as far as they could reach. This made an easy ride for the individual trollies that loaded various boats with wares, provisions, spare parts and scuba tanks. Charlie had built a compressor area at the western end of the Yacht Haven property, acquiring a series of used commercial oxygen and nitrogen bottles from hospitals making a 'bank' for the compressed air to fill Underwaters' daily use of steel dive tanks. The air was filtered, cleaned and pressurised by the old Worthington compressor into the individual tanks seated in threes or fours inside a 55-gallon drum full of flowing fresh water to cool the heating compressed air. Scuba tanks could be filled quickly in bulk instead of one at a time; when the bank reached a certain low pressure the compressor engine kicked in and built the volume back to a selected storage pressure. The area was surrounded with a chain link fence and every morning Charlie could be seen inside letting an alarming loud belch of compressed air to scream across the parking lot as he bled the valves on finishing the fills.

Twice a day when the busy seasons began, a trolley would be parked outside the compressor area where two instructors would load what they dared to balance, maybe two or even three layers of steels tanks, to make the tenuous journey down the dock where the *Queen Anne's Revenge* lay berthed. The trip would be fairly slow as the steel cylinders banged and rattled against each other. The collection chocked with three-or four-pound lead dive weights. Some days inside the office one could hear the calamity of the over weighted trolley falling, steel tanks banging their way down the wooden planking as two unsuspecting dive instructors scrambled to save them going overboard.

As a thirteen-year-old, I am walking past the Bahamian deep sea fishing boats preparing their lines and baits for the day ahead. The summer sun is hot before 9 am. The water is like oil with the light dancing off the smooth surface, reflecting the colours of a powder blue sky and painted boat hulls. I stop briefly to admire a huge tarpon lying motionless in the shade under the dock planking, so large it spans from one side to the other. Within days I learn all the captains' names along with their mates. They greet me each day as I walk the same route dressed in a light cotton shirt, shorts and flip flops, making my way to work the holiday job envied by all my schoolmates. Two divers are loading tanks down to Captain Ronnie – they are older than I by a few years sporting the familiar company black speedo swimsuit, bare feet and great tanned skin. One has a cigarette hanging out of his mouth, shirtless, light blue eyes and a mop of windblown brown hair extending a hand in greeting. The ladies must trip over themselves when they see this chap I thought, comparing him with my scrawny frame.

'Hi, I'm Bobby Mather and this is Bob Nieswander.' I introduce myself, explaining how Mr. Young had told me to get some equipment for the morning dive.

'So you are going to swim safety for us then?' Bobby asked. He showed me the rows of fins laid under the seats running each side of the dive boat.

'Masks and snorkels are in here.' He pointed to a closet in the forward section. It seemed only minutes before we spied Ray leading a small group of tourists followed by Charlie and Gardner. We greeted everyone as they came on board and let them sit where they pleased. Ronnie turned the ignition key and the dive boat came to life.

Underwater Tours left for its morning trip shortly after 9.30 and at idle we glide past *Traveler* berthed toward the end of the dock. Larger *Gulliver* and *Alpha* are on the far side. Passing the tip of Potters Cay, the tide is rushing past the lone pole stuck in the rock and we head east toward Montagu Bay. Rows of casuarinas line Paradise Island eventually seeing the Cloisters posing on top of the hill overlooking the harbour and tiered gardens of the Ocean Club running to the water's edge. Reaching the end of Paradise, a channel making narrows and divide from Athol Island, the tide races through the cut with thousands of long black spiny sea urchins grasping the ocean floor. Years later while navigating my own boat through here I spy dozens of floating objects being taken by the current only to suddenly realise them as bodies lost tragically off a Haitian sloop carrying illegal immigrants wrecking in the dark of night. I talk with Ronnie as he navigates the channel, turning northeast bound to pass tiny Spruce Cay to our right. This little treeless cay lay barren save one small beach just wide enough for one boat to claim.

The crew starts to assemble sets of scuba equipment; each selecting a grey steel 72-cubic-foot tank, placing the black plastic backpack over its top valve. The simple two-stage single hose regulator tightened in place over the 'k' valve and turned on to check for leaks and function. Each tank filled to about 2,200-pounds-per-square-inch pressure, lasting the average diver, in twenty-five feet of water, just under an hour. The yellow shoulder harnesses of these old-style backpacks are adjusted to fit height for the person they have been assigned to look after. The waist straps are checked along with the crotch strap that fit between ones' legs, allowing the waist strap to pass through. Each day we played the game with Ray as he designated which guests were going to be 'ours' to safety swim the dive. Trying to keep a straight face he would introduce each of us to a particular couple or individuals and pair us up according to their qualifications in the water. The dreaded crotch strap was the first challenge in the art of 'dressing' our divers. Ray would have a hard time keeping the smile controlled when he introduced myself, Tom Branley, Bobby and especially Tom Ullery, the most mischievous amongst us, to a sufficiently large lady that had no possible 'gap' between her legs for the strap to travel! He would watch with a wry grin as we would ask the lady to kindly stand up with her tank on, place the regulator over the right shoulder, explaining this strap had to be passed between her legs so that we may thread the waist strap through it and attach. With great trepidation we would feed the strap as close as we dare to her rear end and ask that she reach down between those very generous thighs and pull it completely through for us to buckle hoping the waist strap could be extended far enough to circumnavigate the generous waistline! There were those excessively large enough not able to reach their rear end keeping the loop in a very low position making attachment especially precarious to her private anatomy! With the men, it was easy, 'Just pass this strap underneath for me sir,' we would say, not venturing any further. He can do it up himself. Exceptions to the rule came into play with the gorgeous young ladies that we lucked out being assigned, the procedure of course immediately modified with the guide calmly whispering 'allow me to thread this strap for you' passing the looped webbing with delicate handling and amazing precision through the whole journey, from back to front and of course making it nicely snug in to position in the front, invariably bringing a controlled polite smile to the attractive guest.

'Is that comfortable?' we could ask, Ray would just shake his head stroking his blonde goatee rolling eyes with mischievous approval; dive instructors could be scoundrels at heart most of the time!

Underwater Tours offered half-day dive excursions for the complete beginner who signed up for a scuba lesson at their hotel, having an hour lesson in the pool the day before their day out to the coral reef. The instructor would assess their swimming ability and then demonstrate the basics of how the equipment worked and how to handle the swim and descent under the water. At the conclusion, he would note with a code how each student could be rated for the dive-master to designate to each safety swimmer and guide. Most people were quite able to hold their own after the hour pool lesson was complete. Some really should have stayed at home never seeking a thrill under the sea! Nevertheless, we really gave everyone the chance to experience the adventure.

After watching a few days in the water off Rose Island I could observe the drill and see how one acted as guide. Seated on the stern it was up to the guide to judge each weight of the diver and present them with a weight belt that would counteract their total buoyancy. As the new lad on board, Ray would give me the 'experienced' divers to start with. Those who had been underwater before or those who carried certification to say they had completed a standard dive program holding qualification enabling to dive in the open water alone. Experienced divers, even those holding 'C-Cards' presented daily challenges. 'When was the last time you were in the water, sir?' we would ask. 'Oh just a few months ago down in Aruba,' they would lie. Feeling relieved at not having to watch this fellow too closely I asked how much weight he required.

'Give me about fourteen pounds please.' This seemed a little heavy to me but the man was quick on the reply so I handed the belt to him.

'I see you use the same "respirators" that I have used before.' 'Oh great, the man doesn't even know the correct name for what he is breathing out of!' I noted. Ray overhearing this gave me the wink. Our guest stood on the transom; no swim fins on, placed the regulator in his hand and jumped overboard before we could get a word out. In an instant he disappeared below in a froth of bubbles.

'Better go get him, Paul' Ray quipped as he kicked the divers fins into the water, 'He'll need those when on the bottom!' Our guest sank like a rock, over weighted and no way to tread water with no buoyancy compensators to stay afloat in those early days of commercial diving. He hit the ocean floor with a plume of sand just as I submerged for the retrieval watching his fins float gently.down toward the standing bewildered scuba diver. We wondered how he was able to clear his ears of pressure with that fast a descent? He gave me the 'ok' sign, donned his fins and took off like a Polaris missile breathing so fast I knew this dive would be short one.

As guides we explained how to use hand signals needed to go on their exploration, if they felt ok, when to come back up, how to keep them from straying away from each other; often too engrossed they drifted far from their partners, most would have no clue which direction or how far they were swimming. We were their sheepdogs, constantly herding the flock below paying attention how the tank rode on their backs. As it became empty it would start to float higher making the diver more buoyant and hence more difficult to stay underwater. There were no gauges or dive computers in the early days. Dive guides grew very aware of how a person behaved in the water, what their breathing rate would be and how efficiently they would swim under the ocean surface. We would learn to judge almost to the minute how long each individual would last until they pointed sheepishly at their mouth indicating the air was not coming in as easily as they wanted. It became a science steering them back toward the vicinity of the platform just as their tanks would expire. We would give each person the thumbs up sign that they were now to surface looking for the back of the boat. Clinging on to the wood platform we relieved of the weight belt then releasing their waist straps and harness off one shoulder, allowing the equipment to literally slide off them, some holding insecurely to the regulator mouthpiece so hard that they had nearly chewed through the heavy rubber.

'You can let go now,' we would gently say as we coaxed out the mouthpiece. On one of my early guide jobs I had to administer the 'coax' a little harder and damned when his set of false teeth flew out sinking instantly toward the bottom.

'You pulled out my teethhhh!' he cried with gaping gums watching in disbelief as the complete set of false dentures sank gracefully to the sand below. 'Be right back,' I replied, leaving him hanging there with a quick free dive to twenty-five feet below. White pearly jawfish hovering above their holes on the seabed dove for the safety of their homes as the teeth hit the sand beside them. Easy to spot in the crystal clear water, in one quick scoop I had them in hand returning upward to surface right next to the guest. Very delicately I handed them over so no others could share the scene, except Ray trying to contain himself on the stern above.

This first summer job was a raging success and I looked forward to a call from the office across the street saying they needed a safety diver for the day. Until the winter months arrived changing everything. The weather pattern in the 60s was very predictable, during late fall the first cold fronts would race across the Florida peninsula and toward the Bahamas to arrive within the next couple of days. Our winds would pull from the prevailing easterly flow toward the South and southwest. The days would be warm in the eighties and the ocean on the north side would flatten out for great diving days. With the southwest wind in place it would be only hours before watching the sky from the opposite direction. Unless the front stalled out in the Florida Straights our skies in Nassau, looking toward Andros and the Berry Islands, would take on an ominous dark grey line about an inch above the horizon. A vicious front would carry a dark purple grey. The winds would increase making white caps on the ocean indicating fifteen knots or more. The grey line would be growing in height by the minute and better be under way toward home and a lee side for protection. The westerlies wouldn't be there for long. In an hour, the grey line was high with heavy rains very evident against the sunlit turquoises of the ocean. Dramatic scenes would prevail and be gone in minutes as the squall line raced forward; always a favourite subject I painted in oils. Winds would shift rapidly to the northwest and the temperature would drop ten degrees or more with the rush of cold air passing overhead. Short heavy rains washed the islands if we were lucky during the winters but only last for a short period. The cold winds would blow hard for two or more days before shifting easterly. The water temperatures noticeably dropped several degrees after the fronts passed by. By the end of October and into November the balmy summer waters were a thing of the past. By Christmas time and the winter holidays in Nassau one would get a surprise jumping boldly in to the sea. It was more than ten degrees cooler now. Seventy some degrees water temperatures were freezing to us locals!

The telephone would ring in the William Street apartment and Gardner's growl would come over loud and clear.

'Can you come to work in the morning Paul?'

The *Queen Anne's Revenge* would plough her way against the strong easterly winds that we referred to as 'down the slot': days offering no shelter with local islands facing east and west denying any calm to hide in. Athol Island was the only option tucked up close to the shoreline out of the tidal flow. Tide flowing against the wind would pick up the seas to a nasty chop making the dive impossible to pull off in comfort or safety. The shallow waters of Athol hosted small coral reefs in ten feet of water where the Hartley's could be seen tucked close to shore. Novice divers would not question their location but a serious certified diver hitting the bottom as he plunged into the cloudy stirred ocean did not go down so well! There were many miserable winter days on 'Canon Reef' trying to bluff our way into entertaining divers on the ultimate vacation adventure while blowing a gale after a passing cold front. Even the boat ride changed for the crew, no more days sitting on the roof or lapping up the sun's rays perched on the bow. We huddled pitifully in the forward cockpit of the boat keeping Ronnie company as he steered eastward. In those days there were no wet suits. The company did not own any in the early years and Gardner's policy was that if guests were not suited then the crew definitely would not be.

'Just tough it out for the swim' he would say. The guests would plunge off the stern and then the reluctant safetyman took a deep breath before leaping in. The water in January and February would sting with cold. The folks from Minnesota made fun of us about 75 F water compared to the conditions they had left behind.

I remember well Bobby Mather, Tom Ullery, Tom Branley, Victor Moody and the other infamous crews that worked for Gardner, all in the water together, now forty minutes into the dive with arms folded tight trying desperately to maintain body heat, turning strange colours of blue and purple shivering as the water lapped over our bodies.

'Time's up' we would tell the guest. Their gear was off in seconds and we were out of that water to rinse with the just-as-cold fresh water hose in the rear of the dive boat. Towelled dry and thick sweaters were donned as the visitors smiled at our behaviour.

'You guys need to come north and see what real cold feels like,' they joked.

Gardner's dive company broke new ground with the television and film industry taking great interest in using the fabulous Bahamian underwater locations. The black and white filmed TV series *Sea Hunt* starring Lloyd Bridges used the locations at the end of Athol Island with an old Landing Craft semi-submerged at its eastern end. The show later replaced with another underwater adventure called *Aquanaughts* the starring boat purchased by Captain Lou Kennedy. Those early days saw the first underwater TV commercial ever filmed, shot on location at Rose Island by the Timex watch company. In later years, I too would share the film industry experience, doubling for Mickey Dolenz, lead singer of the pop group 'The Monkeys'. After an hours' makeup and wig I was to sink from the surface, as if fallen off a boat, into forty feet of water, to be caught by two approaching mermaids and hauled off scene in to the depths, a long time to hold ones breath. All went really well until my safetyman was a little late with much needed regulator of air. Everyone else was taking those precious breaths and I suddenly alone, wondering where Captain Emerson Roberts could possibly be? Cameraman and director Lamar Boren waved frantically for someone to save the young 'stuntman'.

Lamar was a large barrel-chested man who only ever wore the old-fashioned small webbed Voit surfing fins. With his huge 35-mm underwater camera housing we all wondered how he would be able to support that bulk and manoeuvre under the surface. Deciding on a free ascent in order to stay alive I headed upward. Robbie, as we all knew him, suddenly appeared halfway up and shoved the mouthpiece in, allowing compressed air to rush in to my lungs!

In the mid-60s the dive company grew, with Charlie and Gardner often working underwater repairing propeller shafts, bent propellers and rudders at Symonette's Shipyard near the outskirts of Nassau town. The yard operated by Roy McKeene who one day brought to the divers attention a rusting 65-foot steel hull sitting up on dry dock in the yard. He exclaimed that this old faithful with her 671 Cummings diesel would cost a whole lot less to run than their gasoline guzzler and carry three times the passengers. She owed the yard $4000 and Gardner could make the sale for just $5000 more. Sealing the deal to work off the owed yard bill with jobs Symonette's would need underwater. The steel hull, named *Gateway Clipper* was one of two ferries that Huntington Hartford had used to take people over to Paradise Island, landing at the world-famous Cafe Martinique. Charlie running true to form with his love of pirates renamed her the *Royal James* after the Welsh pirate Howell Davis' ship manned in 1719. Months later and maintenance completed the modern-day *Royal James*, with her battleship grey hull and red lettering displaying the company name down both sides lay at the Nassau Yacht Haven ready for service. She became a very familiar sight traveling the harbour toward Rose Island. Many of the calls to Underwater were for commercial jobs. Mike Miller, the US Navy liaison officer with Gardner and Charlie who would dive for the AUTEC bases in Andros. He expressed to the dive operators that invoices to the United States Navy headed with Underwater 'Tours' did not fit the profile and maybe they could come up with a more suitable title. In 1963, along with a well-known Bahamian photographer, Gus Roberts, and Gary Moss of Bahamas Customs, they formed a new partnership of Underwater Engineering. Badeau with his artistic flare created the logo of a hard-hat diver holding a slide rule; the sign now hung on the opposite wall of the doorway outside their office at the Yacht Haven. A short solid built black Bahamian with an infectious laugh captained the dive boat. In those days it was near impossible to find locals to work underwater, in general were non-swimmers or dared venture no further that waist high off Saunders Beach.

There were no Bahamian qualified Open Water Scuba Instructors and renowned fearful creatures that dwelled underwater stayed in local memories. Immigration in those early days issued Working Permits for foreign instructors, costing $500 a year. Captain Emerson Roberts had the qualifications and a great sense of humour that went with the commercial dive business. He would brag that the 'fellas in the grey suits would not come and eat him because he would taste too bitter'! The dive crew often frequented an old houseboat down by Potters Cay next to East Bay Marina housing the infamous 'Father Allen's Chicken Shack'. The best-fried chicken-in-the-bag you could find! By the time you walked across the road to your vehicle the brown bag was saturated with grease from the mass of French Fries and fried grouper splashed with hot pepper sauce. The other local delight found on the wharf being delectable stuffed crabs that only Nola could produce. We would hail 'Shorty' the local inebriated dwarf street person who stayed in the East Bay Marina often guiding traffic in the middle of the busy road. Years later and a few too many pints of Bacardi white, found 'Shorty' floating face down in Nassau Harbour.

An early notable day aboard the 'Queen Anne's Revenge' occurred with a private group, chartering the whole boat for the morning's dive while staying at the British Colonial Hotel. Instead of driving through town with buses, the dive boat made its way down the harbour to collect the group from the waterfront. A new crewmember joined us some days that summer who I only knew as Krov. Coming to discover the son of Yehudi Menuhin, probably one of the world's greatest violinists of the 20th Century. Krov became a very renowned cinematographer in his own right and a well-qualified pilot being part of a fun farewell to Frannie's mum in later decades. 'Buzzie' holding vast reputation as a pilot in her own right was cremated after her passing. It seemed fitting that she depart this earth from an airplane, hence her ashes loaded aboard Krov's Cessna and taken above the Exuma Cays. A 'couple' glasses of champagne inhibited the understanding that once the co-pilot window would be opened and the urn emptied, Buzzie would rather flood the aircraft interior than disappear into the atmosphere! What was left of her, it was later that day decided, that she depart off the stern of Frannie's dive boat anchored off Norman's Cay. The old lady went off in style taking Monty Doyle's cell phone falling out of his pocket into the ocean and Fran's $300 sunglasses!

The hotel's dock protruded out in to Nassau Harbour with Hog Island and its picturesque lighthouse in the background, more sets used in the Bond movies. The sea was glassy calm this fine spring morning. Tied to the dock we saw the group threading its way through the palm trees around the pool deck toward the boat. One by one we loaded them on the stern of the boat. I happened to look across the bright turquoise water to see a monster dorsal fin, about as long as my arm, break surface about fifty yards behind us and very visible to anyone's gaze. The three-foot-high ominous fin looked like a nuclear submarine surfacing from the depths. I nudged Krov who tipped-off Ray Moore and glanced toward Hog Island.

'Holy shit, it's "The Harbour Master"' Ray mumbled quietly. 'They see that and we'll never get them in the water!' a 12-foot long hammerhead shark notorious for cruising through the waterway. We loaded twenty people without anyone noticing our local marine legend cruising by. As *Queen Anne's Revenge* backed out from the dock, Captain Ronnie Kemp swung her sideways away from the huge shark that submerged behind us just as quickly as he had appeared.

The first years in the Bahamas my mother's driving tours around the island in that white Ford Anglia allowed me to learn the art of hand line fishing off Clifton Pier. Sitting on a towel draped over the honeycombed rock she sipped a cold Coca Cola watching her son whirl the fishing line around his head and casting expertly out into the water; on weekends when invitations to go boating were not in place my parents would treat me to a day in Coral Harbour. We passed between two native-stone watchtowers where a line of young coconut trees bordered the road headed southward. The coconuts were starting to sprout with the young trees barely five feet off the ground. The community of Coral Harbour was very quiet and laid back, many homes built by commercial fishermen along with airline crews and ground staff with its close proximity to the airport; we loved it and hoped my father would purchase a home here as he would then be close to his work. It never happened, rather fate playing an interesting roll, where this southwestern community entered my life time and again considered in those early days way too far to drive from town. My father's secret personal agenda dominating our lives, repeatedly declining chances of real estate purchases my mother would expose him to while working for Chester Thompson Real Estate, often offering him many first options on beautiful homes around New Providence. He did consider a house called 'AWOL' (Absent Without Leave) on West Bay Street only to hear him back out yet again. Owning property would have allowed us as a family to apply for 'Belongership' status that the Bahamian Government offered expatriates during the years before Independence in 1973. Applicants would sign a declaration showing intention to stay in the Bahamas to reside while retaining home citizenship. Many of our friends had taken the opportunity, allowing them to come and go as they wished without a restriction on their stay within the Bahamas. Mother and I pressed father to consider doing this for us with his reply 'that he would never put his name to something he had no intention of living up to'. Mother and I did not see the relevance to this until just after my twenty-first birthday.

Bahamas Airways would hold ditching drills in the Coral Harbour Club swimming pool for cabin crews often needing volunteer 'passengers'; a chance for a swim surrounded by lovely stewardesses sounded like a reasonable trade for a new teenager. The main Coral Harbour hotel building stretched westward toward the ocean canal entrance and rows of new docks protruded from the canal walls. The club was set within a stand of tall palm trees and manicured lawns bordered with flowering hibiscus and oleander. Bahamas Airways crews would assemble at poolside and practise the inflation of the large life-rafts that were carried on the company fleet. The volunteers would be shown how to don a life jacket and once inflated jump in to the pool with a bikini clad stewardess providing good stories back in an English boarding school.

The crew would climb into the raft bobbing around the pool, practising hauling passengers over the raft entrance. After the drills were completed we all met in the Pub with its cosy atmosphere situated on the canal side of the club building, a favourite weekend watering hole for locals; the aroma of fresh grilled homemade hamburgers made by Chef Otis became infamous amongst the airline staff. Those of us who lived 'out east' would make the long drive to Coral Harbour on a regular basis when we were not boating at Rose Island. While the parents all socialised inside I took a light hand line to 'spin' for pilchards that schooled in masses under the dock pilings in front of the hotel and Pub. The hand-sized baitfish used to bite well at the bear spinning tiny hook that we ravelled with our fingers, making it glitter in the sunlight.

When the fish struck they were hauled quickly in to an awaiting bucket of seawater. After catching half a dozen one would then cut the baitfish in to inch thick steaks and bait a larger hook on heavier line and lead weight. Now we were ready to launch attractive bait in to the middle of the canal system that ran through the whole development, no clue decades later I would live yards from here. The line would sing through our hands when large grey snappers hungrily took the bait, my father joined us and hooked a four-foot young reef shark that gave him an impressive fight on a hand line only to be let go after a picture taken.

The local airline was a subsidiary of British Oversees Airways Corporation and their emblem on the fleet aircraft tails was the BOAC 'Speedbird' mirror-image set on the diagonal. Bahamas Airways fleet consisted of the Handley Page Hermes, Vickers Viking, and faithful DC3s dating back to the 40s along with Aero Commanders, Grumman Goose and Widgeon. Weekends at Rose Island where airline staff used to beach party were sometimes treated to a 'flyby' – a few select Captains returning from North Eleuthera airport would lower the small airliner to a few feet off the water after telling passengers they were being treated to some local sightseeing! Henry Pyfrom on one occasion knew his co-workers would all be sipping a cold brew in the water off McTaggart's Beach. Air Traffic Control in those days was not the sophisticated operation it is with today's radar and those of us swimming could hear the approaching drone of radial engines waving at the passengers as they flew past us almost at eye level climbing out over Sandy Cay inbound for approach to the airport. It was the likes of Henry Pyfrom and Captain Eddie Ballard jesting in the Pilot House Bar, calculated a DC3 would fit on the diagonal for a flight between the pilings of the new bridge being constructed across to Paradise Island! There were some fun crews back in the early days, all possessing that unique love of island flying while gifted with great aviation stories I was privy to. Airline gatherings would be at Frank Salmon's house in Montagu Heights, Henry's place on Winton or the balcony of Captain Eddie's house on East Bay Street overlooking the Yacht Haven. This was the company that kept the spirit of aviation alive inside me as a youngster. One day I was surely destined to fly.

The Police Force in Freeport used one of the Aero Commanders for flight patrol and the fuel attendant omitted securing the fuel caps on both wings. Just out of Freeport the Commander fell silent with both engines failing after having siphoned all of the fuel. The pilot radioed an emergency and using the vast area of shallow ocean made a successful forced landing off Water Cay. My father volunteered his son, who knew how to hold his breath and free dive enough to make the length of the fuselage and back underwater, in order to retrieve the pilots' briefcase and paperwork from the cockpit. I was flown on a regular BAL flight up to Grand Bahama and taken by boat to the crash site. Small reef sharks were swimming around the submerged aircraft and none of the locals would take the plunge to fit in the narrow door. Any chance available I loved to be around aircraft no matter the circumstance; all through childhood and especially here in the islands I felt that familiar tug toward being close to something involving aviation. It would take more than four more decades to make the move from this stage in my life. My father was promoted from flight engineer to Deputy Operations Manager under Captain Phillip Farrington who advanced from Chief Pilot to Operations. As 'staff families' we had the advantage of paying only 10% of fares, to Miami was a mere $2.70 making the departure tax of $3 more expensive than the ticket! Father's duties were to design and supervise construction of a new hangar needed for Bahamas Airways maintenance. Another issue he addressed was that the ageing DC3 fleet needing repainting. John Harding supervised the stripping of paint from some of the older planes to whittle slowly, layer by layer, reducing the already excessive amounts of paint that had added over the years, adversely affecting the weight of each plane. He noted colours of different airlines and cargo services that the old fleet had served. When they reached the Glider Tow colours of World War Two he dared go no deeper. I was always curious why Dad did not want to actually fly aircraft rather sit behind the pilots at the engineer's helm. He responded 'anyone could fly a plane but knowing all the inner workings during flight was another matter that he preferred'. I inwardly disagreed. One day I would be up front in that left seat holding the actual controls to feel the freedom of flight.

The airline had ordered more up-to-date aircraft with the arrival one Christmas of the Hawker Siddley 748. Several families of Bahamas

Airways gathered on the open balcony upstairs at the main terminal and watched Captain Farrington, dressed in a full Santa suit waving from the left seat of the 748, having permission to buzz the Control Tower building with the new arrival. The Hermes, Vikings and amphibious aircraft were eventually phased out but the DC3s kept plodding away for several years. Avro had designed the original Hawker Siddley medium sized turbo-prop in 1958 with its two Rolls Royce Dart engines and STOL, short take-off and landing capabilities, good for Out-Island operation. The first 748 flew in 1960, the same year under the pressure of the British Government Vickers merged with English Electric forming the British Aircraft Corporation. Vickers at the time were designing a jet to replace the ageing Vickers Viscount fleet, called the VC10, which I had the pleasure of flying across the Atlantic as a young boy. In 1963 BAC introduced the One Eleven 300 and 400 series. While I watched Sir Lawrence Olivier play Hamlet on the open new stage of Chichester Festival Theatre, our local airline was talking about jets and the possibility of BAC 111s for the Florida routes. Bahamas Airways was changing hands taken over by the Swire's Group started by John Swire back in the early nineteenth century. The modern companies core businesses held in Hong Kong in the Far East under Swire Pacific Limited, the largest shareholder in Cathy Pacific Airlines. Connecting the dots later, my father's future plan must have started to unfold during these years?

Chapter 8
Death in the Afternoon

Nassau Harbour in the early 60s saw the construction of a modern bridge to span between the mainland and Paradise Island. Huge 'dolphins' made of heavy timbers formed around each massive foundation to protect from accidental strike from a passing vessel. The tide raced mercilessly around the concrete creating whirlpools of saltwater and swirling white caps. The early sixties transformed Hog Island in to modern Paradise Island; a world-class destination, which began its creation a few years later with the completion of the bridge and the first hotel foundation laid by Lowe's Corporation rising on the North side of the island overlooking Cabbage Beach. Paradise Island Hotel and Villas in its infant stages scarred the landscape, where huge stands of casuarina pines once crested the slopes above the magnificent beach. None of us could envision the new development with its wide new roadway lined with palm trees leading off a 72-foot-high bridge rising from the blue harbour waters. Little did I know I would be the first Open Water Scuba Instructor to venture across the new structure every day on my way to work?

As the concrete pilings grew skyward in the harbour in 1963, on the Paradise side, where concrete docks stretched out from the canal entrance to Cafe Martinique, a strange form later would begin to take shape out of metal frame and fiberglass sheeting's. Slowly a life-sized replica British Air Force Vulcan bomber was born. I was fascinated by this aircraft re-creation, as my father in his early thirties had been crew for Handley Page, located in Radlett, a village just north of London in the same county in which I was born. Handley Page produced three bombers in the 'V' Series. The Vulcan, Valiant and lastly the Victor, first taking flight in 1952, formally introduced six years later in 1958, built for high altitude, high-speed penetration of Soviet airspace to deliver a free-falling nuclear weapon. They had a service ceiling of 56,000 feet flying at 650 mph for over 2,500 miles; a total of eighty-six were produced, the last being retired in 1993. The aircraft required the crew to wear a type of space suit. The impressive jet looked and sounded out of a science fiction novel in those days. I was never given the photo portrait of John Harding dressed in full high altitude flying attire holding a flight helmet at his side. The futuristic jet bomber had suffered its losses during its flying era; there was a story recalled about a crew that had to bail out at high altitude with one of father's friends falling near three miles, his parachute safely deploying but landing on a telegraph wire between his legs slicing him as a cheese wire.

Ian Fleming's creation of the James Bond character was to come alive in the Bahamas with the movie *Thunderball*, released in 1965. Almost all of the feature film was to be shot on location through the islands. The brainchild of four friends collaborating in 1958 on a number of drafts for a possible TV series or film using Ian Fleming's British Secret Service character. One of the four, Kevin McClory, born in Dublin, Ireland in 1926, a well-known Bahamas resident. McClory in his early years had joined the British Merchant Navy and torpedoed in 1943, spending fourteen days adrift in the North Atlantic Ocean before being rescued. He started his film career as a boom operator and location manager for the film *Cockleshell Heroes*. He later assisted famed director John Huston on films such as *The African Queen* and *Moby Dick*. He became a screenwriter in the 50s and with financial assistance from the heiress of American A&P, Josephine Bryce, sister of Huntington Hartford, wrote, produced and directed his first film *The Boy and the Bridge* only to fail at the box office. Ian Fleming drifted away from McClory after this and, without permission from the others, novelised the screenplay draft they had all worked on, into his ninth book titled *Thunderball*. A legal dispute in 1961 ensued between Fleming and two of the other writers, with McClory and Jack Whittingham in a London court for nine days. McClory was awarded financially, but more important retained certain rights to the story and characters of *Thunderball* as long as he allowed ten years to elapse after its release. Film producers of the Fleming novel, Albert Broccoli and Harry Saltzman, who owned film rights to most of the Bond books, feared McClory would produce a rival film, which he did much later with the release of *Never Say Never Again* in 1983. He used similar characters and story line shooting the film here in Nassau with opening scenes on the old Oakes Estate in the centre of New Providence starring Sean Connery once again. Free of the original franchise it was opportunity for Connery to make this his last appearance as James Bond with the fitting title. Kevin McClory died in November of 2006 aged eighty and just four days after the release of another Bond film *Casino Royale.*

The underwater footage of the original *Thunderball* film was in the hands of the infamous underwater cinema-photographer Lamar Boren who I worked under in later years very near the identical dive location of the Bond sites. The 1965 film directed by Terrance Young and starring Sean Connery, who came to love the Bahamas so much bought a property in Lyford Cay on the golf course boundary. The underwater finale was the largest underwater fight scene ever shot with over forty divers involved with the production. Fame soon came to a small hollow rock just north of the Staniel Cay Yacht Club, half way down the Exuma chain of islands, near seventy-five miles southeast of Nassau. One of three pieces of limestone that rose from sea floor the most northerly having a hidden feature of being hollow inside. Three small holes in the roof of the cave allowed sunlight to filter through the crystal-clear water creating the atmosphere of an undersea cathedral. Swarms of schooling fish weaved in rhythm as they crisscrossed in front of the various entrances that perforated the cave. Large Nassau groupers lay motionless on the floor in some of the entrances, their large eyes watching visitor's every move while uncountable masses of schooling minnows darted above them, their tiny silver bodies glistening in the sunlight as they moved in perfect unison. On the west side of the rock a huge slice of limestone had cracked away in years gone by, sliding in to the water leaving a long four-foot-wide crevasse for a snorkel diver to carefully navigate in to the main entrance of the mystical structure. On high water one would have to momentarily hold your breath and slide under the entrance guarded by sharp limestone ceilings dipping just under the surface. Reappearing on the inside was a huge cavern, decorated walls with running rainwater from above brushing streaks of green algae. The Bahama blue pastel sky and green scrub vegetation showed clear through the holes in the ceiling, their jagged unyielding edges menacing anyone who would dare the jump from above. A diver could lie on the calm surface gazing at a gorgeous iridescent blue exit hole on the east wall under the water. Pillars of sunlight shimmered their display; a perfect setting for a feature film to leave its name on newly named Thunderball Cave. Years later the famous cave became part of another career where I would treat many hundreds of people to this incredible swim having arrived there by the ultimate means of a seaplane! The 1965 film was the fourth in the James Bond series following the original *Dr No* filmed in Jamaica released in 1962. When John F. Kennedy listed *From Russia with Love* as a favourite, Fleming's book sales rocketed.

The *Thunderball* story was based on the evil empire of 'SPECTRE' stealing two NATO nuclear bombs from a British Air Force Vulcan bomber holding them ransom for $100 million in diamonds. The structure I watched being built on Paradise Island was later lowered in to forty feet of water out near Goulding Cay off the western end of New Providence; the location a favourite for major film productions featuring dramatic underwater footage. The film depicted the villain's yacht, *Disco Volante* anchored off 'Rock Point' on the western coast road near the caves owned by construction owner George Mosko, whose son Jim I flew for later in my career. The film broke box office records that year making more than all three of its predecessors in the series with an estimated $996 million at estimated 2008 financial standards. Nassau had put on a special edition of the 'Junkanoo Parade', our world-famous carnival that occurs just twice a year at Christmas and New Year's, to be featured in the movie production giving the Bahamas unprecedented exposure worldwide.

The holiday weeks spent in the Bahamas flew by incredibly fast and before one could blink it were time to board the Boeing 707 back to London Airport and faithfully awaiting grandparents. The brief intervals at Grey Thatch were always a welcome cushion back to the reality of an English boarding school. Edna Dean began to teach me the art of cooking and preparing various foods which the three of us would enjoy around the tiny dining room complete with black hard wood beams laid on the white-faced flint walls over 400 years prior. I polished the skills of stalking prey, spending early morning and evening hours walking alone through the fields at the northern end of the 400-year-old property. Stealth under the giant oaks would allow an occasional shot at an English wood pigeon. Time alone always illustrated an appreciation of life outdoors, I killed very little, it was simply 'being there' in that beautiful outdoors that mattered. Later school years I joined the Combined Cadet Force, compulsory for all boarders to attend; I became a marksman with both small bore .22 rifles and the large bolt-action .303 Lee Enfield. The game birds near Grey Thatch were large and delicious having fed for months in the neighbouring grain fields. I learned a strict code to only take what we could eat with no desire to take animals. Sport bird hunting only lasted a short while however, participating far less as the years went by and only during my early twenties, eventually giving it up entirely preferring armed solely with a camera instead. I turned my early hobby into a profession that takes me in later years to amazing countries to specialise in nature photography both above and below the water!

The drive to the railway station repeated time and again for the trip back to King James School. So clouded by the distaste of the system that was supposed to be educating me I failed to absorb the beauty of the surrounding countryside on the Isle of Wight. My fellow student from the Bahamas helped alleviate the monotony of classes, with Graham and I in the same platoon in the Combined Cadet Force; here at least we had entertainment being able to get our hands on real weapons even if they were the ancient bolt-action .303 rifles. On the firing range we polished our skills in marksmanship enjoying the loud retort and heavy punch the rifle gave on recoil. The itchy heavy brown material of the army uniforms always to be well pressed with matching boots; scrutinised during inspections by higher-ranking students and teachers while finally elevated to lance corporal with one stripe on my arm.

The year 1963 stands alone. From beginning to end, each month unravelled world events that our age group watched in awe and disbelief. The year opened with the release of an epic film starring the volatile couple Elizabeth Taylor and Richard Burton in *Cleopatra*. Like a runaway train, days clicked by with news snippets from all parts of the globe hitting us in every direction. In the United States troubled racial issues festered with Governor George Wallace of Alabama elected to declare 'segregation now, segregation tomorrow and segregation forever'. Fourteen days later an African American student enters Clemson University in South Carolina being the last state to hold out with racial segregation. In England, the famous steam locomotive and luxury train, 'The Flying Scotsman' made its last run. Northwest Airlines loses an airliner in to the Everglades of Florida, killing all on board. Female suffrage is enacted in Iran. On my birthday, I heard country superstar Patsy Cline dies in a plane crash. She had noted to friends of impending doom, quoting 'she had experienced two bad accidents and the third would be a charm or it would kill her'. She boarded a private Piper Comanche piloted by her manager headed for Nashville. Flying in to inclement weather with high winds the Comanche plunged nose down in to a wooded area. In the middle of San Francisco harbour the world-famous island penitentiary Alcatraz is closed by the Attorney General of the United States, Robert Kennedy. As the first James Bond movie is released in May the world hears of the death of Pope John XXIII and nearby Yugoslavia becomes a Socialist Republic.

In early June President Kennedy delivered his historic Civil Rights address asking for 'the kind of equality of treatment that we would want for ourselves' while Russia launched a Vostok rocket taking the first female cosmonaut, Valentina Tereshkova in to space, returning her to Earth three days later. The United States introduced Zip Codes to their postal system, an idea which later spread to other countries. The United Kingdom along with Russia and the USA signed the Test Ban Treaty for nuclear weapons while a group of bandits in Buckinghamshire, England pulled off the famous 'Great Train Robbery' lead by British criminal Ronnie Biggs; the usual haul for this train in the region of £300,000 in valuable mail but the robbers hit after a Bank Holiday in Scotland having to unload an unexpected 124 sacks with two and a half million pounds in one, five and ten pound notes! In August over 250,000 people from all walks of life march on Washington, DC where on the steps of the Lincoln Memorial Dr Martin Luther King delivered his 'I have a dream' speech.

The Atlantic hurricane season brought a monster across the ocean late in the season on October 4 to hit Hispaniola and Cuba. Hurricane Flora kills over 7000 people. The second Bond movie is released as new car manufacturer Lamborghini is introduced to the world. The President of South Vietnam is assassinated in a coup, which the United States declares later they will support. As a fifteen-year-old, now back in England for the winter term at King James, I am walking from our dormitory situated upstairs down the dark wooden main staircase of Nubia House headed toward the dining room. I was about halfway down. On November 22 1963 we all knew the exact spot we were at 12.30 pm United States Central Standard Time. A motorcade passing Dealey Plaza, Dallas,

Texas is approaching the Texas Book Depository building. Riding in the open limousine is President John F. Kennedy with his wife Jackie, along with the Texas Governor John Connally and his wife. The streets are lined with thousands of cheering spectators. Mrs. Connally turns to the President seated behind her and says,

'Mr. President, you can't say Dallas doesn't love you'. The limousine turns past the Book Depository and on to Elm Street. It was as far as the black and white television pictures covered. No one really reacted to the first shot, thinking it sounded like a car backfire or firecracker. Witnesses declared that they saw a muzzle flash from the sixth floor of the Depository building and could give a description of the white male they saw in the window.

The President and his wife together with the Texas Governor were all acknowledging the crowds to their left side abruptly turned to their right. Connally attempts to turn around to check Kennedy who he does not see only to hear unmistakably a high-powered rifle shot. In turning forward he is hit in the upper right side of his back and is heard yelling 'Oh no no no, My God they are going to kill us all!' Mrs. Connally, after hearing the first loud retort from behind and to her right, turns toward the President to see his arms and elbows raised high with both hands clutching near his throat. The bullet had entered JFK's upper back as he waves to the crowd. It penetrated his neck, slightly damaging a spinal vertebra and a piece of the right lung now exiting out of his throat just below his Adam's Apple nicking his necktie. He leans forward and Jackie tries to cradle him in her arms. The same bullet then travels through the Governor's back and shatters his hand. Nellie Connally hears the second shot and heard her husbands' cries. Turning toward him a third shot spatters her and the limousine interior with blood, bone fragments and brain matter.

The spectators on both sides of the road are stunned, those standing on the grass verges dive for cover to escape the gunfire. Many onlookers still just stand there, not having heard the rifle fire, gazing without comprehending the unfolding events. Suddenly Jackie Kennedy gets up from her seat and is seen trying to crawl backward over the trunk of the limousine as Secret Service Agent Clint Hill leaps from the running board of the car behind; sprinting at full pace towards her trying to protect the President after the first shot is fired. He reaches the Presidential limousine and jumps on to one of the specially mounted steps, grasping a handrail mounted on each side of the car's rear. He believes the First Lady is reaching for something that may have been a part of a skull and sees her crawl back in to the rear seat with her husband crying 'I have his brains in my hand!' The limousine breaks from the line of cars and begins speeding toward Parkland Hospital in Dallas, a medical team awaiting arrival three minutes later. Kennedy's massive wounds showing a large oval portion of the rear of his right skull blown away still held in place by the scalp. American television suddenly broadcast, 'We interrupt this program…' news anchor-man Walter Cronkite, sitting in his newsroom with recognised thick black-rimmed glasses, announced 'the President had been shot in Dallas'.

On the other side of the Atlantic, in an English boarding school near dinner time, troubled shouts from students on the ground floor came clearly audible halfway down the main staircase 'They have shot the President!' We were just schoolboys in our early teen years, impressed as so many young people were, with this charismatic, handsome president whose wonderful humour captured our attention. I can visualise to this day the main staircase as if it were yesterday: I remained motionless unable to take another step for several seconds. I wanted so badly to realise this moment unreal. We had not followed American politics closely and at that age not avid news hounds. Similar with most people on the planet, we had however, watched this socialite family known affectionately as 'Camelot' rise through the ranks of modern American history to produce three young and attractive sons who entered the world of US politics. They were America's counterpart to our Royal Family and covered accordingly by the press; the most charismatic of the brothers now murdered right in front of us. It was disturbingly surreal, nothing close to the fictional death one watches all too frequently on our screens: an unshakeable image, that to this day comes to mind all too easily. This was someone we knew and admired as young people taken with such violence right in front of us. Even at that age it felt like the wind had been knocked out of me affecting our generation as did that fateful September day decades later in New York. The stark realisation of such an act so shocking left an awful empty feeling, no matter one's citizenship over on the other side of the world. The next morning loading in to a bus outside our school for transport somewhere, we saw the senior boys had taken all the copies of the British daily newspapers screaming headlines that jumped off the page, 'JFK Dead'. I was never able to retrieve a copy to keep. The black and white footage shown on television was stark. Later when still photos were printed in *Life* magazine in living colour the event became even more shocking with the moment captured in motion on colour movie film to be played later over and over where one finally had to turn away in repulsion rather than view a man's head explode in living colour. Unlike modern times where major news networks have camera crews in all areas of an important event, the irony of that fateful day in November was marked by their absence. All network stations had sent their camera crews to Kennedy's destination that day where he was scheduled to speak, none to record that fateful few seconds with the exception of one soul who considered himself an amateur cameraman having presence of mind to keep the motion camera motor running.

An immigrant to America, Abraham Zapruder, a garment manufacturer loved taking home movies. Wanting a prime view of the motorcade as his President would be passing from left to right that sunny afternoon in Texas. His original plan was to shoot the film from his garment office building next to the book depository. Deciding a better view walked down to the grounds surrounding the Plaza where standing precariously on the most western of two concrete pedestals, part of a structure overlooking Elm Street. Steadied by his receptionist while holding a Bell and Howell 8-mm-silent film camera he shot a few frames of his nearby friends first for practice and then saw the motorcade turning the corner. He squeezed the shutter of the movie camera with colour film traveling through his camera lens at just over eighteen frames per second. He captured 486 frames of film that lasted just over twenty-six seconds. When the fatal headshot made impact, the President was almost exactly opposite and below Zapruder's line of sight.

That one frame numbered 313, froze the most graphic event in American presidential history; its owner took the film after the numbing event, to the Eastman Kodak laboratory just after 3 pm where he waited for the only developed moving film recording the assassination. This piece of film would become one of the most famous motion film productions recorded by an amateur and the only piece of continuous footage that captured the event from start to finish. Zapruder later went to the Jamieson Film Company at about 6.30 pm and had three copies made. He retained the original, giving the other two copies to the Secret Service for their investigation. He hated the film. The next day *Life* magazine bought the printing rights for $50,000 and dispatched the film to their production facilities in Chicago. On November 24 they bought sole rights to the film for $150,000 payable in six annual instalments of $25,000. Zapruder donated the first payment to the wife and children of the police officer who was killed by the assassin during his attempted escape from the scene. *Life* magazine never allowed the film to be broadcast and in 1975 sold it back to the family for $1, now the property of the National Archive in Washington, DC where the family were then paid $16 million for it. Zapruder never shot movie film again, saying after that event he lost his appetite in the pursuit of his hobby. He died of cancer in 1970.

One hour and twenty minutes after the assassination, Lee Harvey Oswald was captured inside a movie theatre claiming that he was set up as the patsy. Dallas police confirm with a paraffin test on his hands and right cheek that Oswald had recently fired a weapon. On the sixth floor of the Depository building authorities found a Carcano M91 bolt action rifle with three shell casings. The world was glued to their television sets to watch the events unfold. At Parkland Hospital John Fitzgerald Kennedy was declared 'moribund' meaning he had no chance of survival. At 1.00 pm CST the black and white TV picture showed us Walter Cronkite sitting in shirt sleeves in the studio, glancing at the wall clock and declaring the President of the United States had been pronounced dead. Audiences were stunned and sat in silence, news footage showing the general public's reaction of gut wrenching grief.

A few minutes after 2.00 pm Kennedy's body was removed from hospital before a forensic examination could be performed, violating Texas State Law. At the time, it was not a Federal Offence to kill the President of the United States! The body was placed in a casket and taken to Airforce One on the ground at Love Field. A row of seats had been removed and the casket lay in the rear passenger cabin as Lyndon Johnson took the Oath of Office at 2.38 pm on board the Presidential aircraft. Jackie Kennedy stood next to him in her blood stained pink outfit, refusing a change of clothing. After the oath, Airforce One lifted off toward Washington, DC. JFK was taken immediately to the East Room of the White House for twenty-four hours where family could visit in private. The following Sunday a flag draped casket was taken to the Capital for public viewing where hundreds of thousands lined the streets to pay their respects to the fallen President. Representatives from ninety countries attended the State Funeral on November 25. The world watched as Kennedy's casket slowly passed his three-year-old son saluting his father on his third birthday. JFK was buried in Arlington National Cemetery with an Eternal Flame being lit at his grave. The flame burns to this day. JFK died on a Friday. By Monday morning Jackie Kennedy had received 45,000 letters of condolence from ordinary people of all ages and would receive near one and a half million in all.

Two days later on a live broadcast we watched Oswald being taken from Police Headquarters to Dallas County Jail. Coming down a walkway wedged between two Dallas detectives Oswald was suddenly approached from a man in the crowd. Grimacing in pain and collapsing after being shot by a nightclub owner Jack Ruby who declared 'he had done it for Jackie'. On November 29 1963, Lyndon Johnson established the Warren Commission named after the Chief Justice Earl Warren. Several appointed officials to the Commission took their positions with extreme reluctance. The 888-page document was published by The Double Day printing company in Maryland and presented to President Johnson in September 1964. The twenty-six-volume report was made public three days later and has stirred controversy with its findings ever since. It has been criticised for its important omissions, methods and conclusions. The latest edition of the Commission's report contained a forward writing that, 'the CIA destroyed or kept from investigators critical secrets connected to the 1963 assassination of JFK'. It was said, 'the Commissions probe put certain classified and potentially damaging operations in danger of being exposed'. The CIA's reaction 'was to hide or destroy some information which can easily be misinterpreted as conclusion in JFK's assassination'.

Abraham Zapruder's film was not shown publicly until the trail of a New Orleans businessman, Clay Shaw in 1969, tried for conspiracy in the assassination of John Kennedy. The killing had weaved a tangle of theories and accusations of a conspiracy. Through the years and to this day one can visit video sites on our personal computers to watch specialists and theorists take on the evidence that modern forensic science can prove. Trajectory angles, rifle reloading times and as did Zapruder's film show, body angles of the frame-by-frame events as they unfolded. Achieved black and white television and amateur footage taken in all parts of Dallas that day are put together showing some alarming situations that bear questions to be answered.

Volume 18 of the Warren Commission reproduced 158 frames of the Zapruder Film. Frames 208 through 211 were missing and a splice was evident. Frames 314 and 315 were switched and 284 a repeat of 283. FBI Director, J. Edgar Hoover wrote in 1965 'it was a printing error'. In 1967, *Life* magazine released a statement saying four frames of the camera-original had been accidentally destroyed and adjacent frame damaged by a laboratory technician on November 23 1963. They also that year, hired a New Jersey film lab to make a 16-mm copy of the original film.

In 1991 the famed Hollywood director Oliver Stone released his film *JFK* starring Kevin Costner playing the prosecutor Jim Garrison in his case against Clay Shaw. Stone paid the Zapruder family $85,000 for the rights to show Abraham's account of the fateful day in Dallas. Being the first public showing of the footage Garrison played and replayed the 'fatal shot' frames over and over to demonstrate, that a human being who is shot in the head with a high-powered rifle from behind, as the Warren Report and House Sub Committee controversially suggested, does not have his head violently move in a backward direction toward the impacting bullet. Frame 312 shows a rear headshot and half a second later in frame 313 a penetration from the front. It was not possible to fire and reload a round with a bolt-action rifle and re-aim and fire again with that accuracy in just half a second. The frames also showed Jackie's face looking downward as the first round was fired and her husband slumped toward her. Then they show her face raising to her right and looking up at her husband's face as the frontal shot connects. Her head continues moving backwards and behind the President as her eye catches an object leaving her husband's head and landing on the trunk of the limousine, only possible from an impact from the front. She had registered in her mind that she must go and retrieve whatever it was. Hence her attempt to climb backwards as agent Hill sprinted forwards on Elm Street. She had in fact retrieved part of her husband's brain matter and clutched it in her hands all the way to Parkland Hospital where she handed them to Dr Marion Jenkins.

Oliver Stone's film also brings to light the three shell casings found on the sixth floor of the depository seemed to set the stage, for only three shots were fired when there was evidence of marks in the roadway of a shot that missed completely, as line of sight evidence later collected, showed that a horizontal road sign may have blocked Oswald's view of the motorcade at some instant. The second bullet was allegedly found on the Governor's gurney at the hospital. It was photographed and entered into evidence showing it still very much intact and almost perfect in shape after supposedly causing seven entrance and exit wounds in two men? After passing through the president it would have had to stall in mid-air for a split second and take a left and then right turn to re-enter the Texas Governor at the trajectory given in the report? The 888-page Warren Report has 552 witnesses and 3100 exhibits. It was transferred to the National Archives with the unpublished portions initially sealed for seventy-five years being the year 2039 for reasons of 'intending to serve as protection of innocent persons who could otherwise be damaged because of their relationship with participants in the case'. The remaining JFK assassination related documents are scheduled for release to the public by 2017, twenty-five years after the passage of the JFK Records Act of 1992. President Johnson, Robert Kennedy and four of the seven members of the Warren Commission all articulated, some off the record, a level of scepticism about the Commissions basic findings.

1963 left a nasty scab on most of us to this day can be opened to ooze at mere mention of the horrible events. I write in detail of that fateful day as this left a most vivid impression on those of us who were just teenagers in those days. To actually watch the gruesome real murder of another human made stark contrast to the fiction seen on the screen. This figure was one of the worlds' leaders who we, as young people admired. He was so different to the older grey-haired stodgy men we had grown accustomed to in politics; this man was vivacious, handsome and made us laugh with his wit. We could relate and take notice of what he said for it had valued meaning in those insane days of the 60s. He was going to take us to the moon!

The year tumbled forward with another air disaster from Trans Canada Airlines losing a DC8 after take-off from Montreal's Dorval Airport losing all on board. Near the end of the year in December lightning takes down Pan Am flight 214 in Maryland and we watch news reports about the kidnapping of Frank Sinatra's son at Harrah's in Lake Tahoe. The last month continues with Kenya becoming Independent under Jomo Kenyatta becoming Prime Minister. Turkish and Greek Cypriots are fighting each other and on the 22nd the cruise ship *Lakonia* burns north of Madeira losing 128 passengers. Lighter news of the year ended with the phenomena of 'Beatlemania' after the Liverpool group released their two single hits 'I Saw Her Standing There' and 'I Want to Hold Your Hand', that sold millions of 45-rpm plastic records that a tone arm used to scrape across to produce the music we all loved listening to on our old Garrard turntables. No 8-track tapes, cassettes, CD's or iTunes in those days! On June 9 in Owensboro, Kentucky actor Johnny Depp was born, whom later as my client I had the privilege of calling my friend, flying for three years to and from his private island purchased in the Exuma Cays.

Chapter 9
Here comes Betsy!

The Bahamian way of life was now firmly planted in this English schoolboy. Travel back and forth across the Atlantic alone was old hat. I was still trying to persuade my parents that an education in St. Andrews' school on Shirley Street would be a far better investment than the rubbish I was exposed to in England. My mother was enthusiastic for the idea but my father had other plans. Three times a year I made the crossing with BOAC flying it's 707s and then VC 10s. At the ripe old age of seventeen my holiday jobs with Underwater Tours were something to look forward to. Weeks seemed to crawl by all too slowly in England with half-term breaks at Grey Thatch always elevating my spirits. I had purchased a single barrel 12-gauge shotgun to walk the fields of Sussex honing my skills of providing a meal of fresh game for my grandparents. The English woodpigeon would come across the tree lines with lightning speed and with a good lead and two eyes on the bird I could down two or three in a morning, enough for a fine meal with Jorge and Edna.

Finally, welcome news came that Graham's meeting with my parents, that very hot July Sports Day on the Isle of Wight, had finally sunk home to both our respective parents. Both of us were being removed from King James First. I was to choose a different school after passing the General Certificate of Education exams while Graham escaped before me to Dawlish College in the county of Devon. My parents showed me the prospectus for Seaford College, an impressive looking school set in the countryside of Sussex just outside of the village of Petworth lying just north of my grandparents home in the same county. Already I thought this a better choice. The main school building stood on an elevation of manicured lawns overlooking the five 'houses' that comprised the school scattered throughout the grounds; a multi storied grand old estate house from the past with green algae growing on the large stonework with familiar ivy crawling up the walls. Huge ancient conifers dotted the landscape where flowering English gardens provided the smattering of colour.

Behind the main house with its pillared frontage climbed the familiar wooded hills of the Sussex Downs. My interview went as poorly as the first one given on the Isle of Wight. The headmaster repeating again, 'what sport I specialised in and what position I played'? 'Shit', here we go again I thought. Does everything linked with the education system in this country immediately revolve around what sport you play? 'I excel in swimming, sailing and water sports' did not get me any points with the short rotund man with close cropped forward swept hair known as the Reverend Headmaster; his tweed jacket and white dog collar complete with familiar black flowing master's robes. I was assigned to Charmandean Hall down near the playing fields. The senior boys ran the school with teachers acting as council if needed. As one worked his way up the system and became more senior, promotion followed to junior prefect presiding over the other younger lads in your house. The senior prefects ruled each house and were awarded their own private study while junior prefects remained in the common dormitories. Above all of us the head prefect enjoyed his own private study, housing a private bedroom and bathroom. Our senior man was tall, thin, quiet individual with amazing skills in pencil drawings that adorned his walls of gorgeous female models. I always coveted that talent and hoped one day I could draw that well with art a favourite subject in school managing often to be top of the class. Passing exams for GCE however proved more difficult, failing twice to the disbelief of my teachers. The third effort gave me a passing grade to complete the ten certificates I succeeded in where the country average was about five. My English teacher who exclaimed 'your spelling is atrocious Paul, I can't see you passing your finals' was stunned on my achieving a distinction! Writing did return as a part time career later with freelance publications in American aviation magazines and art stayed with me after arriving in the Bahamas to live permanently. During slow days before businesses got off the ground I picked up the brushes to enter exhibitions held at the Buena Vista Hotel with a local group of seventeen talented friends; names such as Rolf Harris, Melissa Maura, Nellie Higgs, Sue Shepherd, Eddie Minnis, Dennis Knight, Steven Malone and Fane Solomon to name a few, selling near all my works completed in oils, watercolour and acrylics. Over three decades would pass before I pick up the brushes again.

The new school's pecking order became very relevant and worked fairly well. There were always one or two bad apples, as in the first institution, but with added seniority my position held more clout from the first day there; being taller reaching over six feet and starting to take better shape also helped without question. I still had to endure the 'apple-pie bed' made up in secret by some fool playing prank on the new boy. That first night I found it impossible to crawl between the sheets; one had to strip the whole bed and remake much to the tittering of the juniors in the dorm. With early promotion, I soon had some control over my destiny and the behaviour of others around me. Time finally arrived for me to stop taking crap from anyone in the system playing a role for unacceptable behaviour all through my life. My juniors came to respect that I took time to talk to them, taking interest, rather than merely bark orders. They competed to be my 'fag', an awfully misconstrued title for a position of merit the junior lads vied for. The lad would polish my shoes daily; display my uniform on my bed, which he made while I taking a shower receiving added pocket money for his labours. There were more pleasant mature oversees students enrolled at Seaford College. Standing out was an American bearing my mother's maiden name of Hood. He knew Florida and the Bahamas, familiar with favourite radio stations such as WQAM that we all listened to as teenagers here in Nassau. Having someone who understood our way of life and knew what we talked about not reacting negatively through jealousy was a warm welcome. I finally had someone to communicate with nearing the end of my schooling saga. The school system itself still had the similar old English educational ways with field sports dominating the itinerary and everyone's time; I loathed being soaking wet where it mandatory to cheer from the side-lines on an abominably cold rugby field in the middle of January. This island boy could only reflect racing over warm turquoise waters off the Ocean Club on a slalom ski pulled by Andrew's yellow fifteen foot Jupiter speedboat over powered with a large 85HP Chrysler outboard; these English lads had no clue what one could call a good time!

Andrew worked for Volkswagen in Oakes Field and became a close companion through the years. We shared the love of the sea and the game of tennis. In later years we made a weekly pilgrimage for much needed extra income on Saturday mornings to the south side of Rose Island in his speedboat holding a fifty-five gallon plastic garbage can between the seats. In a day of free diving, using only Hawaiian slings, we would only head home when the can overflowed with spiny lobster whips and the occasional grouper, yellow fin rockfish or sweet tasting Hogfish. Starting at the East end near Booby Rock Channel we worked our locations westward one reef at a time. One diver would cover the perimeter and the second the interior ledges of the coral growth. Countless dives from the surface would be made in a day covering depths averaging twenty to thirty feet of water. Our diving relationship became a main stay of income in years just ahead.

The herding aspects of school days were still very evident at Seaford. A large school hall was used to congregate all the houses together for general assemblies and special occasions. The only good part about the place was the movies that were shown on a Saturday night. Other general meetings in the huge hall were of great annoyance to many with the music teacher demanding us all listen to music not attuned to teenage boys and at times a ridiculous sing-a-long or recital. Here students could call out names of their comrades forcing them to walk up front to humiliate themselves in public spectacle on stage. School society I was learning had some very strange ways of amusing themselves. I felt way out of place in this country and it played a crucial part in plans for a permanent solution, ridding myself of both school and country. My time was numbered as the students worked their way through the 'privileged' or 'foreigners' known publicly to be extraordinary from the rest of the gaggle. It would be the Bahamian boys' turn next. That Saturday morning I had a plan in place when the chant went out for me to rise. I let the crowd chant in a rising crescendo before making my move. In front of 400 gleeful students and masters, slowly rising out of my seat to the cheers of hundreds waiting for their ultimate humiliation. I raised my middle index finger high aloft bringing silence to the auditorium telling them clearly 'you can kiss my Royal Bahamian ass'! I walked slowly and deliberately out of the building and back to the house study. The silence was stunning as all the heads and gaping mouths stared at my exit. Never in school history had a soul voiced against this ridiculous ritual. He's never going to pull this off they thought in unison; he's in for some real punishment now. You could hear a pin drop as I walked calmly to the rear of the hall, my shoes making a solid noise on the wood floor each step passing venomous looks and out in to the weekend sunshine. No one followed save the American, with a pat on the back and wide grin, 'these bloody Brits are nuts, that was brilliant, good for you!'

The drive from North Bersted village to Petworth was certainly more attractive than the long train journey and ferry ride across the Solent. The weaving country lanes found their way through the Downs descending toward Seaford's impressive entrance. Large wrought-iron gates lay open to the long driveway leading up to the main house. Joining the cue for my first meal at the main building I walked face to face with Rick Roldan, whose parents we had known since arriving in Nassau. Neither family had talked about where their boys were being sent to school, small world. Rick was in a different house, Adair House I believe, and being the accomplished soccer player and track sprinter fit right in with the sports stars of the school. We saw little of each other, two Bahamians in the same location but our worlds far apart on those sprawling grounds. One of the first evenings at the movie hall I suddenly felt deathly ill. Nausea rising and sweat running down my paled complexion, needing to get myself across to Charmandean Hall and a bed; my shaky exit and condition was noticed by the American. He escorted me to the dorm and I crawled in to bed shaking violently with fever. He covered me with an extra blanket and said he would inform the school nurse. I always noted that act of compassion from a fellow student compared to the cruelty of those imbeciles from the previous institution I had attended.

Seaford College was at least a step in the right direction and a more constructive learning curve. One of my house members also an 'airline brat', as we were termed so affectionately, his father working for East African Airways. Alastair Gill similarly had a grandparent living in an old thatched cottage near Chichester. He was an avid and accomplished hunter since early childhood in the African bush. I imagined and witnessed later him dressed with the familiar faded green bush shirt and felt hat, curly brown hair showing under the brim; a freckled face with a wry smile, he looked the part from a Robert Ruark novel. We would become co-conspirators in many escapes off the school grounds at unapproved times with my grandfather acting as a willing accomplice to go on shooting expeditions down at Grey Thatch. Sunday was a good time to sneak away for a day's shoot and some of grandmother's cooking. I had been promoted to Chapel Steward because of my seniority. When duty called it involved preparing the chapel for the Sunday service and communion, in turn giving welcome access to the wine. Seated in the forward pews created quite the stir when needing to relieve myself of gas. The hopefully silent fart proved fatal in odor and noise level as it rattled off the long wooden pew. That quaint old building acoustically had the entire younger audience shaking with uncontrollable laughter as we bent over in prayer. We were collectively behaving only as boys could, scowled ferociously by the Reverend Head Master. Pretending to be on the way to chapel while off duty we would divert behind the old school church, complete with dark green ivy crawling up the grey stone-walls up in to the heavy wooded hills behind the school property. Hidden in the trees a plastic bag with a change of clothing getting us out of the school uniform that would have been easily recognised by any Sussex local spotting us exiting the tree line at the top of the hill. As prearranged, Jorge Dean would be waiting with his car at the roadside summit and we would be off southwards for a day's adventure. Alastair owned a side by side sixteen-gauge hammer shot gun which he left at Grey Thatch, manufactured by Russell and Hilsdon the very long established gun shop in Chichester that we bought our ammunition from. When school days were coming to a close some three years later Alastair offered me his gun to purchase that I still own. Before we parted company he would make another offer that would change my life. 'When we are through with this crap, come to Africa and see what a safari is really all about!'

We would walk through the fields and working together flush partridge and pheasant from the tall grasses. The birds would explode from under our feet and scatter in all directions. I would work the left side birds and Alastair the right flyers. He would prompt me on the 'Churchill style' of using a side-by-side; two eyes on the bird and just follow the target with natural point and lead. A squeeze of the dual triggers let hammers set off each barrel with an ear shattering boom, left first and then a tighter pattern of shot from the full choke on the right while following the more distant birds and bring them down; two barrels only per man per shot.

Anything that you missed was fair game to escape for the next encounter. I soon found a matching Italian hammer twelve-gauge to purchase, which proved a master at the longer ranges, and big birds that we would raise. The afternoon was spent cleaning our catch and having a cold beer and wonderful food with my grandparents while wiping the guns clean with an oily rag. Jorge would then drive us back to the hillside rendezvous point where a change of clothing back in to uniform. We scurried down the hillside full of leaves laying on the ground snapping buried twigs in our hurried decent; making our way in to the main building to join the line of boys waiting for the evening meal to be served in the main dining room.

'Where the bloody hell have you two been?' some would ask as we both slyly blended in. 'Oh just to the library and out walking,' we would bluff to the disbelieving looks.

The summer holidays of 1965 were upon us, another eight weeks of fun in the sun. The welcome approach of the 707 over the familiar aerial view of the Berry Islands with North Eleuthera laying out of the left side windows. Losing altitude, the four-engine Boeing lined up for the approach to Runway 14. The new bridge construction was near complete joining Potters Cay and East Bay Street to Paradise Island. Dark blue waters gave way to sudden turquoise and the orange hews of shallow coral heads off Love Beach. Palms waving on the shoreline in the gentle July breezes made the scene as stunning as the very first viewing. The short stubby control tower passed the left side as the huge main undercarriage touched the runway with blue smouldering rubber. The aircraft let out its roar of reverse thrust and the wing showed all its inner workings as spoilers were deployed. We taxied to the terminal and the large stairway wheeled to the forward entrance of the jet. As the main door opened the welcome hot summer air rushed through the air-conditioned cabin. My father with familiar white aircrew shirt and brown complexion met me at the stair base.

'Welcome back, good flight?' I nodded in appreciation and looked toward the open balcony below the tower building. My mother waved energetically. It really was good to be home. I couldn't wait to walk to the end of the dock at William Street and buy a fresh sixpenny conch that would make salad with fresh lime and bird pepper. When the currency of the Bahamas changed from pounds to dollars that same conch jumped overnight to fifty cents, the equivalent of three shillings and sixpence, my first lesson on inflation!

The welcome drive home along the coast felt more comfortable with road surfaces supporting new tarmac. The bright pink Emerald Beach Hotel still played its part displaying beautiful landscaping next door to the Nassau Beach. The 'Howard Johnson's' sign would become a daily landmark in my early daytime career and the Rum Keg throbbing to the merengue during the hot summer evenings. Through town we passed the familiar traffic policemen standing on the short wooden boxes in the centre of the street, their crisp, white, perfect uniforms showing immaculate creases as they waved traffic through with white-gloved hands. A raised hand to stop traffic meant a photo opportunity for passing tourists welcomed to stand next to them for a vacation moment recorded on film. Passing the Savoy Theatre, the only place in town to see the latest films released; a small hole-in-the-wall building on the north side of Bay Street where the inside resembled an old stage theatre in London with rows of red velvet seats curved to face the stage and screen set far below. Mandatory dress code for the movie theatre in the 60s was jacket and tie for the men, even in the height of the Bahamian summers where queuing outside the sweat trickled down your back soaking one's shirt. Exiting town and near the yacht marinas we turned up William Street where, on the brow of the shallow incline, stood the familiar two story pink apartment building still standing today. The old wooden Pritchard house still stood across from our entrance with its latticed balconies behind Stanley Toogood's studio on Bay Street; a strange crackling sound awakening us one night with a raging fire splintering the old timbers. We recued the frail old couple in time before it collapsed in ruin; no longer did we have to watch out for the old man's antics of bathing in Oxydol laundry powder! The row of coconut palms had grown slightly but still in clear view were the docks of The Nassau Yacht Haven. *Traveler* and *Alpha* berthed in their usual spots with the *Tropic Bird* catamaran still docked on the outside now on the East dock. She had been moved inward to allow her huge sister ship the *Tropic Rover* to lie on the outside.

'She's the largest catamaran in the world' my Dad explained, 'you can water ski under the thing as she is so tall!' Her dark blue hulls and tall masts were impressive.

The *Tropic Rover* was indeed huge in comparison to the *Tropic Bird*, operated by Tropic Cruises Ltd here in Nassau. The *Rover* spanned 145 feet displacing 150 tons. She was designed by Captain Sid Hartshorn to carry 10,000 square feet of canvas, schooner rigged with twin diesel engines for power. He followed the Pacific theory of design where the twin hulls were relatively deep and narrow for directional stability in rough water and following seas. He also had designed the earlier commissioned *Tropic Bird*. The hulls on the new boat were 128 feet long and she drew only five feet, each hull having twenty-two separate compartments. They were constructed out of plywood and fibreglass upside down and then turned upright for the two hulls to be connected with decking. A perfect idea for the shallow Bahamian waters. She was to carry sixty-six passengers who would cruise the local waters of New Providence having been launched in to the New River at the Summerfield Boat Yard in Fort Lauderdale in the spring of 1962 at a total cost of about $100,000.

Nineteen-sixty-five proved to be another tumultuous year where world events played out on both sides of the Atlantic. In January, we saw the State Funeral of Sir Winston Churchill, the British Prime Minister who led the UK through World War Two. Never had so many dignitaries been assembled from so many countries to attend such occasion. While racial tensions flared in the United States, NASA was launching more space flights than any other year. The Russians however did beat them to spacewalking when cosmonaut Aleksei Leonov left his spacecraft for twelve minutes where he could gaze upon the earth from outside his vehicle. The film, 'Sound of Music' premieres and five days later 200 state troopers clash with 500 civil rights demonstrators in Selma, Alabama in what would be remembered as 'Bloody Sunday'. Three days later the first 3500 US Combat Troops enter Vietnam. In March, Gemini 3 launches from Cape Canaveral off the Florida coast with Gus Grissom and John Young aboard. Within two days the news shows Martin Luther King having succeeded a march from Selma to Alabama's capital of Montgomery with 25,000 people. Near the middle of the year large production films such as *My Fair Lady* win eight Academy Awards while the space program opens the doors of modern communication with the successful launch of the 'Early Bird' Satellite. Starting its service in June for telephone, television and facsimile where, for the first time, Europe and the West have almost instantaneous communication.

British race car driver Jim Clark wins the Indianapolis 500 Formula One race and takes the Championship for that year. Gemini 4 launches Ed White for Americas first spacewalk, while Mariner 4 flies past Mars sending back the first close up photographs of the Red Planet followed by another Gemini flight piloted by Conrad Cooper and Pete Conrad on board. Canada unveils its new red maple leaf flag. The hot summer days of July flowed into steaming August. The ocean hosting many oily calm days where one could ride the bow of Underwater Tours dive boat watching reef fish scatter for the safety of their coral homes as the steel hull sliced through the crystal-clear Bahamian water. We would pass through the narrows and hear the steel band playing aboard the *Tropic Bird* as she sailed around Paradise Island's Long Beach to bump her bows gently on to the soft sand of Cabbage Beach releasing her cargo of tourist passengers appearing like lemmings pouring from inside the hull. The pristine white sand now full of footprints as they all walked westward along the empty natural shoreline. While we jumped off the stern of the dive boat into near ninety-degree ocean a huge weather system drifted off the west coast of Africa; conditions ripe for the spawning of another hurricane.

On August 27 1965 Tropical Storm 'Betsy' was named east of the Windward Islands. She travelled up the North side of Hispaniola making a north-westerly turn toward the Carolinas becoming a fully-fledged hurricane. Betsy was large and really well defined. Her ominous, near perfect, circular shape with distinctive 'eye' kept all our attentions fixed on her course, appearing to track the familiar course past the outer Bahamas and curve toward South Carolina. All interests in the islands were beginning a sigh of relief as she passed eastward of the Bahamas on September 5 and by nightfall she lay 350 miles east of Daytona Beach, Florida. That night the huge storm made an unprecedented loop in its path, a phenomenon not seen but this once in all my years in the islands, a full 180 degree turn south-westward heading straight for the northern Bahamas. At 2 am that morning my father bringing me out of a deep sleep awakened me.

'I have to go to the airport and evacuate all the Bahamas Airways planes, I need you to help your Mum get the apartment and patio ready, Betsy has turned around!' No trip to Jamaica this time. We were going to see first-hand what a major storm strike could do to our island.

The morning of September 6 had Betsy clocking winds of 140 mph completing her full circle turn heading directly toward New Providence. Great Abaco recorded sustained winds of 147 mph. In the early light of dawn winds were already bending the palm trees. My father had returned home with the airline fleet scattered in the night. The docks of Nassau Yacht Haven looked skeletal with all the occupants having evacuated during the dark hours. Most had run eastward, about the only choice available, toward Eleuthera with havens of natural hurricane anchorages such as Hatchet Bay. In the early morning hours, the winds started their ominous howl through the power cables down the street, leaves rattled furiously in the trees and loose small debris beginning to take flight. A dull dark grey sky let loose with torrential horizontal rains and westerly winds building their crescendo as each hour passed.

Our patio faced north, offering enough lee side protection to view the natural phenomena in entirety. Starting in the west winds would pull through south and later to east. The hurricane approached the north shore of the capital with raging winds constantly over 140 mph gusting twenty knots higher, her forward speed slowing to a crawl. The noise was deafening and relentless. Palm trees moaned as they leaned precariously from the pressure of the wind, their fronds lashed and shredding with horizontal rain as if needles penetrating their skins. The scene was one seething mass of motion for hours on end. Crescendos of howling winds filled the air, offering no let up and no escape from anything outside. Domestic pigeons could be seen flung through the air to crash helplessly in death to the mass of foliage raging below them. The motion was so violent that the palms became a blur with speed and water all mixed in one weapon. Debris flew sideways, tree branches shearing off, coconuts becoming missiles. Sheets of corrugated iron flew at huge speeds through the air wrapping themselves around palm trunks with consistency of paper towel. Wind gusts screamed as they passed by. One could not imagine it could blow any harder when it suddenly did, effortlessly. Mature trees finally succumbed to the ferocious forces pounding them into submission, their roots having been displaced by raging rainwater; with a merciless crash they broke to the onslaught, shattering their trunks to hit the property walls below. Our street disappeared from view, filled with crippled palm tress lying on their sides in an angry river torrent of gushing rainwater.

Looking northward we saw the sea white with fury as the wind sheared the waves eastward. One or two remaining brave conch boats dipped their bows and stretched their anchor lines to their limits holding their own on the inside waters off Potters Cay, sails once bound tight being torn off the booms they had been lashed to. The casuarina pine forest on Paradise Island leaned and struggled against the salty barrage, their incredible strength enabling most to endure. Some in the waterlogged ground finally gave way. Power lines were snapped as if threads of cotton. All appliances in the house fell silent. Our electricity would be gone for days. Betsy had stalled in her track. Now a stationary monster with its eye wall just north of Paradise Island we took three more hours of roaring wind at its highest velocity. So much rain had fallen that streets were underwater. William Street was a torrential river, a few yards further we could see Bay Street had disappeared under the salt of a high tide. When the wind switched direction, we watched the world's largest catamaran, after mandatory evacuation from the docks where it had laid – having tried safe anchorage in Nassau Harbour – simply glide away absent of any crew aboard. The hurricane played with the *Tropic Rover* as it were a toy, driving the dark blue hulls across the waters to be destroyed beyond the harbour entrance.

Without warning the wind suddenly started to die with brighter light breaking the grim sky. It seemed just minutes before we saw blue skies with a dead calm falling over the island. As if on some magical film set where lights came on and fans turned off we all stood up to gaze on a surreal scene. Hot Bahama sunshine glistened off everything in its wetness. Trees now silent and totally limp lay broken in tattered heaps exposing their massive root systems.

Dead birds lay battered and soaked in a sorry mess on the ground. The forty-mile-wide eye of the storm had brought its calm upon us. My father armed with a machete asked me to go exploring the neighbourhood and waterfront. We knew time had to be heeded but here was chance to see first-hand what those hours of destruction had brought. We would pay strong attention in the opposite direction as the other side of the hurricane still approached. Our shuttered apartment had weathered well as did the neighbouring wooden Bahamian houses. Wood shingles had torn off most roofs showing bare patches of rafters underneath. Television antennas lay in crippled twisted heaps. There was no sign of the driveway or road, every square inch was covered in a layer of debris; broken trees, flowers, buildings and leaves formed a blanket for us to walk on. Our cars were covered with the green shroud of tamarind leaves and branches. My father hacked his way through palm fronds of downed trees that blocked the road to the waterfront. Crawling under the openings he made we reached Bay Street a few yards away. The main road awash with near two feet of saltwater lapping at the doorways of the Toogood building. The sea was dirty looking like tainted milk, every square foot some kind of debris floating in the gentle waves. Pieces of boats showing clue of familiar orange colour once deck planking of the conch boats. Broken water glasses and plastic buckets bumped gently against dock pilings that lay almost submerged by their heavy weight. Bottles in the midst of carpets of Sargasso seaweed added to the mix all over the road. Power lines lay shredded in the saltwater. With power out over the whole island there was no danger of electrocution. Some of the fishermen had brought their vessels into the shallows with the extraordinary high tides allowing them to fall over on their sides as the water receded. They were nearly on the road now some having broken their side planking on the coral shoreline with the incessant battering from the waves. We walked westward towards East Bay Shopping Centre.

Approaching East Bay we could see that there was virtually nothing left. The roaring westerly winds had taken their toll on the frail wooden docks ripping them from the seabed and scattering the planks for miles. Boats that had been left there lay like crippled antiques, torn apart and healing on their sides underwater being held in place by the last remaining mooring lines to the only pilings that had survived. Buildings in the shopping centre were in ruin with sheets of tarpaper torn above their exposed rafters. The calm of the eye was passing as we suddenly felt a gentle breeze coming from the East. Blue skies offered small wisps of cloud that raced at high speed in altitude above us. Over Montague Bay and out toward east end point the sky grew angry. 'Time to head home, here we go again,' my father warned. We waded as fast as possible reaching the entrance to our street as the sunshine disappeared yet again. Within minutes the ordeal started over from the opposite direction. The afternoon saw the hurricane lash our islands from the East; remaining foliage becoming so thin we could see neighbouring houses that for years were hidden from view.

During the rage of the second onslaught we thought we heard human voices over the roar of the winds. They seemed to becoming from our easterly neighbours. With wind driven torrential rains racing through the underbrush the familiar shouts of Captain Eddie Ballard became very distinct. 'Get out of bed Hardings!' the voices jested.

'What the hell…?' my father exclaimed as he saw the Eddie and his wife 'Buzzie' plough their way through the trees toward the stairs of the apartment, soaked to the skin dressed in foul-weather gear they scaled the wall shouting loudly,

'Conditions are critical. We're out of rum!'

They sat for hours telling stories of past storms and boats and Bahamas Airways. The dark rum flowed making tales more vivid. Their excited conversation suddenly interrupted as we watched in amazement a forty-foot ketch sailing down the harbour from the east unaided, with no one on board, apparently torn from its mooring. It raced toward the bridge in a straight course as if being steered. Favouring the Paradise Island side of the narrow waterway off Potters Cay it cleared hitting land. On Paradise Island, we could see the yellow jackets of several men in foul-weather gear standing on the walls of Hurricane Hole Marina. As if a master helmsman were at the wheel the ketch suddenly turned northward with perfect timing against the racing harbour currents, sailed accurately in to the entrance of the marina, the yellow jackets throwing lasso ropes on to the decks hauling her toward safety to a perfect halt without a scratch. I learned years later one of those mariners to save the vessel was Gardner Young, my first employer!

Vessels that had run across to Eleuthera for safe harbour found themselves in more danger than where they had left. Within Hatchet Bay anchor lines proved too short as the water rose with the storm surge. Anchors tore out easily from the soft grassy bottom they were desperately holding, dragging for yards within the gale. Like toy boats were pushed on to shore and stacked upon each other. It was carnage on a grand scale. As Betsy headed toward the Florida Keys the Bahamas calmed and returned to blue summer days. The coast road by The Caves near the airport had slipped in to the ocean leaving no passage for vehicles for days. Flooded streets plagued us as the island foliage rapidly turned black ravaged by the salt air started to die, everything that used to be green now dead and broken. An odour of rotting vegetation would stay for days until fresh rain breathed new life. With amazing 'island spirit' Bahamians rallied. Unlike some major countries hit by disaster taking months or years to get up and running, the Bahamas clean-up was inspiring to watch. Caribbean countries came to the rescue as our nation had done to them in earlier times. Jamaican Electrical workers arrived lending hand to the Electricity Corporation restoring power lines to the grid. During those early days all seemed to recover really quickly. Heavy equipment ploughed the roads out west covered with the sands of Saunders Beach and huge boulders washed ashore out of the ocean. Hoteliers had maintenance crews and landscapers working feverishly making properties presentable again. The coast road was rebuilt allowing traffic to flow toward the airport and Lyford Cay, everything natural so visibly thinner with the major loss of vegetation and trees. There was a noticeable silence in the morning air with no birds seen for months following. The pristine ocean waters now pastel turquoise and opaque in appearance, fine sediment taking days of tidal flow to disperse showing eventual sign of clarity again. There would be no dive business for a while.

On September 7, Betsy passed over Key Largo as a lower Category 3 storm but warmer waters of the Gulf refuelled her back to a Category 4 with 155 mph winds. One mile an hour short of a Category 5 Hurricane Betsy's eye passed over Grand Isle, Louisiana on September 9 crippling every building there. Eight offshore oilrigs were destroyed and a Shell Platform at the mouth of the Mississippi was never seen again. The 'Maverick' platform owned by ex-President George Bush Seniors' Corporation vanished.

Entering the month of August Betsy's eye-wall covered New Orleans from 8 pm to 4 am the next morning with winds of 130 mph that pushed a storm surge in to Lake Pontchartrain, a 630 square mile body of water averaging twelve feet or more deep. Levees in the River Gulf Outlet and Ninth Ward failed letting water flood the houses up to their eaves. Residents trying to escape the rising floodwaters were drowning in their attics. Seventy-six people died and it took ten days for the waters to recede. Home owners were sleeping in shelters and on the streets where possible while having to forage for food. One hundred and sixty-four thousand homes were destroyed. The French Quarter being one of the highest areas survived; in those days populated by the lower income population and not yet fashionable to live there. Not until the 1980s did values begin to rise to what it became today. Evidence emerged that poor construction and maintenance of the levees caused the failures and $1.2 billion in damage. A 2005 equivalent was estimated at near $12 billion. Because of 'Betsy' the US Army Corps of Engineers Hurricane Protection Program was founded building stronger and taller levees resistant that would in theory survive a Category 3 storm. In August 2005 'Katrina' spawned over the Bahamas growing to a Category 5 would prove their efforts futile and history to repeat itself worse than before. The names 'Betsy' and 'Katrina' were retired from the names list of the Atlantic Storms. Betsy's size only repeated twice in history with Hurricane's 'Carla' and 'Opel'. During this edit hurricane 'Joaquin' is lashing the southern Bahamas as the strongest October storm to hit our islands since 1866.

Chapter 10
A Nightmare at Sea'

The 1960s were incredibly turbulent years. As youngsters, we watched in amazement the events of our world unfold. We had witnessed the assassination of a popular American president and times were to get worse. It was difficult for those of us schooling in a sheltered English countryside to comprehend of the severity of war and civil rights violence in the western world; a blessed generation that escaped actual involvement in war through each and every decade. War would surround us, coming uncannily close but our ages and nationalities graced us to not be called to active duty: the daily struggle of different races and creeds elsewhere hard to grasp staying sheltered in day-to-day affairs in our tropical paradise. During vacations in Nassau, hearing American news broadcasts, we comprehended little the consequences of history happening from all directions on the planet, seemingly all at the same time; life's cycle did not gel with us in the teen years. We simply let time fly ignorantly past us. Nineteen-sixty-five had us experience the mighty power of a hurricane here at home but as the year passed world events continued to bombard us from all direction; positive news one minute and disaster the next. We would be awed by Gemini space projects and the launching of some of the world's first communications satellites, then hit with war in Vietnam taking horrendous tolls. Contradictions of men burning draft cards on the grounds of the University of California in Berkley to an air force spreading deadly napalm in war. Dr Martin Luther King spearheads the Civil Rights Movement in America while the World's Fair opens in Flushing Meadows, New York. Police were beating, hosing and killing civilians in the southern states of America yet still we were distracted by the young charismatic prize fighter Cassius Clay, renaming himself Muhammad Ali, knocking out Sonny Liston in the Heavyweight Championship fight. We are amazed at first pictures of the planet Mars thanks to Marina 4 spacecraft, unable to comprehend photographs successfully traveling 249 million miles! Great Britain finally bans cigarette advertising under the crush of evidence and legal pursuits toward the tobacco industry. Our planet is a world of extremes. While the worst race riots break out in Los Angeles the Beatles play their first concert in Shea Stadium on the other side of the same country. While a thousand buildings are badly damaged or destroyed in the Watts Riots we still find time to focus on Gemini 5 with Pete Conrad and Gordon Cooper traveling above us all in the first week long journey in space; later to be trumped by Gemini 6 and 7 performing the first successful spacecraft rendezvous in the dark void above us. The television series *Star Trek* began to capture our imagination as actually feasible with space travel becoming the norm. Here on Earth, India tries to invade Lahore while its neighbour Pakistan enters India's sector of Kashmir. We read of names such as Harold Wilson the Prime Minister of England, Ian Smith of Rhodesia and Charles De Gaulle seeking re-election in France. Russia admitting sending rockets to the North Vietnamese while at home we watch the new epic film *Dr Zhivago.*

It was a calm day on November 12 1965 when one of the three cruise ships sailing weekly between Miami and Nassau, set sail out of Port Everglades Florida to make her 186-mile journey to Nassau, at 365 feet displacing 5000 tons the *Yarmouth Castle* carried 376 passengers with 176 crew members. Her sister ships *Ariadne* and *Bahama Star* crisscrossed the same routes faithfully to all be in the port at Nassau for a busy weekend of tourist activity. The winter season had begun. *Yarmouth Castle* was built in 1927 in Philadelphia christened the *Evangeline* requisitioned by the United States Government as a troop carrier in the Pacific. She ran from San Francisco to various battlefronts as a Hospital Ship. After the war, she was refitted at Bethlehem Steel Shipyards costing $1.5 million to be returned to passenger service in May 1947 between New York and the Bahamas, only to be laid up between 1948 and 1953. The next year she was sold to a Liberia Company servicing from Boston to Yarmouth in Nova Scotia, Canada. In 1955 she sailed to the Caribbean and sold yet again in 1964 to bare her new name of *Yarmouth Castle*, routing between New York and Nassau for Caribbean Cruise Lines, which ended later in bankruptcy. Finally, the cruise ship became Panamanian Registered operated by Yarmouth Cruise Lines carrying passengers solely between Miami and Nassau.

During her maintenance it was common practice to cut corners, shaving valuable time to strip old paint before applying new coats. With time and costs being cut regularly, refurbishments saw excessive coats of paint on the walls and carelessly applied on top of lifeboat ropes and hatches. New paint liberally spread over porthole boundaries helped seal and make useless doors and windows. The superstructure of the old ship was made out of ageing wood. Stateroom #610 was situated just above the ships boiler room where added insulation still proved too hot for anyone to occupy. Panelling on the walls had been stripped off and used elsewhere, as was ceiling material, leaving exposed insulation to the open air; the cabin was emptied of all contents and designated as storage. An old mattress pushed haphazardly against a wall had pressed against an exposed light bulb while cans of paint were strewn across the floor. After the evenings activities the bars and restaurants emptied as passengers retired for the night. The cruise ship sailed through the calm waters of the Bahamas on a perfect moonlit evening, heading eastward to skirt the northern Berry Islands before taking a more southerly course toward Nassau by daylight. Her screws chewing through the dark crystal clear ocean creating sparkles of green phosphorescence in the white water of her path. Stars were bright without the obstruction of city lighting. The moon reflected bright light on the smooth oily surface.

Shortly after 1 am the exposed light bulb had generated enough heat to set alight the mattress. Flames rose quickly and efficiently igniting the insulation of the open ceiling. Thick dark smoke raced across the ceiling crawling downward toward the floor. The paint and mattress fabric fuelled the first flames into a roaring inferno within seconds. Fire streamed upward through every crevasse it could find. Layers of heavily painted stairwells and walls allowed all hell to let loose within minutes. The wooden superstructures were engulfed as *Yarmouth Castle* steamed unawares through the Bahamian night. Passengers asleep in the lower decks would hear nothing as fate's eager fingers raced toward them with disastrous efficiency. A badly burned passenger caught unawares in the mayhem made his way to the upper deck before collapsing and discovered by a crewmember seeing a stairwell full of billowing smoke.

The officer on watch notified Captain Byron Voutsinas who in turn ordered the second mate to sound the fire alarm. Duke Smith, a young

Bahamian lad aboard the cruise ship that night, had been employed as a waiter and crewmember, later offered his first break into the entertainment world as a singer aboard the *Yarmouth Castle*. Very popular and well known amongst the passengers, Duke had heard the commotion outside his cabin. He recalls how mandatory coast guard drills held in the Port of Miami had always run so efficiently and this cruise ship crew was known for its speed of operation during the exercises. He recalls *Yarmouth Castle* on past ventures had been plagued with troubles of her own. She had lost power one voyage with engineers having to be helicopter landed on board off the Florida coast. She had on occasion taken on water. This night when pandemonium broke out all past crew training went to hell. Passengers and crewmembers scattered in all directions trying to work their way upward to the safety of the top decks. The second mate never made it to the bridge being overcome with flames. The radio operator was off duty at the time but when rousted discovered that the radio-room was also ablaze and inaccessible.

The doomed ship was 120 miles east of Miami and 60 miles north of Nassau with no alarms sounding and a failed water sprinkling system to douse a fire; passengers and sleeping crew only awoken by the shouting and screaming of others outside in the corridors. People were searching for life jackets that many cabins did not facilitate. The ship had a natural ventilation system that allowed the flames to race vertically through the wooden panelled stairwells creeping unobstructed across wooden floors. Passengers were trapped in their cabins with paint sealed portholes barring their escape. Some broke the glass as the only way of getting out, slicing them as they slid overboard to bleed in the night water. The fire was more intense and concentrated around the forward section of the boat forcing people to flee toward the rear. Lifeboats were catching fire still in their davits. The ship became stationary in the clear November night. Conflicting stories of bravery and cowardice followed. Lifeboats that were launched first had crewmembers scramble aboard first with few passengers taken to safety. Duke remembers how other crews were amazing in their aid to those badly injured and assisted in the safe descent down the rope ladders thrown over the sides toward the waiting ocean; some crew seen giving away their personal life jackets to passengers who had none to find. Chaos erupted where the panic stricken or injured were manhandled and simply thrown overboard in to the sea below to avoid the overpowering flames and heat.

Six miles in front of the *Yarmouth Castle* steamed a Finnish Freighter *Finnpulp* and twelve miles to her stern cruised the *Bahama Star* also bearing toward the Port of Nassau. The freighter noticed the Yarmouth Castle starting to lag behind in her progress and then saw the distinct glow of fire. Captain Carl Brown aboard the *Bahama Star* at 2.15 am catching up and seeing trouble ahead steered full-steam toward the ailing ship. The freighter turned about and tried to notify Nassau three times by radio with no response from the island, then made the first successful distress call to the US Coast Guard. Problems aboard the burning ship worsened as lifeboats jammed in the winches due to ropes plastered with paint, fire hoses brought in to action did not have enough water pressure to take effect. Boats that were successfully deployed from the burning cruise ship had no oarlocks offering no way of manoeuvring away from peril only to be paddled like giant canoes. Only thirteen lifeboats made it in to the sea.

First to arrive on scene was the Finnish freighter with Captain John Lehto, so outraged when he discovered the first lifeboat with only four passengers on board; the other twenty being crew members including Captain Voutsinas claiming he was there to make a distress call from the rescuing freighter. Lehto took the four passengers and in disgust ordered the captain and his crew back to rescue those who were left behind. Two other lifeboats were found also containing only crew from the *Yarmouth Castle*. Captain Brown eased the *Bahama Star* within one hundred yards of the burning ship and launched his lifeboats, which made their way to the starboard side of the doomed liner. Duke recalls how he held a burned victim in his arms and helped others down the rope ladders to the safety of the *Bahama Star*'s lifeboats now alongside. He too climbed aboard the rescue boats and as they eased away from their burning vessel noticing the hull starting to list. The scene resembled infamous past events in the frigid waters of North Atlantic where *Titanic* met her doom with an iceberg some fifty-three years earlier. This night Duke recalls, was eerily the same except for dealing with intense heat instead of frigid cold. Captain Brown confirmed later hearing the screaming and breaking of glass, escaping steam now forced through the ships whistle sending an awful cry over the panic unfolding. Women were loaded on to the saviour lifeboats, husbands comforting them with the message 'I'll see you later'. The water was littered with deck chairs and debris floating as far as one could see. People on the listing decks were throwing anything they could find from luggage to benches into the ocean so those in the water had something to cling to.

Finnpulp launched a motorboat to assist in the towing of useless lifeboats away from the *Yarmouth Castle* over to the safety of the awaiting *Bahama Star*. The freighter made a daring move pulling alongside the liner where some people were able to step from one deck to the other safely. The heat became so intense however the Finnish vessels paint started to blister and burn hastening a retreat to safer distance.

The dark ocean water, reflecting the dancing fire above, became so hot from the scorched hull of the dying liner that it began to boil. The huge hull listed to port side as the dawn sky started to show. Coast Guard planes flying at 4000 feet arriving on the scene were nearly engulfed in smoke and flames from the burning ship. Duke recalls the deep rumbles from the exploding boilers from within the ship sitting in silence watching her last throws of life in the early morning light. At 6 am the liner finally gave in and healed over. In three minutes with a rush of steam and white froth of seawater the *Yarmouth Castle* disappeared beneath the surface taking eighty-seven souls with her. Everything suddenly lay ominously quiet and empty on the open ocean as another gorgeous Bahamian day began. The *Bahama Star* rescued 240 passengers and 133 crewmembers; the *Finnpulp* saved fifty-one passengers and forty-one crew. Fourteen critically wounded were transferred from *Bahama Star* by helicopter and three persons died later in hospital. Out of ninety victims only two were crew, both renowned as wonderful people, the ship's stewardess and its physician. Both rescue ships sailed in to Nassau Harbour on November 13. Survivors were transferred to the British Colonial Hotel on Bay Street for processing and release. Reports made later confirmed that fire doors that should have been closed remained open, that many cabins did not offer lifejackets and no inflatable boats were on board the liner. There was one radio operator when there should have been two. Passengers were never offered a fire drill or shown evacuation routes.

The captain and crew of the *Yarmouth Castle* were charged with violation of duty for leaving the ship before the complete evacuation of its passengers.

The cruise line business went through major changes after the loss of the liner. Duke went on to continue his career aboard the new arrivals of NCL's ships *Sunward* and *Skyward* that would service the islands after this. In 1976, he and his wife Sue started new careers with the first commercial horse stables in the Bahamas in Coral Harbour calling it *Happy Trails*; the same year 1976 I created my first business in the diving tour industry called 'The Out-Island Safari' with its parent company Diving Safaris Ltd. Canadian singer-songwriter Gordon Lightfoot wrote his famous song 'The Ballad of the Yarmouth Castle' to release later in 1969.

Chapter 11
Africa!

With the dramatic pictures from *Gemini 8* in 1966, docking high above the earth, we started to take space travel some what for granted although the magnificence of Earth from that altitude always inspiring. Unmanned Soviet vehicles travelled distances beyond comprehension to crash on the surface of Venus, with space exploration reaching further than our imaginations ever expected. *Surveyor 1* launched from the United States would soft land successfully on the moon. Cape Canaveral was rocketing craft in to space near monthly as visible orange streaks climbing in the night skies north of our Bahamas Islands. In June, *Gemini 9* allowed Gene Cernan to complete a two-hour spacewalk, followed by *Gemini 10*, the twenty-fourth mission and sixteenth manned flight, in which John Young and Mike Collins set an altitude record of 474 miles above the earth.

The United States suddenly has to admit losing a U2 spy plane over Cuba. Suspects in the Great Train Robbery in the UK were apprehended and the Canadians saw Montreal inaugurate their underground metro system. John Lennon meets Yoko Ono and the actor Ronald Reagan is elected Governor of California. This year brought into the world John Daly who became a golf champion, entertainers Stephen Baldwin, Janet Jackson and Julianna Margulies, figure-skating champion Kurt Browning and boxing bad boy Mike Tyson.

The world became very environmentally aware in March 1967 with super tanker *Torrey Canyon* running aground between Lands End in the UK and the Scilly Islands, spilling an estimated twenty-five million gallons of crude oil, only to happen again in America over twenty years later with the *Exxon Valdez* in Alaska entering world history as major disasters that still affect our planet today. The first tanker destroyed by the Royal Air Force using her as a bombing target in order to sink it while that year ocean liner *Queen Mary* retired from service. The 1960s were coming to a close with achievements that amazed us, still contradicted by nations behaviour at war. Israel shoots down seven Syrian MiG fighter jets as the Six Day War approaches. The Soviets lose their first cosmonaut when a parachute fails to open on re-entry to the earth. *Mariner 5* is launched toward a landing on Venus. The decade would not go out unscarred with yet again two tragic losses of renowned figures in 1968.

On Thursday, April 4 Martin Luther King, renown leader of the African-American Civil Rights Movement, standing on his motel room patio at 6.01 pm in Memphis Tennessee when stuck with a single 30-06 bullet fired from a rooming house across the street. The bullet tore through his right cheek breaking his jaw before traveling downward destroying several vertebrae and spinal cord. The impact had ripped off his necktie and severed his jugular vein. Dr King collapsed violently backward immediately unconscious and bleeding profusely. Escaped convict James Earl Ray was seen fleeing from the rooming house across from the motel having dumped a package holding a Remington rifle and binoculars with his fingerprints on the items. Friends of Dr King rushed outside believing that he was already dead although found to still have a pulse. Rushed to St, Joseph's Hospital he was pronounced dead at 7.07 pm at the age of thirty-nine. He had predicted to his wife Coretta after the assassination of John Kennedy, 'this is what is going to happen to mc also. I kecp telling you, this is a sick society'. President Lyndon Johnson declared a national day of mourning with over 300,000 people attending his funeral. James Earl Ray created a worldwide manhunt ending with his capture two months later at London Heathrow Airport. Ray died in jail in April 1998 of liver failure. Senator Robert F. Kennedy gave a speech on the assassination of Dr King during his campaign for presidential nomination, his audience not yet hearing of the death in Memphis. The crowd's reaction was loud and full of emotion with Kennedy's aides feeling there may be well a violent reaction. Pleading with everyone 'For those of you who are black and tempted to be filled with hatred and mistrust of the injustice of such an act, against all white people, I would only say that I can also feel in my own heart the same kind of feeling. I had a member of my family killed, but he was killed by a white man'. He asked the country, 'to make an effort and go beyond these rather difficult times,' that the country needed and wanted unity between whites and blacks. Two months later Robert Kennedy lay dying on a pantry floor within a kitchen of the Ambassador Hotel in Los Angeles.

On June 5 1968, after winning the California and South Dakota Presidential primary elections, shortly after midnight, a twenty-four-year old Palestinian-Jordanian immigrant named Sirhan Sirhan stepped forward with a .22 calibre pistol and fired several times before being wrestled to the floor by several bystanders, some of whom famous football players and Olympic Medallists, all the while his wild shooting continued in various directions wounding five other people. The assassin broke free from his captors and tried to fire again but the gun was empty when again subdued. Kennedy had been shaking seventeen-year-old busboy Juan Romero's hand as Sirhan fired the first shot. A jacket was placed under his head as he lay on the floor where a .22 calibre shell had entered his head. Still conscious and holding the busboys hand Kennedy asked, 'Is everyone safe, OK?' 'Yes, yes everything is going to be ok' the young man replied. Ethel Kennedy finally reached he husbands side waiting for medical attendants to arrive. While lifting him on to s stretcher he whispered 'Don't lift me' were to be his last words. Losing consciousness he was transported to Central Receiving Hospital near death. His wife could hear through a stethoscope that his heart was still beating.

Robert Kennedy was then transferred to The Hospital of the Good Samaritan where he underwent a three-hour-and-forty-minute surgery after being shot three times. One bullet entered just behind his right ear from about an inch away dispersing fragments through his brain. The other two near his armpit exiting his chest while the third lodged in his neck. With extensive neurosurgery to remove the fragments the senator died some twenty-six hours later on June 6. He was forty-two years old.

Just before we bid the decade farewell, 1969 gave us one more bruising with an awful act of violence, news of which swept around the world of the entertainment business; film director, Roman Polanski in London on a film production, leaving his eight-and-a-half-month pregnant wife, actress Sharon Tate, in California. Followers of ex-convict Charles Manson, under his direction, entered the Tate home on the night of August 8 1969, declaring 'Now is the time for *Helter Skelter*', a title taken from a Beatles song. Tate's former lover and hair-stylist, Jay Sebring; Abigail Folger, heiress to the Folger's Coffee fortune; and Polanski's friend Wojciech Frykowski were all brutally stabbed to death. The word 'pig' was carved on Tate's stomach. The next evening the same fate befell couple Leno and Rosemary La Bianca, also living in a Los Angeles neighbourhood. Eventually Manson and his entire family would be captured and sentenced to death, their sentences commuted to life in prison when California temporarily suspended its death penalty. At eighty-years-old today, his next parole hearing will be when he reaches ninety-two, costing the American taxpayer over $2-million to keep him alive in prison.

In space the Russians are well in to their Soyuz program where crews are transferred in outer space, while on Earth, Led Zeppelin produces their first album. Charles de Gaulle steps down as the President of France and Richard Nixon succeeds Lyndon Johnson as 37th President of the United States.

Joe Namath is voted the most valuable player in the American Football League and Elvis Presley is recording again in Memphis, Tennessee, making popular hits such as *In the Ghetto* and *Kentucky Rain*. The Beatles make their last public performance, filmed on the roof of Apple Records in London. In February, the Boeing 747 makes its maiden flight while in Toulouse, France, the first test flight of the Concorde is completed. The Apollo space program sees the launch of *Apollo 9* to test the lunar module, while the United States establishes its famous 'Top Gun' school at Naval Air Station Miramar. Author Mario Puzo publishes his famous book *The Godfather* and John Lennon marries Yoko Ono in Gibraltar. The infamous Harrier jet is introduced to the Royal Air Force in the same month the first temporary artificial heart is implanted. In March, Golda Meir becomes the first female president of Israel while *Apollo 10* flies within 15,000 miles of the lunar surface in a dress rehearsal for the lunar landing. On Earth, the Oscar winning film *Midnight Cowboy* is released and Hollywood loses Judy Garland, dying of a drug overdose in London. June of that year marks the beginning of the Gay Rights Movement and America starts pulling troops out of Vietnam for the first time.

That last year of the 1960s was a huge marker in my life – in July, I and 600 million people on this Earth watched something only dreamt about; a man setting foot on to the surface of the moon. All over the world television stations carried the saga of *Apollo 11* as it launched into a beautiful Florida morning sky, July 16 at 9.32 am local time from Cape Canaveral.

This was the fifth manned mission and third lunar mission. Neil Armstrong was selected to be the man to take that first step. Born August 5 1930, he was a naval aviator, a test pilot having flown 900 flights in many different types of aircraft while at the Dryden Flight Research Centre. He joined NASA in 1962 and commanded *Gemini 8* in 1966, being one of the first American civilians to enter space. He was commander of the first lunar landing along with Buzz Aldrin while Michael Collins remained in lunar orbit in the command module. The Saturn V rocket was enormous, standing 363 feet high and 33 feet wide comprising of three stages. The first stage engines could produce over seven and a half million pounds of thrust, lifting its six and a half million pounds of mass, together with over 2500 pounds of payload. The first engines fired for a mere 168 seconds after first igniting, seven seconds before actual lift-off. When the first stage shut down, the vehicle was already above 200,000 feet and fifty-eight miles downrange over the Atlantic Ocean, in two and half minutes the Saturn V rocket with three men on top were traveling at over 6000 miles per hour to an altitude of near forty miles! We all stared in awe at this immense spacecraft soaring upward. A huge white cylindrical rocket trailing the same length of flame as it climbed into the blue Florida sky and out of our sight.

One of the tensest moments of the whole flight as the rocket first lifted, for here it would not have safely settled back down on the pad without certain catastrophe. To clear the tower alone took over twelve seconds. At a mile high it was already traveling at over 400 feet per second. Armstrong's heartbeat was recorded at 110 as the thrust took the three astronauts upward. At forty-two miles the first stage shut down, dropping earthbound 350 miles down range to splash into the Atlantic Ocean. The second stage propelled the spacecraft to 109 miles high at 15,647 miles per hour, statistics not comprehendible to the layperson in those days. One second after the second stage cut off it separated from the spacecraft and the third and final stage ignited to burn for another two and a half minutes, taking the craft over 1600 miles down range and traveling at an astounding 17,432 miles per hour to further accelerate and escape Earth's orbit at over 25,000 miles per hour. Twelve minutes after launch the three men entered Earth's orbit and after just one and a half orbits the third stage engine pushed the craft toward the moon. After half an hour, the command module separated from the third stage and docked with the lunar module that was nestled in the Lunar Module Adaptor; four panels about seven feet long opened like flower petals on the top of the rocket. The command module turned 180 degrees, performing a ballet above the earth. Once joined together the new craft sped toward the moon.

Three days later on July 19 the spacecraft passed behind the moon and fired its propulsion engines into lunar orbit. The crew could see their landing site in the Sea of Tranquillity, chosen for its smoother rock free surface first seen by unmanned crafts *Ranger 8* and *Surveyor 5.* One day later Neil Armstrong and Buzz Aldrin entered the lunar module Eagle and separated from Columbia manned alone by Mike Collins. Eagle pirouetted in space allowing Collins to inspect it for damage before its historic descent. The two astronauts found themselves about four seconds ahead in their distances meaning a longer distance for the landing taking them miles west of the chosen point. They were about 6000 feet above the moon, distracted by computer alarms, machines in those days not handling all the information asked of them at such speeds, therefore postponing some of its task; diagnosed later as a rendezvous radar switch being in the wrong position. Mission Control from Houston gave an 'all clear' to continue downward. Neil Armstrong looked outside noticing the computers landing target was now a boulder strewn area northeast of a 900-foot crater. The commander took semi-automatic control while his partner called altitudes and speed. With twenty-five seconds of fuel left they bumped the lunar surface. Engines were shut down and checklists completed. The famous radio transmission from Neil Armstrong came back to Earth that we all were intensely listening to; 'Houston, Tranquillity Base here, The Eagle has Landed.' 'Roger Tranquillity, we copy you on the ground. You got a bunch of guys about to turn blue, we are breathing again, thanks a lot!'

Around the world all eyes were on the little spacecraft standing alone on the lunar surface. A mounted slow scan television camera sent grainy black and white transmissions back to Earth. From Times Square to the Far East, northern hemisphere to south, every public window that had a screen visible shared what we all were watching in our homes that Sunday evening at 10.39 pm July 20. Countless millions all over the planet stood still in the streets of their towns, cities and villages, where furniture and appliance stores had left all the television sets on in the display windows; to stare in awe at those poor quality black and white pictures. Some locations poured with rain and yet the masses stood speechless as Neil Armstrong open the hatch of his craft and began the descent down nine steps toward the lunar surface – at 10.56 pm his left foot touched the surface of the moon. He described the surface as 'fine and almost like a powder'; stepping off the Eagle's footpad he uttered those famous words, 'One small step for man, one giant leap for mankind'. John F. Kennedy's mandate 'to place a man on the moon before the end of the decade and return him safely to Earth' was being fulfilled. Buzz Aldrin joined Armstrong on the moon and we watched in fascination as the two men moved around on the surface collecting, forty-nine pounds of lunar rocks and samples, planting the US flag which had to be supported having no wind on the moon's surface. It was very hard to comprehend this was actually happening on that bright planet we could see so clearly from where we stood on Earth. The astronauts used a Hasselblad camera, shooting two and a quarter square film to record remarkable still-photographs of each other along with the lunar craft set against a dramatically bleak lunar landscape; the tiny blue planet Earth appears just above the horizon while Mike Collins orbited above them. The grainy footage we watched of their departure from the lunar surface resembled a poor black and white science fiction film. One second the craft was blowing debris, the next arising out of sight. During lift-off from the moon Aldrin noticed out of his window the engine blast knock over the American flag they had stuck in to the lunar surface, which they had walked on for near two and a half hours. Later missions back to the desolate planet had astronauts place the flag well away from engine blast so it may remain upright after man's departure. On July 21 Eagle jettisoned to lunar orbit and control calculated that it impacted the moon's surface some months later. On the 24th, some fifteen miles from the USS *Hornet* the command module Columbia, slowed by three huge drogue parachutes, splashed in to the Pacific Ocean at 11.51 am with considerable force and upside down. Floatation bags, deployed from the crew inside, righted the craft and recovery of the craft and crew a success to begin their twenty-one days of quarantine after which three astronauts began a 'Giant Leap' tour lasting forty-five days covering twenty-five countries. The command module is now displayed at the National Air and Space Museum in Washington, DC sharing the main hall with The Wright Flyer and Spirit of St. Louis.

Here in the Bahamas old-timers I knew personally from Cherokee

Sound thinking this piece of history a hoax 'filmed in a dessert here on Earth somewhere secret' exclaiming, 'there was no way in hell that men were standing on the moon's surface, that was all a bunch of foolishness!'

Through all these decades, none has marked us the way the 60s did; massive man-made accomplishments often overwhelmed with incredible strife and senseless acts of brutality leaving us to wonder what on earth would the 1970s bring to our fragile planet?

Life at home during the last years of school was becoming noticeably different. My mother religiously wrote the weekly single sheet airmail letter, arriving at school some two weeks later. She had described the good things that she did during her life in the Bahamas. She talked of her work and occasional short vacations my parents took; about charter boats to the Exuma Cays with Captains Arthur Moxey and Milton Pierce, accompanied by his first mate 'Ghost' Pierce during the Easter Holidays too short for me to fly home. She described the fun they had fishing and the haunted nights at anchor in Waderick Wells Cay. Her letters confirming the stories about crews sneaking off the boats while guests were dining to climb the summit of the hill above the anchorage, dressed in white bed sheets and lighting fires while screams of terror echoed across the water, reinforcing stories of the haunted island. I remember a black and white photograph taken in Beirut traveling to Lebanon while I was in England. They still boated on weekends to the nearby islands off the shores of Nassau. During my visits we always met the Johnstone, Eldon and Raine families up at Green Cay camping over the long weekends to all play on the beaches and swim in the warm shallow water.

My school days thankfully were finally drawing to a close; an era of my life that seemed endless, where mediocre routine remained a constant; the holidays in Nassau ending with transatlantic flights only including one quick stop in Bermuda and on to London by breakfast the next morning. Jorge Dean faithfully meeting me and escorting to Grey Thatch then on to Seaford College for another endless term of 'higher education' for what that was worth? I specialised in biology, zoology and botany, hoping a career in the marine sciences along with my introduction to the sport of diving may allow an escape on to the oceans of the world. My love for animals and a career in veterinary science quashed with mandatory university requirements to pass Advanced Level mathematics in order to gain university entry. I could not even spell the word calculus let alone understand the basic principles. My father had visions of me wearing the proverbial white laboratory coat and becoming some genius in a Florida marine institute. He was in for a let down when I told everyone to stick it as far as further education was concerned? You can keep your damned A-Levels; there were things to do and places to see!

The last flight across the Atlantic departing London Airport stays well imprinted for the one item I wanted to take with me back to Nassau. Writing this story in present day and age the event seems something out of *Mission Impossible* with commercial air travel the nightmare it is today. I had said my farewells to Jorge and Edna Dean at Heathrow and strolled through the crowded terminal building with my carry-on luggage and an assembled twelve-gauge shotgun in its padded case! I checked in at the BOAC counter and proceeded to the gate assigned for the flight to Bermuda and Nassau. No security in those days, pleasantly void of scanners or x-ray machines. No TSA personnel harassing you every six paces or having to remove one's shoes! Earlier flights from school had seen this performance repeated with about two pounds of raw potassium nitrate fertiliser bought at the local hardware store in England; we were after all in the 'rocket manufacturing' business as schoolboy projects during our holidays; many a successful launch off the William Street patio to land on or near the Haitian sloops at anchor in the harbour. This last transatlantic flight however far more interesting as I boarded the 707, where just inside the entrance found the familiar locker for coats and jackets to hang in. I asked the stewardess politely if I might store my gun inside for the flight. She eyed the length and calmly said, 'it would be better if you just stowed it alongside your seat!' I flew the Atlantic with an assembled gun stowed next to me on the floor.

The first journey abroad from Nassau came from the offer Alastair had made as we were departing school. While walking the fields side by side, raising coveys of quail and pheasant in the fields behind my grandparents' property, he had pledged 'you have not really lived until you see Africa'.

'Our parents are airline folks, why don't we trade flights, you come to Nairobi first and then I will come and see The Bahamas? There is no way we could afford it otherwise,' he exclaimed. The seed was planted and after my last term in Sussex I asked my father about the idea. He knew it to be an offer of a lifetime I could not pass down. At 10% fares for airline staff the trip to Nairobi through London totalled $90 each way. The trip was arranged and ticket purchased. Knowing my growing passion of photography father offered his camera, an old Kodak Retinette 35-mm film in a brown leather case that I practised with beforehand on boating days with Roma and Norman Smith joining my parents for a days outing to Rose or Athol Island. Fairly small and compact it would be an easy carry along with rolls of Kodachrome II colour slides.

The Boeing lifted off from Nassau and for the first time off on my own toward a new continent saying farewells to the dive crew at Underwater and my current girlfriend Diane, whose father also worked for Bahamas Airways. The really cute freckled young lady seemed quite upset that I was leaving for a few weeks instead of being able to escort her to the Doubloon each weekend listening and dancing to *The Nassauvians* band. Alas, the price paid was an end to the friendship on my return. She had moved on to greener pastures, a relief to my father with his Austin Healey not been driven all that way to Coral Harbour!

The familiar nine-hour flight to London was long and uneventful. I transferred over to East African Airways flying direct to Nairobi, about the same length flight. A familiar heat, this time from the Kenyan day, rushed through the open cabin doors. Alastair and his brother Angus, also a Seaford senior in his day, met me as I exited the arrivals terminal. I was on African soil for the first time.

'You need some bush clothes,' they welcomed me with. We drove through Nairobi bustling streets of cars, people, open storefronts and street vendors, a whole new experience. Stopping at a safari outfitter I bought three classic green bush shirts and items they said I needed for living in the bundu, native lingo for 'bush'. The Land Rover pulled up to the Gill family hacienda type house with screened porches on the outskirts of Nairobi. A manservant greeted me with a cold gin and tonic, a green slice of lime perched on the rim, his name was Paris and he would be attending my needs while staying as honoured guest.

'Jambo Paris' was my first try at Kiswahili, the melodic native language of Kenya. His faced beamed at my effort showing some crooked white teeth; 'Jambo Bwana' came an immediate reply. My stay in the house was to be a short one.

'We drive this afternoon to the border,' Alastair announced, 'about 140 miles down to Arusha and into Tanzania, bring all you documents for border crossings'. The Gill brothers, like other East African hunting families, rented 'blocks' of land giving sole hunting rights on hundreds of acres. We loaded the Land Rover with basic food supplies and water along with a 9.3 bolt action Mauser rifle and two twelve gauge shotguns with loads of ammunition.

'Don't forget the crap-axe!' Alastair smiled as he packed the small hand axe in to his rucksack. 'I'll explain later.' I squeezed the lime into my drink.

We clinked glasses, 'Welcome to Africa!'

The drive was amazing. Africa played with your soul the minute you stepped foot onto the continent. A similar feeling the stunning archipelago so far away had affected me. The paved roads soon gave way to dirt where dust whirled in reddish-brown clouds behind our aging four-wheeled drive vehicle. It was rough going for many miles and one could travel forever without seeing any other vehicle. Maasai cattlemen walked their cows alongside the roads, their skins covered with a fine layer of powdered dust, kicked up by passing vehicles, classic spears in hand. They were very tall and lean, robed in loose red material, smiling as we passed and raising their arm in a friendly wave. They are a tribe indigenous to Southern Kenya and Northern Tanzania, about 800,000 in numbers with over a dozen dialects in their language. The town of Arusha in northern Tanzania lay on an elevation of 3000 feet surrounded by stunning East African landscapes including the Serengeti National Park to the West and Tsavo National Park to the east, both boasting famous landmarks such as Mount Kilimanjaro and the Ngorongoro Crater. A garrison town formed by German Colonists in 1900 after the Boer Wars in South Africa naming the town after the local tribe 'Wa Arusha'. In 1901 the colonist army built a fortress commanded by a First Lieutenant named Georg Kuster, no relation to the American general. The local tribesmen were not in admiration of the man they called 'Bwana Fisi' or Hyena. Arusha became a thriving European settlement until the British occupied the town in 1916 expelling all the Germans. In the early days, the colony was named Tanganyika where in 1961 became an Independent Nation renamed Tanzania. As a youth who collected mailing stamps from all over the world, only Tanganyika had the most beautiful animal stamp collections. Nineteen sixty-two put Arusha on the map with the Hollywood production *Hatari* starring John Wayne filmed on location in the region.

Alastair pulled up to the border crossing producing our passports for inspection. Armed guards satisfied that hunting permits in order, we were allowed through turning westbound for another eighty miles. My host explained that two to three million years ago a massive volcano estimated to be 15–19,000 feet high exploded so violently that it collapsed upon itself to a depth of 2000 feet down. Over the millennia it became a natural enclosure for animals with the floor of the crater now mostly rich grassland covering over one hundred miles with scattered clumps of woodlands comprising mostly of local acacia trees seen all over Africa. The place we were going to see first was a national treasure called Ngorongoro Crater. Not all species of African wildlife made it down inside the crater, being void of impala, orbis, giraffe and crocodile. The Ngorongoro does however support 'The Big Five', namely rhinoceros, lion, leopard, elephant and Cape buffalo. Here a natural irony emerged for lions where ample supply of food made for successful breeding and creation of large size, extremely intimidating for any new encroachment from intruders. The resulting inbreeding became a detriment to the advancement of the bloodline. Early German land owners had tried unsuccessfully to drive out the competing wildebeest herds but the animal migration that had occurred for generations, along with zebra, had moved south into the region in December and back again north in the month of June. The Ngorongoro Reserve holds the most species of African wildlife in one area, with strong holdings of cheetah and lion populations.

As we drove the eighty miles Alastair recalled the local history where fossil remains showed a Hominid species lived here over three million years ago. Later history shows a tribe called the Mbulu who were hunter-gatherers about 2000 years ago. In the 1700s, the Datooga tribe became prevalent. However, during the 1800s, they were embattled with the Maasai who killed their leader in 1840. The tribesmen, it has been told, planted fig trees on their fallen leaders grave and the giant trees still stand today. Nowadays there are less than 100,000 Datooga in the region.

Alastair was the picture of young East African game hunter. I had always described him emulating Robert Ruark, whose novels of big game hunting read voraciously as a young student in school. Ruark laid the graphic and beautiful scenes of the African bush into print, a favourite being *Uhuru*. For those of us who yearned to walk the open grasslands of this magnificent continent were devoted audience to this writer. My friend was not large in stature but his wiry frame; freckled face adorned with the infamous African felt bush hat captured your whole attention to every detail. His instruction on the old 'Churchill Style' of shooting was ingrained in me from the the days together in Sussex. Alastair reiterated his philosophy about not the killing of one's quarry; merely 'being there' that mattered, taking only what one needed to eat. We drove westward as he continued the history for what I was about to see. No Europeans had ever set foot in the crater before 1892 where two German brothers leased land from the German East Africa Company. One of their clients, a Dr Oscar Baumann, shot three rhino in the Ngorongoro. Soon clients from all over came to hunt the big game found in this region. The famous crater became part of the Serengeti National Park created by the British as a Reserve in 1951. The local Maasai lived within the area until they were evicted in 1959 after constant conflicts about land use. Today it is unique for Tanzania as the only reserve providing protection for wildlife and allowing once again habitation by humans. Land use is strictly controlled so as not to provide any negative effect on the wild animals, the Maasai are allowed to graze their cattle on a daily basis allowed entering and exiting the reserve each day.

Our vehicle came to a stop and we walked up the steep grassy slope still unable to see what scene approached a few feet beyond. Africa lay as far as the eye could see; huge open blue skies, the famous flat shapes of the thorny acacia trees and wildlife meandering everywhere. We reached to top of our climb to peer over a spectacle of indescribable size and beauty.

'How about that?' Alastair gazed forward with me. The rim of the extinct volcano stretched forever. So far were the distances the horizon took a blue hue. Letting one's gaze feast downward in to the never-ending bowl below was something we would later imagine in a Spielberg movie about dinosaurs. We sat there for God knows how long; animals, even massive bull elephant, looking as if they were in microscopic form meandering below in the canvas of dried grass. Trees allowed welcome shelter from the mid-day sun. Predators lay in the shade while some prowled the long grasses. We were so high that we looked down upon huge vultures meandering the warm air above certain death that lay below them. The cycle of African wildlife lay before us in splendour.

'Time to move on.' My host spoke quietly as if not to disturb too abruptly the magnificent scene.

We drove back eastward through the town of Moshi and into the bush. There were no tents, no servants, just a walk through the wild bundu of East Africa. Two twenty-year-old college students who once walked the English countryside fields in West Sussex, sharing mischievous weekend escapes to our grandparents, now here hundreds of miles from any other familiar civilisation. Alastair had instructed that we were to live off the land for a while. We would only shoot small game if we needed meat otherwise only hunt birds, mainly yellow necks and guinea fowl. It was hot and dry. The grasses were brown and crisp. We walked the dirt trails quietly and hand signals came discreetly to show when to stay still or crouch or load for impending shot. Around one tight turn in the path we froze at the same moment. Just feet in front of us stood a mature giraffe grazing the overhead trees. He glanced at us for a few seconds and continued foraging the thorn and leaves off the giant acacia tree. It is hard to even comprehend that here in 2016 there are less giraffe roaming the continent than elephant. The wanton illegal poaching for their meat, hides and tail have placed this gentle giant near the endangered species list. We moved after some time allowing the beautiful animal to turn away idly walking into the bush disappearing in seconds with his natural camouflage; the bush vibrated with sound; a multitude of birds and animals calling; none to be seen unless we surprised them down wind. I asked about snakes. Alastair smiled and said in all the years he had only seen just a few in the wild. It was after all the country for black mamba and cobra. Yet here we were just walking casually through the wild bush, it seemed worth asking! 'Besides,' my colleague quirked, 'if a mamba spotted you he can outrun you anytime!'

His hand came up for us to stay silent and still. Pointing through the open thicket we spotted several dark shapes scurrying across the ground, guinea fowl. Their call was everywhere and very dominant. I was summoned to take the right side and my friend covered the left. As we made another forty feet and an explosion of birds came from beneath. Rule was simple, left take the left and right take the right, never crossfire or stray toward the other gun. Both of us emptied first the left barrel and then the full choke right barrel as the remaining birds took flight further away from us. Two birds each twisted in their flight to fall earthbound with a thud and spray of dust. The bush fell deathly silent.

'There's supper!' Alastair called out. 'Let's find a campsite'.

Further into the bush we found a watering hole, now low in level with the dry season well in place. On the top embankment found a flat area over shadowed by an acacia tree. Not enough cover for big cats to hide in but good enough to make camp.

'We have to clean the guineas,' Alastair told me, 'making sure that we bury all the waste feathers and entrails far enough away from the campsite so as not to attract anyone with bigger teeth than us!

'The hyenas and wild dogs will come and dig them up while we sleep. By the way we will sling the birds that we don't eat today in this string bag, this we throw over the branch above our heads so that if a big cat comes in the dark to steal we can feel the bark falling on our faces?'

'That's what the Mauser was for?' He grinned at my questions. 'We wouldn't kill any cats but the damned thing is so loud, quite enough to chase them away!'

'Sleep?' I thought, 'now there's a thing'! We made a fire from tinder and small broken branches lying around, large enough to create a warning for prey to stay away from us and hot enough to produce warming embers for the near cold African night.

'Watch out for scorpions in the dead wood,' I was warned. A sting out here could lead to a drastic situation. 'Don't forget to bang your boots upside down in the morning, some big bastards love to crawl inside during the night!' We prepared the fowl with a few scant seasonings brought with us searing them cooked to perfection over the flames. The sunsets in East Africa leave a permanent vision in one's soul. The canvas of orange and blue hues swirling above the acacia tress along with the calls of wild-life, teasing one's hearing. As the dark descended sound becomes more acute. The temperature drops noticeably every minute once the sun has disappeared.

'What the hell is that?' I asked quietly feeling as if the ground trembled with the low rumble coming through the woods.

'A lion grunting and that other noise is its stomach grumbling, two distinct sounds.' We roasted two birds over the open flames, as the skin browned they smelled incredible, the night air taking our dinner aroma outward. Within minutes, small bright white lights paired together out of the pitch black surrounded us. The giggles of the surrounding hyenas that encircled the campsite grew strong but they never ventured into the light of the fire, staying just far enough away to remain safe of the men who sat there.

'Now you know the real meaning of 'safari',' Alastair remarked, 'Swahili literally translated for 'long journey', but 'outing' or 'overnight' is close and understood'. The word drove home all that I had lived for. The world of outdoors, the open sky, the wildlife and exhilaration it all encompassed, whether here in the African bush or ventures to the Out-Islands of my Bahamas. We talked about the old school days and how damned glad to be rid of them we were. I told him of the adventures the ocean life had been offering back in the islands and offered him the reciprocal vacation when it came to parting from Africa. I told him how he would have to brush up on the swimming, which they all did here taking holidays on the coast of Kenya at Malindi where the Indian Ocean meets the Kenyan coast.

'We have a lot to cover here first,' he exclaimed. 'Time for shut-eye.' The fire crackled with a dark red glow sending orange sparks skyward. The hyenas lay quiet and the night insects set up their harmony while zebra whinnied in the darkness. Big cats were on the move in the ink-black of the African night. We lay in sleeping bags close to the fires warmth on the forest floor gazing upward to one of the brightest starlit nights I could remember. Shooting stars raced across the heavens. Indeed, I was in the 'real Africa' now! The harmony of crickets lulled us both into sleep in the cool night air.

Dawn's early light awoke me. The insects were silent. Herds of zebra were calling to each other and a chorus of guinea fowl filled the air. I lay full length in the sleeping bag turned on one side facing the now grey embers of our campfire. My eyes focused just beyond the ashes where a small spiral of blue smoke meandered gently upward to what appeared to be a row of black feet? Many black feet indeed, close together and very still. As the bush became alive it became apparent we were surrounded. Maasai herdsmen stood side by side to form a circle, many on just one foot with the other resting on the opposite knee in perfect balance. They were all silent, dressed in the familiar tattered red cloth robes holding their spears with the base stuck in the dirt and sharp shaft upright. They stood patiently, waiting politely for the white men to awake. Alastair rolled over and greeted them in Swahili dusting of his felt hat. 'Jambo bwana,' they all replied in unison. A short conversation ensued and my host explained that they had brought their cattle to the watering hole not wanting to muddy the water before we had chance to take what clean water we may have needed. The hospitality of the bush was duly noted and I gave the apparent leader of the group 'asanti sana', thank you, as we went to bathe. Alastair grinned at my lingual practice instructing in Swahili what to say in order I purchase a real souvenir from Africa. The tall herdsman smiled with a stained row of large teeth as he realised I was the guest in this country and the other man here a local. He told me how many 'shallingies', in those days the equivalent of the English shillings in our currencies, that I could have a set of spears and from under his robe strapped to his buttocks a sheathed knife called a 'Simi'.

'Good price' Alastair said, 'Don't even barter'. I accepted the trade willingly owning a genuine set of Maasai armament. Most of their steel taken from wrecked cars left abandoned. Heated on an open fire and honed into the length of blade they needed. Hard woods cut to make the handle to fit cleverly into each end of the spears foot and blade. The Simi was probably a car spring hammered flat in the fires heat. A file sharpened both sides razor sharp to resemble a short hand spear, the cross between a panga and machete. Two flat pieces of wood were shaved to make a handle on both sides of the blades end. Here they slipped over the top the forearm skin of a fresh killed dik-dik, a miniature gazelle that frequented the bush. The skin dries tight holding the two wood halves ingenuously in place. The hide sheath it came with hand sewn together with homemade thread. The herdsmen bid us farewell, literally melting into the surrounding bush while guiding their cattle to the water after we were finished.

One morning, while heating water over the fire, nature called Alastair requiring a sudden to visit the neighbouring scrub bushes – toilet paper in hand he picked up the 'crap-axe'; my having learnt it was the needed tool to dig a shallow hole then used to lean on while squatting, accompanied with the ever-present side by side twelve-gauge. 'Never leave home without it' was the rule of encampment. Within a minute or two of his discreet pose behind the bush the silence was broken with the thunder of both barrels being fired. Alastair emerged grinning from behind his cover, trousers round his knees, white buttocks on display and gun in hand,

'Damned guinea's ran right in front of me,' he cried out, 'what was I going to do, waste the chance?' The two downed guinea fowl flapped in the grass some fifty feet in front of him. One could only smile as the morning sun suddenly caught his lily-white rear end contrasting with wiry tanned legs. We sat and skinned the guinea fowl, their thick steel blue feathers were very thick and the meat was plump and rich. A sudden careless slip of the knife I felt the blade slice cleanly through my left index knuckle.

'Shit,' I yelped as blood shot everywhere. Alastair grabbed the toilet paper and we wrapped the finger tightly. The wad became soaked in red quickly but slowed the flow until it stopped.

'Just leave it on there and it will dry solid,' I was instructed.

'Lucky it's not your trigger finger and you can still hold a gun ok?' He smiled that cheeky grin. After several days the hard brown blood had the finger healed in place without stitches.

'It will come off soon enough when we have a swim in the New Stanley pool.' The New Stanley Hotel being Nairobi's famous landmark, opened in 1902, frequented by the rich and famous through its days found also within my pages of the Ruark novels. Sure enough, at a stop through the city we took a day by the pool and the infamous toilet paper floated off my finger disappearing indiscreetly down the skimmer drain.

The second half of the safari would be north of Nairobi into the Great Rift Valley and Lake Naivasha, this time we were to camp in the bush mostly fishing for tilapia and bass. The Great Rift Valley, a geographic trench about 3700 miles long, stretching from Syria to central Mozambique in South Africa. Many of the lakes very alkali in nature with the exception of Lake Naivasha supplied by fresh water springs. Its name coming from the Maasai language meaning 'rough water' with its reputation of quickly changing conditions due to developing sudden storms. The lake spreads over sixty miles and another thirty miles of low lying swamp giving habitat to incredible wild life and 400 species of exotic birds. The lake only averages twenty feet in depth but the thick surrounding lily pad fields offer protection to abundant fish schools while supporting large herds of hippopotamus.

'Two guys in the bush you watch for mate,' Alastair talked about as we launched a rented skiff loaded with fishing tackle, 'the Cape buffalo who can turn around in thick bush without moving a twig and the hippo down here at the lake, forget the crocs, a hippo can cut a boat in half!'

We motored though the dark calm water of Lake Naivasha, cobalt blue sky reflected all about us while the history lesson continued:

'Again the Europeans settled the region and started many of the towns. One of them called East Nakuru which later became Naivasha.' Alastair reminded me of Southampton in Sussex, a port town further west on the coast from Chichester where both our grandparents had houses not far from each other in neighbouring Sussex villages.

From this port in south England the flying boats used to depart on their routes to South Africa stopping here on Lake Naivasha between 1937 and 1950. A famous passenger being writer Joy Adamson who wrote *Born Free* about Elsa the lioness, which later became a film; the Adamson's lived on the shore of the lake here; Joy was murdered in June of 1980 in the Shaba National reserve by a former employee. Her husband George also murdered nine years later in Kora National Park, saving tourists from poachers. It was strange how life's history seems performed in circles with notable events crisscrossed in their paths? I would have no clue while casting a fishing line on this gorgeous lake in Africa I too would become an aviator flying floatplanes, yet here I was in the 1970s on the exact place where huge flying boats made their way southward, originating the very town I once schooled.

This romantic chapter of aviation history started when the *Daily Mail* newspaper in England had offered a prize of £10,000 for the first trans-oceanic airliner. The UK and United States collaborated and resulted in the Curtis Model 'H'. The hangars used were ironically the same buildings I used to sail snipes by in East Cowes on the Isle of Wight. Here the boat building company of J. Samuel White set up an aircraft division building the first flying boat displayed at the London Air Show in 1913. The same year S.E. Saunders, also in East Cowes, and Sopwith Aviation Company produced the 'The Bat Boat'; a laminated hull that could operate from either land or water, called an amphibian after the reptiles that crawled in and out of the water. The first craft they built came down the same ramp in Cowes where I witnessed the first hovercraft emerge into the sunlight known as 'Saunders Row'. That first plane could fly as far as five miles, managing six journeys within five hours. The early Curtis planes back in 1914 were pioneering the art of water flying, a new set of dynamics to be conquered where craft aerodynamic in flight had to overcome the effects of a hull at speed in the water first. Design flaws appearing early tended to make the bow submerge while taxiing, also when power added for a take-off roll. Fins were fitted to the underside of the bow for hydrodynamic lift, these were later to become sponsons, a type of pontoon mounted in pairs on either side of the hull adding much needed buoyancy, taking into account the suction water produces hindering flight ability. In 1915 there was the Seaplane Experimental Station at Felixstowe, a seaside town on the North Sea coast of Suffolk in England. By 1917 the underpowered new Curtis 'H 8' was upgraded with 250HP Rolls Royce Eagle engines and another valuable innovation, first called the 'Felixstowe Notch', was incorporated in the design. The rear section of the hull was now sharply recessed to enable the craft to break free of the surface tension much earlier. The notch then was renamed the 'step' an addition that still exists in today's floatplanes both of hull and pontoon variety.

The days on Lake Naivasha were exhilarating with vistas one could gaze at forever. The huge open skies were teeming with wild birds. Huge patches of moving pink showed flocks of flamingo by the thousands strutting in the shallows. The surrounding bush was alive with the fresh spring water feeding in to the lake providing much desired sweet water for the animals to share. We would drift almost motionless on the calm lake water just off the main lily-pad fields where fish hid underneath for the shade and away from predators flying above. The two of us recounted hunting stories and I some fish stories from the Bahamas, describing a near world record Bonito as a youngster, a record that to date I do not think been broken? We cast light spinning tackle into the waters alongside the lilies with great success hooking large bass who hit the lures hard while running exceedingly fast removing yards of line at a time. Rods bent over near double we would bring them to boat side and lift carefully with a hand net. Cooked over an open fire the delicious delicate white meat would fall off the bone. With a swift hand motion from Alastair we fell suddenly silent and motionless. The outer waters within feet of the boat rippled from underneath. A fully-grown hippopotamus surfaced face on a mere few feet from our little craft. His ears flapped back and forth and the enormous nostrils blew water vertically in the still air creating a plume of mist blowing a soft rainbow in the sunlight, the gentle mist wetting our faces; a scene to stay imprinted on my memory. Not daring to move a muscle, 'Don't even breathe' my host barely whispered his voice near inaudible.

The giant looked at us with his pig-like eyes and water streaming off the immense head, much wider that the beam of our dinghy. His enormous body was completely submerged with just a small section of the spine showing near the surface. We never even blinked, daring not to move a muscle. As if suddenly filled with lead the giant sank like a submerging submarine blowing the air first and then closing the nostrils in a gasp for the dive right under our boat. The ripples scattered outward as we too exhaled in relief.

'No sound.' Alastair instructed holding an index finger to his lips as the hippo passed underneath; these enormous animals known to have been upset with people in boats surfacing under their craft to capsize the poor individuals inside toward pending doom.

'He's headed under the lilies,' he whispered again where not the slightest hint of movement of any plant alongside us. The lilies sent roots all the way to the bottom like a tangled forest of telegraph poles, how could something weighing a couple of tons walk through their midst without moving a leaf?

'They do that very well!' Alastair exclaimed.

Africa had indeed left its mark on my soul. For those who share the fascination of wildlife and beautiful places this continent changes you forever – a continent, however, in trouble with the staggering loss of its precious animals. A couple of decades ago there were 420,000 lions in the wild throughout Africa and now those numbers barely stand at 20,000. In the Ngorongoro where the densest population of lion were found there were just sixty-two animals left. Elephants in 1987 were counted at forty-two and again in 1992 at just twenty-nine. In the last century elephant populations massively declined due to habitat destruction, increased agriculture and the bloody ivory trade. Rampant ivory poaching from 1979 to 1989 halved Africa's elephant population from 1.3 million to 600,000 – numbers may be as low as 470,000. Tanzania alone lost 60% of its elephant in the last five years, some 65,000 animals slaughtered. Botswana, Namibia, South Africa and Zimbabwe sold 105,000 kg of ivory to China and Japan; the insatiable consumption by the oriental people for sculptured artefacts and insane belief of aphrodisiac qualities of rhino horn rampantly destroying the most protected animal life to the point of extinction. Poachers butchering magnificent creatures to simply steal a horn sadly misconstrued by Asian society over a material exactly the same constitution as the human fingernail!

Since 1980 the crater's wildebeest population has fallen by a quarter of what it was to near 19,000. The African lion could well reach extinction within the next ten years. Studies show that the total population has declined by two-thirds over the last fifty years and there may be as few as 32,000 left in all Africa; witness to mankind's atrocious behaviour of greed, poaching, corrupt trophy hunting, civil war, population explosion and total disregard for the natural environment proving him to indeed be the pestilence of this planet as Africa starts to implode upon itself. Fortunately, in recent years, with encouraging financial outside support arriving, some of the National Parks are now holding their own; more toward Southern Africa than in the East where many places are just too dangerous to travel to. Tourists in some areas have to be escorted with armed guards and safaris are carefully located to safer areas. Botswana has finally recognised the immense value of their animal population, banning trophy hunting along with the exportation of animals into South Africa for that same purpose. High-end commercial safaris found today are very expensive, offering safe exclusive living in splendid tents for accommodation adding handsomely to local economies with rents paid to the Maasai for use of their lands. Times of walking in the bush alone and sleeping by the open fire long gone. My timing was right to experience the very best always yearning for chance to return. I would wait over forty years before a close friend's kind offer allowed me to set foot on African soil once more. I never heard from Alistair again.

Earliest photo of myself
with cousin Veronica.

Mary Harding as a teenager.

The Hood Family: Mother, Cuthbert with Veronica, James, Faith, Paul.

Major Harold Wilson.

Mother's wedding day
escorted by her father.

Grey Thatch in West Sussex.

Jorge Dean enjoying conch
salad from Nassau.

My bedroom window at Grey Thatch.

The Flying Bedstead at Farnborough Airshow.

Getting acquainted with a boarder of Deanwood Kennels.

Walking the dogs with Jorge Dean.

The Savoy Theatre 1960s.

Bahamas Airways Handley Page Hermes 1960.

Father in front of a Bahamas Airways Grumman Goose.

Bahamas Airways DC3 in the 60s.

Boating off Paradise Beach 1960.

The Tropic Rover.

Nassau Yacht Haven 1960s.

Anchored off Long Beach with
John Howson and father.

1st time driving father's
boat to Rose Island.

First speared spiny lobster, aged 12.

Holding my 1st camera, an Instamatic with Norman Smith.

Lifting the engines aboard 'The Bloody Mary' with Norman.

1st casting lessons with Roma Smith 1960s.

Beach Day at Spruce Cay, Terry Rivet, Mother, Norman, Roma & my father.

1st sighting of friend Melissa Maura.

Beaching at Athol Island with Eleanor Isles, Roma & Norman Smith.

The Coral Harbour Club 1960.

Parents deep sea fishing with Basil McKinney & friends.

Bahamas record Bonito weighing in at 24lbs.

Fighting my record fish aged 12 years old.

John Harding fishing aboard 'Seapie'.

My first Barracuda.

Capt. Ronnie Kemp relaxing aboard 'Queen Anne's Revenge'.

My 1st summer job with MM Underwater Tours 1961.

Melissa's Centaur Magazine debut in her early 20s.

Mary Harding in Exuma aboard Capt. Milton Pierce's 'Blades II'.

Constructing the Vulcan bomber with the 'Disco Volante' of 'Thunderball'. (Photo: Roma Smith)

Parents in happier days during the 60s.

Father aboard a replica of Columbus' 'Nina' in Nassau Harbour.

Sir Sidney Poitier horseback down Cabbage Beach 1970s.

With Lloyd Bridges on Paradise Island.

Lloyd Bridges while shooting 'The Happy Ending'.

Walking the woods over on Paradise Island in the 1970s with Gary Cox.

Deep diving with 'The Aussie', Gary Cox off the wall at Lyford Cay.

Melissa riding her horses in the ocean off Eastern Road.

Portrait of my mother taken
by Helena Lightbourne.

Charlie Badeau of MM
Underwater Tours in the 60s.

Gardner Young (right) with Ed McMahon of the 'Tonight Show'.

Fran & Gardner opening 'Divers Haven' on East Bay Street.

Underwater photo of Gardner using an early re-breathing apparatus featured in Skin Diver Magazine.

The author in final edit with our trusty potcake showing the tension!

Bahamas Ministry of Tourism promotional poster featuring Gardner descending 'The Wall'.

Sighting Melissa bareback in the ocean of Eastern Road, Nassau.

Mary Harding visiting her brother Cuthbert in Yorkshire, England.

1st girlfriend Melanie with my Triumph GT6.

Chapter 12
From Boy to Man

Returning to the Bahamas after an extraordinary month on the other side of the world I recalled to my family and friends the adventures of Africa. Hundreds of Kodachrome slides recorded the adventure only to succumb through the years to the islands moist humidity and mildewing beyond repair. We were far from the digital age back then and only climate-controlled film would survive. Some old film photos can be restored digitally but time has faded the brilliant colours of the day. My spears and Simi still adorn my walls along with hand carvings of craftsmen in the Nairobi Market.

Life in our new country continued its course. The weekly ritual of socialising with the Bahamas Airways associates that my parents had made over the years becomes tedious. My father's contract had been renewed promoted to Deputy Operations Manager under Captain Phillip Farrington, while my mother pursued her real estate career with Bill Turtle and Basil McKinney moving later with Chester Thompson, all of whom she loved to working for. Every now and again she would tell my father excitedly about an extraordinary deal on a property only to be brushed aside by his indifference to the notion of us all staying in the Bahamas. My mother and I shared the love of this country and had no thought of returning to the UK. Our life was here, our true friends mostly Bahamians or expats married to Bahamians. We had progressed from 'required jackets' worn by men to enter the Savoy Movie Theatre on Bay Street to the new air conditioned Shirley Street Theatre at the top of our street boasting swing back seating and a wide screen! Concerts starring Peter, Paul and Mary played at the Cat and Fiddle Club down on Nassau Street; we partied at the nearby Drumbeat Club enjoying Peanuts Taylor's show and review. The Bay Street businessmen retreated daily to the Doghouse Club and Pete Gardner opened a courtyard restaurant just off Shirley Street in the early years calling it 'Sun And...' Stars, celebrities and famous sports figures met in the bar before dining in the courtyard around the decorative fountains and tropical vegetation. Their autographed photographs adorn the walls.

Little did I know that my father's drinking had escalated causing an uneasy friction within our household. His job was always approached with utter professionalism and painful perfection. His intolerance of the 'Bahamian way' things were handled at the airport within the airline drove his frustration to unacceptance. Each evening he unveiled 'Mr. Hyde' within the first couple of drinks. As a young man now in my early twenties I used the evenings as an escape. My friends were all driving their parents' cars to meet at 'The Doubloon' nightclub on west Bay Street; a safe hang out we had as teenagers for the enjoyment of great music played by local talent including David Graham, Stuart Halbert, Tommy Goodwin, Rolf Harris and Frank Scully on drums. Dancing and music of the classic 60s rock and roll mixed with popular Bahamian merengue kept most of us there until the early hours often breaking curfews set by all our parents to be home by midnight. Reluctantly my father allowed me to drive his black Austin Healey Sprite. On hearing I had a lady friend who lived all the way out in Coral Harbour he exclaimed that I was just 'wearing away metal' with that amount of driving. 'Good grief I need my own trans' soon ran through my head.

My father's 'duty' he had explained 'was to carry you until the age of twenty-one'. Not one for birthday parties I did make exception and allow my mother to invite 'all her boys', that is my friends that she took under her wing over the years; all the clan I had known through Bahamian childhood came to the balcony of the apartment at William Street. My mother prepared food of all kinds, her cooking well renowned amongst all my comrades while my father presented me with a Rolex Submariner watch knowing the love of the water and my association with Underwater Tours. He could see clearly the expected career I was about to choose, much to his disgust, after all the schooling he paid for soon to end with a final term.

I learned of a plot from within my schoolhouse that last day at Seaford College to sabotage my leaving in a peaceful manner. Right to the very last a few boys continued their idiotic behaviour toward me. Jealousy had an insidious streak aimed against those of us who bore any form of 'privilege'. To get the last laugh I planned a secret early escape with my grandfather foiling the plot arriving a whole day early at Seaford. I threw luggage in to his car when it pulled up at the front door of Charmandean Hall to speed down the long driveway, much to the disbelief of a few seniors who witnessed the unannounced departure. Watching the main school building on my right speed past my window only crowned by the joy of passing through the huge open wrought-iron gates at the entrance for the very last time. I pledged never look back at the grounds of the school patting my grandfather with praise on his shoulder keeping my face forward, smiling all the way home to Grey Thatch. I was free, free at last!

Gardner Young kept a promise, offering my first job. Completing my training course as a qualified PADI Open Water Scuba Instructor held locally that year in the warm waters off Clifton Pier and Goulding Cay, my first assignment being an instructor at the prestigious Balmoral Hotel on Cable Beach. Needing my own transportation, I saved $700 to buy a used bright red Triumph Spitfire convertible with black leather interior. My mother smiled knowing the jealousy would exude from her husband having her son's car parked alongside his in the driveway. From the halls of Seaford College and the frigid playing fields in England I was driving a sexy red sports car to work by a swimming pool every day in the Bahamas. The lifestyle change soon built a very content twenty-one-year old. There was very little hint in those days of what may have been happening between my parents, they kept personal emotions under wraps for the most part. My fathers' behaviour each evening was on the decline and after work unexpectedly asked if I would join him for a beer at the Pilot House Bar next door. This immediately raised a warning flag having never asked this of me before.

'Son, we need to talk.' I sent a puzzled look at my mother as I walked out of the apartment door behind my father. Seated in the familiar bar looking out of the glass windows toward the pool deck I sipped a cold beer he placed on the table in front of us. With no preamble he came right to the point.

'I am leaving in the morning'.

'Leaving to where?' I asked quite taken aback.

He explained that his time in the Bahamas was up and he had accepted another job in Hong Kong with Cathy Pacific Airlines. Apparently, he had offered to take my mother with him, however that sounded unconvincing in its suggestion. She had declined he told me, saying that the Far East was not her preference and that the Bahamas was now her home as was it for her son with his new career. She knew I would be moving on with my life choosing to remain close at hand in a place familiar with people she loved. Returning to England as a stranger and unemployed at her age was not an acceptable option. I asked my father the details of my mother's wellbeing and financial security leaving her alone in a foreign country. He confirmed 'all that had been well taken care of and we should have nothing to worry about'. The conversation was brief. He showed no interest in my plans or willing to disclose any of his. He paid the bar tab and we walked the hundred yards back to the apartment. Dinner was in near silence as he sat there wavering in drunken stupor. Mother and I shared cautious bewildered glances. The atmosphere very tense and I recall nothing further of that evening. Alcohol was very prevalent in Nassau society and the airline crews and families were no exception. Endless cocktail parties continued common practice where I watched with boredom the drinking and pitiful gestures of meaningless conversation. As evenings progressed certain individuals became more and more obnoxious. My father seemed to slide comfortably in to this niche. Near the end of his tour in the islands I found him at home one night standing belligerently in the middle of the living room floor weaving uncontrollably picking a fight with my mother seated quietly in her chair. I ordered him to quiet down and leave her alone. He was sad to watch. Sweating profusely, scantily dressed and slurring his words: the booze making him a mean drunk. Here in front of me the sad remains of a strong good-looking, very brilliant man, now merely a pathetic staggering fool turning his rage toward me. I stood up from the couch to hold my ground now standing taller than he. Feeling threatened he challenged me 'to hit him'. Temptation was very real. Pulling back by arm and fist firmly in place I readied for the blow right in the centre of his face to vent the frustrations of a family betrayed, I could have floored him with a single blow.

'Go on do it!' he exclaimed with eyes now full of venom, sweat running in rivulets down his face, it made good sense to deflate this upsetting scene. 'I just can't bring myself to hit a drunk,' I said very softly with a sadness never felt before. Picking up my car keys I left the apartment for a drive praying that mother would remain unharmed. Through time as a young man and on to late in life, I never attained much tolerance for drink. Alcohol certainly did not like me, leaving me quite ill on occasion; feeling blessed not having that gene in my system. I do love an ice-cold beer once in a while, or a dark rum and coke with a squeeze of lime befitting many casual relaxation times. Fine wines I really enjoyed educating myself on: a good glass of red or white with a great meal became a perfect complement. My tolerance however for distasteful drunken behaviour from others was minimal at best feeling very uncomfortable when exposed to it having witnessed one's own family pulled apart by its effect. Later in life alcohol came calling again with its insipid destruction shattering everything I had worked for and losing a long enjoyed relationship.

The next morning was a beautiful Bahama day. While having breakfast, we heard a brief honk of a car horn from down on the road below our small kitchen window. My father walked in to the bedroom and picked up a suitcase, kissed his wife of twenty-five years gently on the cheek while she stood next to his twenty-one-year old son and simply said, 'goodbye'. I did not respond. As he walked down the staircase of the apartment we both moved in to the tiny kitchen and peeked over the sink window to watch the head of our household walk out of the driveway. Without a mere glance upward he disappeared behind the branches of a tamarind tree to enter the waiting cab parked on the road so we could not see it. In a second he was gone. It would be the last time in life I saw my father. My mother looked up at me and leaned against my open arms. We whispered to each other 'it's over' now we can be at peace. I felt her relief but saw the wetness in her eyes. A huge part of her life was over. We were totally alone now. Times I learned had been rough for her; on occasion nights of alcohol had brought on physical abuse, intimidating her to a point of fright. She declared there would be 'no legal pursuit against him,' too scared of the consequences he had threatened to take. The relief and welcome quiet within the apartment did not leave much room for sadness. My mother kept her feelings very much to herself but I well imagined the shock of losing her life partner and the eventual emptiness that might creep into her soul. We would become friends offering mutual support in what was to be a whole new start for us both.

Captain Phillip Farrington was not a man to be taken lightly. A strong commanding Bahamian who ran Operations for Bahamas Airways walked his deputy, John Harding, to the awaiting airliner. At the base of the steps, I was to learn later, he shook father's hand and asked about the wellbeing of his wife and son who were to remain in Nassau without long-term status or financial backing.

'Have you taken care of them John?'

'Absolutely Phillip, they have nothing to worry about. I have set everything up for them to be secure.'

'In that case I wish you well,' said Captain Farrington watching his friend walk up the staircase and in to the cabin. The door closed and the engines started. John Harding left the Bahamas for the last time never to be seen or heard from again. The only truth he told was whom he going to work for. The same corporate personnel, the Swire brothers who owned Bahamas Airways had offered him a position with their entity Cathay Pacific based in Hong Kong. My father we soon learned, then liquidated all his properties and bank accounts held with his wife to disappear to the Far East leaving her in the Bahamas without any legal status and penniless. His son 'was on his own' being of age and therefore not his responsibility. I soon found out that Captain Farrington learning of our dilemma was shaken and furious at the deceit. I heard through time that Jorge and Edna Dean were planning to leave the Grey Thatch property in England to me knowing how much I had cared for that 400-year-old cottage and the near ten acres it stood on. They had plans of retirement in Malta where it was warm and comfortable for them. My father having strong hold over his mother persuaded them not to give up the Sussex property gaining further control of everything they had in the UK and eventually all they had in Malta.

Once my grandparents left the UK, I simply let go of our relationship. It was a regrettable mistake, wanting simply 'that period and all it entailed, gone from my life'. These lovely people had been the only two who showed constant kindness and guidance through my younger years learning so much more from them than my own parents. A letter arrived in our post office box recognising Edna's handwriting. Carefully slicing open the envelope a small passport picture of Jorge fell to the floor. I knew instantly the letter would bear sad news. With heavy heart I read of my grandfather enjoying being outside in his garden while Edna went to make tea. His heart suddenly failing for her to find him lifeless, the shock must have been devastating being inseparable all those years. I had lost a true friend who would have been proud of his grandson's journey after school days and a youth under his care. Tears of loss welled up quickly and I sat quietly reflective for an hour. I hope I still have the letter somewhere. I never heard from my grandmother again. Nor did I ever learn of her fate other than my father placing her in a nursing home. How long she lasted remained a mystery. My mother and I moved forward to more positive and peaceful times with her partaking in charity work for the Red Cross and Humane Society, keeping her well occupied and later becoming my partner in business. With my first work permit in hand our rent in William Street was $400 a month paid from wages earned in my first job. Life had new beginnings and the Bahamas was unquestionably home. Little did we know that local politics were rapidly reshaping and changes were on the horizon? Our futures would take some interesting turns with fate dealing strong lessons in survival lying just ahead.

Chapter 13
A Shift in the Wind

Life in the real world lay ahead for me in the 1970s. I had finished college, started my first job, bought my first car and supported a household now with just the two of us; a peaceful time no longer having to haul across the Atlantic three times a year subjected to the trials of life in an English boarding school. Year's later fate would hand me different cards to play involving another trip to the UK meeting my mother travelling earlier to visit her family that she had not seen us in decades. I felt compelled to give my birth country a closer look from fresh eyes untainted by the distaste of an unsavoury educational experience. It was June and a friend of mothers who had worked for Resorts International kindly gave me centre-court seats at Wimbledon; a tennis fan's dream that I was not passing up. That memorable day included a pass to have lunch in the players' lounge seated between Yannick Noah and Gabriella Sabatini. Yannick smoking like a chimney I asked unabashed 'how the heck do you run around the court for so long?' He laughed it off and was very cordial. Watching the matches live a real treat, the court looked so much bigger on television and yes, Gabriella was just as attractive! The weather worsened while we both stayed with ex-stewardess and best friend Sue Shepherd from Bahamas Airways now living on the banks of the River Thames. The setting was gorgeous but the damp and cold days of June soon gave my mother a change of heart about visiting the north of England.

'You've not seen your family in years' I exclaimed. Mother replying without hesitation. 'I am not that keen to be honest and I miss our dog, let's go home!' We changed our tickets and were in the warmth of our Bahamas within forty-eight hours.

During the 60s and 70s the Ministry of Tourism advertisements portrayed the Bahamas as 'Playground of the Western World' and the first year of work at The Balmoral Hotel, commuting every day in an open red Spitfire convertible lived up to the Ministries message. In those early days, a drive through town and along the coast road took less than twenty minutes even in traffic hours. All of us working the water-sports entertainment on that Cable Beach resort strip met daily at Howard Johnson's restaurant in the Nassau Beach Hotel each morning. Our waitress, Mildred Sands or Millie as we called her, knew us well saving us a booth by the window. Hotel guests took note of the four very tanned lads dressed in instructor jackets each day where attention of single girls was a piece of cake! The Balmoral was a beautiful private hotel away from the main commercialism further along Cable Beach with its own private island across the bay. My duties were to open the booth on the pool deck leased to Underwater Tours. I would display sets of masks, fins and snorkels along with a set of scuba gear showing that instruction was available. Snorkelling over on the island was beautiful and I rented gear daily to those taking the hotel ferry across for the day. Very quickly I started honing the skills of teaching, naturally winning students' confidence about being under the water and actually able to breathe. Visitors from all over the world were traveling to the Bahamas, many whose homeland void of water to swim in let alone oceans. On occasion, I could practice very broken foreign language skills or gently coax those who could barely swim into the water conquering their fear of being able to put their head beneath the surface. Many rewards lay ahead such as teaching a clinically blind young man to Scuba dive. Succeeding in his pool training all done by feel, I escorted him to Rose Island and the world underneath the surface. Again taking his arm as guide into near thirty-feet of water I took his hand to touch the soft corals, sea fans, sponges and hard corals. On surfacing he was ecstatic about his experience asking 'what did you not want me to touch?' sensitive that I had withdrawn his hand all too quickly from touching a well-camouflaged and highly poisonous Stonefish. Great satisfaction lay with those who could barely manage to swim but game enough to let me show them the art of snorkelling in the pool first. With added confidence in how to handle fins on their feet or tread water to putting their head under the surface without a mask; scuba became so much easier for them to grasp. We could teach a complete novice enough skills to dive for the first time in twenty-five feet of water, under close supervision, within about an hour.

On occasion, we were elected to work the dive boat to Rose Island an added treat from long hot days on hotel pool decks. One morning an unexpected visitor arrived just off the beach, surprising some of my new snorkelers practicing for the first time in the shallows. A very young bottle-nosed dolphin apparently hit by a boat propeller came amongst us unafraid. It was about four feet long with a nasty scar just behind the dorsal fin not yet healed. Fellow instructor from the Nassau Beach, Dave Andrews joined us coaxing the dolphin to play soon allowing a gentle stroke down his body. Our new friend became accustomed where we could swim and touch without hesitation adopting us to stay in close proximity for weeks. Every day we would pat the surface of the water and in seconds see our young friend racing towards us. The hotel guests were captured by his presence and my snorkel equipment would rent within the first hour. Having a boat available the young porpoise followed us as far as Rose Island some ten miles away. Very quickly he grew over six feet long and by the end of the summer with his wound completely healed we guessed a young lady porpoise was in the making for he was suddenly gone.

I was promoted to the Nassau Beach Hotel a more lively location where Dave and I put on pool shows for visiting conventions in the early evenings after work. Clown acts off the springboard, dressed as waiters we would mingle amongst the hotel guests gathered around the pool deck. Stunts revealed received laughter and a round of applause as the party entered full swing under the colourfully lit coconut palms, accompanied by a steel band playing in the warm Bahamian evening. Guests were dressed to the hilt in those days, jackets and ties proving uncomfortable for the men who perspired uncontrollably in the tropical heat reminding us the similar trials of dress to attend the Savoy movie theatre on Bay Street. Food heating trays uncovered by chefs in starched white uniforms and familiar toque blanche hats allowed aromas of conch chowder, grouper fingers and fried plantain to drift over the hotel grounds; the island music hypnotically sending charismatic melodies against the gentle lapping warm waters on the nearby beach; a scene bringing travel-brochures to life.

The Nassau Beach was the centre attraction on Cable Beach with its sister hotel The Emerald Beach next door to the west. Cable Beach was stunning in those early days, sixty feet of white powder sand as far as you could see in either direction, decorated with small thatched huts for guests seeking cool shade. Small gold coconut palm trees dotted the beach and pool deck, very attractive to stay there let alone have it as my daily office. The dive instructor's booth adored the pool deck with concessions on the beach for sailboats and water skiing managed by Sea Sports owned and operated by Doug Pruden, Jimmy Lowe and Leny Feldman; the front desk run by Kathy Snow and Pat Ruffin with Mr. George Myers as night manager. One day I was approached by fairly elderly lady who asked if I would be able to teach her how to scuba dive; at 78-years-young, showing for the appointment at the pool with the huge rubber bathing cap covered in bright plastic rubber flowers. I had a hard time keeping a straight face. In a two-piece bathing suit displaying the powers of gravity over time and managing barely to hold a set of heavy scuba gear, I assisted her in to the water. Across the other side I noticed a guest sketching on a large drawing pad. At the end of the ordeal he presented me with the finished drawing of a cartoon depicting the two of us in the shallow of the pool. I believe his last name was signed Winn, introduced as the cartoonist for the New York Times.

Lowe's operates the first phase of the new hotel constructed on Paradise Island, a theatre corporation in the United States, naming it Paradise Island Hotel and Villas. Gardner sent me to be the first dive instructor on Paradise meaning a considerably shorter commute from the William Street apartment. Proverbial 'Murphy's Law' struck the very first busload of tourists I picked up at the hotel for the morning dive. Racing over the new 72-foot-high bridge to Paradise Island in one of Gardner's ageing Volkswagen buses, I arrived at the hotel dead on pickup time at 9.15 am. Mr Ottis King, a well-loved familiar character who used to tend bar at the Bahamas Airways functions, surprisingly greeted me as head doorman of the new resort and ushered my clients aboard the vehicle. Years later his son Percy would steer me home many times as an air traffic controller with his distinctive voice reassuring 'Radar contact Pablo!' Reaching the apex of the bridge, headed towards Bay Street I readied the old bus for the descent. The brake pedal went hard to the floor with a thud I could not conceal. 'Oh that's great,' said the guest in the seat next to me placing his hand on the dashboard to brace for impending doom on fast approaching Bay Street. Quick down shifting gears and pulling the handbrake got us out of an interesting situation where others in the bus had no clue what had happened. For the next year I worked the pool deck at the new hotel, getting to know all the waitresses up at the snack bar, meeting the welcome face of Millie Sands who used to make the greatest milkshakes at

HoJo's while teaching me all about 'bush medicine'. I met the pool-deck crew, Gerry, Tony, Major and old man Roberts, adopting me as 'family' where during slow days we could all sit under the pavilion and swap fishy stories or dreams experienced the night before that they would look up intently the meanings in their 'dream books' stuffed into back pockets for playing the numbers! 'I played your birthday Paul and won $200!' Gerry would exclaim.

I was about twenty-four years old driving along Eastern Road spying something in the water that had me pull over and park the Spitfire under the shade of a casuarina tree. A beautiful white horse, maybe sixteen hands, swimming in the crystal clear shallows of the northern shoreline, most of his body submerged, mounted by a young girl in a small bikini riding bareback accompanied by two dogs. Her long dark hair waving in the gentle offshore breeze with a smile that captivated many of us who knew Melissa Maura, an island scene all too surreal with composer Frank Mills serenading her with bagpipes while standing on his seawall.

My mother and I had known her father well while at Nassau Tours on East Street near the cruise ships. Michael Maura the charismatic character who added initials 'MM' to Underwater Tours in partnership with my bosses Gardner and Charlie; Michael later working with Mackey Airlines at the airport and on to Chalks Airlines on Paradise Island where the Grumman Mallard often dipped its wings after a harbour take-off over the Maura house on East Bay Street. Melissa and I would soon meet as fellow artists involved with exhibitions with Brent Malone and at the Buena Vista Hotel managed by mutual friend Stan Bocus.

My skills in art produced extra pocket money. I completed my first water colour in 1969 branching into oils and later acrylics, with canvas and frames bought from an American couple, the Wasilles' owning Nassau Art Gallery on Bay Street's waterfront. Paintings took hours during the evenings and days off to complete enough work to share chance of showings with seventeen fellow artists at the Buena Vista. Displaying our paintings for the exhibition Melissa would always flash that warm generous smile, each having a twinkle in our eyes from way back, never having opportunity of furthering the relationship. A familiar fine thread however did weave through my story for years entwining both our lives in an enchanting way. We met later sharing photographic awards or flights to rescue birds or count iguanas in the outer islands. Rendezvous often unappreciated by partners of the times asking, 'What is it with you and Melissa?' I would simply smile knowing nothing ever happened. It would take near thirty-five years for that fate to travel full circle.

I began my first underwater photography with disposable film cameras that Kodak marketed at that time. On the shore of Cabbage Beach in front of the hotel were a group of huge flat rocks, smoothed by the waves over the years providing reef-like lodgings for a large variety of fish; grey snappers, sergeant majors and schools of small permit that we locally called 'Old Wives'. Collecting discarded bread and hamburger buns from the snack bar every day I had a good venture going with my snorkel gear rental as I had done at the Balmoral, each morning taking food down to the beach feeding the fish population. My hotel guests lay quietly in the water surrounded by a feeding frenzy bring the ocean surface to a boiling action of hundreds of fish. It caught the attention of passing local fisherman, Tony Maillis, a Bahamian of Greek decent, being our local 'Old Man of the Sea'. For years he had taken tourists out on his wooden Bahamian motor sloop to fish and snorkel off Paradise or Athol Island and on calmer days as far as Salt Cay and Rose Island. The boat held a live-well built in the hull so his catches could be kept alive. He had an amazing voice that could be heard far away over the water as he serenaded his clients with opera while steering the tiller perched on the stern, continuing eastward. His dark weathered skin and deep wrinkles had seen years of life on the sea. A familiar black Greek beret, faded now with years of sunlight, sat slightly askew on his grey curly hair. Seeing the surface boiling with my fish feeding Tony decided to troll as close as he dare off the hotel beach where he could strike some nice sized pompano.

'Carry yourself Tony,' I would call out, 'I need those fish for my business, give me a break'. He would wave in acknowledgement and smile while sitting on the transom, one hand casually guiding the tiller and bursting into song.

Unusual opportunities presented themselves when film companies started using the new resort as a location. I finally met my childhood TV idol, Lloyd Bridges from the television series *Sea Hunt* having watched religiously all those years ago in England; a real gentleman who I fortunately spent quite some time with over the days he was on location. Katherine Ross who had starred in *Butch Cassidy and the Sundance Kid* was involved, it appeared, with the lead cameraman. Jean Simmons and Shirley Jones also a delight during the production of *A Happy Ending* filmed in Nassau and Paradise Island over the next few weeks. One-day Bahamian actor Sidney Poitier came riding on horseback down the beach to where we were feeding fish off the shoreline of Cabbage Beach. Meeting him another real privilege and perk of the job; a fellow Bahamian from Cat Island became and Awards Oscar winner later knighted. I was now using a new 35mm Pentax camera and glad to have caught some good images of stars I met through my job developing my own film in a blacked out kitchen above William Street. With hands covered in developer I was sure I heard my GT6 start up down in the driveway? Rushing out of the apartment to chase my own stolen prized sports car out of the driveway on to Bay Street. As if I could catch it on foot? Pulling up behind me came friend Carey Leonard driving an identical white Triumph. He opened the door letting me in while saying, 'I've always wanted to say this line: "follow that car!" Unfortunately Carey being fairly conservative behind the wheel lost the pursuit. Other friends later that evening, catching the culprits in the Harbour Club parking lot stealing fuel from another car! I did not hesitate to prosecute the two boys sending them to Fox Hill Prison.

I was quickly being introduced to new lifestyles we all had simply read about in magazines becoming very enamoured with my career. Those fools I had schooled with would never believe these stories. I made little money but times were certainly fun. Returning home one evening I explained to my mother the next day I would not be at work because Rod Taylor had chartered a helicopter to take us to Rose Island as it was too rough by boat!

'How on earth did you get that invite?' she exclaimed, with Taylor being her vintage screen idol.

'We just became friends on the pool deck and talked about diving and spearfishing, and being an Australian; he would like me to guide them to a picnic spot on Rose Island.' Sure enough the next morning a Bell Ranger was waiting for us accompanied by new girlfriend Melanie, who had previously persuaded me to do a walk-on extra part for the Lloyd Bridges movie; we loaded and flew the short ten minutes to Rose Island. Picnic baskets were unloaded and the beach party began, a strange sight where all the locals wore woollen sweaters while guests in bathing suits taunted us. A strong cold front had passed through with temperatures barely climbing above the sixties making the campfire the place to be with rough surf pounding on the beach. Melanie was the lovely young lady that shared a magic experience we all remember as 'being the first'! Our turn would be on a warm moonlit night under the palms in the swimming pool of Grosvenor Court apartments; young lovers nearly getting caught later by her father returning home unexpectedly. Fortunately the familiar sound of his MG-GT saved the day by seconds!

Our salaries in those early days were by no means sufficient to support the pleasures we aspired to enjoy. Golf, boating, water skiing, photography and spearfishing were the order of the day when off duty. During lunch hours Tim Horton, Tom Ullery and I would try to sneak in a few holes of golf while in the Cable Beach area. We had no clue what we were doing. The game would come on a more serious note later where I played weekly while also pursuing tennis, a game landing me in various competitions organised within hotel clubs on Cable Beach where Vicki Knowles was tennis pro. We spearfished with her husband Sammy while young son Mark would soon have Wimbledon in his sights! Tim was saving money to begin training as a commercial pilot. He drove a silver Lotus Elite we all coveted. When ready to leave Underwater Tours he kindly gave me his training books knowing that I had a craving for aviation. There was no way my father would support the idea in those early days and I had no funds of my own to pursue the career. Running a sports car and buying that ice-cold Heineken while playing nine holes during lunch would suffice for now.

Additional income was to be made from spearfishing selling fresh lobsters and fish fillet to hotels and restaurants around Nassau and Paradise Island. Not a pastime to pursue on one's own, I needed a partner to dive with. In 1968 an Australian lad had befriended Brad Lightbourne, a Bahamian traveling through Australia. They met in Sydney and after spending time 'down under' the invitation to come on over to the Bahamas was extended to the adventurous Aussie. In June of 1969 Gary Cox landed for the first time in Nassau. The world of Underwater Tours soon had the two of us introduced where he too landed a part time job as a fellow safety swimmer for the novice scuba divers. We both recognised immediately a great new friendship forming with added bonus of a reliable dive partner creating many ways to survive financially without having to leave the country in years to come.

Times in the Bahamas were changing politically. A new era lay just around the corner with tensions underlying the political surface in both Nassau and Freeport, with whispers of Independence. As expats we felt the need to pay attention to the world around us especially here in the capital. Things were not as fancy free and relaxed toward foreigners as in the old days of first arrival under the old United Bahamian Party; a white dominated political group of influential local businessmen. The Bahamas are a successful democracy under a two-party system emulating the Westminster Political structure led by a prime minister over his cabinet and opposition with a governor representing the Queen: the country remaining a member of the British Commonwealth. The old-school government and business clique that ran Bay Street commerce here in Nassau were on the way out. As early as 1953, Lynden Pindling joined an Opposition Party known as the PLP, the Progressive Liberal Party. The public majorities were leaning heavily in the direction of the everyday Bahamian who rightfully wanted their fair share of the pie. Pindling was born on March 22 1930 in Masons Edition here in Nassau. His father a native Jamaican had immigrated to the Bahamas joining the Royal Bahamas Police Force as a constable. He graduated from the local Government High School in 1946 and worked as a clerk in the local Post Office Savings Bank. Later he went to London to study law and received his degree from King's College in 1952. He was called to the English Bar in February 1953 and again to the Bahamas Bar in June of the same year. By the end of the year he joined the newly formed Progressive Liberal Party as its legal advisor. In 1956 he became the parties Parliamentary Leader after Henry Taylor, leader of the party, was defeated in that year's general election. Sir Lynden taking majority rule on the January 10 1967 with his PLP Party enjoying an unbroken reign of power until defeated by Hubert Ingraham's FNM in 1992.

On April 27 1965 Bahamian history notes a day called 'Black Tuesday' where Pindling delivered a speech in the House of Assembly situated in Rawson Square, town centre of Nassau where a statue of Queen Victoria stoically kept watch. He accused members of the United Bahamian Party of tactics to perpetuate the white political hegemony in the Bahamas. To emphasise his conclusion, Pindling picked up the Speakers Mace, a very treasured ceremonial artefact in the Westminster system, and threw it out of the window to land in the square below under the unchanged gaze of Queen Victoria. He exclaimed, 'This is the symbol of authority, and the authority in this island belongs to the people, the people are outside and that's where the Mace belongs too!' Fellow member Milo Butler followed suit by adding the Speaker's Hourglass to items ejected out of the House windows. Milo Butler, in an ironic twist of like and dislike involving the English parliamentary system here, ended up receiving a knighthood from the Queen, later becoming Governor of the Bahamas. An up and coming group of black Bahamians started the long process toward gaining power in their Opposition Party and the dreams of an Independent Nation. In 1967 they won control of the Government by at first equalling the eighteen seats of the United Bahamian Party receiving the swing vote from elected Independent, Alvin Braynan, who agreed to be the new Speaker of the House with Randol Fawkes, the only Labour MP, who voted to sit with Pindling's party. With the first black government of the Bahamas now in power the outside would take note, that major transitions in Bahamian power were always peaceful, demonstrating time and again its stability as a nation. Our islands began enjoying an increase in banking industries, tourism, and offshore investing offering equal rights for all Bahamians led into independence from Great Britain.

Prince Charles, representing the Queen arrived on the British frigate *Minerva* on which he was serving. That night of July 9 1973, hundreds of residents made our way by boat to anchor in the harbour before the midnight ceremonies began. The dark night waters were littered with marine craft secure in the cruise ship turning basin just north of Fort Charlotte, having no idea years later I would be landing seaplanes in this very spot. The night sky illuminated with powerful floodlighting of the independence celebrations that entertained an estimated 50,000 people just below the old Fort, once guarding the harbour entrance, never having fired a shot in hostility. The British flag barely fluttered in the night air. Celebrations were filled with pomp and circumstance, the police force band, scores of dignitaries and the excited mass of locals filling the night with vibrant electricity. At midnight, we watched with mixed emotions the Union Jack being lowered and a minute later the black, turquoise and yellow flag of our new nation rise to flutter gently in the dark early morning sky. A huge roar erupted from the crowds as the new era began that night; a proud moment.

Slowly but surely the repeated re-election of the same Government nurtured corruption, where in the 1970s familiar political cracks began to appear in the leadership. Later years started the political downfall of the 'Father of the Nation' when in 1983 investigative reporter for NBC Brian Ross aired a show entitled *The Bahamas – A Nation for Sale.* The report alleged that Pindling and his Government along with other Bahamian officials had accepted bribes from Colombian drug smuggler Carlos Lehder, co-founder of the Medellin Cartel, a famed report that still airs today on the internet.

Carlos Lehder, born on September 11 1949, became co-founder of the infamous Medellin Cartel with Pablo Escobar, Carlos' father a German engineer and mother a Columbian schoolteacher. His shady career started out as a stolen car dealer from vehicles taken in the US and Canada. Caught and jailed he befriended bunkmate George Jung, later played by my client Johnny Depp in a film about the cocaine trade involving islands in the Bahamas. Lehder revolutionised the idea of moving cocaine in light aircraft to the United States that had travelled from Columbia up through the Caribbean to Normans Cay in the Exumas just forty miles southeast of Nassau. Normans had been the island destination for famous celebrities with its marina and clubhouse on the hill overlooking a small airstrip, a playground for the likes of Elizabeth Taylor and stars of that era. In 1978, Lehder starting buying as many the properties on the island as possible after his arrival in 1978, living in a renowned house on the northeast corner of the island called Volcano. Those who would not sell he intimidated with violence, forcing them to vacate their homes and flee the island. One stubborn holdout owned a houseboat, returned to find his home lifted from the water and placed in the bush strategically near the islands highest point completely unmovable, easily visible as an example. It is estimated Lehder invested more than $4 million in the island becoming his lawless 'kingdom', forcing Jung from the partnership with a rumour of fugitive Robert Vesco joining forces. The cay operated successfully from 1978 through 1982 as the Caribbean's main drug smuggling route. The story goes about a large smuggling plane making a poor approach into the island during dead of night. The Curtiss C 46 hit something on the threshold of the runway damaging gear and forcing a go-around. Deciding a water splashdown was the safest way to keep the aircraft in one piece and crew alive without blocking the valuable airstrip. Landing in the shallows of the eastern side of the island the Curtiss stopped short of the deep channel by fifty feet and all aboard was saved. Planes, boats and people were all expendable in those times. Up to 300 kilos of cocaine arriving on the island each day would be reloaded onto light aircraft or fast race-boats for the 200-mile hop over to Florida, Georgia and South Carolina during the night making the drug lord's wealth climb into the billions where invited guests were often greeted in a Land Rover of naked girls down at the runway for party-time up at Volcano.

Rumour reached all of us in the boating business here in Nassau 'it not advisable to venture near or especially land on Normans Cay'. We had heard of an aircraft declaring an emergency landing unwanted on the island, to be forced airborne again by submachine-gun-toting guards, the plane barely reaching Eleuthera. Another fun story emerging – member of parliament Norman Solomon disregarded the warnings wanting to see for himself if rumour were true, drove his boat from Nassau to land on the beach near the airstrip. Pretending to casually swim and lay in the sand, he was soon approached by the armed guards ordering him to leave immediately. Arriving in Nassau gave information to the US Coastguard and Bahamian police force where raids were soon instigated ending Lehder's reign on the island in 1982. He managed to escape but after the NBC interview with Prime Minister Lyndon Pindling, Lehder was unable to re-enter the Bahamas and later captured in Columbia, extradited to the United States where he was imprisoned to life without parole. In 1992 with sights set on convicting Panama's Manuel Noriega for trafficking, the US made a deal for Lehder's testimony, reducing his sentence to fifty-five years.

A year after the change of Government in the early 70s we saw a massive sweep in the expulsion of expatriates. The irony of Pindling having a Jamaican father, the sweep with immigration targeted many Jamaicans residing here along with the British. Rightly, if a Bahamian could do the job then the expat would lose his or her working permit and be asked to leave the country within a certain specified amount of time. It was not made public what certain families were undergoing, where radical stories of Gestapo-type tactics became whispers, especially in Freeport where Prime Minister Pindling had given his famous 'Bend or Break' speech and some expats given just twenty-four hours to vacate the country.

Freeport, situated on one of the largest islands in the archipelago was destined to be the nation's second city, thought crucial to the growth of the Bahamas founded by Wallace Groves and the Grand Bahama Port Authority in 1955. Groves had come to the Bahamas after serving time in jail for mail fraud in the 1940s purchasing the Abaco Lumber Company in 1946 selling his interest nine years later for $4 million. The UBP Government having given the Port Authority many concessions and complete control over the casino under the Hawksbill Agreement. With Immigration and Customs also under their control the Port could issue licenses and work permits acting a quasi-government within itself. Many white southern Americans with racist attitudes emigrated to Freeport, discriminating against local black Bahamians wanting residence or jobs there. Local outer communities on Grand Bahama often displayed run down surroundings while suffering a lack of running water or electricity, whereas in Freeport times were prosperous. The arrival of the PLP Government finally offered access to the new city for all Bahamians much to the disgust of the white expatriates ensconced in business there. On July 26 1969 at the official opening of BORCO, a huge oil refining company, Prime Minister Pindling warned the Port and its licenses his government would end discriminatory practices, warning if they did not bend to these wishes then he would break them. Expats began bailing out of Freeport in droves taking the island into recession reflecting off the American financial decline of the 70s. The nation's second city never fully recovered from its peak of the 60s.

The Immigration Department, under the command of Loftus Roker, Minister of Immigration was situated on the top of Hawkins Hill and steered with an iron fist by the deputy prime minister's sister, another irony with her married to a Haitian national. It became a street that we as foreigners avoided traveling at all costs. The net spread wide and deep to take all unwanted expats off the island. An added irony continued in that we, as a part of that targeted group, had discussed amongst ourselves the real need to 'get rid of all these whining Brits' – this clique that only read the airmail version of the *Daily Mail* while eating lunch in Ben Warry's Green Shutters every day; complaining constantly about Bahamians and the Bahamas, saying 'they couldn't wait to go home'. Question was 'how do we get to stay apart from them and prove our differences and loyalty to the Bahamian people?' We had heard an average of about 400 a week being shipped back to the UK. The difference in my field of work that black Bahamians in those days really did not venture far in to the water, let alone scuba dive in to the deep ocean. There were no Bahamian instructors with exception of characters like Emerson Roberts our fun Bahamian captain; Instructors Working Permits back then near that of a garbage man costing only $500 annually. Time however finally runs its course and one day Ray Moore, our office manager, called me in to the office at the Nassau Yacht Haven. Ray-Ban sunglasses perched on top of his head solemnly slid an open letter across his desk toward me. My heart sank reading the title header on top of the page, 'Bahamas Immigration Department'.

'With reference to the renewal of Mr. Paul Harding's Work Permit please be informed the application has been denied. Signed, The Director.' No mention of 'requested to leave the country' as were in other letters I had heard of being received. Some foreigners had thirty days, some ten days, some twenty-four hours? Nothing here? Ray apologised for the loss of employment and asked that I hang around as long as I could to see if there were any changes in policy. He too was in a sticky position as all the main crews for the water sports industry here in the Bahamas especially the field of scuba diving, were mostly foreigners.

Walking out of the Yacht Haven parking lot back across to William Street to give my mother this news was very difficult. It was a numbing feeling of loss. Now we were both in the same boat, no status in a foreign country, with no financial support and very little in the bank to keep us afloat for even a short period of time. Looking at the waterfront where pristine yachts lay berthed, the calm harbour waters reflecting the colours and young palm trees still in the morning air the decision to 'stay put, come what may' very much in my psyche. This is home and we are staying!

'Good God Paul, what are we going to do, we will have to go back to England?' my mother cried with despair, her eyes saddened at our prospects.

'No, that's what that son of a bitch wanted to happen to us,' referring to my father's plan. All during my relationship with him, I suspect starting with my birth, a subtle streak of jealousy toward me? When I returned from schooling in England I lived at home for a while in order to get started on my new life. I was informed that I would be contributing financially toward household expenses and could maintain use of my own room in William Street. However, the arrival of my first sports car did create a stir. My father soon sold the old Morris Minor wagon, now full of termites in the wooden frame, replacing it with a convertible Austin Healey Sprite. The competition was on it seemed between father and son. Within those first few months I was quite successful and heard about a flashy Triumph GT6 for sale at an irresistible price. I tried without success to keep its license tag number of 69, well suited maybe for an aspiring scuba instructor. My father's jealousy was evident when I pulled into the driveway in that white sports car, resembling a small version of the Jaguar E-Type. I could see the gleeful expression in my mother's face standing behind my Dad as if needing to give me a 'high-five' in victory, the two of us here years later in the dilemma of how to keep life afloat. I had creative ideas racing around my imagination. I felt no fear, only confidence in my ability to succeed.

'We both have nothing in common with England, no home, no friends, no connection. If we are going to be poor, then it will be in a pair of shorts!' I declared with new authority.

'But how in the world do we survive here?' mother asked. I knew instinctively the ocean could be my source of living. I had met the Australian and together we would make things happen.

'We will survive off the sea, mum,' I replied quietly reflecting our options. 'There is good money in seafood, coral for jewellery and tropical fish for aquariums. Gary and I have the connections to sell everything we catch.' With my official letter from immigration having not mentioned any request to leave the country I simply stayed, not leaving the island for the next several years. If I had left for any reason, there would be no getting back in other than as a tourist. There was no need to travel, quite happy to be in the Bahamas; it was the only real home we knew and we were going to hang on tight, whatever it took? Our only friends were here, many of who were 'family' to us, both black and white Bahamians all supporting our decision to stick it out. Even a few immigration officers who knew us well from the old Bahamas Airways days, telling us 'this was a load of foolishness' and 'not to go anywhere!'

Chapter 14
The Aussie

The immigration 'crunch' as we termed it, under the rigid enforcement of the Minister and his subordinates, spread noticeably through Nassau and Freeport finding both Gary and me in the same political situation and lack of legal status. Neither of us had received official notice to vacate the country, he residing with Frank and Mary Pritchard and two daughters, a Bahamian family and me still sharing the apartment with my mother, each having a roof over our head yet needing a way to pay our weekly expenses. Any thought of saving money out of the question with life becoming simply a matter of day-to-day survival. Our skills in the water were excellent. Both very confident and no fear about making a living from the wild, with practise could now free dive up to sixty feet of water to spear fish and lobster. We were well qualified to scuba dive specialising in deep water work if required, both having past experience with underwater film crews and engineering projects. We shared the same interests of filming, either stills or video, similar music and all things with the ocean. 'All we need now cobber, is a friggin' boat!' the Australian quirked in his broad down-under accent. Making calls to a few friends it was Graham from the boarding school days offering a welcome suggestion. He was fortunate to be living here legally after his parents had the good sense applying and granted 'Belongers' status offered in earlier years by the Bahamian Government. My father had not been so generous. Graham recalled seeing in his travels throughout New Providence an old wreck of a boat in Coral Harbour. Once again the southern residential area came back in to my life with hope of a vessel to rebuild. The three of us drove from town twenty odd miles south towing a boat trailer passing through the twin towers that stood proud at the entrance of the community roundabout. On one of the side roads next to one of the many canals lay a poor excuse for a 'boat'. About fifteen feet long and full of dirt with three feet of grass growing inside, one side completely torn from the gunnel to the chine.

'How in hell can we fix this thing?' I asked in dismay. 'No wonder someone dumped this!'

Graham smiled, 'Well, I can teach you two how to fibreglass and repair. I have an old McCulloch 14HP outboard that should push her pretty good'. He produced a shovel from the back of his car and we started excavating the growth of weeds and dirt from inside. We worked in turns soon in sweat-drenched shirts hauling the wreck aboard the trailer. It was the sad-looking remains of an open skiff obviously abandoned years ago. We pulled the boat back to William Street where it sat under the trees for my first fibreglass tuition. Graham explained which fibre cloth, matt and resin to purchase along with disposable brushes and acetone for the clean-up. He leant an electric sander and instructed how to sand groves each side of the tear in the hull creating a valley for the new glass to be laid in layers creating a new seam. However one tried to dodge the fibreglass dust that bellowed in to the air there was no escaping the itching skin; the obnoxious white power getting in to one's hair and skin under the clothing especially a nightmare, only long soapy showers finally rid one of the torment.

Over the next few days the hull came together with the magic of the glass repair. Each layer sanded and built upon created a sturdy finished hull. We turned the boat over, painting the bottom with antifoul paint, an expensive item for very little money to our names. Donald and Sydney Brown, owners of Browns Boat Basin on East Bay Street helped us with all the pieces of the puzzle needed for this resurrection. With a couple quarts of marine paint we brushed the aqua-blue interior and mounted the old outboard. Having secured a small space by the fuel dock at Brown's we launched my first boat! We were in business. The hull rode well in the calmer seas out past Athol Island and over to Salt Cay. Gary and I used to dive every day weather permitting, agreeing some days we should never have left the dock, for it was no hull for rough water. We gained approval with restaurant owners throughout the island such as chef Ronnie from 'Sun And...' and our friend Glen Pritchard from Island Seafoods off Wulfe Road along with Tyrone Darville opening Portion Control on Fowler Street, on occasion driving to Oakes Field selling to Echo Bahamas. Taking a share each and a share for the boat we could now make a living and maintain the boat with its expenses at Browns. We set out each morning enjoying the friendship talking of previous adventures we had both shared passing Tony in the harbour as he trawled a yellow feather behind his boat, still serenading his clients on board.

Our first anchorages on calm days were over 'the cars'. In the early 60s, old wrecked cars around New Providence were collected off the roadsides and taken by barge to the South side of Salt Cay where a crane dropped them one by one in a long line to submerge in about thirty feet to a clear sandy bottom. In years to follow, corals began to grow as the junked cars corroded, a new ecosystem created in each vehicle with schools of snapper and yellowtail swimming through the wreckage. Within time, spiny lobster, or crawfish as we knew them in the Bahamas, found their way in to their new home under the hood or trunk of a crumbling Chevrolet. Hard to reach, some of the crawfish grew to huge sizes we nicknamed 'hairy legs' as their appendages big enough to make a meal by themselves. Boiled and split open with melted butter a delicacy for our tables. The tails were selling now for about $5 a pound; one would only need a few pounds making the day profitable. The Australian and I developed a method of diving, taking turns to search the wreck or coral head shelves while the companion stayed above spotting runaways that crawl away in a hasty escape out of view from the diver below. If one needed to attract the others attention we would take the Hawaiian sling and bang the spear shaft rapidly, sound travels efficiently through the water and is easily noticed. With hand or arm signals each diver knew instinctively what the other needed. Very little escaped us once working together. The code was simple, the diver who spotted prey made the first dive. If needed the partner would make a second dive for the kill shot and retrieval; large fish that were hit and escaped would be immediately followed by the diver above. Almost no prey would escape our pursuit with each day presenting adventures one could only smile about later eventually bringing us close to serious trouble. Every spear fisherman knows fish stories come with the territory.

The first outlandish incidents found us diving for the same huge lobster under ledges located off Paradise Beach known as 'the caves' lying in forty feet of water. The top of these underwater ridges easily spotted from the surface once bearings from the land were remembered. Down to the sand below one could swim inside these holes finding large crustaceans hiding along the back wall. Some of the 'caves' far less accessible with narrow openings too small for a man to manoeuvre inside. Yet there we could see massive orange legs reflecting the light from outside. 'Shit that's a monster!' Gary would exclaim on the surface knowing a few tails like this in the boat would be a handsome day's work. I was much smaller in frame than the barrel-chested Australian. 'Mate, you crawl in there and bang him!' he would instruct. 'Oh great Aussie, and how the hell do I get back out?' I yelped. 'I'll follow ya down and when you plunk him kick your ankle and I'll pull you out!'

We found other holes on the ocean floor further down by the lighthouse. We also found cannonball crusted into the coral bottom only possible from the guns of Fort Charlotte directly opposite. 'That's a hell of a distance for a bloody piece of iron to travel' Gary would remark. Again, huge crawfish hid in the far rear of these holes and the tactic would be repeated. No sooner than I had crawled inside by a few feet did I find myself propelled backwards into the sunlight.

'What the hell, Oz?' I barked as we tread water on the surface, 'I didn't have chance to take a shot!' He smiled saying quietly 'go have a squizz just inside that hole my friend!' I took another good breath of air and submerged downward. Just inside the entrance an enormous green moray eel thrust his head aggressively toward me warning of his home, an eel so large it had to lay on its side with a body over six feet long and thick as my two thighs. Even underwater one could feel the hair stand on your neck, damn: snakes and eels taking me by surprise are my fear. Once a spear fisherman there comes eel stories, especially with the big green morays fending their territory. Partnered with the Australian while diving off Clifton Pier a large green came rapidly all the way out of its home forcing a hasty retreat rather than tangle face to face. Later with Andrew Barr diving lobster over the wreck of the Mahoney, off Paradise Island, a huge green eel, a good two feet thick, came charging out of its hiding place following us all the way to the surface! We entered over the gunnel of his Jupiter 15 boat with speed and grace to see the open-mouthed head protrude out of the water. Never had I experienced such aggression scaring us both silly!

An odd occasion did present itself after successfully shooting a Nassau grouper in about forty-five feet of water. The fish barely moved as the spear found its mark. Feeling I had sufficient air held I kicked forward for the retrieval suddenly seeing a monster rockfish racing through the soft corals to steal my catch: a fish as long as I and much wider, as big as my motorcycle, weighing in at ninety pounds its huge gaping mouth would have swallowed my fish in a gulp. I had a barbless spear in hand when the massive form closed in allowing me to reload and let fly. With inertia that high the sharp point penetrated the large skull between the eyes causing the massive fish to stop in its tracks. It turned about face swimming away in slow motion, making just a yard or two before healing over resembling a unicorn lying on its side. My dive partner passed me for the retrieval as I sped upward for desperately needed air. The spear had collided with such force neither of us could extract it until back at the dock; slicing off the mammoth fillets weighing in at sixty-four pounds paying fuel and expenses that day with salary left for each of us.

The art of stalking the fish in a dive to the ocean floor perfected with practice. Large Nassau groupers would eye us from the surface, eyes dancing like a chameleon watched us drift stealthily downstream; diving quietly to the bottom and safe distance from the prey, one would very gently kick a fin stealthily through the soft coral feathers. All the air within the snorkel tube had escaped to the surface in a stream of small bright silver bubbles leaving nothing to alarm the unsuspecting fish watching keenly as the strange shape drifted ever so slowly toward him. Forty feet on the bottom one would very quickly feel the desire to take another breath but chance of a shot not to be lost. At any given moment, the fish decides this was close enough and makes a turn to swim away exposing the side of his head. Drawing a line behind the eye and from the first gill slit upward, where the lines crossed a guaranteed brain shot. The diver with sling rubber stretched to breaking would release the spear in a fluid motion to keep the aim. Six feet of steel would find its mark and the fish would shudder in sudden death instantly changing colour to pale; now the perilous journey back to the anchored boat hoping not to attract the attention of predators able to detect the slightest signal of sound and smell from miles away.

The worst offenders for sounding the dinner bell were hog snappers. The locals called them hogfish, a beautifully decorated scale fish that fed solely on the bottom. Its long snout and distinct front teeth used for excavating and crushing small shellfish giving the apt name. The kill spot was small on these fish. Many times, with a skilful approach, the hogfish would turn sideways and display his dorsal fins in a show-off fashion offering generously a side view to shoot at. Every once in a while, we got lucky with the fish instantly losing its colour on impact quivering in instant death. Other times the salmon-coloured fish would dart away incredibly fast leaving the hunter no choice but to rise upward for air. Their jerky swim patterns and lightning speed more often caused a long swim away from the boat, trailing them from the surface while they hauled the heavy stainless steel hanging out of their side. These fish were very strong, capable of traveling a hundred yards without stopping, many simply escaped into the void. Sharks love to eat hogfish and we had many a battle to keep our prize. Losing fish to predators was rare but when it happened things could turn dangerous very quickly.

I was dating a former runner-up to the Miss Bahamas Pageant working for Bert L. Roberts real estate business downtown for son Larry Roberts. Kathy was a lady of the sea with her family heritage from Abaco. One weekend we took her diving with us on a spearfishing expedition to the North side of Rose Island. The ocean was flat calm and the oily surface a joy to ride over. Sitting on the bow of our skiff my wife to be watched familiar sea life pass under her spotting thin-lipped conchs lying in the dark turtle grass, starfish scattered on the white sand sea floor. Rainbow parrotfish dashed for cover while schools of blue tang rushed away from the small bow wave we pushed. We headed east past Sandy Cay and Green Cay to approach a small barren coral island rising from the sea called Iron Bound Rock. There were no Global Positioning Satellites in those days. We had to mark waypoints the old-fashioned way placing this lone rock against another part of Rose Island in the background. Adding the old Montagu Hotel on the eastern shores of Nassau with Rose Island's western shore one could place a cross-reference to the site finding lobster-hiding places often within feet of where we needed to be. This system working well for us until one day the abandoned hotel was blown up with explosives to clear the property for further re-development – our waypoint references gone in a cloud of concrete debris.

Our skiff travelled to Booby Rock Channel at the far eastern end of Rose Island. The infamous piece of water known through our fishing community as a very precarious place to swim let alone spearfish. Big creatures swam through this channel from both sides of the island with the fast streaming tides allowing passage to the deep ocean water on the

North side. This folklore was more than we both could stand. Gary looked at me with mischievous grin and with a nod we slowed the skiff to idle anchoring in the middle of the channel. Tide was easing and the Danforth anchor bit hard under a ledge.

'You fools are not swimming here, please tell me you won't spear anything?' Kathy pleaded.

'No worries, love,' Gary replied with that wry smile and a cautious wink of the eye in my direction. We donned our snorkel gear in the hot Bahamian sunshine. With no Bimini-top to shade us, keeping the sun at bay impossible, with salt and sunshine our bodies became dark with tan. I had bought an early model Nikonos underwater camera from Pat Turnquest at John Bull improving my new love of photography. Chances like this warranted carrying the camera over my neck in case of finding something really unusual. We both slipped quietly in to the warm ocean water, spears in hand. Strong currents running through this infamous channel did not allow large coral growth and the bottom lay fairly flat some twenty feet below. A few rocky ledges and turtle grass adorned the seabed with an occasional long body of soft coral that would lean gracefully waving with the tidal flow. Small wrasse fish darted between the weeds. Kathy sat in the bow while the Australian and I drifted apart by a few yards. Within a few minutes the familiar clanging of the sling against the stainless spear meant I was being summoned. Gary was motionless on the surface and his steady breathing could be heard clearly through the big-barrelled snorkel. He was pointing forward and below him. A large Nassau grouper with its familiar brown camouflaged colours lay on its side looking upward. It must have weighed a good thirty pounds.

'What a ripsnorter!' he exclaimed in his familiar Australian slang as we plotted the strategy of taking the fish, treading the water as quietly as possible. The grouper was no fool and had grown that size from experience in dodging trouble. He swam lazily away a few feet then effortlessly sliding sideways under his hiding place, a narrow ledge of flat rock grunting at us in defiance that could be heard on the surface.

'That's not such an easy shot mate,' I said as we trod water.

'I'll plunk him while you keep an eye out for any beasts?' he remarked placing the snorkel back in his mouth. Kathy could hear everything well in view of the two of us a few yards away staring in disbelief what we were planning.

The water is crystal clear with the high tide flowing in from the open ocean, visibility at its peak. She watched as Gary doubled over and gracefully slid downward away from the surface, his fins barely slicing the water so as not to cause disturbance. With two or three wide kicks he was horizontal on the bottom, watching him draw back the sling with steady aim while drifting silently toward his target. The fish lay on its side with the smooth head visible under the narrow crack in the rock. He released the sling and the sharp point of the spear penetrated just shy of the skull bone, missing the vital kill spot. Groupers and rockfish are big-mouthed fish and one of their defences is the art of opening their mouth as wide as possible causing the gill plates to wedge against the surrounding surface. The wounded fish thrashed violently sending a cloud of powdery sand out of the hole. Strong grunting added to the noise while Gary jumped forward thrusting the spear securely into the prey. Gill plates opened the grouper held firm in his hideaway. There was no budging it just yet. Dark patterns of blood, appearing iridescent green at this depth, wafted outward into the current below. The fish would slowly start to deplete in strength while sending that well-known distress signal through the clear waters. In the world underwater this was a loud and clear summons to eat.

Out of breath, Gary pushed off the bottom and headed upward for a gulp of fresh air, dropping the mouthpiece out of his mouth and exclaimed a frustrated '*Shit!*' across the surface.

'Bloody hell Gary you are crazy, I told you don't shoot anything here!' Kathy added to mix. It was time to take the next dive and repeat the process until the fish was retrieved. Sometimes we would work for near an hour in retrieving our quarry; whatever it took, we very rarely left our fish to be the meal of others. I stayed close by watching all directions as the cloud of sand and blood increased from the bottom drifting off in the direction of tidal flow; my friend made another dive beginning to force the fish outward, the large head appearing from under the ledge, my attention suddenly catching the unmistakable large form racing in to view from one side across the bottom. In a split second a very large bull shark, eight or nine feet in length, appeared out of nowhere, its destination without question directly toward Gary with frightening speed. I banged my sling furiously against my spear in warning and rushed forward offering defence obviously needed. Gary hearing the frantic signals looked up instinctively in the right direction as the shark was nearly on him. Leaving the speared fish in its place the Australian pushed off the bottom just as the big fish reached him. The huge head rolled over on its side exposing the light cream colour of his underbelly skin, its wide pectoral fins grasped downwards and toward each other in the act of aggression, like a muscle man flexing his strong arms to display the power he possessed. The huge fish opened its mouth for the first bite at the diver's waist, exposing its rows of perfect triangular teeth. With a good dose of adrenalin Gary's reaction was lightning fast, successfully punching at the shark's nose hitting it square and hard on its side; an area full of sensitive nerve endings the large flat head pulled away in defence for a few spilt seconds making a continuous turn around the ascending man's body. Gary turned in unison sending a second swipe at the huge head coming at him for another bite. He had turned maybe two full rotations as I reached him with the bull shark trying continuous bites at his torso. The punches were clean and hard so as not to abrade on the shark's skin, composed of thousands of dermal denticles, a similar composure to that of their teeth can tear human skin like a cheese grater. Round and round they turned during the climb upward.

The ocean appeared as if through a looking glass, it was that calm, the scene playing out just feet away from the boat. It must have been frightening to watch as Kathy's hysterical screams carried clearly as far as Rose Island.

'You two fucking idiots get out of the damned water!' this polite, well-mannered young lady hollered. If we needed any prodding of urgency she certainly made her point in an instant! I made a dive toward Gary and his aggressor reaching both in a few strong strokes. Within a few feet of the surface I rammed my spearhead into the sharks' gill slits. Suddenly distracted the huge fish shook free and turned its attention to me allowing my friend to launch himself with one graceful motion into the boat. I braced for the head-on impact, a bull shark habitually bumping its prey first, unexpectedly opening its mouth to clamp down on the shaft of the spring steel spear held in front of my torso for protection. Refusing to relinquish my weapon, I held on tight as the desperate tug of war began. The big fish was very strong and very pissed at both of us. His head twisted aggressively side-to-side, tail thrashing the surface sending white saltwater spray in every direction while trying to pry the spear from my grasp, its pectoral fins arching downward again in signalled aggression. With every ounce in me, I yanked the spearhead out of the clamped mouth, bending the barb backwards giving a valuable second to ram the point against that sensitive snout. It bounced off as if I had hit granite but in an instant, the bull was gone. I too ejected myself out of the water landing in a pile inside the bottom of the boat, two divers hysterically laughing, the fear of the moment with adrenalin flowing tuning us like a stretched piano wire.

'What a rip!' the Aussie cried. On seeing me lying there still with the Nikonos draped around my neck he then added 'Did you get the photo?'

'Photo?' I questioned in disbelief. 'You have to be friggin joking you crazy bastard, I was trying to save your ugly arse!' Kathy was even more furious at our warped sense of humour shaking her head in relief, tears flowing that we both were safe inside.

'If ever that happens again Paul, you take the damned picture first!'

'Right,' I thought just staring at him, 'like this would ever happen again?' We had been spearfishing our whole lives without incident. That's how rare this moment would be. Little did I know history would repeat itself in another location not far from here; and yes Gary, I did get the photo!

'Damned if I am leaving that lovely grouper and me spear down there for that bastard,' the Australian mumbled. We waited a few minutes watching the waters below from the safety of the small boat. 'Tell me you two fools are not going in the water again?' Kathy pleaded quietly. Feeling more confident the large grouper had succumbed its injury we slid very quietly back in to the water. The nice-sized fish was indeed motionless, collapsing the large gill plates allowing the spear and fish to slide smoothly from under the ledge. The unease of the situation stayed with us voting to move location a mile further westward off Iron Bound Rock to continue the hunt hauling again the small Danforth anchor overboard paying out line until secure in another forty feet of water.

The soft corals and ledges were clearly visible and large parrotfish could be seen grazing on the hard corals held firm on the ocean floor. Once in the water with surroundings so very quiet that day one could hear their teeth scraping off the delicate coral tissue from below us.

'You two idiots aren't going to spear again are you?' Kathy still pleading knowing the answer.

'Keep your eyes peeled, mate,' Gary said, knowing full well sharks can hear a commotion from miles away and no guarantee the same bull shark would not hear the dinner bell go off again. Within minutes we spied a really nice male hogfish; the sweetest fish that we all loved to eat, cooked in any style the preferred take home catch of anything we could hit. I made the dive to bottom several yards away from the fish while he stopped his forward swim to stare in curiosity at the approaching diver. It was one of their downfalls. While stalking very slowly through the waving fan and soft corals to hide my presence the hogfish turns sideways to present all his dorsal fins in a show of defiance. In smooth motion, I draw the sling until the spear tip is near the shooter handle. The sling's rubber near to breaking, I drift still further toward the target with a mere motion of one swim fin kick in slow motion. Two eyes affixed on the target area just behind the eye and above the first gill slit. My brain is now screaming for fresh air but the adrenalin is holding everything in check forty feet down on the ocean floor. Within inches of the displaying fish I let the shaft fly. Six feet of spring steel meets its mark but does not penetrate the body even with all that force applied. With a strong kick forwards, I reach the struggling fish and make that important thrust forward to push the spear through the body and set the barb on the other side. It is vital, if at all possible, to grab the shaft and fish in the swim upward for that much-needed breath. The anchor line in view resembles an umbilical cord stretching upward to the small hull floating above me. Leaving the fish to trail under ones ascending body would create too much drag on the diver's ascent providing a tempting target for an imposing predator; we would position the fish close to us and in the most streamlined profile for the long swim to the surface. Once the surface was broken we would hoist the fish out of the water to stop the thrashing body from attracting attention; a swim back to the boat and turn of the spear so the catch could slide down the open end of the shaft safely in to the bottom of the boat. I was about twenty feet from the surface when the banging of spear against shooter had me spin around in a circle to see why the warning sounds were being made from my partner above.

A large reef shark maybe six feet in length was hurtling toward me and impaled hogfish. This fish was more streamlined in design than the heavy bull giving far more speed. The tail hardly seemed to move and yet it propelled through the water like a torpedo honing in on its mark. The Australian already had the big fish in his sites. He kicked furiously downward to intercept us. I saw his spear fly forward and hit the body full force in the centre body making its contact exactly on the lateral line resembling the sensitivity of a spinal cord. The steel bounced outward and spiralled downward toward the bottom as if hitting a concrete wall. It had been a fluke of a shot meant only as warning; all through our diving career we never intended harm toward these denizens of the deep. We did not fear them in any way, simply respected that we were intruding their world and taking heed of the beautiful creatures they are. Sharks are a valuable asset to our ecological system and so often abused by so many cultures; again the Orientals take first prize with their abusive slaughter for shark-fin soup. Criminal waste where the dorsal fin is sliced off and the still-alive torso thrown shamelessly back overboard to sink helplessly to the bottom and perish. Gary's sharp point left a tiny white scar but the damage enormous; as if a gyro out of control the big fish arched its body in jerky motions corkscrewing awkwardly downward in a deathly dive. Around and around the big fish turned, portraying a crippled acrobatic aircraft in a flat spin to the ocean floor. I made the surface gasping for the breath of fresh air while watching Gary free dive the forty feet to retrieve his spear appearing a silver toothpick lying in the soft corals. The shark shook in smaller throws and reached the bottom in spasms. Disappointed in causing loss I again hauled myself over the boats gunnels and lay in the bottom waiting for my friend to repeat the entrance amongst the dead fish and blood on the floor. We laughed in nervousness like two clowns in a show. Kathy now quite distraught, 'You two fools just don't know when to quit?' We lifted yards of rope and anchor back inside. The engine came to life and we headed back to a beach on Rose Island where the rocks on shore acted as our cleaning table. More work ahead with sharpening stones and large commercial fillet knives we cleaned our catch for sale on the mainland. Several grouper and hogfish gave us some handsome fillet to sell at prime price to Ronnie, whose menu boasted fresh catch of the day. A couple of choice fillets for our families and the day were done. It was not all easy street and wild fun, there were times when the seas were so rough, days so very cold during winter or fish so sparse after expenses we split as little as $7 each for near eight hour's hard labour!

We heard of an offer to join a commercial fishing boat operated by heavy-equipment operator, Brian Stevenson, called the *Maty Sein* moored in the canals of Coral Harbour. The boat would be gone for three weeks at a time trying to fill its freezers with lobster and fish in the prolific waters off South Andros. Brian had assembled a crew of divers with a cook from Abaco and first mate 'Gully' who we knew training as a pilot later senior in Trans Island Airways. The first breakfast of plain boiled fish heads cooked without sign of seasoning or vegetables brought near mutiny on board. To survive in one piece, the elderly cook soon developed new skills. Brian was also new to the commercial fishing game knowing roughly where to look in the Grassy Cays for the coral heads holding swarms of lobster, but his knowledge of tides and depth quite rusty finding us healed over aground one morning. We were awoken by loud country western music blaring from external speakers mounted aboard a passing Spanish Wells fishing boat broadcasting verses of 'Stand by your Man' by Tammy Wynette clear across the water. 'Got to love those Sigilians!' Gary exclaimed shaking his head as we partnered once again into one of the outboard skiffs early that morning in search for the corals that lay inside circles of turtle grass. 'I'll check this first head,' I volunteered rolling backwards of the gunnel as divers did in the movies. As the froth of white bubbles dissipated I saw instantly having landed literally on top of a nine-foot hammerhead shark following underneath the boat. I was back inside the boat having hardly become wet! 'What the hell are you doing?' Gary disbelieving the manoeuvre 'Take a look my friend,' I instructed as he leaned over the gunnel holding a mask to his face. 'Shit that will wake a bloke in the morning!'

The diving in those cays amazing, finding coral heads near eight feet tall infested with spiny lobster. On one head alone, appearing like locusts crawling over everything, Gary and I collected 210 in about an hour's diving. We left the last lobster under a ledge being too small and illegal in size. For three weeks work we were given less than $500, with piracy alive and well with the owners of the boat pocketing our hard-earned income. It was a clear signal that this kind of work would not be repeated and time to find something new?

We were into the decade of the 70s. The Aussie and I stayed as a team becoming creative about making a living in the land we loved. I was still living under my mother's roof as the breadwinner with my Australian friend living about a mile away off Shirley Street. We stayed financially afloat for four years without having to leave the country. There was nothing we would not try to produce income from the ocean. There was demand for black coral from some of our jeweller friends on Bay Street, so we volunteered to harvest some. Between us we owned four sets of Scuba gear and could always buy air from Gardner or Bill Whiteland who had now created Bahama Divers on the ground floor of the Nassau Yacht Haven. Our tanks were the old heavy steel 'K-valve', seventy-two cubic inch capacity, having no reserve valve making us pay attention to time and depth carefully. I had bought the original Dacor Decompression meter that worked by gases forced under pressure through a piece of ceramic. The meter's gauge climbed as depth and time increased, showing the diver the limitation points of a particular dive. In its day, the decompression meter was quite the ingenious piece of gear. Computers were decades away. This piece of equipment substituted the Navy dive tables that we had to adhere to, give or take! Pushing the time-below envelope allowed nitrogen gases to accumulate in the body that had to be purged with slow ascent, and stops in certain depths until the meter registered an all clear to continue upward. Failure to do so created the soda-pop cap scenario; popping the cap too quickly allowing fizzy gases to expanded over flowing the bottleneck with bubbly froth. So too would nitrogen behave in the blood stream causing severe pain in the joints and possible permanent damage known as the Bends. Black coral was found in the depths off what we all knew as 'The Wall', the edge of that underwater precipice surrounding the northern shoreline of New Providence. Directly off Lyford Cay Marina entrance was a particularly shallow section of the wall. The edge found in about forty feet of water dropping instantly to 3000 feet of deep clear indigo. A dive to 200 feet could only last four minutes without a mandatory stop to surfacing. We found trees of coral in about 130 feet allowing us slightly more time to play making sure to preserve the large specimens having taken generations to grow for sport divers to admire. Finding an isolated tree, we could cut branches that offered chances of fine jewellery and haul them upward to an awaiting line hanging off the side of the boat. It was messy work pruning unwanted small branches with feathery ends before hauling inside the boat proved the only way of avoiding the brown slime that it exuded. Many a dive we exceeded the boundaries of safe sport diving. The decompression meter needle rose rapidly with deeper dives and we found ourselves sucking harder through the regulator to get the air we needed. We had no gauges to show depleted air pressure in the tanks; there was only so much equipment we could afford back then. We did have one old Voit depth meter I had owned from my instructor days, where constant hand signal communication kept us both at the same depth and time below. After 100 feet down the wall, one would start to experience nitrogen narcosis, an equivalent high that one could get from a couple of stiff martinis. As the depth continued so did the level of narcosis; feelings of utter euphoria and wellbeing known to overcome divers without experience. As time went on in our careers both of us built a noticeable resistance to narcosis able to dive deeper and longer without experiencing any effects.

One gorgeous quiet morning we anchored in deep water abeam Lyford Cay Marina entrance – the day panning out to be one of those picturesque brochure Bahamian days. Gentle blue skies and calm, clear inviting ocean water reflecting the occasional white cotton-ball clouds that hung gracefully overhead. With a whisper of south wind, not enough to ripple the surface, we could see the sand bottom in between the rocky crevasses leading down to the wall. Paying out the anchor rode we could clearly see it laying on the sand allowing the small boat to tail out over the edge of the deep indigo water, the sun's rays dancing in parallel perspective through ocean as if in tune to some hidden symphony.

'What ya say we do a real deep one to start with, cobber?' the Australian hinted with that mischievous grin. I picked up the challenge.

'How about we make the pin peg all the way around?' I said. Looking at the old Voit meter he exclaimed, 'Shit Paul, that's 255 feet down … bloody right, you're on!' We donned our scuba gear and rolled backwards off the gunnel in to the sea. The mass of white bubbles cleared and one could see how we were suspended, as if two astronauts, floating in midspace in 3000 feet of water. We gave the 'ok' sign to each other and began the free fall downward. Both of us so relaxed after countless deep dives we simply exhaled to become negative buoyant, sinking in silence down the face of the underwater cliff. We were slow motion skydivers floating in inner-space. Pressure building in the ears after so many feet had to be relieved quickly and repetitively, the same way one would pinch your nose in an airliner and try to blow gently, so as not to damage the eardrums. There were rare times that one of us would have a head cold and clearing ear pressure impossible. We never forced the ear that could easily end a diving career. The depth gauge needle started its turn around the far side of the meter. We passed 150 feet and slowly some effects of narcosis were apparent. As depth increased so did the ease of the free-fall, buoyancy disappearing in the depths. At 200 feet, we looked up, able to measure our still visible boat hull with an out stretched arm, at about the size of our thumbnail. Compressed air rushed in to one's lungs at the mere suggestion of a breath. We were six times the surface atmospheric pressure. Past 230 feet, I remembered oxygen under pressure now considered poisonous to a diver and the narcosis severe. The needle fast approached the far side of its limitation peg. At 255 feet, we were 'narked' badly enough to where I was trying to concentrate on which gauge gave me what reading. Was that my depth gauge or was it the decompression meter; the brain betrayed with nitrogen. How much time was on my watch bezel from the surface descent? Detail became hazy and unreliable. Senses dulled intensely to make me frightened about the noticeable lack of control. Time to get the hell out of here! Gary was well below me by another twenty feet or more with seemingly no care in the world, his attention obliterated with narcosis, damn him being close to 300 feet! I banged on my tank furiously and he did not respond at first. Going further down just that fraction more was beyond my comprehension at this point. I banged furiously again so the alarm was heard this time. The crazy man casually gave me the ok sign and carried on as if on some casual swim sporting a silly grin around his loose regulator mouthpiece. I emphatically gave the thumbs up sign repetitively and started kicking with wide strokes of my heavy swim fins. We had no buoyancy compensators in those days that would have made an ascent effortless. Swimming vertically that far was work. Finally my partner followed suit and began the long ascent. Our air was running low and breathing became laboured all too quickly. We stopped twenty feet below the boat grasping the anchor line. Here we could hopefully be rid of the accumulated nitrogen that must have been rushing into formation within our bodies in the dark deep water. The decompression meter suggested an additional stop at ten feet that we ascended attempting to suck the remaining precious air very slowly out of our tanks so empty they floated high off our backs. The last possible breaths were taken and we surfaced.

'Now that was bloody amazing mate!' my friend exclaimed in exhilaration as he trod water.

'Bloody right Oz, but that's the last time we play that game ok?' I confirmed, feeling especially good to feel the sun shining on us again. We had watched the changes in both the coral life and the fish we had observed every dive taken on that wall. At 255 feet, seven atmospheres, there was little to see except some stunning trees of black coral, huge dome shaped sponges, and once in a while really large amberjacks cruising past us in ultra-slow motion. The colours were all opaque illustrating the same shades of dark blues and grey. In later years Gary and I returned to deep diving almost every day catching deep-water tropical fish for Bill Whiteland who exported them, in Styrofoam boxes holding plastic bags with little seawater and mostly pure oxygen, to London and faraway places to sell in exotic aquarium shops around the world. Being paid by the fish sometimes a single dive could take home quite a few dollars between us. It sure beat punching sharks for a living!

We became very creative in this new art of deep-water tropical fish collecting. Fish brought upward from depth can damage their swim bladder, an organ used for balance if they rise too quickly. We devised a way of collecting often over a hundred feet down and storing them in a gallon mayonnaise jar with a long line attached. Special nets we designed gave only precious minutes to perform any capture. As we ascended letting out the line attached to the jar leaving it suspended in space below us, with maybe twenty dark blue Black Capped Basslets lying in the bottom of the jar. On the surface Gary and I would remove scuba gear and slide it inside the boat sitting in the warm sun for an hour or more while my friend smoked, slowly raising the jar toward the surface, chattering like schoolboys on the days adventures. Smoking for me was so rare and alien to my body feeling nausea with every puff as a schoolboy in my day, a habit as were drinking that thankfully did not agree. So disgusted at feeling poorly after accepting that much desired 'after dinner ciggie' in New York one evening, I extinguished my light never to pick one up again. The fish bladders would expand safely enough to slightly protrude from their bodies where we carefully inserted a fine hypodermic syringe instantly relieving the air pressure. With twelve hours recovery in an aquarium the prize collectables displayed their incredible iridescent purple colours as if nothing had happened.

In Europe and New York aquariums our fish fetched handsome prices, payment to us mere dollars each. The rest of our day spent in shallow waters finding the more common salt water species, the tropical fish business more lucrative compared to the long arduous hours of spearfishing. We learnt how to construct the all-glass aquariums that had come into fashion. Gone were the old familiar glass tanks framed with steel. We gambled with some of our savings that Nassau Glass on Mackey Street could supply us with various thickness of glass, cut accurately enough to construct various sized aquariums depending on gallonage a client wished for, the larger the tanks the thicker and heavier the glass. The living room floor in William Street became the construction zone with mother shaking her head muttering something about 'what next would you two think of?', stepping gingerly over sheets of glass, rolls of masking tape, tubes of clear silicone cement and rolls of paper towel. The end result was impressive. Carrying the finished heavy product down the outside staircase and loaded into a car another matter. I had discovered an outside filtration system, through Bill's business venture, called Eheim from Germany, filters so efficient in moving large quantities of water allowing saltwater aquariums to become reality for home or office. We could build and install the tanks, decorate with local dried corals and fresh sand, fill with ocean water carried from Montagu Bay in plastic jerry cans. This new venture came to be a saving grace, opening doors later where I could return to making a living with legitimate paperwork to stay in the country.

Time was running out for Gary's stay in the Bahamas. There was little chance of him becoming a legal immigrant into the Bahamas with the short amount of time he had accrued in the country. The immigration purge of foreigners was full on in the 1970s where dreaded squads from Hawkins Hill rounded up illegals within the country escorting them to the airport for repatriation. At all costs we circumnavigated that street to get to and from Palmdale. My friend never possessed the paperwork as I had done, with little choice he said goodbye to the Pritchard family. I shook his hand and wished him only the very best as he left the Bahamas for his homeland of Australia. Internet was a long way off. Staying in touch would be a challenge with only regular mail service taking near a month to arrive or exorbitant telephone oversees calls. We hoped one day to reunite and tell some stories. Decades later with the wonders of Google my Australian found me once again. A phone call came one day while with my dogs in the garden in Montagu Heights. 'G'Day Pommie' came the familiar voice! We have visited each other's countries since that day and still in touch reminiscing our adventures planning to meet somewhere in between.

A walk one day down the shoreline of East Bay Street – I went to check out a new pet supply store that had opened in the East Bay Shopping Centre. A very tanned distinguished gentleman met me inside. His salt-and-pepper, swept back, thick head of hair and curved pipe became Ray Claridge's trademark as CEO of Claridge Enterprises based in partnership with Jude Kemp over in Nassau Village. He was extremely cordial and we struck up an interesting conversation discovering my qualifications in saltwater aquariums fascinating. There were no pet supply shops in Nassau dealing with saltwater fish and was interested in my ability building all-glass tanks being able to service and supply them. I explained my immigration status and how I had lost my work permit as a dive instructor in the immigration crunch throughout the country. Ray offered immediately to regain my status, needing desperately someone in his employ with my qualifications. We shook hands creating an accurate title for an immigration application that no Bahamian could hopefully fill. There was not one inquiry to the advertisement in the classifieds. With my own boat for harvesting and knowledge in all-glass construction we created 'Aquarium Systems Manager' offering installation and service in commercial and residential residences supplying them with saltwater fish for display as well as keep Nassau Garden and Pet Supply in full inventory of tropical fish. The application was granted in short order with Ray's connections and dedication to the farming industry of the Bahamas. My mother was ecstatic along with my steady girlfriend Kathy still working for Larry Roberts in his downtown real estate office. We became engaged.

One of my first clients lived off Brace Ridge Road on the eastern part of New Providence. With an appointment one morning I was greeted by a tall slender jet-black-haired gentleman smartly dressed in slacks and Polo sweater. Financier Robert Vesco, having taken up residence in the Bahamas, escorted me through his home to an open-plan living room showing me where he wanted a huge fish aquarium to be displayed. He was very cordial introducing me to his wife Patricia and two sons. I took the measurements and calculated his aquarium would hold well over a hundred and twenty gallons, a big project of half inch glass and a monster to carry for installation. After leaving a healthy quotation I found out who my client actually was. In 1970, Vesco began a successful takeover bid for a mutual funds investment firm called International Oversees Service with holdings of $1.5 billion created by financier Bernard Cornfeld. Born in Turkey, 'Bernie' had been taken to the United States when four years old. He suffered a terrible stammer in his youth but possessed a gift for selling things. In 1955, Cornfeld left America for Paris where he started selling mutual funds from a mere few hundred dollars he had saved. In its prime IOS employed over 25,000 salesmen scattered all over Europe. The bear markets of 1969 turned the tables with IOS funds taking a serious tumble, and by March the company was near out of money. Little known American Financier Robert Vesco entered the scene with an offer of $5 million to bail out Cornfeld's troubled corporation. Vesco saw the opportunity to assume control and evicted Cornfeld from the top position while transferring over 200 million cash belonging to IOS funds into layered shell corporations based in obscure locations around the world. The monies made only available to Vesco and well hidden from law enforcement. Stories flourished that Vesco hid his funds in dummy corporations linked to prominent people in global finance and even European royalty? For fifteen years he lived in countries with no extradition treaties with America but in 1973, with criminal charges levied against him for securities fraud, he loaded $200 million aboard his private jet and fled to Costa Rica and on to the Bahamas.

I was in Vesco's living room setting up his aquarium while he sat on the sofa in quiet conference with another gentleman I learned to be President Richard Nixon's nephew. After Watergate, scandal charges linked Vesco with illegal funding for a company owned by Donald Nixon. In 1973, hoping to stifle security investigations and five outstanding indictments of fraud, Vesco routed substantial contributions to Richard Nixon through his nephew. Fleeing to the Caribbean, Vesco attempted to purchase the sister island of Barbuda from Antigua to create his own autonomous country having its own national law protecting him from extradition! This acquisition failed with Vesco ending up in Costa Rica contributing

$2.1 million to a company allegedly founded by the countries president Jose Figures, who then passed an anti-extradition law guaranteeing protection for Vesco. The president's term however expired in 1974 where the incoming President Rodrigo Carazo repealed the 'Vesco Law' in 1978 forcing him to move on. Countries were accepting Vesco for considerable financial contributions but increasing pressure from the United States kept him on the move. The Bahamas became the next viable option.

During my visits with the Vesco family the two sons learned of my boating background here in Nassau. Their father had provided them with all the toys needed to live the high life in Nassau. One gift, a '42 Cigarette Powerboat, one of the boys wished to race in the upcoming racing season naming it *Oye Como Va* after a popular *Santana* piece of music. The world-famous Bahamas 500 was still in existence and an offshoot race comprising of four circuits around Paradise Island and neighbouring cays had been organised, offered to local racers as well as the international community. Vesco's son Tony needed a navigator, preferably a local who knew every inch of those familiar waters and one who could guide the boat as close as needed to shave off valuable distance. After watching these boats race through the entrance of Nassau harbour as a young lad of twelve years old the offer coming my way a dream coming true!

Race day was as exciting as it gets. The harbour on both sides packed with spectators. Bahamians lined sides of the bridge going over to Paradise Island. Helicopters from the United States press fizzed up and down the harbour passing Hurricane Hole under the bridge itself. There were many boats entered. We suited in elaborate floatation vests on the docks of the Nassau Harbour Club where most crews were staying and their boats moored. Robert Vesco with his wife Patricia and friends aboard his latest acquisition, a huge dark green Cigarette powerboat with a bright green frog painted on both sides named *Jeremiah*. Race crews were given notice to 'start their engines' and meet in the middle of the harbour for the race start line off the point of Fort Montagu. Countless local spectator boats bobbed in the waters of Montagu Bay awaiting the flag to fall and our throttles to be pushed full forward. It would be full power come what may around every inch of the course.

The race boats lined up across the bay, very surreal to be actually part of. The committee boat flag raised and in an instant we were all accelerating through the pristine waters of Montagu Bay, headed eastward to the far tip of Athol Island and Porgee Rock to make a westward turn around the north side of Paradise. The Cigarette race boat sliced the water easily and I guided my driver close to the rocky shoreline and tip of Athol passing the familiar waters I used to work in with Underwater Tours. Tony Vesco never flinched, trusting my judgment every second. Other boats unfamiliar with the waters seeing shallow coral reefs near that point all shied away for a wider turn. We gained a huge distance with this manoeuvre knowing that on lap two the other boats would follow us through this shorter course. The wind raced passed our faces as we accelerated out of the turn around Porgee Rock, with its familiar corroded beacon mounted on its barren centre. Westward now towards the inside of Spruce Cay where shallow grasses lay on the bottom, most boats again taking the safer outside course favouring the visible channel near Salt Cay. We gained distance yet again now leading in our class. The only boats ahead of us the larger professional Cigarettes and Donzies. At the end of Spruce Cay we charted over toward the East tip of Paradise Island and the public point of Long Beach. Missing jagged rocks by mere feet we raced parallel to the shore of Cabbage Beach inside the two rocks that lay near the canal entrance where we used to water-ski through as kids. Local spectators lined the rocky shores of Paradise Beach all waving us on enthusiastically. We raised a wave back. The entrance of Nassau Harbour beckoned with our familiar white lighthouse guarding the entrance. Committee boats bobbed in the small ocean swells welcoming our arrival keeping local traffic away for us to make the high-speed entrance. I guided Tony very close to the shoreline for a dramatic tight turn through the channel marker buoys where cruise ships docked at Prince George Wharf. The harbour lay in front of us with Paradise Island Bridge spanning the far end. The water calmer here and the wind rushed passed our bodies more forcefully as the race boat flew eastward, spectators becoming a blur of colour along the rocky shoreline. This was the leg of the race I had anticipated most. That first harbour bound turn threw vast sheets of white frothy water, brightly lit by the strong sunlight, behind our speeding race boat; it was here as a youngster I had sat on the rocky shore exhilarated by the shear speed of the boats as they sped toward the finish line at Hurricane

Hole having departed 186 miles from Miami some five hours earlier. As the years passed and technology changed race boats to become larger with faster efficient catamaran hulls that doubled and trebled the old boats speed; for me a surreal moment racing the same course in the footsteps of Don Aronow and Richard Bertram. Our Cigarette flew passed *Jeremiah* and the gleeful look of proud parents cheering us on. The crowds went wild on either shoreline as we approached the seventy-two-foot-high bridge. A Bell Ranger helicopter sped behind us at low altitude filming our boat from slightly above. Tide flowed against the wind in this narrow part of the channel, throwing a lateral swell about four feet high. Our race boat sprinted like a flying fish from one crest to another throwing showers of white water out to each side of us as we flashed under the bridge with a press helicopter thumping the air just above us. Past Hurricane Hole the cheers grew louder even above the noise of our full out engines racing again the South shoreline of Paradise Island for the second lap. With four laps completed we headed that last time for the finish line across from the Nassau Yacht Haven. With arms flaying in glee both driver and navigator crossed the line in fourth position. Dreams came true that day!

Political pressure and proximity to America became too much for the Vesco family. They left Nassau shortly after landing next in Antigua and on to Nicaragua while the Sandinista Government was in power. Only his vast looted wealth gained him entrance to these countries and as the contributions ended so did his welcome. In 1982 Vesco's health was deteriorating and entered the island nation of Cuba for medical treatment and promise of no extradition. In 1990 Vesco became involved again with Donald Nixon who wanted to partner with the Cuban Government in conducting clinical trails for the drug Trixolan claiming to boost the immune system, Cuba's health system renown for being advanced over other countries in the region. Vesco introduced Nixon to brothers Fidel and Raul Castro who agreed to provide laboratories, equipment and doctors to administer the trails. Results claimed to be positive, but in May 1995 Vesco slipped up trying to defraud Nixon and Raul Castro. The Cuban Government seized control, arresting Vesco along with his second wife that he married in 1982. Nixon was also detained but released thirty days later. Vesco was charged with 'fraud and illicit economic activity'. He was convicted and sentenced to thirteen years in a Cuban jail scheduled for release at the age of 74 in 2009, but died in prison of lung cancer in November 2007. He was buried in Havana.

My time with Ray Claridge was fruitful and a very valued friendship ensued. We shared the love of farms, agriculture and animals. I arrived at East Bay one day spotting immediately a new face staring at me from a wire cage. Dark brown trim surrounded the black face of the German Shepherd puppy. Its ears were pricked up and massively out of proportion at this early age. Since arriving in Nassau as a youngster my father had made us part company with our Golden Labrador in England, during his tenure in the Bahamas had forbidden a dog to be part of our home, 'not wanting to create an obligation we had to keep' in a foreign country. That thought ended that morning. This gorgeous little girl was to be mine. I agreed on a price with Ray and took her home to the William Street apartment. My mother was well pleased for additional company. On arrival in our garden the puppy christened the grass with a poop the size to astound! 'My Lord girl that looked like a rhinoceros passed through' I exclaimed, naming my new friend the Swahili for rhino, 'Faro'. We began a very loving bond gifted with a magical way with animals that my grandmother had spotted years ago.

Within weeks of buying Faro, change came to my work place. Ray had entered a partnership with the owner of East Bay Shopping Centre, Neville Roberts. I was introduced one morning and knew within seconds this relationship was going to be short-lived. Neville was a huge, chain-smoking man weighing in at well over 300 pounds. Sitting in his manager's chair up in the office section of the shop he soon dictated radical changes in staffing and ways to slash costs any way possible. Ray often looked at me with sheepish acknowledgment that the end was nigh for all of us, partnering with this man a regrettable mistake. As an expat on a work permit I was one of the first to go. Ray agreed for his part to keep my work permit in place as if I was still employed. This gave me months of freedom to move around without the worry of being illegal once more in the only place I wanted to live. Nassau Garden & Pet Supply failed shortly after Neville Roberts' takeover and closed its doors under his leadership. Ray returned to his beloved farming on Cow Pen Road. I had no choice but to return once again to the sea for my income alone in diving for fish, an unnerving venture at best. Kathy introduced me to some friends of hers, one of whose husband was searching for a part-time dive partner to make some extra income. An instant friendship formed yet again with the same name at my side. Gary worked for a lumber company on Wulfe Road. His Canadian wife managed a local shoe store. We became close friends and the diving adventures started almost immediately, spending a couple days each weekend diving the south side of Rose Island for lobster and the ocean side for fish when the weather allowed. The days not spent on the water I took Faro over to the grounds of Fort Montagu for training. The dog grew into a beautiful animal and exceptionally smart. For fun I entered her in the local kennel club obedience trials. The venue was difficult for any animal with that amount of distraction on all quarters. Spectators leaning over the railed enclosures, we had to work with other dogs yapping and causing troubling distraction nearby. We completed one challenge after another with near perfection. The hardest trial kept to last where our dog was to remain sitting off the leash with its owner leaving the arena for two minutes to return and stand in front of his or her animal. On command the dog could finally move and come to walk around the owner and without promoting sit of the left side at heel. Faro completed her task winning Best in Show every year for three years running. Every year we showed up at the trials we could hear the moan of 'oh no they're back'!

My faithful young German Shepherd was only about three years old becoming suddenly very ill. Our local vet Patrick Balfe having a small surgery in Marathon Estates we had known for years took an x-ray showing suspected foreign objects in her stomach. His lovely receptionist, Mrs. Rolle, peeked from behind her little office window that looked into the waiting room. Doggie cartoons adorned the walls supporting Patrick's great sense of humour along with small advertisements for puppies for sale. The vet's dark curly hair would look around the surgery door dressed in ever-familiar Rugby shirt, long shorts, knee high socks and brown street shoes.

'Yes Paul, bring her through.'

I would go through the door and into his surgery letting my dog sit quietly in heel at my side.

'Did you hear the one about …' Patrick always began with a new joke leaning against the tile wall. His repertoire was amazing. But with today's more sombre situation he just asked me to lift my lovely animal on to the stainless-steel examination table to inspect her.

Behind up on the shelf of many medicines was an impressive display of repaired dog and cat bones showing Patrick's creative fixes for some terrible accidental breakages using stainless steel that he would home manufacture in his workshop at home in Sea Breeze Estate. He saw me looking at them and smiled.

'Good fixes eh'? He confirmed with confidence. 'The deal is when the animal finally dies I get them back!' He said with a smile; his gentle voice now talking assuredly to the Alsatian who we could feel trembling in anticipation. My vet's strong hands gently felt her underside, experienced fingers exploring for something foreign inside her body.

'Don't feel anything Paul, let's get her in the back room for an x-ray.'

There on the screen was something clearly looking like a stone inside her. 'I need to get that out of her,' Patrick commanded. 'Can you help out in the operating room Paul?' My Zoology major at school had me slicing and dissecting preserved animal bodies so showed no hesitation I could handle this?

'It's different when it's your pet, Paul' Patrick instructed gruffly. 'If you feel you are losing control put your head down and don't look.' Faro was sedated and lifted as if lifeless on to the stainless table her soft pink tongue sliding uncontrollably out of the side of her mouth. My friend shaved her tummy and took out a new scalpel.

'I can do this' I muttered to myself. I must help my animal. As the blade travelled down the skin opening the stomach to her visible insides the room suddenly went round like a spinning top.

'Shit' I said very softly seeing white flashes in front of my vision and the room begin to spin faster; putting my head down knowing I was about to pass out. Some surgeon I would have made. Patricks' hands gently explored the inside cavity of my dog to find nothing solid but showing us the clue to her illness.

'That was a freaky shadow on the picture Paul but this lovely dog has Parvo Virus.' A disease speeding amongst imported puppies not usually seen in older dogs.

'There is a wonder drug Paul called Gentacin but very expensive my friend.'

'Go for it Patrick,' I responded without pause. 'Please save my dog.' We fought the battle for three or four days, one night both Patrick and I lying prone on my mother's apartment floor next to a dying Alsatian. Dealing with the death of one's animal, however practiced you become, always *the* worst day in our lives. To part with that unconditional love a gut wrenching experience. We lost the battle as her lifeless body lay on the apartment floor. Tears flowed free as I held my champion friend one last time. Dying naturally of old age is one thing but this kind of loss is excruciating an experience that would come back to haunt us again, me swearing 'no more dogs'. I should have known that would not last.

Chapter 15
I have an idea ...!

Survival was becoming a required art form in my life. Long-time friend Robin Brownrigg proclaiming in his office one day, 'I have never seen anyone with the ability to survive as you Paul! Life just bombards you from all direction and you get right back up to stand tall again'. Every turn I took seemed something or some event that would have me sit and think things through as to how to stay alive in the Bahamas without a regular source of income or legal status, yet each week I was able to put food on the table and never late in rent payment. To increase income, I kept my Saturday spearfishing vigil with Andrew also partnering him in tennis challenging friends Tommy Kemp and Timmy Sands to pound the hard courts at the Grand Hotel on Paradise Island two evenings a week. I ventured later into mixed doubles entering local competitions with Ann Parnell, a superior player than I, playing at the Emerald Beach Hotel. She introduced me to the game of golf at South Ocean Golf Club. I loved to walk all the courses in Nassau and when I traveled to places such as Torrey Pines in California. A back injury later forced me to retire from the two sports I so enjoyed. Each Saturday Andrew and I met at Browns Boat Basin to race up the South side of Rose Island in his yellow Jupiter-15. The big 85HP Chrysler outboard took no time making the outer reefs of the long narrow island; the rigorous dive plan working the reefs in succession from the far end of Rose toward home in a westerly direction. Each reef scoured with precision with one diver working the centre section of corals while the other swimming the circumference. The free diving was intense and non-stop. If there were a lobster on that reef we would find it.

We had split up by many yards one morning, each diver making the descent to bottom turning upside down to look under the dark ledges for those tell-tale whip antenna waving at you from the back of their hiding place. Once the carapace was pierced satisfactorily the spear would be pushed hard forward to make the complete penetration allowing the barb of the spear to open on the other side as we did with fish. The struggling crustacean would then be dragged outward and up to the surface in one breath. Finding lobsters in over thirty feet of water all day long quite the challenge; as the day wore on our breath holding however became more efficient and bottom times improved impressively.

This day a shallow part of the reef yielded a huge spiny lobster sitting in the open outside his domain. The sunlight and dancing waves above giving him a psychedelic colour show of oranges and reds. His two long antennas waved an inquisitive warning at me. I took the breath some distance away so as to approach the crawfish straight on. The spear let fly and pierced the shell between the eyes. I swam upward with my catch aware of something forbidding fast approaching near head on. The unmistakable shape of a very large juvenile tiger shark barrelled toward me with wide sweeps of his tail. I had never been in the water with a tiger until now. The predominant dark stripes down the side of his steel grey body, jet-black eyes set in a broad head identifying the young beast without doubt. The only other I had seen alone out by Salt Cay where it charged the back of my skiff, the huge wide head showing triangular white teeth trying to bite the rotating propeller of my outboard engine! This strikingly beautiful creature came forward at great pace with no hesitation in wanting my catch. It took split seconds to be on me where baffled at its aggression never hearing of one eating lobster off a spear! I kept the spear well in front of me for some semblance of defence, hoping to hold off the huge shark with what looked like a toothpick compared to its size. The tiger's mouth gaped open showing daunting rows of perfect teeth and the roof of his mouth. The jaw crunched down on the huge lobster, crushing it effortlessly as if a paper bag while I held the steel shaft for dear life. One quick swipe sideways of the broad head shred the lobster off my spear and within seconds the great fish was gone. 'Holy *Shit*,' I cried out as my snorkel dropped from my mouth, gulping in fresh air above the surface. My yell carried far over the surface that calm August morning.

'What's up, me old bean?' Andrew retorted from yards away, not having seen a thing.

'You won't believe what fuck just happened!' I yelled. The dive continued but every few minutes would find ourselves cautiously gazing into the void around us, an incident this dramatic tends to stay for a while! An image such as that does not leave easily. We worked well as a team, spending at least six hours in the water without a break keeping our bodies in peak condition. When the fifty-gallon plastic garbage bin was brimming with lobster antenna that was a cue to stop for the day. The journey back would be at a fast idle, letting the Jupiter steer itself while the two of us twisted tails braking the whips off each lobster used to clean the tails of the centre-gut while discarding the heads overboard. In those days, we sold crawfish at going market price of about $5.75 per pound; already double from when I had started making a living from the sea, quite the increase again some thirty years later!

It had been over three years not leaving the islands for fear I would never re-enter legally. The phrase to my mother 'I'd rather be poor in a pair of shorts' gave me the self-support and satisfaction I needed to stay alive and happy in the Bahamas. The alternative of living somewhere else other than our islands gloomy at best. Working the sea nurtured a welcome work ethic, along with stubborn persistence to reap good reward in turn gave back the self-esteem boarding school had shredded from my personality. There was nothing to stop me now from making a pronounced mark here in these islands. My strong-willed personal philosophy of 'making a living doing the things I loved to do' would all come to fruition. In return I could promote these islands to thousands of people with the expression written on the back of my company T-shirts sold at the end of each day, reading 'Come see the Real Bahamas!'

Having my relationship well-established with Kathy along with permanent future planned together, I expressed an idea after supper one night in the William Street apartment.

'I have an idea,' I began. 'I think we should start a Bahamian business, where I take tourists out for the day making a living doing what we all love doing on the weekends at Rose Island. I am willing to bet that visitors will pay handsomely to arrive on those beaches, deserted and quiet during the week days, given snorkelling lessons and swim off those fabulous reefs. I could spear a couple of lobsters or a grouper and cook over an open campfire for lunch! We could introduce scuba lessons later and underwater photography? Mum could take the phone calls here at home and I could go and pick the guests up in the morning and drop them back to their hotels after the trip?'

The two ladies could only nod in agreement, smiling in support and boldness of the idea and especially of me not having to leave the island on three week spearfishing expeditions in South Andros working a commercial smack boat to raise enough money to live. The journey to Africa had stayed large in my imagination. Using the Swahili word 'safari' for an overnight journey, I thought I could alter its interpretation slightly becoming a day's journey with diving in the Out-Islands.

'I want to call our venture 'Diving Safaris Ltd' with the day tour named 'The Out-Island Safari,' I concluded.

The year was 1976 and our company formed and listed with the Registrar General through Peter Higgs at Higgs and Johnson on Shirley Street; Kathy our company president I later married in St. Annes church in Fox Hill at the ripe old age of twenty- eight living in a rented house from Norma Sawyer in Tuckaway. I applied for and was granted a new work permit for our Bahamian owned company. In essence, working for myself for the first time. The journey begun here would last over forty years! First pricing matched the very few similar day excursions at a mere $25.00 per person including transportation to and from their hotel in my Austin Mini station wagon. Food would be speared and cooked each day, including refreshments along with snorkelling equipment free of charge. 'A bargain of a day!' read the first quotes in my new guestbook that I asked our visitors to sign at the end of their experience. With a pack of 500 brochures I distributed to every hotel on Cable Beach and Paradise Island. In those early days there existed a lone table to display in each hotel lobby or space on the Bell Captain's desk; all of whom I knew from my days as a dive instructor based in each of their establishments. I had a great relationship with each captain welcoming a new local attraction placed on their desk where loyalties such as Mr. Deveux at the Ocean Club lasted over twenty years.

'Your excursion is exactly the quality guests staying here are looking for Mr. Harding.' The response so positive that many visitors also wrote praises to the Ministry of Tourism resulting in a win of the Pride and Joy Award a few years later. The mode of transportation however didn't last long. Pulling up to the exclusive Ocean Club foyer in an old Austin Mini wagon did not quite fit the profile of guests staying there! Arriving at the Sonesta Beach

Hotel one day to pick up a couple that had booked a place on the day trip set the stage for change. Stepping out of the car I called their name to see which of several couples waiting there would respond. My two people came forward and we all broke out laughing at the same time. Thank God for a great sense of humour. They were huge! Both weighed in at near 300 pounds, and heavily tattooed. To stereotype would have them climbing off an enormous Harley motorcycle, he with a generous red beard and headscarf and her with tights that defied the art of clothing.

'Looks like we are spending the day here,' the large man beamed. 'I am so sorry,' he continued holding his hand out for a shake.

'We should have said something about size?'

'I am truly sorry about this tinker-toy car,' I added. They would not have fit in the door. Within days I hopped a Bahamasair flight with Andrew also on the hunt for a new car in Florida, finding a nine-passenger Chevy station wagon in a used car lot in Miami for $700. The growth of Nassau traffic eventually snuffed that part of my business needing the services of Bruce or Charles Rolles' taxi service for guest transfers.

In 1976 a couple of day-trips recently entered the market resembling our new product, the 'Keewatin' sailboat, and artist Rolf Harris also operating a sailboat charter as a day adventure. Ours would be the only 'small group dive business' in existence. An American, Robert Major, married also to a Bahamian had started a more commercial boat trip called the 'Robinson Crusoe' taking folks to nearby Sandy Cay. I was only operating a 19-foot 'Seabreeze' outboard boat that I again learned to fibreglass from Graham's instruction. Morton Turtle, or 'Moke' as we knew him, had created an outboard repair shop called Sunpower Marine, whose realtor father Bill had employed my mother in earlier years. Morton let me trade in my small outboard and financed a used Evinrude 125HP engine he had rebuilt for sale. Installed homemade wooden bench seats enabled me to carry up to three couples for the day making an exciting prospect of $150.00 income a day income normally taking a week to produce! The phone started ringing immediately. It was a gamble each day taking perfect strangers out to the middle of nowhere convinced I could provide a fresh catch each day while guests watching me spearfish. One morning in the early 80s, I recognised Captain Nigel Bower at the fuel dock of Browns Boat Basin aboard his bright red Scarab race boat. He had purchased the confiscated drug boat to start his new day trip into the Exuma Cays called Powerboat Adventures. In his advertising he used the word 'safari' which I had copyrighted under the advisement of Peter Higgs forming my company. Still raw from a friends earlier plagiarism of my advertising, I approached him from the dock reaching out a handshake, unfortunately omitting to explain what I was about to ask; 'Hey Nigel, Paul Harding here, do me a favour and not use the word safari in your advertising!'

'Well good morning to you!' he exclaimed at the rather abrupt introduction. We have been close friends for 41 years and counting coming to find we shared similar pasts of a lousy boarding school, film production, Africa and so it went on.

Both our excursions succeeded right from the start with Powerboat still in operation as I write today. In 1976 my guests take a swim with me with good fortune always finding a couple of crawfish antenna waving at me or a grouper hiding under a ledge; later to the beach and anchor the boat to establish everyone on our site under the shade trees. Some would walk off alone down the endless stretches of white powder sand on MacTaggart's Beach. Some simply floated close to shore gazing through goggles at the marine life below them. Our advertising claimed there were lots to do on the island or guests 'could enjoy doing simply nothing at all'. I was winging it from that very first day, polishing the mistakes and honing the timing of each event. Every day venturing behind the campsite, collecting dry wood and make the fire with a grill hidden under the pine trees. Timing was of the essence. It did not take long to have the day so strategically prepared where all flowed beautifully, until the rains came. There was no shelter out there. We were roughing it on a deserted beach; clothing and towels hastily hidden in the bench seats as the huge grey squalls moved down the islands on the easterly breeze. As the ice-cold rain pelted us, we hid in the warm ocean water by lee of the boat. I had found and kept hidden, pieces of plywood that had washed ashore to place over the fire saving it from being drowned and lunch lost. An amusing aspect of those first day trips was the inevitable American lady who would ask out loud, 'Where are the bathrooms?' I had to ad-lib something instantly reciting a made-up poem: 'Here is the islands where we don't all behave, water is something we have learnt to save. So let's keep a secret between you and me, do us a favour and pee in the sea!'

The work was nonstop but our guests loved every minute, raving about their experience on return to their hotel. Word of mouth advertising was a wonderful thing and the days filled with reservations. We had to buy a diary with days in advance now being requested. The savings account slowly grew and time came for a huge investment, a factory new boat that could take the present engine we owned. A boat that could hold up to four couples supporting a Bimini top for shelter. Weekends had been spent spearfishing from Tony Trecos' 20-foot Dusky, diving with Gary and Godfrey Thomas: a deep-V hull that sliced the water efficiently and showed great value at $3000. I placed the order direct with the factory for my third boat shooting a new colour brochure, having met Greg Higgs at Nassau Paper Company, working wonders for our advertising. Life was good. Course was set to build a prosperous future from that never-forgotten day, unable to find twenty-five cents between us to buy the *Nassau Guardian* newspaper for my mother to read. We could afford to go to the movies at the new Shirley Street Theatre, watching Stallone in *Rocky* and Streisand in *A Star is Born*; *All the President's Men* with Redford, and De Niro in *Taxi Driver.* Peter Sellers was still producing the Pink Panther series, while director George Lucas began filming his new idea of *Star Wars* in March of this year. The summer Olympics are held in Montreal. Howard Hughes dies on April 5 in Houston, Texas having earlier occupied the whole top floor of the Britannia Hotel on Paradise Island sealed off on Hughes' arrival to live in the Bahamas during his last years.

The 1980s came within sight all too soon. The 'Out-Island Safari' had become Nassau's leading small-group day charter service already boasting repeat clients enjoying the Rose Island experience. New timeshare units were under construction on West Bay Street with the concept of people buying 'weeks' of vacation time becoming increasingly popular. I had a pickup one morning at Westwind-1 with a couple from Grand Rapids, Michigan, Jim and Jo Schaafsma spending the day with me snorkelling with their young son Scott enjoying my famous bar-b-q chicken and fish. There are those times when friendships for life are formed in an instant. They do not come often. The connection with this couple has endured through the writing of this story near forty years later. In all our little company's history, I computed that about 50,000 guests had spent the day with us yet a mere handful became family friends, traveling to each other's home to spend holidays in faraway places together. Jim and I would laugh from the minute of shaking hands. He would introduce his close friends Chuck and Margaret Henry, a doctor from the same town and later their young son Charlie earnestly wanting to stay and work for me. I had recently purchased four sets of scuba equipment enabling me to offer added entertainment to the day, income that would pay the days' expenses. Operating on my own I safely taught all these families and their friends how to scuba dive; introducing them to their first open water dive on the spectacular coral reefs just offshore that afternoon. With a Nikonos 35-mm underwater camera I offered to record all aspects of my guest's diving adventure, above and below the water. This produced yet another additional fee while non-divers passed time choosing whatever activities they fancied. I would announce to meet back at 3.30 pm for departure or 'we will see you tomorrow' No one ever missed the boat!

Success came from absolute dedication and damned hard work. Life in paradise had its price. Jim, Jo and the good doctor became the annual friends promoting my trip every chance they could. Purchasing a unit in the new Westwind-2 complex on Cable Beach my mother would gleefully announce every March 'they are back and have another whole group taking the day!' Often two or more groups would spend the day enjoying the reliability of the same product over and over again. Jim would become my volunteer boat crew, cementing our friendship. There were days when a predicted cold front would arrive sooner than expected. 'Not lookin' good out there buddy!' he would quietly exclaim. We would all be well established on the beach on the north side of Rose Island, lunch was over and finishing the scuba dive when skies to the Northwest took an ominous appearance with that familiar dark purple line expanding as you watched the horizon.

'Time to up anchor everyone!' I would shout down the beach. 'Weather coming, we must leave *now*!' A quick headcount and Jim would be up on the bow ready to pull anchor. Running home westward past Sandy Cay the frontal line would be catching us fast. Prevailing winds were east to northeast. Movement to the South providing maybe one or two days of calm waters on the more attractive north side of the islands where we preferred to locate. A wind pulling to the Southwest signalled a cold front imminent. Winds pulling westerly announced the arrival of the system from the northwest passing Florida within hours. I estimated the wind would pick up very quickly as we skirted through The Narrows, that small channel between Athol and Paradise Island. Weather from the very beginning of my career always the most stressful aspect of every day operations where one became very astute in the art of forecasting. In the early days of really crappy television reception and no such thing as internet, getting accurate information was scant at best.

That dark line Jim and I saw those days was the leading edge of the front barrelling toward us where winds produced strong white capping waves and a sudden drop in temperature by several degrees, to howl out of the northwest up to twenty or thirty knots. Rain often accompanied the first part of the arrival and then over in minutes. With stiff northerly winds and returning sunshine forced us to use the south side of Rose Island in Lower Harbour; overcast days killed any chances of guests having an enjoyable day and was it best we cancelled? As locals we would drive the boat in sweaters and long pants dreading the thought of having to strip down to a bathing suit to set the anchors on the beach, our friends from Michigan and Minnesota making fun of our thin skins thinking seventy degrees just wonderful.

As the years clicked by we became very aware of our climate changing. News stories began to take headline with some scientific authorities and politicians vehemently contesting global changes as they continue to do through these modern times. In the islands, it was undeniable. We saw winds hold in the west for days never noticed ten years prior. Weather patterns became so unpredictable the art of accurate forecasting became a task until the arrival of weather satellites and infrared imagery from thousands of miles in space. The amount of lost business through failing weather became very disappointing during winter months, holding the highest tourism figures. We had full boatloads on the diary and with one swipe of the pen a line would appear diagonally through the page noting a cold front, strong winds or rain. Losing valuable funds proved frustrating as the self-induced pressure to succeed grew. Even when my career changed later from going down every day to up in the air I still remained at the mercy of the weather.

Chapter 16
Once in a Lifetime!

Aged twenty-eight I had married my girlfriend being the last single of our local group in Nassau to tie the knot. My friends all recently married and it seemed time to make commitment to my partner. We were good friends and enjoyed peaceful times. It felt right. Gordon Lomer worked at the Ministry of Tourism and friends with us while working for Gardner Young in the early years, tragically lost his wife in a car crash pulling out on to Village Road one fateful day. Gordon was devastated and decided to return home to Canada. We made an offer on his house in Woodland Road after renting in Tuckaway some two streets away off Village Road; Kathy was still downtown working reception for Bert L. Roberts Real Estate. Our business was flourishing and success tasted sweet after a long hard climb from absolutely nothing. The first mortgage with FINCO was paid within two years. While we were riding the wave, we would keep going having no clue that wave would last through two careers over four decades! A honeymoon in Mexico gave my first break where we loved climbing the pyramids and exploring silver displays in Taxco while walking out of the ghastly bullfight our tour guide insisted taking us to. Working weekdays were more preferable as boating weekend warriors, resembling a small Armada each Sunday, invaded our peace up at Rose Island; producing that magical 'desert island feeling' hard to pull off with MacTaggart's Beach resembling a parking lot for boats; tranquillity spoilt by water-skiers fizzing passed our location making snorkelling hazardous for our guests.

Awarded by the Ministry for 'the business bringing most repeat clients back to the islands'! I was presented the award downtown by Sir Clement Maynard, Minister of Tourism. Our business in later years was nominated again by the Ministry for the coveted Cacique Awards only to be beaten by one of the more ancient mariners and bonefish guide over in Andros.

There were few sources of day-excision entertainment back in the 70s. The very few that were operating day charters suddenly found ourselves with a quandary on our hands. A few taxi cab drivers suddenly had the idea of starting their own 'tour companies' where relatives could be placed behind a desk inside every hotel lobby paying a monthly rental fee using our literature as their new source of income. With visitors selecting our trips the tour operator would charge us 20% of our gross income in commission for the privilege of making that phone call. Bell Captains were at the mercy of the new tour operators and lost their valuable source of income from those of us who rewarded them for their loyalties. The problems began all soon enough now liable to accept the terms of the tour desks. Our daily cash flow instantly dried up, with guests presenting us with a voucher redeemable at the end of each week along with a submitted invoice. Very few companies honoured a timely repayment, loosely termed 'Bahamian Time'. There was always excuse to delay us. 'The cheque is ready but not signed'; 'this weekend was a public holiday'; 'the owner is off the island this week could you come back next Monday' and so it went. Meantime, we were obligated to pay our vendors fuel costs, maintenance and dockage on time at the marinas; we had to pay transfer services daily along with the costs of food and refreshments purchased with valuable extra cash earnings brought in from activities not included in the voucher. Our ventures into tourist entertainment had created a monster that now had tight hold of every hotel in Nassau and Paradise Island. Enter that magic word, 'corruption'.

It was time for us to expand. Numbers became the issue although I had every intention of staying 'the smallest day-trip operation in the Bahamas'. My ploy starting early on with arising competition to be the most expensive! That old adage very apparent in this new game I was playing – 'you get what you pay for' – seemed a great tactic and all through my boating and flying career it worked. Guests sometimes calling from their hotel rooms to ask 'Why are you more than the others?' 'Simply put, you can be with four or five couples on a beach of your own or a few hundred people all packed like sardines on to one boat.' Americans mostly were shy of reserving over the telephone, preferring to ride down the elevator to the tour desk to buy a ticket. With that little coupon in their hand they felt secure with their reservation losing us 20% of income.

We calculated through time that with the per person fare in those days of $35 we took home about $8 for all that service provided. Numbers had to be increased by the purchase of a larger boat. I could sell the 20-foot Dusky open-fisherman easily with market for weekend pleasure boats on the rise. I spied in an American Boat Trader magazine, a 23-foot Formula inboard-outboard boat for sale in Miami. I had saved the money in reserves for the purchase so made decision to give it a try owning a well reputed ocean going hull. The seller was a Miami-Cuban who lowered his price just enough to seal the deal. A good friend at the time, Don Maclean, owning Ziebart Rust-Proofing in Palmdale, and fellow fisherman, married to friend Wendy Bethell, said he would love to come on over and accompany me for the return ferry-trip back to Nassau if I bought the airfare. Our ladies were a little timid about two lads going over to Florida, purchasing a strange boat and successfully surviving the 186-mile journey home.

I eased their concerns slightly by telling them we planned to install a Citizens Band radio in the boat before departure, allowing us to stay in contact with our growing group of amateur radio operators within the islands. Citizens Band was a fad that came and went in those days. For a couple of years our islands had many operators with these communications in their cars, boats and houses. We could sit on the Montagu foreshore at night and talk clearly with our friends in Spanish Wells, where Andy Higgs and friend Brian Hunt had created a local CB radio club. In later years I progressed to passing an exam for my amateur radio license, useful for both a boating and aviation career. New and complex antennas sprouted all over the islands discovering signals at times would 'skip' in huge directions all over the world. Every now and again someone from distant shore would call our names and we would be talking with Australia, Canada and huge audiences in the USA; a favourite amongst some Bahamians were a truck-driving couple from South Dakota!

The sale went well in Miami and the Cuban gentleman trailered the boat to a local ramp near Government Cut. We were loaded and fuelled for the journey home. Weather was favourable for several days and the seas calm. Leaving the Florida coast, we took a compass bearing for the islands of Bimini some forty miles away. There was no GPS in those days. The northward pull of the Gulf Stream current took hold and we estimated compensation for its deviation. A sliver of land soon appeared on the horizon. Not knowing our compensation accuracy, we headed for the target slightly to one side of the bow. An early lesson came in to play finding our 'land' to be a tanker, headed north! Resetting the compass course and making the adjustment for poor navigation we kept the Formula across the ocean at comfortable speed. This deep-v heavy hull rode beautifully needed exactly for the business to expand with a dozen or so passengers fitting comfortably. We spotted the islands of Bimini this time without question, being our first destination to clear Bahamas Customs. As the islands came closer the starboard engine suddenly changed note in its regular hum of cruise speed. Temperatures were rising on the gauge and I immediately eased off on the throttles. The small-cabined boat came off the plane and idled toward Bimini.

'*Shit!*' Don exclaimed. 'Not this far out please! We haven't accomplished a quarter of the journey yet?' Lifting the engine cover we could see the engine struggling. We had basic tools on board, but this was something internal. Voting to keep going as far as we dare to reach safe harbour where help maybe be found.

Inside the safety of North Bimini the engine seemed to take life again. Maybe a thermostat in the cooling system freed itself allowing the flow of seawater around the risers and manifolds? We took on more fuel to make the long run over the shallow Bahama banks toward the Berry Islands, some eighty-five miles further eastward after clearing customs. From here onward the shallow waters are a wide open; only an occasional lone sponge would break the monotony of the vast sand bottom. After passing north Andros Island we encountered that three-mile-deep Tongue of the Ocean, light turquoise giving way to the deepest indigo separating the Berry Islands and Nassau. Halfway across the banks we made our first radio contact with our friends, all eagerly tuned in to hear our progress. Warren Russell who worked at Maura Lumber Company on Shirley Street came over the air with that friendly familiar voice calling himself 'The Lone Ranger' as his 'handle' was referred to. He acted as relay to the rest of the crew in the further islands with someone making a landline phone call to our families letting them know 'Deep 6' or Andy's '77 B 66' was still alive out there. The island grapevine worked so very well in those days.

Approaching Chub Cay, one engine died suddenly. We kept a forward movement at really slow idle speed with the remaining good engine. Lifting the engine cover we found split water hoses had sprayed the entire little Chevy engine with salt dried to a white crust. My kingdom for a roll of duct tape! Don and I talked over the gamble of making Nassau on the remaining engine. The journey would take us well into the night. We could have left the boat at Chub Cay and hired a charter flight to Nassau, safer this way, or just keep plodding away at least getting the boat delivered to Nassau where it could be worked on by a professional ready for business? With a really calm sea and radio communication working even better as we drew closer to home we opted to keep going. The setting sun on an open sea cast a barrage of magnificent colour reflecting perfectly on the smooth surface while we snacked on packets of biscuits and junk food washed down with lukewarm fresh water. As the night became pitch black, the Formula kept her pace at reasonable idle speed showing us the glow of Nassau's lighting downtown while throwing beautiful luminous green phosphorescence in our wake behind. It was a long day. Hours clicked by slowly, where the city finally came well into view in the dark early hours of morning; that welcome revolving beacon on Nassau's water tower flashing on top of the hill above the city. Rounding the harbour entrance guarded by that familiar old lighthouse to our left felt a real accomplishment with the sparkling lights of dockside cruise ships decorating the scene with shimmering reflection in the night waters. Warren had stayed with us on the radio well past midnight. He said that's where he planned to stay until we were safely tied up at Browns Boat Basin. Thank God he did. Approaching Paradise Island bridge the second engine died just as quickly as the first. Don scrambled onto the bow of the Formula and threw out the large Danforth anchor to save us from the strong tides flowing rapidly under the bridge; ebbing at the time would have taken us back toward where we came in. About opposite the old ferry docks of Paradise Beach the anchor bit and our silent vessel pointed into the tidal flow. The Lone Ranger, how appropriate was that, came to the rescue calling our other CB friends, Tony Collins and his father coming out with a tow into the safety of our marina at two o'clock in the morning. We were home.

Entering the Brown's family owned marina on Bay Street the next morning I asked Donald Brown who he recommended to take care of our repairs.

'There is only one man you need Paul and he is out there on the dock now, look for Hartley Parotti and tell him I sent you.'

'Thanks Donald, will do,' I replied with thanks. I crossed East Bay

Street from the office at Browns making my way down the floating docks finding Hartley lying down inside an open engine cover actually on top of an engine cursing out loud at the black Mercruiser he was working on. I clearly heard a spanner slip off its mark causing a man's knuckle to tear open, 'God damn you bastard,' he yelped vehemently toward this chunk of metal, blood spilling freely over the black engine.

'Morning, Hartley!' I bravely interrupted not daring use the word 'good'!

The fairly heavy-set man grumbling out loud with dark blue shirt, matching trousers and work boots, sporting jet-black curly hair and heavy eyebrows, rolled over to see who had the audacity to interrupt his day. A small stub of a thick cigar, barely an inch left clenched between his teeth. Dark eyes and very tanned skin showing his Italian heritage clearly.

'What can I do for you?' he said grumpily wrapping his injury with an oil-stained rag.

'Donald tells me you are the only man I need to keep my new business going. Hartley we have a 23-foot Formula with twin Mercruiser engines, will you be my mechanic? We came in last night from Miami and had to be towed in losing both engines!'

'Well, I'm kinda busy right now but I could have a look I guess, where are you?'

'Over on the other floating dock by the gas pumps,' I instructed.

'Ok, let's go see what you've got yourself into,' he said still wiping filthy grease and blood covered hands on yet another old rag hanging out of his pocket and shaking my hand. A moment remembered here marked the beginning of a long and loyal friendship, staying with us all through my boating career. The same demeanour as my vet, he also would start the conversation with, 'Did you hear the one about …', also having a miraculous repertoire of jokes. Hartley stepped aboard the Formula with his heavy black work boots and lifted the engine cover.

'No friggin' wonder you had problems my friend, no-one paints Mercruiser's green, that's just fucking sacrilege!' he exclaimed in horror seeing the home-style paint job the Cuban had performed allowing one to spot oil stains should they appear?

'Mercruiser's stay black, Paul. Let's get her out of the water and to my daddy's yard in Palmdale. I have a complete workshop there and we can go from one end to the other on this piece of shit!'

Fortunately, with the extra money saved, the long partnership began with a major overhaul. I had thrown out the offer to my new mechanic – that if he gave me preferred treatment as a commercial operator in return would get paid immediately, an attractive offer in comparison to other clients who he had to chase for payment. He accepted with work beginning right away. After a few days, I checked back to the small workshop in Mr. Parotti Senior's garden. The old man would let me in the side door of his house, never having a shirt on, his lean old tanned body topped with a thick head of white curly hair and few precious teeth left in his mouth, a cigarette tucked into one corner. Daddy used to be the specialist at fixing our cameras in Nassau.

'How the hell did you get this piece of crap from Miami to here?' the younger Parotti scoffed in the back garden with my Formula sitting on a trailer a garden hose attached to each of the lower units of the newly painted outdrives.

'That lil' Cuban saw you comin' my friend!' he retorted with a wry smile supporting the ever-present cigar stub.

'The engines were all fucked up! Those outdrives are really creative! He had four cylinder Chevy engines driving 165 Outdrives holding 188 gears in the lower units and the wrong props!' 'Never seen anything like this before!' He gestured for me 'to come take a look inside'.

Climbing up the small ladder alongside the boat I peeked in. Two shining black engines greeted me with their matching newly painted outdrives and new stainless steel propellers. The man was a perfectionist when it came to rebuilding engines. The black greasy boot-marked decking was a Parotti signature we all thankfully lived with!

'Turn on those garden hoses' he asked pointing to the taps on the side of the building. Fresh water squirted from the boots wrapped around the lower units forcing fresh water to flow around the engine block manifolds. He turned both ignition keys and the engines started first crank. They purred as if new sewing machines were running a few feet away.

'Jesus Hartley, you are a friggin' genius,' I complimented.

'Now you are ready for business!' he proudly retorted. He smiled with the cigar stub firmly in the corner of his mouth adding, 'Get out the cheque book!' We joked in later years that with all the work I commissioned him to perform during that career I put both his daughters through college!

It was 1980 and the world around us was changing rapidly. This year we could watch two Olympics with the Summer Games in Moscow and Winter Games in Lake Placid, New York. This year witnessed the insidious onset of terrorism creeping into world affairs taking many shapes and forms. The Mafia assassinates the President of Sicily while American hostages in Iran have their fate decided by the Iranian parliament so decreed by the Ayatollah Khomeini.

Early in the year, US President Jimmy Carter, a peanut farmer from Georgia, proclaims a grain embargo against the USSR and bails out the Chrysler Corporation for $1.5 Billion. Moscow citizens enjoy their first rock festival! American census finds there are near 227 million people in the United States, while the fifth George Lucas film in the Star Wars series *The Empire Strikes Back* is released. In April, Iranian terrorists take over the embassy in London only to have the British SAS take it back a few days later with only one terrorist surviving. The personal computer age is just beginning with Pac-Man coming out of Japan in May 1980 as one of the first games played. The coming year would see the emergence of Paul Allen and young Bill Gates introduce the Microsoft Corporation. We would have to wait four more years for Steve Jobs to place his first Macintosh 128 K on the market, the brilliance of invention coming from two different garages. In June of 1980, television greets the first 24-hour news broadcast from CNN in Atlanta, Georgia, created by millionaire Ted Turner later to marry actress Jane Fonda.

October gives us the first remarkable high resolution pictures sent back from Saturn by Voyager 1 near 77,000 miles from the ringed planet. That same month a huge earthquake rocked Algeria, killing 2600 people. As the year comes to a close the American elections welcome in Ronald Reagan the ageing Hollywood movie star defeating Jimmy Carter on November 4. The year ends in tragedy for the music world on December 8 in New York City where lone deranged gunman David Chapman comes up behind John Lennon while outside his apartment and shoots him dead. We are at a loss in trying to conceive why someone would kill one of our greatest modern musicians.

In the Bahamas, our friend King Ingraham is running his Treasure Island day trip over on Sandy Cay after Robert Major vacated the island, suddenly losing his creation to his transportation company, the largest on the island who kept the Robinson Crusoe name and moved the operation to a newly purchased property in Lower Harbour on the south shore of Rose Island. Roberts' partner Inez started an offshoot of their creation calling it Sea-Island Adventure. No honour amongst thieves, Major the foreigner and powerless vacates the country. The Keewatin schooner was still in full function with friends Eryn and Randy Varga starting their Barefoot Sailing Charters with 'The Out-Island Safari' now a well-established day excision here in Nassau. I had raised the price to $38 per person remaining the most expensive day trip by $3.00 still with everything included as far as transportation, food and refreshments. The couple who I had befriended and husband becoming my dive partner months earlier stayed close for several years. On his days off or on the weekend selling our catch to his contacts in the seafood industry at Burrows Seafoods, owned by brothers D'Yenza and Doyle Burrows and Tyrone Darville still running Portion Control on Fowler Street – we had good outlets to sell our fish fillet and fresh lobsters. With the Formula we could now work in comfort even in rough ocean waters on the North side of Rose Island as far as Six Shilling Cays toward Eleuthera. I had no clue there would be lessons on betrayal ahead.

Our first major adventure together brought an event never repeated within my lifetime. It was July 31, the day before lobster season opened. We had planned a spearfishing journey over to the Berry Islands, having heard of some good crawfish locations on the shallow bank side of the cays. Taking time off work we departed the day before opening of the season on August 1 every year. The ocean treated us to a classic flat calm Bahamian day reflecting the stunning pastel blue sky of that midsummer; an ocean so quiet there appeared no horizon, sea melting perfectly into sky. We loaded basic camping gear planning for a site under the pine trees of one of the cays. The boat never moved off course. One could sit and chat to each other without touching the steering wheel. The two four cylinder Chevy engines hummed and the journey would take just under two hours. About half way across the Tongue of the Ocean, with land in sight, a huge plume of white spray drifting as a fine mist back to the surface suddenly broke the surface of the water. A whale blowing between breaths. We approached with slowing speed seeing how close the beautiful creature would allow us to come. Closer and closer we drew. At idle speed the Formula was very quiet with the huge beast allowing us to approach closer than imagined. Slowly, ever so slowly, as if frame-by-frame in a reviewed motion picture, the huge sperm whale rose and fell alongside our small boat. Our vessel was a mere 23-feet, and this lovely animal over twice that. The whales' dives were submerging thirty or forty feet underneath our hull and clearly visible from above with the suns rays dancing into the bottomless indigo depths. Sperm whales are the largest toothed mammal growing up to 67 feet weighing in at over 45 tons, capable of diving over 3000 feet chasing squid to eat. Such a dive would have the animal holding its breath for up to 90 minutes. They have the largest brain of any animal known to exist, capable of consuming a ton of fish and squid every day. This more likely a male as females travelled in pods. Victim of over hunting they are now protected. We stayed for several minutes leaving the engines in neutral, our guest staying with us as if offering a welcome swim. I had always been fascinated with whales and dolphins, feeling an uncanny affinity toward these creatures with the ocean playing such a huge part in my life: mankind's really poor behaviour toward these magnificent animals striking a hostile chord within my soul. The ancient trade of whaling always leaving a foul taste as the harpoon stuck home creating a gush of blood staining the ocean. Mother's bodies pierced as their calves swam alongside. I hold extreme distaste for the Japanese fishermen and people of the Faroe Islands for their wanton annual slaughter of whales and porpoise. Why the general populations of these countries don't raise their own protest with the rest of the planet voicing such disgust over the wanton slaughter is beyond comprehension. In the nineteenth century the whale populations were decimated where three million animals were killed. Yet the killing continues with these two countries totally disregarding the world's plea to cease, even though whale watching generates over $2 billion in revenue, far more than whaling ever produced!

Underwater photography had become a growing passion over my years at sea. There were so many amazing sights I deemed a privilege to witness leaving them unrecorded seemed such a waste of opportunity. Fortune today had me bring the right camera; an opportunity here not to be missed for moments as this may pass but once.

'Let's take a swim my friend,' I said almost too casually to my dive partner.

'Not friggin' me! That water is over 10,000 feet deep!' he exclaimed emphatically. 'There are some big nasty creatures that swim with these things you know!'

He was right in thinking about the huge creatures; very large tiger sharks often travelled close to these whales during their migration northward through our waters, seeking moments of distress or the birthing of youngsters. Knowing I would be alone on this adventure I donned my snorkel gear on the swim platform at the rear of the boat. Spitting in the mask and wiping the saliva around became an automated ritual, keeping the glass lens from fogging. A quick rinse and I slid silently into the blue abyss. The ocean water appeared intense deep indigo blue. The sun's rays danced all around my vision, eerily in perspective pointing toward the bottom some three miles beneath me. Suddenly, within seconds, my forty-foot host made a turn and approached me head on. Vision magnified by two-thirds in the underwater world this massive animal weighing in at several tons kept coming, appearing the size of a school bus! I froze as if suspended in space. Audible clicking noises filled the sea. My companion was communicating, as did the dolphins I had played with in past years. Closer and closer the huge creature came, head on, mesmerising me to forget having a camera hanging close to my body. The scene far too distracting to record the moment, I missed capturing the approach. This stunning sight was quickly filling my vision, and apparently no intention of stopping. I reached out my arm, stretching its full three feet, imagining boldly I could actually bring something so huge to a halt. With my wide-open fingers straining as if to widen the distance, the two swimmers made contact. A surreal picture played out before me. The whale touched gently as if a spacecraft delicately docking in orbit. His skin, soft as silk to the touch, indeed did stop in an instant. He rolled over in weightlessness on his side, allowing the huge pectoral fins to relax as if in a wave of greeting while I held the massive snout. More clicking sounds with a graceful turn, offering me to join in the encounter. The huge tail flukes near ten feet wide each side, near the length of our boat in total. They rose and fell as if in effortless ultraslow motion as my two swim fins pedalled as fast as I could to keep up. Too close to this massive tail and the turbulence would bowl me over in innocence like a small toy. Senses restored I clicked off a few frames of film but the size and effect was going to be lost in these pictures. I needed to be close alongside for any chance of dramatic perception. The boat was still close with my Bahamian friend leaning over the gunnel watching the spectacle in the deep water below.

'Gary, do me a favour and get your gear on, this is too good to miss!' My tone clearly pleading over the surface of the oily calm ocean.

'Oh what the hell …' he finally succumbed. Sitting on the stern platform of the idling powerboat he slid the large fins over his neoprene booties and in one graceful motion, without a splash, he too slid into the blue. Removing his mouthpiece, he uttered in near whisper 'Unbelievable!' We swam together while the sperm whale continued its slow-motion exercise of diving below the surface down forty feet, followed with the slow rise again for an explosive exhale of white mist in a very audible blow from the hole in the top of its head. I caught Gary's attention with a gentle touch on his arm; he near jumped out of his skin in surprise looking up for brief conversation. Almost whispering, I explained the plan needing him to follow in order to capture the possible picture of a lifetime. We separated in the warm water and with a single hand signal we took one good breath for our descent, able to stay easily to depths of forty feet. The huge Sperm Whale with a newfound trust allowed to me swim close enough to touch the massive head, his gentle eye perversely small to the huge body, pivoting in its small socket watching my every move. Utter silence in that deep abyss let me hear the unmistakable audible click of the camera shutter.

Our gracious host from inner-space had set a course northward swimming away from our drifting boat. Distance out here all alone becomes very apparent instilling sudden uneasy fear. My partner was showing concern in his body language and frequent glances above and below the surface. We both ascended to the calm surface exhaling about the same time, as did the great whale.

'Your turn?' I tried persuasion.

'No bloody way my friend! 'Better get our asses back to the boat?'

The whale now oblivious to the two humans in the water, our encounter had ended, going our own ways in this beautiful very warm ocean.

Glancing up we noticed the Formula's hull uncomfortably quite some distance away, near a hundred yards looking visibly very much smaller. The two divers taking comfort in each other's close presence for the swim back to safety. Our fin stokes plunging deep and noticeably quiet so as not to create splash and noise of vibration. Stealth out here was a good thing and we looked behind and under us in jittery caution every few seconds. Swimming out here left one incredibly vulnerable and one's heartbeat certainly increases at the thought of the unknown approaching silently from underneath; to be alone drifting after some emergency quite unfathomable but to be witnessed years later. We reached our idling boat and heaved aboard with one graceful motion together onto the swim platform.

'Well, what do think on that one!'? I exclaimed with the rush of exhilaration still within my body. 'Wow!'

'I hope I got that photo,' Gary confirmed. 'Just clicked the one!'

Gear thrown on the floor of the boat, we towelled off the seawater avoiding the itchy salt crystals dry on our skin in the hot August sun. Fine white mists still blew as our companion stayed on course. Clutches slid gently forward commanding the two four-cylinder engines clunk into gear. A slow push of the throttles and the Formula reacted with grace again to speed smoothly toward, ironically, Whale Cay lying just ahead over a glass-calm ocean. We stayed on a flat desolate cay camped under the pine trees as planned finding many cracks and ledges while diving in the uninteresting shallow waters off shore littered with occasional small coral heads and fields of waving turtle grass. Lobster antennas were everywhere. Much smaller in size than anywhere we had fished but still legal. The tails were twisted off and our coolers of ice already starting to melt. The ice water would preserve the catch until home in two days.

After that expedition, there was little hesitation taking the film to Ricky Wells's photo studio in Palmdale. That one photograph came out to perfection. Perfectly framed portraying me alongside the sperm whale illustrating the huge bend in my fins with the extended effort needed to keep up with my companion. I showed it to famed underwater photographer Stan Waterman who filmed *The Deep* starring Nick Nolte and Jacqueline Bissett, while he gave a symposium in one of the hotels a few years later. He marvelled at the picture but more so the opportunity we had to swim with this magnificent ocean traveller.

'That only happens once in a lifetime, Paul. I doubt you will have chance to repeat that experience,' he added. He was absolutely correct. I have seen many whales since both from a boat and while flying but none offered the gift of that unforgettable Bahama day. From that experience I have formed a special intuition about a whales' presence nearby. Very often while flying I would have the feeling one of my companions close by somewhere. Sure enough, more often than not, within minutes I would spot the familiar white plume of exhaled spray.

We made several expeditions to the Berry Islands over the years with successful catches of crawfish taken from the cracked rocky bottom in the shallow inside waters of those cays. An evening of note where Gary's wife had joined us for the three-day adventure. Nights sitting around the campfire saw the appearance of a bottle of tequila and fresh lime. Drinking was still a poor practise with me but this evening watching the flames dance against that still ocean water lapping the sands each sip went down far easier than the last. I needed to pee but standing was not going to be successful this night. With tears of laughter my two companions watched in glee my best imitation of a loggerhead turtle returning to the water! The tracks that following morning lay as proof of my accomplishment. I fried eggs over the morning fire, feeling perfect as my friends groaned in their sufferance from inside the tent.

Chapter 17
'Hello Natalie!'

The failure of my first marriage came as bitter disappointment. I had been the last of 'the gang' to wed. Kathy had been my best friend and changes between us came fairly quickly after the second year. In Mexico, we were two young people exploring abroad together for the first time. My mother introduced Kathy to a Canadian friend who was Bill Claridge's accountant at the headquarters of Kentucky Fried Chicken in Palmdale. Terry Rivet was retiring and needed a replacement. Advancement in career was well received and Kathy never looked back. We knew the Claridge family well from back at the beginning of our lives in the Bahamas where week-end boating meetings at Green Cay commonplace where I swam with children Steven and Diane closer to my age. I put the failure mostly on myself. Maybe I was too immature at this age but Kathy had changed also, and her 'Miss Bahamas' appearance soon lost. I thought inwardly that we were way too young to change physically, it was important to stay attractive to ones' mate? I remember later chatting with male friends in times of trouble we, as men, 'don't know our arse from a hole in the ground during our twenties'. The physical attraction was gone and I was simply living with my best friend. One day at work I strayed toward a very attractive French-Canadian single girl who had come for a second day out with me to Rose Island. There was no denying the attraction and clearly she had the same intention, eventually later becoming the mother of my child. To make the break as honourable as possible I walked away with just what I was able to carry. Leaving my wife with a lovely home fully paid for. We stayed friends ever since, I was lucky Kathy had class and kind temperament remaining director of our company for years after. My mother's friend before retiring gave me a stern warning about what I had done more so about whom I had done it with. 'Watch out for those damned French-Canadians Paul, they are trouble, I too married one'. That phrase came to haunt me all too soon.

I found another potential home further up Village Road in the prestigious area known as Montagu Heights. Homes here were set on larger lots of land and tended be where the up-and-coming younger and more established business people of Nassau preferred to live. For me the empty, overgrown home I discovered while driving through Windsor Avenue would be perfect, offering a quick short cut across Shirley Street to the marina where my boat was docked. I tracked the vacant property belonging to Emmet Pritchard of Asa A. Pritchard, the wholesale food business. I knew his two sons Hugh and Robert really well. Taking bull by the horns I walked into Emmett's office one day asking boldly if he would be interested in giving a private 'Bahamian mortgage', a fairly common practice with established businessmen. He graciously accepted asking for a 10% deposit and terms to be drawn with monthly interest and principal paid. I was short on the deposit by a couple thousand dollars but his generosity shined, waiving the amount to pay down. I gave the good news to my mother living in an apartment in Rose Lane, Palmdale that I had a new home with monthly payments of just over $1000 a month. She went ballistic.

'How the hell are you going to afford that?' she cried.

'No worries Mum, I can do this and pay it off in about four years!' Mr Pritchard told me not to push that goal seemingly impossible to achieve. On year four, to the day, I gave my mother the final payment to deliver on my behalf. Emmett was staggered on my timing, later helping my return to his office asking for a second mortgage for the adjoining vacant land ending at Montagu Avenue. I would own from road to road making it only one of three double properties in that neighbourhood. There was no stopping having the taste of success rewarding me with assured self-confidence. I was to never look back. From here with a new relationship I would begin the longer journey of greater success. Working near 24–7 as they say, I climbed the financial ladder looking once again for a bigger boat to run my business. I had a buyer for the Formula and found a 25-foot Flybridge Bertram belonging to Herbie Knowles, owner of Lorenes clothing stores, at the Nassau Yacht Haven, named *Vicky* after his daughter. The purchase of this new addition was the starting point of new expansion within my company and my life's quests as a whole.

The world was witnessing images that shape us today in aviation, film, music and politics. The first Airbus A-300 is certified while in February Freddie

Laker's airline flies its last flight. My father had worked for Freddie back in the UK. The famous Thunderbirds acrobatic team are grounded when four T-38 Talons touch each other to crash losing all four pilots. Argentina lays claim to the Falkland Islands and Great Britain responds rapidly with the deployment of its two aircraft carriers, Hermes and Invincible along with an Avro Vulcan bomber on its way to the Ascension Islands, where it attacked Port Stanley in East Falkland Island on May 1 1982. It was the longest bombing mission to date, over 8000 miles and sixteen hours round trip. Argentina retaliates sinking the British destroyer HMS *Sheffield* with an Exocet missile. In civil aviation we see some milestones where American Airline flies its one-millionth passenger and British Airways flies its last Boeing 707 from Cairo to London. The airline has a real scare on June 24 with a 747 flying through volcanic ash south of Java to lose all four engines. There is silence aboard the airliner with crew managing a restart and safely land at Djakarta. Pan-Am is still in operation, loses a 727 out of New Orleans killing 145 and eight souls on the ground. Later in the year the airline inaugurates the first and longest distance nonstop flight from Los Angeles to Australia. In Romania the BAC III flies off the production line and becomes the first jet Bahamas Airways brings to its fleet. World politics are becoming explosive with Israel starting the Lebanon War against the Palestinian PLO, ending later in September of that year.

Those of us following music and film remember 1982 as the debut of some well-known artists of our present time including Madonna, Hugh Grant, Angelina Jolie and Eddie Murphy. Michael Jackson releases *Thriller* becoming the highest grossing album of all time selling 110 million copies. He begins to subject himself to radical facial cosmetic surgery destroying his admired good looks over the next few years; Michael eventually dying as a fairly young man from a controversial drug overdose. We lose many extraordinary talents of show business to this same fatal choice during the next few decades. We enjoy movies such as *E.T.* from director Stephen Spielberg and amazed by Richard Attenborough's epic *Gandhi* – winning Best Film and Best Director at the Academy Awards – while having the wits scared out of us with *Poltergeist.* I remember the end of the year for it is here I learned I was to be a father that coming July.

With the Flybridge Bertram, I am able to host seven or eight couples comfortably with the price of the excursion slowly climbing from $38 per person to $45. 'You moving up in the world' Hartley would say as he began maintaining a larger vessel. It was still my policy, as other competitors stated raising their tariff, to remain the most expensive, a tactic that stayed in my favour all the way to the end. On one of my day trips out to the island I met a guest from Beaumont, Texas joining us while staying on Paradise Island with his son. They had booked direct from their hotel room, still a rarity in those days and asked for the additional attraction of being taught to scuba dive with me photographing their experience underwater. Pulling the car up to his hotel lobby there was no missing that familiar southern American accent. His voice, although loud, very commanding and friendly, learning later a voice often requested as a radio announcer on Texas radio stations.

'Hi Paul, my name is Jeff Hughes and this is my son Jeff Junior.' They sat on the bridge of my boat for the drive up to Rose Island and we hit off a good friendship from the onset. He was fascinated by my very pregnant French-Canadian partner seated on the very bow of the boat with her legs hanging over the edge of the deck above the racing water beneath.

'Good Lordy, I hope the bumping of the boat ride doesn't start her labour!' he exclaimed. The day was gorgeous and their dive went well after the short introduction lesson on the beach that morning. Seeing my abilities in the water taking pictures while holding my breath he soon revealed his profession and made an offer that brought another exciting unexpected dimension to my life.

'I'm in film production Paul and have a television series that I am about to start up which could be as much as fifteen shows on the newly formed Discovery Channel. It's called *The International Outdoorsman* and I would like you to film for me!'

'Wow, Jeff' I replied with enthusiasm. 'I must tell you up front I've not shot much video and have no equipment' I explained.

'Don't fret the small stuff my friend, I've seen your talent with boats and under the water. I will get you the gear. By the way, do you snow ski?' he asked. I told him of learning in the Austrian Alps in a small town called Zell-am-See several years earlier with my first wife along with dive partner and his wife. We skied Kaprun and the glacier of Schmittenhohe. 'I'm no pro Jeff, but could probably hold my own for filming needs?'

'Wonderful' he added, 'we will be getting up to all kinds of mischief then! I have some plans for deep diving in a submerged lead mine in central Missouri, jumping out of airplanes and we need some sharks!' He had my attention on this last one, explaining that he would like me to film the first shark film for the Discovery Channel preferably right here in the Bahamas, and wondered if I could set something in motion? I had heard of the resort in Stella Maris in Long Island run by Peter Kuska and Jorge Friese having a renowned shark-dive taking a bucket of fish parts amongst their divers to watch feeding at close hand. It was a ground-breaking entertainment idea that caught on later all over the globe.

'Perfect!' Jeff said, delighted with the prospect of a successful production. He returned some weeks later to the Bahamas with his producer and friend introduced as 'Uncle Harold' a long-time family doctor friend, presenting me a complete underwater Sony video unit. Special VHS was the latest technology of the day with the housing and lighting to complete the equipment needed over the next few weeks to become familiar with and ready to start production on *The Sharks of Stella Maris.* Soon after release the cable channel introduced an annual series called *Shark Week* which successfully airs to this day featuring friends Stuart and Michelle Cove, out of their South Ocean location where underwater film techniques evolved way past expectation, including today's use of drones for impressive effects above the dive sites.

Jeff had an original approach of producing television shows. They all were in essence a 'travelogue' where he would approach well-known destinations or famous personalities owning high-end resorts, asking a trade of a promotional film on television for all expenses absorbed by the host. It worked. We were to explore to all points of the globe where airlines and the host resort all received lengthy promotion allowing us to stay for free with all amenities offered for the story we were to put on film. 'We won't make much money Paul but we can have a hell of a good time!' Jeff would retort. Sure enough, every now and again with little notice an airline ticket would arrive via Federal Express courier asking to meet him in the mountains somewhere or in Houston for a get together before traveling to other beautiful dive destinations in the Caribbean and as far as The Red Sea. The ticket would be the best he could muster. 'What the hell my friend, first class is the only way to travel, we just pay a little longer!' his well-known motto.

I followed an unexpected discovery while having dinner one evening on the patio of the Poop Deck restaurant over at the Nassau Yacht Haven. Gone were the old apartments that housed Underwater Tours management replaced with a balcony restaurant owned by Eloy Roldan, first friends of my parents back in 1960. Eloy still manages his success story some forty-six years later! Seated on the balcony and waiting for a cold beer to arrive I looked downward to the docks, where I used to walk and work as a young schoolboy, noticing a rather nice 28-foot Flybridge Bertram chained to the dock. That seemed strange enough until noticing a 'For Sale' sign up in the forward cabin window. Investigation led me to call the listed number on the sign to be told by a local doctor handling the sale for friend Juan Fernandez who raced powerboats with my boss Gardner Young. Small world. The chain was holding the boat in place because the owner owed dockage to the Yacht Haven to be paid by the purchaser before it would be released. The sale of my 25-foot boat paid the cost of the new 28-foot model enabling me to carry up to ten couples on my day excursion, my final target number to have on board. Twenty people paying $48 for their day and scuba an additional $25 each made the trip quite profitable with average work days at least five a week. The outdrives which required as much labour as the engines would be gone, my maintenance bills climbing monthly from Hartley who endorsed the idea sighting 'a really good investment'. Now I owned straight drive shaft, eight cylinder engines providing ample power to move that amount of load up to my new private location on Rose Island rented from an old acquaintance Captain Bill Pemberton. Bill had bought a piece of the island in Lower Harbour which ran from one side of the island to the other where he built a native-stone house on the top of the hill overlooking his dock on the South side. He too owned an identical Bertram. His location gave me the advantage I needed to run daily trips being affected by rough seas on the windward side of the island. Rough winter days on the beachside meant I had calm water and a dock on the lee side to the South. It was worth the rental investment and a warm friendship evolved with Captain Bill being my old school friend Graham's father-in-law. The island was indeed a small community! Within weeks Bill approached me about 'dying for something to do and wife Edna wanting him out the house some days, what were the chances of him joining forces with me to run two boats to his property?' Diving Safaris was to grow one more time on a part-time basis when demand came evident during the higher season of business. It is 2015 and I learn with sadness at Christmas time about Bill's death following soon after his wife Edna. He was a true gentleman and close friend.

Walking into a Le Mars class is not way up on the to-do list of a charter boat captain! It is something persuaded by one's partner and partaken to appease! We seated ourselves on the floor next to another couple whose husband smiled a sheepish acknowledgement. Harvey and Diana introduced themselves becoming friends since that fateful June afternoon some thirty-three years ago. It took about a minute for both men to let humour fly with deadly looks from our partners lying prostrate on the hard floor blowing for all their worth. Their son Gavin was born five weeks ahead of my daughter and shared boating adventures to the Exuma Cays when both children were still very small. Their young baby boy decorating my 28-foot Bertram aft deck with projectile vomiting while Harv and I sipped a cold rum and coke up on the bridge!

Later years saw our friendship weave its way through a rag-tag group of island lads annually gracing Highbourne Cay's South House during springtime. 'The Rough Boys' gathered for a fishing tournament usually over a long weekend during dolphin season; a brightly coloured game fish known in places as Mahi-Mahi. Two boats full of fishing tackle and beer made their way across the shallow banks from Nassau to Highbourne; stragglers in the group meeting at Crocodiles to board the seaplane for the short eighteen-minute flight to Cheap Charlie Beach. Tim Revington, Ian Mabon, Mick Bancroft, Harvey and his Dad, Theo Tsavoussis and myself would compete in the dark indigo waters of Exuma Sound to catch the heaviest fish while trying to survive Theo's wild gaffing techniques that had us all diving for cover aboard the open-fisherman boat! The cuisine each evening was outstanding in taste and creativity. Man-time enjoyed to the max. July 3rd 1983 started in the very early hours of the morning. My daughter was on the way. I knew it was a girl although never told. I had not considered otherwise. The bag had been packed and car ready. We barely made the front entrance of Doctors Hospital and in the early light of day saw Suzy's water break outside the doors on to the ground in a puddle. Within an hour or two I watched in awe as that little wet body slid into the waiting hands of a Wellington-booted Doctor Achara about mid-morning. 'Hello Natalie!' I said softly.

I was a fairly typical inept male when it came to babies. Scared silly of being a klutz and maybe dropping the tiny soul, holding my little girl however a spiritual delight not ever forgotten. At this very early stage it's a 'mummy thing' I was convinced knowing well my stomach failings toward a fully loaded diaper! Inwardly I knew that this lovely child was definitely going to receive far more from this father in her childhood than I was ever offered. Sure enough, as she grew into a little person and just starting to walk a fabulous bond began to flourish. Nats, as friend Martin Isles nicknamed her early on, would share some very special times with me. Since moving into Montagu Heights I always had dogs, German Shepherds at first then Dobermans both having mutual adoration for our little girl watching them follow and 'protect' her down our long garden was heart-warming. As a little person she would grasp some of the ripe cherries from the tree at the bottom of the garden, ones within easy reach and feed each dog that stayed protectively close to her side. Within time we renovated our carport, rear workshop and maid's quarters to a lovely modern apartment for my mother to live in. Paying her rent in Rose Lane seemed ludicrous and with her staunch independence the close proximity seemed a safe bet and worked well. She kept far stricter boundaries than we did. Natalie had 'Nanny' in the same garden next door so both parties revelled in the easy visits. The discovery of Natalie's clever breakfast planning soon became evident when searching for her some mornings only to find a grinning four-year-old sitting up in her grandmother's bed with breakfast tray on her lap.

Natalie shared our daily lives with the business as well. In her early years, she loved being on the boat and within no time was sitting on my lap up on the Bertram bridge holding the steering wheel as guests chatted below deck on their way for a day's adventure. While trying to correct her steering, my hand was forcefully pushed aside as she was bound to be the sole captain in charge. At two years' old she had no fear of the water as we had her floating in the warm summer ocean as a baby from the first week since birth. She soon enjoyed a tiny swim mask and size one flippers. Before long Nattie, as friends of her age would call her, could handle herself in any depth of water and started to free-dive, learning how to clear her ears of increasing pressure by squeezing her nose with two fingers trying to gently blow. When she felt that squeaking noise and relief down further she would dive. She was undoubtedly an 'Island Baby'! At this stage she would come on the afternoon dive with me to watch the tourists Scuba diving below here. She met and had a close relationship with 'Uncle Jeff' who came regularly from Texas to have a few days on Paradise Island where he could play in the casino and day trip with 'The Out-Island Safari'. Evening dinners with us all at Cafe Martinique were mandatory. I watched with a smile as my daughter and producer swam together off the shore and over to the close by corals, the little swimmer often nudging the older man to come see a parrotfish or blue tang. On a dive near the shores of Green Cay one afternoon my lovely daughter informed me 'that she had to go!' I could hear Jeff utter quietly 'Oh Lord!' as he would say in that Texas drawl. With no working bathroom on the Bertram I whispered for her to swim way downstream from our visitors below. We watched as her little body swam away from the boat past the rising bubbles reaching the surface from below. But alas the distance was not far enough before she shamelessly dropped her tiny bikini bottom and sent a huge offering into the sea. 'Good grief' Jeff spluttered with laughter watching the long snake-like deposit descend toward the sandy bottom below. We prayed our guests did not discover this unfamiliar creature lying in wait. Natalie returned beaming to the dive platform very proud of her accomplishment.

'You taught her well.' Jeff aimed the comment my way.

'What do we tell the divers if they find *that*?' he asked the beaming young lady.

'Tell them it's a sea cucumber!' my daughter exclaimed without hesitation.

'We have to put this sea-nymph on film Paul,' was Jeff's reply.

On his next visit to the Bahamas Jeff brought a gift set of miniature scuba gear manufactured in Texas out of an emergency air supply, called in the business, a pony-bottle. To add to the attraction of my near four-year old he had it painted bright pink. The small backpack fit a little large for her tiny frame. She floated like a cork and needed at least four pounds of divers lead weight added to the waist strap to have her submerge. In the dive industry there was a strict age limit to children learning the art of scuba. This daughter of an Open-Water Instructor was however quite unusual in her marine abilities so we decided to let her 'have a go' in the very shallow waters off the beach at Rose Island. The regulator mouthpiece was the smallest we could find, still large for that little mouth to hold. From flying in airliners to going snow skiing she had mastered early on the art of clearing her ears of the pressure changes we are all familiar with when airborne reminding her constantly to equalise pressure so as to avoid early ear damage. To distract her we placed a series of shells and starfish in a straight line along the bottom of the seabed in about five feet of water. Regulator in her mouth she allowed herself to sink to the sand for the first time breathing beautifully underwater. Cameras were rolling above and below the surface. Her first 'dive' recorded.

Being well versed with the underwater camera housing and contracts in place with the Discovery Channel Jeff wanted the first production to be about his little dive companion, calling it *The Child and the Wonders of the Sea*; a story of a four-year-old who's life above and below the water living in the Bahama Islands. We filmed the land-based scenes with a huge heavy old Ariflex camera and the underwater work with my SVHS unit Jeff had given. Her actual dive would be in twenty-five feet of water above the staghorn corals near Green Cay. With her Dad holding hands she jumped fearlessly into the clear ocean water while another friend of Jeff's handled the camera work. Set with lovely music we later laid in a Texas sound studio the piece was a hit. The Japanese bought the work sometime later I learned, showing on national television. From here soon after Natalie's life would soon take a drastic change.

Living in a foreign country is difficult enough. Living in a small island nation working as a foreigner is illegal without special permits. My French-Canadian girlfriend, mother of my child, found island life closing in on her. She had made eerie mention of a past boyfriend and her city life in Montreal where family were. Home life was good for the most part but with family responsibilities weighing heavily on my shoulders I had ratcheted up my business to makes ends and financial obligations meet; success wields a two-edge sword. The work was long, hard and continuous. When the Bahamas gained independence that warm July night in 1973 I was one of the first foreigners to apply for citizenship under the new constitution. So new was the idea that even the national newspaper did not have the wording for the advertisement I was requested to place announcing my intention. It took all of thirty years to get my citizenship in the country

I had adopted as my own since boyhood. A proud day it was standing in that room on top of Hawkins Hill raising my hand to swear allegiance to Her Majesty the Queen and her heirs after been forced to hand in my British Passport! Nagging me that day was the company, surrounded by Haitian women who had married Bahamian men being bestowed the same honour in less than a handful of years after arrival in my country and still not one understanding a word of English. The tide of Bahamian way of life would soon be changing.

There was an underlying current in Nassau toward 'foreigners' that became personally volatile with a despicable act from a local Bahamian businessman blowing my second relationship wide apart. Landing on the South side of Rose Island my guests gathered on top of the hill as we did daily, giving them a welcome and a few minutes chat and instruction on where they could go and swim in safety, showing them the trails through the trees that led down to the beaches. Here lay many vacant undeveloped pieces of private land with lovely sand to sit on where guests could snorkel off shore to the nearby corals. The law in the Bahamas states clearly that *all* beaches are public up to three feet above the high-water mark, so walking and sitting posed no trespass for my clients. Some walked further to far coves enjoying real privacy on a mostly desolate nine-mile island. The day was panning out smoothly while I cooked the lunch over the homemade bar-b-q built of upright fifty-five-gallon steel drums. Guests were gathering for lunch where Natalie's mum was helping to prepare the large salad we brought with us daily. Our daughter now attending Mrs. Munroe's kindergarten school in William Street with Shirley our housekeeper who cared for her until we arrived home.

One of our guests came running through the woods exclaiming, 'Captain Paul you had better come down to the cove. There is someone being really rude to us there!' I reached the beach in seconds to see a small centre console outboard skiff pulled up to the beach. Sitting on the console seat was a woman screaming abuse at the top of her voice as if in some deranged state. The driver and apparent husband standing over a young couple sitting in the sand near the water's edge ordering them 'to get off his property.' I approached the scrawny looking man who I saw of Chinese descent but clearly local with his foul mouth spewing Bahamian slang.

'What on earth is your problem?' I asked in firm tone.

'Your people are on my beach' he screamed. 'They are trespassing!'

'I'm Bahamian my friend and telling you within the law these people are perfectly entitled to sit here. If this is your property they need to be three feet *above* the high-water mark to be on your land'. 'Besides that you can see they are tourists to our country and your attitude will destroy all the good work we are trying to do here!'

Standing very close to him now I towered with intimidation over the little Chinaman as he retreated rapidly into the water with his still screaming wife on board. It was hard to distinguish which of those people was more demented. They pulled a small anchor starting the engine and raced off toward Nassau. I apologised to my guests explaining that in all my years and thousands of clients I had never seen such behaviour from a local, and as a Bahamian ashamed of their bad manners offering profuse apologies on their behalf. My girlfriend sat in her usual perch on the very front of the boat as I drove homeward the mood on board flat and sombre.

Pulling in to Browns Boat Basin and docking stern in was always an interesting challenge. The twin screw Bertram however made the task an art form. Standing with my back to the controls I could spin the boat on its own axis and make her slide into the small space relatively with ease using just the engine clutches. A technique I had watched time and again as a small boy as the fishing charter boats returned to the Yacht Haven dock. I noticed a couple of local Bahamian men approach my space and offered to pass the dock lines to my girlfriend as she was there to help my other guests secure the Bertram while I scaled down the bridge to set the spring and bow lines. Before I could react the two men had taken hold of my startled partner by her arms in front of all my guests, informing her 'she was under arrest for working illegally in the Bahamas!' My guests were dumbfounded as they watched her being forcibly led down the dock with me in hot pursuit.

'What the bloody hell is this all about and who are you?' I shouted in panic.

'We are from immigration and we have had a complaint against you and that your girlfriend is working illegally on your boat! You have until five o' clock to get her out of jail otherwise she is there for the weekend as it's a holiday weekend tomorrow!'

'*Shit!*' I said out loud. This was July 9, and it was Independence weekend tomorrow. How the hell did they get this information was my quandary, and who the hell can help me with less than two hours to go and help my distraught partner?

They shoved her cruelly into the back seat and slammed the doors which had locks removed as I tried to open the door. She was crying and rightfully very frightened as the car sped off out on to Bay Street.

In panic, my mind was racing. Taxi, I need a taxi to take all my guests home who had now started to walk up the dock on their own to see if they could assist me. I ran over to Dexter, the fuel dock lad who I saw every day. He too was very disturbed at what he had watched. I asked him to call taxis for me while I hastily said my goodbyes to my clients shaken by a scene from films about foreign authorities throwing their power.

I needed some real weight with this situation and immediately thought of Kathy's office in Palmdale where Charles Carter, Member of Parliament worked for Bill Claridge. I raced over in about five minutes driving like some road-raged maniac. Running upstairs to the offices I desperately asked for him personally saying there was an emergency in progress finding thankfully he was there. We had known each other from his radio days at the local station of ZNS. Charles could see that the situation was desperate and reacted accordingly to my story as it spewed out in shaken panic. He was clearly aghast on hearing the news taking me inside his office to call Barbara Pierre, Director of Immigration who took his call without hesitation.

'Your bloody people are acting like the damned Gestapo,' he said loudly. 'Get this lady her freedom immediately and I want a formal apology!' Small dialogue continued for a few seconds and he put the receiver back on its cradle visibly furious.

'Paul, go down to Central Police Station in Bank Lane and ask for the officer in charge where you can pick up your girlfriend immediately. I am so very sorry this happened to you both, it's a damned disgrace which I will pursue!'

'Thank you Charles,' I near wept giving a hug farewell. I gave Kathy a quick hello on the way out who understood my frantic behaviour. 'Go get her now!' she added as I left.

Within minutes I was in Bank Lane parking in the first reserved space I could find, not caring about a ticket at this point. Entering the green painted old building with its stagnant air and noisy cellmates from inside, I saw Suzy standing there visibly about to come apart at the seams. I put an arm securely around her and led her out of that awful place into the warm sunshine of Bank Lane.

'They strip-searched me!' she exclaimed with a shaking voice to my horror and disbelief.

'*For what?*' I cried 'Fucking assholes!' I yelled in frustration over my shoulder. 'What the bloody hell was happening with this damned country?' adding, 'We need to be out of here!' Reaching home we fell into despair. It was shades of the 1970s all over again, with that dreaded regime on the top of Hawkins Hill. How could we live in this place if the locals were to behave like animals? I called Charles back and explained what they had done to my partner inside the police station. He was incensed and apologetic for his government's behaviour.

'For an Immigration offence Paul that is unheard of, this sounds like a vendetta to me, someone has made 'the call' as it was termed. It's a well-known Bahamian weapon against expats here, just call Immigration who will act first and inquire later. I will follow through on this for sure,' Charles replied graciously.

In days ahead I was given the name of the caller, a weasel of a Chinaman who's relations ran small convenience stores on Wulfe Road, had requested they put a strong squeeze on me by abusing my girlfriend. 'Get rid of her and he will go as well.' I dug my heels in on this one hoping one day I would see the nasty little Chinaman before he saw me coming. I wrote to the papers making the issue public eventually receiving a call from Immigration for me to attend a meeting at their headquarters. A very senior officer met me and in a private room offered the most profuse apology for their poor behaviour and said that it would never happen again to pass this to my partner – alas, irreparable damage was done.

We talked it all over many times at home deciding to look for somewhere else on this planet where people behaved in a normal fashion toward each other. For my preference, I always leaned toward beautiful scenery. Those of us who have grown up in beautiful places become very visual in nature. Our spirits in the worst of times kept aloft by the surrounding scenery so pleasing to the eye. It was here that my home country of England could not compete. There are some gorgeous places to be found in the UK but living in common suburbia with that climate would break my soul. I was very adaptable but the setting in which I was to live would play an immense part of a basic need coming to haunt me again later in life. Here lay the ultimate irony of me waiting all those years for Bahamian citizenship and now I may have to leave the country I loved. Having a Canadian lady, I offered a trip to the west coast of Canada to explore a favourite location in British Columbia I had spied on television travel documentaries, Montreal and its freezing months not an option having experienced first hand that province during the long cold winter and standing on top of Mont-Tremblant in minus 50 degrees! My offer was most welcome so we headed to Vancouver, a beautiful city with our good friends the Hyatt's having moved there from residing in the Bahamas several years earlier.

A drive up the Sea to Sky Highway and arrival in Whistler Village showed right away this certainly was a beautiful location, one that would keep my soul well content surrounded by such vistas of magnificence; postcard scenery of the two massive mountains of Blackcomb on one side and Whistler on the other. I spied a fabulous location for owning land overlooking the two mountains with the quaint village below, an advantage living in a resort location one learns how to distinguish its advantageous areas to reside in.

'You have a good eye, Paul,' our real estate host noted. 'That piece will be developed one day and I will give you first shot!'

In the meantime we need to make a living so as to afford an investment there, and the Bahamas was going to be our ticket out. The business was established and the income good enough to produce another home in a relatively short span of time. We decided to return and give my country another temporary chance. I started the day trips up upon arrival home working feverishly to produce income. Natalie and her Mum never stepped foot on board my boat again. I followed through on my promise of a new location and jumped at the offer of a Whistler property when the call came.

My mother had a long-awaited trip back to England planned to see her family after years of absence. With the home situation in delicate shape she was reluctant to leave, extremely perceptive in fearing our family teetering on the edge of disaster with something not appearing well within our household. I persuaded that she should make the journey with the ticket already purchased and her family eagerly waiting. 'You may never see your mum again,' I added. I showed understanding asking she give us time to heal from this ordeal. She left the next night on British Airways for London with plans calling for a visit on arrival with her long-time friend, Sue Shepherd, who used to be a lead stewardess with Bahamas Airways, now living alongside the Thames near London. The next morning as my mother arrived in England I bid my family farewell leaving for work saying I would call from the island on our radio system that I had set up in both the apartment and the main house. This way we always had communication and could talk at times through the busy days.

My guests were situated and off toward the beaches for their swimming. I prepared the food for lunch being alone once again up on top of the hill at Rose Island. Using my hand-held radio, I called the house to say hello and make sure all was well. Silence. I tried again and again. Silence. Strange feelings washed over me not able to shake the feeling of dread all through the day. Caring for twenty visitors and having divers that day I tried concentrating on their wellbeing as paying guests. After lunch I tried my radio again. Silence.

The trip homeward toward Nassau could not have gone fast enough. I dropped visitors to their various hotels and made a beeline home to Montagu. The front gates were shut with no Cortina parked in the driveway, a car I had bought for my partner. Hastily I parked the station wagon and opened my front door. My German Shepherd dog lay quietly on the bare tile living room floor. She stared mournfully up at me as if telling clearly something was awfully wrong. There was no wagging tail, no coming to greet me. Racing to Natalie's room I saw cupboard doors open revealing a vast array of empty coat hangers, those pretty little dresses gone. No shoes. Drawers empty. Into our bedroom, closets empty, ladies clothing gone, everything gone, my family gone. I could feel my spirit shattering.

I raced outside unawares of where or what I was doing, flooded with distraught emotion I made it to the road where I collapsed in a heap in the middle of Windsor Avenue wailing in grief out loud, my cries loud enough for my neighbour across the street, headmaster of Queens College, to hear me. Reverend Sweeting knelt his large frame down beside me in the middle of the street and asked what had happened. 'Gone … they've all gone,' I wept.

'Dear God I am so sorry, Paul,' he comforted. 'Come inside and let me call for some help.' He led me on to his patio and called friend Dr Timothy McCartney who came within what appeared to be minutes. Dr Tim knew my family well referring to Natalie a 'love baby'. He said she was a gorgeous little girl with lovely parents questioning deeply what on earth had this mother done to kidnap her own child and desert the marital home. He stayed with me for seemingly hours. I wept openly not understanding why this woman would desert the man who provided a lovely home, worked his heart out to give the very best of everything to his lady and child without question. Our lives had been harmonious, full and pleasurable with travel and the ocean which all of us loved dearly. There had been some normal up's and down's, as most couples have. Tensions with business related issues, the recent betrayal of friends making me angry. But any anger had never been directed at my family. It was my rule. The abuse of authorities recently was unforgivable, questioning why I was the one to pay the price? Tim's words soft and reassuring advising me to give my partner time to settle within herself and for me to leave the island as soon as I could for somewhere completely away from all this trauma. All I could think of was a call to my mother who needed to hear the news from me directly. She cried in despair saying, 'I knew it … I knew she was up to something really awful.' I told about what Dr Tim had advised and offered to get on the plane tonight and come to England. We could go to York together? I spoke with numbness well set in. Like some machine with its guts torn out I barely functioned rationally managing to close the business down with tape recorded voicemail on the phones about a 'family emergency' and found disbelieving friends to look after my dog. I called our closest friends who lived over in Little Blair Estate, my friend Andrew who I spent years diving and playing tennis with. Our ladies were close friends asking them if they knew of anything about the planned secret move. They too were shocked to the core that Natalie had been taken, for their little girls were close friends. The once beautiful family picture had been blown to pieces by a mother's selfish action. Coincidentally they too were booked on that evening's flight to London for a holiday in the UK. 'Come join us on the flight!' they exclaimed. I did just that. Sleep was out of the question. The dark hours of droning across the Atlantic aboard BA's Speedbird seemed endless and the morning decent through the grey skies of England were very apropos for my temperament. My friends were very supportive and their kindness softened the ordeal fractionally.

Walking toward UK Immigration I spied Sue who was an airport employee at the time standing behind a barrier to escort me through the terminal. The officer at the end of my cue was a tall smartly dressed Sikh Immigration Officer sporting a maroon turban. I handed him my passport that he studied for several seconds before exclaiming in the deepest cockney accent I had heard in years, 'How long you stayin' then?' I was taken aback by both question and accent, not expecting either with my entry back to my country of birth with a British passport! 'As long as I like officer,' I replied curtly not having an ounce of patience with Immigration officials after the mess in Nassau. 'You don't live 'ere so I'll give ya three weeks!' his reply. Sue was visibly giving the 'zip-it' sign behind meaning I could be in for a battle had I pursued. My mother waited outside the terminal at Heathrow and she cried on seeing me walk toward her. Our two lives so abused by the actions of another. We drove to the small Thames-side cottage and had tea outside; it was June and noticeably cool. Mother spoke of a call from our close friends the Hirschorn family telling them what happened. Her best friends' husband Alan had set up a day for me at Wimbledon knowing my love of the game. Being host of the casino here had fabulous connections with all the concierges around the planet. I was to have lunch with the players of Centre Court. He was always very kind to us and offered all the help he could in providing distraction from the horror of finding that empty home. Alan retired years later after working in Las Vegas and we tragically lost him to a brain tumour in 2015.

The days dragged by, with the day at Wimbledon really good medicine. The grandeur of the place came to life after I had watched the famous tennis facility on television all those years; enjoying the rants of McEnroe and Connors became so real when actually sitting there in Centre Court; the public's dress code very grand that June day, the champagne, strawberries and double Devon cream quite marvellous. Recent memory of the personal drama of my home life remained heavy on my mind those remaining days in England. We should have made the effort to venture north to York but neither mother or I could muster the emotional stamina to do so. We left early for a flight back to the warmth of Nassau and loving company of our faithful dog facing that house together to pick up the pieces.

Weeks crawled by having finally opened some communication with Natalie's mother, well-entrenched back in Quebec boasting how 'her daughter had learned to speak French fluently in just six weeks'. I learned later on arrival in Montreal no one would converse with my four-year-old girl in English save a few words sneaked from her grandmother. I could not imagine taking a child away from her family, her birthplace, her home, her school and friends to somewhere totally foreign, not speaking to her in the only language she knew. I was to learn about cruelty and deceit in more ways than I had ever encountered at boarding school. The lady who bore my child had emptied a joint bank account before her exit and under some pretence obtained a new birth certificate for our daughter in her mother's maiden name with birthplace forged as Montreal, changing the spelling of her Christian name. All mention of her father eradicated. Natalie soon obtained a Canadian passport and then citizenship taking my name off all official records. Oh, how the wheel of time would come back to bite those actions. Then came the last straw of applying in Quebec for sole custody; the fight was on with arduous legal battles and horrendous expenses just beginning. I learned about that thin line between love and hate being sucked repeatedly through the court system for over ten years, in sheer principle not backing down at any cost. Hiring a well-known legal firm in Montreal I flew to Canada laying claim to my daughter. It took thousands of dollars, months in time and emotional toll on my mother, my daughter and myself. I won my case and slowly, ever so slowly, regained some semblance of a relationship with my little girl.

Mother and I travelled in turn to escort Nat back to Nassau for holidays. She played with friends again enjoying the ocean she had grown to love. Jeff came when he could and gave us holidays in Aspen and Beaver Creek where Natalie could be seen racing down the ski slopes at the tender age of five and six. She dined in the finest restaurants in New York enjoying the views from the top of The World Trade Centre, a highlight being the helicopter ride around Manhattan and ballet at Lincoln Centre while I dated a fun loving corporate Israeli lawyer living on the Upper East Side. Natalie was back in our lives on a temporary basis for a few scant weeks at a time. The Quebec influence was hard and cold as ice. My lovely young lady took on semblances of her Quebec peers living most of the year in her new homeland. My warm, laughing and fun loving Bahamian baby was gone, for now.

Chapter 18
Lights, Camera, Action …

With flexibility in career and single status I took chances of travel offered by Jeff, easing the raw emotion of losing my family. The emptiness of a once vibrant household became a very stark and cold existence. I worked every chance I could and relieved when a ticket arrived from Texas to fill the void eager to explore new horizons. Our first film, *The Sharks of Stella Maris* had been planned for Long Island, sanctioned by Peter Kuska and Jorge Friese, owners of the renowned resort. Designated cameraman it was my privilege to enter the water first capturing the water entry of the divers from above. The dive boat anchored in forty feet of pristine water over a broken bottom of small coral heads and white sand patches, Bahamian water so clear one cannot stop gazing at it. Within seconds of the engines falling silent and the vessel tailing downwind several large reef sharks gathered at the stern, idly swimming a few feet under the surface. They knew it was dinnertime and their slow methodical swim pattern so close to the dive platform visually quite ominous with dorsal fins slicing effortlessly through the surface, a fun opening shot. Jeff assisted me with Scuba gear while standing on the rear platform waiting for a gap between the near dozen sharks now gathered.

'Go get 'em partner' Jeff said with a wry smile knowing that first step really intimidating. We had planned for me to have three minutes to descend, settle and position myself for the water entry shot. As I hit the water the reef sharks scattered for a split second and then regrouped around me through the descent. They looked magnificent with shining metallic steel-grey, torpedo efficient bodies moving faster in excitement through the crystal-clear water, mouths slightly agape allowing the salt-water to rush over their gills for oxygen. I touched the sand bottom with a puff of silt as if landing on the moon in a lunar lander. As I readied the video housing I spotted a huge shape barrelling toward me. The very familiar unmistakable large bull shark was headed toward my body at full steam as if some over bloated torpedo. I powered the video to life and held the housing firmly in front of my head aiming at the charging fish more for protection than capturing a really opportune few frames. Within milliseconds we collided very hard. Near eight feet of speeding shark smashed into the dome lens of the housing, coming to an instant halt nearly knocking it from my grip. Contact with its snout was hard with sensory cells concentrated here. Its huge body arched with the impact sending the two side pectoral fins downward as if speed brakes on an airliner wing. Hitting that round snout with rows of razor sharp teeth underneath sent an alarm through its sensory system turning the beast on its own axis to speed away. Looking through the eyepiece of the camera I noticed the abrasive skin of the shark had actually scarred the polished lens. We were now stuck shooting all the underwater scenes with a tiny scar well visible. I aimed upward and captured the divers step into the water. White foaming bubbles dissipated the silhouette shapes swam down toward my waiting lens. I kept the scene in motion with the dive master swimming toward the sand grasping a white bucket to place on the ocean floor between the grouped divers; no sooner the bucket touched the bottom it as if someone rang the dinner bell. The sharks went berserk into a feeding frenzy, a free-for-all to bite pieces of fish out of that small container. I eased forward on my knees within mere feet of the target, the viewfinder full of twisting fins, tails, bodies and teeth. Pieces of fish scattered all around me while huge gaping mouths filled the lens as they raced over the shoulders of this invading cameraman, knocking me from side to side in the commotion. Fifteen or more six to eight-foot-long sharks provided several minutes of exhausting action. The bucket suddenly emptied and their swimming instantly serene. Graceful bodies changed back to their slow-motion glide through the water as the spectacle wound down to absolute tranquillity. I shot several close-ups of Jeff and other divers along with other scenes of groupers feeding to tie the piece of film together allowing the story to unfold. We gave each other the 'ok' sign and swam gently to the surface. Hanging on to the platform our crew reached down for camera equipment and then removed dive tanks and weight belts.

'Wait 'til you see that opening scene Jeff!' I said with a laugh. 'Got rammed by a big bull and the film was rolling!'

'Oh Lordy!' Jeff followed through. 'Can't wait.'

The Sharks of Stella Maris was well received by the Discovery Channel and they gave us the go ahead for the rest of the *International Outdoorsman* series. We played a part of television history with this feature creating a series that continues today known as *Shark Week*.

With approaching winter the business was flourishing between cold fronts that screamed through the islands after leaving the Florida coast. Our weather patterns still predictable with Bill's house providing added opportunity to work during the northerly blows that previously would have been days lost. All we needed were blue skies to make the excursion work; sunshine was the key to success. I paid for the Whistler property in full and the house in Montagu looking an impressive property from road to road. Tragedy struck again without warning taking my mother and I down for the emotional count once more. Back in the days of mother's Rose Lane apartment I had surprised her with a purchase from England to keep her company. A top breeder in the UK had bred the winner of Cruft's International Dog Show producing a fabulous female Alsatian for sale. 'Journey' arrived on British Airways one afternoon. I went out to the airport to collect her not believing the size of this three-month-old puppy, already bigger than an English Cocker Spaniel. Moving into Montagu this fabulous animal actually stopped traffic in admiration as it passed. Fruit finally stayed on the citrus trees I had planted year's earlier inviting theft over our wall at any given time. Now a hundred pounds of Alsatian flew down the garden causing thieves to become instant Olympic champions in high jump over the wall topped with razor-wire onto the safety of Montagu Avenue.

Our thoughtless neighbours decided to combat their growing rat problem baiting their back garden without informing those of us with animals next door. One dying vermin managed to carry a piece of bait through the chain link fence allowing our beautiful animal to pick up. It took all night for the poison to corrode her intestines. In the morning, my mother, distraught, called me over to find our dog huddled under the shrubbery having found her place to die. I carried her inside the apartment and called Patrick Balfe. He checked her over and seeing the sadness in his face knew we were too late. 'Damn these inconsiderate stupid bastards!' he exclaimed as the precious life slipped away. I buried our beautiful friend in the back garden of Montagu under a full tangerine tree. My mother was drained with sadness and alone once more. 'No more dogs Paul, I can't go through this again, that's two we have loved and lost'. I watched my mother sit many a day in sad silence of that apartment knowing we could only last so long before four-legged friends would again nourish our spirit.

Filming with Jeff was indeed an adventure not be turned down, but my business would suffer as result of closure while I gallivanted all over the planet shooting video, the price of self-employment and a one-man-band sometimes a high toll to pay. Needing to find help I approached Steve Kemp having known from work with Ray Claridge partnered with his father Jude in the years of Claridge Enterprises in Nassau Village. Working closely together I showed Steve the ropes about running a day-charter boat service. He was a quieter, more private man but very qualified to drive the Bertram, a man of the sea and great in the water soon learning the art of cooking a great bar-b-q. Guests liked him and it gave me chance to escape the island pursuing a side-line career while keeping the income flowing.

In the heart of the winter months Jeff had two productions he wanted to finish. He called from his Beaumont home.

'Paul we have two great invites. One is in a submerged lead mine in Bonn Terre Missouri that has become a real hotspot for divers. The attraction of this place no matter the time of year the water temperature stays at fifty-eight degrees. We will descend down into the rock formation chambers 400 feet below the ground and then enter the water. When the mine closed and the pumps silent it flooded with a million gallons of fresh water. Time has stood still down there and the fun part is you will be following in the footsteps of Cousteau who was the last cameraman they allowed into the deep chambers. 'Those are big footsteps to follow in my friend, how do we get around down there?' I asked excitedly.

'Good question, they have a full dive facility in the main chamber with full lighting and platforms featuring rows of underwater scooters like those in *Thunderball* you used!'

He added, 'You'll need your woollies again because we are headed to Deer Valley in Utah with a fabulous invitation from the 1952 Norwegian Olympic Champion Stein Eriksen to come stay at his ski lodge for a week!'

My film career was certainly off and running with Jeff offering chances of directing when chance arose. Many of the action scenes I was able to hone from imagining new angles of filming to push the daring side of camera technique.

We arrived in Missouri with a hefty snowstorm in full swing, needing to shoot the first scene immediately having director credits on this production – a scene so surreal not to be lost with possible weather changes the next day; opening footage of divers carrying their tanks over the shoulder to approach a cave entrance in the blowing snow during darkness was too good to miss. It came out beautifully. We did dive as planned the next morning, descending carefully down flights of stairs cut into the stone over four hundred feet below ground visually stunning.

In magnificent panorama, the huge cavern opened before us where voices carried in booming echoes across the rock faces. The scene resembled a James Bond movie set where immense walls of stone rose out of the dark still waters with artificial lighting enhancing the cavern's beauty. Mysterious tunnels disappeared into the background begging to be explored. A huge wooden deck had been constructed just above water level at the base of the steps where impressive rows of underwater scooters lie waiting for us. All our dive equipment and lighting was neatly displayed with heavy wetsuits to keep us warm in the fifty-eight-degree fresh water. We were introduced to our hosting crew who went through their safety procedures asking what methods I would like to incorporate in to my video shooting. Setting up all the camera equipment took little time having been prepped the night before. For those of us used to the warm water diving in the Bahamas climbing into heavy wetsuits complete with hoods a new experience. The amount of weight we had to wear daunting to the usual six or eight pounds of lead we normally carried to compensate the buoyancy we were about to experience.

Ready for the water entry, the cameraman once again had the pleasure of the first plunge in order to capture the rest of the teams entry and descent. Acting as director I also went through the action techniques I needed each man to perform while making the descent and the exploration of the mineshafts. I stepped off the platform, instantly covered in the cold crystal clear water of the mine. Shocking chill slides through narrow spaces beneath my suit. My body takes a couple of minutes to heat that thin layer, a dramatic change to the warmth of the Exuma Cays. I am suspended in outer space, dark liquid giving way to a feeling of utter weightlessness. I dump air from my buoyancy compensator, sinking in a free fall to about forty feet downward, camera aiming vertically I signal the crew to step forward. A mass of white foam appears with dark silhouettes of frogmen looking spectacular in the cavern lighting above; the scooters follow hoisted into the water by the surface crew. We climb aboard our machines resembling the familiar 007 motion picture set shot in 1964 at Lyford Cay Bay diving in single file with beams of torchlight leading the way downward into the pitch-blackness. Time certainly stood had still in a moment it seemed.

One could imagine the sounds from below echoing through the tunnels of rock. Mine equipment rumbling on rails, men shouting instructions to each other over the din of drilling. Hammers hitting steel as it shatters solid rock. Their tools now lay where they dropped them that last day frozen in history. Motionless trollies intact, still mounted on rails of shiny steel rusting brown over decades. The massive iron framework of the shaft elevators beautifully draped in delicate shards of orange rust, held in suspension having succumbed to years of submergence looming out of the black waters. I descended to about eighty feet allowing me to capture the beautiful vista looking vertically upward as motorised divers eerily darted across the scene in dramatic silhouette their exhaling breath streaming bright silver bubbles against the lighting of the caverns overhead while the main shaft disappeared in perfect perspective.

That first dive we filmed the necessary POV, point-of-view shots required to tie the story together. Our hosts had been watching us vigilantly assuring them our expertise sufficient enough to allow the next adventure through deep space and solid rock way below the earth's surface. The horizontal mineshafts connecting the tunnels offered no hint of illumination from above. Without lighting we were in absolute blackness, encased near 500 feet underground. I was the second underwater cameraman to record this fantastic voyage through a tomb set in inner space. Diligent to not stir the silt from the floor of the tunnel, I swam ahead of my team and turned to signal them approach and swim past me. Only the straight white beams of torchlight showed the yellow wetsuits of our submerged astronauts looming out of the void. At the end of the long passageway we suddenly entered a vast underwater cavern lit by the Bonn Terre crew. The surface sparkled from above beckoning us to rise and wonder at the scene displayed all around us, magnificent stalagmites and stalactites climbed and descended from the walls of rock. Eons of time had rainwater from the heavens creep through the earth's surface finally dripping to the floor of endless caverns underground, their tiny particles of sediment eventually building these stunning monuments.

The mid-eighties saw financial security set well in for the first time in my self-created business life. It came however with heavy prices. Self-employment demands a mind set of dedication and relentless pressures of presenting the product to the very best of one's ability at all times, it takes years to build a reputation and moments to lose; in the public entertainment sector there are no real days off, weekends blend into the week, time off becomes scarce. Stark reality dictated *I* had become the product. That quiet boarding school lad long faded from the scene, replaced with a self-confident teacher and host of Nassau's leading, award-winning, small group day charter business. My success came with the belief in the product I had to work with. Who could not absolutely *love* being out on the ocean exploring gorgeous beaches for the day and actually being paid for it; swimming, spearfishing, cooking a bar-b-q over an open fire and teaching visitors how to dive for the first time? This kind of canvas would give anyone the needed confidence rich in the reward of watching and hearing positive remarks from people of all walks of life who never before experienced such sights. Friends and visitors made similar remark about 'how lucky I was to have a job like this', failing to visualise what lay behind the scenes for those of us who created these playful tours. The hours were arduous, the work and pressure of responsibility of making it all work in utmost safety overbearing at times. As business owners, we had mortgages, school fees, boat, car and equipment maintenance: we had created the vicious cycle of success. The days often relentless where the only time off duty were those in which the weather turned really sour, confining us indoors, difficult to bear. I belonged outside, in the sunshine with the sound of water thrown by my wake; I held firmly to the familiar adage 'make hay while the sun shines'. It was hard for a family structure to function 'normally' under these conditions. Work became God. With most of us who were self-employed, the draw of making our career the number one priority a very easy pitfall to be drawn to, a two-edged sword making sure recipe for failure in some form or other. Weekends normally were family time spent together but work the great distractor. That telephone kept ringing and the tour desks loved the feedback. The frenzy of producing ploughed on through the weeks into years.

Those of us who pioneered the day-charter businesses soon found every man and his dog seemingly jump on the bandwagon. Local Bahamians tended to copy rather than originate. Tour desk operators noting our sales formed their own tours creating monopolies. Large boats came on the scene calling themselves 'booze-cruises'. Sales could boom one week and stop overnight. On investigation soon found the wonderful world of corruption had leached into our way of life. Some operators chose to bribe sales girls behind the tour desks with round trip tickets to Miami or colour televisions for the most sales in a week or month. Those of us who did not partake suffered sudden silence in our telephones. Business would come to a trickle. Desks still charging 20% commission on sales forcing us to raise prices with rising operational costs. We formed an association with the hopes of creating some semblance of unity and agreement about behaviour, the original dream corroding rapidly away with the influence of corruption. There were a handful of us, mostly the originators of the outdoor entertainment, refusing flatly to pay under the table. I maintained the lead still the most expensive day-trip on the market at $48, proving way too under-priced in the Caribbean market where similar tours were selling for at least $75. No one saw fit to raise the standard in the Bahamas while facing monopolies able to produce larger volume. When unscrupulous operators started removing our literature from the hotels at night I resorted to a new form of advertising in local tourist newspapers where bookings and inquires could only be completed with us directly. With these new ads and my faithful following at time-share units around Nassau and Paradise Island we barely stayed ahead but the writing was on the wall. I felt the time to change careers just lay ahead.

In the midst of the changes two other events altered the course of everything I had believed dealing with trust. Through communication with my daughter and her grandmother in Montreal I learned that Natalie's mother had resumed a relationship with her Canadian boyfriend and given him a daughter. Their life however not turning out as planned with their relationship soon failing after the birth. I learned whispers of regrets and wishes to reunite. Overpowered by the emotion of having my family back intact and unable to see a possible manipulation I travelled to Montreal to see where all those stories lay. Naivety took hold and I bonded again with Natalie's mother. This time I would offer more security in marriage with me now a

Bahamian citizen. My mother was well pleased having us united again with the added pleasure of another granddaughter who we took as if our own. The pages of life unfolded back in the islands and hurt put aside for new beginnings with two small girls entering St. Andrews school.

The Bahamas Kennel Club called having given my name from our vet explained how they had mistakenly donated two German Shepherd dogs to the Royal Bahamas Police Force, admitting their young history not fully explored beforehand. They were two brothers about three years old raised by a loving family in the States suddenly thrust into the hands of Bahamian policemen thinking they could 'make them vicious attack dogs'. The atrocious training methods had the animals beaten incessantly in ignorant cruel attempt to change their temperament, beatings where one of the brothers suffered internal damage discovered later. The force decided 'they were useless', requesting the Kennel Club take them back finding a more suitable home. I drove to Police Headquarters in Oakes Field asking the sergeant to bring them both to me. He explained one was much stronger than the other and potentially a better dog yet I may pick which one I liked. From two separate cages the two Alsatians came out to greet me. Having not seen each other in weeks the two dogs went berserk to be together again. I opened the big station wagon rear door saying, 'put them both in there'! With all the rear seats folded they leapt inside without hesitation lying down instantly, eyes bright with excitement, tails wagging.

'Let me wire them up for you,' the sergeant exclaimed.

'Why would you do that?' I queried as the two beautiful animals watched me intently.

'To keep them in place, they may not sit like that when you are driving? I also have to tell you Mr. Harding these dogs are so useless they don't even bark!'

'I tell you what Sergeant, you come to Montagu heights a week from now to my back gate on Montagu Avenue for a look see?'

He laughed, 'ok, will do' he promised as I shut the rear door. A week later he did show up at the back gate met by two very loud barking Alsatians trying to eat him through the heavy wire. It was good to have animals again.

The years in this new decade saw President Ronald Reagan, a former Hollywood movie star elected in 1980, holding talks with the new regime of Mikhail Gorbachev. Reagan gave a famous speech asking the soviets to 'tear down this wall' and in 1989 maybe the most noted event of the decade occurred with the fall of the Berlin Wall. The soviet city of Chernobyl came into our daily lives in 1986 with the nuclear meltdown of its facility making an eerie ghost town for scores of miles. At the beginning of this changing decade the first personal computer from IBM was introduced in 1981. Wars in the Middle East were raging with Iran and Iraq losing over a million people. The new 'Holy Wars' raising their ugly heads with Islamic extremists haunting us through history to the day I write this biography and beyond. The word 'jihad' entered our vocabulary to stay. In 1985 we hear names such as Abu Nidal supported by Libya attacking El Al airlines in Rome and Vienna. In 1983, the barracks in Beirut bombed with two trucks loaded with high explosives killing 299 American servicemen, an organisation calling itself Islamic Jihad claiming responsibility. George Orwell's 1984 saw unrest in India after the assassination of Indira Gandhi by a Sikh militant. Hindu militants rioted killing thousands displacing untold thousands of Sikhs. Canada did not escape the wrath when Sikh-Canadians in June of 1985 destroyed Air India flight 182. It became the largest mass murder in Canadian history. Another famous airliner became tragic history on December 21 1988, with the loss of Pan-Am flight 103 blown up over Lockerbie, Scotland having left Heathrow for New York killing all 270 people from twenty-one nations. Commercial air travel would be changed forever.

We witnessed the flights of the first space shuttle 'Columbia' from Cape Canaveral. This massive spacecraft inching upward in the first few seconds off the launch pad in a mass of orange flame and an Earth-shaking roar, a vehicle that would return safely to Earth later landing either on the Cape in Florida or California mounted on the top of a Boeing 747 weighing in total about 488,000 pounds for transport back to the Cape; aviation of this sort very surreal out of science fiction memories.

The morning of January 28 1986 was one of those days once again where you knew exactly where you were on hearing the awful news from Cape Canaveral that very chilly crystal clear day. Seventy-three seconds into flight of the space shuttle 'Challenger' there was a sudden catastrophic explosion disintegrating the entire spacecraft. We watched news broadcasts earlier in that week highlighting the first schoolteacher to ride into space. Christa McAuliffe was to teach lessons from outer space to her class back in America. An O-ring in the right booster rocket failed due to the extreme cold blue Florida morning. I was outside the British Colonial Hotel driving through town after undertaking a brochure run to the hotels on Cable Beach. The car radio came alive with a special broadcast. The effect numbing while sitting in traffic uncomprehending the loss of all seven crew on board the shuttle. Reaching home, I watched replay upon replay of the horror that unfolded. The school teacher's parents bundled up in warm clothes staring upward, exhaled breath very visible watching their daughter soar off the launch pad then questioning the massive white cloud that ensued above them in the bright blue sky not understanding what they just saw.

The brittle O-ring allowed pressurised burning gas from within the solid rocket motor to sear its way into the massive external fuel tank. The spacecraft had travelled down-range from its launch site over the Atlantic Ocean. Pieces of wreckage eventually recovered from the ocean floor after a lengthy search and recovery operation. The exact timing of the death of the crew is unknown; several crewmembers are known to have survived the initial breakup of the spacecraft. The shuttle had no escape system, and impact of the crew compartment hitting the ocean surface too violent to be survivable.

President Ronald Reagan ordered a though investigation with The Rogers Commission finding later NASA's organisational culture and decision-making processes key contributing factors to the accident. Managers had known about contractor Morton Thiokol's design containing potentially catastrophic flaws in the O-rings since 1977, failing to address them properly. They disregarded warnings with a fever of 'go for launch now' from engineers fearing low temperatures of that morning while failing to adequately report these technical concerns to their superiors. The disaster resulted in a 32-month shut down of the shuttle program where the Commission report did not highlight the vehicle ever certified to operate in temperatures that low.

It was as if the world was going mad at an elevated level. The Soviets were entrenched against the Mujahedeen in Afghanistan, the United States invaded the small island nation of Grenada triggered by a military coup; the war in El Salvador reached its peak in the 80s taking the life of over 70,000 El Salvadorans. Israel invaded Lebanon in response to an assassination attempt on its ambassador to the UK, occupying Southern Lebanon. Iraq's Saddam Hussein is accused of using chemical weapons against Iran and his own Kurdish people while America carries out an aerial bombardment of Libya in 1986 in retaliation for attacks in Germany and Turkey. The news spews on about the Iran-Contra Affair spurred by the US intervention in Nicaragua resulting in members of the US Government indicted in the same year; stunning pictures on television from Tiananmen Square in China in 1989 with pro-democracy demonstrations crushed quickly by The Peoples Liberation Army, a lone soul standing defiantly in front of a military tank is fixed upon our memory. In the Caribbean, Haitian dictator, Jean-Claude Duvalier is overthrown by a public uprising on February 6 1986. Africa has trouble spots in Nigeria with multiple military coups whereas in South Africa the long-standing border war with Angola, Zambia and Namibia comes to an end.

Mother nature showed us her extraordinary powers in May 1980 with the spectacular eruption of Mount St. Helens in Washington State, killing fifty-seven people and destroying thousands of acres of natural beauty. At the end of the 80s while Game 3 of the World Series was playing in San Francisco, the Loma Prieta earthquake struck injuring thousands and killing sixty-five. Structural damage to gas lines, buildings, and highways mounted over $13 billion. Heat waves and droughts killed thousands in the United States while the Caribbean suffered terrible losses with major hurricanes, Allen, Alicia, Gilbert, Joan and Hugo decimating islands and yachting destinations.

Airlines suffer awful losses of flights during the 1980s. Dan-Air, Saudi, Pan-Am, Delta, Aero México, Arrow Air, Northwest, South African Airways, and August 12 1985 saw the worst single air accident with Japan Airlines Flight 123 losing 520 people. The most remarkable saving of life came with United Airlines flight 232 carrying 269 people experiencing an in-flight engine failure forcing a crash landing in Sioux City, Iowa. On July 19 1989 United's DC-10 suffered a catastrophic failure of its rear tail-mounted engine. Eighty-five minutes into flight pieces of the engine severed the hydraulic system of the aircraft resulting in loss of flight controls. The flight crew commanded by Captain Alfred Haynes, first officer William Records and Dudley Dvorak as flight engineer feeling an explosion in the rear of the aircraft. After notifying the passengers of the engine failure, passenger and off-duty DC-10 training captain, Denny Fitch went up front to offer assistance in managing the failing aircraft using differential throttle adjustment. The plane could only be steered to the right not left. This kind of emergency was unprecedented taking all of the cockpit crew to keep the plane flying for more than forty minutes while trying to find some solution as to how to land. Later investigation revealed a lack in maintenance procedure should have noticed minute cracking in the fan-disk due to impurities in manufacture. High speed shrapnel hurled from the spinning engine penetrated all three of the independent hydraulic systems aboard the airliner causing loss of control to nearly everything needed to fly the passenger jet. The crew however managed amazingly to maintain some semblance of control with the only two working systems left on board, the two remaining engines. By using each engine separately, they managed to hold a form of steering and rough ability to maintain altitude. With emergency procedures in full force the crew guided the crippled jet to Sioux City Gateway Airport lining up with turns in one direction only to the approach runway. Without flaps or slats they managed to slow the airliner down for landing, but not slow enough for safe arrival; their approach would be at 250 knots descending at 1600 feet per minute. They had only one shot at the approach and were too fast with a high rate of descent and inability to flare. The right wingtip touched the ground causing a cartwheel where the aircraft broke apart on touchdown and rolled over catching fire off the runway into a neighbouring cornfield. The ferocious crash allowed 185 souls to survive. All the cockpit crew also survived with serious injury. Both hospitals in Sioux City were in the middle of a shift change so fully staffed when the accident was reported. This tragedy resulted in the dramatic changes in design of the hydraulic systems aboard the DC-10 and its predecessors with changes in regulations about 'lap-infants' requiring seats of their own after a successful campaign from the chief flight attendant who survived the crash. Denny Fitch who managed the throttles of the McDonnell Douglas was injured but returned to flying duty with United Airlines later to be diagnosed with brain cancer in 2010, ending his life in May 2012. Captain Al Haynes tackled even more, losing a son to a motorcycle crash then his wife to a rare infection. His daughter needing a bone marrow transplant would not be covered sufficiently with insurance but hundreds of people, some from the airline crash and some from families who lost love ones on board that day, all donated over half a million dollars in her name. Seeing the amazing water landing in the Hudson River, Captain Haynes contacted 'Sully' Sullenberger expressing 'a kinship' with his fellow airline pilot saying, 'Wait until you are ready and then go back to work. You are a pilot. You should be flying'. Advice I too would also heed one day.

The ocean suffered a major ecological disaster in the late 80s. On March 24, 1989, with oil tanker Exxon Valdez running aground on Bligh Reef in Alaska's Prince William Sound spilling an estimated equivalent of 750,000 barrels of crude oil. Although not among the largest oil spills in history, its remote and sensitive location in the beautiful region of Alaska made it one of the most devastating ecological disasters. Thousands of wild birds and sea life animals were destroyed with scores of clean-up crews hired by Exxon costing the company millions lasting for years after.

The late 1980s saw a few more television film productions under my belt. Some made it on to the Discovery series and some stayed in the studio never finished. I travelled to the Red Sea, invited by my Israeli girlfriend touring through her country witnessing the magnificent streets of the Holy Land, the Wailing Wall and vibrant city of Tel Aviv, fascinated by the friendly interaction of Israelis and Palestinians living and working alongside each other in Jerusalem, selling their wares and eating together while their governments waged eternal war against one another. We drove across the border into Egypt at Sharm-el-Sheik to dive Ras-Muhammed. Stopping at small cafes in the desert it was commonplace seeing patrons sipping coffee with submachine guns placed on their tables. The Red Sea was not as warm but clear as we knew it in the Caribbean, corals predominantly of the hard species showing a definite lacking in the soft waving fans and massive sponges due to the noticeably high salt content. The dives were all underwater canyons, their ocean falling rapidly away from the shoreline into deep indigo water. We had to carry cumbersome equipment over long rocky pathways to enter the ocean. Washing off camera equipment took ages with the hot sun baking white crystals hard on the housings. I smiled seeing a famous photograph taken here of the schooling hammerhead sharks remembering it used in the book *Turning the Tide* about the 70s' drug cartel of Norman's Cay in the Bahamas, incorrectly saying these were the sharks found in Norman's Cay Pond!

British Honduras was very similar to the waters of the Bahamas, shooting film in Roatan. Noticeably missing were the large food chain fish such as snapper and groupers. The locals had decimated the fish with the legality of hookah rigs; floating compressors that the local divers manipulated to pump high volumes of air through expended hoses, allowing them to hunt the deep waters where large fish inhabited; their ignorance wiping out the adult egg-layers, leaving nothing for their futures. When this equipment began to appear in the windows of Bahama Divers for sale and legalised within our country I knew it was the beginning of the end for Bahamian waters. The Hondurans were paying a heavy price for their greed. A divers average life expectancy was less than thirty years old pushing boundaries of safe deep diving; their bodies often severely bent with nitrogen narcosis killing many from decompression sickness. As a film crew arriving in British Honduras our Producer was armed with a fistful of hundred dollar bills. I questioned Jeff about this and he smiled quietly asking me to 'watch and learn' about Central American corruption. Sure enough, the authorities, seeing all our equipment, immediately impounded it all saying we would have to provide certain documentation showing we could shoot a film production within the country. Jeff took the official to one side and with a heavy roll of currency sliding out of his pocket the equipment became suddenly available. Transportation outside the terminal not what we asked for having another roll produce just the vehicles we needed. It went on and on. Halfway through production the locals suddenly decided their wages were not sufficient. The corruption finally overflowed our producer's tolerance and in one swift sentence from Jeff, 'We are done here, wrap it up as we are going home!' We hired a Cessna 206 at the airport to get us out of Roatan back to the capital city of Belize in order to catch an American Airline flight to Houston. While loading the small aircraft the pilot with his impatience and lack of care shoved the tripod through the rear window sending a shower of shattered Perspex onto the tarmac. He was about to cancel the flight but another roll of hundred dollar bills persuaded him otherwise providing an interesting flight of rushing air whistling through the gaping hole as we passed over acres of banana plantations.

'That was interesting: no surprises with the Central Americans!' Jeff exclaimed on landing home. 'We'll do better with Utah but first we are going to throw you out of a perfectly good airplane 15,000 feet above Texas!' I just stared at him in disbelief.

My producer with all his wit had organised another story idea called *Dive If You Dare* involving those of us who knew each other in the underwater world of the Bahamas laying challenge to a skydiving school near Beaumont, Texas. We would let them throw us out of airplanes and while meeting our parachute instructors back in the Bahamas we would nudge them off a dive platform to awaiting sharks swimming below. The first parachute descent was tandem at near 15,000 feet. Being at the mercy of an expert that you are strapped to is not as terrifying as stepping outside an aircraft by one's self. That first free fall was very exhilarating, watching the altimeter on our arms unwinding rapidly as we fell toward the earth at 125-feet-per-second, the explosion of the chute opening and the glide to Earth something to experience. Classroom training followed and afterward suited with our own chutes. The climb to altitude in the Cessna 206 took forever, about 7500 feet, with hearts jumping out of our chests. Again, the cameraman gets the first honour. I was instructed out on to the step of the aircraft holding on to the wing strut, this time truly frightened. 'What the bloody hell have I got myself into this time?' I muttered. My mouth was parch-dry, heart thumping and adrenalin racing through my body. This was surely the most insane act I was about to perform. The Cessna pilot slowed just above stall speed, the air still rushing past me faster than any motorcycle I had been on. The landscape seemed miles away below, fields appearing very small in their patchwork on the Texas floor. Jeff and the others watched in silence as the instructor raised his arm for me to ready myself to release the strut and fall away. His arm fell and my fingers didn't move a millimetre. He raised it again and again it fell. I said, 'yes' to myself but my hand stayed firmly locked on the metal structure of the plane. I could not make myself let go of that strut. He raised a third time and yelled 'You got to go, Paul'. So, with another muttering of 'fuck it' to myself, I suddenly saw my ride disappearing above me as I fell earthward instantly not believing I had jumped out of a perfectly functioning aircraft! The small radio strapped to my chest came to life and the chute opened. They were talking to me from the ground telling me which way to steer downward to my landing zone. Suddenly the ride was pure fun. Silence and floating as I drifted downward turning the chute exactly where I needed to be; the fields, growing larger by the second and aerodrome clearly visible almost beneath me. The ground rushing upward as I could hear 'flare, flare, flare!' from my radio; I pull down hard on the rigging to land while lifting my knees with a comfortable thud on the turf letting out a hoot of exhilaration and incredible relief to find myself still standing upright.

'Great job Paul!' my young instructor praised as I watched Jeff come down with the same look of expertise. We laughed and joked about what a rush one feels with this new sport. I could see where the expression 'adrenalin junkie' came from. I watched my other instructors pack their chutes as if casually packing a bag of clothing. In what seemed minutes we reloaded the Cessna for a second time where smiling stopped once again during the take-off roll and climb skyward: this feeling of dread returning all too quickly. It felt as if standing on the outside ledge of the tallest skyscraper looking down toward the street below. That strange sensation in the pit of your stomach; I am not normally afraid of heights. Sitting on the lip of the Grand Canyon, perched on the edge of a huge boulder with feet dangling into space was a piece of cake compared to this. The second dive went as the first with only two delays before I let go of my ride. The third leap out changed in a second. The parachute was tangled with the rigging spiralled close together. 'Oh shit, here we go,' I dismayed out loud to myself, looking upward to see my canopy fluttering in a bunched up mess; the rushing air quite noisily through the fabric against a stunning blue sky as background. The radio attached to my chest remained silent. Without panic, to my surprise, I realised it was only up to me to sort this sad situation out with simple logic. The lines all showed a twist in the same direction. I immediately made myself spin around in the harness in the opposite direction to the twist and watch in amazement as the lines untangled and the chute fly open in beautiful array. The radio came to life with typical Texas humour.

'Shit Paul, we thought you were going to be our first PP?' On landing safely, I asked what the hell a PP was? Out here we call them 'Pancake Person!' my instructor laughed.

'Enough of that shit, Jeff Hughes, this island boy is going back to his sharks!'

I returned to the Bahamas resuming my normal way of living before another airline ticket arrived taking me to Salt Lake City in the winter months. I met Jeff for the drive into the mountains of Utah and a famous ski resort called 'Deer Valley'. It was a blizzard and he asked me to drive, a Bahamian fresh from the island trying to manoeuvre blindly in a white out. Our hosts were Stein Eriksen, wife Francois and young son Bjorn. Stein was a very elegant gentleman with that familiar 'sing-song' Norwegian accent still very present. He was the first male alpine skier outside the Alps to win an Olympic Gold Medal in the giant slalom during the Winter Games of 1952 and again three gold medals in the 1954 World Championships. He moved to America with a career instructing in Sun Valley, Idaho also in the states of Michigan, Vermont, California and Colorado. In 2007 he celebrated his eightieth birthday in Deer Valley. Watching Stein descend the mountain is sheer poetry in motion. Only his nine-year-old son Bjorn able to emulate his fathers unique style of snow skiing. Our host met us in the lounge of the lodge offering a warm welcome with gracious hospitality offering every facility the establishment could to offer in order to produce a first-rate documentary about the resort bearing his name. I learned that Stein Eriksen died 27th December 2015 aged eighty-eight at his home in Park City, Utah.

Our rooms were suites and the food exquisite. Deer Valley is a fully groomed resort with all qualification of ski runs available from the widest of 'blue' to the trickiest of 'black' runs. Our host provided snow-cat and heli-skiing taking us to the far slopes of Utah's finest scenery. We filmed children learning the skill for the first time and enjoyed the warm hospitality of all the instructors at our beck and call. I was given directorship of this production and well pleased the footage we captured during some pristine days on the slopes of Deer Valley. The show again well received on Discovery Channel.

Life was taking on a celebrity surreal atmosphere. Flitting from country to country with new adventures at every turn only to come home and roost in our wonderful Bahama archipelago. Life was blessed but changes were imminent.

Chapter 19
'You ordered *what* ...!!?'

By 1989 the writing was on the wall about our future in the day-charter boat business. Gone were the beautiful days of cruising to Rose Island, passing the classic magnificence of the schooner *Keewatin*, hailing King Ingraham and his lady Ushi on their houseboat full of patrons spending a day on 'Treasure Island'; a wave to Randy and Eryn anchored with their guests off the first beach on Rose Island, some snorkelling off the stern. Gone were days able to spearfish the abundant sea life under the surface. It appeared today as if an armada headed out of Nassau Harbour each morning to invade the peaceful little islands a few miles to the Northeast. Corruption was rampant and the quality of the products deteriorating; large crowds of visitors packed aboard vessels like cattle, subjected to loud offensive music mutilating the quiet of a Bahama day. I overheard a tour desk representative telling an inquiring visitor holding my brochure 'this trip was boring because there was no music'! Bahamian culture, in the boat business and public events it seemed, only deemed things 'fun' if one was continuously bombarded with noise so loud you could barely hear yourself speak accompanied with as much cheap alcohol as one could consume. During a recent stay in the islands at the new Melia Hotel on Cable Beach that theory still played out all the way into 2014. While enjoying the tranquillity of a clear picture perfect Bahamian morning listening to the small waves breaking gently against the pristine sand, green palms set against a power blue sky, the pool deck suddenly erupted into the blare of loud music from huge speakers mounted on the terrace above. It was incessant and abrasive, lasting for hours until late afternoon. The local staff disregarded our plea to 'turn it down'. We left the island in disgust knowing the 'good old days' of that tasteful steel band gently playing over the grounds of the Nassau Beach were long gone. Even on private property up at Rose Island leasing the hilltop weekend house from Captain Bill Pemberton, other visitors from neighbouring 'cattle trucks' encroached our peace and quiet. With Bill operating an identical 28-foot Bertram, the sister ships could easily transport thirty or more guests each day. Visitors still loved our day especially after passing the over-crowded party boats, expressing relief they had not been booked on this kind of day. The costs however were climbing where I was lucky to produce near $10 per person in profit. Similar excursions in todays' market are priced near $140 per person! With workloads higher and rewards lower, the process for change was imminent.

It was a bright clear day and while out at the island I spot a small float-plane fly overhead. I could not escape my gaze upward. A spark of delight rushed through me with a fun idea becoming very clear in an instant. Aviation, an idea that had been dormant from a young boy, was indeed alive and well. Wanting desperately to pursue a flying career since finishing school in Sussex, along with my father not budging in support of entering his career. 'It's fools game' is all he could add to my pursuit and refusal to offer any financial assistance in attending flight school. The subject with him was closed, not spoken of again. Making an aviation career self-happen at this early stage seemed impossible so decided to make 'going down' another fun alternative way of making a living; here we were, seventeen years later in 1989, opportunity finally knocking. It had been near the end of this decade when a young couple staying at the Sonesta Beach Hotel had booked a day's excursion with scuba diving included. On picking them up Colin and I became another instantaneous friendship. With his sharp wit and zest for having outdoor fun I learned he was a flight instructor. After I taught him to 'go down' he responded with an offer to teach me how to 'go up' by hiring a Piper Arrow from the local Flying Club now based at Windsor Field. Fizzing at low altitude down the whole length of Eleuthera he smiled with satisfaction saying, 'you have the touch my friend, go do it!'

Without hesitation I implemented my two personal philosophies; 'as opportunity races past my window I will reach out and grab life whatever the consequences', and 'make a living from something you love to do'. Most times it had paid off with huge dividends, rarely landing me in a heap of trouble. To not at least try was chance lost. From the sale of my property in Whistler, British Columbia, I was able to double my investment. Canadian taxation on vacant land was high unlike our laws in the islands where it tax-free. Building had begun on that gorgeous mountainside showing clearly I was way out of my league with extravagant log homes under construction worth three quarters of a million dollars or more. Twice in life I recognised this dilemma knowing to exit without hesitation. My property sold quickly allowing funds to return into my savings account with handsome profit paying the purchase price of a factory new seaplane.

My two friends in the Exumas, Marcus and Rosie Mitchell, who owned Sampson Cay Marina both flying Maule seaplanes often carried on the top deck of their salvage vessel *Sampson*. Rosie, I had known since childhood, walking the docks of the Nassau Yacht Haven, saying good morning to her father Captain Lou Kennedy with wife and three young daughters living on board. The freckly one was my favourite! Marcus was acting agent for the Maule family and offered help with the purchase of my new aircraft adding, 'It is without doubt the safest airplane you could find and perfect to configure as a seaplane!' After guiding me through all the specifications that I would need in a floatplane I wrote a cheque for $85,000.00. Never in wildest imagination could I have envisioned being able to pen to paper for such an amount; from not having sufficient coins to buy the local newspaper to buying a brand-new plane, a day never to forget. My mother knew immediately upon entering her apartment something was brewing by her son's radiating demeanour. With a wry smile on my face trying to act nonchalant I suddenly announced,

'Mum, I just ordered an airplane!'

'*Ordered?*' she nearly choked on the word. 'You mean as in *'new'?*' She added in real shock, the colour fading from her face.

'Yup, a brand-new seaplane!' I touted proudly.

'*A seaplane!*' she almost hollered. 'But you don't know how to fly!' her stammering English accent reaching crescendo.

'I know. While the plane is being built I am off to Florida to take lessons and get my license!'

'Oh dear God!' she slumped in her reclining chair as if the air suddenly emptied her lungs. 'I knew one day you would do something with airplanes, it's been in your blood since a little chap!' 'What about the business?' she pleaded defensively.

I explained that November was 'out of season', a quiet time of the year and had offered my close friend Gary and his wife chance to make some extra money while they too were on holidays from their jobs. Gary had his own boat for years and I knew that between both entertaining tourists for a day would be an easy and enjoyable task. They were a little strapped for income so the arrangement very welcome and our business would not have to shut down. My mother would continue taking reservations and preparing the food for the day. They would return later that evening with the income where splitting the profits all would be satisfied. I had researched flight schools finding a small organisation run by an American couple in Rockledge, Florida near Cape Canaveral. I could live on site and the fees very reachable, costing under $3000 for a Private Pilot's License. During my stay I would progress over to Winter Haven where staying at a famous seaplane base on Lake Jessie I could pass the additional rating for flying floats.

Within a couple of days Marcus was in Nassau stopping by the house to confirm the order with the factory in Moultrie, Georgia, just north of the Florida border. My mother immediately put him on the mat asking in a mock stern voice bathed in pronounced English dialect:

'What have you got my son into, Marcus Mitchell?'

He smiled saying calmly with all the charisma he could muster,

'This will change his life Mrs. Harding! He will be just fine. Boat captains like us make great seaplane pilots.' After he left I talked more with my mother about my plans to change the business completely, a dream seeded long ago.

'I have been beating my brains out for seventeen years, Mum, it's been a load of fun for the most part but it's not what it was when we first got off the ground. We have won awards and made some money, enough to buy houses and boats and land and planes and motorcycles! It costs us a fortune to run twenty or more visitors up to the island taking home only a few dollars per person. With a plane, I need only take four passengers to make more income than it did with twenty. Time for something new and I feel sure people will pay me to take them flying through the Exumas for the day?'

Being of that generation where things were more set in their ways, the thought of giving up on an established business sent an element of fear running through her. It was easy to see her point of view. We had come from literally nothing to heights never dreamt of. To let go of it now must have provoked a real fear. I had no such thought, only positive vision that a day excursion flying over the most beautiful part of our country could only succeed? To soften the blow, I explained that all this would take time; I would need to build the hours required for a Commercial Rating while applying for a local business license in aviation.

I knew the seaplane owners on Lake Cunningham and in the Exumas, privately owned aircraft, some making occasional income but none holding the commercial license needed to run a fully-fledged legitimate operation. We would be the first in the country and located in Nassau would be all too visible under the authority's scrutiny, especially operating from busy Nassau Harbour. Our neighbour in Montagu Heights, Bertram Knowles, who we had known for years as tennis pro here in the capital at the once stately Montagu Beach Hotel, ventured recently into the restaurant business with a waterfront cafe called 'Coconuts', a property next to Sir Roland Symonette's house on the harbour. It had a small beach near forty feet wide perfectly fitting a ramp for a seaplane. Bertram was excited about having an additional tenant and one offering such an attraction while his patrons dined overlooking the water. With the aircraft ordered and paid for and location it was to be kept now in place, all that was needed was me get qualified to fly the thing, and lest I should forget, permission from the Bahamian authorities to fly it within the islands out of a harbour location. Minor details I thought with amusement, maybe putting cart before the horse?

Ahead I would need to conquer the Civil Aviation Authority, the CAA, along with the local Port Authority and, compounding the issue further, involving the FAA from the States. Three bureaucracies to tackle at one time would prove quite the challenge. No one had ever ventured into this territory with a light aircraft operation where almost immediately I met resistance. Members of the CAA here in the Bahamas were tied in affiliation with Civil Aviation in the UK, back in 1989 comprising of British representatives as well as local Bahamian CAD management that I had to persuade to allow me permission for a commercial business license. The aircraft was to be under American registration making an easier market to sell later complicating the issue involving the FAA for my maintenance program. The paperwork would prove a daunting challenge reaching nightmarish proportion for any neophyte entering this game.

Armed with a mountain of statistics from the Seaplane Pilots Association supporting the idea of commercial operations found in Canada, Australia and Alaska; countries where seaplanes were the local lifeline water taxi holding exemplary safety records, I ventured before a panel of Civil Aviation management officials with rules in the Bahamas to date stating only twin-engine aircraft should operate a commercial business with single engine planes deemed unsafe. I was asked by one renowned Bahamas Airways captain if I was prepared to climb to at least 5000 feet on a flight between Nassau and Chub Cay, some thirty odd miles, in order that I may glide to either if I lost an engine. I answered chances of loss minimal and my craft could land on the water put quiet to the question. The paperwork illustrated the attractive safety record of commercial seaplane operations throughout those countries comprising of vast bodies of water; I presented our archipelago, being 700 islands spread over 100,000 square miles of ocean. Here were countless communities far away from land-based runways and I would be able to reach 'their back doors'. I was eventually granted permission to apply on condition that the Port Authority gave me it's blessing also. Having operated a commercial boat charter service for near twenty years, the Port Authority knew me well from the annual inspections they had given my vessels each year. I brought to light Nassau Harbour, renowned as an approved landing zone in the past for its seaplane service by Pan-Am in days gone by, their old terminal building still standing as a green police station next to the air-sea rescue group called Basra. Recent years saw permission granted to Chalks Airline out of Florida operating service into Paradise Island with Grumman Mallards. Permission was granted in writing to Civil Aviation with mention that I coordinated with Chalks sharing a radio frequency enabling communication with each other on arrival and departure from the harbour waterways.

November came all too quickly. From one day to the next I was driving a 28-foot Bertram through the Narrows of Atoll Island to arriving at Orlando International Airport on the way to flight school. Exiting the arrivals terminal, I was met by Dave and Danielle Stevenson who owned and operated Rockledge Air Park. They were extremely friendly and well accustomed to meeting Brits attending their school. I was their first Bahamian. The drive through central Florida heading eastward toward the coast took an hour or more. The autumn season had set well in with the oppressive heat of a Florida summer washed away with the first cold fronts bringing cool Canadian air southward, welcome temperatures in the seventies with clean air blowing across the flat countryside. The small town of Rockledge lay close to famous Cape Canaveral where we had watched launchings of the space program on our televisions. The airpark comprised several small outer buildings with a flight line of small Cessna's facing a narrow 2000-foot hard surface very narrow runway. At the north end a fairly tall commercial plumbing building sat nestled within a clump of trees. The south end offered a clear flight path out to the vast wetlands of the Florida Everglades lying to the west. The administration building housed the ground school and outer buildings were residences with a kitchen for those of us staying and living on site for the few weeks of flight training.

On arrival there appeared several new students mostly from the UK. The few flight instructors intermingled were all Americans. Dave and Danielle introduced me to all the crew, Chris Schubert, Jim Kelly, Greg, Dale and Brian from New Zealand, Andy the helicopter instructor. Most students and instructors barely in their twenties, all aspiring future airline pilots here earning precious income and hours required toward their Airline Transport Certificates. We talked and introduced our plans. The room went very quiet when I told of my plans to fly a seaplane operation in the Bahamas and my new seaplane was being built as we speak. One could see instant scepticism in the room toward this forty year old save one grey haired gentleman from Kent in England who was a fraction older than I immediately voicing a 'Good for you, Paul'.

'The name's Ernie Ford,' as we shook hands, 'looks like we are the two old farts here!'

Ernie and I became friends instantly that first day, still well in place as I edit this piece ensconced in my villa on the Turquoise Coast of Turkey in early 2016! I admired his fortitude in late start following a dream, telling of his childhood days watching the Spitfires and Hurricanes crossing the English Channel during the war, always wanting to fly showing it never too late! A young Irishman with a heavy brogue introduced himself as Alex Corcoran saying confidently he was aspiring to fly for Aer Lingus. After introductions, we listened to a short talk from our hosts about Rockledge and the plans set out for our Private Pilot Training. The course would be about forty hours in flight training with ground school commencing early the following morning. The course completed the ground school first followed by a written exam requiring an 80% pass rate before actual flight training began. An average overall pass for the Private License would take about four weeks or more with a final daunting check-ride from an outside FAA examiner.

The next morning we assembled in the classroom overlooking the flight line. Ground school began with all the basics of flight and new books to study. No computers in those days so everything completed on paper with a multiple-choice questionnaire at the end. About three days in we were all near ready for the written. There were no failures in our group all eager to climb into aircraft for the first flight. My flight instructor was a much younger American chap named Chris Schubert. He had all the traits of a young professional aviator building his own hours training others toward a career in commercial aviation. Sporting a flashy leather flight jacket with familiar white aviator short-sleeved shirt and Ray-Ban sunglasses crowned with a mop of blonde hair and fun cocky attitude, Chris fit the profile flight instructor image to a tee. He believed that learning to fly should be nothing but fun and exuded that attitude every time we walked out toward our aircraft. His heavy American accent and constant laughter made the days enjoyable from the very start. He was fascinated in my plans for an aviation career not quite believing that a brand-new seaplane was already under construction for this rookie pilot to simply 'fly home'. The little Cessna 150 was to be my chariot for several weeks, a light high wing trainer reliable and easy to fly with controls so light it seemed a toy. We walked around the aircraft in the same pattern every day performing the pre-flight inspection. Peeking under aileron hinges, feeling the free motion of the control surfaces and tugging on propeller blades to feel them securely in place, then taking fuel samples checking for water contamination. Opening the cowling port to check the oil level while looking at tyre pressures. Every day this ritual was performed ensuring the plane became a part of us. On the flight line one morning we could hear a commotion in a broad excited Irish brogue as Alex had given his propeller a really heavy tug to make sure it was secure and the damned thing actually came loose grounding the plane for major inspections. We all became aggressively vigilant after that with pre-flight checks becoming far more anal than usual. I had not stepped inside a cockpit since mentor Colin Budenberg took me for a ride in the flying club Piper Arrow back in Nassau; the little 150 a squeeze with two grown men over six feet in height. Chris ran through the simple instrumentation on the dashboard explaining a start and a stop procedure once re-parked after flight. Without much further chatter he told me to have feet on the brakes, master switches on, throttle about a quarter inch, mixture in and turn the key. The Cessna obeyed and came to life first crank. He casually told me to taxi down toward 'the plumbing building' that I had seen at the far end of the strip, its roof providing many a near miss for us all on short final approach for landing from the north to the short runway below.

'There are only about six lights working at any time,' he adds flippantly 'so night flying later on will be fun to find when returning home from a bar-b-q dinner in Orlando!' At the far end of the runway we performed the engine magneto checks and one last flight control check before easing the small plane onto the hard surface.

'Go for it!' he calmly instructs, asking for a take-off after a radio call announcing our intentions. There was no instruction on how far to run or speeds to reach before rotation taking for granted I knew all from the manuals. Full throttle and yoke neutral we picked up speed down the runway. Slight back pressure and 2000 feet seemed to come to an end all too soon so I ease back on the yoke allowing the Cessna to become airborne; the ground falling rapidly away; a nice angle of climb with a right turn taking us out toward the orange groves and cattle country of central Florida for training. I am flying! We all remember that first flight and feeling of the freedom flying allows us to have, the exhilaration of making this machine do what I request of it. This aircraft is very light and responsive. Away from the crowded airway corridors along the east coast we are quite alone now over flat grasslands. Chris has me practise all the basic manoeuvres of climbing, descending and turns. It's damned good fun. Returning to Rockledge we make the approach pattern to the runway and practice the first of many close calls over the plumbing building roof in a dive for the tarmac, Chris not really giving any instruction on technique rather simply saying, 'put her on the numbers' presuming I pull off the landing without a hitch. During my career, I was always fascinated with various instructors I encountered, through all the various ratings, noting they never actually taught the art of flattening the plane out just above the ground, bleeding off the speed before a slight flare and waiting patiently to allow the craft to actually land itself with near perfection. It became a self-taught skill over time. Having been an instructor in the underwater business I knew that good teaching technique could relieve the stress of 'not knowing'. Why did aviation instructors seem to fail in that regard learning immediately flying proficiently 'was an art' to be acquired over time? That first landing, with Colin whispering in my ear, I went with pure intuition putting the 150 nicely down without ramming the landing gear through the tarmac as some fellow students were performing on a regular basis creating shameful bounces down the hard surface.

'Good job, Paul!' Chris exclaimed. 'You are going to get this quickly,' he reinforced. We talk in the cockpit after the propeller had come to a stop and the engine shut down, Chris running through some of the specifics of our time aloft. We exit the little trainer and walk toward the office building to fill in the first entry of many log books, my first hour of flight is there in writing. In my wildest imagination I could not have envisioned over fourteen thousand more to follow!

Flight training usually had us airborne for an hour or two in the morning and again another hour in the afternoon depending on the allocations of the aircraft to all the students. On the second and third hours, we were taken away from the field heading north-eastward toward Merritt Island, proving a favourite training airfield relatively close by with its runway protruding into the Indian River. The radio work heading this direction close to Cape Canaveral became a complex affair having to talk with military Patrick Airforce Base close by. Air traffic was heavy here and one had to really pay attention. We lost one of the 150s that first week to a fellow student losing control after touch down skidding off the runway into the ditch running down one side of Merritt. No injuries but bent landing gear and a prop strike onto the ground put that little aircraft in the shop for weeks. The rest of us pissed at the young pilot for this aircraft a favourite in the flight line.

Finding our way back to Rockledge was a challenge at first. Everything on the ground looked so alike with our small narrow airstrip becoming lost in the sprawl of Florida suburbia. How the hell would we find our way back in the dark I thought having to complete three compulsory night flying hours for one's license? There were no GPS or Loran in these little trainers, simply an analogue VOR navigation aid and compass with a DG, directional gyro. After flying westward, we were given instruction on stalls really holding our attention. Feeling that aircraft straining to stay airborne with the nose being held aggressively high while a screaming stall warning indicator yelled at us, we held the plane as level as possible until insufficient airflow over the wing had the nose suddenly pitch forward toward the ground. After learning how fast recovery actually happened our confidence returned, not a favourite manoeuvre by far. Simulating a loss of engine power proved entertaining one morning with Chris pulling the throttle full back to where the quiet became an unusual whisper of the propeller idling quietly through the air.

'You've lost an engine, find a spot and prepare for an emergency landing while you try and sort out the problem of a possible restart,' Chris calmly instructed.

I lower the nose a fraction to attain the best glide speed and fascinated how long the small plane can stay aloft simply gliding gently toward the ground. I am simulating my list of things to sort out, fuel on both tanks, placing the emergency 7700 code into the transponder so air traffic controllers would instantly recognise an aircraft in trouble, then suggesting that I would re-crank the engine all the while looking for a nice flat space to soft field land the plane where at the very least just climb out and walk away in one piece. Getting in the mind set one would probably lose the machine the 'walk away' being most prime outcome to look for. It became a valuable principal I would always adhere to, witnessing a couple pilots later in life not willing to sacrifice the aircraft, believing they could 'make it back to the field' at all costs. Turning with a failed engine, turning too steep, dropping the landing gear, both lost their lives with their aircraft plunging earthward. Both incidents had vast open spaces of flat calm water readily available that would have made a perfect splashdown enabling a wade to shore. There was a primal fear it seemed among landplane pilots about water being an alternative runway. A prime example later in history seeing a commercial passenger jet land safely in the Hudson River in New York without losing a single soul. Little did I know this valuable strategy would come into play many years later in my own career, also saving the day?

Training over the Florida landscape I had my simulated landing site picked out, talking out loud so Chris could hear my thought process and logic. I had the aircraft pointing into wind for the landing confident any second my instructor would give the quick order to 'go around!' 100 feet, 50 feet, 20 feet, nothing said. Chris was thinking he would have fun watching how low I would take it before giving power back to the engine. We were near clipping the tall reeds that rose from this piece of wetland when Chris gave the order with a laugh. I pushed the throttle in hard and the engine died with a cough. I heard *'Oh shit!'* from my instructor as he grabbed the throttle and pulled it part way out again. The small engine regained composure coming back to life just before an actual touchdown.

'Lesson there Paul, squeeze the throttle in slowly; even when in a desperate situation so as not to choke the engine!'

'Thanks a bunch, Chris, *now* you tell me!' as we climb back up for the flight home.

The flight hours clicked away, still not in double digits accumulating all of nine in my logbook. We landed back at the Air Park and I taxied toward the parking spaces on the grass alongside the narrow runway.

'Hold her here, Paul,' Chris said. I looked puzzled at this request short of our parking spot on the grass unaware as to what he was up to. Before realising where this was going my instructor was outside the aircraft beaming with a smile as he closed his door. He shouted above the drone of the engine,

'You're on your own now Paul, take her around with one touch and go then land to a full stop!' Solo flight I grasped. 'Hell no Chris, nine hours total, I'm *not ready* for that yet!' I pleaded.

'Oh yes you are my friend, go for it and enjoy!' Before I could say more he turned and walked away from the idling Cessna.

This is a day all pilots hold dear and never forget. The door closes and you taxi the aircraft away from your instructor. The prop wash blowing his hair as he holds his sunglasses securely from the wind you create. A nonchalant wave and thumbs-up sign from him and you head toward the far end of the field. The adrenalin kicks in as you line the little airplane up on the runway looking down those 2000 feet of tarmac. On the radio, I nervously call out my aircraft call sign to 'Rockledge traffic' on their Unicom frequency, saying I am departing to south with left traffic, already nervously tongue-tied and octave higher, I squeeze the throttle and the Cessna obeys with gaining speed. Without my friend sitting next to me the small plane is ready to fly much quicker than I expect. A slight ease backward on the yoke and I am airborne. Alone. At about 500 feet into the Florida blue sky I do what most solo pilots admit, we look to the co-pilot seat and then behind us in the cabin. No one there! 'Shit, it's really up to me to make this thing come back down in one piece!' That lovely fear disappearing in an instant; the training kicks in as if second nature already and I fly by everything I learned in those precious nine hours and under Colin's tutelage. The 150 is fabulously responsive and flies the pattern around the field perfectly. I approach for my landing to the South always remembering 'nice approach, nice landing' down to that familiar roof and power off to the runway. A few feet above the ground level out, slight nose up and wait. Touchdown! Power smoothly in I rotate again seeing Chris standing by the flight school building watching his student's every movement in the sky. I waggle the wings in salute to him and he waves back as I progress around the pattern with a longer downwind leg this time. 'Damn I don't want this to end!' Left turn to the base leg, radio work calling out to thin air 'I am turning final to land full stop'. Taxiing off the runway and onto the grass to park I have the plane perfectly in line with the other aircraft while pulling the mixture to hear the engine die, the propeller suddenly motionless. Master switches off and keys out. Chris opens my door before I realise the moment in full.

'Congratulations buddy!' Mr Solo did good up there!'

We walk around the Cessna using ropes lying in the grass, attached to secure buried metal hoops as tie-downs, used against any wind gusts that could so easily move our machines causing immense damage. Together we approach the waiting students lined up outside the building all clapping and yelling 'congrats' toward me. One cannot help but smile. What they are really waiting for is the ritual all students go through after their solo flight. From nowhere a pair of scissors appears and from behind the whole of your shirt is cut from your back. Everyone writes something and signs the torn material as their trophy is pinned to the public noticeboard inside the school. It will hang there for the week joined later by Ernie, Alex and some of the others shirts making a patchwork of colour, design and good humour marking the moment in a student's achievement that once was just a day-dream.

Chapter 20
Winter Haven Traffic

The crisp November mornings offered a serene landscape. Small training aircraft stood obediently in a row showing elegance in the early misty light. Dew trickled down the sides of each fuselage and windshields leaving sparkling clear trails as if little snails had crept downward through the delicate wetness to fall on the ground. The air was absolutely still as the sun slowly rose above the eastern horizon. The stillness here was very noticeable compared to the islands where trade winds blew constantly off the ocean in the morning hours, moving the palms in graceful unison and capping our turquoise seas with white. Florida seemed wonderfully quiet and serene in the early hours with water so calm it offered perfect reflection. Planes welcomed easier lift off their runways in the cooler air. It was a beautiful time of day to fly and revel in the thrill of being airborne while soaking up the wondrous panorama below. Those of us who booked the first-light time slots met in the schoolroom for coffee that steamed in our cups in the chill surroundings. We chattered excitedly like young schoolboys undertaking a fun expedition about the plans for this flying day. With our gained experience in double-digit figures it was time for map work and navigation, flying our cross-country requirements to airports far away from the coast. One of these would be a compulsory 250 miles in length, a favourite being a straight westerly line across the state following the familiar Alligator Alley Highway, a narrow ribbon of dead straight asphalt drawn with rule-like precision carving its way across the Florida Everglades, vast marshlands neighboured with huge cattle pasturelands leading into the city of Naples. This easy navigation simply following the road below gave time to be distracted within the cockpit, practise using the Visual Omni Range or VOR navigation aid, an instrument when tuned in to the destination airfield frequency showed a needle centring itself on the dial and small flag indicating, 'To'. If controllers asked our location, we would dial the VOR where the needle again centred with 'From' flagged on the face. Now we could read the radial degree we were located on estimating distance from his station. So that's how these pilots find their way around up here! We smile in relief of a simple secret revealed, calling Naples air traffic controllers giving notice of our approach and intended pattern of entry to their runway. Here we would land and refuel with a stop at a nearby local restaurant for lunch before attempting some serious map reading north-eastward across the state to the small airstrip of Okeechobee alongside the seventh largest freshwater lake in the United States covering 730 square miles. Hard to miss even for a novice flyer!

Adding to the fun of flying an aircraft by one's self we often paired up for the company and thrill of flying in tandem. It was natural for the two old codgers to get together and let the younger lads sort themselves out. Ernie being the older I designated as the 'Wing Commander.' A nickname that carried to this day and created a fun morning when the postman arrived at his Kent home some months later. I had addressed the envelope affectionately to 'Wing Commander Ford'. The postman who had delivered there for years did not simply drop the mail through the letterbox this day, instead knocking on the door exclaiming 'in all these years he had no idea that you was a Wing Commander!' Ernie roared with laughter knowing exactly whose letter this was!

The early mists succumbed to the warmth of the sun leaving the air sparkling clear with a powder blue canopy above the cloudless landscape. Both pilots pre-flight our Cessna's and climbed aboard to taxi out together for take-off. The familiar scent of ageing leather seats and slightly sweet acidic smell of aviation fuel that had dripped steadily from the overflow valves on the underside of each wing greet us each flight. With an exaggerated exhale to calm the adrenalin we each turn the ignition key to hear our faithful Cessna spring to life. While the engine warms its thick cold oil we turn on instruments and check flight controls, reading our checklists to ensure nothing forgotten. We gave radio notice over the Unicom frequency for Rockledge and with a squeeze of the throttle Ernie's aircraft rolled southward down the runway. Satisfied that both magnetos are functioning as required we prepare for lift off. As he neared the end I was already lined up to follow his rotation and right turn to the West. Away from the busy suburban sprawl below the flight of two soon found ourselves in open countryside speeding still westward at near a hundred miles an hour. The air was still stable at this early hour with the sun at our backs. The heat of the day would soon warm the air for upward thrust creating bumpy thermals that could toss our aircraft around making flight more arduous. We both tuned in to the chitchat frequency of 123.45 where we could talk freely without interrupting other flyers.

'How about taking a look a little lower Wing Commander?' I asked, mischievously.

… 'I'll follow you' Ernie replied knowing full well what 'a little lower' meant. We descend from our cruising altitude of 1200 feet until the two light aircraft are fizzing across the vast expanse of grass. The Everglades came into view making the flight really exhilarating as massive reed beds whizzed underneath us sending magnificent white egrets exploding out of their hiding places amongst the tall grasses. Climbing skyward again we found Alligator Alley and flew alongside each other all the way to Naples. This kind of travel was so surreal at first. One could just climb into your own aircraft to fly all the way across the state for a lunch somewhere. Then fly to another airport in the centre of Florida and a third leg all the way back to your home base. This navigation stuff really works! A journey not easily accomplished by car now taking only a few hours in the air. The fuel costs in those days minimal with our machines barely using eight gallons an hour wishing even then, it back in the days before the OPEC Embargo toward the western nations in October of 1973, allowing cost of aviation fuel a mere sixty cents a gallon; here in the late 80s still below a dollar a gallon.

There were some fun cross-country stories. Flights where map reading a little rusty some students becoming quite lost having to land somewhere to make a desperate phone call back to the school. No cell phones hooked up to Bluetooth in our headsets back then! One young lad called saying he was 'somewhere up north' and needed directions back to our neighbourhood. One of the instructors taking the call realised the fellow was near the coast so told him 'just keep the Atlantic to your left and call us when you recognise a renowned landmark close to home' Some time later that afternoon the base radio came to life with a familiar voice calling in to 'Rockledge Unicom' an octave or two higher than usual. He was flying southbound along the coast and suddenly recognised a very long runway close to the ocean and 'this huge square building nearby'. Another higher squeal over the speaker exclaiming 'that a rocket just took off in front of my view!'

'Holy shit!' our instructor cried. 'There's a Notam, notice to airmen, out today about a launch at Cape Canaveral and all air traffic restricted within miles of their area'.

'Turn immediately ninety degrees to your right for five miles,' he barked bark at the student pilot. 'Then fly due south again and you will see Merritt Island to your left close to Rockledge for your inbound radial.' Within thirty minutes the young pilot approached our narrow little runway, home to the nest safely. The Cape in later years of the space shuttle became very stringent on air traffic with that particular coastline littered daily with student pilots.

After landing at Okeechobee Ernie and I had an idea to make a stop at Winter Haven to find world famous Jack Brown's Seaplane Base run by two brothers, Jon and Chuck Brown.

'I need to check in with Jon as we had talked earlier from the Bahamas about my water ratings. This looks like the day to make a slight detour and get the task done.' Ernie was up for anything in those days. As long as we could fly there was no destination he was not up for. Looking at our charts and noting the VOR radial off Lakeland Airport a few miles to the west of the seaplane base we could then cut some corners and fly into the airstrip at Winter Haven. The flight went as planned talking with Lakeland Tower issuing vectors to fly direct to the seaplane base. Here we found reading a map and flying in a strange area could become extremely intimidating for still low-time pilots, the landscape below a continuous mass of lakes, towns and highways all looking similar in appearance. Having the discipline to navigate with the aids aboard the aircraft and talking to Air Traffic Control let the journey unfold, as it should. Taking the radial from Lakeland eastward we soon found Lake Jesse where familiar yellow J3 Piper Cubs parked at the North end of the lake displaying the seaplane base: the original manufactured Cubs were built between 1937 and '47. Talking with Winter Haven Unicom we hear no response, signalling the traffic pattern is clear for us to go around and explore from above before landing. We see there is a taxiway down to the seaplane base from the main runway. Lining up on final our two Cessna's follow each other to land. After touchdown, we follow the narrow taxiway down to the line of seaplanes behind the base. A Twin Seabee sits parked by the fuel pumps and we find a space to park pulling the mixture to stop the engine. On the side of their wooden office and reception building there are three or four different models of seaplanes on straight floats having no amphibious wheels. They are pulled into the shallow reeds on the edge of Lake Jesse all facing toward the water. One is an impressive twin Aztec on floats and the others single Cessna 185s. To the west of the hangar is another line of yellow floatplanes all 85HP Piper Cubs that Brown's use for their flight school. As we walk along the planked walkway toward the office door a tall moustached man exits a door holding out his hand in greeting,

'Welcome, gentlemen, I'm Jon Brown, how may I help?' I introduce myself and Ernie reminding that I was the one from the Bahamas who contacted him a while back expressing interest in getting my float rating and here completing our PPL, Private Pilots License, over at Rockledge. Jon had an inch or two over me so I knew flying with him in a Cub where the instructor sits in the front seat would be an interesting challenge!

'Great news Paul' he exclaimed 'do you know all the other float crews in Nassau, Marcus, Jimmy, Tommy and Charlie?'

'Yes, I know all those pirates well!' I jested.

'Come on in and meet my brother Chuck'.

We followed Jon into the office where a few patrons sat in large leather lounge chairs reading aviation magazines. Chuck came from behind the glass counter and introduced himself with a cheeky smile. 'So you are the fellow from the Bahamas who ordered a seaplane from Maule without knowing how to fly? That was pretty ballsy'.

'That's me,' I confessed. We all talked in length about the aircraft I had ordered with Marcus and they expressed what a great choice it would be. The two brothers very interested in how I planned to tackle the Civil Aviation Authority and our Port Department about opening a local commercial floatplane operation in Nassau having never been done before by a private citizen. I told the story of my father being with Bahamas Airways providing an introduction to some members of the airport authority, along with my seventeen-year career operating a commercial boat business out of Nassau Harbour giving familiarity with all those who could walk me through permission. The two men expressed enthusiasm about my undertaking bringing attention to needing a base of maintenance in the United States under the FAA Part 124 Program. Browns Seaplane Base was a perfect location for me to fly into having no wheels on my first seaplane. An amphibian was way too expensive for my undertaking. 'If ever you went that route Paul, you may well want to talk with Harry Shannon over in

Bartow, he specialises in amphibs and understand that Tommie's girlfriend Elle is also starting the paperwork so there could be two of you out there!' We talked about the procedures of flying in an out of America from the Bahamas. The flight would be just under three hours from Nassau to Winter Haven with a stop in Fort Pierce on the coast for US Customs to clear me in.

'Just call them ahead of time' Jon explained, 'Give them your estimated time of arrival and that you will meet them in the waterway near the base of the causeway bridge or better still at the 'Pelican Marina' beach. They will pull up in a customs vehicle and do the paperwork with you right on site, Tommy does it all the time!'

'Sounds great Jon' I answered. 'Let's keep in touch and I will come back in a couple weeks for my water rating!'

We parted company with Ernie off my right wing flying in formation back to Rockledge having completed our long cross-country flight requirements.

The days clicked by with an occasional break in flying due to cold fronts passing through the region as they did at this time of the year. Not strong at first with wind shifting to the Southwest and then a familiar dark line of clouds ominously creeping toward us from the Northwest. The same pattern we all knew well in the islands that would have arrived a day or two after passing through central Florida. The temperature changes with a frontal passage were very noticeable up here compared to Nassau. The high eighties quickly replaced with twenty degrees cooler with the winds dragging cold air all the way down from Canada. Poor weather days had Ernie and I borrow a school vehicle and go food shopping. We noticed most, if not all the students, were surviving from canned food not having honed their culinary skills yet? The two old farts were wiser toward their nutrition and returned later with fresh vegetables and ground beef for homemade spaghetti sauces. The welcome aroma from our cooking piqued the interest of the other student pilots.

When the flying resumed, more difficult manoeuvres were to be completed, one being unusual attitudes. Chris with his flippant ways and wanting some fun took me westward and up to about 3500 feet.

'This time Paul I need you to close your eyes and lower your head. When I tell you, open your eyes, check the instruments, assess your attitude and correct accordingly!'

'Ok' I muttered, having no clue what he was up to. Eyes closed and head lowered. The aircraft changed attitude with a manoeuvre so smoothly executed giving no premonition what attitude we were in. Usually this would be in a climbing or descending steep turn I thought?

'Open your eyes!' Chris sat there smiling.

'Bloody hell Chris we are upside down!' I yelled at him.

'Yup, fix it then mate!'

I rolled the little Cessna to the right maintaining level flight where the attitude indicator did not have the darker half on top and blue on the bottom! As I completed this the whole scene suddenly started to visually spiral. The aircraft was stable but my balance was gone completely with vision spiralling uncontrollably.

'You ok?' Chris's smile suddenly vanished seeing his student in apparent distress colour draining from my face. 'Want me to take it?' he asked.

'No, I have it. I want to see if I can manage to get her down in this condition,' desperately wanting to prove I could keep control while nausea overflowed my senses.

We flew back to the airpark and landed safely taxiing the aircraft off the runway prematurely and pulled the mixture. After the engine shut down I near fell out of the plane on to the grass with the world whirling above me.

'Holy shit Paul, I am so sorry,' Chris feeling badly about the stunt seeing my face in pale pallor.

'Not to worry' I added quietly 'something has gone adrift with my balance. That drastic a manoeuvre must have turned something loose in my inner ear?'

Slowly, ever so slowly the sky stopped rotating above me. When it stopped, I stood up slowly and we walked over to the school visibly pale and shaken.

'I guess acrobatics are out for you my friend?' Chris said quietly. Quite true I thought feeling disappointed some affliction could affect my career at some time.

Just as well I found out then with fate soon stealing Chris's best friend Carl, who taught aerobatics in the 150 Aerobat used to instruct at Rockledge. Thoughts had been considered to giving acrobatics a try certainly useful honing flying skills in unusual attitude but learned Carl, losing control with a student over the ocean, seen in a downward spin toward the water never to recover. Both pilots lost their lives, Carl leaving a wife and child.

Chapter 21
Time to Get Wet

The month was over all too quickly, the logbook filling with entries of flights accomplished in all required quadrants save one. Night-flying. The school made this learning experience fun. Our first night flights off our airstrip at school ventured over to Merritt Island a few minutes away returning after a few touch and go's. Merritt's airport was always up to specification with all the lights working perfectly, we marvelled at the technology of flying over in the dark and not being able to see the runway. A few clicks of the radio transmitter and the airfield exploded with visible lighting allowing a fun approach more often to the end of the runway stretching out in the waters of the Indian River. From here we knew the flying time back to Rockledge and with much needed instruction able to pick out the dimly lit six little white landing lights of our home. Putting the small trainer down nicely in the dark required much more finesse but soon we became proficient enough for adventures further afield. The idea of flying to Orlando International in a Cessna 150, having a meal in a local restaurant to then fly home sounded all too decadent for this group of novice pilots; let alone accomplishing this at night – it made the task appear quite daunting. We set off resembling a small squadron of five or six aircraft catapulted off an aircraft carrier. Re-grouping over the night waters of the Indian River we talked with air traffic control all the way to Orlando International. My approach became quite the conversation piece as I lined up on final for the one of the main runways my controller asking casually if I 'could expedite your approach speed having a 747 "heavy" behind you!' 'I'm pedalling as fast as I can,' I replied, flying all the way down to the runway before lowering any flaps that would have slowed me down to a crawl. 'Heavy on short final,' the controller prompted with more urgency. 'Exit the runway when able,' he said. I touched down and almost skidded off the first available taxiway, uttering an audible sigh of relief as the very large airliner screamed passed me for landing. 'Damn that was close!' I spoke out loud without hopefully keying the microphone. Switching over to ground control I asked for a 'progressive taxi', not having a clue where I was on the airfield or how to navigate around all these little white and blue lights on the ground, or how to find the Fixed Base Operation, FBO, that we had planned to meet up at. Five or six of us all parked alongside each other to find transport over to the restaurant. Excited chatter as if straight out of a school outing occupied the evening, swapping aviation stories of an approach into a major airport hub at night. Within a couple of hours we regrouped at the FBO, pre-flight our Cessna's once more, then armed with ATIS, the aerodrome information, we all started our machines to taxi down to the departure end of Orlando's runway in use. Flying on a clear night is one of those remarkable experiences, aircraft in America are allowed to be flown visually at night but not here in our islands with their lack of runway lighting and navigation aids. There is no turbulence found with the hot rising air of daytime. One can see for miles to the horizon in any given direction with the city laid out underneath you in a vast twinkling of lights resembling a moving map, the mass of stars and other aircraft lights around you all set in vast inky blackness. The white headlights and red tail lights of vehicles threading their way along the highways like filing ants passing huge neon lighting of advertising billboards. The aircraft instrument panel displaying the gauges I need to monitor the engine and navigate home. We are all alone up there in the night sky trying to find one's home airfield and landing safely brought a real sense of accomplishment for new pilots with little over thirty hours of experience.

I was approaching the required forty hours of flight time in my logbook when Chris announced that he had arranged the FAA flight examiner to come to Rockledge that following weekend to give our final flight exam. Ben Quinn was a large man, my height and generously supporting more weight than Chris or I carried. Squeezing into a Cessna 150 with two larger men is even more a challenge. Nerves were at their peak. Here was the check ride that we had worked so hard for, definitely not wanting to repeat if at all possible. It is here that we must allow the skills of flight control to become second nature and concentrate on recollecting that vast amount of learnt information at any given moment, lest we fail. Mr. Quinn asked politely for a soft field take-off and left turn over to Merritt Island. 'Yes, Sir!' I answered through my newly acquired David Clark headset adding small take-off degree of flap. At the end of the airpark runway I inquired if there was any traffic inbound to Rockledge over the radio Unicom frequency and asked my passenger to secure his seat belt. Phew, remembered to do those I thought! Stick back and feet hard on the brake pedals I allowed the small engine to rev up smoothly. At full revolution, I released the feet off the top pedals and allowed the trainer to run down the runway where with yoke held in back slight pressure she would rotate prematurely as if simulating off a grass field. Once airborne I urged the yoke level to allow the plane flight through ground effect just a few feet off the tarmac. Remembered that! Once enough airspeed was gained, I pulled back gently to climb out towards Merritt Island easing away flap to cruise level. With a couple touch and go's we head westward over the flat Everglades of Florida to complete air work including dreaded stalls with and without power, steep turns around a point of reference – with a wing nearly vertically downward on one side with co-ordinated rudder – and simulated engine failures which I remembered all too well after Chris had me near chopping reeds in the swamps below.

'Let's head back,' Mr. Quinn said quietly, showing no sign of any emotion. I felt fairly confident about the flying even though nerves were playing havoc. 'May we have a short-field landing please?' Mr Quinn requesting. 'Yes Sir' an instant reply. The landing at Rockledge was impressively short squeaking the tyres gently raising my confidence for the hopes of a passing grade. I taxied off the airstrip to park on the grass where the long questioning of the oral exam was to begin while sitting on one of the outside benches of the flight school. The groundwork seemed to last forever when my examiner finally said, 'Good enough, congratulations Paul, you now have a Private Pilot's License which from here is a license to learn'. My father's words from long ago echoed from within, 'You'll never amount to anything,' scorning after I rejected the idea of going to university. His generation attitude carried forward by ours, that if you did not hold a university degree one's chances of success in life were deemed dismal. With the right fortitude my philosophy of 'make living from something you love to do' seemed to be paying off well on my chosen path without that higher education drummed into us as a requirement. A dream came true watching my examiner sign my first logbook with a passing check ride, thoughts immediately turning to Winter Haven and that long-awaited seaplane rating. Chris was very happy to see the smile on my face, signalling his student had succeeded. Dave and Danielle offered congratulations along with all the students gathered in the school that afternoon. I watched Ernie pass me as he headed out to his Cessna and an awaiting Mr. Quinn.

'Go get 'em Ernie, you'll be fine,' I encouraged the older friend. I could see he too was a bag of nerves. A couple of hours later I saw him again walking from the flight line with the same broad smile. He too had achieved that well-earned piece of paper from the Federal Aviation Authority. The following day I packed my belongings and had Ernie, now legally able to carry a passenger, fly me over to Brown's Seaplane Base after bidding farewells to my hosts and the other students. Chris walked us out to the Cessna and asked about my seaplane under construction.

'No one actually believes you have a brand-new plane being factory built' he jested.

'Well,' I confirmed, 'In about a month or so I will come back over this way from Georgia and call you inbound'. I pointed to the familiar plumbing building 'I'll come down the strip and buzz the lot of you in that brand-new Maule!'

'You do that Mr. Harding!' he shook my hand. 'A real pleasure flying with you, keep in touch,' he asked with that mischievous smile.

In Winter Haven I bid farewell to my wingman Ernie Ford wishing him well as he would be headed back to the UK within a day or so. We vowed to keep in touch and near thirty years later have fulfilled that promise living a short train journey away along the south coast of England while in neighbouring counties.

Jon Brown welcomed me back to the seaplane base with a firm handshake and established me across the highway in the small waterfront motel called Lake Marianna. It is here that I would return during my new career skimming the large trees to descend to the dark lake water landing gently on the calm surface, taxiing slowly to bump the shallow embankment behind my room aboard my own new seaplane. Now it was time for more ground school in the classroom at the seaplane base built as part of the dock stretching out into Lake Jesse. It was unusual to be taught in a classroom with the sound of water lapping underneath.

Jon's father, Jack Brown, founded the base after flying seaplanes during the Second World War afterward beginning an extensive career as a flight instructor in Florida. Finding a large parcel of land on Lake Jessie just outside the small holiday town of Winter Haven, Jack started a civilian seaplane school in 1963 flying an estimated 24,000 hours in the aircraft he loved to fly, the old classic yellow J3 Piper Cubs. The base was neighbour to over a hundred fresh water lakes within a five-mile radius of its location. Tragedy struck in 1975 while ferrying a Seabee to North Carolina where he experienced a fatal loss of elevator control. Survived by two sons, Jon and Chuck, the world-famous seaplane base carries the legacy of Jack Brown to this day. Both sons accumulating thousands of hours flying experience becoming qualified flight examiners. Jon became the mainstay of the seaplane base while Chuck pursued other careers in aviation flying commercial airliners and corporate jets all the while maintaining a strong presence as a flight examiner with his father's creation in Winter Haven; the torch now carried forward with the third generation of Browns becoming qualified in water flying. Travis Gaines became a master in the art of fabric work reconstructing the J3 Cubs needing a refit while acquiring his Private Pilot's License; Emily Brown also completing flight training. The seaplane base became the busiest operation in the Western hemisphere after Seattle and Alaska.

My first flight instructor was Billy Smith from the neighbouring town of Auburndale, Florida. He was living now in Alaska as commercial pilot with Air Alaska and working part time for Jon. With dark well-groomed hair Billy was one of those strikingly handsome souls who never lost his looks, having us all rib him about, through all the years we knew each other. His quiet, unassuming demeanour made him a great instructor. We enjoyed the bond of fellow pilots staying friends through the decades of our careers, later to actually meet again up in Homer, Alaska where he lived building a home while I had travelled on holiday to film the wild bears. All those years later he looked like the day we met; lucky bloke, I joked with him. I noticed very early on that vast differences in flight experience had no bearing in the camaraderie between the men and women that flew airplanes, even with those who only shared the interest and not taken the actual controls. Everywhere one travelled in aviation there was a welcoming acceptance not found in many careers. Marcus had been right. Aviation was changing my life and broadening my vision in ways unimagined.

The class was small, just three or four of us having signed up for our Single Engine Sea Rating met in the wooden classroom. My immediate thoughts were of the sheer enjoyment of this new learning experience compared to the boring drone of mediocre teachings during my early schooling. What a difference it makes when the subject matter has your full attention and flight school having thus far no use for the word calculus! Our flight instructors made very clear all the intricacies of flying a water plane, the point that caught my ear about 'boat captains making good seaplane pilots and not necessarily the other way around'! I clearly saw the truth in this expression having seventeen years Class-A Captains experience under my belt; knowing intimately first-hand the behaviour of water, wind, wave and climate. To my real advantage was the experience of ocean waters compared to lake flying which most of the students coming through this school were going to be subjected to. Many students arriving here would have no knowledge of tidal flows, wind against tide and ocean swells and narrow spaces to land. A large percentage of students coming through Browns Seaplane Base were long time pilots just wanting that water rating added to their licenses with no real intention of taking the qualification much further, simply having that rating on the wall sufficient! Some were long-term airline career pilots itching to get their hands on the single stick control of a J3 Piper Cub for the shear fun of it and really feel the art of flying once again.

On the second day, we took our written exam, all passing with ease. Three bright yellow Cubs waited patiently on their wooden ramps for a push into Lake Jesse. Inside the small hangar two more sat on their floats undergoing various maintenance procedures with Travis and Mark, the base mechanics. The walls of the hangar displayed wing spars in different stages of repair or rebuild. Two of the fabric-covered seaplanes were turned on their heels tied securely from the aft cleats while we received some basic instruction on the flight controls and the plan of first flight. The black painted interior of the old planes offered a tiny cockpit where two pilots tightly fit one behind the other. Billy offered me the rear seat being the student while he stood outside on the float. He went through the procedure of starting the small Continental engine. With magnetos turned on he took hold of the two-blade propeller pulling it sharply downward. Hand propping, as it was called, with an engine void of a starter motor, usually took two or three tries before coming to life. Sure enough, on try three the engine fired having us immediately pull away from the shallow reed beds of the lake, no brakes on a water plane! I had been instructed to hold the stick fully back and steer the plane with rudder pedals as Billy climbed in up front to lower the water rudders. We each put on headphones found held over a hook above our heads. Simple instrumentation lay displayed on a panel up front. We used no radios only observing any traffic arriving or departing the neighbouring airport of Winter Haven. I practised several methods of water taxiing, upwind, downwind and crosswind. With added power, I gave the seaplane a straight course down the lake to the far end on the step where the little Cub confidently sped across the calm surface as if water-skiing.

'OK, Paul,' Billy called through his microphone 'let's do that power up to the step and this time keep full power. You will feel when she wants to rotate so stick gently back and she will come off the water!'

Facing the seaplane base from the far end of Lake Jessie we headed northward in our take-off. I feel sure every pilot who runs along the water's surface for the first time remembers that rotation and climb out? The sheer exhilaration of flying these old classics whether on water or off the land, especially with an open cockpit, is incomparable to any other flying. It is the real thing! The base passed under us and we gained an altitude to about a thousand feet leaving the main airport played out below us, over large Lake Marianna where I was staying and into the wilds of central Florida. Up here one could see endless lakes with small towns scattered in between. Billy instructed clearly and precisely all the air work I was to know for the flight check that would follow three days from now. Flying with just a stick for controls without two hands holding a yoke became very familiar quickly. The Piper Cub is sensitive and responsive to every move, a very fun aircraft to fly. With stalls, slow flight, turns about a point, and emergency descents to landing where each flight became more enjoyable than the last. Learning how to spot wind direction from observing the calm shiny leeside of the lakes or simply a flock of birds at rest on the surface all facing into wind. Landings on the water were always fun and always different, paying attention every landing essential, as seaplanes soon were to show they could bite an unwary pilot. Billy was an artist at his job demonstrating the finer points of water flying. One-float landings and take-offs always impressed me. How to glide gracefully over the water's surface bleeding off valuable airspeed and allowing the floats to touch the water so very gently let one hardly knowing if we were actually flying any more.

'The Maule will be a whole other story, Paul,' he talked while taxiing along a lake one day. 'She will be a handful at first. Loads of power compared to these little girls and will certainly ask a lot of you. It won't take long before she will talk to you!'

I recalled these words many months later after being able to land my own aircraft with the same precision while studying at night a textbook called *The Art of Instrument Flying*. It is an art in every sense of the word and its mastery takes hours to perfect resulting in the pleasure of man or woman and machine behaving as one.

My last day in Winter Haven had me experience another check ride. Nerves were faint compared to the experience of that first examiner with barely 40 hours under my belt. This time it was Jon himself as my examiner. At six-feet-four-inches Jon fills the front seat of a Piper Cub making the students view quite the challenge from behind him. He hand propped the Cub and we taxied across the lake with me leaning hard to one side in order to see where we were going.

'All right, sir,' he always instructed so politely, 'a take-off please with a course to the north'. We flew for near an hour when he pulled the power all way off to where the small engine gentle purred in quiet idle.

'We've lost an engine, sir, please take us down to safety,' he said.

I immediately lowered the nose slightly downward so we could comfortably glide slowly through the air all the while talking my way through the headset the required checks an airman would go through to see if the aircraft power could be restored, demonstrating to my examiner how I was sorting out the problem while still flying yet planning a landing somewhere safe. With fuel selectors and magnetos checked a simulated restart performed I gave instruction that we were to land in a lake coming under us. One could clearly see the glassy calm water running alongside the shoreline so I banked gently to gain valuable distance downwind, leaving enough height for a final turn back into the wind. Reaching within less than ten feet off the surface I levelled the yellow aircraft with the water's surface and allowed its speed to bleed off. When sufficiently slower I eased the nose slightly and waited to hear the floats make contact with the surface. The landing was perfect and relief shown with a quiet exhale from the student in the rear.

'Very nice, sir!' Jon exclaimed 'let's do a plough turn downwind to ready us for a taxi and take-off and back to base'. Landing in Lake Jessie always a great experience where other students could be seen perched on the end of the dock watching fellow pilots return. Before reaching Jon draws my attention to a huge log lying on the surface of a large lake underneath us, 'look at the size of that alligator!' he exclaims. I bumped onto the vacant ramp looking at the hangar. Travis was a young linesman back then, stepping forward with a line to secure the front cleats. Hanging up my headset while Jon vacated the Cub he turned and offered congratulations on a pass of my Single Engine Sea rating.

'Nicely done Paul.' he smiled, 'time to go and learn now. I'll see you back here soon for your Commercial rating, have fun in that Maule!'

Good grief I thought, that's over 250 hours away!

Powerboat racing with Tony Vesco.

Teaching Jim Schaafsma & son Scott to Scuba dive at Rose Island.

Swimming with a 40 foot Sperm Whale in The Tongue of the Ocean. (Photo: G. Pinder)

Daughter Natalie's 1st Scuba lesson at Rose Island. (Photo: Jeff Hughes)

Flight to Perth, Scotland with friend Colin Budenberg.

Golf with Colin at Gleneagles, Scotland.

First seaplane arrival at Winterhaven, Florida to show Jon Brown.

Meeting fellow student 'Wing Commander' Ernie Ford.

1st day at Rockledge Flight School with instructor Chris Schubert, 1989.

Arrival Chub Cay, Bahamas in the 1st Maule seaplane, 1990.

Meeting Rosie Mitchell in her Maule N77627 at Waderick Wells Cay.

Donated notice sign for Park HQ with Marcus Mitchell & Warden, Peggy Hall.

PAUL HARDING working on location in Deer Valley, Utah, with The International Outdoorsman TV series, featured on "The Sporting Life", currently showing on The Discovery Channel and networks in 35 other countries!

Newspaper article about my joining 'The International Outdoorsman' TV series.

My 1st film shoot as cameraman for 'The Sharks of Stella Maris'.

Filming with Olympic Champion Stein Eriksen & son Bjorn in Deer Valley, Utah.

Film Producer Jeff Hughes on location in Utah, USA.

A day's skiing on the slopes near Boise, Idaho.

1st Skydive jump in Beaumont, Texas. 1980s.

Last day's location shoot for 'Dive if you Dare'.

'Neddie' takes care of me down the Grand Canyon, Arizona.

Sitting on the rim of the Grand Canyon.

Shooting video for television production in the canyon lands of Arizona.

Vacation skiing in Idaho, USA.

Early magazine film shoot with the 1st Maule seaplane in the Exuma Cays.

Flying over Powerboat Adventures at Ship Channel Cay. (Photo: Alan Wardle)

First seaplane charters to the Iguanas of Alan's Cay, Exuma.

One of countless magazine covers featuring the Maule seaplanes.

Bahamas Ministry of Tourism promotion poster photo.

Poster photo used by the Bahamas Ministry of Tourism.

Flying frequent flyer customer, Sandy MacTaggart, owner of Soldier Cay.

Early days of Mega Yacht charters into the Exuma Cays.

Twin-Engine Land & Sea rating at Browns Seaplane Base in the Seabee.

Purchasing our Piper Navajo, N577PC in Nashville, Tennessee.

First flight after meeting Suzanne in Stella Maris, Long Island, Bahamas. 1994.

Suzanne with one of her horses in North Carolina, USA.

Suzanne at her North Carolina cottage in 1994.

Shooting 2nd camera with Hal Lee in Cat Island, Bahamas.

Refueling in Great Inagua, Bahamas while shooting for Hal Lee.

On location shooting film with Hal Lee in San Salvador, Bahamas, 1994.

Flying TV host Regis Philbin to the Exumas for the day.

A day's flying with Col. Charles McGee of the Tuskegee Airmen with Ethel Finley, WASP.

Riding friend, Larry Wassong's 'Cappie' in North Carolina.

Re-visiting an old poster still displayed on Bay Street, Nassau.

Under The Golden Gate Bridge in San Francisco, early 90s.

On location with Capt. Nigel Bower with 'The Regis & Kathy Lee' TV show.

My mother's last seaplane flight with Suzanne & friend Margaret.

Long time friend Jim Schaafsma watching sharks in the runway at Highbourne Cay.

Teaching friend & mentor Capt. Colin Budenberg to fly the seaplane.

An overnight stay with friends Bruce & Kelly Griffin aboard their yacht.

Meeting Colin at Browns Seaplane Base in central Florida.

Grandson Jacob's first seaplane flight off Lake Cunningham, Nassau.

Adding fuel for an extended flight from Tiamo Resort, South Andros Island.

Jacob always did love my old 1986 Honda Shadow 700 motorcycle.

The 3rd Maule, N294SM arrives at a small cay off Normans Cay, Exuma.

Single-hand sailing my 34ft Gemini Catamaran off Shroud Cay, Exuma.

'Wilson' often flew for a vet visit along with owner Barbara Thrall.

Many a reunion with friend & flight examiner Jon Bown.

Last commercial flight for Sandy MacTaggart at Soldier Cay, Exuma, 2012.

Chapter 22
Career Change!

With a seaplane rating added to my pilot's license I returned to Nassau in early December to restart the boat charter business in time for the holiday season. We were in the cold front passages once again during the winter months so days had to be well chosen for running the trip to Rose Island; I was planning to leave one business for another where, like it or not, weather always ruled. As captains and owners of charter companies one had to be very savvy about forecasting weather. Knowing what would be approaching, how fast a particular system was traveling and the effects it would bring to our region quite vital, in this career it became part of who we were, and fast learning the uncanny knack of prediction. Simply stepping outside and observing sky and trees gave clue what the day would bring. Over a month's flying had spoilt me, giving taste of what the future could hold and less enthusiastic preparing that boat for a long day's work. Gary returned to his job at the Wulfe Road lumber company, having thoroughly enjoying himself with time on the water making good income as bonus. He had experienced a taste of what he might have done having the imagination and fortitude to create his own product. For me it was back to the madness of fighting tour desk operators who 'lost' our brochures and continued delaying payments. The inclement weather patterns making Bill's house in Lower Harbour a Godsend location during rougher days of northerly winds. The boat business was getting old after sticking with it for near seventeen years compared to being airborne. Besides damned hard work, long hours and constant maintenance with Hartley, recent years were taking an emotional toll. I was torn between calling it quits or maintaining responsibility of a family to house, feed and educate played heavily on my shoulders. Pulling the plug now would be a risky move but risk was nothing new in my life.

The wind was gentle out of the east one morning with the day trip underway during a clear blue day. The boat was full of guests with a couple of repeat clients sitting alongside me on the bridge while I drove the Bertram toward Rose Island. Passing the golf course on Paradise Island the lady next to me started the conversation with a surprise statement, 'I guess next year we will be going with Gary and his wife?'

'No, I'll still be here!' I replied in ignorance, a little startled at her opening remark. Plans to run the seaplane commercially were definitely on the table as well as keeping the 'Out-Island Safari' alive with Steve as captain.

'I don't think you know what I mean,' the lady interjected. 'Gary has started his own day-trip business called "The Rose Island Adventure"!' There was a noticeable silence as my mind grasped what she had said.

I was floored and couldn't find words fast enough to reply.

'Oh dear,' she hesitated to continue. 'I see you didn't know.' A strange feeling of dismay came over me. Driving that wonderful boat over these blue waters on a fabulous day only saw the joy drain out of my body. How the hell could a close friend be so sneaky having trusted in him with my livelihood? The day couldn't go fast enough and the emotion of betrayal grew by the minute. By days' end I was furious.

I drive that evening around the hotels to see for myself if this rumour is true. Sure enough there were new brochures on every tour desk. My friends had been very busy while I was away. The photographs and text were almost exact copies of my literature right down to the rear panel pictures of 'Your Hosts' showing the two of them as I had done with Bill Pemberton and myself. I saw red that night and demanded an immediate explanation. Taking a new brochure I arrived at their house to confront them with the betrayal. I banged aggressively on the front door. The son opened and I pushed past him in dismissal slapping their advertisement down on their dining table.

'What the hell Gary?' I near shouted in frustration. The room fell silent. They were lost for words not expecting this kind of forceful surprise entry causing the wife to start crying quietly in shame.

'I trusted you as a friend to run my business and you decide to clone it calling it your own while I am away?' My friend was mute while his young son instantly took up their defense being far more aggressive in nature than either parent.

'There's not a damned thing you can do about it!' his immaturity snarling at me.

'If you had bloody waited for me to come back and discuss it I would have offered it to you anyway in a partnership as I have new plans for our future'.

The son's aggression growing he came closer to face me, 'Why would we want a partnership when we can have it all?' he replied belligerently.

'You people disgust me! You just ended a long-term friendship' I said more calmly turning on my heels to walk quietly out of their home leaving the front door ajar. It would be our last time together; my thoughts racing about self-preservation in an already dog-eat-dog business. The name of their new creation was so very close to another day excursion run by Inez operating the 'Sea Island Adventure', maybe I could pit her with the closeness she had with the girls behind the desks, against my former friends. The ploy worked. Inez tackled them head on about the title being too close to hers and insisting all the brochures be removed, they complied reprinted later as 'Island Fantasy.' My attitude toward quitting now more intense as days went by. I could feel myself becoming angry by the continuous bombardment and pressure of this way of life. What started out as an incredible way to make a living had deteriorated to maddening competition coupled with poor behaviour from fellow operators and incessantly corrupt tour companies holding us hostage. Operational costs were rising with none of the independent excursions having the fortitude to increase prices accordingly. The large conglomerates were now quite able to supply themselves huge daily volumes ensuring survival, leaving us smaller tours to choke under heavy costs. I was not alone with these sentiments. Those of us who created the industry would soon throw in the towel out of sheer frustration, losing the countries vital tourism market some of its most valuable products. I managed to last another year while Steve ran my boat allowing me to fly the seaplane from my new location in Nassau Harbour, building the needed hours for a commercial operation to open. Gary and his wife had purchased a larger vessel from a family relation and passing it each day on our way to Rose Island was a bitter pill to swallow. The one satisfaction I had with ability to speed past that ageing slow boat with two fully laden Bertram cruisers leaving them buffeted by our wake.

A few months later Steve approached me one morning looking a little sheepish and embarrassed. 'Paul I have sad news,' he said quietly. 'I am quitting as of this week.'

'What on earth happened Steve?' I asked with obvious disappointment, the plan for future business instantly bleaker.

'Your "friends" who run Island Fantasy have asked me to come and work with them as the son is opening a new small group scuba business. We know each other well and I would like to give it a try.' I was again dismayed at the lack of loyalty by my employee leaving to work for my direct competition. He knew the hurt he had just delivered and I dismissed him on the spot to watch him walk quietly away down the floating dock, he would be missed.

The story takes a good turn some time later, proving true yet again the old adages true, 'what goes around, comes around' and 'karma is a bitch!' Needing something from the lumber company I walked through the store noting a familiar face mixing house paint behind a counter, the belligerent son who had displayed that cocky aggressive attitude that fateful evening, the bold young entrepreneur appearing very unenthusiastic about his new position in a hardware paint department! The family's boat charter business and sons' diving tour had both failed miserably causing Steve to lose his new found job and forcing both father and son to return to the retail business they had once been employed. Exiting the building patrons had to produce a receipt to be checked on exiting by an employee. My ex-dive partner could barely look up from his new career checking customer receipts as they vacated the premises! He initialled the paper seated on his little doorway stool. 'Well, well' I thought to myself, 'that's about where you belong', how the wheel goes around I reflected with utmost satisfaction. Having been handed a fabulous business opportunity on a plate, with all the secrets of success given freely, he still did not have the character to make it succeed.

'Long drop from being a charter captain,' I said quietly, not looking back as I walked away. It would be the last time I saw any of that family again. Steve I am glad to report went away to school and now qualified in marine electronics, coming to help with a job on my catamaran many years later. The day-charter business had been a project of passion, an idea taken to fruition and blossoming into one of Nassau's leading tourist attractions. A vast learning curve of how to make something one creates from scratch into a finely polished product. 'The Out-Island Safari' taught me the discipline of maintaining finesse where visitors experienced a day always remembered. This would be reinforced more than once along with 'Safari Seaplanes' that would follow. I received a call from a long-past client. 'We were with you many years ago Paul' the conversation began.

'My wife recently passed away from cancer. I was with her to the very end, talking about our life together. She said the one-day that stood out above all others was that day we spent with Paul on his boat at Rose Island and our scuba dive while on holiday in the Bahamas'. His voice began to break describing his wife's last request. 'Would he take her wedding ring back to the reef we dove on and place it there in my memory.' On arrival back in Nassau I took him out to Green Cay and what I believed the reef they explored. He watched from the surface as I free-dived the 40-feet to the bottom, sliding the small gold ring over a long soft coral where it would remain secure. The experience repeated years later, with a similar request to land in the seaplane next to the plane wreck at Normans Cay, here I would witness the scattering of ashes to drift in the warm current over the crumbling cockpit of the old Curtis lying in the shallow water.

Work began on my new ramp needed for the seaplane's arrival. Long two by twelve timbers that hung out of the back of my ageing nine-passenger Chevy station wagon were laid into the water at each low tide, joined across with two by sixes secured with stainless steel hardware. While the ramp was under construction and aircraft nearing delivery, paperwork was still incomplete and I unsure of any Government approval, a good time perhaps to pursue Civil Aviation and the Port Authority for my base of operation? My workplace, thankfully, would be located minutes away from home making a welcome commute with only a minor problem becoming clear. Choosing a location in the saltwater produced the need to be well versed in the varying tide-table for any given day. Prior planning required untold trips during the night commonplace needing to tie off the plane at the end of the ramp or be high and dry when required the next morning!

Word came from the Maule factory in Georgia that my seaplane was ready for collection. I telephoned Marcus down at Sampson Cay with the news having volunteered to come with me and assist the delivery back to the islands. On his recommendation I would accompany him for a stay in the Exumas with he and his wife Rosie while teaching me the intricacies of flying in short spaces and handling the seaplane in ocean conditions. Marcus estimated a weekend would suffice for my training. We flew into Tallahassee Airport met by his friend Robert McFadden who worked for Maule at the time as production manager. A tall, slender-built, quiet spoken man sporting a very RAF type moustache, looking even more the part sporting and old English deerstalker hat, Robert knew every inch of a Maule and could fly one accordingly. Seeing the brand-new seaplane sitting on the factory floor is quite a sensation for someone, who as a small youngster, had always dreamt of flying. I had to pinch myself to make sure it was true for there was a brand new blue and white Maule M7-235 on matching Aquafloats, gleaming under the fluorescent lighting of the huge factory hangar.

Belford D. Maule creating a family-owned enterprise founded Maule Air in 1941. 'B.D.' as he became affectionately known in the early years designed his own aircraft, the M-1, starting at just age nineteen. He started his original company Mechanical Products Co. in Jackson, Michigan marketing his own engine starter design. In 1941 The B. D. Maule Co. was founded producing tail-wheels and fabric testers. In 1953 he started design work and aircraft production with the 'Bee-Dee' M-4 model. Aircraft built today by Maule Air are tube-and-fabric designs, popular with bush pilots, known for their very low stall speed, light gross weights available with tundra tires and very forgiving oleo strut landing gear. Their reputation as a STOL aircraft, Short Take-off and Landing, soon becoming famous, with B.D.'s impressive demonstration of flying an aircraft airborne from inside a hangar out through the doors, a stunt not performed before! He was born November 4 1911 in Old Fort, Ohio to farming parents. Not caring much for farm life, he left at the age of fifteen to live in Salladasburg, Pennsylvania with an aunt and uncle who owned a garage and tearoom. There he demonstrated his mechanical ability, building a tractor, motorising an ice cream freezer and an ice saw among other inventions. He joined the Army when he was eighteen, assigned to the 19th Airship Company at Langley Field, Virginia. While working there he designed and built his first airplane, a single seat mid-wing monoplane powered by a Henderson 27HP motorcycle engine, known as the M-1. Having an early passion for water planes he started with the airplane on floats and later on wheels at the Salladasburg farm teaching him self to fly! He married June Aderhold in 1934 after his time in the army with her birthplace midway between Lock Haven home of Piper Aircraft and Williamsport the location of Lycoming Aircraft Engines. This was a perfect area in keeping with B.D.'s interest in aviation; starting working for Lycoming designing in 1939 'The Hummer', a low cost mechanical starter for light aircraft.

In 1940, the Maule family moved to Jackson, Michigan where in 1941 the B.D. Maule Company was formed in the town of Napoleon, building a light tail wheel airplane of his design, a steerable, full-swivelling tail wheel plane still manufactured by Maule in an improved form today.

In 1946, with the help of their two oldest children, they converted the Napoleon property to an airport, levelling a dog-race track once operated by Al Capone. The airport flourished for flight training during the initial post-war aviation boom. In the Fifties, B.D. decided to apply his design and engineering talents to improve the new industry of television, designing and marketing special antennas, towers and rotator parts.

In 1955 many airplanes were still being produced with organic fabric covers that deteriorated rapidly to the sun's ultraviolet rays creating damage requiring an annual strength test. The existing test procedures at that time involved cutting out sections or punching holes in the skins of airplanes; a traumatic and expensive experience for aircraft owners! The Maule Fabric Tester invented by B.D. was soon accepted by the FAA as a viable alternate and is still in production at Maule Air, Inc. along with the famous tail-wheels.

Bedford Maule began designing the first production Maule airplanes in 1952 as a high-powered tail-wheeled airplane for serious pilots who fly for the sheer love of it. He envisioned the need for a four-place aircraft that could be used as a multi-purpose machine for bush flying in rugged environments. His first prototype was completed in 1957 taking an award at the EAA Convention. Testing for certification of the new plane started that same year with the first production model known as the Jetasen M-4, delivered in April 1962 after FAA approvals a year earlier.

B.D. Maule now needed to expand searching for a larger space incorporating an airstrip suitable for test flying. In 1968 his family moved the company to the disused military Spence Air Base in Moultrie, Georgia, where the company and family still reside today. The Georgia location offered better flying weather with labour costs lower than up north. New manufacturing buildings were constructed and a spacious home designed by wife June. B.D.'s original irresistible passion for seaplanes prevailed even though the Moultrie location had no water close by. Undeterred he climbed aboard a D8 bulldozer near his house and started digging a hole in the ground! The soil was removed in a line westward taking a slight curve as far as the property boundary would permit skirting the main road to the south. Deeper and deeper the hole became until, story has it, B.D. lost the dozer down a sinkhole. Fresh water seeping in from below filled the huge hole aptly named Lake Maule. With his first aircraft mounted on straight floats these models were very capable of a safe take-off, successfully climbing out over the tall pine trees close to the house. It was here I was to taxi my first seaplane alongside the reed beds where serene swans would glide gracefully to feed.

In the years that followed, the Maule planes gained good reputation as a superb aircraft at a very reasonable price. My first seaplane landed a price tag of $85,000 and near twenty years later my last and fourth model, a fully equipped amphibian with a larger 260HP engine fetched over $350,000! All through the decades into the 90s, B.D. and his sons kept improving the Maule Aircraft. Model changes when approved became the M-4, through to M-7. In 1990 the model he called The Super Rocket was approved being my first aircraft purchased that same year.

Under B.D.'s guidance, the factory aeroplane supported a variety of engines, with recent years utilising a 420HP Allison Turbine Engine, enough horsepower to climb an amphibious plane beyond 1900 feet per minute near vertically skyward! The structural design has remained the same with the original fuselage jig still being used. Only a few turbines were ever sold to some celebrity actors and musicians, one later acquired by special client of mine that offered me the pleasure of flying briefly. New model Maule's now exist powered by a diesel engine!

In 1995, Maule was the third largest producer of single engine aircraft in the USA and by 1996 the factory produced sixty-four aircraft annually employing some seventy-six people. Some employees have stayed with the company over twenty-nine years producing over 1800 aircraft since its inception, Maule's are found in every continent as trainers and workhorses from the mountainous regions around the planet to the palm tree beaches of the Bahamas.

Unusually, through a span of fifty-three years, B.D. remained in total control of the operation of the company as well as the technical development of the product, until his death in 1995, having successfully survived regulatory and product liability problems through this industry, being a notable achievement for that length of time. He continued to fly his airplanes quite frequently even into his eighties. When I arrived at the factory for the first time, Marcus found him sitting in one of the many rocking chairs he had strategically placed in locations around the factory floor. Here he would ride his bicycle around each station of the work force checking on the daily progress of manufacture. When he tired the bicycle stood on the concrete floor while he sat and rocked in one of his chairs. Here we could stay with him and chat about his beloved airplanes as his brother Ray operated the maintenance facility named Maule Flight next door on Spence Field while his young grandson Brent was still at school, later becoming an integral part of Maule sales and a friend.

I spent many a visit with B.D. through the years where he always asked with interest how his machine was performing in the warm salt water. My early models not faring well to the 'warm battery acid' I described that we all flew in down there. I would pester him about finding coatings to protect the delicate steel frame tubing that corroded in the aft sections and complain bitterly about the lack of reinforcement of the underbelly fabric that would always split due to water pressure from take-off's to landings. The aircraft leaked profusely through the doors during rainy season suffering worse corrosion from rainwater than the salt she landed in. He would grumble in agreement, not comprehending the amount of hours we in the islands were flying commercially. His seaplane designs were tailored more toward the usage of private aircraft operating in fresh water and used far less frequently. In time, with persistence from each of us flying floats in the islands, veteran pilots such as Tommy Goodwin with his lady Elle and Tim Wrinkle off Lake Cunningham with Marcus' wife Rosie flying out of Sampson Cay, the aircraft came through different protections sprayed or painted over the frames. We all proved 'powder coating' looked pretty but served no protective barrier compared to a better two-part epoxy coating that I pressured for later. New corrosion-proofing sprays were being introduced and no product we did not time and test over the years! In time, with the help of great maintenance facilities in Florida that we used later, along with our own inventive protections, we finally added precious hours of service to our planes from the first lasting barely four years to doubling that in the last production aircraft. We often referred to winning a few battles but for certain eventually losing the war against salt. Both FAA and CAD authorities giving a winked approval when they inspected our machines knowing well our 'improvements' were only there to bolster the safer operation of our aircraft in the extreme corrosive environment we all flew in.

Marcus laid out a chart in Robert's home near Moultrie Airport. He showed the course that we would set back to the Bahamas with a fuel stop in Winter Haven to see Jon and then off the Florida coast toward Bimini. I added that without question we had to divert over toward the east coast in order to fulfil a promise of buzzing my old flight school in Rockledge; both friends' acknowledging a very appropriate manoeuvre. The next morning, with great anticipation, I watched the new Maule hoisted onto a trailer by a strong chain block and tackle from the hangar beams above then towed into the clear Georgia sunlight. It was all very surreal and emotional for me. Recanting inwardly from being told by one's father that 'you will never amount to anything', that 'flying was a fool's game' and all the negativity endured through my years growing up, to finally succeed in seeing a dream come true with your own brand new aircraft being towed through the South Georgia sunlight, a very long way from not being able to buy a newspaper! This gorgeous new machine was the gift of hard work, endless persistence to succeed and the will to make things happen in life. Lady luck had travelled alongside me a lot of the ways giving me chance to reach out and grab life firmly as it whizzed by, a secret I found early on, where at the very least, you give it a shot come what may!

The Maule M-7 Super Rocket model came with a 235HP Lycoming normally aspirated engine utilising a carburettor at first and fuel injection coming later. The seaplane was mounted on straight floats built by Terry Claggert, owner of 'Aqua Floats' in Minnesota. His design was exactly what I needed with strong flat decks and a proven record of endurance in commercial use on a Maule. These South Georgia days were clear and calm as the tractor towed the seaplane slowly toward the lake after being fully fuelled in front of the large factory hangar. Reversing the trailer carefully down to the water's edge Bob McFadden and some factory crew eased the seaplane for the first time into the murky fresh water. Floating free of her ride the airplane was turned and heeled onto the shallow bank. Marcus climbed aboard after going through a pre-flight while I watched patiently from the shore. I was to witness the first test flight before finally setting off home. The large black three-bladed propeller turned obediently as Marcus engaged the starter motor. The Lycoming coughed into life with a small puff of blue smoke from her exhaust giving the seaplane momentum into the centre of the lake. The paint gleamed as he taxied toward the far end of Lake Maule allowing engine oil to warm while turning into the very gentle breeze that had arrived in the morning air. Marcus eased the throttle forward where higher revs allowed a check of the propeller feathering. Within a couple of minutes the seaplane suddenly jumped forward quickly settling on the step to plane rapidly across the glassy water giving us barely time to read the registration number, N783SP. A number celebrating the month of July in 1983 when my daughter was born. Passing the men standing on the embankment Marcus pulled back on the yoke coaxing the plane off the flat surface. Gaining airspeed down the lake the floats let go of their grip gaining a few feet in ground effect as the pilot pulled harder back on the controls allowing the machine live well up to its name of Super Rocket. The Maule roared skyward clearing the trees without hesitation to circle the factory where most of the employees had now assembled outside in ritual gathering to watch one of their machines airborne for the first time off the lake; a round of applause as the blue and white Maule banked steeply overhead. It was a moving moment to witness the factory crew spectating with exhilaration and pride, one of their machines having patiently progressed its way along their production line during the last few months. They often took little notice of Ray Maule testing a new land plane whereas a seaplane launch always drew attention; a phenomena I was to soon learn throughout my whole career, where seaplanes held fascinating attention and the source of many photographs wherever one would be seen.

'She sounds fabulous Pauley!' Robert always called me by his given nickname, a generous smile showing through his very British moustache! My new plane turned onto final approach for the lake with the engine barely whispering now at low speed for touchdown on the glassy calm fresh water. One could not hear a Maule on final with a gentle purr as it came overhead. With one float held over at a slight angle Marcus barely grazed the water as the seaplane came to rest, settling in an idle taxi back to the grasses on the water's edge. Climbing out of the pilot seat his smile told the tale about his thoughts on the seaplane. 'She flies beautifully Paul, let's go home!'

We loaded our scant belongings and I climbed into the left seat to familiarise myself for a couple of minutes with controls, instrumentation and simply the feel of sitting there before starting my new machine for the first time. As the engine fired I had not yet reached fifty hours total flying time. Taxiing to the end of Lake Maule headed eastward I squeezed in the throttle allowing the seaplane to jump onto the step across the serene lake waters, forcing the swans stay high on the grassy banks. My heart was racing with the excitement holding the controls of my own machine. Adrenalin flowed freely allowing all my senses to come very noticeably alive. Inwardly I knew it would take some time before we really got to know each other, that special relationship pilots have with the machines flying on a regular basis, day in, day out, eventually becoming as one in the skies and on the water, feeling as it were each other's pulse and behaviour. Heading towards B.D.'s house I could feel the seaplane wanting to fly. Marcus had shown me the trick of pumping the flaps as the yoke was pulled back asking the plane to hop off the surface sooner than it wanted. Staying in ground effect the airspeed rose rapidly as the pine trees approached quickly. Another pull of the controls and the seaplane rocketed skyward to clear the treetops. Full of fuel and two grown men with luggage this airplane lifted effortlessly. The sea of cotton fields gracing this area of South Georgia passed below us, a mass of white soon ready for harvest as we climbed south-eastward towards the state of Florida up to 5500 feet; leaning the engines' fuel supply to become more efficient and economical for the near three hour journey to our first stop homeward bound. On arrival in Winter Haven we could top up the fuel tanks at the seaplane base allowing Jon Brown to see my machine for the first time. I purposely flew over the office and hangar making a right turn at the end of the small lake aligning up for a final approach to the water. Hearing the familiar tone of a Maule, Jon strode out of his office and through the hangar to meet us at the ramp where fuelling was easiest. Pulling the mixture killed the engine while I turned off the ignition keys and steered the drifting seaplane to bump accurately onto the wooden ramp. My flight examiner, with rope in hand leaned forward to secure the machine by its forward cleat on the float. 'Very nice Paul, congratulations!' he exclaimed stepping back a few yards to admire. We took a photograph together standing on the floats for posterity and the beginning of a long friendship well intact some twenty-five years later.

After departing the seaplane base we edged our way over the East coast of Florida where I was to fulfil my promise to the flight school at Rockledge. Calling their Unicom frequency, 'Rockledge traffic, N783SP, a seaplane inbound, any traffic Rockledge?' I heard the familiar voice of Danielle Stevenson. 'Is that really you Paul?' she asked excitedly. 'Get Chris and all those pilots out toward the runway!' I commanded back 'I promised you a flyby!' Within minutes I could recognise the familiar thin 2000-foot runway with the plumbing building one end. We both could make out clearly the group of people streaming out of the school buildings to await the approaching aircraft. Marcus flipped on the landing lights for added effect making us more pronounced again the midmorning sky. I dropped the Maule below the treeline so the students and instructors lost sight of us for a few seconds. Then, in total surprise, we roared over the roof of the plumbing building dropping dramatically within a few feet of their runway seeing waving arms as we raced by the line of small Cessna's and Andy's helicopter. At the end of the concrete I pulled hard on the yoke making the seaplane race skyward at a dramatic angle of climb waggling my wings in a wave of recognition to my friends below. 'That was fabulous Paul' came the call over our radio, 'Congratulations, she's beautiful!' 'See you in the islands and thanks for everything!' I replied into the microphone, high-fiving my co-pilot while climbing again to altitude and talking to Melbourne Approach for flight following back to the Bahamas. We had planned to land in Chub Cay to clear Customs with Marcus' friend Mr. Whylly and proceed on to the Exumas for my few days training out of Sampson Cay. 'That was well worth the diversion Paul!' Marcus said smiling as we climbed into the blue adding, 'You must be feeling very proud to have reached this milestone!'

Watching the intense dark blues of the Gulf Stream turn into swirls of bright turquoise was always the most exhilarating feeling for us who fly aircraft in this part of the world. There is no accurate wording to describe the colour schemes that played out below our aircraft. I often called the whole scene 'my very own Van Gogh painting' to the tourists I was to be flying in the near future. Anything that would describe in some inadequate way the magnificence of the swirling blues, greens and turquoises with creamy sand bars painted by the tides among the canvas of our world famous Bahamian waters. Flying each day became a surreal exciting experience that never grew old. From British Columbia to Alaska and Rocky Mountain bush pilots, those who traversed the Mara Plains of Africa and outback in Australia, we as pilots always marvelled at the dramatic scenery flown over. The Bahamas offered our very special and unique equivalent. I descended towards Chub Cay having cancelled our flight plan with air traffic controllers in Nassau and switched over to the Unicom frequency of the islands to listen for any traffic coming in or out of the airstrip at Chub. Making my first approach to the waters of the clubhouse beach lying to the west of the marina after just over two hours of flying en route. The sea was calm here with gentle wind from the east allowing us to land gently in the shallow sea in between a few scattered sail boats lying at anchor in the lee of the island. 'I can see you are going to get the hang of this pretty fast!' Marcus said gently as we removed our headsets for the taxi in to the beach. We unloaded our light baggage to wade ashore after setting the small Danforth anchor in the powdery sand; one could see why those of us who flew floats wore short shorts and no shoes, the ladies loved our dress code! Nathaniel, the Club driver, was there to meet us and drive through the casuarina pine trees towards the airport, where our friendly customs officer waited in his office. Marcus brought out a couple of aviation magazines from his briefcase and gave them to the appreciative officer knowing his love of airplanes and the dream of flying one day, a fatal choice for the young officer with dire results some years later. Formalities in order we returned to the seaplane sitting patiently at her mooring just off the beach. Stowing the anchor, we would dry our feet faithfully on a towel always carried over the back of our seats. No salt inside this plane! Flaps were lowered all the way so as to catch the wind pushing us in reverse far enough out to crank the engine back to life. This technique of 'sailing' a seaplane backwards I often used when looking for conch on days off. Holding the tethered airplane I would slip into the water with snorkelling gear on allowing the heavier aircraft to pull me along with wind catching the lowered flaps. Spotting large thin-lipped conch on the bottom I would dive down holding the Danforth anchor and set it in the soft bottom to collect dinner in a very unique way, only a Bahamian seaplane pilot pulling this stunt off!

Take-off down the creek lying north of the marina provided a beautiful runway. I climbed over Whale Cay clearing the airstrip of Chub turning south-eastward again for a high-altitude flight over the top of New Providence toward the Exuma Cays. We contacted Nassau Approach announcing ourselves a seaplane departed Chub Cay for Sampson Cay requesting flight following. With this in place we knew that the controllers would be keeping an eye on us as we passed through their airspace where, after about twenty-five miles to the south of them, radar service would terminate and on our own.

Ship Channel Cay lay to our left side with Normans Cay seen just ahead. Passing close to Highbourne Cay with its small marina tucked behind the beach we could see a few boats tied to the docks. A small group of people standing just outside the infamous 'Oar House' where Harold Albury administered the marina office. They looked up as the seaplane passed by them just a couple of hundred feet high now and different colours to the yellow and white Maule that everyone knew Marcus flew; his wife Rosie having a matching plane, N77627 in green and white with the famous emblem of the witch on her broomstick painted on its tail.

We flew passed Little Spirit Cay where friend Tim Revington lived as caretaker, seeing clearly the little island separated from its parent, Long Cay with the little known fresh water well lying amongst its sand dunes below sea level. We would often visit Tim spending a day spearfishing and a welcome rinse from the cold fresh water scooped to drink or wash from the well; story had it a source of water for pirate ships in centuries past. There was a lot to learn with this becoming my new neighbourhood in years to come. I would be learning of tides and sand bars that disappeared at low water, where thousands of baby conch shells would clutter shorelines in just inches of water, easily puncturing delicate aluminium skins of pontoons if not careful. I would be taught over time to distinguish all the depths of various approaches to the different islands and small cays, a lot familiar with over seventeen-years-experience as a commercial boat captain; where to land and hide when the weather suddenly turned sour threatening the safety of both plane and passengers. Entering the Exuma Cays Land and Sea Park with the northern boundary designated by Shroud Cay Cut the panorama below was utterly distracting. One could not help gaze in awe at the swirling vista of colours between Hawksbill Cay to the South. For twenty-three years I passed over this one location in all types of weather and light, the spectacle always holding me spellbound. Cistern Cay where the same MacTaggart family from Rose Island days had a single lovely home, tucked back into the trees painted in vivid orange to one side by a magnificent Royal Poinciana tree; the necklace of islands takes a slight south-easterly turn towards Waderick Wells. Here the mythical haunted anchorage clearly showed snaking through the northern boundary where Park Warden Peggy Hall's little tugboat *Moby* sat faithfully at her mooring in water so crystal clear it appeared airborne. A few more seconds of flight we pass the large vacant island of Hall's Pond and its smaller uninhabited sister, Little Hall's Pond neighboured by yet another MacTaggart owned island of Soldier Cay, offering protection to the East. Little Bell and Bell Island lay next defining the southern boundary of the park with Conch Cut boasting its deep centre channel of dark indigos descending over forty feet to the bottom. The formidable size of Bell Island still untouched with all it's perfectly sculptured coves and bays offering safe shelter for visiting sailboats spending their days laying in the calm pristine ocean, so clear from above boats appeared to be suspending in mid-air above their blue heavenly waters below. It was scenery from a *National Geographic Magazine*.

Just when one thought you had experienced the zenith of sights, we enter Pipe Creek. Here lay the jewel of the Exuma Cays. Island boundaries flanked with deep ocean indigo waters meeting the westerly chain of cays on the shallow bank side. Strong tidal flows in between each of the islands carved with years their magnificent trail of channels. Fast moving waters sculpture the ocean floor changing direction every six hours. Scattered coral heads lay on the bottom providing home for the vast fish population; in between huge beds of turtle grass lying flat with the racing overhead waters providing sustenance for the huge thin-lipped conch that inched their large shells for food each day. Life on the ocean floor, even deep below, clearly visible from the surface as the flawless saltwater appeared gin-clear.

'What a stunning place to live Marcus!' I exclaimed through my microphone.

'We love it here. Life at the cay is very special. Our home is a salvage ship aptly named Sampson', he pointed as we circled over the marina. Marcus had been a dive instructor, as I had been when first starting out to make a living in the world, located first in Eleuthera rather than facing life's bustle in the capital. He later became involved with the marina business in Exuma opening his own salvage business operating throughout the islands. Answering calls of distress commonplace in the middle of the night from visiting yachts having misread their charts to run aground on shallow sand bars or ending in mishap attempting to navigate between our complex jagged coral shorelines. Insurance companies would pay good benefit for his knowledge of retrieval especially after a passing hurricane wreaked havoc with boaters caught in the wrath of foul weather. *Sampson* was an impressive steel-hulled vessel that could carry their two seaplanes piggy backed on her decks. I landed safely in the lee of his island and let him guide me through the menacing narrow entranceway of his marina passing the fuel dock to our right. Colours here defy description, an iridescent bright turquoise only seen in a few places other than our Bahamas. An ocean so crystal clear it shimmers as a flawless diamond with sparkling sunlight dancing off our small bow wave. The light is so crisp that every detail of emerald foliage noticeable against the powder blue sky. Detail is in sharp focus. The waters race through this small opening as if a waterfall waited on the other side. He warned firmly, 'You only get one shot here so make sure you line up well with the flowing water!' A slight misjudgement would see my frail airplane crushed on the jagged razor-sharp rocks bordering each side as we raced through the channel entrance to the awaiting calm water, heart rate bumping now under my light cotton shirt. 'Now watch as the tide drags you sideways here!' He expertly navigated the drifting seaplane into the protected cove on the inside of the cay. I could see this would be a sharp learning curve from the onset where a strong mixture of aviation meets nautical ability. Mistakes here would be terribly unforgiving.

Darkness fell over the islands beginning with the symphony of cicadas buzzing they're rasping tune in the thick bushes. The sunset painted the Out-Island sky with such dramatic brush stokes it was hard to break our mesmerised gaze. We sat in mutual silence captivated by the spectacle of bright turquoises mingling with iridescent orange swirls of high cirrus clouds. Minute by minute the colours changed until the glowing orb disappeared below the horizon. We await the legendary 'green flash' but see no such phenomena. The evening air was warm and humid slipping comfortably into one's lungs. The hiss of a bottle cap being removed broke my spell. We sipped an ice-cold beer as darkness descended, speaking of seaplane stories and past adventures the ocean had graciously given us. Life was good. One slept early here to awaken with the soft powdery light of dawn caressing the small cays with barely a sign of breeze, a lone mosquito whining its shrill note too close to my ear having me swat the air hopelessly. The ocean mirror calm reflecting the cloudless sky set in opaque baby blue. Seagulls drift gracefully overhead before heading eastward over the deep ocean to seek their morning food chased toward the surface by racing schools of tuna or dolphin. Fresh steaming mugs of coffee wafted welcome aroma through the main cabin of *Sampson*. We ate breakfast together on the small dining table talking of the day's lessons in float flying. 'You will be doing a lot of your work in very small spaces Paul' Marcus started instructing quietly. 'Runways out here are most times very short or narrow where only a Maule will keep you safe! The 206 just doesn't cut it in these parts, rule of thumb with that seaplane simply "don't take off with anything in front of you!"' he mocked with a wry smile, recalling wistfully, 'we did a take-off competition once with Jim Buchanan in his 206 with our Maule at a 1000-foot while the Cessna was still on the water! I'll show you some tricks and then its up to you to take your time, think things out and play by the rules to stay safe'.

My friend was a master with his Maule. Both he and Rosie could make these airplanes talk. I coveted the day when I could perform the same as I taxied out into the clear Bahama morning. After two hours flying within the confines of Pipe Creek, both landing and taking off in very restricted spaces, Marcus caught me off guard by reiterating my friend Colin's words 'Paul, you have the touch my friend. Go on home to practice when you can. Never take these machines for granted as they can bite awful quick without warning! The Maule is a damned safe little airplane that will look after you. Just make sure you fly her and not allow her to fly you!'

We shook hands firmly and parted company in the midmorning sunshine. The journey home would take about forty-five minutes to cover the seventy-five miles. I called my mother briefly before departure to come and meet me at 'Coconuts' restaurant in the harbour. Being alone in my cockpit for the first time was a splendid experience, the same as that day I soloed for the first time. All the juices are flowing. The cabin and upholstery having that 'new' smell, the gauges only just reaching double digits on their time recordings, so much to pay attention to with just over ten hours' seaplane experience. Having back-taxied the pristine harbour of Sampson Cay, the Maule turned automatically into wind gentle now out of the southeast. I squeezed the throttle feeling this performance seaplane literally jump onto the plane racing toward the closed end of the marina. Well before reaching I ease the yoke feeling the easy climb away from the surface. I looked again behind me yet again to see in disbelief if anyone else inside the cabin, exhilarated to confirm flying a seaplane quite alone! I weaved back and forth in slow graceful turns above the small islands and cays letting the aircraft and myself become more acquainted. Flying at about 1000 feet north-eastward I left Highbourne Cay behind to cross the Yellow Banks. My instrumentation was a simple analogue display on this first aircraft, a compass and VOR navigation aid, no Loran or GPS in those early days as an aviator. This new pilot, well versed in reading the ocean floor, would note certain location hints now being able to observe from above. Out here I was very much at home as a licensed boat captain recognising the western end of the Yellow Banks tapering to a white flash of sand; learning to cross this perpendicular would give a course directly to Montagu Bay. Near twenty-five miles out of Nassau I nervously keyed the microphone, not wanting to sound amateur in my radio work. I remembered the lessons. Give them who you are, where you came from, at what altitude and your destination. Keep it simple. Nassau Approach Control on hearing I was a seaplane enquired if I were landing in the lakes, being long accustomed to hearing Jimmy, Tom and Charlie, all owning property there for their seaplanes to be based. 'Sierra Papa landing in the harbour,' I clarified. 'OK Sugar Pop' – the controller enjoying my call sign, 'Let me know landing assured?' I would come to know this voice so very well over my career. Tony Dean, a senior controller, becoming a good friend.

Nassau Harbour was a very busy place to fly in and out of compared to the idyllic quiet waters of Lake Cunningham. Certainly not the ideal place to learn the ropes of float flying in congested areas. The lessons here would be thrust upon me on a daily basis testing my wits second by second. How the hell I did not get into more trouble with so few hours under my belt? Choosing a landing zone, void of activity, landing safely to taxi in between the moored sailboats, compensating a tidal flow suddenly pulling me sideways was the first of many close encounters. Adding the challenge one of my first clients was number four in seniority flying British

Airways 747s. My co-pilot that day was Captain David Goodyear and the landing approach with a northerly wind had me had me dodge past the steeple of St. Matthew's Church heading directly at the Chalks' Ramp on Paradise Island a narrow pathway rife with marine obstacles. Timing was everything to miss the wake of glass-bottomed boats going under the bridge and westbound traffic out of Hurricane Hole Marina while weaving through the maze of anchored sailboat masts and very lucky having tide flow calmly with the wind. I greased the landing on to the harbour surface to approach the concrete ramp in front of me a little too fast. 'Oh crap!' I thought with immediate panic taking hold, 'this will be a fuck-up if I don't get creative.' Obviously I was going to hit the hard surface with some force – I pulled the mixture and exited the aircraft in one seemingly serene motion; extracting six feet two inches out of that tight space in seconds becoming a required art form. Taking a graceful lunge off the bow I managed to stop the float from touching bottom. With one motion spinning the seaplane about face and heeling it on the ramp. Re-starting the engine, we taxied across to Coconuts Restaurant.

'My word, that was impressive!' David exclaimed. 'You are a lot busier in this cockpit than I am on final to Heathrow in a 747!' I acknowledged the compliment having pulled off early in my career one of the great 'saves' float pilots are faced with, making it look as if this were just another normal landing with a heart rate thumping away within my chest wall.

My mothers' small frame on this first landing into the harbour became clearly visible as she sat patiently on the top step of my new ramp awaiting the first of thousands of approaches. I bumped the seaplane in the centre allowing the float to bite its wooden support firmly before pulling the fuel mixture. The three-blade McCauley propeller stopped abruptly as I listened to the instrument gyros spooling down. I secured the interior before exiting the door onto the deck on the left float. Mooring lines already in place on the ramp allowed me to secure both floats on their front cleats, a ritual giving familiar hand movements from near twenty years of boating coming in to welcome play yet again.

'I never thought I would see this day!' Mum said proudly, coming forward for a welcome hug feeling very small in my arms as I towered over her. 'I can't believe you bought a brand-new plane having no clue how to fly! God, I wish your bloody father could see this!'

Chapter 23
Safari Seaplanes

Limiting operation of the dive charter business only to days of favourable weather I was able to build flying hours quite quickly. It took little excuse to pre-flight that seaplane so receiving an unexpected phone call one morning from a yacht owner at anchor in the Exumas peaked my interest.

'Paul this is Viktor Kozeny down at Hall's Pond Cay, I understand you have a seaplane?' I acknowledged that I did, and how may I be of help? I knew of Viktor from recent island gossip. Born in Prague 1963, educated later in the United States, graduating from Harvard in 1989 with a bachelor's degree in economics. I knew that he had acquired a large home in Lyford Cay.

During the privatisation of Czechoslovakia, state assets were to be handed over to Czech citizens through a system of vouchers, with Viktor starting his own mutual fund using the renowned name in part calling it Harvard Capital and Consulting. Success came quickly. Thousands of Czechs were signing over their voucher books to 'Harvard', with promises of an incredible 1000% rate of return on their investment. Harvard Funds then bought shares in a number of companies, stripped their assets and transferred the money abroad to offshore tax havens such as the Bahamas. This scam grew like wildfire and Kozeny along with colleagues made millions. In the early 90s it is said that Viktor ran one of the great scams of the post-Communist era earning him the media title of 'The Pirate of Prague'.

In 1994 he planned to conduct a similar transaction in Azerbaijan, another country privatising its state-controlled oil company. Viktor's services were accepted having American investors such as AIG and Columbia University handing over more than $400 million. The government of Azerbaijan suddenly reconsidered their privatisation, however the investments were not returned, instead hidden in the tax haven of the Bahamas. Viktor bought his estate in Lyford Cay complete with private yacht and his own private island called Halls Pond Cay in the Exumas with justice finally catching up in 2005.

Viktor had a likeable side to his personality. I got along with him well and he started to use my services regularly. Interesting I thought, first Vesco and now Kozeny. What was the attraction to these 'bad boys'? Probably from being a fellow pirate at the time anyway, accepting 'charters' that he said would liken to 'contribute to my cost of fuel'; a satisfactory agreement in a very grey area for accepting financial reward for flying! The first flight for reward certainly presented a huge carrot waved in front of me, asking I deliver a flat of fresh raspberries and the *New York Times* for a nominal fee of $600! 'I'll be there within the hour' I replied eagerly. 'Damn' I thought with a smile, 'it would take me days to earn that boating'. The charter business to Rose Island had a lifespan severely numbered after this.

With barely four pounds of freight on board the seaplane I turned the ignition key of the Maule letting her idle out of Coconuts Restaurant turning an immediate left to taxi westward down the harbour. The convenience of this location to begin an aviation career was a great choice but in time I would learn an expensive lesson with chunks of revenue disappearing toward maintenance, for here was a brand-new seaplane costing some $85,000 sitting twenty-four hours a day in some of the saltiest water in the world. I had ample supplies of fresh water on hand from the property I was renting to find 'city water' here full of impurities insufficient in ridding the aircraft of its entire corrosive environment. The winter winds blew like hell some of the time, gusting through the harbour leaving films of salt all over the aircraft where running one's finger across the new fabric found a gathering of sparkling white salt crystals. I could wash until kingdom come knowing well eventually I would lose the war against corrosion. Marcus had been kind in his tutoring but not mentioned in enough detail the need for precaution using corrosion barriers *before* departing the factory. My first landing in home waters became the beginning of the end with unprotected steel bathed in warm salt, a learning curve that would last my entire career. For now, the excitement of flying a water-plane over rode all the downfalls. Prevailing easterly winds dictated almost daily that I taxi the length of Nassau Harbour toward the cruise ships for a take-off. In front of the restaurant one could see the roll of waves created by strong tides under the bridge flowing against the wind. Take-off here would be impossible into swells this high and one of the contributing factors I felt sure in the demise of Chalks aircraft in the tragedy they suffered out of Miami one fateful day. Commercial boat traffic was busy and congested within the confines of the harbour. Every day we would watch in amazement how Chalks Airline taxied their Mallard amphibians down that concrete ramp on Paradise Island into the water, turning immediately eastward to venture under the bridge for a take-off roll. On days of tide flowing with the wind offering calm water the procedure worked well. Even here as pilots pushed their throttles forward to full power, cascades of white salt spray completely engulfed the amphibian with its radial engines drinking gallons of salt until managing to climb on to the step safely, planeing the water like a mammoth speedboat to rotate near the golf course into Montagu Bay. Rough weather days bellowed the awful noise of huge waves washing through their propellers. The maintenance on these planes became inconceivable to imagine and only time would tell if they survived the onslaught of salt into their fragile alloys. It was disaster waiting to happen.

The amount of time it took me to taxi near the cruise ships consumed many hours of valuable total time on the engine, keeping in mind a mandatory engine replacement or certified rebuild in 2000 hours. The M-7 Maule 235 had a carburettor engine that accepted regular vehicle high-test petrol as well as Avgas. Fuelling became my daily physical workout, filling five-gallon Jerry-Jugs at the gas station across the road in the back of my old Chevy Station Wagon. These had to be laboriously carried to the rear of the restaurant building and stacked on the ramp. On days of a required speedy turn around I often marvelled at Suzanne sitting there with full jugs of fuel having carried herself to await my arrival. There seemed nothing she could not accomplish with flying floats in mind. Two at a time, weighing near sixty pounds carried down the slippery wooden structure to precariously balance on the front of each float. Being long in the leg really helped the stride up the side of the engine cowling while balancing a foot on the wing strut to heave the heavy container aloft onto the wing. A large metal funnel allowed the jug to rest on its lip while the fuel raced into the wing. This laborious process was repeated many times daily during the course of a busy day, I would stay in good shape with no need to subscribe to a gym with this career!

I needed time once in a while to escape and spend time with Natalie. During her breaks from school I was able on occasion to travel to Montreal and take her somewhere fun for a long weekend. A memorable time was had in Manhattan riding horse-drawn carriages through Central Park and dining in some first class restaurants in Greenwich Village while enjoying the company of my girlfriend's huge black cat called Magus. Other trips saw us enjoying the ski slopes of Colorado and Utah where I could watch a five-year-old in full ski suit fly past me after exiting a chair lift on her own with instructors having given slack reign to the little expert on the well-groomed slopes.

My daughter surprisingly hinted in conversation that things were not going smoothly for her mother and stepsister in Canada and that, 'Mum had broken up with her boyfriend and was living back at home'. She hinted in her fun cheeky way 'maybe you should talk with mum again', hinting broadly there might be chance of reunion. A golden rule I had learned was 'never go back' with relationships, seemingly a recipe for failure in a second innings. My daughter's heartstrings had an influential pull that no father could refuse try a family repair. Arriving in Montreal to hold that new baby girl was magical, even though not my child there was something incredibly compelling to 'give it a go'. My paternal instinct surprising even myself, let alone the rest of the family, saw in seconds that something good was about to come out of this reunion. I explained to Natalie's mother life for me was changing rapidly, now a pilot with a new seaplane my career had changes planned with a new staff member running my boat business while working with Jeff on film production meant me traveling from time to time and away from home. Days of being together up at Rose Island would be fewer than they had known in the past. The new foundations of possible life together were well received and within a month they all arrived back in Nassau. The house in Windsor Avenue would breathe new life.

The new decade of the 90s saw changes everywhere. On February 11 we watched Nelson Mandela walk out of his twenty-seven year prison life as a free man, with F.W. de Klerk, the South African Prime Minister announcing the unbanning of the African National Congress – South Africa had finally taken bold new steps. An agreement was reached in Germany with a plan to reunite east and west as we witnessed photographs transmitted from 3.5 billion miles away from Voyager 1. The UK and Argentina resume relations after the Falklands War eight years earlier. There is a massive riot in London starting as an anti-poll tax demonstration; over 400 people are injured in what was called 'The second battle of Trafalgar'.

The environment takes a horrible hit in Alaska with the grounding of super tanker Exxon Valdez wreaking havoc and natural loss in the region that would last for decades. Our computers are loaded with Microsoft's new Windows 3.0 and President George Bush Senior signs a treaty with Mikhail Gorbachev to end the production of chemical weapons and begin the destruction of their nations respective stockpiles. A terrible earthquake in Iran kills thousands in June and Kenya suffers rioting against the monopoly of the Kenya Africa National Union. On August 2, Iraq invades Kuwait beginning the Gulf War where eight days later Egypt, Syria and ten other Arab nations vote to send forces in to Saudi Arabia to ward off invasion from Iraq. By September the United States warns of intervention against the invaders.

African turmoil rekindles with the beginning of the Rwandan Civil War, taking an immense civil toll of over 800,000 souls. On November 22, another milestone is made this infamous date, with the resignation of Margaret Thatcher as prime minister of the England. By the end of the year workers from the UK and France meet forty metres below the English Channel with the first joining of the two countries estimated in over 8000 years! A new amateur writer begins scribbling a book idea on a napkin in a local coffee shop in England, an idea that makes J.K. Rowling the richest woman in Great Britain next to Her Majesty the Queen. We lose a lot of familiar actors such as Arthur Kennedy, Terry Thomas, Barbara Stanwyck, Ava Gardner, Sammy Davis Jr, Jill Ireland, Rex Harrison, Jim Henson, creator of the Muppets, writer Roald Dahl and American composer Leonard Bernstein.

After Steve's resignation as boat captain the days operating the Out-Island Safari are seen coming to an end. The day charter business had become so ravenous in nature we soon would fold our operations; pioneer services would fade giving way with Bahamian Tourism losing some quality entertainment. Within two hours of driving around the hotels on Paradise Island and Cable Beach, I was able in one night, to remove every scrap of promotion for the 'Out-Island Safari'. After seventeen years and entertaining near 50,000 visitors, the Ministry of Tourism Award Winning excursion closed down with the unceremonious dumping of a brown paper shopping bag full of brochures into a fifty-five-gallon garbage drum outside a hotel on West Bay Street. The drive home felt liberating. That daily grind of preparation and providing transport to each of the hotels for clients was over. Time now to move forward with this brave new idea of a full career in aviation. The dream a young schoolboy had found its time. Shortly after my closure, friend King Ingraham followed suit with the termination of 'Treasure Island Cruises'.

The next months see my pilot logbook starting to fill pages. Finding any excuse to fly I begin to build hours of experience in order to approach Civil Aviation with application for a Charter License. I need 250 hours in order to travel back to the Seaplane Base putting me through the paces for my Commercial Single Engine Sea rating. Before the family arrived in Nassau I took opportunity to travel to southern California and take up a Multi-Engine Rating with American Flyers staying with a new girlfriend I had met aboard my boat trip one day, living in La Jolla while flying out of Montgomery Field. I had decided whatever opportunity opened for me in aviation I should at least have the ratings in order to pursue any new opportunities in the future. 'June Gloom' is a well-known phrase in California and flying in visually impaired conditions a near daily event. For several days I mastered the Piper Aztec through the busy traffic patterns finally passing my check-ride first time. With this rating in hand I could ask Jon Brown to give me time in the Twin Bee for a Multi-Sea Rating addition. Before leaving my lady friend treated me with a ride through the magnificent desert country of Arizona, passing the famous 'Four Corners' highway intersection arriving at the stunning El Tovar Hotel perched on the edge of the Grand Canyon, awakening to that view was beyond description. Walking a small path along the rim I found an outcrop of boulder offering a surreal seat to one of nature's most splendid scenes. 'Please don't venture too close the edge' my friend would plead. Funnily enough the same phrase repeated verbatim while walking the cliff over Beach Head many years later by another lady!

Carved over near two billion years by the Colorado River the canyon is 277 miles long and up to eighteen miles wide in some places reaching depths of a mile deep. My host had surprises in store with the famous mule ride down the canyon for the day. Perched tentatively on the back of 'Neddie' I watch my sure-footed mule navigate perfectly down the narrow rough pathway descending into the magnificent vista below, the animals feet often inches away from the rock wall edge as my steed knocks loose pebbles thousands of feet downward! Following this adventure the next day I surprised my hostess with a ride in a new Aerospatiale helicopter. Sitting in the front seat with headsets playing exhilarating music we lift off over pine treetops whizzing underneath. One cannot visualise where we are until the canyon rim appears without warning. The helicopter dives into the abyss for one of the most thrilling rides I have experienced weaving through miles of steep canyon magnificence.

Flying back to Florida in those early days was really fun. We were advised by US Customs in Ft. Pierce to give twenty-four hours' notice of our arrival calling them twenty miles out allowing time for an officer to drive from the airport over the causeway bridge meeting us at the Pelican Marina for customs formalities. I topped the main fuel tanks on the Maule and ten gallons in each tip tank as reserve securing at least four hours of fuel. The trip would take about two hours and forty minutes from Nassau Harbour to Winter Haven with the stop in Ft. Pierce as the Point of Entry. Climbing out to 6500 foot and passing the North end of Andros I could ask for flight following from Miami Centre. It was always worthwhile having this service with the amount of traffic flitting back and forth between the Florida coastline and the Bahamas. My route taking me almost direct north of Palm Beach traversing over the Berry Islands and just west of Freeport, Grand Bahama; the view from that altitude resembling a Google Map displaying the amazing swirl of unique Bahama colours. The prominent straight line of the Florida coast with its vast beachfront properties and towering concrete etching its way northward became clear after passing West End, Grand Bahama. Air Traffic kept me offshore headed parallel to the shore toward Ft. Pierce. The familiar and very prominent power station just south of the city was the check-in marker for calling Fort Pierce tower, beginning my descent saying farewell to the controllers in Miami and Palm Beach. Explaining that I was a seaplane checking in with customs, the tower made the phone call for mc and relayed I would be landing in the waterway for the Pelican Marina. The large causeways across the wide expanse of waterway quite visible and I soon found the marina from Marcus's description. Circling once to check a good landing zone I prepared for my touchdown to taxi across the brown waters of the waterway toward the small slice of sand next to the marina facility. No sooner having bumped the bottom of the shallow water I noticed a government vehicle pull up just across from me. The customs officer familiar with Bahamian float pilots gave a beckoning wave so I walked up with all the paperwork ready to clear. He was very cordial and the procedure in those early days of flying went smoothly with chats about the flying from the islands and what I would be doing up at the seaplane base.

Within minutes I would be reloading the seaplane and turning it about face with the heels of the floats sitting firm in the shallows. Restarting the Lycoming was easy with it firing on the first turn of the ignition key. Taxiing out into the middle of the waterway I checked all around for any boating traffic. It was a weekday and fairly quiet on the water. Squeezing the throttle full forward the Maule jumped obediently onto the step where it begged for flight within seconds. I again called the tower and told of my intention to pass south of the airfield and head westward. Aviation for private pilots works so efficiently in America. It's as if the whole country is geared to making private air travel an everyday convenience, the days of commercial airliner travel far less attractive after the treatment of flying one's own aircraft. I bid Fort Pierce tower farewell 'departing the traffic pattern to the west' speeding across the vast orange groves of central Florida. Fields of cattle-grazing lands soon blended with visible waterways and all too soon the immense area of freshwater lakes lying south of Orlando International Airport came into view. Following the Florida Turnpike made navigation straightforward with the aeronautical chart folded in front of me. I could see the main roadways laid out on the chart and with clear view from 1200-feet in altitude I followed the map waypoints below me. Out here navigation required I be underneath the busy Orlando airspace that reached far out into the countryside. Lakes by the hundreds as far as the eye could see of differing sizes and shapes clearly recognisable on the chart and from above could estimate the most direct line to Lake Jessie with its familiar seaplane base lying on the North shore. It was as if I were coming home.

Talking with Winter Haven traffic, I swoop over the base to say a hello from above flying downwind to set up the welcome fresh water landing. A couple of students stood on the veranda of the school overlooking the lake watching with keen interest how the Maule performed on its approach. Making a flawless landing scrutinised by one's peers always a must during one's flying career! It was one of those understood statements pilots crave, if not to spectators for the simple self-satisfaction of squeaking those tyres onto the runway or floats touching the surface without being able to feel it, affirming clearly 'we have mastered the art' I am beginning to feel this aircraft becoming an extension of me flying as if one. To the east of the building lay a reed bed where I find tie downs for securing the seaplane while here at school. Pulling the mixture, the seaplane glides to a halt in inches of water in the knee-high reeds. Stepping off the float I nearly land on a baby alligator sunning itself in the warm Florida afternoon.

The written work for the commercial seaplane rating was all familiar territory under the guidance of my new instructor, Scott Slay. I had been forewarned this rating would probably be the most fun of all the ratings a pilot could sign up for. They were right with Scott and I forming a friendship that would last through the writing of this book. He made flying fun also gifted with the knack of making a Maule 'talk' as well as being a master of the violin. Pilots from all over the world came to this little seaplane base wishing to add that ticket to their logbooks and fly those classic yellow Piper Cubs. The check ride in my own aircraft was slated for the third day of training with Jon's brother Chuck. He often came to the base in between his commercial career now flying the executive jet for Publix Supermarkets. Chuck's flying skills were always enjoyable coupled with his good sense of humour, making the ride a fun challenge throwing all kinds of emergency scenarios at his unsuspecting student. With the Maule ride over a successful pass of Commercial Single Engine Sea is signed off in the logbook.

Next came a real challenge, flying the Twin Bee for my commercial multi-engine rating. The 'ugly creature' as it was affectionately referred to having a designator of UC1, a tail dragger, having the familiar main wheels with a small swivelling tail wheel under the aft end of the fuselage. Taxing this beast up the narrow taxiway, from its parking space next to the fuel pump, onto the main runway of Winter Haven Airport proved a fun time dodging tree limbs inches from the left wing. Chuck instructed I perform a take-off with a climb northbound after rotating. With a fist full of throttles above one's head I eased the Bee into a take-off roll. The cockpit offers full view of the round nose that falls away underneath the pilot seats feeling as if you are almost outside. No sooner I had rotated off the runway and put the landing gear up when my trusty flight examiner pulled one of the throttles backward. A wide grin with the words 'you lost an engine' to watch gleefully what reaction I would execute. 'Oh, thanks Chuck!' I exclaimed immediately pulling the next throttle backward to balance the lack of power. The sudden flood of adrenalin making thought and vision exceptionally clear. At this low altitude, the twin seaplane would not have sufficient strength to climb out in safety on one engine. 'Pick a landing zone' came to mind within a heartbeat. There is none with the runway falling behind us and houses and traffic all around! Bushes and minimal flatter area are all I have, no wait, water in front of me! Wind streaks on the lake's surface display I was in good direction for approach to the water with enough time to put in a degree of flaps to soften the touchdown. 'Oh, very nice move Mr. Harding!' Chuck praised. 'I haven't seen that done in some time' approving my flattened approach to the water. The Bee had little flair to the landing with the hull sitting in the water instead of pontoons feeling as if on a Disney ride about to submerge on touchdown. With confident relief, I knew immediately this exam was going well. Some more air work and water landings showed I had command of this aircraft. It felt exhilarating to fly a heavier complex airplane and get it all right, a new pilot could easily understand ambition in his early career wanting to climb into something larger and more responsive to fly. The downwind leg to the airfield felt very comfortable again putting in the correct flap settings and gear down just at the correct segment of the approach. A smooth touchdown had Chuck reach over and shake my hand; 'well that's your multi-sea rating in the bag!'

Chapter 24
A Demon called Andrew

August of 1992 was the usual hot, steamy month with calm, clear tropical days lying over the Bahamas, clammy air thick with humidity, the expression 'could cut it with a knife' so apropos. Far away in the eastern Atlantic a tropical wave of disturbed weather falls off the African coastline. Strong wind shear in the upper atmosphere at first prevented any serious weather from maturing. By August 17 things changed dramatically with conditions allowing the first tropical storm of this hurricane season take foothold. Six days later it grew to a minimal hurricane christened with the first letter of the alphabet as 'Andrew' this year. This storm was unusually small in perimeter size and we paid little attention as it worked its way across the warm Atlantic waters. The first storm of the season historically fails to mature into any major threat however its unwavering course in a direct line toward us definitely caught all our attention. Established in the boating business and now owning a light aircraft sitting very vulnerable in the waters of Nassau Harbour, my agitation grew by the hour. Each passing day this storm would grow some thirty knots in intensity. High water temperatures this year reached into the deep ocean hampering chances of cooler water disturbed to the surface making hurricane fuel abundant, the upper atmosphere favoured anticyclone conditions above the developing storm allowing a deep drop in surface pressure. Air inside the eyeball would be rapidly rising. The internal engine of this ferocious hurricane was perfect. It had both Bahamian and Floridian's utmost attention now.

We all became glued to the Florida weather stations, especially WTVJ, the NBC station, having Bryan Norcross at the helm of their weather department. He had moved from ABC in 1990 and had a natural flair for portraying all the pertinent information those of us with outdoor careers needed at this important time. We watched him guide us through the expected path of this storm. Very quickly it had all the appearances of travelling in a straight line instead of the usual curving course from the southern Caribbean up toward us. This nasty piece of work looked as if headed straight at the Bahamas and into South Florida. By the August 20 there was no doubt this storm was ours for taking a direct hit. The house in Montagu Heights lay on a slight hill letting me feel at ease with the thoughts of flooding in our area. The family would be safe within the old solid concrete building but the hardware afloat needed immediate attention. The boat was hauled at Browns Boat Basin and hopefully safe sitting on the hard surface out of the water. The little seaplane would not survive. Having no choice, I gave notice of an International VHF flight plan to Winter Haven, once here I would be able to see where the storm was heading and if necessary fly northward and away to the second choice of hiding, Georgia at the Maule factory. It took little time to secure the household. Aluminium shutters already fitted to the old windows were easily lowered and bolted within an hour. Andrew tightened in its shape staying the same diameter as a dangerous intense Category 5 hurricane, a very dangerous phenomenon headed directly for us.

Leaving the family was a difficult decision but the only one available. To lose our source of income made little sense with an ounce of prevention at hand. The familiar flight to Florida was accomplished with ease with my American customs officer meeting me once again at the Pelican Marina very understanding of my early return.

With sustained winds of 157 mph or higher this little monster would holds gusts inside sometimes 50% higher than sustained surface wind and making matters worse contained tornadoes that could shear three foot trunks of old Casuarina trees as if they were toothpicks. Three days later on August 23 the centre of Andrew hit beautiful Harbour Island and Spanish Wells direct with devastating forces clocking more than 200 mph in gusts and a record surface pressure of only 922 millibars. I watched in utter helplessness from my motel room in Winter Haven while winds and embedded tornado's shredded everything in their path with tearing salt that pierced the heart of every living thing. Ancient trees buckled at the relentless forces, roofs peeled from houses like over ripe banana skins. Boats of every size ripped away from their moorings or off their safe dry land storage battered by tearing forces mangling everything into tinder. Shopping centres collapsed while huge freight boats mounted the land to be dumped like rubbish in the bush. Nothing remained untouched and scarred or destroyed. As the eye-wall passed directly over the small settlements an eerie stillness gave way to brief sunshine. The ocean waters on the shallow bank side of Current Island receded hundreds of yards leaving virtually dry sands where the shallow pristine waters had once laid. As the next side of the storm raced over the water an ominous dark purple wall of weather approached like a roaring freight train. Gone again the welcome light, sparkling blues and turquoises traded for ink black and swirling menacing greys. The wind screamed mercilessly once again as the ocean piled back onto the shallow banks in tsunami like destruction. Houses filled with saltwater residents described later, near beaten to death by floating refrigerators acting as if a battering ram within the room where they cowered in fright. Some would not survive only to drown within their own home. The swirling mass of weather ploughed westward to leave the small island communities in utter destruction and still death of the aftermath. Nassau lay ahead but fractionally south of the path. By miracle the storm stayed true to its course with its small circumference only bombarding the capital with sixty mph or more winds.

The Berry Islands however were not to escape the same fate as North Eleuthera. The clearly visible eye of the storm tracked directly over the southern cays. Alder Cay, a private island development owned by Paul Tudor, a New York commodities broker I had started flying for, took the full brunt of the hurricane first. His caretaker John Davis, who I had befriended over my many flights, lived aboard a houseboat moored to the new concrete floating docks within the small harbour the owners had developed. Seeing the path of this storm, he did not hesitate in fleeing in a small outboard to the larger safe haven of Little Harbour just north of his location. Barely making it to his manager friends who had a home on the hill overlooking the tiny harbour, he secured the skiff and hammered on their door asking for sanctuary. Pieces of the house started to fail in the onslaught and finally collapsed from above, pinning John under of the lady of the manor now buried with a pile of broken timbers. John with his twinkling blue eyes and Carolina wit made light of the situation by describing afterward how easy his escape from the cay was compared to being peed on by the petrified woman he was trapped beneath, not able to move for what seemed hours!

Within minutes the marina at Chub Cay would be under the gun ravaged beyond accurate description. Across eighty miles of shallow hot water the hurricane fuelled itself as a Category 4 storm, slightly weakened by the small landfalls it had to traverse now aligning Cat Cay it its sights. Queen Victoria deeded this beautiful little haven in 1873 to Captain William Stuart for his service as lighthouse keeper over on neighbouring Gun Cay. Pirates such as Edward Teach, well known as Blackbeard, were known to use the cay earlier on. Various private owners bought and sold the island that was badly damaged back in the infamous 1929 hurricane. In 1931, a New York businessman bought the island for $400,000 constructing some guest cottages while turning the island over to architect friend Mike Smith having a passion for Bahamian and English style houses. In 1935 he made the island into a Club Resort with annual dues of $500 a year. Fishing around the neighbouring Gulf Stream waters became popular attractions through the next several decades sporting the famous Cat Cay Tuna Tournament. A small nine-hole golf course was constructed playing host to the rich and famous during its years. The late Duke of Windsor while Governor of the Bahamas played there naming the course Windsor Downs and thought it a grand idea to have a small casino on the island for guests, to which he granted license. In 1963, with the death of the owner Louis Wasey, the license expired. Hurricane Betsy hit in 1965 causing enough damage to close the island. Some time later Al Rockwell of Rockwell International and a group of investors revitalised the island as a private resort with high-end businessmen from Florida starting to invest in vacation homes being situated a little over forty miles from the Florida mainland. Cat Cay became an official Port of Entry for the many yachts that visited and harboured there. With Bahamas Customs in place it made a great place to touch down with our seaplanes and clear custom formalities.

That summer of 1992 saw the destruction of nearly every home on Cat Cay along with its natural surroundings and infrastructure. This strange storm with its unique size damaged the neighbouring islands of Bimini but not to the level of neighbouring Cat Cay. Now it was South Florida's turn to lie in the treacherous path. During the early hours of Monday, August 24, Bryan Norcross held a marathon TV and radio broadcast being the only contact Floridians had during their ordeal. While his station was being badly damaged during the battering of hurricane Andrew, Bryan stood his ground with backup generators and stayed with his audience through the night. Morning heard an uncanny stillness over the region.

A popular adage of 'looking like a nuclear bomb having dropped' seemed the only way to describe the flattened twisted neighbourhoods that were left. Corrugated iron metal impaled into trees, vehicles overturned and mangled, what little was left of them. Nothing was unscathed. Vast neighbourhoods, as far as the eye could see, in Homestead, Miami and Dade Counties, completely wiped off the map with ships sitting on top of rumble blown miles from their watery hideouts. The scenes later broadcast were difficult to comprehend. Over 63,000 homes were destroyed and over 100,000 other seriously damaged estimating 175,000 people homeless. Hurricane Andrew became the costliest hurricane in history to this date with four lives in the Bahamas lost and damages of $250 million. In Florida, forty-four souls were lost with $25 billion in damages. Leaving Florida, the epic storm travelled across the Gulf of Mexico taking thirteen oil platforms with it entering the state of Louisiana devastating the freshwater fishing industry and another 23,000 homes.

With the storm exiting the west coast of Florida, I was refuelled and airborne for the flight home. Carrying enough fuel, I could easily fly direct to Cat Cay and on to Nassau Harbour in one flight. Leaving the Florida coastline behind I headed direct to Cat wanting to clear customs there first. I could see land ahead but not recognisable as anywhere I knew. Maybe I was just south of course and this was the small rock line south of the port of entry? Speeding overhead it suddenly dawned on me, 'Shit, *THAT* was Cat'. I banked the Maule over to the left in a hard reverse course and started the video camera I had taken along for the ride. Circling the cay, I shot several minutes of footage showing the stark blackness of the landscape below. Houses were shattered and the marina destroyed with docks stretching out in the shape of undulating waves where the water had lifted the pilings from the seabed in graceful pattern. Nothing moved. There was no life visible. Landing carefully to avoid floating debris and taxing up to the beach by the marina entrance I threw out anchor and secured the plane. I carried my passport and video camera but nothing else. There was an eerie silence in the still clear heat. A stale smell of decay lay stagnant in the hot morning air. It carried from buildings, broken vegetation, from animals and birds that had succumbed the onslaught of flying debris. The air thick and moist as one drew air inward. There was nothing left of the facility to clear customs. It actually took a while for me to even recognise where the building that I needed to visit had been. I was totally alone on the entire island. Life had ceased to exist here. The decking and docks in front of customs had been lifted and placed upside down on top of the facility. It was the casuarina trees that really caught my attention. I had seen giant trees in Nassau hit full on by heavy vehicles in an accident that utterly destroyed all the metal in an instant leaving barely a scar on their trunks; these Australian pine trees gave appearance of solid iron, yet here were giant limbs near three feet in diameter twisted off as if a mere twig and thick trunks shattered a few feet off the ground, it was inconceivable – what force could possibly do such ferocious damage? So unique was this storm that its complete small circumference would fit inside the 60-mile eye of another monster called Floyd.

There was nothing left standing on Cat Cay taller than ten feet high. I recorded the devastation on film as a sudden movement ahead of me caught my attention. A lone battered rooster with little feathers left on its scraggly body scuttled in front of me to hide under the mass of wood debris. Graham Bruce had been manager there with his wife Anne but no one was in sight. All had evacuated the island with no time yet to return, I was the first soul there after the hurricane. I finished filming the ghost town and climbed aboard the seaplane heading for Chub Cay where our Customs Officer had often cleared Marcus and me. Heading eastward across the shallow bank waters a noticeable phenomenon came immediately into view. A large vessel passing over shallow water can stir the bottom silt leaving a trail behind it; so did this powerful hurricane. After many hours since its departure from the Bahamas I could still see the trail about a half-mile wide in a straight line toward its path from the Berry Islands. Approaching Chub Cay I called on the marine VHF radio several times only to hear an ominous silence. Flying over the island I could see it fruitless to even land with damage catastrophically the same as Cat Cay. Better to circle and shoot more film that may be of interest to the local television station showing our nation what was left of our precious Out-Islands. Leaving the same spoiled black twisted landscape under my wing Nassau came quickly in to view. The noticeable first sighting was that of green: an island saved.

I called Michele Malcolm, a newscaster with ZNS TV on arrival telling my story and she asked I immediately come to the station to lay up my video report for that nights evening news broadcast, insisting I try to complete it with one take. As we played the tape back with my commentary a silence fell in the control room the scenes before them proving too shocking to voice. My home and family were safe having found them visiting another friends home for the company and children able to play together rather than be distressed by the trauma heard outside. The Montagu property had little mess and the roads of Nassau already cleared. Now was the time for the seaplane to come to the aid of those in need in the Out-Islands. Greg Higgs from Nassau Paper Company, who always printed my brochures, called and requested the seaplane take as much fresh water supplies as I could carry up to his family community of The Current in North Eleuthera. Removing all the rear seats, we carried as much as able flying in thirty minutes to land on the water near the small Out-Island community. The hotel built near the shoreline was completely gone, only the flat concrete pad where the foundation had been remained. All the houses were badly damaged or removed from the landscape completely. People were simply sitting around staring at the ruin in shock while others had started cleaning up the debris from their houses and some trying to clear the road for incoming help. The welcome was very moving when residents came down the beach to meet us. I flew for several weeks with needed supplies to various communities, the seaplane having advantage of landing right to their back door instead of additional transportation from the nearest airport sometimes miles away, the very point I had made before the Civil Aviation Board not long ago. It took months for our island nation to recover the wrath of this freak storm and during this long operation the reputation of my seaplane grew immensely. Many times I flew over the *Sampson* anchored in middle of nautical mayhem where yachts and cruising vessels had been at the mercy of hurricane force winds. The magnitude of which blew them as if toys into heaps along the shorelines of supposedly safe anchorages. Millions of dollars worth of boats were total losses, splintered hulls and twisted rigging piling on top of each other in abandon forming a very macabre sight. The salvage operation would remain in full swing for weeks afterward, Marcus often giving a wave from the deck seeing my new career taking off rapidly as I dipped my wings in reply. His words to my mother echoing in memory, 'flying a seaplane will change your life'.

Chapter 25
A Decade of Change

Captain Danny Trainor from the UK was to supervise the Operations Manuals mandatory for approval of my charter license issued by Civil Aviation.

'You will need an Operations Manual, Paul, and it has to fit all *your* requirements' appearing as if one of my schoolteachers sitting behind his desk peering through reading spectacles balancing on the end of his nose. 'This is *your* manual,' he echoed. 'Next you will also need a Maintenance Manual under the supervision of the FAA Part 129.14 Program which has to be approved by authorities in America first owning a U.S. registered aircraft. There are standard manuals you can acquire and model your operation and airplane around those requirements.' Complex paperwork is not my strong point and it took weeks of work to compile, print and bind for presentation of approval. The FAA wanted to first come over to Nassau and inspect my base of operation seeing first hand where the seaplane would receive maintenance. They arrived at the ramp to look at the aircraft and my facility also to meet my Airframe and Power-plant mechanic. Under recommendation from the other float pilots on the Lake I was able to persuade Christopher Scott who worked at the airport to be my maintenance facility manager. We became good friends in this new career. The head FAA inspector wanted to know where we would be doing maintenance? 'Well, sir,' I replied, 'right here as we have no wheels it has to be performed on the ramp'.

'You mean out here in the open and in the water – what if it rains?' I could see their imagination thin and were just picking points to show superiority and maybe dampen my chances of approval?

Stating the obvious, I replied, 'We will not be performing maintenance on days of inclement weather sir, nor will it be in the water. We have six hours of low tide where the aircraft will be high and dry on its ramp.'

'Oh,' came the feeble response. 'I see. Well, you will have to manufacture an awning to cover the aircraft while being worked on.' He was just not going to let me get away without inflicting some requirement. I thought it better to just agree and present a drawn sketch of the awning that would be manufactured. The aircraft being brand new passed inspection offering nothing they could find needing attending to. At great expense, I produced the awning that in my entire career was never unwrapped. The maintenance program was issued shortly afterward.

Next came the presentation of the Operations Manual to CAA at the airport; no success here. It was nowhere near the required specifications reminding Captain Trainor 'this was *my* manual' but that did not wash. I had to start the tedium all over again with paperwork satisfying all the standards of the authority in the UK. Another few weeks of cutting and pasting information, diagrams and charts to compile what was needed for acceptance. Finally one day I received a call to come and collect the approved license that had just been signed by the Director. All that remained from Civil Aviation was an inspector to look over the Maule before the final sign off even though the FAA had just passed an identical procedure. 'Good morning,' the soft English voice said arriving at the ramp one day. 'My names Keith, Keith Riches, not like the Rolling Stones!' It was one of those instantaneous friendships once again. He had just arrived in Nassau and interested in learning about boating, learning of my past career on the water. We have shared adventures above and below the water in some beautiful places with a friendship still in place at the time of this edit. Safari Seaplanes was the first legitimate single engine seaplane operation in the Bahamas. Within a week or two Ellen Payne, Tommy's partner on Lake Cunningham, opened Bahamas Seaplane Service to be second. We were both off and running agreeing from the onset not to compete on price, warding off patrons attempting to play us against each other. We also agreed to both operate at an hour minimum so as not to compare with land-based aircraft operating solely on tachometer time enabling them to offer far cheaper rates. Elle and I both concluding the work involved preparing a floatplane for flight and the aftermath of washing it down certainly not worth a few minutes 'tach' time compared to counterparts in Aztecs, simply locking the door to drive home! For the convenience of taking clients almost within yards of their destination rather than the nearest airport often miles away requiring taxi fares was no contest in our pricing.

The Bahama Out-Islands were under a huge real estate boom. It was as if the world was playing this giant game of Monopoly within our islands and cays. Every week we would receive charter requests to fly real estate agents and their clients to look over potential purchases. Islands that were bought for thousands decades before were now selling for hundreds of thousands and in to the millions. With sales confirmed new owners hired local construction crews for their development in turn retaining the services of our seaplanes for transportation. On Bay Street, Jim Mosko, along with father and brothers, owned Bahamas Marine Construction: Jim knew he could drive one mile to the seaplane and be on site somewhere in the islands within minutes; their companies work was meticulous and his reputation for results kept us all hopping from Alder Cay in the Berry Islands to Little San Salvador recently purchased by Holland America as a cruise ship destination.

Environmental impact studies became a large part of the equation, calling Keith Bishop one of my early 'frequent flyers'. Private Island developments seemingly paid far more attention to the environment than huge conglomerates. We all watched in disappointment the destruction of Cable Beach where hotels grew from foundation set too close to the water casting shadow over sands relying on sunshine for their patrons. An insane behaviour repeated again on Paradise Island with the Holiday Inn casting shade soon after lunch over a magnificent cove. Experts from out of the country tore up the shoreline in front of the Crystal Palace, a hideous piece of architecture painted purple of all colours, making a poor resemblance of a lagoon. Nature fought back stagnating the water and denuding the beach of sand to massive areas of coral rock. It would take local knowledge with players such as Keith who would advise on the safe development of our shorelines. In time nature won the war with both establishments failing and succumbing to the demolition crews. Cable Beach and the cove on Paradise Island came back to life with removal of the designer blunders. Bahamas Marine Construction ran near the whole length of my career making it clear policy I would be taking care of my local clientele before all others. Everyone became a winner. The islands now had the loyal air charter service they had so long needed and our telephone never stopped ringing. Everywhere I landed I left business cards and introduced myself demonstrating with just a phone call they could have engineers, architects, guests, supplies and medical evacuations if needed. Some projects required weekly provision runs where a shipment would be delivered to my ramp full of groceries then loaded piece by piece and flown to the construction sites. The blue and white seaplane soon became an established sight with the Bahamas.

My old boarding school friend, Graham had purchased Nassau Plastics from retiring Peggy Hall who was to become our new Park Warden in the Exuma Cays. Graham had kept up his new flying career with occasional flights out of Oakes Field in a Cessna 172 off the private airstrip in the centre of New Providence still in operation mostly for the local Flying Club. He expressed interest in acquiring a twin-engine rating and talked of us both investing in plane for our respective businesses. He could move the plastics company freight from Florida and I could expand the charter service with a larger land plane. The idea was sound and having no fear of taking the plunge we flew to Nashville Tennessee exploring a Piper Navajo we found for sale. She was an old 1968 model with the forty-degree flaps that offered short landings in some of the tighter runways. Finding her in great shape and test flying we made the offer. With the deal in place we paid a ferry pilot to bring the Navajo, N577PC, back to Nassau. Flying this more sophisticated machine was an added joy I seemed to be getting the greater advantage of. Graham took the check ride proving a little more machine than he was comfortable with. To pay its expenses I used it on occasion for some additional charter work with one outstanding early offer from a film producer working off his yacht down in Long Island. He asked if I would fly him all through the Bahamas, from Walkers Cay to Inagua filming all the islands for a promotional video production he would edit and produce from his floating studio. Hal Lee had learned of my camera experience with Discovery Channel and asked if I could be an additional 'shooter'. Here was an offer I could not refuse. The chance to see my entire country and be paid for the privilege!

Business boomed and I seemed to be calling Chris Scott for the required fifty-hour seaplane maintenance more often than ever imagined, religiously changing the oil and performing the required inspections according to the new manuals all repeated again the next fifty with a more complex 100-hour inspection. Flight hours clicked away in my logbooks now in a second volume and in turn off the total time of the engines life. The seaplane was near four years old by now and with an average of 500 hours or more a year the mandatory engine re-build or replacement was rapidly approaching. I was nearing 2000 hours of logged flying time. Chris explained that he too was becoming bogged down with work at the airport and he would like to introduce me to his friend and fellow mechanic, Wilfred Clarke. Willie, as everyone affectionately called him, had worked for the old Bahamas Airways when my father was employed there. He was well versed with water plane maintenance having taken care of the old Grumman Goose that was part of the old BAL fleet. One day, while performing a fifty-hour check from around the corner arrives Willie sporting his ever-present baseball cap on backwards. He greeted me with warm smiles and eager to work with us on the Maule. We have been friends now for near twenty-five years.

We accumulated more stories working together than he could recollect with any other pilot. 'There are no pilots that want to turn wrenches with us Mr. Harding, you are the only one!' Willie would explain all the procedures with me bound and determined to learn every nut and bolt on this seaplane. I pestered him constantly about what he was doing hoping to learn the inner workings of my machine. There would be times out in the wild that something would go wrong and at the very least I could give it a shot at repair in order to make it home. There was not an inspection I missed, already knowing how to change the oil and filter, clean the spark plugs and look over the engine to spot broken tie-wraps and strange leaks of exhaust stains or oil streaks giving hint of a new problem. Willie had the patience of Job. I never heard him raise his voice even when things were going badly. A slip of the wrench had most of us yelp in frustration as the blood flowed off torn knuckles; not a sound from Wilfred, he took it all in patient stride.

With the approach of mandatory engine replacement or major overhaul I began to explore the options I would be facing. A factory-new engine was priced near $50,000 and I was nowhere near saving that amount of money. Those first three or four years I made it our dream to rid ourselves of outstanding debt. A very new concept that was most attractive to see unfolding. The day finally came where I could fulfil my promise to Emmett Pritchard and pay off my existing mortgage. My mother was so excited at this milestone asking if she could be the one to go and plop the last cheque on his desk. Emmett was very kind and complimentary saying I did not have to stretch myself to that degree, but outstanding that I achieved a goal he did not foresee happening. Montagu Heights with its extended property was paid full. The vision of aviation for a living had changed everything; gone were rents and having to survive off the ocean, gone were days earning a mere $7 for eight hours' work, no diving to dangerous depths fighting off sharks or grubbing around in a freezing cold Montagu Bay on a January day for sea urchins to sell for aquariums, arduous work hopefully behind us. We should be at last saving for a future?

Natalie and her mother were due for a visit to her French-Canadian family in Montreal while I continued running both operations here at home. Something was amiss. There was an air of indifference within our household. The magic seemed to have disappeared. Once enamoured with life in the islands while offering all the perks of flying, boating, travel and security for us all I had the feeling my wife's heart was in another place once again. She returned a couple weeks later with the two girls walking up the driveway displaying a dramatic change in her appearance. My mother came out of the apartment to greet them. Gone was the straight attractive hairstyle, now full of perm curls and exaggerated make-up spoiling the once natural attraction. She uttered a muffled 'Hi' and walked past us into the house, the two little ones saying nothing. My mother glanced at me saying quickly, 'who the hell was that?' as she walked back to her apartment in disappointment.

In days following the atmosphere of change became very evident, a sudden financial discovery was about to unravel everything. In four years of flying I had barely achieved the $16,000 or more needed to re-build with Zephyr Engines in Florida. What the hell had gone wrong? While checking the math over and over my bank accounts displayed frightening condition with insufficient funds to replace the engine on the plane. I was guilty in the first order of not paying close attention on the home front details and too liberal in my control of accounts. I discovered a lot of money missing. Sitting in shock on the top step of my ramp one day not fathoming how I had let this happen. The restaurant chef came past me saying, 'Mr. Harding you ain' lookin' so good?' Disappointment gave way to anger. My mother shattered with the news about being defrauded and incredibly perceptive, 'She came back on a mission, son,' her only thoughts. Both girls now old enough to attend St. Andrews school, one of the best on the island. I felt confident inwardly of always being a good provider but it always takes two to tango and two to fail. It became apparent that with the Canadian relationship failing and another baby to care for I became the rebound relationship offering a port of safe haven. The thought of not having my daughter and this other gorgeous little girl in our home took the very wind out me. I was emotionally at wits end knowing there can be no repair of financial betrayal. I could not on the other hand live the lie. I attempted analysing 'my part in all this' a plague that tends to stick. Overworking, guilty I am sure, for rising out of the ashes of nothingness work can become God all too easily. Life in the Bahamas is expensive with children to educate and a business to keep afloat; the demand to stay successful can be vicious. Maybe the expressions of frustration with the other betrayals in business a contributing factor? I was scrutinised for expressing anger. Life was tense in the wake of success having travelled and lived life to the full. This was, in my mind set, perfect time to make space and both able to breathe apart for a while? Call it an escape but the phone call, perfect in its timing. Hal, the producer beckoned from their anchorage in Joe Sound in Long Island. 'Any chance you can fly that Navajo down and start that shoot through the islands?' 'Good timing Hal' I breathed relief 'I will be at Stella Maris in the mid-morning tomorrow'.

A blue Bahama day greeted me as I drove to the airport and pre-flight the blue and white Navajo parked at General Aviation. I was not able to afford being based at an FBO, fixed base operation, just yet. There were two here at Nassau International – Millionaire at the far end of the field and Cleare Air just getting organised where the large hangars lay designed by my father. With fuel tanks topped I climbed aboard and closed the aft cabin door. It was very surreal and exhilarating to sit in that cockpit of a sophisticated twin-engine aircraft and know I could handle the complexity of this lovely machine. My mother's expression echoed gently that familiar phrase in the background about 'wishing her husband could see me now' after his demeaning of my abilities.

Both engines started with ease and hummed in synchronicity. I worked my way through the fairly lengthy checklist item by item. There was a lot more to do up front in this beast compared to the Maule. Flight plan filed with 'Radio', I release the brakes as a linesman guides me out of the row of aircraft on to the main ramp behind the fire station. Having listened to the ATIS, the airport information pertinent to that time, ground control gave permission to taxi to the active runway. There is something very satisfying following a large commercial airliner or just taxiing past the main terminal buildings where I used to watch aircraft as a boy. It's just 'pilot stuff' to those of us sitting up front, something unique to feel really satisfied about. It's simply 'being there'. 'Good aviodomy!' a fun word my mentor and friend Colin had created and used to exclaim. Aligning up on the departure end of Runway 14 and seeing 10,000 feet of concrete tapering in perspective away from you leads way to a smile of enjoyment. 'This is what it's all about'. Tower controllers speak clearly through my headset. 'Cleared for take-off Papa Charlie.' With a handful of throttles gently pushed forward to their full power position the Navajo responds quickly to race down the centreline. Reaching rotation speed, I ease the yoke backward and the twin climbs gracefully off the runway. Gear up gives a welcome sound underneath and three green lights extinguish to indicate all is well with the departure. The streamlined Piper climbs effortlessly to 7500 feet, a long chore for the seaplane. Here I level into cruise flight with both engines purring in unison I drift peacefully above the pure white tops of the scattered cumulous clouds that paint the scenery below. Graceful towers of white cotton floating as if weightless dirigibles above the brilliant turquoise canvas beneath them. Flying is everything wonderful and the true expression of pure freedom. The trails and tribulation left on the ground peel away from my insides, my mood as bright as the pure blue of the skies ahead of me. To be alone in this blissful solitude is a wondrous feeling to experience and for those of us who fly, a privilege to enjoy.

Passing at high altitude over the magical chain of the Exuma Cays is hard to put into words, the scene passing me underneath spectacular. Three hundred and sixty-five islands and cays, one for every day of the year, lay in a gentle curve to the southeast of Nassau stretching their spell on all of us for a distance of 120 miles. Curving away from the main island of Great Exuma I could see Georgetown with its thin accomplice of Stocking Island lying a mile to the East offering protection to over 400 cruising sailboats at anchor in the lee of the islands. From up here they appear as white specks suspended over a bed of turquoise. Nearly overlapping, on the Atlantic side, lay the northern tip of Long Island. Deep inviting indigos gave way to a sudden burst of bright iridescent turquoises circled in the centre with shades of warm creamy sand bars boasting their very shallow water. I trimmed the Navajo to a slight nose-down attitude of descent easing the power from both engines. Changing radio frequency to Unicom 122.80 I called 'Stella Maris Unicom' for a traffic advisory. A welcoming voice answered with 'No traffic at this time Papa-Charlie cleared to land, winds 130 at ten'. Lovely I thought, right down the runway is a perfect start to this adventure. The stunning shallows of Joe Sound pass to my right revealing Hal's white hull of *Tremalino*, a 65-foot motor-sailor floating in the ribbon of deep indigo water. I spot the narrow strip of the airport runway just ahead. With checklist in hand I made the approach by the book. Gear down for the familiar sound of the wheels leaving their snug hiding place under the main hull of the plane, a transition landing gear light turning once again to the always welcome three greens. Flaps down and approach speed reached, the runway gaining on me far faster that I am used to with the seaplane that could seemingly hover above its landing site. Power off as I glide gracefully over the trees to the runway threshold, slight flare and wait, yes wait for that touchdown of a gentle squeak of rubber against the hard surface. Colin would be well pleased to see his students' progress within his world of aviation.

I secure the plane on the ramp near the small terminal building and talk briefly with Bahamian Customs issuing a Transire, the document I will keep on board all our flights through the islands, showing our places of origin and landings. A small courtesy car takes me up to the main lodge that I had not seen for years since last filming the *Sharks of Stella Maris* for the Discovery Channel series. The familiar faces of Peter Kuska and Jorge Friese greet me just inside the lobby doors. 'Good to see you again Paul,' in a light German accent. 'Hal is just inside the bar waiting for you.' 'Thanks Peter good to be back. We can talk more later!' I walk through the lobby and into the main area where everyone meets for planning their days diving or activities. A small bar lay at the far end of the room. Hal was sitting there nurturing a glass in front of him, seated next to a young lady both seemingly in deep conversation. Sensing my approach across the room he swivelled on his stool to stand and greet me. With outstretched hand gesturing to his guest, 'This is my pilot! Paul, I would like you to meet Suzanne!' Sparkling turquoise eyes met mine and with a warm smile, she shook my hand nearly crushing my fingers. 'My, that's quite some handshake!' I exclaimed. 'Good to see you again Hal.' I felt flustered and uneasy for some reason. The effervescence from this lady with long waving blonde curls catching me unawares; she was stunning. 'I just need to go and clean up,' I stammered like a schoolboy. 'Be back in a while', a slight panic and unexplainable need to vacate this introduction.

'Great,' Hal said, 'see you for dinner, Suzanne is joining us'. His loosening dentures clicking back into place when he spoke.

I walked briskly outside the building, that old familiar feeling of an intimate connection sending a wave of knowing through my psyche. Looking upward in prayer-like stance, voicing clearly while motionless, 'Not now! Why now?' How could this attraction come at this untimely stage of my life? We all met later for dinner in the lodge dining room, where after dessert, Hal could see that his pursuit of this lady was in vain, and cordially left the scene, having invited her to come flying with us through the islands. 'See you in the morning you guys, about nine am?'

'First stop, Pitts Town Point, eh Paul?' My heart sank. Back in those days the shortest runway in the Bahamas especially for a twin and my early skills in this aircraft would be put to the test with a landing on the north end of Crooked Island. The plan had evolved over dinner to fly through the southern Bahamas first for several days and then meet back in Nassau where *Tremalino* would berth at the Yacht Haven. From here we could cover the northern islands and cays. Hal Lee had been a professional cameraman in the film industry, working at times on the early Bond films. It was here he was badly injured in a helicopter crash while filming, which ended his career. Recovering in time and receiving handsome compensation, he invested in the motor yacht *Tremalino*. Aboard, he had installed a fully functional film studio in the main cabin, enabling him to edit for commercial productions selling freelance while on his travels.

Morning came all too quickly after spending a late night in deep conversation for hours that cemented a new relationship in an emptying restaurant. We walked the moonlit pathways where light danced off the dark palm fronds. It was as if nature was conspiring to breathe new life into our souls, neither of us resisting the inevitable attraction. In the early hours, I plan flights to places never seen while living in the Bahamas and a letter of thanks to my new companion, delivered thoughtfully by Peter that night. Suzanne had explained her being there to accompany her North Carolina landlady on shelling expeditions and an occasional scuba dive for herself. I had reiterated the invitation making the line quite attractive, 'hoping that rather than go diving you will fly with me through The Bahamas!' Hardly a line to resist for here I learned was a lady who had lived previously in Freeport where her son was born. She had loved Grand Bahama and island life not wanting to leave when her then husband was transferred working with Eastern Airlines.

There were many well-travelled local Bahamians met later in life having been to New York, Europe and out as far as Australia, yet never visiting a local Out-Island. The prospect of experiencing my whole country was slightly overshadowed by nervousness concerned about competency of flying and navigating a more complex machine. So much to consider compared to flying the seaplane. Time on route, distances, and fuel consumptions just the beginning. Navigation without the luxury of GPS in those early days was purely by compass or an occasional VOR signal: if one was fortunate enough to be within range. Time indeed to stay acquainted with our trusty E6B flight calculator. An ingenious piece of equipment developed by U.S. Naval officer Phillip Dalton in the late 1930s. The name coming from its original part number for the U.S Army Air Corps during World War II. After resignation Dalton became a Navy Reserve pilot tragically dying in a crash with a student practicing spins. With prevailing winds out of the east-southeast, this important first day at least offering favourable conditions. We all met under the shade of palm trees, fronds waving gently in the ten-knot breeze, appearing is if in some destination brochure. Several passengers milling about awaiting the arrival of the scheduled Bahamasair flight back to Nassau, tourists casually dressed in bright coloured Hawaiian-styled shirts, shorts and flip-flops, exposing their crimson, sunburned skin, chatting loudly in strong American accent. Hals' Cuban wife, Isis, had joined us from their evening aboard their yacht. A tiny-framed thin-limbed girl with long dark hair dressed in a short thin white cotton dress, weighing less than a hundred pounds I calculated. I loaded my three passengers and camera equipment, with Hal sitting in the rear of the plane where he could shoot video from either side-window as we made ready for departure, our new guest from South Carolina, in welcome close proximity, sat in the right seat up front. Suzanne had flown before with her father in Piper Cubs. Losing him to a corporate air disaster where a Mitsubishi fell out the sky in a thunderstorm, now took considerable courage to come and fly in a private plane. She laughed aloud and placed the headset on without hesitation, trusting my ability to keep us safe. The week spent together renewed her love of flying so emphatically on returning to Florida she enrolled in flight school. I had discovered quite by fate's intervention a true partner in life.

Full power at the departure end of Stella Maris runway, the Piper responded as if there were no additions of weight, lifting effortlessly upward in a climb toward Crooked Island. With a few circles around the northern tip of Long Island Hal was able to capture the aerial footage of our lodgings and his yacht, with captain still on board, seemingly afloat on a mirror of crystal clear ocean. At 5500 feet, the clear Bahama day showed the northern tip of Crooked Island quite quickly. I was still amazed at how fast this light twin could fly.

The famous and very prominent white lighthouse of Pitts Town Point came into view. I glanced back at Hal, sensing he would give me a signal what he needed to film before landing. He saw me turn and with index finger drew several circles. There were few buildings here on this end of Crooked Island making up the small resort facility that offered very casual lodging in a dozen small cottages, mostly for visiting pilots in private aircraft. Several planes lined the narrow tiny strip. 'There must be a fly in,' I commented to my guest next to me. All the small aircraft were single engine Pipers mostly, Cherokee Sixes, Saratoga's and a few Cessna 172s. No twin engines. As we went around the runway I noticed the surrounding waters here even more turquoise than I had seen before, inexplicably more intense. This fast approaching landing suddenly took all of my attention. This magical little facility hidden in a grove of coconut palms was so small and runway so very short. I would have to touchdown on the beginning of this hard surface that protruded slightly into the ocean offering a stingy 1600 feet of good landing surface with the far end a meagre 400 feet of slightly cleared underbrush. I lined up on final a fair way out into the sea, treating this approach as if I were in the Maule coming into somewhere very tight. I reached across to my guest and gently squeezed her hand. Suzanne smiled as if really enjoying this experience. Gear down and with the full forty degrees of flaps this old Navajo offered, I neared the surface of the water. The approach from the back of plane must have appeared daunting, only feet off the waves. Pulling off the power as the aircraft slid over the stubble grasses at the beginning of the runway I allowed the main gear to squeak nicely onto the tarmac. Applying brakes fairly quickly the twin came to a stop quite short of the end. I think that's when I finally exhaled. 'Very nice!' Hal called out from the rear. I raised one hand in an 'ok' wave with my fingers as reply. As we pulled up on the ramp area the manager came over to say hello. 'That was pretty impressive,' he smiled, 'you only used about 1200 feet! Come on in and have some lunch'.

None of us had ever tasted creamy conch chowder before. With aromas of very warm fresh locally baked bread, the welcome meal slid down comfortably. The plan made around our lunch table was to navigate Crooked Island working our way back up to Rum Cay with a landing on San Salvador to film the famous site of Columbus's landfall in 1492. We became very aware that our predecessors for lunch were actually all waiting for us to finish the meal and leave the restaurant; wanting to see how this twin engine was going to actually get *out* of here now that they had got in. Re-seated on board, and cabin door closed, I began the start-up procedure. Both engines kindly behaved with class and distinction, firing up almost instantly. No restarts here in front of an audience, no long grinding of starter motors with an engine nearly flooded. Thank you Navajo!

I taxied to the departure end making the turn so close to the edge that Hal's seat was hanging over the waterline. Sixteen hundred feet in front of us looked awfully short from here with ominous broken greenery at the far end. I eased both throttles full forward, stepping hard on both brake pedals. Everyone had exited the restaurant building and now lined up on the side verge of the runway to witness how this lad who wore only shorts, tee-shirt and no shoes, was going to pull off such a short field take-off. Reflecting back on some of these departures or landings I really became very aware how incredibly bold or full of folly human beings are at times. That undying faith we have in our flying machines unmatched, taking for granted in unquestioned faith that every nut, bolt and moving part of this complex collection of machinery is going to perform flawlessly; that the laws of lift will always come into play without question and we will rise in safety off our runway, however ridiculously short it may be. Years later, when all these factors stayed in place, save one, I would have only split seconds to stay alive.

The Piper strained to gallop forward under the thrust being put upon it. The engines spooled upward in RPM and just when I felt it impossible to hold any further, I slid both feet off the toe pedals to take firm hold on the main rudders. The Navajo leapt forward to race down the runway. I could feel myself swallow and hold my breath, waiting for the bushes to come frighteningly close from the far end seemingly forever before gaining ample speed. I pulled back with authority on the yoke, now slippery from the moisture of my palms, and I was aware of a thumping in my chest. My subconscious hearing clearly those pilots watching so intensely as we run out of runway, whispering 'Come on baby, fly!'. And fly we did. The gear came up obediently and I turned the aircraft in a right climbing turn. Once completing the circle, I lowered the nose for a rapid descent toward the line of planes. 'Go for it!' Hal squealed in exhilaration from the rear, knowing that buzzing the audience a mandatory manoeuvre. The pilots froze watching our aircraft swoop down the runway from the far end to race past at over 100 mph only about ten feet off the surface, a strong amusement park climb and waggle of the wings in salute to our friends below. The radio came alive, 'Very nice, thank you Papa Charlie!'

Some 524 years ago Columbus had been rowed ashore by his crew aboard one of the tenders off his flagship *Santa Maria*, his first footsteps on this side of the Atlantic sinking into the finest talcum powder sand on San Salvador Island. Some historians claim the original landing was on *Santa María de la Concepción* or an island we know well to be Conception Island neighbouring Rum Cay. The flat lonely cay in the middle of the ocean far more desolate than San Salvador may not however have supported a local tribe? Today we walk barefoot near the water's edge, hardly feeling the smooth surface touching the soles of our feet, where local light-skinned Lucayan-Arawak Indians first greeted the explorer, the spot marked here by a white stone monument. The open ocean continues to the West and it would have been here, on the calm lee-side of the island, back in 1492, where three wooden ships would have lain at anchor. From traversing the vast open Atlantic, Christopher Columbus was amazed at our crystal waters, finding I am sure with alarm, how an open ocean could suddenly go from extreme depth to mere inches above beds of treacherous coral reef. He called this land 'Bahia Mar', Portuguese for 'shallow sea'. There are records of Columbus' logs that have interesting entries about the Europeans observance of the peaceful island inhabitants and the immediate intension of abuse.

Saturday, 13 October 1492: ...They brought us sticks of the cotton candy thread and parrots and other little things, which it would be tedious to list, and exchanged everything for whatever we offered them. I kept my eyes open and tried to find out if there was any gold, and I saw that some of them had a little piece hanging from a hole in their nose. I gathered from their signs that if one goes south, or around the south side of the island, there is a king with great jars full of it, enormous amounts. I tried to persuade them to go there, But I saw that the idea was not to their liking...
Sunday, 14 October 1492: ...These people have little knowledge of fighting, as Your Majesties will see from the seven I have had captured to take away with us so as to teach them our language and return them, unless Your Majesties' orders are that they all be taken to Spain or held captive on the island itself, for with fifty men one could keep the whole population in subjection and make them do whatever one wanted.

Centuries later three replicas of the explorers' ships sailed the same route with the smallest of his fleet, *La Nina*, Spanish for 'The Girl' (being her nickname to the chosen traditional name of Santa Clara given in the day). Notably known as Columbus's favourite of the three ships, the first replica laid anchor within Nassau Harbour. A second replica was constructed in 1988 in Brazil with her construction techniques of the 15th century, using only axes, saws and chisels. In 1991 she was sailed to Costa Rica for the filming of *1492: The Conquest of Paradise* using my friend Marcus Mitchell and his team as film support crew aboard his salvage ship *Sampson*. In the mid-60s, my father took me by boat to tie up alongside *La Nina* and climbed aboard. Immediately noticeable was the definite pungent aroma of wood, pitch and hemp rope, as the vessel had been constructed in every original detail; its smallness shockingly apparent – although weighing an estimated sixty tons and near fifty feet in length, with less than a sixteen foot beam, the boat must have rolled easily in the ocean swells for the original fleet had been designed to sail the Mediterranean, not meant for the open ocean. The twenty-four-man crew lived aboard this tiny space eating below in the cramped darkness, while sleeping on the decks for that first voyage to America. The use of hammocks came after seeing the Native Americans utilising them. They had set sail leaving Palos de la Frontera on August 3 1492, to arrive for a stop in the Canary Islands, nine days later before heading westward again into the open ocean where many of the general population feared they would fall off the edge of the horizon.

It would be two months later on the dawn of October 12, that Columbus made landfall within the Bahamas. *La Nina* sailed back to Europe earlier the following year nearly being capsized by a storm east of the Azores to arrive safely back at her departure port on March 15 1493.

The smooth clear waters radiated a thousand points of light as the Bahamian sunshine danced off its surface. Hal and I filmed the surreal landscape that we felt confident keep an audience spellbound, for the Bahama Out-Islands, in our estimation, deserve to be classed as one of the world's wonders. We drove through small settlements filming local Bahamian ladies balancing on small rickety wooden stools while weaving their straw, shaded by tattered fading umbrellas advertising Heineken beer outside their stalls. They were no means camera-shy, smiling generously with missing crooked stained teeth set in dark crinkly faces while their talented gnarly fingers weaved the straw in automated motion from years of practice. The friendly banter most often beginning with 'Baby, gimme five dollar for a lovely hat!' As we approach they try another line, 'Tree dollar for a place mat?' the strong local dialect always misplacing the 'h' in our language.

Our flights around the southern Bahamas provided valuable lessons in our countries culture, ways of life, and geographical beauty; an appreciation of being able to witness the real Bahamas, where even the light of day had a magical clarity, making everything we filmed appear surreal in iridescent colour. The settlements found in Cat Island, Long Island, Inagua, and San Salvador all clustered in those southern regions offered the simplest of rewards, a warm welcome from small populations sharing their love of being locked in a time warp, where it seemed as if I had just arrived in 1960 or even decades earlier. Everyday folks going about their business of weaving straw or mending fish pots or caulking wooden sailing craft, all taking the time to acknowledge our presence with a warm Bahamian smile saying, 'Good Morning' as we passed. Here they did not lock doors and there were no keys to our hotel rooms. We hoped selfishly progress would stay hidden. The footage we captured here became a fabulous hour-long postcard that Hal would edit with melodious 'island sound' music, steel drum, guitar, trumpet and vibrations of the merengue. After several days of production, he realised that his immigration time allowance in his passport entry was expiring for this visit and asked me to plan a flight down to Providenciales in the Turks and Caicos Islands. Here we could stay for the required 24-hour period out of the country and return again for their re-entry into the Bahamas. The flight went well and, approaching the most southern of our island chain, we could see that Provo, as it was locally known, was surrounded with similar gorgeous colours of the ocean and powder white beaches although the island noticeably flatter and more arid. Flying that couple hundred miles further south gave noticeably warmer temperatures. Exiting the plane and checking in with the local customs and immigration we felt a definite change in hospitality; the hotel check-in confirming a surlier attitude than our last few Bahamian days. Our time here would be spent casually taking the day off from filming. With a return to Stella Maris time had arrived to pack for a flight back to Nassau. The last night's dinner aboard *Tremalino*, we recounted stories and viewed some of our work while making plans to meet back in the capital for a continuing second phase of the project into the central and northern Bahamas. Hal's captain needed a lift into Nassau to collect needed boat parts so took opportunity to ride in the right seat back with me. I bid farewell to my three friends and felt the definite tug of sadness having to depart from a developing new relationship that offered a God-sent escape from a poor situation on the home front. There was however little doubt this would be the beginning of something very special, having us partnered for over eighteen years! The next few weeks after leaving here were going to be a tough journey for my soul to bear.

Several weeks later I learned that Suzanne had made the bold move of signing up for flight school. Paul Tuzio at Fort Lauderdale Executive Airport being her private tutor flying a Cessna 150, as we all had done in the beginning. Helping Paul instruct was a mere slip of a girl with long blonde hair. Teri could fly anything that had a propeller and became my first instrument instructor later herself entering the cockpit of commercial jetliners where I imagined those large crew seats would have near swallowed her whole? I was so enamoured with Suzanne's fortitude in sharing my new career I offered her a seaplane rating at Browns Seaplane Base as a birthday gift, a qualification she aced the first time with a higher score on her written than I. Within a few weeks of our meeting she calls me with an invitation to Normans Cay where she, Teri along with boyfriend Dirk and her son Jay and girlfriend have rented the house on Pyfrom Cay. They have rented a Piper Cherokee 6 that Suzanne would fly in order to obtain her long cross-country qualification. The low-wing single was indeed a truck of the skies loaded to the max with the group carrying coolers and baggage. I met them at the cay flying in to land in their waterway with the new Maule where I would stay a couple of nights learning outrageous stories of times past about this famous island of ill-repute.

Ralph, the caretaker was one of the many off-the-chart characters that inhabited the infamous island once owed by the king of cocaine, Columbian drug lord Carlos Lehder, co-founder of the Medellin Cartel. Ralph had arrived by sailboat one day in years past having run away from New York with his babysitter hiding in the balmy waters of the Exuma Cays in the Bahamas. His young partner proceeded to run off with another visiting yachtsman laying anchor inside Normans Cay Pond. Ralph stayed on making a life caretaking and general help around the island with the local residents who returned after Lehder's purges in the takeover. Island folks keep in touch on the local marine VHF radio with his fun call sign, 'Okay-fine-right'! Carlos Lehder had a chief pilot for his drug operation who in turn had arrived on Normans with Michelle, his under-age girlfriend also having run away from home. The parties at Lehder's private home 'Volcano' were infamous within themselves often with more ladies of the night flown in from mainland Florida. Lehder was known to drive around the far side of the island where he gated that section from anyone else being allowed. Guarded with sub-machine gun toting characters and guard dogs the drug lord's private laboratories were said to have created the first crack cocaine.

Michelle returned years later to strike up romance with Ralph, a match made in heaven we all hoped. Lehder's chief pilot, now due for parole sent word of returning to Normans Cay. It is here the story ended with the happy couple boarding a chartered King Air for direct flight to Panama with laden suitcases never to be heard from again!

Idyllic days were shattered once again on arrival home. It was as if I had thrown a hand grenade into the room allowing it to shred our household. Everything that had made us whole as a family now spattered into fractional pieces with feelings torn and hurting. I had new courage to confront my spouse with my lengthy financial investigation and all too soon emotions overflowed. How could something that started so beautifully turn so sour? Relationships, even good ones, are inevitably hard work at times, and here we failed, a fine example of two people seemingly not able to help themselves make life less complicated than it already is. The remaining downhill spiral was fast. Recovery at this point impossible, as if we were in a flat spin headed for imminent impact with the ground. We all lived inside that home for a while longer but not together, I refusing to relinquish my roof to someone who exercised betrayal. It came to simple principle, stubbornly holding my ground at whatever cost.

The 'coup de grace' to an emotional flogging was administered with my mother opening a morning's conversation, 'Can you drive me to hospital tomorrow, I am going for an operation with Dr Earl Farrington to have a lump removed from my breast?' The strength in my legs suddenly drained away and I sagged into her sofa in the apartment, mother and son just looking at each other from a few feet apart with empty expressions, grasping to find adequate words. Finally, she broke the silence speaking softly. 'When Olive was here a long time ago, she told me she had a lump and was going to a Harley Street specialist to have it removed, I had found one also and could have gone with her but not wanting to be a bother, I said nothing.' Her friend had been a long-time acquaintance and stewardess with Bahamas Airways. 'Mum, that was years ago!' I nearly cried. 'She would have taken you with her!' 'Not wanting to be a bother? Really?' My voice near breaking. There was no reasoning with my mother now. Her heart set on her doctor, who she liked and trusted, having set her broken arm years before from a car crash, with my father probably driving drunk. Not versed in this chronic ailment I could offer little argument. The operation went to her satisfaction with the tumour removed. I collected my mother outside the hospital entrance, she appeared so very frail, the years suddenly showing, that strong English wit lay quiet. My wife on hearing the news of the catastrophic disease told the children 'Nanny was very ill' and they would walk around to the apartment daily to keep their grandmother company. 'I want to be a nurse,' Natalie confided in us one morning, 'I could look after her'. Her mother on the other hand retorted in frigid tone, 'I hate taking care of old people,' having had nothing to do with her dying father in years past as he succumbed to lung cancer.

Natalie never wavered from that career choice, becoming a qualified RN and moving back to her Bahamas after a Canadian education, recently qualifying further as a Certified Emergency Nurse here with Doctor's Hospital, the very building she was born in.

Time had slid by in a stale unfriendly speechless atmosphere. I received an occasional glare of contempt and no real contact from the children. They had been well instructed to stay clear of their father. There may have been room for healing earlier on but repair now seemed utterly futile. Returning home one day from work my mother met me outside her door. 'They're gone!' My heart sank, but no real surprise, as with my father it was a relief. The black Ford Cortina I had bought we found within an hour, knowing without question where I to find it, spitefully parked in the short-term parking at the airport, vandalised in the interior with spilled nail polish. With the children's belongings removed left a house once again empty. My study used by all three now filthy. 'Hell hath no fury…' I reflected in quiet empty sadness, a noticeable silence in those tiled rooms, void of children's laughter with a heart-breaking illness to keep company next door. Slowly, very slowly, day at a time, I put life back in some semblance of order, becoming a robotic machine making work my distraction. I kept in close contact with a new fresh relationship flourishing from the Carolinas, selflessly offering loving support so I leaned shamelessly hard. The Bahamas and these southern states seemingly joined through time in one way or another. Robert Wilder's classic novel *Wind from the Carolinas* really coming into play. This new health crisis would put us together in permanence. My job demanded I became a first rate actor, giving visitors to our country a day they would never forget while emotions inside ran amok. In a call from my new companion came news, 'I have requested a transfer to Florida!' she exclaimed 'I have found a great apartment in Del Ray Beach.' We needed help desperately and I felt confident there were answers abroad. Within a day or so I received a call from Suzanne saying she had done some homework with her close friend Maggie in West Palm Beach, who in turn was friendly with Florida's top oncologist. He recommended my mother come immediately over for a check-up, a move that should have been done in the first place. Armed with more information I put my foot down insisting mother would fly over to Florida and pursue further treatment. She knew of the new personal relationship that had developed while shooting film with Hal and not happy about it. 'I'm not staying with *her*,' she exclaimed.

'Oh yes you are,' I said with stern conviction, taking my mother by surprise with resolute firmness. She saw no way out of the argument having jeopardised her life with poor decision of 'not wanting be a bother'. 'How will I recognise her?' she enquired, feigning control. 'You just will,' I tried saying with quiet compassion. I ended the conversation asking her to pack enough for a lengthy stay. Emerging from her bedroom with an overnight bag I could have held in the palm of my hand. 'I'll go for the weekend,' she stated firmly. At this point I was not going to argue further, just glad I was putting her on a plane. On arrival in Florida I was told later, my mother walked into the terminal building and marched straight over to my new partner, 'Take those sunglasses off!' she nearly barked, looking into her sparkling light blue eyes Mary Harding simply said quietly, 'Now I understand,' linking arms with her new friend. The weekend stay lasted six months.

An infuriating fact about American Healthcare came to light. The costs of cancer treatment were going to be astronomical requiring a kind of care that could be paid over time. The oncologist was a compassionate, sympathetic surgeon with fabulous demeanour, swept back salt and pepper hair tied in a short ponytail. My mother's humour shone through once more when she saw the care and facility offered her. It was explained 'if she had landed on American soil *illegally* she would have been offered totally free health care!' 'Since you entered the country legally we are obliged to charge!' An explosion from my partner erupted in the reception of the cancer facility. 'You mean I pay all these bloody taxes and can't get assistance for my mother-in-law who is willing to pay?' From within the ethers of medical bureaucracy a reduction was soon discovered, realising she had no insurance coverage; a luxury in the early days we were unable to afford with her age. A few times each week mother would lie obediently under the huge machinery that radiated her body. Two more tumours were discovered; one in each breast of differing types of cancer, one more aggressive in nature than the other. We learned that by opening her body in Nassau the surgeon had not removed enough damaged tissue, creating a disastrous runaway train allowing her ailment to spread rapidly through her lymph system. The lessons of this ugly disease were being learned daily, giving us understanding of the dreaded words 'aggressive' and 'metastasised'. Each visit, the once vibrant English lady came out with some fun remark in effort to lighten the seriousness of her situation. 'It's like being on *Star Trek*!' she exclaimed about her experience under the radiation equipment.

I was working in Nassau through the week commuting to Del Ray Beach every weekend in the Piper Navajo landing at Boca Raton Airport, my two ladies forming a very tight bond with real kindness, sympathy, love and understanding being the adhesive. Further surgery became necessary to remove large areas of threatening tissue. Mother became a fighter and bound to come through this invasive bombardment. She rallied to point of feeling much better and spoilt with daily breakfast in bed. Radiation ran its course with nasty scar tissue from operations healing well. Within six months she stated clearly, 'I want to go home now!' I could see the time was right after having spent a Christmas in Florida. The Navajo seemed a fitting ride for her return. We planned the journey where suddenly before leaving she put her foot down, almost stamping the floor as if an adolescent, 'I'm not going without Suzanne!' There was no argument; with notice given in her job and apartment I loaded the two ladies on board the twin-engine aircraft for a flight back to Nassau. Clearing in Chub Cay with Mr. Whylly, our friendly customs officer, seemed the way to go with an aircraft brimming with personal furnishings from the apartment. On loading at Fort Lauderdale Executive it became very evident that two flights were needed to fit all the belongings left from the move. Mother sat proudly in the cabin behaving as if the Queen of England while she watched her son start the engines of her private charter to Nassau. 'So much for your father saying, 'you will never amount to anything!' she whispered with an assuring smile to me as I walked forward into the cockpit touching her shoulder in reassurance.

How could we be half way through the 90s already? Time has mysteriously accelerated compared to those tedious boarding school days seemingly crawling by with a never-ending wait for the holidays in the Bahamas. In the blink of an eye our fortieth birthdays were behind us. I would be forty-eight years old when life would have me face that inescapable darkest moment, the loss of a parent.

The doomsday word came back to haunt us. Cancer. Mum started to have repetitive headaches where nothing offered relief; the invasion of toxic cells now racing uncontrolled throughout her body through the lymph system and into her brain. We had the gift of life for nearly a year and a half before serious trouble returned. Another hasty visit to the Florida oncologist had her back under an MRI machine scanning her body. That sombre and all too familiar scene we have seen played on television hospital series became stark reality; the doctor in his starched white coat and stethoscope draping his neck asks the family members to 'meet him urgently in his office'. I was filled with a gaping emptiness that flooded through me with the knowing of what was coming. The surgeon, as if on script, slid the large x-ray under the backlit panel for us to see. No need for words. There, plain as day, an ominous black shaded area on one side of my mother's brain, a death sentence in a picture. 'How long?' words barely audible crawling out of me. 'A few weeks,' came the quiet reply. 'With a more rigorous treatment of chemotherapy and radiation we may get longer?' 'The spirit is alive and well but old chassis is just worn out,' he offered in affection. The news was relayed gently where my mother announced clearly, 'No Chemo! That's enough now'. She did however accept a stronger radiation treatment in Nassau to alleviate the head pain. Arriving back in the Bahamas, we drove home in sad silence, looking toward me simply saying quietly, 'I think I am on the long road now?' I knew she was confused.

'I fear not so long Mum' is all I could muster in reply, reaching to hold her cold hand on this hot summer day. Her body paid dearly from Dr Lund's burning radiation with clumps of hair staying on her pillow each morning. I watched in disbelieving numbness as my mother's spirit was being taken from her leaving her body a withering husk once so full of life. My kind compassionate new partner took daily care of the lady she had become very close to. The only food source we were able to get down her these days being fresh vichyssoise made lovingly by Suzanne, nothing solid. Natalie had arrived from Montreal for her holidays where each day she spent time nursing her grandmother, along with Karen, a professional full-time nurse we had hired to help us through this incredibly difficult time. Natalie's last day in Nassau, before returning to school, brought the stark reality of what was coming next. The bright sunshine gifted us a beautiful July morning, powder blue sky with still coconut palms glinting the light off their fronds. The dogs played unawares in the back garden, a mocking bird singing atop the satellite antenna oblivious of the sadness this side of the house.

'Go say goodbye to Nanny' I said with all the braveness I could muster, for the word 'goodbye' this time meant certain finality; those simple words difficult to pronounce, without question she would not be seeing her grandmother ever again. I walked my daughter to the apartment door and sat outside at the concrete round garden table, the grass taller underneath where the mower could not reach. This was their alone time; a precious moment where a young granddaughter gave her grandmother a goodbye letter to open after she left. Now I broke. It was here that the very true sensation of heartache finally weighed down my body. My head sagged forward unable to sit upright, a flood of tears welling up to run freely down my face, liquid falling from my nose in a bubbly mixture. My shoulders shook in uncontrollable grief picturing the scene inside that small bedroom. I was mourning our loss before the event. My thirteen-year-old daughter came quietly outside a little time later, wetness streaking her suntanned flawless cheeks, compassionate eyes full of water. They had talked briefly finding a way of parting for the last time. It is a profoundly sad time to witness. A week later, having slipped into a coma almost immediately her granddaughter had left, at 10.50 am on the August 6 1996, Mary Harding waited for me to leave her momentarily and allowed her last breath to escape quietly. Suzanne came and sat with me at our dining table laying a hand over mine, 'She's gone,' saying with breaking voice. I walked as if in a trance through the back door to the apartment to sit gently at the foot of the bed. One never can fully comprehend what it is like to gaze at a lifeless parent. There is no movement and what little colour remained now draining away each second, her small frame lying in surreal stillness as I searched the room fruitlessly to feel her spirit. I said goodbye to my special friend and mother of all these years. Grasping for something to comfort myself I reflected that her journey for the most part had been a good one. Her happiest days spent in the islands of our Bahamas. She had hated the cold weather of her birth country and loved her countless Bahamian friends. Not questioning the sudden need for male company, I walked outside with a portable phone to sit at the same garden table dialling my friend Robin who worked not far from here at Bahamas Realty. His mother had been taken the very same way also too soon in life. He would know what I needed now. As if in the next minute he was at my side. I am not sure how he arrived so quickly. The scene played out as if in slow motion, a silent film in colour, the ominous black hearse backing through open gates into the driveway. Two attendants going into the bedroom with a stretcher and emerging with my mother's little body covered with a sheet. My friend's arm holding me by the shoulders as the large vehicle pulled away. The scene here fades. I cannot remember what followed. The memorial service was kept simple with my same friend, one of 'Mary's Boys' as she called him, giving a moving eulogy. The church is quite full but only in a blur. Sitting in that front row where 'the family' is seated the only person I remember seeing, his eyes wide with sadness, in suit and tie, our faithful friend and plumber, Robert Johnson.

Fulfilling mothers wishes, she was cremated, asking us to spread her ashes at the last place she went swimming, Whales Tail Beach on Norman's Cay. Keeping her humour somehow alive within us we also kept her wish of 'not being in a box, you know I'm claustrophobic! Put me in a Baggie so I can see out!' The Ziploc bag stayed in that apartment for weeks perched in the faded blue chair she once sat in each day waiting for the right time to say a final goodbye. We had no earthly idea that day would have an added immeasurable sadness added to it.

The lessons of death come to us all. A natural unfolding of life, as tragic as it is, facing a debilitating disease or awful accident; to lose those we love too early is how life unfairly plays out for some of us. We experience abandonment. We have no choice but to accept the loss hoping time will have us heal, never completely. The thoughts of those awful days do finally fade, replaced with memory of good times and scenes that make us smile. Their souls live on through those left behind recalling those familiar pages of a journey travelled. One also learns there are those who's journey is far more painful to bear. Tragic death welds a much heavier sword; it rips through the toughest tissue, tearing vein and shattering bone, penetrating all the way to one's soul. The gaping wound it delivers would be felt a few months later.

Chapter 26
Tragedy and New Beginnings

Two thousand hours appeared suddenly one morning on the tachometer in front of me. It felt the blink of an eye since arriving in Nassau with less than fifty flying hours under my belt and here I was having timed out my first engine. The Maule had provided such faithful service and time had arrived to rebuild the engine in accordance with commercial specifications. Replacing with a factory-new engine always a preferred choice, putting the clock back to zero and having the reliance of extraordinary tolerances under that cowling to fly safely another four years. I was flying about 600 hours a year, the boat business long closed and behind us. My friend since childhood, Kevin Cartwright, had found a management position over on Little San Salvador for Holland America lines and wanted to buy the Bertram. He had taken over his father's business, Marine Diesel planning to install my hull with diesel engines. The sale was agreed and for the first time in eighteen years I was without a boat, a very strange feeling for a man of the sea in this land surrounded by water.

With my financial situation in disarray there was no choice but ask Jon Brown's friend, Charlie Melot owner of Zephyr Aircraft Engines to rebuild my engine. The cost would be about $16,500 and take a couple of weeks to complete the overhaul, giving me needed time off to travel in the States on invitation to ride horses and play in the Nantahala River in North Carolina with Suzanne and my daughter; time also to reflect on all the experiences of four years flying. One relief did come unexpectedly with valuable insight from Walter Evans, one of our favourite inspectors from Civil Aviation Authority. He never failed to open a conversation without asking 'How's the Madam?' On seeing the number of hours accumulating in my engine logbooks he pointed out, 'Total time, from his days of flying, was recorded from applying throttle for take-off and ending on landing at destination; taxiing the airplane at idle would not be counted.' I calculated that within a lifetime of 2000 engine hours some 200 or more were spent in manoeuvring down the harbour to a safe take-off zone. I had removed the engine for overhaul way too early; time lost would have paid for a factory new engine, an expensive lesson not to be repeated! Mr. Evans was always fun to watch inspecting the Maule never allowing me a perfect pass. He never took interest in looking under the cowling rather asking for something minuscule to be changed such as the 'Exit' decals on the doors being too small or life raft coming soon for repacking! Having recently lost him we all recall his presence with affection.

Wilfred Clarke was now my full-time maintenance mechanic with Chris Scott working mostly at the airport. Religiously we met at Coconuts Restaurant where I would arrive ahead of time to remove the cowlings of the Maule sitting high and dry on its ramp with a low tide morning. I had learnt all the details of dropping the oil into a container for disposal, changing the oil filter and removing the spark plugs to be cleaned of small lead contaminations found inside. Willie would arrive, baseball cap always on backwards, smiling to say, 'Good Morning'. 'You'll soon be ready so sit your Airframe and Powerplant exam,' he joked seeing my progress in preparing the plane for his inspections. We had both become very familiar with this flying machine, learning every nut and bolt that made her work. The 100-hour inspections were more complex. Compression checks of each cylinder mandatory to show there were no leaks of air pressure that we pumped inside from a compressor Wilfred had brought with him. The Lycoming engine was always well within specification, through my whole career a really sound investment. I learned how to check the tightness of valve covers, safety-wiring all those pieces that had been removed and replaced. Changed air hoses and checking oil and fuel lines. Getting to know my aircraft a must, for there would be rare times when she would fail, for certain always the most remote of locations. Broken battery leads, cooling hoses having vibrated off their mounts or failed solenoids inhibiting a restart. Being able to perform a fix in the field would be a valuable asset. Ziploc bags hidden under seats and in the floats stored a few small spare parts and a scant amount of tools. Sitting on a lonely beach with a plane out of service, miles away from help and agitated tourists wondering if they are to sleep there not something I would recommend. One recalls Out-Island stories from Charles Bethell Jr over on the West side of Andros Island where he carried ownership of his grandfather's creation of

Flamingo Cay, a bone fishing lodge of world repute. Royalty from many countries used to visit and hunt over here. In those early days, the old pioneers found their way by sailboat often getting hopelessly lost in the maze of waterways and cays, having to survive by eating crabs and lizards; the west side proving a whole new world within the Bahamas. Full of wildlife, amazing creeks and miles of open space where green water signified salt and white milky lakes being fresh. Wild boar tracks threaded the whole area looking as if our version of Africa. Nowadays Charlie would fly guests over on his single de Havilland Otter floatplane landing on his homemade grass airstrip. I learned early to carry a hand-held marine radio having been stranded to hike through dense scrubland to the summit of Hawksbill Cay, high enough to get signal out asking Jen and Stan for assistance from neighbouring Cistern Cay! To the north I had Peter and Alison at Highbourne, to the south, Ray Darville, Park Warden at Waderick Wells. Having good friends in the islands a magical asset for a floatplane pilot, along with several plastic jerry cans of spare aviation fuel hidden in the bushes of various islands.

The first seaplane was very light having straight floats equipped, unburdened by the weight of heavy landing gear, easily accommodating the fourth seat in the rear holding an average weighted passenger, totalling five of us on board. Tourism flying being the first business venture became a huge success, a natural transition from the boat to a plane. One of my first full loads cautiously flown with four Japanese visitors, smaller in stature and heavily armed with cameras slung around their necks, each excitedly climbed aboard the seaplane chattering incessantly like exuberant school kids. We taxied all the way down to the cruise ships for the longest afforded runway facing east toward Montagu Bay. In those days, I had emulated the helicopter flight taken earlier inside the Grand Canyon where guests were provided headsets. Hearing a running commentary from the pilot a novel idea I thought would work well for a flight through the Exumas; difference being no microphones, we could only listen. In the seaplane, with live microphones listening to four Japanese jabbering away at the same time became a lesson learned. I could not get a word in sideways. Easing the throttle forward the Maule leapt forward without hesitation flying easily off the water heading directly for Paradise Island Bridge spanning the harbour. A yelp of glee erupted from my passengers as the 72-foot span came ever closer. 'Hell,' I thought with mischief, 'let's fly them underneath'! The tall concrete pilings of the bridge flew past our windows. My passenger in the co-pilot seat in his best English leaned over saying, 'We do again?' For their good humour, I circled the hotels on Paradise while they clicked away hundreds of frames again lining up for another direct flight under the bridge. I could see a few spectators standing by the railings at the apex knowing this little seaplane would rush underneath. The visitors exploded into applause. 'Better head away,' I thought, 'Civil Aviation will not be so happy'. I smiling to recall Captain's Henry Pyfrom and Eddie Ballard from Bahamas Airways had calculated a DC3 could fit under the bridge diagonally! We lost them both some time ago 'That one was for you, Henry and Eddie!'

The tourist flights became very well known throughout the more high-end hotels. I had created a new three-page brochure that Greg Higgs printed for me. With photographs of the seaplane sitting in crystal clear water off an Exuma beach, pictures of huge iguanas and underwater caves with my guests' snorkelling in front of an anchored plane, there was no going wrong with my promotion. So successful was the product I still have copy of the famous promotional photo used by the Ministry of Tourism. An enormous relief having no further dealings with tour desks, although on rare occasion a few still hungry for commission tried to persuade us *they* had promoted a sale knowing full well a brochure had sparked the interest. I explained clearly 'this was not a commissionable product, guests will have to call direct'. Mr. Deveaux from the Ocean Club and a handful of loyal bell captains had my information for the more adventurous high-end clientele never failing to call expressing gratitude 'for giving their guests the experience of a lifetime!'

The phone never stopped. In those early days of the new 'Seaplane Safari' guests were treated to about six hours of excitement. A flight over to Allan's Cay to feed grapes to the large iguanas, followed by an hour's snorkelling off the teeming coral reefs just off southwest Allan's Cay. Once dried off and re-seated on folded towels, another lower altitude flight saying 'low hello' to friend Captain Nigel Bower in his Powerboat Adventure trip with Alan Wardle crewing; on to the Land and Sea Park where I served a picnic lunch on the headquarters balcony at Waderick Wells. Coolers and snorkelling equipment had stored easily in each float compartment. Visitors would marvel at the clarity of our Bahama waters, with aerial views boasting a line of sailboats sitting on their moorings appearing as if floating on air. A group of small bananaquit birds would tamely sit on their fingers sipping sugar we placed in their hands, while Ray Darville gave introductory speeches about the park. Here was opportunity to provide income for the Bahamas National Trust with guests purchasing books and T-shirts as souvenirs. Over my seventeen-year career with seaplane tourism and emergency life flights I became a noted Life Member with my name plaque mounted on a balcony wall just under that of actor Tom Cruise.

After lunch the last flight would have our guests enjoy another water landing into the quiet leeside of Staniel Cay, splashing down to anchor off world famous 'Thunderball Cave' where the Bond film had been shot in 1965. Securing the aircraft here became a swift lesson in tidal flow and timing. The first few ventures had me scared silly, nearly losing the plane against the intimidating rocky shore. Halfway through a swim inside the submerged cave I noticed the strong tide had suddenly slackened to change direction. My seaplane was now being pulled toward the island on the racing outflow of ebbing tide! In a wave of panic and a sprint swim to retrieve the small Danforth anchor I had to pull, with every ounce of strength crying 'shit, shit shit!' through my snorkel in effort to manoeuvre the seaplane through the water sideways avoiding certain destruction against the jagged coral island. The wingtip missed the razor-sharp rock face by mere feet. Climbing on board and starting the engine would have not offered enough time; sitting inside soaking wet a totally unacceptable option with just seconds available to save the day! Guests returning from their adventure had no clue what their exhausted captain had just been through, not noticing their craft in an entirely different location, acting classes once again in this new career becoming a necessary art form. That charade only happened a couple of times before I practiced Suzanne's father's old acronym of the 'the six Ps'. Prior planning prevents piss poor performance! Knowing where that tide is flowing and anchoring accordingly certainly gave the day a more expert appearance with the pilot seemingly knowledgeable where to placc his machine out of harm's way.

With a heave, most swimmers made it back up on to the float deck. Some passengers could not grasp the manoeuvre however they tried, finally requiring quite a push from underneath. Having been comfortably dry I was obliged to slide back into the water in order to administer a well-placed hand placed in the correct part of anatomy. With a pilot anal about his aircrafts appearance, entering the seaplane even damp was no option. Passengers had to be dry with Rosie taking it a step further and washing their feet with fresh water first, and I thought I was anal! Europeans had no inhibitions about being naked and would stand on the floats wringing out their suits but the Americans with their long soggy bathing attire it became quite a task. As careful as I was the wear on my aircraft was beginning to show after four years work entertaining hundreds of clients. Within time over the next few years the swim at Thunderball was phased out except for special private charters, picnic lunches were replaced with a stop at Staniel Cay Marina, where lunch of cracked conch or grouper fingers were included in the more expensive trip I had created, bringing welcome revenue to the Out-Island Resort. I would generate as much income in two days compared to a whole week's work at Rose Island gaining new clientele like James and Louise Sollins, calling from New York preferring an arriving flight almost to their back door of their recently purchased beautiful home on the waterfront of Harbour Island. I would approach close to North Eleuthera Airport flying down to the trees at the far end of the island for my touchdown just shy of the Government Dock. Letting my friends paddle in shin high water with water shoes they left with me in my float compartment each trip. I would about turn the seaplane hearing a call from the dock and that slender familiar frame of Melissa hailing me with an excited wave and long hair flowing loose in the breeze as I taxied for take-off back to Nassau. I called across the water a familiar island response: 'Hey gorgeous! I'll catch ya later!'

The joy of putting an airplane in seawater becomes an expensive learning curve. Every day new lessons, some hard learned. Just as self-confidence peeked that little seaplane would jolt me back to reality. Taxing back into the harbour ramp one fateful day my approach quickly became a hazardous navigation through several sailboats inconveniently moored directly in front of my base. Weaving one's way through a maze of masts and bow rails with wings spanning just over thirty-three feet no easy task for a low time float pilot, especially if failing to account for a fast flowing ebb tide to drag you sideways. Once in the pack of sailboats I recognised trouble in a fraction of a second. Either pull the mixture now or risk a higher speed collision. Within a couple of seconds I was out of the cockpit and on to the float, a quick climb up on to the wing to shuffle in great haste to the wingtip where I could maybe hold off from hitting the steel bow railings? A distraught boat owner flew out of his cabin making a speedy run along his deck also trying to fend off. The collision was imminent and a brand-new seaplane suffered a dented leading edge. The yacht I hit escaped unscathed. I was devastated seeing a nasty crease in the shiny metal of a near new aircraft. While the yachtsman tried desperately to hold me in place I reversed the manoeuvre to restart the engine before the tide dragged me hopelessly amongst the other anchored sailboats wreaking certain havoc. With Wilfred's talent, he managed to pull the dent out and use plastic body filler to redo the finish. In time, I would take the protective attitude, this was a 'working truck', not some show-case model that should remain flawless. I did however find use for the familiar verbal expression 'shit, shit, shit!' voiced in rising octaves several times through my career becoming more graphic as the situation at hand became increasingly worse. *Caribbean Travel and Life Magazine* placed me on the cover of one issue with an article about 'The Five Best Jobs in the World'. If only the general public knew what float pilots have to face behind the scenes!

The more I flew over all the islands the more word spread about this new seaplane business based in Nassau Harbour. Private islands, anchored motor yachts and commercial marinas all finding my business cards strategically placed. Flights home would deliberately have me at low altitude fizzing down the cays where appreciative spectators could see the small floatplane speeding by. This form of advertising worked like a charm. The brochure eventually reached the end of its usefulness as I began replacing tourism scenic flights with passenger or freight charters on demand. There was more income to be made flying by the hour than babysitting visitors for a six-hour day, yet even after raising the Exuma excursion where costs would equal charter flights lost, the phone still rang! Month by month I began supplying various islands with more regular flights. Yacht owners realised all too quickly they could save a small fortune no longer having to move their vessels miles in order to meet guests arriving by land plane onto islands with runways; guests and family members were met in

Nassau by my driver Charles Rolle who promptly brought them to Lake Cunningham for a departure on the seaplane. In thirty or forty minutes they would land conveniently next to their awaiting yacht. An inflatable tender would motor over to pick them up, everyone expressing 'that was the only way to travel!' News spread fast amongst mega-yacht captains talking to each other at anchorage about having the seaplane fly for them. They could provision their yachts without moving. Tourism soon slipped to second choice of my business income with the price rising immensely to make it worth the effort involved. In 1990 my first fees began at $275 an hour. Twenty-three years later I left the business in new hands with the fare more than double, with maintenance and mandatory insurance premiums contributing the main cause of inflated prices.

The Nassau Harbour waterfront restaurant had changed ownership to my friend Dave McCorquodale, buying from Bertram Knowles who moved on to pursue other business ventures. Dave's name, unpronounceable at his first school earned him a nickname he now gave to his new restaurant calling it 'Crocodiles'. This next story deals with the subject of 'afterlife'. The restaurant decor was being upgraded with a carpenter he hired daily creating new wooden benches and tables for patrons to sit. I saw a potential for using his woodwork skills after work in our Montagu home. I needed a system of shelving in the garage for storage. I forget his name but remember the ponytail hair and scruffy thin frame. He needed lodging, as his apartment lease was due. We agreed on a trade where he could stay in the apartment next door while the job was underway. On completion, he would have to vacate, as I wanted Natalie to have a place of her own when visiting from Canada. There was something about this character that did not sit well. Mary Harding would not be pleased at this stranger in her place, more especially her bed! The first morning after his settling in there was a frail knocking of my front door. Standing outside holding a huge bump on his head explaining in a shaken voice, 'that heavy painting hanging above the bed had come loose of its mount in the night, hitting me direct on his head knocking me senseless!' Oh Mum, I smiled; you made your point. Nicely done!

I have always been sceptical about the afterlife. One can romanticise about life after death and what happens to us. The picture of the ascension into the heavens created by a wonderful imagination seems a realistic explanation and reasonable doubt for some of us dreading descent down into the flames. Astrophysics professor Carl Sagan had portrayed all too well that 'out there were billions upon billions of stars'. Certainly no seventy virgins waiting for some religious martyr want-to-be's! I fly for a living and watch spacecraft ascend into the heavens showing me the blackness of space, surrounding our beautiful orbital globe suspended in the darkness. There is no one sitting on the clouds just above to welcome some of us up there and St Peter surely overwhelmed at how many thousands dying each minute here on Earth? Maybe heaven and hell are what we experience right here in life on Earth? It seemed to make better sense. I often pondered why the good Lord would create such a beast as man who ravaged his planet mercilessly and showed such intolerance of difference in such violent ways? There is a brilliant interview with Stephen Fry on social media recently about his thoughts on God. His first answer certainly stirs provoking thought. 'Cancer in children? Really, what God of compassion would create such a monster, for that is not a manmade scourge? For all the pain and suffering on this planet we are to spend a lifetime on our knees saying thank you?' A valid observation while visiting Guadalajara, Mexico, a scene having me perplexed to observe the poorest of the poor literally crawling on their knees in humility across the Plaza toward the entrance of the cathedral for worship. Inside that building treasures beyond description where everything was covered with gold. An untold fortune belonging to the Catholic Church with its patrons in rags, an obscenity of religion I find difficult to accept. The Native American belief of worshipping Mother Earth and all she offered for our existence stuck a chord within me early on, the beautiful outdoors becoming my church. I quickly grew intolerant of religious fanatics, from early times through to today, promoting so much abhorrent killing and destruction; religion itself merely a convenient way to control the masses? I sometimes have mused about *the* ultimate irony, what *if* there is truly nothing beyond this existence, we really are 'ashes to ashes … ' and untold millions have died in God's holy name' for nothing, a fitting end for the behaviours of mankind? Where in fact biblical prophets indeed were just men of influence in their times. The Testaments are a record of history. Stories told over eons of time passed by man in the form of writings; stories easily imagined, embellished or changed as they passed from mouth to mouth, having us wisely not take as verbatim? We can be assured there was a man named Jesus of Nazareth, a man to be admired as a peace-loving messenger spreading goodwill. A man brave enough to offer himself at a young age to the inevitable death lying ahead having voiced against the violent regime he lived under; a man making his quest to deliver hope for the rest of the poor mortals of that turbulent time. What the Romans did to him I feel sure true depiction of the atrociously cruel times he lived in. One only has to watch any of the countless depictions of his death to believe how awful mankind can behave. Near flogging a man to death and driving a spike through is hands and feet in crucifixion is about as barbaric as we can go? Leap forward over 2000 years and our technology shows evidence never dreamt. Now we see images from the Hubbell Telescope showing with define precision that our planet is merely a pinprick in size spinning within one small galaxy, one of uncountable millions comprising this massive universe. There is certainly no being as we know it here sitting just above our sky caring for all of us? As pleasant as that might appear, whoever it might be would certainly have their hands full with the madness he created down here?

For me the souls of humans are kept alive by those of us remaining, its our love, the reminiscing memories we share fondly of those departed; passing their stories and images through generations while we bury their chassis here on this earth or scatter their ash over sand and ocean or into the very wind that caress our faces. My mother's ashes remain part of the fine powder caressed daily by a crystal clear ocean lapping that gorgeous beach on Normans Cay. A favourite spot where I cleaned fish and lobster from a day's spearfishing with Doug Fitts and Steve Rudski on reefs off shore; using the rocks in that far corner with a piece of driftwood as a cutting board. Hopefully I too will end up there one day and ask this small task of my loving partner. For out there is my 'church' where our spirit can join those who walk those soft sands and swim in that warm shallow water, making quiet love or eating fresh mangoes with juice running down their chins while gazing northward toward Highbourne Cay while Ospreys watch from overhead?

When the carpenter finished his work, he asked to stay another month or so and pay us rent. After the first month he failed to pay and was promptly evicted. The apartment was thoroughly cleaned by our housekeeper and painted where needed. Friends, Jim and Jo visiting from Michigan would stay here and my wife's parents from the Carolinas on occasion. One day Suzanne came back into the house from preparing for her parent's arrival next door saying, 'you have to come into the apartment quickly, there is something I need your opinion on'. Not given any clues, I walked next door seeing her enthusiastic haste. Immediately there was an undeniable aroma of a very familiar perfume. The apartment had been emptied of all mother's belongings months ago. We had discovered her personal papers and her life savings that she wished I had, all $800. After the housekeeper left there was no trace of anyone having lived here as the small bottles of Chloe had been given months ago to her granddaughter as keepsake. Yet here it was, that unmistakable perfume filling our senses, not a mere waft of scent rather a prominent aroma. 'She's happy about Ruthie and Murray staying compared to that damned carpenter!' We smiled. Any belief of afterlife suddenly became starkly apparent to think about and very hard to discard this message, finding no other acceptable explanation in this mysterious universe. It would however be one of two signs that we would receive.

The seaplane engine rebuild in Florida was complete, reinstalled by Jon's mechanic at the seaplane base. Plans were made to fly commercially to Orlando and drive the thirty-five-minute journey westward to the base. We would stay once again at the old Lake Marianna Motel across the field just minutes away from Jon's hangar. The rooms were comfortable but in fairness I could only award a couple of stars as a rating; a place to lay one's head with your plane anchored outside the door. We ate out in the local cafes and restaurants filled each morning with local patrons who worked the nearby orange groves. Strong coffee aromas mingled with light blue smoke drifting silently through the restaurant often described as 'a greasy spoon' occupied by dark tanned unshaven men in tattered plaid shirts and stained baseball caps with bent peaks. The seaplane was nearly ready to be test flown and the stay this time a short one.

Nights in central Florida were very still and humid where prevailing breeze succumbs to approaching darkness. Crickets filled the night air with song. You could feel the thickness of the air and smell the purity of rain. The afternoon heat built towering cumulous clouds seen growing from their white billowing peaks thousands of feet above the flat terrain;

some appearing to have explosions of light coming from within their core, beautiful in form yet menacingly ominous and dark at their bases. Greys are shaded with purple as a sudden clap of thunder shakes the ground displaying impressive forks of lightning making contact with the ground. Some so close you could sense the sky being ripped in two before the actual explosion of sound reached us. The sweet smell of static electricity filled the air blown now by a rising wind. Rains were torrential, blinding one's view as you drove, car wipers unable to push the sheeting water sideways off the glass fast enough. In an instant, it stopped. The black roads steamed in brilliant sunshine. By dark the show was over. Cooler night air calming the towering monsters that seemingly collapsed from within leaving stars and moon to paint the darkness with a million of points of light.

Sleep was disturbed with a persistent knocking on our door. The Canadian motel manager stood outside looking very serious. 'Sorry to wake you Paul, an urgent phone call for you on our house phone in the office'. I stumbled quickly into shorts and t-shirt leaving a bewildered spouse still in groggy sleep. 'Be right back,' I said gently. Inside I picked up the old-style telephone receiver. 'Hello?' I asked. 'Paul, its Suzi,' came a trembling voice, 'I needed this call to come to you first.'

'What's up, are you alright?' I asked my daughter-in-law. Her voice shaking uncontrollably, 'Jay's dead. He hung himself in the public park today and they found him a while ago in the tree,' her shaken voice becoming barely audible with the loss of her brother.

'Oh dear God *NO*!' My voice faltering; We all had known this fabulous looking young man, just twenty-one years old with dark neat hair and blue eyes, suffering terribly with bipolar disease. He had attempted several times in his youth to end the turmoil within but not in the short time I had been with his mother. The last time we had met him was in Greenville, South Carolina where he announced that he had gone AWOL from the Navy, first entering as a submariner, now running away to marry his girlfriend; another manic episode taking him on a wild emotional ride that affected all of us who loved him. We had asked to meet but he only agreed to find us in a public place, a parking lot to the shopping mall not too far from home. Mother and son talked for several minutes and then he came to me, encircling with strong arms holding me close to whisper in my ear, 'Take good care of Mum for me'. 'Jay *please* don't do anything silly,' I pleaded in whispered reply holding him close until he pulled away.

His eyes were vacant and left me fearing for his welfare as we watched him walk away, the last time to see him alive.

'We are on our way right now, Suzi' I said quietly into the telephone replacing the receiver in slow motion, dreading the walk back to our room. The motel manager sensing that tragedy had struck. 'Don't worry about the bill or anything you need to leave. We'll see you when you come back.' Walking across the tiny parking area of the motel in the darkness my eyes filled with water, blurring vision as I opened the door slowly and sat at the end of the bed. Suzanne seeing my slumped shoulders knew instinctively what I had heard. 'It's Jay, isn't it?' I barely nodded unable to say anything. How does one tell a mother she has lost her child? Family history had been really cruel. The father lost in an air disaster, the older brother killed in a highway accident now the son to suicide, all the men being taken tragically. I held the bereaving mother until she could take air into her lungs again. 'We must go now,' she sobbed. Packing the car took minutes and we were on the highway heading north in the middle of the night to reach South Carolina by morning. Flashing blue lights from behind, a Highway Patrol car pulled us over somewhere in Georgia. The officer was huge with thick muscular arms. 'Sir you were speeding, step out of the car.' Standing outside I explained briefly our predicament and offered apology. The policeman examined my Bahamian driver's license and sensing our situation was real, left us with a warning and a compassionate understanding of bearing such crisis.

One wonders why two people are put together. Why they find each other at the times they did? At the time we had met, my personal life was in utter turmoil. Bringing a total stranger into one's personal mess is risky business but if meant to be nothing stops it. Over eighteen years later it would happen, to my utter amazement, yet again. While driving that night we both knew the reason for our meeting. This terrible year of 1996 would have the two of us back-to-back fighting together the demons of personal loss. I had received all the support I could ask for in August and now the tables were turned a couple months later. To see this attractive young man lying in a coffin, the rope burn slightly visible on his neck was tragically surreal, bringing to light the preciousness of life. A mother said goodbye to a beautiful son racked from within and brought his ashes home wanting to take him back to the one place he loved more than any, Normans Cay.

'Mary can handle him from here. We'll put them together on the beach,' she said with a brave smile. That day did not come for several more weeks both needing to feel time was right, one of those 'goodbyes' you have to ease into. One day the sky was flawless, the air still. 'Let's go today,' we agreed, taking a small container of ash and mother, still in her Ziploc bag, with us on the seaplane. A majestic blue Bahama postcard day allowed us landing on the north side of Whales Tail beach. We both had dressed in respect of our loved ones myself in Captains whites and shoulder bars. A simple service administered by the two of us with the style our loved ones deserved. Mum's close friend Sue Shepherd, now living in England, had sent a small box of rose petals from the garden where the two ladies had tea together by the River Thames. We scattered them with the ashes running gently through our fingers, some touching the shoreline sand some drifting on the calm warm water. A sudden familiar cry from the skies above had us marvelling at a pair of osprey's soaring closely together directly overhead. What timing, enough to convince it was one last sign?

Personal loss stays in the forefront of our relationship for quite some time. We thoughtfully try to put feelings in private places but I could feel the tragic loss of a child understandably outweighing the natural loss of an ageing parent. One can offer support in all ways possible but the process of sadness often leads way to anger and resentment toward the child, not considering what devastation they leave behind. It takes large amounts of time to heal and feelings to fade; not fast enough to stop the beginnings of corrosive behaviours seeping surreptitiously into our relationship. There is anger and frustrations lying just below the surface. Death, divorce, betrayal, expense, all start ripping the fragile seams of paradise apart, constant ringing telephones disrupt so needed quiet, personal time, acting as a trigger having me often unexpectedly explode. My partner escapes into alcohol. We are trapped by reaction and fault in not seeking help. Work provides my grand escape setting new financial goals that may well exceed our capability. Leaving the island is good medicine and seeing Australia and the magnificence of New Zealand soothe the wounds temporarily. We had arrived in Auckland with only a car rental planned. From here we would wing it day by day driving the circumference of North Island, exploring the magnificence of the Coromandel Peninsula to find the most amazing fish and chip shop on the eastern shoreline. I fly-fished for trout near Lake Taupo and explored the hot springs of Rotorua. Arriving in Wellington to take the ferry across to magnificent South Island arriving at beautiful Picton where another car awaited. From Queenstown in the south we ventured over to the fiords discovering Doubtful Sound. Captain Cook had ventured in here against advise of his navigator knowing the winds could hold him inside, doubtful of his ability to sail out. Visiting Australia reunited the Aussie and I for the first time since we had parted years ago. We took opportunity to visit the famous Australia Zoo owned by nature expert Steve Irwin and his wife Terri. The couple had spent their honeymoon trapping crocodiles together with footage taken for the first episode of their television show called *The Crocodile Hunter.* A show debuting on Australian TV in 1996, later in the United States and on to 130 countries. I was fortunate enough to photograph Steve at work with a massive croc while Suzanne fulfilled a dream of holding an adorable koala bear. On September 4th 2006 Irwin was on a film location near Port Douglas in Queensland, filming a portion of the new series *Ocean's Deadliest.* While snorkeling in shallow water Steve approached a large stingray from the rear so that it may swim away toward the camera. Being too boxed in unexpectedly the ray rose defensively on its front and started wildly stabbing many strikes on Irwin within a few seconds. The poisonous barb penetrating his heart causing him to tragically bleed to death. All copies of the only existing fatal attack ever filmed were requested by the family to be destroyed. Returning to Nassau I resume the fight with my daughter's mother in court, for nine long years her quest to completely destroy me took a weighty toll. I would fight to the bitter end thankfully having my partner's consent and support to do so. There is a time to put an end to poor human misbehaviour? Judge Longley who had first presided on our case had been transferred to Freeport about half way through the saga. On the ninth year, he returned to Nassau aghast that we were 'still at it'. In a matter of minutes, he ended the proceedings with a dismissal that 'parties that should settle out of court', knowing we were hopelessly deadlocked. I walked away with relieved smile knowing it was finally over with my wish granted. There is justice every now and again I just wish it had not taken so inexcusably long to arrive.

Wilfred, being off the island could not perform the next 100-hour inspection so I arranged with Chris Scott to meet at Crocodiles on the last day of

August. He had arrived before me and the cowlings were already lying on the top of the ramp while he stood on the float draining the thick black oil. 'Morning, Chris,' I greeted him. His reply caught me off guard. 'Did you hear that Princess Di is dead. Killed in a car crash!' 'What!' I exclaimed not having heard the news that would send a shockwave around the planet. Another day where you knew where you were on hearing the news. It was the last day of August 1997 when the Princess of Wales and her boyfriend Dodi Fayed fled from their French hotel in order to elude the hounding press photographers. A high-speed chase had their driver Henri Paul take their Mercedes into the Paris tunnel. Inquiries later showed the crash ensued because of reckless drunk-driving from the chauffeur, having previously goaded the press outside the Ritz Hotel where he was head of security. Dodi's father, Mohamed Fayed, owner of the hotel, claimed that their deaths were result of a conspiracy orchestrated by MI5 and the Royal Family. Losing control of the car at about 12.23 am in the tunnel they collided with a concrete column at about 65 mph. The Mercedes spun around hitting the wall from the rear. The press soon caught up with the devastating scene, some taking pictures of the injured passengers while others tried to pry open the doors. Diana was heard to murmur 'Oh my God' and when the police arrived 'Leave me alone'. Fayed was dead at the scene along with the driver. Diana's bodyguard, Trevor Rees-Jones was still alive and survived the crash. The front airbags had deployed successfully with occupants not wearing seat belts. Massive internal injuries had displaced her heart tearing the pulmonary vein, Diana may well have lived if wearing a seat belt.

The funeral for the Princess was held at Westminster Abbey and the public expression of grief in Britain was extraordinary, bringing over three million onlookers to London. The event was broadcast to an estimated 2.5 billion people worldwide in over forty-four languages. Her London home in Kensington Palace inundated with over a million bouquets of flowers five feet thick by September 10. Criticism was later raised at the hysterical and irrational 'sentimentalisation of Britain' fuelled by media. Ten years later the event was quoted as by a journalist as being an, 'embarrassing memory… we cringe to think about it'. The reaction from the Royal Family produced public resentment and outcry – while on holiday at Balmoral not immediately returning to London. Protocol rules no standard should fly at Buckingham Palace while the Queen is not in residence hence there was no flag flying at half-mast. A Union Jack was however later flying at half-staff above Westminster Abbey as Elton John sang the famous 'Candle in the Wind' during the service.

Not too long after sharing that day with Chris I received a phone call from Wilfred breaking news that, 'Chris has had a nasty accident at the airport and in hospital'. While working on a Piper Aztec he broke precious rules with handbrake holding a plane in place and one engine running, not paying attention walked forward into the propeller blades. One's mind visualises the horror of a human body coming into such deadly contact. I rushed to the hospital finding my mechanic friend alive and badly injured. It would take months of operations, therapy and healing for him to firstly be able to walk and then be at work once again with savage scars to show for his ordeal.

While in town for the day and near my ramp, Marcus stopped by to say a quick hello and look at the seaplane he had helped order. 'It's been a few years sitting in this lovely saltwater' he said sceptically, 'How's she holding up?'

'Pretty good,' I replied, 'it's like the San Francisco Bridge, finish maintenance at one end and go back to the beginning!' He nodded in agreement. 'It never stops my friend,' stepping on to the rear end of the right float to have a closer look. While I watched he suddenly made a slight jumping motion to put pressure between the float and the hull of the plane, a trick only a long-time Maule owner would know. The fabric at the lower end of the rear passenger door crinkled showing a tell-tale break in the fuselage tubing. 'These things leak like a sieve Paul, rainwater is a worse enemy in places than salt!' Sure enough the fresh water had seeped in through the poor top seals of the door trickling downward to lodge along the fuselage tubing in places where our inspections could not see. 'Come down to Sampson and let my mechanic go through the plane.' It was more like an order than request but I respected the expertise of my friend. While at the cay an inspection was carried out with Jim Buchanan exclaiming, 'I am grounding this aircraft!' Horrified at the thought of business coming to a halt I had no argument at the findings. In those early days, the battle against corrosion was young and we had very few products to fight against the deterioration of our aircraft. There were sprays and misting products one could apply but here in the islands with the most corrosive saltwater one could wish for they proved futile in our fight. We used nasty brown goo called Black Bear applied with a brush where possible drying to a waxy film keeping water away from the metal surface although unable to reach the inside surfaces the outer fabric was stretched over, water would inevitably find its way in and the destruction of metal soon underway. Our aircraft frames were filled with linseed oil at the factory and worked well keeping corrosion from the inside. The outer surfaces however were helpless to the onslaught of trapped salt. We would scrape, sandpaper and wire brush brown rusting spots that suddenly appeared, recoating with the best primer possible with two or more coats of finish paint. The next week a brown blemish would have returned. As we had tested scuba regulators in the old days to find the best models to survive our harsh climate, so it became with our aircraft. As new anti-corrosion products emerged later we would share valuable findings in freelance articles written for the Seaplane Pilots Association, a writing career in progress.

Safari Seaplanes had to close its doors temporarily while the Maule was headed to Florida for rebuilding. What we thought would be a few weeks out of service turned into six months. Wheels would have allowed us to choose our maintenance facility based at Bartow, for now little choice but to fly back to Winter Haven and have Jon's crew disassemble my aircraft in his hangar. From here the damaged fuselage would be hauled by trailer to south Florida where we had discovered a couple who specialised in aircraft restoration at Ft. Lauderdale Executive Airport. Jerry Stadtmiller's reputation was strong enough to have his work in the Smithsonian Institute where irreplaceable fabric antique aircraft had been restored for exhibition. His partner at the time was a tiny freckled red headed girl called Lynn Zaro, who's meticulous detail workmanship with aircraft fabric proved a valuable partnership. They agreed to take on our project and build a brand-new frame from the husk of what remained. In hindsight, we should have asked the Maule factory for a new frame, but time and expense was not on our side. Our friendship grew over the next few months where they agreed to finance the project for us with the bills mounting handsomely every week. Stainless steel took the place of some structures and a new spray coating that was an aerosol form of Black Bear had come onto the market. SP400 made by the CRC Corporation became a standard protection for my aircraft over the years. One could spray several coatings with time between for drying and months later there would be no trace of bombardment from the elements gaining us precious airframe hours during the life of the seaplane. With the frame completed on the hangar floor at Fort Lauderdale Executive we sprayed the protectant over the entire metal work before Lynn began to stretch the fabric over the outside. Slowly the new Maule began to take shape. The white silky Ceconite fabric was glued in place with Poly-Tac then warm-ironed slowly pulling it taught like a drum skin. Layer upon layer of coatings, up to eight in all; applications of Poly-Brush sealant turning the fabric in to a strong outer skin. The last silver coat for ultraviolet protection and then the painting would begin.

While the fuselage was prepared the elevators and horizontal stabilators that completed the tail surfaces were also re-skinned. Glacier White made the new seaplane shine. Blue stripes then finished the effect. On the sixth month, we loaded the new fuselage onto the trailer for its reverse journey back to Browns Seaplane Base where N783SP would be reassembled. It would take about six or eight of us to hold up each wing while the head mechanic affixed the main spar bolts. My second Maule was now complete. Clientele in Nassau were screaming for my return desperately missing our convenient services. Bahamas Marine Construction calling every other day with their lead engineer and friend Keith Bishop pleading for my return. 'Paul Tudor has given the go-ahead for Alder Cay's development and we need you almost daily!' The island development would prove a major contributor to my growth over the next couple of years where the successful New York commodities trader pumped vast amounts of investment into his little paradise over in the Berry Islands. Within a day I was back in the harbour loading Keith and Jim for several flights each week to the site. Landing inside the tiny harbour of Frozen and Alder Cay becoming an art form in itself when frontal winds made the eastward approach to landing impossible. Take-offs proving even more of a challenge where we would taxi to the far southern wall of the harbour barely missing the jagged coral rock face, to about turn into the wind for a crosswind race across the water. Just as we would meet the choppy exposed waters I would pull hard on the yoke while pumping the flap handle, a trick taught from B.D. Maule to Marcus and passed now to me. The seaplane would literally jump off the surface allowing me to speed across the water just in ground effect keeping the aircraft in flight while building precious airspeed. Only a Maule could prove herself in such tight spaces.

One special crosswind experience well worth a story happened after the passing of Hurricane Floyd in 1999. A familiar voice came on the phone during the storm. David Craig from Scotland, a long-time friend was a leading insurance adjuster for some of the major companies in the Bahamas. He was on his way to meet me once again in Nassau after the storm had passed. We had spent hours flying together using the seaplane to hop from one disaster area to another. While other adjusters flew together in land planes often getting stuck in locations that had not been cleared of debris, David successfully took care of hundreds of people by using the efficiency of the floatplane service into the storm struck Out-Islands. We had just finished a survey of damage up at Great Harbour Cay in the Berry Islands. Trees had been stacked like broken matchsticks; yachts and small boats piled into harbour corners now in ruin on top of each other like mangled toys; buildings with torn roofing badly damaged from flying debris. We taxied out of the small-protected harbour, the entrance squeezed between perfectly cut coral rock leading to the open water on the lee-side of the island facing westward. Easterly winds still blowing with some strength gave way to a decision to take a near ninety-degree crosswind take-off to the south allowing us to avoid the choppy water further away from the island. Here was enough lee from the wind offering attractive calm water for a comfortable runway accommodating the light load of just David and I on board. Squeezing in the power the seaplane performed as expected rotating easily from the flat shallow waters. Within a second, maybe two, there was a loud bang from behind us with the aircraft instantly pivoting sidewise into the wind. Flying seaplanes for years accumulates hundreds of hours aloft where an experienced pilot becomes naturally in tune with his machine. One becomes extrasensory; the slightest noise, even above the drone of an engine, can be heard or felt in milliseconds. Through a career spanning over twenty years, rest assured there are going to be noises and this one caught both our attentions in a split second!

I had heard before something quite wrong with the power plant in front of me where my passengers remained oblivious. On this day, I was barely off the water yet my reaction time was impressively instantaneous; so dramatic there would be not hiding it from my client. We are taught repetitively at flight schools about emergencies, repetitively instructed to emulate solutions to produce the very best outcome documented from past incidents and experiences. This one was not in the book. One can scoff at that expression of 'doing things by the book' but more cases than not with this rule we survive. We were only ten feet off the water heading at 80 mph straight toward a frightening scene of inhospitable jagged rock face with its torn shrubbery on a craggy apex. Added to our plight towering above an electric cable appearing as if a tight-rope wire held taught by its wooden poles running the length of the cay, the approaching height of it all seemingly impossible to clear. Split second reaction had me hit the opposite rudder pedal so hard that I broke the metal toe piece of the pedal clean in half. Nothing happened. We were headed to certain disaster at this altitude with no directional control and mere seconds to play with as the rock face began to fill our vision.

There was zero choice; not enough distance remained ahead to land safely. If I pulled the power now momentum would crash us into the base of the rocky shoreline and death. I must keep the seaplane flying flat enough toward the solid rock allowing it to gain valuable airspeed. Did we have enough time? When things are going horribly wrong the scene appears to take on an appearance of slow motion. Panic is no option; it becomes think, think, think. Those remaining precious seconds lasting forever giving time to react. In a flash of memory I remembered the manoeuvre that B.D. Maule made world famous in aviation history. The climb out of an aircraft hangar! I could see David's body language shuffle awkwardly, bracing his hand on the interior windshield support that ran from the roof of the cockpit through the instrument panel, something, and anything solid to hold on to. We raced unabashed toward the land with its threatening wires above. I heard a slightly shaken brogue 'Oh Shit!' from my passenger as we came within the last few yards. I heaved on the yoke and pumped the flap handle in that familiar movement from flying in tight places. The little seaplane obediently leaped skyward, like its name the factory had declared on its tail, 'Super Rocket'! The wire whizzed inches underneath and a very audible gulp of air coming from both occupants through their headsets. 'Damn that was a close one!' David nearly shouted in excitement. 'I'm really glad I had an insurance adjuster on board,' I replied. 'I thought I might have been calling my insurance company on that one.' Trying to make light of the scary situation at hand.

'That was an amazing piece of flying, Paul!' David exclaimed, visibly inhaling.

'You can thank this fab little plane for that one' I said with conviction. 'Now comes the fun part…'

'What do you mean?' he asked, facial expression becoming instantly serious, thinking all was saved and we could just go home.

'We have no rudder, my friend,' I added gently not wanting to raise further alarm. I demonstrated by showing him what happened when I pushed the rudder pedals from side to side, nothing.

'Flying without a rudder is one thing but this aircraft is a "rudder plane", that is to say one that you lead with your feet and follow with aileron control to co-ordinate,' I explained. 'We can fly sort of straight but I'll need rudder for the precision needed to land straight ahead, especially on water; slightly crooked with the floats and we could cartwheel!' 'Oh crap!' came his short reply. 'We can land somewhere out here and try a fix but if it doesn't work we could be stuck. I say we go home and use the harbour. At least we will be home and near help if I screw up'. I knew that the only part of Nassau Harbour we had available to try this risky manoeuvre would be the large turning basin used by the cruise ships near the lighthouse entrance. The seaplane flew all the way back to Nassau slightly skewed to one side. It was incredibly strange to have no rudder control and this next landing was going to really test my skills. The flight home gave us time to talk about what had happened and how things can go incredibly wrong in a blink of the eye. The subject of accidents naturally came up. This incident was one of those mechanical freaks that required split-second decision-making. The fix in these cases can either work or fail; I have experienced both. I made point of so many losses of life avoided if only the pilots could accept the imminent sacrifice of their aircraft to save the souls on board. Aircraft accidents in recent years around the islands that proved fatal in hindsight could have possibly saved those on board. Landplane pilots have an inherent fear of putting an aircraft into the water. Those who braved the choice executed great landings in the shallow waters south of the airport or the vast expanse of Lake Killarney offering miles of friendly flatness, each saving their passengers from harm except a good soaking and loss of pilot ego. A pilot in command, bound and determined to make it back to the runway before fully regaining control after engine failure, more often has perished in awful crashes, adding in factors of overweight, dropping the land gear and difficult weather another recipe for disaster. Twin-engine planes notoriously do not survive dramatic turns with the loss of one engine. There is a procedure that if executed correctly under that amount of pressure will save the airplane. Running out of fuel gives no option but an immediate choice of flat open space whether wet or not. It all comes back to that old lesson of 'by the book'.

Those of us who fly water planes have a distinct advantage wanting to keep our machines in one piece with multiple choices of 'runways' in most cases and downright scary in others. More often we get to choose our spot, a large wide-open flat space heading directly into the wind. When I flew the twin engine Navajo the thought of ditching never really intimidated me, with exception of being over a very rough ocean knowing this affects every aircraft, equipped with wheels or floats. With knowledge of water behaviour, winds, tides, lee-side v's windward side, there are in most emergency cases, precious seconds to make a possible survivable approach exampled by the recent and now world famous event with the ditching of USAir flight #1549 out of LaGuardia, New York. An airliner losing all power to bird strikes and crash landing safely in the Hudson River, saving all one 155 souls on board. The event inspired a movie portraying a cold January afternoon in 2009 when the Airbus A-320 on initial climb out from take-off, suddenly striking a flock of Canada geese three minutes into the flight. With zero thrust from the engines returning to an airport quite out of the question, offering the only visible long, flat and open landing area as being the Hudson River. Precious seconds gave the crew barely enough time to communicate with air traffic controllers their choices and for setting the aircraft up for an emergency landing. Gliding in for a water landing, Captain 'Sully' Sullenberger and first officer Jeff Skiles managed to miss the spanning bridges of the Hudson River ending with a splashdown in midtown Manhattan. I am reading at present his autobiography *Highest Duty* having had the distinct pleasure of being introduced to both pilots at the Oshkosh Air Show in Wisconsin. On finding out about my career Sully told me with a smile, 'I just wished the water had been as warm as what you put down in!'

There seemed no point in declaring my emergency to the air traffic controllers in Nassau. They were more than familiar that I was a floatplane, not ever landing at the airport where emergency serviccs could be offered. When I reached the harbour the last thing I needed were additional watercraft from the Harbour Patrol or Police Force that could impede my landing zone. I had quite enough on my plate having to deal with the constant daily traffic of a busy commercial harbour. Glass-bottomed tour boats, water-taxis, racing jet-skis, government tugs, booze-cruise party boats, private yachts all entering or leaving the harbour. That thin body of water presented some unique challenges for a seaplane pilot; one's eyes had to dart in every direction absorbing the movement of water traffic and the wake they all produced, also noting effects of wind direction in that tight area, all the while maintaining safe performance of the airplane. Here was a crucial difference from those coping with landing on a concrete runway. Quoting Captain Goodyear of British Airways, my co-pilot on an across the harbour landing early in my career, after seeing me dodge the steeple of St. Mathews, weave carefully through the cluster of anchored sailboats while taking into account the boat traffic under the bridge, said 'you are a lot busier in the cockpit than I am in a 747 landing at Heathrow!' A seaplane's landing surface could be so disturbed simply from water traffic that has already cleared the area; wake, swells, tide and wind can add untold hazards often forcing me to fly around until settled suitable enough to safely put down on a calmer surface. Accomplishing this without a rudder was going to take a load of luck and all that I could muster from thousands of hours in the air.

'Landing assured' I declared to Roscoe Perpall, my well known friend and senior air traffic controller bidding me 'good evening, Paul'. We were on our own from here. Circling the turning basin, I could see clearly the wind lines drawing their clue of direction on the surface favouring slightly to the northeast, a directional advantage displaying the longest stretch of water to put down, praying the wind hold us straight as a weather vane. Added visible problems suddenly became all too clear. There was a large cruise ship preparing to pull away from the wharf for its departure to Florida and those marker buoys lining the entranceway of the channel where the ships followed the deep water. I had to draw a mental line directly into the wind, not a degree off and free of any obstacles such as a twelve-foot-high ton of floating metal chained to the ocean floor! There was no time for us to wait for the ship to leave as that could have taken valuable time with fuel remaining on board.

I aligned the aircraft into wind keeping the image of my chosen runway. Down to the water we flew with one degree of flap set in. Closer, and feeling confident, I applied the second notch of flap carefully, slowing the approach down safely. It looked as if I would nail this first time with my feet trying in vain automatically for some rudder control that did not exist. Very near the water and a sudden slight gust of wind slightly from one side had us careening toward a tall green marker buoy. 'Damn it,' I muttered unable to control direction adding full power immediately with a go-around my only option. 'This is how we must keep trying it,' I explained to David through my headset microphone, watching and wondering our chances without saying a word. I climbed out successfully over Randy Hall's house on the Paradise Island side of the harbour making a crude skidding left turn to set up the approach again. Back down to the water, repeating the procedure for hopeful touchdown the small seaplane this time staying true into the wind. A quick, yet smoothly applied third degree of flap while we floated a few feet above the water, setting up the slight nose high flare that would ensure an admired touchdown. There were several instances during my flying career where the ending could have gone horribly wrong. There would be such a day coming. Today's landing however was executed with perfection. Recalling each instance and time allowing, I would demand of myself the procedures of finessing an airplane to its landing surface. Flying is an art form; strangely, landings in particular, the intricacies of which not often taught by flight instructors or examiners during the learning phases of my training, all simply insisting simply I 'put it on the numbers' rather than allow the aircraft to bleed of speed and let itself settle gently on the surface. These days, while showing a keen passenger or fellow pilot the fundamentals of flying seaplanes, I always experience the joy of demonstrating a really clean landing where one could barely tell, if at all, when the pontoons touched the water's surface, or the wheels kissing the concrete with barely a sound. That short sensation of floating and wait, wait, wait, without moving the controls more than a fraction. A favourite manoeuvre being the one-float landing, where the aircraft is slightly tilted with one wing leaning into the wind and waiting for the single landing surface to meet its mark before allowing the second float to lay down softly; a reaction of appreciation and added 'wow' factor with no sensation whatsoever of touchdown is achieved and little wonder airline passengers sometimes applaud their touchdown! This harbour emergency landing I instinctively strived for that effect with power all the way off and the sudden sound of gentle slapping water against the metal floats. Success!

'Well done, very nice!' David sighed.

'More fun coming my friend, this time it's you who will save the day!' I smiled at him. 'What now?' he asked as we taxied forwards.

'Well, we still have no way of controlling this thing. The rudders are linked to the water-rudders which steer us on the water!' 'Oh crap!' came the familiar response in a Scottish brogue.

'I need you to exit the plane and crawl on your knees the back of the float to push the rudder in the direction I yell out to you!' Without hesitation, he took off his headset and started to exit the door. 'Do me a favour David,' as he looked back at me, 'please don't go for a swim because I won't be able to come back for you; it's only about eighteen inches wide down there and you have an audience of several hundred people!' pointing at the large cruise ship that had cast her lines. He rolled his eyes and headed aft, smiling in confidence as we both saw the humour of this insane method of getting back to the beach near the Hilton Hotel. 'Ready,' I heard his call.

'Push full left,' I yelled out of the open window of his door. The plane obeyed and turned around. 'Straight now!' I barked another command. Straight ahead we went. David now on all fours facing backwards, recognising he had full control of where we were going. We taxied across the waters of Nassau Harbour much to the amazement of hundreds of passengers watching from the deck railings of their ship as she passed behind us. They must have all been asking the same question, 'what the hell was that crazy man doing kneeling on the float of a taxiing seaplane?'

We approach the beachhead on and I pull the mixture to shut fuel flow. The propeller suddenly stopped as we bumped gently onto the soft sand. Ignition turned off, I could hear clearly the instrument gyros spooling down from under the panel inside my cockpit. 'Good job crew!' I called back to my balancing passenger. Carrying small articles needed for 'that quick fix' was a necessary part of bush flying. I searched inside the passenger side float for something we needed, a small length of stainless safety-wire to repair the easily spotted culprit. A broken rudder turnbuckle that now fell limp under the rear of the plane. An approved aircraft part no less! Temporary fix in place, we restarted the engine with both of us inside the cockpit, taxied eastward the full length of the harbour, pulling successfully onto my wooden ramp at the restaurant. We smiled at each other shaking hands in celebration of a really good ending of a shit situation. The ice-cold beer found just a couple yards away went down very easily. The aviation turnbuckles were replaced with heavy nautical stainless steel substitutes that the FAA inspectors once based in Alaska simply smiled at. David Craig recalled to me in later years of retelling that story several times in many bars around the world during his career. He exclaimed with glee in broad Scottish brogue 'I nay had ter embellish it either!'

Flying seaplanes appears from the outside as probably the most romantic job imaginable in aviation? For those of us who put in countless hours of pumping water out of floats in the wee hours of the morning, washing off our aircraft way after the sun has gone down, desperately trying to rid the machine of saltwater contamination and what seems endless maintenance, we still marvel at that incredible view from our seat up front. That first flight of the day when Judy has called from Bell Island asking for a 7-am pickup, I have crawled out of bed at 5.30-am, still dark outside, to make coffee and a quick bowl of cereal. My film producer always made light of my eating choice first thing in the day, 'Damn Paul, how can you eat those bark and twigs?' On the beautiful mornings, I would straddle my 700 Honda Shadow motorcycle. An old classic 1986 black and chrome street bike that always brought a stare with its throaty sound. My friends often ribbed me about 'how my insurance agent must love me' for riding a big motorcycle to work then flying a bush plane for a living and diving with sharks on my days off!

Nassau Harbour these days was becoming intolerable to work from. The boat-traffic, hardly heeding the 'no wake' rules of maritime courtesy, made life for a seaplane quite hazardous. Bahamian commercial boat captains, for the most part, had little care about rules of the road and it was becoming a free for all on the water. Time on the engine grew preposterously having to taxi to the far end of the harbour in order to offer the added security of ample space. The 2000 hours of engine time had gone by quickly where the rebuild had taken all my savings. I was now on my second seaplane having had the first completely renovated along with the engine. The day came when the final straw broke the camel's back. Leaving Crocodiles restaurant for a tourist day trip one of the government tugs came roaring under the bridge heading westward. This heavy displacement hull pushed a wake over three feet high sending anchored sailboats into hazardous tilting angles as the wave hit their sides. Frustrated yachtsmen raced out of their cabins to yell abuse of the carelessness. I could see trouble racing across the harbour surface and made a grab for my marine radio microphone. Verbal abuse over Channel 16 was not good behaviour but I knew the captain would have his radio tuned, as would the Port Authority officers on duty. Someone had to hear about this idiot causing damage with his reckless driving. Nothing happened, having me take evasive action of approaching wave at a forty-five-degree angle so the floatplane would not capsize with the flooding water that would flow over her decks. I forewarned my passengers to hang onto loose objects such as cameras as we were in for a tilting experience. The wingtip barely missed the surface as it dipped over by a couple of feet. 'I'm done with these fools,' I thought angrily. Time to move over to the lake.

On first arrival into Nassau with a seaplane it was not long before I received a phone call from one of the other floatplane owners over on Lake Cunningham summonsing me to a meeting at Charlie Bethel's office in town. Apparently, the other seaplane owners on the lake wished to meet with me and discuss my flying off the harbour. All the pilots there I knew well from over the years; Tommy Goodwin from his band that we all loved playing at the Doubloon night club, Jimmy Sands who worked with his family at Butler and Sands and owned that gorgeous old de Havilland Beaver hangared at his home at the far end of the lake, and Charlie who owned Flamingo Cay bonefish resort on the west side of Andros and hangared his Cessna 185 with Tommy's Maule living next-door. They announced that their 'association should have been notified' I was bringing another seaplane to the Bahamas and talking with them first would have been the thing to do. I was sceptical about any 'association' but could see really they were concerned about my operating commercially. I made it clear that being so visible at my location all would be done above board by the FAA and Civil Aviation at the airport. There was little choice for them to accept me in the water plane community as I was now well established. Several years later with tables turned, I needed to be over with them on Lake Cunningham. A long narrow lake running alongside the airport road on the western side of New Providence with private estates along its north shoreline who accepted for the most part the idea of seaplanes taking off and landing near their houses. There were no vacant lots available for purchase over there. In the centre of the lake another small peninsular ran to the far western end where two more seaplanes sometimes ramped there. Timmy Wrinkle also owner a Maule and Stuart Cove flying a small ageing Cessna on straight floats. I asked both, as friends of mine, if they ever wanted to sell their vacant land with wooden seaplane ramps already in place, would they give me first offer? Both pieces of property eventually sold without either remembering to call me.

I had to find an owner who may be partial to having a seaplane based there. There was one. My mother used to work in real estate and knew Bahamian broker Lester Brown really well, who used to own and fly a Cessna seaplane from his lakeside property. Lester had passed away several years ago and knowing his son Ian quite well decided to approach him about my prospect. In consultation with his lovely Mum, also named Mary, and déjà vu about a floatplane being there again, I was allowed to construct a new ramp at the bottom of their waterfront alongside a small wooden dock already in place. It was private and perfect for what I needed; giving Ian added income with an agreement on a monthly rent. All I had to do was install a fresh water pipe in the ground and reconstruct the old tool shed to house my 500-gallon fuel tank that had been installed a couple years earlier in the harbour location. The days of carrying five-gallon fuel cans from the gas station got old eventually although keeping both Suzanne and myself in great shape! With a long hose that reached the aircraft I could now gravity feed fuel by climbing onto the wing strut of the Maule. The hose turned out to be perfect length for the lake location with an added electric pump and meter making the sophisticated system a lot easier to cope with aviation fuel delivered by Sam Brown owning an independent fuel delivery service at the airport only about fifteen minutes away. 'Hey, Pauley' he used to call me always with a smile. 'How are you today Sam?' I would ask 'Oh, catchin' hell and calling it a good time!' he always joked.

The lake location was beautiful. Quiet surroundings and calm waters to work in and best of all, no tides. With my first landing onto Lake Cunningham, while taxiing to my new ramp, I noticed the dogs from up at the main house running across the grass to greet me. They walked onto the ramp and starting drinking the water. What a great sight that was. Fresh water! Gone were the days of keeping a seaplane floating in some of the saltiest waters on this planet. A young lad I knew from the Montagu home remodelling, Stefan Brozozog, nephew of renowned Lenny who ran Pipe of Peace, a famed tobacco shop in town, came to build my fuel shed. Once three of the four wooden walls were finished we hired a crane truck to lift the large metal fuel tank from its foundation over at Crocodiles and lower it carefully through the open roof of our new structure. Nicely in place, Stefan closed in the last wall and constructed the roof overhead affording shelter from the rain and weather where I could keep tools, snorkelling equipment and spare parts.

Not long after completion we received a frantic call from Stefan's family that he was in hospital after an attack at his home. On opening his front door, a stranger suddenly plunged a large knife into the centre of his chest penetrating his heart. A mistaken identity from his attacker left him dying. Rushed to Princess Margaret's Hospital the surgeons saw no time for selective surgery; his rib cage was opened wide and his heart successfully repaired. Doubts about the abilities of our local surgeons put to rest after that miracle. I went to see him in the public ward and brought several gifts to keep him company. He smiled saying cheerfully 'that was a close one Mr. Harding!' displaying a huge purple scar down the centre of his chest.

The early morning motorcycle rides along the coast road with the soft light behind me and an early summer warm wind in my face was a great start to any day. The low growl of the Honda purring in low gear, the beaches all vacant and the ocean calm and inviting as I pass 'go-slow bend' on West Bay Street. The ageing Nassau Beach Hotel still stands across the bay where it's neighbour, the Emerald Beach having burnt to the ground years ago. The Sonesta is still there, changing name in later years to Breezes, an all-inclusive resort similar to Sandals that took over the old Balmoral property where I had my first job as dive instructor. Cable Beach is starting to show its age and rumour has it there may be changes one day here to compete with the rising new Atlantis Resort, dream of South African, Sol Kerzner and his son Butch.

With my flying career in full swing I would fly Butch on occasion and deeply saddened with his sudden death on October 11 2006 in the Dominican Republic, along with three other passengers in a helicopter hitting a building on the north coast of the island in poor weather while flying over prospective development sites. His father Sol Kerzner began with a single hotel on a deserted beach in Durban building the famous

'Sun City' near Johannesburg in 1979. In 1994, father and son purchased the hotels on Paradise Island from American entertainer Merv Griffin for an estimated $125 million. The luxury resort of the original 'Ocean Club' was included but refurbishing every room cost millions for the Kerzner International Holdings. Butch, born in 1964, launched later another Atlantis resort in Dubai costing near $1.5 billion. He was a known risk-taker, often jogging for miles through the Kruger National Park where predators roam free. Nervous companions he assured would be safe 'as long as they did not lag behind!' Butch was survived by his wife Vanessa and two young children.

I had lost another prominent passenger of mine also to an air disaster a year earlier on December 19 2005. Chalk's Ocean Airways flight 101 from Fort Lauderdale made an unscheduled stop at Watson Island in Miami to pick up Sergio Danguillecourt, great-great grandson to the founder of Barcadi, and his wife Jacqueline, along with his yacht captain, on their way to collect his boat in Bimini. Mystery prevailed with Sergio being the only passenger found not strapped into his seat. Everyone was found in the wreckage in their seats whereas his body was discovered last by fishermen nine miles away from the crash site, either thrown from or trying to escape the falling plane. All eighteen passengers and two crew died that day. The well-known Grumman Mallard, registration N-2969, had been featured on the television series *Miami Vice*. It was the first passenger fatality for the oldest operating airline but second to crash due to metal fatigue. Those of us who lived within sight of Nassau Harbour used the amphibious airline many times from its base over on Paradise Island traveling over to Miami, knowing well how waterlogged the aircraft behaved on landing and take-off. Vast sheets of saltwater would envelop the plane as throttles were applied. The propellers would zing with the sound of ocean water flying through their blades. It was common conversation about what a monumental task it must be washing the planes off after each flight, and what effects would be on the metals inside?

Witnesses saw white smoke billowing out from one engine after take-off from the waterway in Miami before the right wing actually tore off completely sending the remaining hull in a spiral toward the ocean's surface. Michele Marks, thirty-seven years old had received her captaincy a year earlier and her first officer, Paul De Sanctis, thirty-four, had joined the company just eight months earlier. Later in 2007 the National

Transportation Safety Board asserted Chalk's Ocean Airways had failed to identify repair fatigue cracks on the 1947 Turbo Mallard. Grumman had produced fifty-nine models of this type and ceased production in 1951 leaving operators eventually with no source of spare parts. Chalk's had resorted to purchasing several un-airworthy Mallards in order to cannibalise them for spare parts needed to maintain their remaining fleet. The doomed aircraft was fifty-eight years old accumulating 31,226 total flight hours completing over 39,000 take-offs and landings. The remaining fleet was grounded and found also suffering similar fatigue problems with pilots voicing concerns about maintenance; seeing elevator controls snapping but the flight saved and a number of engine failures reported. The Bahamas lost eleven citizens that day and left the country mourning their loss from the island of Bimini. I had lost my frequent flyers often taking Sergio and Jacqueline over to Highbourne Cay where their yacht would be berthed and owning part of the island known to us all as North House, used as a popular rental destination. They were always really nice to have on board the Maule, especially loved by Barbara Thrall and Ian McBeth managers of the cay along with the entire staff over on Highbourne.

Passengers became close to us over the years, we had worked hard for their trust and became really good friends. Losing them was always difficult. Barbara contracted cancer later in my career so I would fly her for treatments along with her beloved potcake dog 'Wilson' named after the film *Castaway*. Wilson often travelled alone with me for a vet visit met by Julie Kimble for personal transportation; it was still mandatory to clean those paws of sand! Losing Barbara eventually took the wind out of all who knew her. Ian retired back to Oregon and for our life long friends, Kevin and Carolyn Cartwright, we connected the job for them as replacement management, able now to relocate away from Nassau.

The big Honda swings left turn over the golf course on Cable Beach, always remembering my friend Ricky Wells, the photographer who was killed in a car crash here at the intersection. I miss his laughter. Arriving at the Lake I used to park the bike under a large palmetto tree by my fuel shed. Removing my helmet the sweet smell of wet grass prevailed. The Maule sits serenely in the glassy calm fresh water at her new home. Early morning mists rose daintily off the cool fresh water while Coots called from inside the rushes and fancy-guppies pick at the sides of the floats. Ian Browns' Macaw parrots call from their cages outside his house on top of the hill Pre-flight was easier now with no tides in the lake. Water levels remaining constant eliminated the late night visits to the restaurant where the plane had to be positioned for being afloat in the morning. Dock lines were permanently in place where and all I had to do was release them from the pontoons and climb aboard for the start. Taxiing down the lake gave the engine time to warm the oil and perform propeller and magneto checks. A call to Nassau Radio at the airport was fruitless with their inability to receive my call from so low on the water. Far better communication was made with Departure Control who kindly issued us squawk codes for our transponders. Once rotating off the water the familiar voices of our many air traffic controllers would issue 'radar contact' as we headed outbound toward our destinations.

My clients based in or near the city were not so happy at my moving west losing their transport convenience, soon forgiving they faithfully continued using my services. Tourism clientele and guests of the private islands and yachts were still transported by our faithful timeless driver Charles Rolle. Retired as maître'd of Buena Vista restaurant, 'Uncle Charles', as we affectionately adopted him, was loved by all who met him; well into his seventies now, he never changed. Always a smile, always gracious, a real 'old school Bahamian' rarely found these days. He would recant many of his restaurant stories of all those hundreds who used to patronise the old classic Bahamian mansion in town. A building whose history started back in 1789 when the Earl of Dunmore granted 150 acres to John Brown, president of King George III's Council. Twenty acres were deeded to Stephen Delancey, a loyalist slave owner from New York who had distinguished himself as lieutenant colonel in the New Jersey volunteers of 1782, rewarded by the king with the position of Chief Justice of the Bahamas. The area around the site of the mansion being named Delancey Town and in 1801 the land was divided into eighty lots and sold to well to do freed slaves. The next fifty years of ownership becomes a mystery until 1851 when the Nassau Guardian articles the property being owned by the Reverend William Woodcock, remembered in the Bahamas for his advancement of education amongst local Bahamians. The property is again advertised in 1896 being now occupied by the Honourable Charles

Walpole, another Chief Justice of the Bahamas. Various occupants lived in the Buena Vista until 1918 where title was granted to a Canadian, Harold Petrie from Hamilton, Ontario. The family owned the house until 1922 where it passed to Madison, New Jersey resident Edward Tooth whose widow opened the house as a restaurant in 1947 on what we know now as Delancy Street. Through the 1960s, while Charles was employed there also as shareholder, under the management of our friend Stan Bocca, the list of famous patrons became extensive under the ownership of McAlpine and Sons, the renowned construction company. Hollywood stars from Robert Mitchum to Sidney Poitier and Eddie Murphy, celebrities Ed Sullivan and Bobby Kennedy all dined in the best-known restaurant within the Caribbean. Much to our disappointment the establishment finally closed its doors in recent history and its infamous maître'd retired to purchase a taxicab working well to this day in his eighties with most of his local clientele always calling him for service!

Charles could still recall almost every patron's favourite specialty from the menu and how they like it served and where they had been seated. From the early days of our living in the Bahamas 'Table 8' over in the far corner was our place to reserve. Here we enjoyed the fine cuisine and company of friends seated around the familiar round table with special guests that visited our islands year after faithful year.

Chapter 27
A New Century!

The end of the twentieth century was nearly upon us. Our world changing on a daily basis, bombarded relentlessly with news of secular wars in the Middle East and Eastern Europe. Bloody unrest seemed never-ending with history seemingly offering no lessons whatsoever. While Shiites and Kurds were killing each other we cringed at the atrocities committed by the Serbian militia's 'ethnic cleansing' of Muslim villages in Bosnia, a war that had broken out in 1992 lasting for three awful years, a country where ethnicity between Croats, Serbs and Muslims apparently incapable of living alongside each other. Muslim persecution so ingrained it became part and parcel for two of the attackers on September 11th 2001. I was staggered by the harsh lessons of the Second World War failing to make an impression on the peoples of these Eastern European countries having lived generations alongside each other within the same borders; mans' insane intolerance displaying its utmost stupidity with leaders of all sides, emulating the recent filth of human behaviour from Nazi Germany only fifty years earlier. It was no longer a faded German memory, rather belonging recently to so many countries in these new decades all over the globe; races of people behaving in atrocious manner and using violence to solve. Monstrous personalities such as Slobodan Milosevic emerged slurring history with the name 'genocide' once again entering our vocabulary.

In a statement on September 23 2008 to the United Nations, the head of the Bosnia and Herzegovina delegation estimated 200,000 people were killed, 12,000 of them children, up to 50,000 women raped, and 2.2 million displaced from their homes. It seems that many sectors of mankind (perhaps I actually mean men-kind) are indeed saddled with the incapacity of learning to improve our way of dealing with our conflicts. We do not appear to have evolved in the slightest, beyond the dismal attempt to deal with any sort of disagreement by killing one another. In the Middle Eastern regions, they have been 'at it' over 4000 years, so why should we expect an end now? I am fortunate in our generation, not conscripted into war; however there is not a month or a year that goes by where peace has prevailed across our world. Instead, our television screens are full of predictable murder, conquests and bloodbaths that have raged for centuries; every religious sect committing atrocities in the name of God, Mohammed, Allah, none are exempt; Christian, Catholic, Muslim, Arab, Jew; all creating images of children walking aimlessly through an epitaph of twisted steel and shattered concrete. This period in our lives it is the radical Muslim's turn to wreak havoc. Suppression, invasion and the west forcing its unwelcome democracy spawns resentment and retaliation from a British Empire that audaciously drew lines on a map, forcing millions from their homelands. Superpowers flexing their muscle and weapons to rid us of miserable dictators, a blessing to those who suffered under them and a curse for creating a vacuum in power that followed, spawning worse pestilence such as ISIS. Now we face a scourge that not only displays atrocious acts of violence but also begins the actual destruction of ancient civilisations systematically destroying irreplaceable preserved historical sites from the face of the earth. We ask is it possible to strive for and achieve a sort of consciousness that might allow us to see the perspective of others and so allow compromise?

War these days, as I tap computer keys, is shattering the cradle of civilisation, displacing millions who flee their homeland for the trek toward Europe, which opens its arms in compassion; many who enter vulgarly attempting to impose their religious laws and radical way of life onto their hosts, arrogantly not learning their new homes' language threatening those country's identities that may change forever. Belgium will be majority Muslim in four years, maybe the wheel going around for the Belgium disgraces of the Congo? Recent times show new evidence of host population resentment and regret of their hospitality, having to deal with rape of their women and immigrant demonstrations, demanding more for themselves and creating a financial burden on already trying economies, eventually aiding the fall of the very leaders that showed compassion. Europe will never be the same and the UK votes out of the Union that history may prove, done too late?

Africa still had its troubles. I just finished reading the book *Dangerous Beauty* by Mark Ross, a safari guide known to friends and pilots we met recently in

Kenya. In this last year of the century he was guiding tourists through the Ugandan forest to see the mountain gorillas, when a band of Hutu rebels ambushed them, taking all hostage, marching them toward the Congo boarder. Mark negotiated that the women be allowed to return to their campsite along with some of their partners all of whom were exhausted by the walk, some barefoot, through the harsh terrain. Eight foreigners from Britain, New Zealand and America were bludgeoned or hacked to death with machetes. As many as 150 rebels had suddenly materialised from the forest, seeking out British and American nationalities in retaliation for their respective countries supporting the Ugandan military, while sympathising with opposing Tutsi tribesmen. The initial onslaught to the encampment began with automatic weapons fire and grenades where thirty-one tourists were captured. Uganda was just on the mend after years of political turmoil and war from Rwanda where the Hutu rebels had mass murdered over 500,000 Tutsi and moderate Hutu members.

The last years of the 1990s saw violence from Mother Nature as well. Earthquake activity became very pronounced, with Taiwan losing over 2400 people and twice in northwest Turkey a massive quake took over 17,000 souls in one episode and another 845 in another. Late in the year a super cyclone devastated the state of Odisha, India. The huge storm named 'Orissa' ploughed across the Bay of Bengal in October reaching maximum winds of 180 mph in its destructive path, killing over 10,000 people.

People in the news made headlines with the impeachment of President Clinton coming to an end, with his acquittal after a sex scandal in the Oval Office of the White House with an intern. He did however leave office later, leaving a legacy of America's surplus not achieved since 1969 and the first Democratic President to win two terms since Roosevelt. He had the highest approval rating of over 65% at the end of his last term, not accomplished since Eisenhower.

Assisted suicide was taking the forefront of news with Dr Jack Kevorkian in Michigan finally prosecuted and convicted for aiding patients to die. Bill Gates of Microsoft is declared the richest man in the world. King Hussein of Jordan succumbs to cancer in February with his son Prince Abdullah taking the throne. Student teenagers who were bullied in an American school retaliate with a mass killing in Columbine School in Colorado, killing twelve classmates and one teacher. A new wave of school tragedies, not only in the United States but in Britain, Norway, and other countries in years to follow, with easier access to guns and automatic weapons. On a visit to America recently, a country being strangled by gun violence with a citizen's right to bear arms written in the 1700s, a country just forming, I was stunned seeing rows of military assault rifles on display for sale in a sporting goods department of a popular superstore, making one wish for a return to the simple musket in use at the time of writing their Second Amendment!

The largest corporation on the planet is formed with the merger of Exxon Mobil. London has terrorist troubles with nail bombers hitting a popular local pub, while the Millennium Dome is completed within the city as an exhibition centre, opening with the turn of the approaching new century. In the art world, a twenty-two-year restoration of Da Vinci's 'Last Supper' is placed on display in Milan. There are a fewer air disasters in these recent years as airline maintenance becomes more scrutinised, and ever more cautious about weather, with the use of modern detection instruments in the cockpit. One tragedy stood out with the loss of an Egypt Air flight that departed New York for Cairo suddenly plummeting into the ocean off Nantucket, Massachusetts, killing all 217 people on board. It was discovered that the pilot left the cockpit, leaving the co-pilot at the controls that abruptly put the airliner into a vertical dive. As I write today the news is filled with similar tragedy where the young German co-pilot, on being left alone in the cockpit of an Airbus, locked the security door from inside the cockpit, not allowing the captain to return. Then he placed the autopilot into shallow rate of descent impacting into the French Alps, taking a terrifying eight minutes. All 150 people died with him. After 9/11 all American airliners were enforced to always have two-crew inside the cockpit at all times, whereas Europe did not follow suit. This tragedy may surely instigate changes?

In 1999 we lose yet another prominent member of the Kennedy family. The Kennedy Curse, as it is termed in the media, took another tragic turn with John F. Kennedy Jr dying in a private plane crash. Since 1941, all the way through 2012, this renowned American family has seen over seventeen memorable deaths or tragedies, starting with Rosemary Kennedy's mental challenges, ending with her husband Joe Sr, taking his wife for a lobotomy. During the millennia that followed Kennedy family members would succumb to plane crashes, airline disasters, car wrecks, amputations, stillbirths, suicides and assassinations.

In 1998 John Kennedy Jr., began a lifelong dream of taking his pilot training in Vero Beach, Florida, passing his Private Pilot's License that year. In April, he purchased a Piper Saratoga, a high-end single engine aircraft. On July 16 1999, wanting to attend the wedding of his cousin over at Martha's Vineyard, his journey would start late in the day. It is reported his flight instructor volunteered to accompany him as he was taking his wife, who was a reluctant flyer, with him, and her sister as passengers. Kennedy fatally declined the offer and loaded the two ladies and luggage for the evening flight. The weather was not categorised as 'Instrument Conditions' that evening, where in America one can fly at night with Visual Flight Rules in effect. JFK Jr was not instrument rated and yet would have needed that expertise once darkness descended, with his course taking him over the open ocean where visual references would have been lost. He finally lost control of his aircraft due to spatial disorientation; no longer able to maintain visual reference to the ground with city lights showing below, the darkness losing his ability to know his planes' attitude, coupled with his inexperience of flying with the use of cockpit instrumentation; the aircraft appeared to have stalled, plunging downward into the sea: Air Traffic Controllers saw the aircraft descended at a rapid rate near 5000 feet per minute. On his failure to reach his destination they put out a call for search and rescue. On July 19 the NOAA vessel *Rude* found debris on the ocean floor with the use of sonar. Divers found the pieces of wreckage in 120 feet of water, with the three bodies still attached to their respective seats. Three days later the ashes of JFK Jr, his wife and her sister were scattered over the sea off Martha's Vineyard. Losing the tiny three-year-old we all watched saluting his father's horse drawn casket in 1963 ended the Camelot legacy America lived with all those years.

This last year of the century would have the Bahamas, Caribbean and east coast of America threatened by a monster called 'Floyd'. On September 7 1999 the tropical depression 1000 miles east of the Antilles became a hurricane on the tenth, intensifying rapidly through the thirteenth. By the time it had reached Eleuthera and Abaco the storm was so abnormally large the outer bands could be seen from satellite images touching Cuba to the South and the Carolinas to the North. The eye alone big enough to encompass the whole outer perimeter of Hurricane Andrew! I decided, with the projected path of the storm, to weather this one out by tying the seaplane down to the heavy wooden ramp it was sitting on. Keith Riches, my friend from Civil Aviation helped secure the aircraft with his invention of control locks that held all the moving surfaces in place. We removed the front hatches of the floats, filling compartments with water making the Maule extremely heavy resembling something secured in a spider-web of rope lines. My only fear being nearby coconut trees blown over crushing my aircraft as if a toy. They had all been well sheared with only three or four fronds left, leaving me confident they would remain standing. The thought of flying all that way to central Florida and back enough to take chance this time around.

The storm passed New Providence to the north leaving us without power and the usual filthy mess a hurricane causes to our natural beauty of the islands robbing us the beauty of long established trees. Once again everything turned black and died, with salt racing through the foliage driven by hurricane force winds. The airplane survived unscathed although nearly sinking with rising water in Lake Cunningham raising challenge in the art of re-floating. The Out-Islands to our north came off worse, especially Abaco, and the seaplane played its part once in helping so many communities needing emergency supplies. David Craig returned once again to assess the insurance claims but the flying adventures paled to match our past experiences.

The second edition of N783SP worked well, with her new fuselage custom built the way I needed in order to survive the cruel salty environment I was operating in. With each hour flown there was a calculated 'reserve fund' set aside for the future purchase of engines, propellers and possible new planes. My prices were beginning to rise with increased demand and wear and tear of my machine. The FAA inspectors stayed away for the most part, visiting my location a few times while in town from Miami, soon learning my paperwork meticulous enough and the aircraft displaying my anal attitude toward its upkeep. The Civil Aviation crew comprised of the few remaining Brits that headed management and its long-time Bahamian counterparts. With tedious revisions, my Operations Manual that Danny Trainor insisted was 'my manual' became word for word what CAA demanded of me. My new inspector from the UK, Keith, showed keen interest in floatplanes, scuba diving and fishing here in the Bahamas. He was on a three-year contract and searching for the same brand of boat while wanting to learn the waters and its dive sites. A good friendship ensued, with him taking occasional flights in the Maule which all too soon developed the craving for him learning to fly. He attended flight school in Crystal River on the north-western coast of Florida, passing his Private Pilot's License several months later. We spent time together once in a while with both Bertram's cruising side by side over the Yellow Banks and into the Exuma Cays. One Christmas spent in Normans Cay Pond, where spectacular weather that year presented us calm blue days of diving, catching dolphin fish in the Sound and certainly appealing for that swim on Christmas morning. Being the first crew of the two boats to rise in the unusual calm winter morning, Suzanne and I headed out to the ocean in our small 11-foot Carolina Skiff: the tender based securely in the shallows of Crystal Beach that she had driven the 42 miles across the open water from Nassau to Normans by herself! I had a favourite fishing spot just off the north end of Little Spirit Cay, where the edge of the blue water came close to the tip of the island. The ocean was so oily calm we could see the emerald greens and flashes of turquoise as the schooling dolphin drifted under our little boat. Armed with a yellow and green feather and piece of jackfish strip-bait, a big bull male dolphin hit hard and fast. Seeing my rod bent near double other larger fishing vessels came closer to drag their lures through our school and share the prized fish. Some captains and crew were enthralled watching us haul in this large game fish into such a small boat. They knew once on board these fighting fish suddenly erupt with one last strategy of trying to escape with a huge leap out of the vessel they have been brought aboard. Question was 'how was this man going to keep such a fish in his small skiff?' Taking my time and enjoying the fight, the gorgeous colours soon came to the surface. My gaff bit hard through the strong head and I hauled the beautiful fish over the shallow gunnel and inside the boat. I could see the intent on the spectator's faces waiting for the explosion of fish that would have easily taken it back into the water. My old trick of a soaking wet towel thrown quickly over the fish's head and body worked miraculously. Nothing further came from my catch, with a quiet, large body lying still on the floor as life slowly slipped away. A round of applause came from across the waters and I raised my rod in salute! Keith finally arrived on scene where we paid out our lines for another catch. I had fished the Bahamas all my life, never fortunate enough to hook a billfish. When I finally landed a spectacular sailfish, we took pictures and quickly released, only to watch in disappointment the exhausted fish keel over and sink to the bottom. Having drifted out of the deep water we could see the silver body lying still on the ocean floor. Not wanting to waste the prize donned our snorkel equipment in attempt to free dive the fish back to the surface. It proved to be near 70-feet of water but with a couple practice dives made bottom taking two of us to hoist the sail to the surface later mounted for my patio wall. This Christmas morning Keith applied the brake carefully to his spooling line, set the ratchet and immediately struck his first fish, a 7-foot sailfish, proving yet again the myth of 'beginners luck' and success with a release to watch the beautiful fish swim slowly toward the indigo depths. We only ever took enough to eat unlike so many fishermen who selfishly slaughtered as many fish as they could pull in. His wife Denise cooked roast lamb for dinner, whining constantly about not wanting their boat used for fishing and messy from fish blood proceeding to drop the dinner on the floor! It tasted great all the same.

Our century, the one we were born in, the one travelled through from birth to adulthood was coming to a close. We are well into the computer age with fears suddenly becoming very apparent our automated world was about to face a crisis, simply how would all the world's computer systems manage to recognise a radical change in the numerical change from 1999 to 2000, the abbreviation for the New Year, 'Y2K'. It was conceived that without corrective action, long-working systems would break down when the ascending numbering, of two-digit abbreviation, 97, 98, 99, assumption suddenly became invalid not recognising 00. There would have to be massive system changes and upgrades worldwide and the number of failures that New Year's morning is not known, with the reluctance of organisations to admit. Credit and debit card transactions were disrupted and many institutions relied on paper transactions until the machines corrected on January 1. On New Year's Day problems were actually regarded as minor, yet worldwide estimation in the year 2000 costs spent on Y2K remediation exceeded $308 billion.

For most of us, this year ending would amount to a massive celebration and welcoming in the twenty-first century. The fireworks displays around the planet were going to be extraordinary. In Nassau, we decided that the newly completed Atlantis Resort on Paradise Island would certainly be the display to watch, but from where? A group of us came up with the idea of viewing from a boat in the middle of Nassau Harbour as we had all those years earlier for Independence. The night was clear and the explosions started at midnight with an amazing display that went on seemingly forever. Champagne flowed and thousands of people could be seen on both shorelines also crowded on the bridge above the harbour. It was strange to accept the 1990s were now behind us.

On average I was flying over fifty hours a month. It seemed only days since Wilfred and I had changed the oil and re-cowled the Maule with my mechanic filling out my Adlog maintenance records. However I paid attention to the maintenance, the second Maule was now showing its age. The first had survived just three years before becoming critically damaged with corrosion and now this second edition was running out of years also. With Marcus's advice of paying close attention to saving a reserve fund we had enough in the bank to order a new Maule. 'Sugar Pop' as Tony Dean affectionately called her, would have to go on the market to help recoup some of the costs. The new engines from Lycoming sported separate magnetos ridding us of the constant frustrations to maintain that temperamental dual magneto. The last straw with that ignition system came on a flight to Highbourne Cay with Peter and Alison, then managers, returning to the cay from a break in Nassau. I had flown my friends many times, having faithfully used my service for flights needed to and from the island throughout the busy seasons of the year. We were about halfway across, well over the Yellow Banks, when I heard a sudden change in the tone of the engine. My attention in an instant went to the RPM gauge, showing a clear loss in power. I knew instinctively that one side of that damned dual magneto had failed, probably the points or a condenser? Question was, had my passengers noticed? Peter was up front with Alison behind neither showing any change in expression. I decided to stay silent, stealing a careful glance sideways in order to gauge my two friends' reaction and not make the dilemma known, giving me time to assess options – continue or turn around and head back to Nassau? Returning to the mainland had the advantage of the wind behind me making the journey a matter of minutes, but the disadvantage of the water below me getting rougher as I approached land. To keep going meant that I would be entering calmer waters with the islands offering protection and very favourable radio communication with the cay knowing help was at hand if needed. If luck held out I could keep the airplane flying and land my passengers at their destination with none the wiser? Seeing Highbourne clearly in sight I decided safer on the latter choice. The Maule was still flying but dropping airspeed from 120 mph down to a 100 mph. I smoothly reached down to my right and slowly pulled a notch of flaps to stop the rate of descent due to the fairly heavy load we were carrying. Peter glanced at my movement and maybe thought this was a tad early for an approach, but we maintained level flight without losing altitude for another several minutes. I called the cay to let them know where we were and my ETA to landing. The winds were gentle that day and the approach into the calm waters just off 'Cheap Charlie Beach' played straightforward. I jumped the seaplane over the two small rocks in the channel landing smoothly inside the bay adjacent to the sand much to my inner relief, while taxiing onto the beach where I could turn the aircraft placing her heels on the sand allowing my passengers to simply walk ashore. We unloaded the groceries and luggage they had brought along, giving hugs and handshakes we said goodbye. Now came another decision, whether to fix the problem here in Highbourne or take the ultimate gamble and fly some forty miles home on one magneto? Fixing in the Out-Islands could only mean calling Nassau and arranging a flight for my mechanic to get into Normans Cay, or lucky enough to find Ellie who had formed Bahamas Seaplane Service about the same time as I had gone commercial. Flying with her coming direct to Highbourne an attractive thought with my mechanic and spare parts?

The day was gorgeous. A real 'blue Bahama day' as we called them. The winds remained light and if I took this chance a forced water landing almost anywhere would have been reasonably safe. I decided to at least restart the seaplane and while taxiing perform a magneto check with the ignition key, selecting left or right side to find out if my hunch was correct. Sure enough, when I switched to the left position the engine tone remained constant and turning to the right side gave sudden silence, dead. Now came the big question, would the plane be able to perform a water take-off with only one side of the magneto functioning with just myself on board? I decided the very least I could do is give it a try and if unsuccessful the decision would be made for me, having to cast pride aside and return to the cay asking for help. If she flew then how would it feel in the air? Again, if unsatisfactory I could simply land again and proclaim my problem to Peter and choose to stay. The taxi out on to the bank side of the island was uneventful, offering an attractive long flat runway to see if the Maule would perform. With her very light load compared to the incoming flight I managed to get onto the plane quite easily, skipping along the calm surface building enough speed in order to lift off. This run although noticeably slower than usual finally rotated off the water. I circled with a right turn keeping safe over the shallow bank waters offering loads of landing choices just seconds away had the need arisen. Confidence mounted quickly where I felt good about giving the homeward flight a try. The Maule flew quite easily with just me aboard and the mainland of New Providence to my relief came quickly into view.

In those early seaplanes, I had installed a two-metre ham-radio that I could talk with my house where a base unit was installed. This gave me the privacy to talk business over the airwaves. I called home and explained the situation about limping back to the harbour, a message not well received. Then the aircraft radio came alive with Ellie, who was based on Lake Cunningham, flying her Maule back to Nassau from Little San Salvador; an island we all flew for under development by Holland America. I asked her to go to the chitchat frequency 123.45 that we all used to have idle talk in the air and explained my dilemma and a try for home. She said she would keep an eye for me as she approached from behind to make sure I made it safely. Within about five miles from Nassau the other side of my magneto decided that was enough and also started to fail. My luck was fast running out and some more quick decisions to be made. The seas below were calm enough for safe water landing so I told Claudette, my air traffic controller on duty, that I wanted to land 'out here to check something out on the aircraft', avoiding a declaration of emergency which might have given Civil Aviation something to hold against us with a commercial business. She knew me well with several unusual requests coming from 'Sugar Papa' over the years, 'you be good out there!' she answered. I knew I had 'landing assured' which told ATC I was safe in my situation freeing them of responsibility. While at altitude I made the call to home for a tow and my position. Ellie now had me in view and watched as I slowly descended down to the water, trying desperately to stay aloft as long as possible making the inevitable tow home as short as possible. The engine was running but roughly losing valuable power and altitude. The surface came all too quickly for my liking and touchdown went well. I pulled the mixture and all went silent. The shore from this low perspective looked miles away. Some friends were called who had a boat, promising to set off for a long slow tow home.

'You look awful lonely down there,' Ellie's voice came over the radio. 'Glad you are safe Paul, nicely done.' 'Thanks Elle, see you soon and thanks for staying around.' I watched as she flew overhead wagging her wings to say goodbye. The slight breeze was drifting me westward; there seemed no need to throw an anchor, I might as well drift off a couple more miles before help arrive? Gazing at infinity there was no sign of a boat; I was quite alone on the ocean, save the gentle slap of water against the sides of my metal floats. Thank goodness for seaplanes, recalling my boast about flying water-planes; 'lots of runway!'

My rescuers finally became visible on the horizon; speeding toward me able to see my location aided by my flashing wing strobe lights turned on for a few minutes. I secured my anchor line to the spreader bar; a strong metal structure holding the two floats together and tossed the open end to my friends. The slow trip home took near two hours to complete. It felt very strange passing under Paradise Island bridge being a spectacle of an aircraft towed by a small boat. A scene repeated some years later with Jimmy having to put down his de Havilland Beaver off the south shore of Nassau with an oil line rupture only to be towed by a sailboat of all things! We approached Crocodiles restaurant and when close enough they released their end of the tether turning me lose. From here I could practice the art of 'kedging' where one would coil the rope at your feet and toss the anchor forward to pull yourself through the water yard by yard to safety. 'Time for that new Maule,' I vowed, placing an order with Brent Maule now sales manager at the factory that week; a new M7-235 on straight Aquafloats to be ready the following year displaying my well renowned blue and white colour scheme and new registration of N294SM.

Chapter 28
New Era – New Plane

My first seaplane rebuilt for a second lifespan sold as 'a project' airplane for $50,000 in the States to an enthusiastic soul wishing to repeat the task of restoration in a private hangar tucked away on a private airstrip during the long winter months. The frame had been extensively rebuilt those years earlier with engine and avionics all very usable. The money from our sale would be placed in savings for part payment on the new M-7-235 that Maule Air were building for me, costing near double the original purchase price. In conversation with Marcus and Rosie I learned of a very reputable broker for Morgan Stanley in Fort Lauderdale who could accrue considerable savings percentage on my investment. I had always been shy and distrusting of investment brokerage houses and an awful gambler when it came to matters of finance. Grandfather's words always echoed loud and clear never failing with 'always put your money into bricks and mortar!' With Marcus's astute reputation for money management in this case it seemed due diligence to at least talk with this broker rather than a sum of money earning next to nothing these modern times within the regular banking system. Gone were the days where my mother and I reaped benefit in Jersey with bank interest rates earning 14%. I introduced myself and put out my friends' names as recommendation. I explained emphatically that I had a set lump sum saved for the down payment on a new aircraft; that he may invest as he wished as long as the principal stay in place absolutely secure. He assured me this was possible and I could look forward to at least 10% or more on my savings during the time it would take the factory to finish my production aircraft. Suzanne's past career as a mortgage banker gifted her way more financially savvy than I and after mulling through all the options with the man we made payment. Monthly statements followed all looking promising, until way into the investment things took a sudden dramatic turn downward. Approaching 2008 there seemed to be a feeding frenzy within the investment industry in the United

States and we questioned sudden losses that appeared on our statements, only to be assured that the market was acting fickle and we should 'hang in there'. There began an ominous period of blank communication from his Florida office until one day a statement arrived showing not only all the interest being consumed also a chunk of the principal disappearing as well. Panicked, we called him immediately. His disobedience of our instruction left us no alternative but to sell out with a loss. Fortuitously a few days later, while watching the CBS Sunday Magazine *60 Minutes* airing an article about Morgan Stanley misleading a single mother out of her life's savings and finding a way of arbitrating her case. Now in the 'information age' with the wonderful world of the Internet at our fingertips, I found this same program segment on the CBS website offering a list of legal advisors in various parts of the United States, including the state of Florida. Suzanne had diligently saved every piece of documentation since the first conversation with our broker that we described during first connection to a lady lawyer in Fort Lauderdale. She was ecstatic at saving our meticulous paperwork and invited us to come over to pursue arbitration against the investment giant; she especially keen after finding our we had sent all the details via Federal Express to the CEO of Morgan Stanley in New York to which there had been no response.

The day in court came several months later with another visit to south Florida. Walking the corridors we witnessed people from all walks of life sitting patiently in the waiting rooms and corridors, leaving a daunting feeling as if a truckload of 'Davids' were here to take turns against the proverbial 'Goliath'. All good working folks from all walks of life in those hollow rooms looking broken by financial loss. Our names were called separately when our case was called. The panel of about eight arbitrators sat behind a few school-like lunch tables all pushed together in a row. Most were men and fairly elderly. The broker looking rather sheepish was seated to one side simply to observe not included with testimony. Two single chairs stood in front of the board, one for our attorney and one for each of us taken individually to make sure the stories and facts were similar. Both our statements were so on track offering little difference in detail, expressed separately yet delivered with totally different emotion, neither intimidated by the proceedings, showing a resounding determination in having a wrong corrected. The only misgiving I had while testifying was the most elderly of gentlemen fell fast asleep right in front of me! The board thanked us for appearing and informed us that we would be hearing from them in due course with a decision. It came unexpectedly quickly. We were awarded our total investment plus all the interest that it had accrued before decline. It was a grand win. To show that even the small, everyday person can take on the corporate giants if you have the will and evidence to support your claim. The broker was censured and our attorney received her percentage leaving us further ahead than when we entered this precarious game of investment. We celebrated with a fine meal and champagne in Miami's Capital Grill. In 2008, the markets and banks began failing with some of our friends losing near all their life savings, an epidemic financial crash that spread globally, lasting several years. Having had a financial close call, I never touched the game again. My grandfather's sound philosophy proving true all through my life with several investments in real estate, whether it be raw land or houses in various countries, I always made a well-earned comfortable profit.

The new Maule looked gorgeous sitting on the factory floor. The glacier white and blue stripes complimented each other in my well renowned colour scheme recognised all through the islands. Locals knew those of us who flew floatplanes mainly by our colours; the green and white familiar as Rosie flying in from Sampson Cay, the witch on a broomstick as her tail emblem. The yellow plane everyone knew was Tommy, often flying off Lake Cunningham to his little island, a flat piece of rock with small surrounding beach decorated with sea oats called Tabletop Cay, a fraction southwest of Highbourne. Jimmy's red trimmed de Havilland Beaver unmistakable with its large rumbling radial engine pulling the old classic along at about 90 knots. Charlie's red and white Cessna 185 on straight floats often departed south-westward towards his bonefish camp at Flamingo Cay in the far stretches of west Andros. We flew commercial up to Tallahassee in northern Florida where Bob McFadden met us for the drive over to Moultrie in South Georgia once again enjoying the traditional pull out of the factory hangar and trailered to the long and narrow hand-made lake that B.D. Maule had sculptured out of the flat cotton field landscape. The swans made way for us once again to enter the shallow water, as they had done near eight years prior, gliding in total silence as if pushed by the gentle breeze. N294SM slid off the trailer elegantly floating beautifully in the morning light, boasting a brilliant new paint job against the powder blue sky, the stifling dread of summer heat gaining temperature rapidly as we prepared the aircraft for the flight southward to include a stop in Winter Haven to stay with our new friends for the night who had invested in a small motel in town on the tiny body of water called Lake Ida.

Paul and Margaret Jackson were from the UK; Margaret from Ireland, a qualified seaplane pilot had invested in a Cessna 185 on straight Aerocet floats, a new concept in pontoons, no longer made of metal but all one cast in fiberglass, catching my attention as welcome insulators against the saltwater influence to the metal aircraft frame, something to seriously consider for the next aircraft should I last that long in this business. Margaret had kept her plane heeled in the shallows next to Jon's seaplane base, and her personal story quite extraordinary. Both she and husband Paul were avid skydivers who had retired from the UK moving to invest in Florida. Paul first on the ground one day watched his wife exit the aircraft for her free-fall to Earth. The parachute partially opened becoming fouled as it deployed. Unable to rectify the situation he watched helplessly in despair as his wife plummeted in to the ground, destroying most of the bones in her body on jarring impact. She was alive facing months of recuperation and corrective surgery, being warned that she may never walk again. Hundreds of pins and stainless steel pieces managed to put her broken body back together. In her thick Irish brogue and great sense of humour she swore that 'not only will I walk again, I will fly a fuckin' airplane!' And fly she did. Paul, a stocky very strong man, was able to carry her on board her Cessna where, once strapped in, she could fully control the airplane. After the flight was completed her husband would retrieve her from the cockpit carrying her ashore. Months passed where she became strongly involved in the local wing of the Seaplane Pilots Association under the Presidency of Michael Volk, Margaret becoming the principal Florida organiser of 'fly-ins', where avid aviators came from all over to enjoy a day's get together, often with bar-b-q lunches by a Florida lakeside. Slowly she healed enough to fly solo from Florida all the way northward to a fly-in organised in Maine. She would stop for fuel in known far out places marked on her route, staying for days before returning south back to Paul holding the fort with their growing popular motel business.

We arrived in Winter Haven after a couple of hours flying securing the new Maule at the seaplane base and made our way to the new recommendation of a place to stay with Paul and Margaret. We often would shop here for supplies found cheaper here than in the Bahamas, and spend some quality time with our hosts. In the mornings, I would see Paul walking their dog around the small lake with a healthy firearm strapped to his side. 'There's a huge gator in this lake and if we are not careful we could lose the dog!' he would explain. Enthusiastic gun owners, they had a fine collection of firearms enjoying the freedoms of ownership not possible in the UK.

That evening our hosts invited us to 'a night on the town' to experience an authentic local restaurant. 'The town' actually involved a ride into Florida's bush land near the famous Everglades far from the lights and traffic of civilisation, an American National Park consisting of 1.5-million-acre wetlands preserved within the southern tip of the state. Vast miles of open, grassy, slow-moving waterways, the park is made up of coastal mangroves, sawgrass marshes and pine flat woods, home to hundreds of animal species; abundant wildlife including the endangered leatherback turtle, Florida panther and West Indian manatee. We weaved in and out of small dirt roads tightly hidden between the vast orange groves that spread for hundreds of miles in the centre of the state. How our friends knew where to go was beyond us in the pitch black without signage anywhere. Eventually we reached a clearing in the thick bush, an open area with wooden-framed buildings supporting corrugated tin roofing and screened porches: a hidden society in the middle of nowhere. Several cars and mostly trucks and four-wheel drive mud-coated vehicles filled the dirt parking area. The stark neon lighting spilled out of the main building, as did the fairly boisterous country music just overpowering the hum of close by generators. The night was thick and steamy, tropical air that felt as if we were inhaling syrup where large insects danced in our headlights. Stars shone clearly overhead being so far away from the city. Crickets and cicadas hummed in harmony and crescendo through the dense foliage all trying frantically to compete with Loretta Lynn's 'Coalminers' Daughter'. The night was black and intimidating in every direction, introducing the creepy feeling of a horror movie set. We walked in through the entrance double screen swing doors; as if acting in an old western film the audience inside suddenly falling silent as all heads turned to watch the outsiders enter their sacred place. In an instant I knew where George Lucas came up with the idea for the alien bar scene filmed for his infamous *Star Wars* production.

The barstools were all occupied. Patrons of every description were seated, balanced or leaning over the pea-green peeling paint of the cluttered bar top. Light blue smoke hovered in spaces of still air, the place smelled heavily of carelessly spilt beer and human sweat. The ageing jukebox standing in the far corner came alive with a Waylon Jennings ballad; his chorus phrase of *Wrong!* made us raise eyebrows and smile at the timing of our entrance. Once we had been studied for half a minute everyone turned back around, quickly uninterested, continuing as if we suddenly didn't exist. Some of the barstools could barely support the huge-bodied women; the small round seat disappearing within the folds of human flesh that draped well over each side. Their badly faded light fabric tunics barely covered oversized discoloured braziers with twisted shoulder straps fluttering in the breeze of pedestal fans gently blowing the hot night air through the restaurant. Next to some of the ladies were their obvious partners, tiny men with stick-like frames, clad in dirty plaid shirts hanging over loose shorts, displaying scrawny hairless tanned legs that pushed close against their massive cellulite-laden neighbours. All wore filthy baseball caps; some turned backward showing the faded emblems of the Miami Dolphins football team. The men nurtured beer bottles that they sucked on ferociously, at times making them belch loudly and expertly without losing the smouldering cigarette hanging from one corner of their mouth. They laughed coarsely with enthusiasm at each others' jokes, slapping each other's back while turning slightly we could see their last remaining tobacco-stained teeth.

The waitress approached and seated us on a long picnic table with the familiar red and white-chequered plastic tablecloth, pockmarked with brown cigarette burns and uncomfortable bench seats; the familiar greasy-spoon centrepiece comprising of the worn plastic ketchup bottle with its yellow mustard counterpart. The once cream-coloured mayonnaise squeeze bottle now stained with dark finger marks. She took our drinks order; the men all asking for the local beer, really cold please, the ladies risking a glass of house white wine. 'Here's the menu y'all,' she said in the thickest redneck southern accent, while sliding dog-eared pieces of laminated menu paper onto the table. 'Specials are on the board over yonder,' she spoke, chewing gum loudly making that infuriating 'click' with her mouth, while she pointed to the chalk blackboard at the far end of the room. Paul and Margaret hooted with laughter at our reaction to this place. 'Food is fabulous!' Paul whispered discreetly to me from across the table. 'You have to try the fried alligator!' He added to watch our doubtful looks and slightly mouth agape expressions with raised eyebrows. The drinks arrived and sure enough the beer was icy cold. Barely had the conversation started when the double saloon doors burst dramatically open. A wiry man, near six feet tall, entered dressed as all the other males in the room except for filthy long pants soaked about half way up and strands of green swamp weed clinging in places. His baseball cap was slightly askew and clearly not shaved in days. Holding a high-powered scope-sighted rifle in one hand he shouted at the top of his course southern voice, 'Y'all got to come outside! We done shot us a giant gator! He's in the truck!' The restaurant came to an instantaneous grinding halt where staff and patrons poured outside into the open parking space. The jukebox had run out of tunes. Curiosity getting the better of us and we followed suit, to find an old dented Chevy truck parked with the rear facing the restaurant doors and its tailgate folded down. Spattered with stinking black mud and decorated with small mangrove branches wedged in its grill, the old vehicle was adorned with a set of steer horns mounted on the bonnet, and a gun rack in its rear window. The whole bed of the vehicle was taken up with a massive alligator lying dead inside. All four feet were tied with cord and secured to the sides of the truck with the huge snout draped out of the back. An impressive hole in the centre of the broad flat head oozed dark treacle-like blood. 'That's the biggest gator we dun shot this season!' the proud hunter, exclaimed spitting a huge wad of brown slime chewing tobacco juice onto the ground near our feet. It was hard to pull one's gaze away from the menacing ivory coloured teeth of the reptile that caught reflection in the restaurants artificial light. The scaly amour-plated body over three and half feet wide in the middle of its belly, and a huge dinosaur-like tail coiled around so as to fit inside the filthy bed of the vehicle. It smelled of stale swampy acrid death as the mosquitos suddenly found us.

'Maybe I'll have the chef's salad?' I said smiling with my hand on Paul's shoulder as we walked back inside, 'Gator just doesn't do it for me right now'.

Years later, after not seeing our friends again for several years, we learned of Margaret's further medical expenses, more surgeries and then financial woes after selling the motel business and opening a restaurant venture in a new location with failing results. Tensions within their household led to a disastrous chain of events and confrontation with local authorities one day. Facts were scarce about a possible speeding offence involving a police chase ending tragically with Paul making known he had a weapon in his car. Maybe it was a sudden wrong movement or possible gesture of aggression that led to our friend being shot dead on the spot?

Chapter 29
September Morn

By the year 2000 it was very evident that not all dreams and aspirations come to fruition, life's roller coaster having habit of showing us constant highs and lows. In older and wiser years, one learned that a step backward indeed wise to look long and deep into what will and will not work for our wellbeing. Impulsive investments historically had worked incredibly well for my financial growth and appetite for adventurous ways. Hard work, fruitful decisions and risk often separated me from many of the friends I knew in the Bahamas. I felt occasional twinges of envy for me when success flowed in my direction. My third philosophy of 'nothing ventured, nothing gained' stands firm even as I write this piece. We had a dream of moving eventually to live in an Out-Island away from the tedious growth of the capital city. Flying over Norman's Cay one day I spied a piece of land that fit all our requirements; hilltop, away from the pounding waves of the ocean side and water frontage along the shores of the inland pond where we could moor our boat. I had no clue whether it was available but put the question to my client and long-time friend Larry Roberts as we whizzed overhead.

'I can answer that easily Paul, I own it!' he exclaimed. Surely then it was meant to be and accepted my offer of appraised value. 'If chance arises Larry I would also like the piece adjoining?' The investment made in property at Normans Cay was a sound one but gave rise to conflict with a small group of local white Bahamians that had arrogantly declared themselves 'the owners' of the island, nicknamed in past eras as 'Bay Street Boys'. Past school days displaying attitude of being told 'you can't do something' all the while knowing clearly you are perfectly within your right, gives welcome opportunity to enter a scrap that yields great pleasure in squashing pompous aggression.

This small gathering of local businessmen, lawyers and accountants, had taken over the responsibility of land sales belonging to a failing

Canadian Corporation that owned a large balance of lots on Normans Cay in the Exumas, the same island of ill-repute occupied by Columbian drug lord Carlos Lehder years ago. Managing a majority of land, they presumed authority to be management of all, even ones who were not governed by the existing covenants and restrictions set in the law. The two lots I had acquired did not fall under their jurisdiction but that did not to deter them from trying to bully their way into my ownership and legal rights there. In short they were furious at missing the sale of two very prime hilltop waterfront pieces of 'their island'. We were summoned to their offices on Bay Street for a meeting of minds, deeming it wise to reinforce my position I asked acquaintance and Member of Parliament, Elliot Lockhart, also in the law profession, to accompany us. We walked into the boardroom of their law firm and invited to be seated at the far end of their long wooden table. The room was adorned with the usual legal library sprawling across the walls decorated with an interesting model of Normans Cay mounted above their doorway.

Noticing my glance, 'This is our island,' the leading attorney declared while gesturing toward the model, opening the conversation with in his best imitation of an upper-crust English accent. Elliot and Suzanne immediately looked uncomfortable as I smiled quietly in defiance of what was to follow. 'Really, since when?' Elliot asked.

'Since we own the majority of the remaining land on the cay,' came the reply, adding with a tone of absolute authority, 'you are therefore required to submit all plans for building to us for approval! We own the whole perimeter of waterfront on the island and your proposed docks are forbidden. There will never be docks inside the Pond'.

'What a load of rubbish,' I retorted. 'Our property has nothing to do with the lots you have under control and as for owing the perimeter is without question the most ridiculous claim!' My partner unable to retain her silence jumped into the ensuing argument that earned an arrogant retort from the leader, 'you, madam, don't even fit the profile for who we want on Normans Cay!'

That was the last straw for Elliot. He exploded with 'We are leaving this fiasco!' signalling to the doorway, asking us to exit with him down onto Bay Street. Once outside we saw him visibly shaken, taking several seconds to compose himself. 'I thought this country was rid of these UBP dinosaurs!' he exclaimed, apologising to us for such hostility. Soon after title was clear and in my name, after the finances had been completed, my building plans were drawn by a local architect Crestwell Stuart who worked for town planning in Nassau. A classic 'conch house' as it was termed locally: a large open planned house in wood with classic vaulted ceilings, dormer windows and screened porches bearing semblance to architecture introduced into the Bahamas back in the 1700s from the South Carolina homes that frequent many of our Out-Islands. Standing on large greenheart timbers the view toward Whales Tail Beach lying the East with the Pond and shallow banks to the West. I confirmed that the waterways and land up to three feet above high water indeed was public with any structure needing local Government approval. It was at this early stage, a dream now on paper and approved by local government both in Nassau and Black Point for a home and two docks into the Pond. We walked the land many times, exploring the hidden treasures of the scrub bush land that covered over 600 feet of water frontage, to discover gorgeous air plants and wild orchids forming circumference around a deep natural fresh water well. Plans for a seaplane ramp in the protected corner of one boundary and the placement of two docks, one for each of the lots; constructing these first a priority in utter defiance of the orders from the boys that declared the island as theirs. A friend of mine in the marine construction business was going to be in the area soon and offered to deliver the lumber and green heart pilings needed for dock construction. One bright morning the barge sat easily in place inside the Normans Pond hammering in the pilings. Unbeknown to us in Nassau, the father-in-law of one of the 'boys' residing on the island at the time made a phone call reporting the beginnings of construction inside the pond. Karma 'really is a bitch' they say, the family suffers awful tragedy later and their house near destroyed in a recent hurricane. Under threat of immediate legal action the barge owner was ordered to remove the pilings from the seabed the next day. Wielding their legal powers, my pilings were suddenly gone. To prove my point and stand my ground I immediately ordered four by four lengths of lumber to be delivered by close friend Nigel Bower on his private barge after dropping supplies to his site on Ship Channel Cay.

A group of friends flew down to the Pond on the seaplane where the front deck of my Carolina Skiff afforded enough height to sledgehammer all the pilings into the seabed. Two by six pieces of treated lumber made up the lengths bolted with stainless steel hardware. We all hammered in the two by six planking and the docks stood proudly in their place. They were the first approved docks inside Normans Cay Pond, much to the utter disgust and frustration of the arrogant representatives who tried in vain to overpower me.

My flying career was steady but did not alter the hard truth that we would be about a million dollars short if going to complete this building project. Here in the Out-Islands one had to consider uncountable details concerning the infrastructure needed to support life as well as the buildings themselves. Without any close settlement nearby power, water and sewage all needed to be installed. Labour would have to be housed while on site. The logistics began to mount making the whole task more daunting. As with the dream of building on the side of a British Columbia mountain I faced the reality of maybe selling out allowing pursuit of other reachable avenues of residing in the islands one day? Maybe a sailboat where one could simply drop anchor in a beautiful location to then move on when the urge set in? Dreams, I always felt, harboured nothing wrong in their pursuit?

Word soon came of a lovely couple from Illinois who were frequenting Highbourne Cay while staying on board their yacht *Harvest Moon* and in search of property in the Exumas somewhere. Recent years had a run on real estate within this gorgeous island chain, leaving very few pieces of land available. The last island that I heard selling was Andre Runte's special place down at Little Halls Pond near Bell Island and across from Sandy MacTaggart on Soldier Cay. Andre had purchased the cay some years ago and he and his wife Connie had camped out on the island, slowly clearing the land in places on top of the hill for construction of their little round house. Stone by stone, timber by timber the couple's house grew skyward, the views from their terraces emulating a travel brochure. He was an avid helicopter pilot and a couple years later while practising an emergency manoeuvre with his dog on board in view of his completed house, his small camera had slipped out of his pocket falling beneath the selector control. Initiating the procedure, he suddenly found the selector jammed sending him into a spiralling descent toward the water. He and dog hit the water, fortunately escaping unharmed, leaving his prized machine a total wreck.

Thoroughly disheartened they packed up belongings and vacated their island leaving friends of ours Chris and Mary from the States to manage and care take their property. Those of us who knew Chris Cloud had given him a nickname of 'MacGyver' after the television show, for his amazing ability to resurrect almost anything from a pile of junk into a viable working machine. Some time later I received a charter from a group in Los Angles to take them down to Little Halls on a purchase reconnoitre. The forty-minute flight was uneventful and landing in the calm waters we taxied up to the beach where Andre had constructed a lovely thatched gazebo and where another small group were seated awaiting our arrival. They walked down the beach to greet us. Joel, who had chartered me, gestured to his shirtless friend looking very comfortable with the beach surroundings. I notice a few tattoos on the pale skin while the face very familiar with a recognised smile.

'Paul, I would like you to meet Johnny, Johnny Depp.'

'Pleased to meet you Johnny; love your work and welcome to the Exumas!' I replied. We shook hands while he inquired quietly, 'May I talk more with you later Paul?' The men all made their way back to a meeting on the comfortable sofas that furnished the gazebo that Andre had built to relax on the beach. Johnny was born in Owensboro, Kentucky on June 9th 1963, the youngest of four children of Betty Sue Palmer a waitress, and his father John Christopher Depp a civil engineer. While talking together his English diction is near perfect without trace of a 'southern drawl' of his birthplace. The actor is of mostly English ancestry, his surname descending from a French Huguenot immigrant, Pierre Deppe or Dieppe, who settled in Virginia around 1700. He moved frequently during his childhood living in more than twenty locations eventually settling in Miramar, Florida in 1970. Johnny's parents divorced in 1978 when he was 15. With the gift of a guitar from his mother when he was 12, he began playing in various garage bands. After his parents' divorce, he dropped out of high school to become a rock musician. He attempted to go back to school two weeks later, but the principal told him to follow his dream of being a musician. He played with *The Kids*, a band that enjoyed modest local success, setting out together for Los Angeles in pursuit of a record deal but the group split before signing a contract. Johnny told me, that similar to my story of starting from scratch, he walked the streets with that guitar on his back until in 1983 when he married Lori Anne Allison introducing him to actor Nicolas Cage, born a year after him. Through Nicholas' father Cage was nephew of famed film director Francis Ford Coppala. With these connections and friendships Cage advised Johnny to pursue an acting career:

a break having him never look back. His first roll was part of the horror film *Nightmare on Elm Street*. Later signing with Disney Productions Johnny secured the lead roll as Captain Jack Sparrow in the highly successful franchise of *Pirates of the Caribbean*, based on Disney's theme park ride of the same name. With prolific film producer Jerry Bruckheimer and a fun cast of characters the first film was released in 2003 grossing $654 million worldwide. The second film of the planned trilogy released in 2006 grossing the studio $1.1 billon at the box office. With total sales exceeding $3.7 billion another tale is due for release in May 2017 after my final edit here is complete. I tended the seaplane and set the anchor further out into the water as tide was falling. Within a few minutes Johnny came to chat with me at the water's edge about flying and the island. He was a pleasure to talk to, very unassuming and polite. A friendship was easily in the making as he asked my opinion on the island for purchase.

'It's a jewel, Johnny' I remarked, 'there are so few left in the Exumas, especially here inside the national park where everything is protected. This one has some gorgeous private beaches and the house is quite lovely sitting on top of the hill'. He seemed really interested in my opinion and I reinforced that with the market behaving as it was I did not think he could go wrong. I explained about his island being protected from storms off the Atlantic lying inside the outer cays owned by Sandy MacTaggart, a real character who I affirmed he would enjoy meeting. His spoke of his mentor Marlon Brando who he had known well and his purchase an island in the Pacific, inspiring a personal wish to emulate his famous friend.

'I can see years from now when you need a place to escape this little gem would be perfect!' I added. He smiled and agreed that sooner or later when time allowed he had dreamed of following in his mentor's footsteps.

'I am not a huge fan of flying, Paul,' he said, 'but this little machine you have looks like a load of fun to fly, maybe one day you could show me the ropes?'

'That would be my pleasure. When next here and the day perfect I will give you a call,' I offered. The sale was secured and I learned how gracious a person he was in the years that followed. His plans for the island were simple and unobtrusive, not wanting to invade the local environment. There were no ostentatious plans for huge buildings and in months later his classic old-style yacht would be seen laying at anchor on the calm lee-side of his island: the Jolly Roger symbolizing the Disney character from his pirate movies, flying from a flagstaff of driftwood on the hill top gave notice of his presence on the island.

I received a call from the owners of *Harvest Moon*. 'Hi Paul, this is Bruce and Kelly up at Highbourne and I would love to come and see your property down at Normans Cay!' He explained that he could be there in his tender and looked forward to meeting me after landing in the seaplane up at the North end of the pond. I threw out the small Danforth anchor that bit easily in the soft sandy bottom. Walking into the knee-high shallows Bruce taxied up to me in his light blue open fisherman tender. We idled out together into the middle of the pond where I asked him to turn around to face the shoreline.

'The property runs from there in the north lot, 600 plus feet southward to that point there,' I gestured to a mark on the coral rock just below the hilltop.

'Wow, that is gorgeous Paul, can we go ashore?'

We tied up to the North dock that we had constructed some months earlier and walked the narrow rocky pathway to the summit of the hilltop. Gazing in all directions there was not much conversation needed for him to shake my hand and seal an agreement.

'I will make your dream a reality here, Paul. You will be an honoured guest anytime my friend!' he kindly exclaimed with bright turquoise eyes and generous smile, another fabulous friendship made in minutes. Once again Marcus's words still quietly echoing about flying changing my life. From one minute to the next aviation introduced me to new people and places never imagined.

With the sale of Normans Cay new possibilities were suddenly available; chance to explore another aircraft that could accommodate four passengers along with their luggage, something the Maule could not accomplish. The dream of owning a comfortable sailboat could act as a second home floating here in Normans Cay Pond was an exciting prospect. My philosophy about boating had changed with retirement from a commercial dive business. Now I did not need the speed to get from 'a to b' because time was of the essence. Now the joy could be held in 'just getting there'. I had sailed small boats such as the Snipe while at school near the Solent and years later received an invitation to deliver a 40-foot ketch from Freeport to Nassau with the magical experience of holding watch through the night water. To reacquaint my plan for a sailboat we accepted an offer from my brother-in-law to meet him in the Virgin Islands where he often bareboat chartered for a couple weeks sailing around the Caribbean, a trip aboard a 40-foot French vessel made by Jeanneau. For days we sailed in the strong trade winds racing between Tortola, Jost Van Dyke and Anegada. The Jeanneau sliced through the waves and sailed close hauled to the wind nicely. The first tack sent my camera flying to break against the inside of the cockpit, while heeling over at an impressive angle played havoc with my old back injury. The advantages of a more comfortable catamaran became very clear in a short space of time. The bars and local restaurants of the British Virgins were a fun holiday, the local exotic drinks dangerously potent! People were friendly with some places resembling our Bahamas, especially devouring succulent fresh lobster, anchored in the shallower waters of Anegada or in Foxy's Restaurant and Bar on Jost Van Dyke. Many of the islands showed disappointingly the cancerous neglect of rubbish alongside the roadways along with rusted skeletons of abandoned cars in the bushes, a disappointing Caribbean phenomena where local populations seemingly cared little about their surroundings, contrasting with gorgeous blue waters lapping gently onto beautiful palm tree fringed beaches with mountains in the background.

Decisions were reached about planes and boats. The Canadians in Parry Sound, Ontario, were re-manufacturing a fairly new seaplane called the Found Bush Hawk; an aircraft within financial reach seemed just the ticket to solve my passenger with luggage problem. Two sailboats came into the running, one a 42-foot catamaran manufactured by PDQ whose factory was also in Ontario. Second choice being a 34-foot Catamaran manufactured by Performance Cruising in Annapolis, Maryland. The Ontario boat seemed a great idea to explore first as it was on the way to the Found factory up in Parry Sound. Our flights booked, arriving in Toronto on the evening of September 10 2001.

The next morning was textbook perfect as far as weather was concerned. Looking out of the hotel window one could see the city of Toronto spread out in front of us with unlimited views of the far horizon. The sun had started to climb in the cloudless powder blue skies over Ontario presenting one of the most gorgeous pristine September days over the entire northeast. Checking out of the hotel was effortless and we climbed aboard the shuttle bus that would take us over to the rental car agents. We were the first passengers from the hotel to board, so seated ourselves in the front two seats across from the driver. We waited for other passengers to exit the lobby and listened to the radio playing quietly just in front of me. Not listening too closely I thought I heard a commentator break in saying something to the effect that a small plane had crashed into one of the towers of the World Trade Centre in New York City. It was just before nine in the morning. I reached forward to turned the volume control upward where the commentary speech gained speed and emphasis. The world-renowned landmark that I had taken my daughter to the top of, and not too far from where we were in Canada, was indeed on fire. The bus filled and conversation was buzzing with a sense of shock about some terrible accident that had just occurred in New York at 8.46 am. A few short minutes after 9 am the radio came very much alive with the news of a second plane hitting the South Tower of the World Trade Centre. Our driver climbed aboard hastily and exclaimed, 'We need to get you all out of here as the airport will be closing down shortly. New York is under attack!'

This statement was too surreal to even comprehend in that moment. 'Under attack?' From whom, how and why for God's sake? The bus sped away from the hotel and arrived at the rental car offices in short time. We unloaded luggage without speaking and walked swiftly to the counter. A gentleman reiterated the wish 'to get you out of the terminal as fast as possible!' saying that we could be stranded if caught with the airport closure during this aviation emergency. He offered us a Chrysler PT Cruiser, a brand-new car that he said we may have. Without any conference the credit card transaction was complete and the representative gave us the keys and driving instructions to exit the airport area. He advised we not stop for some time giving enough distance avoiding possible street closures? Leaving the airport behind us we safely negotiated the highway westward toward the PDQ factory listening to the radio about something incomprehensible that had just happened. Someone was attacking the United States?

The news declared that it was no private plane that had flown into the first tower but in fact a commercial airliner followed a few minutes later by another crashing into the second tower. Both buildings were now engulfed in thick smoke from the upper floors. New York was in chaos. Every television and radio station was on the story. American Airlines Flight #11 had departed from Boston's Logan Airport at 7.59 am bound for Los Angeles. On board were eleven crewmembers, seventy-six passengers and five hijackers. Overpowering the crew, the hijackers were headed by an Egyptian national Mohammed Atta, who took over the controls after fellow hijackers subdued and killed or injured the pilots and attendants with box-cutters, various hand tools with blades, mace and tear gas. Atta, after flight training in Florida, piloted the Boeing 767 fully loaded with fuel for the long flight across the continent, into the North Tower at 8.46 am; the South Tower was impacted by United Airlines Flight #175, also a Boeing 767, at 9.03 am. This airliner had followed the first off Logan Airport just minutes after take-off also bound for LA. It was rapidly evident that this attack was very well orchestrated, and executed with precision.

Thirty-four minutes later a third airliner, American Airlines Flight #77, a Boeing 757 with a crew of six, fifty-three passengers and five hijackers had departed Washington Dulles International Airport at 8.20 am, again on route to LA, impacted the Pentagon at 9.37 am. America was watching their national morning television shows when interrupted by the attacks. The events were now being transmitted live to the world. A fourth airliner, United Airlines Flight #93 had departed Newark International Airport at 8.42 am bound for San Francisco with a crew of seven and thirty-three passengers, who became aware of the terror against New York while airborne. Several members having made cell phone calls or using the cabin Airphone service to loved ones learned of the fate of three other commercial planes. Tom Burnett calls his wife and learned the news, 'Oh my God it's a suicide mission'. He ended the call to her with 'don't worry we're going to do something'. Todd Beamer attempted to call his wife but the call was re-routed to GTE phone operator Lisa Jefferson, a call retold by Lisa afterward where Beamer had described the pilots lying on the floor dead or dying. Not conforming to the orders of the four hijackers who took control, some of the passengers formed their own assault on their captors. Lisa recounted Beamer ending his call with 'Let's roll!' as their retaliation began. On realising the possible loss of control the hijackers first rolled the airliner from side to side trying to unbalance the attacking passengers using a catering trolley as a battering ram against the cockpit door. The cockpit voice recorder is heard to record 'they want to get in here! Hold, hold from the inside. Hold from the inside'; the nose of the airliner is pitched upward and the recorder captures sounds of screaming, crashing and breaking of glass. A voice saying, 'Is that it? Shall we finish it off?' Another hijacker retorting, 'No! Not yet. When they all come, we finish it off!' A passenger is heard yelling 'In the cockpit. If we don't we all die!' At 10.01 am Jarrah, the hijacking pilot asks of another, 'Is that it. I mean shall we put it down?' A voice confirms, 'Yes, put it in and pull it down'. A second later the airliner began its plummeting toward the ground near Shanksville, Pennsylvania, impacting at 10.03 am. It was believed that this aircraft was to target either the Capitol Building in Washington or possibly the White House? The telephone systems around northeast United States and almost globally were becoming clogged to capacity

Having travelled far enough away from Toronto Airport we felt it time to pull over and take a break somewhere to maybe view what was happening across the border in America. A roadside restaurant came into view and we parked to go inside. It was just before 10 am, where on entering, saw the place packed with Canadian locals, who were mostly standing in the restaurant glued to the television that was mounted up in one corner. They immediately recognised we were visitors to their country and offered condolences on the emotional sight on the screen. The South Tower had just collapsed in a cloud of shattered concrete, glass and dust; some fifty-six minutes after impact. We stood with them utterly dumbfounded by the events, unable to say anything. It was impossible to comprehend that such dramatic conflict had been brought to our part of the world. This was something that we had watched on the nightly news for years on the other side of the planet, nothing to this immense scale. This did not happen over here. This happened in Beirut and other Middle East countries, not America. The broadcast replayed with never-ending repeat footage of the impacts of the planes into the magnificent buildings I had visited some years earlier. My daughter and I had stood at their base gazing upwards with necks craned as far back as we could in order to see the structure soaring above us over a hundred floors. I had held her hand as we walked through the huge lobbies to the fast elevators that would take us to the observation deck on the 102nd floor, 1250 feet from the ground. Here we would both marvel at the scene of New York City played out below us from this staggering height. Now where we had stood was engulfed in thick black smoke with the outline of an airliners shape ominously carved as a gaping hole at a slight angle dipping to the left near the top of the enormous structure. Hot fire raced out of the building's interior. White shards of molten metal spewed from some of the windows, the shattered aluminium skeleton of the airliners melting within running downward toward the street below. We all stood motionless inside that restaurant with sudden gasps as camera lenses zoomed in to show us the horror of human beings jumping outward into space from 110 floors up plummeting to their death on the ground below.

For the first time in US aviation history the Plan for Security Control of Air Traffic and Air Navigation Aids, SCATANA, was put into effect. All air space was immediately closed grounding all non-emergency civilian aircraft within the United States, Canada and several other countries. Thousands of commercial airliners and their tens of thousands of passengers all over the world would be stranded. Canada would accept 226 diverted flights. Airfields would become parking lots for landing planes. Fighter jets had been deployed from Langley Air Force Base ordered by the Vice President to shoot down any known inbound hijacked airliner. Many of the warplanes were unarmed which had meant that pilots would have had to use their aircraft to hit a passenger plane, hopefully being able to bail out ahead of impact. Having received only nine minute's notice by reaching New York both towers had already received devastating impact. All international flights were banned from landing in the United States for three days after September 11. Thirty-five thousand flights were cancelled because of attacks on 9/11.

At 10.28 am we watched in horrified awe as the North Tower finally succumbed to the onslaught, having burnt for a 102 minutes, suddenly toppling to one side at the top of the structure, followed immediately by the implosion downward toward the street again in an enormous shower of concrete, shattered glass and acres of thick grey dust. The buildings and streets were packed with rescue personnel from the New York fire brigades and police force. Almost all would perish in the next few seconds that it took for the entire structure to disappear from the New York skyline, now empty of the world-famous buildings that commanded lower Manhattan. The streets below were engulfed for blocks with a huge bellowing white cloud of acrid dust and scattered fragments of the two towers, racing through streets at enormous speed with tiny figures of human population scattering for cover as fast as they could run. Those two monumental structures that had dominated the skyline had literally disintegrated into pieces below leaving a mountain of burning twisted steel and concrete known for weeks later as 'The Pile'. We all sagged into the nearest chairs inside the restaurant watching that massive grey cloud contaminate the Manhattan skyline. Canadians were coming over to us with tears streaming down their cheeks to say how utterly sorry they were to see us watch our country under attack. Not realising that I was merely an 'island boy' from the Bahamas, my partner was the American; it made no difference, those buildings felt a part of me, a part of all of us from that era for some reason. The loss was profound. We bore witness to watching the deaths of 2996 people, 246 being passengers aboard the four planes, 125 souls perished within the Pentagon; 72 law enforcement officers, 343 fire fighters and 55 military personnel. The last attack on American soil had been in Pearl Harbour on December 7 1941. All that was left today in the blue morning sky were millions of pieces of paper scattered like confetti in the gentle morning air, the last remaining contents of the towers floating down to settle in the mess below.

The nineteen hijackers were all affiliated with al-Qaeda, fifteen of whom were citizens of Saudi Arabia and split into four teams lead by one who was pilot trained. Three or four others in each team would act as attackers who could subdue flight attendants, passengers and crew. In mid-2000 they underwent pilot training in South Florida talking their way into access of airliner flight simulators with comments reported that they 'wanted to learn how to land an airliner,' they were never questioned further about their unusual requests. The plan originated with Khalid Shaikh Mohammed, plotting to kill over 4000 passengers on board twelve airliners flying from Asia to the United States with plans to also crash into the CIA Headquarters. The plans were foiled in 1995 with a fire resulting in Filipino Police arresting an arson suspect with a laptop containing the plans. The plot escalated later with the approval of Osama bin Laden, founder of al-Qaeda in 1988. Son of Saudi billionaire Mohammed bin Awad bin Laden, studied at university in Saudi Arabia until 1979, when he joined Mujahideen forces in Pakistan fighting against the Soviet Union in Afghanistan. Heir to great wealth he helped fund the Mujahideen by funneling arms, money and fighters from the Arab world into Afghanistan gaining popularity among many Arabs. He was banished from Saudi Arabia in 1992 making his base in Sudan, until U.S. pressure forced him to leave in 1996. After establishing a new base in Afghanistan, he declared war against the United States, initiating a series of bombings and related attacks. Three of the pilots originated in the

Hamburg cell of Al-Qaeda, training first in camps within Afghanistan and chose by Bin Laden for their knowledge of western culture and language skills. All hijackers were in their twenties except one at the age of thirty-three. It would take ten more years to hunt down Osama bin Laden, finally killed by Navy Seals on May 2 2011 in Pakistan. It was supported unsurprisingly by 90% of the American public, United Nations, European Union but condemned by two-thirds of the Pakistan public. Surveillance and intelligence determining the inhabitants of a compound called Abbottabad had been custom built to 'house someone of importance'. The property had no landline phone connections, no internet and burned all their refuse, unlike neighbours who put it out for collection. The CIA rented another house within the area to survey the compound also accomplished with the aid of drones. Operation 'Neptune's Spear', from the insignia of the Navy Seals, was launched. Inside information suggests this was a 'kill operation' from the start. Bin Laden, three other men and a woman were killed, including bin Laden's son. The raid had taken forty minutes to execute and the leader of Al-Qaeda was weighted with 300 pounds of metal and slid off a board over the side of the navy ship, to be buried at sea as it was said no other country would accept his remains.

Leaving the restaurant, I drove the PT Cruiser westward to arrive at the PDQ factory. They greeted us with sombre hellos and again offered condolences toward the horror we had all watched over the last hours. How could such a gorgeous morning turn into something etched forever in our minds? We would all remember exactly within feet of where we were that fateful September morn. We heard news that Toronto Airport, as most others, had been closed within minutes stranding near 4000 people unable to leave the complexes. Making that hasty escape was good advice. Walking around a boat factory after such a traumatic experience seemed nearly fruitless. Coming this far seemed the right thing to do but concentrating on the production was hard to focus on. The PDQ was very attractive but structurally different to our preferences for a Gemini that could sail in twenty-seven inches of water, perfect for our shallow Bahama waters in the Exuma Cays. With a quick mutual decision easily reached, we bid the factory goodbye and drove on toward Parry Sound and a new concept in seaplane design.

Walking into the Found factory I could see the near completed frame of their Bush Hawk fuselage. It was very impressive. Strong sections of steel beautifully crafted and much more sturdy in appearance than the lighter Maule's I had flown. The Found wing was huge as it lay on the floor, its cantilever design quite different from what I had expected. Engineers described it as a 'speed wing' that could lift a heavier load off the water and cruise faster than what I had been used to and their sales pitch very convincing. The shape was more elliptical than I expected with no flat underside and rounded leading and trailing edges, small signals that raised question about its claims. That famous Maule wing with its flat lower surface allowed the incredible forces of lift to make it a short take-off and landing aircraft. This seaplane looked entirely different. There were no wing struts for me to bang into or have to stoop under moving heavy freight or suitcases. The pilot doors open forwards to latch onto the cowling. The interior space for three middle seats and a large baggage compartment certainly had my attention. There was space inside for 55-gallon fuel drums, not that I would be carrying any, but demonstrated what the Canadians were able to carry up north into the bush. Instrumentation was up to the buyer and I could see a big Garmin GPS and instrument rated panel a huge advantage. The engine was a Lycoming-300HP with a Hartzell three-bladed propeller, approved for flying in the United States, its scimitar blade design for noise abatement. I would learn in good time its disadvantages. The flat floor even with the edges of the fuselage meant no added lifting in and out of the aircraft. The improved downward visibility with huge window panels in all four doors meant that my passengers would be afforded fabulous views of the islands.

In 1946, Nathan (Bud) Found and his brother S.R. Found created Found Aviation with it in mind to develop a lighter more affordable utility aircraft for use in the Canadian north. The company made it through six decades, parting company in 1966 with financial troubles. New management tried to keep it all afloat but once again in 1968 the company ceased operating and sold to auction a year later. Over a span of twenty years they had produced four models yet only thirty-three aircraft, a number that came back to haunt me, number thirty-three. In May 1996, Bud Found, still pursuing the need for a new utility aircraft began acquiring designs from John Eaton, the significant shareholder in Found Aircraft. A subsidiary company, Found Aircraft Canada Inc. was set up in Parry Sound, Ontario, and Number 26 came into production, a prototype called the Bush Hawk. It flew on October 4 1998. This aircraft had the 300HP engine with the fore half of the fuselage manufactured of steel and the aft of aluminium. Transport Canada approved the aircraft composed of over 3500 pieces on my birthday in 1999. The closest competitor for the Found from Cessna producing over 1110 of their popular 206 series aircraft, while Found could only produce some fifty units.

The seaplane version of the Bush Hawk XP that I was interested in would be fitted with the new composite floats manufactured by Aerocet. I had seen these on Margaret's Cessna 185 moored at the seaplane base in Winter Haven, and was very attracted to the fact that now the airframe would have some insulation with fibreglass construction separating the metal fuselage from the saltwater. This plane was becoming very attractive by the minute. Meeting with the management they learned of where I would be operating their aircraft and the experience I had acquired during years of commercially operating a seaplane service within the Bahamas. With the flying magazine articles, television and film productions I had been involved in they could see the added publicity that I may be able to provide their seaplane.

Management was very accommodating and offered to give me a test flight to see what their aircraft could do, introducing me to Mike Henrick their test pilot. He explained the straight float version that I could fly needed to be launched from the lake by the factory but he would have to fly it over to a larger lake nearby where we would all meet up to load aboard. I thought this a great opportunity to see how the seaplane would perform in a limited space so not allowing me to fly from here raised a warning flag. Remaining polite, I went along with the plan and was driven over to the large lake nearby. Three of us met Mike tethered to the floating dock and I was offered the left seat to fly. Starting the Bush Hawk was impressive, she sounded throaty and solid to the touch. I taxied out into the centre of the waterway with Mike issuing brief instruction. I noticed the fuel tanks only about a quarter full and was disappointed that we were not afforded too long a demonstration; I needed to see how she performed under with a considerable load. The aircraft was far heavier to the touch than the Maule but flew with a nice solid feel to it. Flight manoeuvres were straight forward and the scenery around Parry Sound simply gorgeous, spying below us the company president's 'cottage' by the lake. I joked with the sales rep sitting behind that Tony Hamblin and fellow Canadians in this part of Ontario put a whole new meaning to the word 'cottage', seeing the sprawling gorgeous estate homes appearing slightly more than the name they gave it. We splashed down and taxied up to his dock for refreshments overlooking the lake. Flying back, I was guided back to the lake I had departed from, being denied a short landing in the smaller lake by the factory buildings. Sitting in the offices after that flight they made a really attractive offer for my purchase price that at the time outweighed any of my performance queries. With finances in place from selling the land on Normans Cay I thought this a good chance to invest in this slightly bigger plane that in all seemed to offer what I needed to move up to four passengers with their luggage. Performance was going to be different and require me to adjust my flight habits while the Maule was losing valuable business when inquiries from families of four or two couples with baggage forced me to support the Piper Aztec operators that I was friends with.

We shook hands and the production of Bush Hawk #33 was underway. The new seaplane would be delivered on wheels to Winter Haven the following year for the Aerocet floats to be fitted which Found would order for me and match my chosen colour scheme. Here Mike could fly with us back to the Bahamas for some further training before turning me loose on my own as part of the deal.

Our accommodation in Ontario had been arranged prior to leaving Nassau staying in a lovely local B and B owned by retired couple Bill and Mary Tannahill, tucked into the woods by Lake Muskoka. Driving the PT Cruiser through the forest toward their house showed the postcard surroundings of upper Ontario. On arrival, they met us at the front door with open arms and once again condolences for what had just happened in New York. Canada went out of its way that fateful September day to embrace all outsiders with a warmth and compassion not experienced before. Everything in America and Canada was shut down tight as far as commercial airline travel was concerned. Transport Canada had instigated Operation Yellow Ribbon where, for the first time in Canadian Aviation history, Canada had shut down its air space. In all, 255 commercial airliners had been diverted to seventeen various airports throughout the country. Near 500 flights had been en route to the United States that day at the time of the attacks; planes that were at least halfway to their destinations were allowed to enter Canadian airspace to land at the nearest airports entering at a rate of two every minute. Most aircraft were diverted away from Canada's major hubs for security, allowing them to land from

Gander to Halifax and beyond. Secondary airports became parking lots and the Canadian locals voluntarily took in stranded passengers by the thousands. Bill and Mary explained on checking in that we had booked our stay for three days and after that we were to be 'their guests'. The Canadian evening news called *The National* with Peter Mansbridge was probably the classiest news broadcast I had ever watched. It was delivered with such sympathy and style that all of us who were in their country that day received an outpouring of hospitality never to forget, estimated there were between 30–40,000 of us affected that September morn. I wrote a letter of appreciation to the CBC news station.

It took days to reopen US airspace and for airlines make up some semblance of a schedule. As passengers trying to get back to Florida in order to pick up our seaplane in Winter Haven we had to keep in close contact with the airlines. Day after day nothing moved. Nearly a week later and after being thoroughly spoiled by our hosts with fresh peaches and cream, along with Mary's amazing culinary skills, we made it back over to Toronto Airport to witness thousands of people trying desperately to find a flight home or willing to arrive somewhere even near home. We had shared a special time with our new Canadian friends, watching each evening as New York tried some semblance of healing with the 24-hour search and rescue of anyone that may still be alive within that awful pile in lower Manhattan. There were few miracles of survival. We are left with haunting images of that mass of rubble with protruding twisted steel frames once the huge structures of the World Trade Centre. News footage showed row upon row of photographs of missing loved ones posted on fences in downtown Manhattan. Streets all through that area covered in that fine grey dust that we had watched explode outward as if a volcanic eruption from Ground Zero as it was now named. We had seen people walking out of the cloud covered from head to toe in grey filth helplessly covering their faces trying in vain to stop the poisons from entering their lungs, a scene from the darkest of science fiction. The fires burned for days while remaining New York fire crews that had survived worked relentlessly to find others alive or recover bodies buried; the wail of emergency locators seemed unceasing. That mass of humanity and twisted building material would take weeks of clearing. New York and all of us who witnessed that day will never forget the scenes that unfolded. Our world would be forever changed and aviation never the same.

Arriving back in Florida, a relief only to find the federal Aviation Authority had imposed a ban on all private flying for an extended period again stranding us for days, with special flight rules slowly being introduced. I stayed on until finally there was some movement of private aircraft being allowed only to fly under Instrument Flight Plans only. Pilots were told that when given a specific time slot to depart from an American airfield, they had a specified number of minutes to start their planes, take-off and make radio contact with Air Traffic Control. Failure to meet this requirement would result in the cancellation of permission to fly. No special aircraft including floatplanes or other unusual craft were to fly. I decided to call in to Flight Service as a standard Maule departing from Winter Haven bound for Chub Cay, Bahamas, not mentioning I was on floats and my lift off would be from a lake next to the airfield. Permission was granted for my Instrument Flight Plan and the clock started clicking. It was as if I were in a Le Mans car race dashing out of the seaplane base having to use a landline only as cell phones were not permitted. I climbed aboard the Maule, pre-flight previously complete, engine warmed and luggage loaded at the lakeside ramp. I raced down Lake Jessie and rotated with a turn south-eastward. Once over 1000-feet in altitude I was able to contact St. Petersburg Flight service and initiate my flight plan. The day was gloriously clear blue with an occasional white towering cumulus cloud rising in the hot Florida air. Cruising at 5000-feet I was on the way home at last. Leaving the Florida coast behind me I could see the coastline of Vero Beach heading toward the western tip of Grand Bahama staying exactly on the airway I was assigned. As the bright turquoises of home soon came in to view I realised how fortunate we were to be living within the tranquillity of our islands. The world was going to be a crazy place for years ahead with retaliations, invasions of suspect countries and more death with the new millennium unable to resemble anything we had lived through in years past. Countries that were America's friend had now become foe. We would see tyrannical leaders of the Middle East weald their powers until death from the West took them down one by one. Radical Muslims would rise to pull the tiger's tail. History would repeat itself over and over making us wonder if mankind would ever figure out how to live alongside each other? The younger George Bush was re-elected where the English newspapers mocked with dread at four more years their headlines reading 'They did it again!'

Arrival of the 4th seaplane C6SEA,
a Found Bush Hawk from Canada.

The short lived Canadian seaplane
on Lake Cunningham, Nassau.

Jim Schaafsma, once a guest to
become long-term friend takes
us to the U.P. of Michigan.

Tracy loves flying my seaplane
so buys a turbine Maule!

Lessons on STOL flying for Tracy in Normans Cay Pond.

C6WET becomes a popular way for the bride to arrive.

Sailing the catamaran with
Bruce Griffin in the Exumas.

Not many sailboats had a seaplane
tethered to their stern!

Portrait of Suzanne and I in Montagu
Heights, Nassau. (Photo: Gary Cox)

Sharks in the runway at
Highbourne Cay, Exuma.

A visit to Doubtful Sound, South Island, NZ to see the waterfalls blow backward.

Meeting Tracy with his new Citation at Odyssey Aviation in Nassau.

An invite from Tracy to fly with the Aeroshell Acrobatic Team at Oshkosh, Wisconsin.

Honoured to meet Capt. 'Sully' Sullenberger & 1st Officer Jeff Skiles of the famous water landing in the Hudson River, N.Y.

President Kennedy's Boeing 707 preserved in Seattle, Washington.

A similar Super Constellation that I flew the Atlantic in 1960 taking 19 hours.

Another invitation to join Tracy & Rae at King Pacific Lodge in British Columbia, Canada.

The Maule arrives at Browns Seaplane Base for Annual Inspection.

One of my last commercial flights in the Maule M7-235 to Alder Cay. (Photo: Jamie Middleton)

Meeting friend Paul Baker for an Alaska adventure aboard 'Single Star'.

Sailing the Gemini catamaran was always a great escape.

Our Alaska host and Captain, Lee Robbins. Ex-bush pilot, Anchorage, AK.

The late Steve Irwin I had photographed feeding one
of his crocodiles at his 'Australia Zoo'

'Lydia' weighs in at 400lbs and walks within feet of us in the wild!

My 5th and last Maule M7-260 amphibious seaplane, C6WET on the factory floor 2007.

We meet friend Doug Craig who will also take a check-ride.

With Ray Maule, an icon of the Maule family giving me a check-ride.

C6WET arrives in the Exuma Cays for the first time on charter.

The amphibious seaplane becomes the most photographed in the Caribbean!

The stunning aerial views above Shroud Cay in the Exumas.

Beautiful Highbourne Cay, one of my major clients for charters.

Long time friends Carolyn & Kevin Cartwright with daughter Jessie became managers at Highbourne.

Meeting Harry Shannon at Whale Cay, a special friend who maintained my amphibious seaplanes.

Harry was a master of seaplane maintenance in his hangar at Bartow, Florida.

One of the countless film shoots that featured my seaplanes.
Featured here for Ralph Lauren clothing.

One of the large iguanas on
Great Guana Cay, Exuma.

Wilfred Clarke became a
great friend while my A&P
Mechanic for over 20 years.

Natalie gives me three grandsons,
Jacob, Ethan & Joshua.

An engine change at Amphibians Plus
in Florida assisted by Ron and John.

Flying one of the many flights for
Johnny Depp to his private island.

Johnny's beautiful island in the
Exumas, Little Halls Pond Cay.

Johnny became a good friend and very
gracious host to us while in the Bahamas.

Flying Miss Australia on a film
shoot through the Exuma Cays.

The late Marvin Hamlisch, brilliant composer & friend of Barbara Streisand.

David Copperfield became a frequent flyer after buying a private island.

Always a pleasure to fly TV host Montel Williams.

Flying Steve Forbes to Little San Salvador to meet a cruise ship.

Michael Keaton loves to fly-fish at Kamalame Cay in Staniard Creek, Andros.

Presidential hopeful Mike Huckabee vacations in the Bahamas.

Good friend Graeme Brown was Johnny's personal yacht captain.

Every 50 hours we serviced the seaplane in the Odyssey hangar, here with Keith Riches turning wrenches.

Tracy allows me co-pilot duties aboard his latest Citation jet through Europe & Africa.

First stop over we enjoyed lovely Prague, capital of Czech Republic.

Exploring the magnificent ancient city of Petra as we passed through Jordan.

Seeing Lawrence of Arabia's cave I had to exit the city on a camel!

Our guides on The Mara Plain in Kenya, East Africa were brilliant.

My nature photography gets honed yet again on the Mara Plain.

Drama in the morning with a new-born giraffe.

Last day in the camp on the Mara Plain.

A helicopter ride around the Cape of Good Hope in South Africa with Tracy & Rae.

Natalie gets married in a Nassau garden starts my return to the islands.

Reuniting with Melissa now a member of Sea Shepherd Conservation.

On the way to Carnival in Nassau with Melissa.

My trusty driver & long time friend Charles Rolle.

Exploring the ancient city of Tlos in southwest Turkey.

Magnificent views from my villa in Kalkan on the Turquoise Coast of Turkey.

Scuba diving in the Mediterranean with friend Ron Guest from Nassau.

Reuniting with close friend Capt. Nigel Bower in Nassau.

C6WET flies the three Paul's on a training flight to Normans Cay.

Last commercial flight for Bell Island in the Exumas. (Photo: Tom Barbenitz)

My last charter in Shroud Cay Cut before retiring from Safari Seaplanes.

Savouring the moment of the last flight in 2014.

I pick up the brush again in Turkey
to begin a new phase of painting.

Taking the tiller on a writing
visit to Cornwall, England.

Harry Shannon gets me current
again in a Lake Amphibian, 2017.

Time to relax and return to the sea
in Hope Town, Abaco 2016.

A professional photographer sends me a memory from
one of the 'tough days' seaplane flying!

Chapter 30
The Crash of '02

There are moments in every aviator's career that are seared in memory, some humorous and some very scary, some awfully emotional. I always smile when thoughts of a flight down to Georgetown turned into something from a comedy sketch of which John Cleese would be proud to portray, although his far superior height than I would have him bent over to fit inside a Maule cockpit! Talking of height, I had another well-known client, actor Tyler Perry, who I admired and often had the pleasure of flying down to his newly acquired island in the Exumas, not far from Johnny's lovely cay, barely fitting inside the Maule's cockpit.

Tyler was born in Louisiana having a difficult childhood exposed to molestation and abuse. Another unassuming polite gentleman, Tyler was always soft-spoken, open and interesting to be with, I always enjoyed his company. He recounted to me while in the cockpit, discussing our difficult times as youngsters about crawling under his house to a secure hiding place when times got rough. In his early twenties while watching the *Oprah Winfrey Show* he heard about the therapeutic effects of writing inspiring him to begin a career in writing starting with a series of letters to him self. In 1990, he moved to Atlanta and two years later produced a musical based upon his letters, *I Know I've Been Changed*, able to be performed through self-financing with his $12,000 life savings. He continued his television and acting career developing a large following within America. In 2005, Forbes reported him selling $100 million in tickets, $30 million in videos and another $20 million in merchandise. His 300 live TV shows a year brought an audience of 35,000 each week. In October 2012 he formed a multi-year partnership with Oprah Winfrey. I asked a favour of him when next together with her and apologise on my behalf for being unable to fly Oprah after she called wanting a charter to his island as I had previous commitments that day! A career in flying seaplanes so often led to meeting interesting souls who made well out of life having started with barely nothing to their name, especially as with Tyler who also became a licensed pilot himself owning a Cirrus.

The comedy of errors began this day where I was to fly a couple down to Georgetown, Exuma for lunch. I was to wait there for them and fly back in the afternoon to Paradise Island. I explained that I was based at Lake Cunningham and my driver, Charles, would pick them up at the Ocean Club. The Italian gentleman agreed to this arrangement but asked if the location at the lake could offer some privacy as the young lady accompanying him was 'just a friend' who he had to be discreet about. I assured him all would be to his liking and no one would be able to see them together here in Nassau. Charles arrived near 10 am the next morning coming down the hill past Mrs. Brown's house very slowly as he always did. The Italian, well dressed, mid-fifties and quite little fellow, walked over to my ramp and introduced himself along with his very much younger companion. We loaded the Maule and arranged with Charles, who could not refrain from smiling broadly, about a time to meet back here at the lake. Take-off was smooth and we climbed out to 5500 feet toward the Exumas. It was summertime and the heat intense with thick humidity that came with this time of year. The engine and passengers would enjoy the cooler air found at altitude. The Italian sat in the co-pilot seat with his young friend behind him. She was unable to keep her hands from caressing all around his head and neck. Leaning forward every now and again she whispered something quietly in his ear while nibbling his lobe. He smiled continuously at the attention like an old contented dog.

Just past Normans Cay his expression radically changed to one of seriousness. He leaned toward me as if needing to speak in confidence.

'I need to pee!' he exclaimed. 'We must go down, *now*!' the urgency taking effect while suddenly holding his crotch firmly. His girlfriend sat back laughing at the idea of an ensuing emergency.

'You see how high we are? We are at 5000 feet in the air!' I retorted, 'it will take several minutes to get down and land, you have to hold it!' thinking that a water landing would have him evacuate the seaplane to relieve himself off the side of the floats? The little Italian was having no part of waiting.

'No time,' he cried in desperation, 'I have to go *now*!' To enforce his statement he started to unbuckle his trousers and take down his zipper. Oh crap, I thought, he's going to piss inside my plane. In desperation, with his lady laughing hysterically out loud at this comedic scene I thought she might pee herself as well while I began searching for something my co-pilot could pee into. Behind his seat I always kept a *Yachtsman's Guide to the Bahamas* sealed safely inside a Ziploc bag for protection. I grabbed the bag and tore open the zip just as the little penis came poking out of his pants.

'Here, use this,' I pleaded. Within a spilt second the bright yellow stream of liquid started filling the bag while the Italian's glassy-eyed expression of relief was undeniable. The liquid however just kept coming and coming, he must have drunk four or five cups of coffee for breakfast? 'Oh God,' a second thought, 'the man can piss like a racehorse, he is going to overflow'. The stream of pee finally stopped in the nick of time shaking his tiny equipment of the last drops sighing with relief and broad grin as he passed the bag for me to seal. 'No I am flying an airplane!' I said firmly. What did he think I could do with a full bag of pee? 'Seal it for me and put it down by your feet,' I instructed. Damn, that was a brilliant save I thought just as the bag turned in his hand sending a small stream of warm urine into my lap. The fucking bag had a hole in it! Damn! Behind my co-pilot was a towel folded over the back of the chair. I ripped it forcibly from behind his weight and wrapped the Ziploc bag inside then placing it by his feet. 'Don't step on it!' I ordered. His girlfriend was uncontrollably shaking with laughter in the back seat, enough to maybe have her pee herself by accident? In Georgetown as they walked down the road entwined arm in arm to dine inside the Peace and Plenty hotel I emptied the depleted yellow bag into the sea and washed the towel with saltwater to store in the floats for the trip back. Flying floats had its romantic moments I smiled. I should really write about it one day!

Winter came quickly where the cold fronts returned with their blustery northwest winds and more difficult flying conditions; the seas around New Providence now choppy with whitecaps all over the bays. A welcome call from Mike Henrick in Ontario proclaiming his imminent departure south bound with C6-SEA broke the monotony of the weather. He informed me of his ETA in Winter Haven and that I should meet him there for the float installation having confirmed their safe delivery from the Aerocet factory. He sent a photograph of the impressive new plane sitting out in the snow, complete with her original paint scheme that I had designed as a hawk along the side of the fuselage. Aerocet were very excited about their floats being given the exposure of my commercial flying, as these would be the first in the Bahamas. Jon's hangar housed his Piper Cubs leaving little space for the larger Hawk so we arranged space on the other side of the field. Hoisting the airframe up on chains to the hangar ceiling we removed the wheels and slowly, very slowly, the floats were unpacked from their crates to be mounted and rigged. A process taking a small team of men to accomplish along with Mike's expertise the new seaplane took shape. She looked huge compared to the Maule. That evening I spent several hours spraying the inside of the rear fuselage with anti-corrosion inhibitors preparing the airframe for its intrusion of saltwater before it even left its hangar.

The small tractor pulled the trailer carrying the Bush Hawk into the Florida sunshine. The new blue and white colours gleamed in the new morning light. A slow ride across the airfield took us over to the ramps of Browns Seaplane Base. Reversing carefully the trailer slid into the fresh water of Lake Jessie and the seaplane floated proudly on the calm surface.

'That's an impressive looking machine' Jon said quietly coming up behind me. 'Looks like she will do the job for you,' he added. We fuelled the wings and turned the airplane around for her first test-flight on the new composite floats. Mike insisting that I take left seat from the onset while he sat next to me very used to flying from the right side. The big 300HP Lycoming engine came to life immediately after priming the cylinders with the electric fuel pump and turning the ignition key. We taxied around Lake Jessie for several minutes to warm the oil and check magnetos and propeller. Up in Ontario with the extreme cold, warming the engine oil could take considerable time to see the temperature gauge even move a fraction. Here in warm central Florida conditions soon saw the small needle climb. We taxied to the far end of the Lake, used the new electric fowler flaps adding a take-off degree while raising water rudders to allow the plane to weathervane into wind. Squeezing in the throttle gently the big seaplane jumped to life and raced along the surface. Her engine sounding strong and smooth as we rotated off the calm water to climb out northeast bound for some practice water work off the larger lakes that surrounded this area. Mike was a seasoned bush pilot and knew the aircraft well with his teaching precise and clear. I soon adjusted to the new visual lines of reference that we take inside the cockpit. The yoke design was quite different to anything I had flown and the instrumentation very elaborate, planned to be my 'swan song' in the aviation game. The new Garmin 530 with all the latest analogue gauges granted the aircraft instrument rated just in case I ever need to use my qualifications. Visual flying was a luxurious part of daily life in the Bahamas. Our clear days with almost unlimited visibility meant flying by instruments was rarely needed spoilt compared to the pilots from up north! In truth, I never actually became totally comfortable flying without visibility, as these conditions were scarce in the history of our day VFR operation. It always felt alien ploughing into the clouds where nothing can be seen creating an intimidating environment losing spatial awareness in a split second without the luxury of an autopilot. The human body having no sensation of what angle or direction you are facing, and lack of paying immediate attention to those instruments in front of you can be fatal. My thoughts always returned to my instrument check-ride in the twin engine Navajo over at Fort Lauderdale Executive. By the time I was finished after shooting an approach with a simulated engine loss on one side I swore that flying visually was the way to go given chance.

Test flying proved interesting when it came to stalling the aircraft. Raising the nose and keeping the wings level with power full on and again all the way off would simulate too steep an angle of flight during take-off and landing. Airflow would eventually be insufficient to provide lift and the aircraft would fall abruptly making swift control necessary to recover the airplane flying again. The first stall saw the right wing drop dramatically. I recovered quickly.

'Whoa!' Mike exclaimed, 'what was that? You need to keep those wings level, Paul,' he instructed.

'I am sure I did,' I answered. 'Let's try that again.' Once more with wings kept level the Hawk dropped her right wing leaving Mike convinced it was I who was at fault but did not press the issue. The landings were perfect and I felt confident that I had mastered the approach angles well. Another factor jumping to our attention was the published cruise airspeed on straight floats. Found advertised that of 125 knots, which had been a big draw for me at twenty knots faster was now unobtainable. At best, Mike could only produce 105 knots, the exact same as the Maule. The ground roll on floats was proclaimed to be 1200 feet but it appeared now to be more as we took up a good portion of Lake Jessie to get aloft. We taxied back to the seaplane base and loaded our entire luggage along with a generous amount of Florida shopping.

The useful load of the Bush Hawk was published at 1475 lbs., a big attraction from the less than a thousand the Maule could lift off the water. Baggage weight allowance on my small seaplane had been just 125 lbs. in the rear compartment. Now I was offered double that. The maximum take-off and landing weight of the Found was an impressive 3800 lbs. with a climb rate of 820 feet per minute. The Maule could certainly out-climb this seaplane but with these advertised performance figures I felt confident that carrying larger loads safely was a huge advantage. Now full of fuel the Hawk was again taxied to the far end of the lake and this time our take-off would draw an audience from the seaplane base, all wanting to see how this unusual seaplane would perform fully loaded. We raced across the water and headed for the wooden buildings at the far end where two yellow Piper Cubs sat one on each ramp. Mike gave me an approved nod to lift the plane off the water, as the distance remaining was getting smaller by the second. Once airborne the struggle to climb was very evident with three of us on board and full of cargo and fuel reinforcing this test I had wanted to see at the Ontario factory. The seaplane struggled to get 500 feet per minute in climb taking what seemed forever we managed to attain 5500 feet headed back to our Bahamas. There was a lingering sense of disappointment in this new aircraft's abilities, compared with what I had been told and indeed publicised. The deed was done with no turning back now.

This February day was getting late and having lost daylight-savings time months earlier the evening light approached quickly as we came toward Chub Cay. A call on the marine VHF radio to our friendly driver, Nathaniel, who told us Mr. Whylly, the Customs Officer had gone home for the day. Now we had a dilemma on our hands; not having wheels we did not have access to Bahamas Customs at the International Airport to clear inbound from being out of the country, leaving no choice but to land in Lake Cunningham and then drive to Nassau International and make ourselves known to the authorities. There could be trouble doing this? The sun was setting as we proclaimed to Air Traffic Controllers 'we have departed Chub Cay and landing assured'. The wind was gentle out of the Southeast and my approach took us over Jimmy Sands' roof at the far western end of Lake Cunningham. He and Claire must have seen the new seaplane swoop down toward the water and taxi into Ian Browns property; by the time I pulled the mixture and the propeller stopping, they drove down the hill to produce a bottle of champagne and glasses for celebration in the twilight. A fun gesture to which we all enjoyed absorbing the scene of a large new machine perched on my ramp. Cutting short the celebration we thought better of driving quickly over to the airport in the darkness and throw ourselves at the mercy of Bahamas Customs having a US Citizen with us on board. They were surprisingly very understanding of what had happened and appreciated our integrity of driving over with our luggage for them to inspect.

I produced my Charter Certificate, which exempted me from the newly created duties that were being imposed on aircraft being imported into the country. The declared cargo however had remained on board the aircraft, which we returned later to unload. It was strange to see this impressive seaplane tied up at the ramp. Not having landed in saltwater at Chub Cay, the Hawk did not need washing down having departed from a fresh water lake. The moonlight glinted off the shining new fuselage as we drove home.

After breakfast the following day Mike and I met Keith from Civil Aviation at the lake arranging for another check-ride. We loaded the seaplane and taxied out for the first take-off here at the home base. Calling 'Sierra Echo Alpha' was a bit of a mouthful to air traffic and soon we found it better to just use the letters S.E.A. Keith mentioned with a smile through his headset that next time to make it Whiskey Echo Tango, little did we realise what was to come! Mike asked that we do more air work and took us south of the airport airspace to climb and practise steep turns and more stalls. Again, the right wing dropped first with Keith confirming from his rear seat that the wings were indeed level as I climbed to induce a stall with power on. Without power the seaplane did behave properly however and flew next over to Andros for a trial in the most difficult of my runways, the tiny spaces inside Staniard Creek where Kamalame Cay resort was situated. This would be all the proof I needed that this airplane could support service to one of my leading clients. The Hawk did draw slightly more water and I figured for now using the main creek seemed best to stay safe. It was the available distances that had me concerned. Flying south on a take-off would have us meet the small bridge at the far end and very shallow grass beds that converged each side of the creek.

One would have to know well how to navigate the not so straight line of flight, a take-off with curves in the runway! Leaving to the north was less concern, as we would face the open ocean with only choppy waters as our obstacle. The Bush Hawk while carrying light fuel and three of us on board performed satisfactory. It was time to take Mike back to Nassau as he was due to leave for Canada that afternoon. We shook hands and he congratulated me on flying skills saying he felt confident that I could handle this new machine safely.

Winter gave way to springtime and the approach of another busy season for Safari Seaplanes. We were very well established now and our clients, on learning of our increased space on board, applauded the choice of a new plane. The first full load to Little San Salvador for Holland America was however an eye opening experience. My long-time friend, from childhood days, with parents all knowing each other, Kevin Cartwright, had become the Holland Representative on the beautiful island that sat between the South end of Eleuthera and north end of Cat Island. A perfect cruise ship anchorage with the deep ocean sound coming close to shore, Holland America had purchased the island some year's back. From its inception as a cruise ship destination I, and the other Maule owners, had flown charters for the engineers and owners as the development progressed. Now complete, my charter company was awarded most of the flights needed in and out of the island over the next several years.

KC, as we all affectionately called him, was a big man, an inch or two above me but quite heavier in build and strong as an ox. With him and three other smaller men we loaded the seaplane while it was tied to the ramp on Lake Cunningham. With near full tanks of fuel, we were near maximum approved weight. I thought it prudent with a gentle breeze coming down the full length of the lake to taxi all the way to Jimmy's house in the far west corner; no chances today, make the runway as long as possible. Power applied allowed the Bush Hawk to struggle forward feeling very heavy this take-off roll, merely pushing water in front of the floats and burying her rear end down. I pushed the control yoke full forward encouraging the aircraft to get onto the step and run freely across the surface. It obeyed ever so slowly as I asked, allowing the larger seaplane to gain speed before easing back the yoke asking the plane to fly as we neared the far end of the lake. KC looked warily at me from the right seat seeing the mangroves of the East end fast approaching. I was reaching my 'go-no-go' decision point when suddenly we were airborne. Passing low over the mangrove bushes I felt the airplane struggling to maintain any height. We were flying with ten degrees of flaps but barely making any altitude and at a precariously slow airspeed with tall pine trees scattered within the bushland ahead. Both of us in those front seats were now concerned at this poor performance. KC was well versed in the Maule take-off but this was a whole different story, he glanced quickly my way with a raised eyebrow of concern. I was very aware of shuffling in my seat, a conscious movement to alleviate stress. I kept the nose flat steering gently away from the path toward any high objects out toward the sea and any open space barely feet above the foliage. At maximum weight this aircraft was a 'dog' as we termed in the industry. A wave of disappointment came over me. This was not what I had bargained for. Most of the performance numbers the factory had quoted and published in its approved manuals were now proving in the field to be unquestionably incorrect and unachievable. Adjusting all my computations my charters would change drastically with lighter loading. This seaplane was no Maule. It was an extremely brief meeting with fellow Maule owner, Tommy Goodwin, based further east down the lake, coming down the hill on his antique motorcycle that first morning to inspect my new plane; summing it up in a phrase. 'That ain't no lift-wing, Paul,' he said, emotionless and obviously unimpressed to simply turn and drive away.

As the weeks and months passed by I slowly learned what my new plane could and could not do now being stuck with each other. With very light fuel and just two passengers on board I could still land and take off on my very short 'runway' facing east inside Staniard Creek on a high tide. Anything heavier would require crosswind executions off the main waterway facing north and south. The study construction void of wing struts to crawl under became a welcome plus. Loading without doorsills a pleasure when heavy boxes or baggage needed to be hoisted on board, the flat wooden floors where one could slide cargo around most welcome. All four doors having huge panes of Perspex gave fabulous visibility above the gorgeous views we flew over every day. Not having pilot windows that could open in flight did limit my abilities in aerial photography that was becoming an integral part of the business. Landing in slightly choppier water was solid and easy to perform. The floats had huge compartments for added waterproof storage. The aircraft had its good points but in all still left that bitter taste of disappointment.

Springtime always meant the seaplane charter business would enter its busiest season. Fly-fishing was at its peak and I would be heading toward Andros more than the Exuma Cays most weeks. The small boutique resorts such as Tiamo in South Andros and Kamalame Cay in the north kept me working at all hours of the day. On the last day of May I had a reservation from the Bahamas National Trust to fly Eric Carey and two of the ladies that worked with him at the headquarters on Village Road, to a meeting with Ray Darville, the Park Warden at Waderick Wells. An approaching late cold front had the winds that morning gentle out of the Southwest. Having loaded my passengers with light cargo on board we taxied along the north shore of the Lake, eastward toward Charlie Bethell's hangar. This take-off would be across the Lake toward the far corner where the airport road came close to the shoreline. A nice long open space to make all on board feel comfortable in an aircraft they had not flown in before. Rising off the water I headed southeast in a direct line to Waderick Wells laying about a third of the way down the beautiful Exuma chain.

Flying my new machine was becoming a real pleasure allowing its shortcomings to be forgotten and accumulating some 200 hours' experience under my belt, bringing confidence my choice of changing seaplanes for this larger model a good one after all. It was an impressive airplane; heavier to handle it felt as if I were flying 'the truck' compared to 'the sports car'. Now I owned a real workhorse that would outlast any Maule with its more sophisticated construction and new composite floats that would not corrode. Eric commented how nice this seaplane was to ride in and the two ladies had ample room in the passenger compartment. Their cargo so small left ample space to spare. The large panoramic windows were always a popular item and the flight this day was just as gorgeous a view that I could offer. The Bush Hawk with its flash paint scheme was receiving much publicity throughout the islands and featured in both aircraft and float manufactures advertising.

Ray met us in the shallow waters of 'Whale Beach' just below the Park HQ building. Mounted at the top of the sand a complete skeleton of a young sperm whale that had washed ashore up at Shroud Cay months earlier. Those of us who flew that route regularly had spied the dead whale in the shallows one morning, surrounded by many sharks there for a meal that would last for days. Word got back to Ray who monitored the progress of the whales demise to the competitive sharks that were consuming it chunk by massive chunk. One shark had slithered in so shallow water trying to reach the far side to eat, becoming stranded in the inches-deep water, washing on to the beach also perishing. In weeks to come the huge body was nearly stripped of all its flesh. Then came the horrible task of taking the skeleton apart and cleaning all the components. It took Ray and volunteers weeks to perform where eventually reconstructed on the beach at Waderick for display to visitors and students that would visit the facility years later.

We unloaded the passengers and being the only flight of the day booked I would wait at the cay for the return that afternoon. During the balance of the day I stayed up at the headquarters building sitting on the wooden patio, gazing as I had so often done at the marvellous colours that the anchorage displayed, swirls of light turquoise water barely covering the shallow sand bars with a dark blue ribbon of deep indigo that threaded its way through the anchorage. Moorings were strategically placed in the ocean bed, each had yachts of various makes and size tethered at their bows and all facing the same direction with the fast-flowing tide that raced through the channel each day. The anchorage was full. Small yellow bananaquit birds flew into my hands holding small offerings of white sugar, only to be displaced by a large tame mockingbird that occupied this lovely place, a comforting thought that animals and birds still approach me comfortably.

The weather was slowly changing pulling the freshening wind to the west and noticeably quite choppy and white capping on the outside of the cays. The spring tide was high by the time Eric and his crew came back for departure. I would be able to taxi the Bush Hawk around to the east side of the anchorage using the shallows to offer the longest ample take-off area diagonally toward the opening at the northwest end. Threading one's way through this anchorage with its many boats and fast flowing tide as obstacles always an art form during my flying career. I had accumulated over 6000 hours of seaplane experience by now and well aware of the drift a seaplane would be exposed to. Shaking hands with Ray we climbed aboard while he held the rear of the plane allowing me to start up without drifting precariously toward the rocks as I had done many times on my own. Before boarding each passenger having to sit on the struts of the floats first to dry their feet before entering the aircraft. It was a prerequisite ritual I had done from the very first day of owning a seaplane. There would be no saltwater inside my planes unlike other commercial companies I witnessed pilots and passengers simply climbing into the cabins of multi-million dollar seaplanes soaking wet. It was unbelievable to me that some pilots had total disregard for the well-being of aircraft they flew?

While I taxied toward the take-off zone I went through my checks as one did every day, every flight, using that old familiar acronym F.A.R.T.S. Flaps, Area clear? Rudders, Transponder and Seatbelt check. The Hawk had electric flaps that took some getting used to, where in the Maule one would simply reach down to your right side and lift the flap handle rather like a handbrake in a car. My runway was clear, offering loads of distance with my light load of passengers, zero baggage and remaining fuel. The balcony of the headquarters filled with spectators always keen to watch a floatplane fly off the water. I squeezed in the throttle and the seaplane jumped to life soon racing toward the other side of the anchorage into the freshening wind now slightly quartering to one side. To my right were small rocks with little growth on their summits so kept them safely to my right side. About halfway across, the Hawk was ready to fly and with little coaxing it became airborne. As I lowered the nose to stay in 'ground effect', where an aircraft can remain airborne using the proximity to the ground below adding to the force of lift, the right wing suddenly dropped dramatically sending us careening toward the water at an awful angle. I was shocked but reacted in instant by keeping the nose firmly forward and straightening the wings back to level. I did not have that precious single second to exclaim '*Shit!*' that ran through my brain. I did see Eric make a quick grab at something to hold on to. One can count out loud the next timeframe; one and two and … *Bang!* I was suddenly staring at a shattered windshield, a propeller bent double, palmetto trees draped over the engine cowling, a broken screen of that lovely Garmin GPS and silence. I have fucking crashed! Heart now pounding audibly in my chest; adrenalin exploded inside my body taking me into programmed automation.

'Everyone *OK*?' I called loudly as I turned to see the ladies sitting stunned and expressionless with a door jammed open showing the cruel rocks outside. Turning to Eric he said, 'I'm good'. The training manual requirements for a crash landing kicked in without further thought. I reflected later how amazing we react after learning the discipline of a career such as flying. Pilots in serious trouble go to this place in their mind automatically and use they're training to bring the situation, however bad, under best possible control. Captain Sully Sullenberger's book about his ordeal of landing an airliner in the Hudson River describes beautifully this very situation, where he and First Officer Jeff Skiles just went through 'what had to be done' allowing them to save all 155 people on board that USAir flight. Actor Harrison Ford, an avid experienced aviator, lost an engine in California one morning recently and chose his landing zone on a golf course in split seconds to survive the landing.

'Everybody *out now!*,' I said with clarity. 'Be careful where you walk, its rough out there. Meet me over there on the rocks,' – pointing to a flatter rock formation thirty feet away – I commanded, while switching off the main fuel lines and master electric switches. It was all very surreal. I became this robot going through the motions to keep my passengers safe at all cost. I too opened my cockpit door seeing the grey sharp coal rocks right at my feet. No longer was there a beautiful new float to step on to with clear seawater lapping against its side. Now all I noticed was shattered pieces of fibreglass and pieces of twisted airplane filling the potholes of the shoreline. The broken seaplane lay perfectly straight, not one degree out of kilter. I had kept the machine absolutely level and its angle of flight spot on what it should have been. I had simply run out of space that would have allowed the plane to recover flight and instead ploughed onto the jagged coral rocks of this outer cay. The Aerocet floats had taken the brunt of the collision, where by the time we stopped going forward at about 60 mph, the fuselage now lay torn on its underside. Boats were racing toward us.

Ray Darville jumped onto the coral shoreline and straight toward me standing next to my bewildered passengers. The emotional release of the moment suddenly hit hard. I fell against him and unashamedly wept quietly while staring over his shoulder to look at what had been a prized possession, now a crumpled machine of twisted steel and shattered fiberglass.

The loss was one thing but the tears of relief in having not hurt anyone most prominent together with the immense anti-climax of all that work, planning and money into making a new aircraft work for us. I had totally destroyed this lovely new machine without putting a mark on anyone, save a tiny scratch on one of the ladies which she dismissed bravely 'as nothing' while giving me a hug of thanks for saving their lives.

We climbed aboard the small motorboats that had raced out to help us. News flew through the islands at the speed of light. Marine radios had come alive about a seaplane crashing at Waderick Wells. My good friend Chris Cloud who was managing Little Halls Pond Cay raced out of his house and sped toward the Park Headquarters as fast as his boat would go with throttle pushed hard forward. The crowd of spectators stood quietly on the balcony as I walked up slowly with my passengers and Ray in the lead. We had to notify the authorities in Staniel Cay of the accident and then inform Civil Aviation back in Nassau. Ray also offered to organise another flight to get us all back to Nassau but the shaken group declined the offer asking if a boat was available instead. Chris arrived upstairs and gave me a strong bear hug of support asking what on earth he could do for me. We walked back outside for some fresh air and gaze northward at a pile of broken seaplane sitting forlorn on the rocks with its nose in the bushes.

A gentleman unknown to me approached asking to shake my hand.

'That was the most amazing save I have ever seen!' he exclaimed telling he was a retired US Air Force pilot on holiday here in the Exumas. 'A really nice piece of flying,' he added generously, 'That airplane let you down.'

'Thank you,' I said quietly.

I took Chris's offer of help after learning that Glen Wales, who flew a Cessna Caravan for Mr Dingman down at Little Pipe Cay was due to head back to Nassau from Staniel Cay. I needed a ride home and was not about to pound my way across sixty miles of rough ocean by boat. I called home keeping it very short and to the point. 'I have had an accident in the plane, everyone is fine and I am heading back to Odyssey with Glen.' There was a tense and shaken, 'Thank God you are ok' from the other end of the line. 'I'll meet you there,' then silence.

Glen held out a supporting hand for me to climb aboard the Caravan. I had never flown in this huge seaplane before. He offered me the spare Bose headset on the co-pilot side. 'That's an exclusive club you have joined,

Paul,' he said gently, 'I'm glad you are ok. Do you mind if we fly over your plane to see what happened?' he asked. 'No, go ahead,' I replied quietly. That was all we said for the entire flight. My friend knew I needed the time to be quiet and reflect. The turbine spooled up and ignited, pushing the large plane forward. I loved the way Glen flew with such ease. Some pilots make such a meal of flying, pulling constantly at the controls in jerked fashion as if the machine really warranted this behaviour. 'Leave the damned controls alone!' I barked at one pilot whose flying I found irritating to watch, 'the plane will fly beautifully if you let her!'

Within minutes of flying northward we approached Waderick Wells. I felt very strange and very empty staring down at my wrecked airplane sitting alone on the rocks. We turned northwest toward Nassau and I listened without saying anything as Glen spoke with air traffic control. It was Percy King on duty that afternoon, recognising that familiar voice in a second. I walked stoically through the lobby of Odyssey Aviation where Susanne's teary eyes expressed the relief and disappointment to the end of our saga. I learned that one of the visiting yachtsman anchored at Waderick had quickly found my insurance company, laying claim to the salvage rights before I had arrived back in Nassau. The vultures were out within minutes. I had no chance or offer or bid on my own property, rather informed I would paid in full for my loss, reinforcing evidence of exorbitant annual aviation premiums sometimes a good thing to have done.

On reaching my house I suddenly kicked in to practical mode. I needed my Maule back from Jon Brown who was selling her for me. I needed to stay in business, to 'get back on the horse'! To date Jon had received only offers, none sufficient to meet my price. I called the seaplane base and spoke with him right away explaining the accident and that the Hawk was a total wreck.

'Paul!' he exclaimed, 'I have a buyer in front of me now writing a cheque as we speak!'

'Then tell him to tear it up and that I am very sorry to withdraw the sale!' I pleaded. It could take months to find another seaplane to keep me alive in business and better the devil one knew than another aircraft I did not know?

'I had a strange feeling about that airplane, Paul,' Jon added as he dismissed his buyer. 'I am glad you are safe. Come and get your Maule!'

Climbing back into the smaller familiar cockpit felt disappointing. Not that a Maule was that much less of an airplane, it just felt as if I had regressed back to my training aircraft, that of a Cessna 150 compared to flying my Piper Navajo. Gone was the sophistication of an advanced instrument panel, gone the conveniences of design and feel of something really solid in the air. Gone was the newness of everything. The old Maule was looking scruffy compared; she was tired and I could not imagine getting many more years out of her. But she was reliable, trustworthy and therefore safe. Over the years one learns certain aircraft can earn a pilot's respect allowing them to trust implicitly; the Maule held firm that title. It was certainly time however to deregister this seaplane ridding myself of the Federal Aviation Authority. The Bush Hawk had arrived from Canada as a Bahamian registered aircraft and having only one bureaucracy to deal with was certainly more attractive. The straw that broke the camel's back was sudden notice from Tom Roper, my FAA Miami Field Officer informing me of his arrival in Nassau along with an Avionics Inspector who requested meet me at Lake Cunningham the next day for an inspection of the aircraft and its logbook. I had always prided myself on keeping the aviation records in current impeccable condition. After a while it kept the authorities off my back as they could see I was consistently complying with all the required standards. An avionics inspection however was new experience but inconsequential with this aircraft's simplicity.

I arrived at the Lake earlier than they were due making sure the seaplane was open and tidy for viewing. A hire car came down the hill and parked on the grass with Tom at the wheel, his passenger obviously the avionics inspector. He looked like a miniature of the actor Donald Pleasance, very short and bald, a little man. I offered him my Adlog, an up to date combination of all the required logs of the seaplane divided into the relevant sections, a very efficient system of aircraft logs had everything the authorities needed to see in one volume. Tom and I always got along well, a very pleasant man with a great disposition and knowing of how to treat pilots going through inspections. He took me to one side saying quietly,

'Bear with me Paul on this one.' As if a warning to give this little man all the room he needed. 'The plane looks in great shape. You work hard with this one, I can tell.'

The avionics, that is all the instrumentation of the Maule, were standard simple analogue systems. Nothing had been changed or replaced in the aircraft's history. The paperwork reflected this and was a fairly bland entry compared to the engine and airframe, which had hundreds of written entries about the work that had been routinely performed. The last written entry had been about a 500HR check inspection performed on time with the appropriate logbook entry reflecting this.

'Mr Harding I need to talk to you about something here,' the inspector calling me over to where he stood against their vehicle using the hood as a desktop.

'Yes, Sir, what can I do for you?' I asked suddenly feeling a little uneasy by this aggressive little chap. To not appear intimidated I stood quite close to him peering down at his face.

'You have a violation here!' he exclaimed, almost with a smirk of satisfaction.

Tom immediately sensed that something was going amiss here and took a position behind his associate, making careful head movements and a raised hush-index finger to his lips as if asking me not to respond too heavily.

'I am going to impose a fine of $50,000.00 on you for an incorrect entry in this logbook!' he demanded.

'A *what*?!' I cried out loud uncontrollably at this insane statement. Tom waving his hand now pleading that I stay calm.

'$50,000.00 *for what*?!' I near shrieked at the insanity of the threat.

'The verbiage in this last entry is incorrect. Although you carried out this inspection the wording does not include or make reference to the Federal Aviation Regulation that is relevant here!' he said firmly.

'Surely sir, that could be just corrected and we consider this a lesson learned?' I tried to reason with him.

'You can plead your case in court,' he ended the conversation climbing back into the car. I was not sure who had the most astounded look on his face, Tom or myself. They drove away leaving me speechless. These incredibly silly men with their badges of authority came into our islands throwing with seeming pleasure the book at someone who had performed all that was required but phrased something incorrectly? That was it. They have to go I decided. My dealings and exposure to the Bahamas Civil Aviation Authority on the other hand a far different story. These men were polite and very willing to teach us the methods and manner to which the regulations demanded. To hell with the FAA, I would fight them in court over this violation of common sense.

It took only days to finish the paperwork with Flight Standards at the airport and submitting the US de-registration to Jon over in Winter Haven to hand in for me. Stripping off the American registration letter and numbers was a symbolic gesture of 'good riddance'. My friend Keith's suggestion from months ago came to light, the Maule would take on her new identity and C6-WET was born in the summer months of 2003.

I fought the case against me in Florida with aviation attorney Ed Bush I knew well from year's prior. Ed said it was preposterous to what the FAA had imposed and sure enough the case was dismissed, still costing me just over $5000.00 in legal fees and court costs. The little avionics inspector was removed from his Florida posting and stationed in the middle of Central America somewhere way out the Miami office for his troubles. Tom called me later after learning I had gone from US registry, 'I don't blame you Paul, that was taking things way too far,' he offered as an apology.

The early years of the new millennia turned history inside out, from watching that awful day in New York we bear witness to some astounding events. Vladimir Putin is now the president of Russia in the year 2000 and George W. Bush is elected president of the USA the following year. Europe introduces a new currency in 2002 called the Euro, while we watch Apple becoming a mega-corporation giving us a small piece of electronics called the iPod, having us listen to music in very different ways; vinyl records were out dated years ago only to return in style by 2014; our parents 78s to our 45s and LPs followed by the eight track cassette, reel-to-reel tape, the small cassette to the CD and into the digital age. Space travel is becoming almost blasé with the first tourist flying into the heavens. American businessman Dennis Tito had been accepted to fly and meet the Russian Station Mir badly needing extra funding to cover its costs. Plans had to change after Mir was going to be de-orbited and in April of 2001 he managed a seven-day stay aboard the International Space Station despite major opposition from some of the management of NASA. An irony after watching many years earlier, a science fiction movie called *2001: A Space Odyssey* thinking at the time how outrageous this could all be, the thought of living above the Earth? We watch with regularity the space shuttles lifting off in their magnificence from Cape Canaveral flying into outer space to return days or weeks later landing in either Florida or California, then piggybacked aboard a Boeing 747 bearing a total weight of near 488,000 pounds!

On February 1 2003 the Space Shuttle Columbia reminds us all so tragically the perils of this pioneer travel. Returning to Earth that clear morning with a missing piece of insulation from the main fuel tank having fallen off on launch. Insulation had been lost before without incident but this time a fragment had broken away damaging the left wing. On re-entry to the earth's atmosphere over Texas and Louisiana the white-hot atmospheric gases penetrated the wing structure causing catastrophic destruction leaving the shuttle to become unstable and break apart. Again glued to our televisions we watched our newscasts, one more time, as this beautiful piece of machinery disintegrated in fiery pieces that bright blue morning, killing all seven adventurous crew members on board bringing the shuttle program to a screeching halt yet again for the next two years. More than 2000 pieces of debris were recovered over sparsely populated regions of the Southern States. The investigation showed the crew having no time to prepare, some not wearing gloves and one not having a helmet on. The program began again in July 2005 with the launch of Discovery which also lost a piece of insulation but not critical to cause catastrophe. The last shuttle to fly being Atlantis in July of 2011 and I saved a memorable photograph shot from the Space Station of the orbiter as she flew over the Southern tip of the Exuma Cays.

The aircraft insurance company came through for me with flying colours. A cheque arrived for the full replacement amount. I renewed my relationship with my old seaplane and flying a Maule again feeling like the old comfortable pair of gloves. I submitted a full report online to the Seaplane Pilots Association about the questionable publicised performance figures from Found; receiving countless responses from pilots all over North America, especially bush pilots in Alaska who were not enamoured with the Bush Hawk. Since the accident I learned that the owners of the next model produced from mine, production Number 34 suffered the same fate with a similar departure stall accident that tragically took all their lives. It sealed any doubt of my claims in the aircraft's poor performance giving relief knowing my flying skills had been enough to save the day along with loads of good fortune. More than a dozen years later at a dinner party an acquaintance hugged me saying 'my good friend on board that day is convinced she would not have survived if it weren't for you flying'. Over the coming months there was a noticeable disappearance of advertising for the Canadian aircraft and I decided that something really constructive should come from this accident in a material way that could seal my security for retirement. I purchased another condominium in the same-gated complex as my first investment close to Cable Beach in Nassau. With two on rent I would be fairly secure to call it quits one day soon.

Flying from Lake Cunningham presented very much less pressure than that of being based in Nassau Harbour. No matter what winds were the Lake offered a usable runway in almost any direction compared to uptown that presented a logistical nightmare for departures and landing. I could refuel with ease and efficiency to perform quick turn around flights increasing the revenue dramatically. I was flying some 600 hours a year and the engine total time lessened, having eliminated that long tedious back-taxi down the harbour. Wear on the airframe decreased, operating within the calm fresh waters of the Lake allowing Wilfred to enjoy his servicing off my ramp only ten minutes away from the airport. After months of persuasion he finally started working in the water with trousers rolled up and boots off to work on the underside of the engine barefoot. 'Damn Wilfred, you are looking like a real seaplane mechanic now!' I joked with him. I still heard the occasional 'Oh no!' from him as he occasionally dropped something while working above the engine. Without low tides the item, be it a nut, washer or tool would give a familiar 'plop' as it hit the water somehow always sinking between the planking of the ramp. In warm season I would strip down to bathing suit and with mask and snorkel to slide underneath the water recovering the lost item. During the winter, I did not volunteer that easily and we enjoyed working together for over twenty years! One day soon, I promised, we would be located at the airport with an amphibian that could live out of the water where both of us could work dry within the shade of a hangar.

The next few years would have my flying career remain constant with time aloft running into thousands of hours. Safari Seaplanes maintained its popularity and the mainstay of business soon swung over to my local charter clients residing in the Out-Islands, people who I had known since childhood or wonderful new friends who came to be island managers.

These folks were my bread and butter who needed my service on a regular basis, offering a more consistent income through the off-season months away from tourism. Day trips became second priority ages ago as I was tiring from the daily entertainment business. It was far more interesting and far less stressful flying provisions to some gorgeous mega-yacht at anchor or catering to some emergency situation where I could really be of help to those in need. A call from Highbourne Cay one day had me evacuate good friend Jack Cash, suffering terribly from a large fishing hook snagged through his foot while out in the sound catching dolphin. Followed with a call from Little San Salvador about a possible heart attack victim on board a cruise ship visiting for the day. Some amusing requests coming from the managers of Cistern Cay with the owner running out of his favourite yogurt: make sure it's *only* cherry flavoured Yoplait! The small blue and white seaplane became a common fixture with almost daily flights over the Exumas or down the coastline of Andros to the bone fishing resorts. There were occasional long distance flights, mostly guest evacuations from large mega-yachts anchored out near Cat Island, San Salvador and Rum Cay or southward to Long Island. For these I would slide along the wings with fuel hose in one hand having to fill the tip-tanks for lengthy flying times; a great feature of the Maule where the flip of two switches a pilot could transfer fuel from tip-tanks to mains while in flight. These flights would provide enough daily income where the rest of day I could be comfortably off duty. The trails of self-employment in the service industry once again allowed no weekends off. The busiest day of the week usually would arrive on a Sunday.

The demand for flights became trying at times where recreation plans often cancelled last minute, bringing tension within the household. We desperately needed time off to play and enjoy the fruits of Bahamian living only to be pulled away time after time by our regular clients who notoriously called with urgency to disrupt our plans. With the sale of Normans Cay and the insurance payment after my accident had secured the purchase of our 34-foot Gemini catamaran to be ready the following year at the factory in Annapolis, Maryland. A mono hull showed clearly there would be too much strain on my back, an injury I attributed to hours pounding around a competitive tennis court years earlier with Andrew Barr, my doubles partner. My mixed doubles partner Ann suggested I try the game of golf learning slowly on the course at South Ocean. Walking golf courses was wonderful and as I became quite proficient time went on to play some beautiful courses abroad such as Torrey Pines in California and with my flying mentor Colin Budenberg up in Scotland at the world-famous Gleneagles estate, a totally different game to anything I had played before. We had flown in a rented singe engine Piper Warrior flying through the Lake District to Scotland where I landed at Perth. Pulling up to the main building of Gleneagles in a brand new rental Ford, the huge Scot doorman looking distastefully down his nose instructing us with a firm brogue, 'Ya can nay park *that* here!'ordering us around the rear of the magnificent building well out of sight from all the Rolls Royce's and Bentleys. Astoundingly beautiful landscapes adorned the famous course with the longest fairways I had ever played, intimidating rough and greens flatter than my dining table and as long as my house. Standing on the first tee proved a nerve-racking experience with two old local Scots gentlemen perched on the bench to watch our drives.

'Ya can nay take a divot off this tee, Paul,' Colin whispered in his good Scottish brogue while smiling at the challenge. I took careful aim, a slow breath and swore inwardly that I would not look up allowing the ball to fly straight. It did so beautifully, sailing down the centre of the fairway as I walked behind my partner exhaling quietly with relief sporting a look of satisfaction to put pressure following suit, which Colin could manage effortlessly. On the home course of South Ocean, playing with long time friend Harvey Skolnick one afternoon, I was taking a three-iron shot of the third hole fairway when next I found myself with face in the grass lying flat on the ground. I had not felt the sudden drop. Harvey walked on past thinking that I was fooling around, when after reaching twenty yards away realised I was actually injured. The pain in my lower back so excruciating I was driven carefully home unable to move. For a week an ambulance had to come and collect me for recovery therapy where even getting to the bathroom proved an impossible task. After several days I managed, inch by careful inch, to slide out of bed crawling across the tile floor to relieve myself. In time I would visit the Spine Institute of Tampa to find an arthritic collapse of a joint in my hip. 'Arthritic *at forty*?' I questioned in disbelief. Flying would be achieved very carefully each day until I healed, getting inside the cockpit a task in slow motion where once seated flying with ease. Arrivals on to a ramp with a straight floatplane well calculated to make sure the seaplane would remain stationary without sliding backward adrift with a pilot unable to exit with speed. Every once in a while one wrong turn or movement while handling luggage would have me gasp in agony as my back injury reminded me, 'it is still there'.

I watched years later my lovely fellow seaplane pilot Elle suffer the same fate with her lower back, being part and parcel to her having to walk away from flying. Manhandling these seaplanes alone in 15 to 20 knots of wind on a beach can be a real workout. I have been fortunate through life not having, to date, broken a single bone. My family tree had males living well into the nineties on my father's side. Mother's side suffered the intrusion of cancer losing both her and her brother to that awful disease. Health has been kind to me in all; save kicking an occasional conch shell that poked just above the sand, tearing flesh from the front of my toe, finally with age gave up bending! Natalie soon shared this fate regularly with us joking about how we seemed to alternate the same injury involving our feet not wanting to wear shoes of any kind. I never could feel comfortable flying with footwear, even entering the land planes I kicked of both shoes to 'feel' the rudder pedals. I became known as 'the barefoot pilot' in magazine articles not to be confused with the young 'barefoot bandit' years later that entered the Bahamas evading the law in America to steal planes and boats in the Bahamas, eventually apprehended in Abaco. Time came to succumb to Dr Debbie Raine's knife, a long-time acquaintance who had played together as children when our parents all met at Green Cay on a Sunday: here she was later, our local foot doctor, who's skill now removed all the bones from a little toe painfully inhibiting the rare wearing of closed shoes! 'Now you have a sugar banana, Paul, we humans gave up using that appendage years ago!' she smiled on completion. With an order 'not to get wet for a month' made good timing to venture north and purchase a new catamaran in Annapolis. We shut down the business, taking time away from work and arranged with friend Steve Rudski from Normans Cay, who had introduced us to the Gemini catamaran along with Doug Craig working for Boeing and airline pilot Tom Pelczynski years earlier, to meet us there to be our guide and teacher for the sail southward. Steve was in Annapolis when we arrived and drove together to the Performance Cruising factory. Designer Tony Smith, a British sailor who championed the Around Great Britain race designed this 34-foot catamaran so it could be single-handedly sailed and fit into a standard size mooring slip at any marina, sailing easily in just twenty-seven inches of water with retracted centre boards. We met son-in-law Will Hershfeld who escorted us outside to the docks where our new boat lay tethered. On completion, I had requested the services of outfitter Peter Kennedy to complete the special order that we had specified needing a boat that could be self-sustaining away from marinas, able to generate enough solar and wind power to make ample fresh water. Additional luxuries that we got incessantly teased about by the old-hand 'yachties' such as satellite television and single side band radios came as finishing touches; the brand-new catamaran lay quietly afloat boasting an impressive shiny new gel-coat and beautiful lines. Peter had taken a few extra months to complete the order and now she was ready to be sailed home to the Bahamas. Steve helped in programming the GPS and inspecting the boat meticulously to make sure all was in working order, his expertise was more than welcome and made fun company with our adventure through the inland waterways of the east coast of America. A bottle of Veuve Clicquot was tapped gently on her bow so that we may enjoy the ice-cold bubbly christening our boat *Cat's Away*. A play on the word catamaran and insinuating we were to be the proverbial 'mice at play'!

We provisioned our boat fully and headed away from the factory marina. The journey south would take near a month, sailing when we had chance of venturing 'outside' to the open ocean and manoeuvring the waterway through the narrow canals of the Dismal Swamp cut by George Washington for transport of cotton from the South back in the early history of the States, venturing on through Virginia, North and South Carolina with a stop in Beaufort to visit old clients from the charter boat days in Nassau, staying the night to enjoy a fabulous meal of 'Frog Moor Stew', a local seafood brew with a spicy kick to the flavour. Marinas always commented over the radio about liking our name. The ocean presented some fun challenges where Steve was able to save the day, freeing us from an entanglement of crab-pot lines wrapped tightly around our out-drive with the approach of powerful thunderstorms from the open ocean. We raced for the nearest natural harbour in effort to hide from high winds and torrential rains while anchors dragged helplessly through the silt bottom. Southward we sailed through the state of Georgia and into the warmer days of North Florida waters. Dolphins raced under our bow as the Gemini sped beautifully through the sea leaving a muffled roar of white water wake to our stern. Steve needed to get home with his family having used up the available weeks he kindly gave us recommending our other sailing friend from Normans Pond, Doug Craig also a Florida resident accompany the two 'novices' in to South Florida. With our time away from work come to an end we let Steve's family crew across the Gulf Stream to Nassau as my foot was healed enough to fly seaplanes again.

'Television!' retorted Doug as he inspected the main cabin. 'On a boat!' he jested. Near his last days aboard I did have the satisfaction of catching him fully reclined in the salon watching the World Series in baseball. *Cat's Away* arrived with Steve once more at the helm, with his family crewing to sail into Nassau Harbour on Independence Day, July 10. After finding a Customs Officer who was working that holiday weekend in the Port Department we paid the Bahamas Duty and watched our new boat sail on toward the Exumas where I had laid a new mooring in the Pond having received prior permission from Local Government in Georgetown. For several years, I would often touch down in the calm of the Pond, anchor the seaplane close to my boat and swim over to climb on board for a break in flying. There were countless highlights to sailing that beautiful boat. Fizzing along the sparkling turquoises of Shroud Cay in a broad reach, the wake almost roaring behind the stern; under a full moon running with the wind back to Nassau one night and then a challenge from Steve – a master at the helm – asking me to follow his older model Gemini, strictly under sail, into Normans Cay Pond from the ocean side. Here lies only one chance to get it right; retracting the centerboards to avoid the shallows and running with the wind through a very narrow rock entrance. A sudden right turn for a broad reach along the extremely thin waterway, both in width and depth, to a final run with the wind into the deeper blues of the anchorage ahead. Steve raises his arms in salute! There were times when having a boat at anchor offered me a place of refuge from awful weather that foiled a safe return to Nassau, one particular storm that angrily approached from the northwest catching me on the way home with friends Jim and Jo, my Westwind friends staying at McDuff's Resort on Normans Cay out in a small skiff. I landed hastily seeing the dark purple line getting uncomfortably close. The seaplane was secured to my mangrove mooring lines and I swam to board my boat in safe anchorage. With hot coffee brewing on the galley stove I heard the winds howl outside and driving rains lash the cabin roof. Jim had tried to make it back to the resort but got caught in high waves and a failing engine, they near capsized both having to swim ashore to safety losing the skiff. After the weather passed there were no other boats lying in that anchorage during the summer months, none that I have ever seen in the Bahamas with a seaplane tethered from their stern!

Chapter 31
Time to Get Out of the Water!

Every once in a while, I really enjoyed meeting special clients who stood out from my list of regulars. I found in all, guests who booked a day's flying over the Exuma Cays were exactly the type of personalities one would hope to meet, people from everyday walks of life, to those with extraordinary occupations. They would range from airline pilots, to folks who had never seen the open ocean before, from scholars and millionaires to the Hollywood celebrities and persons who left a mark in the history books. On rare occasions, I would hear an ominous silence compared to the usual expressions of glee or wonder at what passengers were seeing from above. Looking over my shoulder I would see someone asleep or reading a magazine or thumbing through the content of an iPhone, leaving me disappointed at how some are totally unfazed at what I was showing them. Why on earth did you ever leave home I would wonder? In contrast, we who lived here never tired of the incredible vistas laid out before us from either the bridge of my boat of cockpit of my seaplane; I always thanked my lucky stars I was privileged to live in this stunning place, let alone make a living from it.

One couple that caught my attention was a fairly elderly black American man accompanied by an equally aged white lady. Both were full of effervescence and thoroughly looking forward to flying in the seaplane for the day. I found them to be Colonel Charles McGee of the Tuskegee Airmen and Ethel Finley, one of the few WASP female pilots of World War II. In 1941, Floridian pilot Jackie Cochran and test pilot Nancy Harkness Love, separately submitted proposals to the US Army Air Force to use women pilots in non-combat missions ferrying aircraft from their factories to military bases freeing up the men needed in combat; the women would also be able to fly tow-planes for aerial targets and drones. Some 25,000 women applied but only 1074 were accepted as WASPs, Women's Air Force Service Pilots, all having prior flying experience and being fully licensed pilots. The first classes held were in Houston, Texas and composed of just thirty-eight women, all having over 200 hours experience. Twenty-three of them graduated in 1943 with their first fatality occurring in March of that year; thirty-eight would be lost in all and at the conclusion of the program 915 women would be on duty.

Charles E. McGee was born in Cleveland, Ohio December 7 1919, and enlisted in the US Army in 1942 becoming a member of the Tuskegee Airman having earned his wings in 1943; flying his first mission escorting B-24 Liberators and B-17 Flying Fortress bombers over Germany in his P-51B Mustang fighter. The following year on escort again over Czechoslovakia he had his first engagement of Luftwaffe fighters, downing his first enemy aircraft. Promoted to Captain he flew 137 combat missions returning to the States as an instructor with the Tuskegee Airmen until 1946 when the base was closed. Through the Korean War he returned to fighter duty again completing over 100 missions flying Lockheed F-80 and F-89 Scorpions as rank of Major. During the Vietnam War, he flew McDonald RF-4 photoreconnaissance completing another 172 missions. In his thirty year active service he flew more fighter missions, 409 in all, than any other Air Force aviator; as Colonel he holds several awards amongst which the Distinguished Flying Cross and, by President Bush, awarded along with all surviving Tuskegee Airmen, the Congressional Medal of Honour, the nation's highest award.

I was honoured to have Colonel McGee sit in my co-pilot's seat and watch him fly the Maule down the Exumas. He was thrilled to hold the controls again, both wonderful company while flying beautifully as he said, 'never having ditched an airplane it's fun to now land in the water!' After our day together in June of 2006, some weeks later I received a signed copy of his autobiography.

Flying a seaplane led to many fun acquaintances and very gratifying to hear visitors voicing an experience of high point in their lifetime, the best reward one could ever hope for. The souls I had found lost at sea always remembered. The ones I did not find linger with you for weeks haunting one's memory as to what more we could have done to save them. There were many heart related emergencies or sustained injuries that I had brought out of remote locations to Lisa's awaiting Air Ambulance Lear jets that I worked with based in South Florida always making a day's flying very meaningful. The Lear would be waiting at Rock Sound or Governor's Harbour depending on the winds that day that favoured an easy transfer from the seaplane to the waiting jet. One unusual call always stays in my mind, with the captain of a Holland America cruise liner anchored at Little San Salvador, an island the company had re-named 'Half Moon Cay' upon purchase, called me personally on my cell phone while on a holiday anchorage aboard my catamaran in Normans Cay. 'Guests on board have received a distress call from home that their daughter had been kidnapped, would I be able to come and pick them up for immediate transport home?' There was no way I could refuse that kind of request. The seaplane was tethered to a mooring I had made next to the shoreline in the South anchorage of Normans Pond, a short dinghy ride over from my sailboat. 'I can be there in about thirty minutes' I instructed. Suzanne would stay aboard monitoring the radios for my progress, the captain was very grateful at help being so close by and offered to have the guests ready for pickup in the lagoon of the island under the supervision of managers Wayne Scott and Kevin Cartwright. The Maule's engine came to life and with ample fuel on board for the short hop over to Little San Sal as we locally called the island, I was on the way in minutes for the 30-minute flight across the deep water.

The passengers were ready and waiting as I taxied up to the shallow beach in the lagoon. Both very relieved that a seaplane had been so available. I loaded one up front and one behind with little luggage that they had brought. I expressed how sorry I was that they had received such awful news, telling them they would soon be home to hopefully find a happy ending to this disturbing story that had interrupted their holiday. Within minutes we were airborne and heading west for Nassau, this flight with a tailwind would take about forty-five minutes and I would arrange for Charles to meet them at the Lake for transport to Nassau International Airport. Nothing was said all during the flight back.

I could see Ship Channel Cay just ahead and Normans Cay to the South where my boat lay at anchor. Suddenly, without warning, someone pushed a white-hot soldering iron into my body from behind on the lower left side of my back. A pain that I have never experienced even compared to the excruciating twinge of that old back injury. I gripped the control yoke desperately, knuckles turning instantly white under the pressure while sucking air as hard as I could through a clamped jaw trying not to let my passengers notice their pilot was in real distress; that's all they needed right now. A terrified cold sweat broke out knowing I had turned white with perspiration trickling down my face. This was a pain I had heard about, unmistakably a kidney stone. There was no question in my mind as wave after wave or torturous pain shot through my lower rear left side. The scorching soldering iron was being turned furiously having me turn my head to lean against the window hiding my expressions from the two passengers seated so close by. I had to keep flying no matter what state I would end up in as it sucked the very breath out of me with each wave of agony that truly frightened me to the core. Having this much agony on the ground was one thing but while flying an airplane with passengers something else. There was a short break from the attack on my body, enough to give chance to make a distress call to my boat where I briefly told of my plight requesting help in making phone calls to anyone we knew living near the Lake who could meet me in and take me to hospital: hopefully being able to land safely under these chronic conditions. A call came back with Suzanne's shaken voice again saying that a Dutch friend, Jan who owned a house on Cable Beach would be there. I called air traffic control very glad to hear Tony Dean on duty. I explained that I was in a spot of personal health trouble approaching with passengers that needed a priority landing. He guided me down clearing air traffic for my approach to the water recognising a change in my usual flippant demeanour when he was on duty. 'Sugar Pop cleared to land, radar service terminated and good luck Pablo!' Tony would end. As I edit this years later, I learn sadly we have lost Tony this week to a stroke at age sixty. Gingerly I reached down to pull the flap handle in slow motion trying hard not to give the game away about my poor condition. The stone was aggressively moving inside my body, with not crying out in relief near impossible. Determined to make this landing good enough the first time, there would be no going around, I approached over the trees skirting the Lake to land north-eastward, heading directly for my ramp. I could see Charles parked there for my passengers and my friend coming down the hill to meet me in. It was not a perfect landing by any means, a little crooked with a small bounce as the Maule settled on the water. Bumping with authority onto the wooden ramp my Dutch friend had the presence of mind to secure both bow cleats with their ropes and help the passengers off the plane being familiar with the doors. I eased out of the cockpit and the grateful couple made mention they had no cash or credit cards, just a US cheque. At that point I did not give much care accepting payment in any form to bid them farewell.

'Maybe you just pulled a muscle?' Jan inappropriately diagnosed. 'I wish,' came my weak reply with good manners disappearing. 'Just take me to the fucking hospital,' I barked in frustrated pain. The agony persisted, unable now to hold in the vomit as I leant out of my friend's car window displaying the urgency of my situation. There were no more questions or silly statements as we drove immediately to Doctors Hospital and into the emergency care of Dr Cates, brother of Chris who I had known all those years in the dive business. He administered a pain relief drug that seemed to only last minutes. 'Give the big-M,' I soon pleaded and vomited uncontrollably again onto the floor, with my daughter the nurse coming to see her father's distress. With morphine coursing into my body, oh how sweet this feeling was, awash with relief and able to smile about this ordeal especially hearing the 'clink' of the exiting stone as I peed into the toilet. Captain Lindy Wells had brought Suzanne back into Nassau where I recovered quickly. The clients who I had brought in sent messages back to Holland America saying the desperate call had been a hoax from the boyfriend of their daughter who was safe. Their cheque bounced, leaving us unpaid and trying to recoup funds from the cruise line.

About two weeks later I had a call for a guest pickup down in South Andros at Tiamo Resort in Lisbon Creek. Rotating off the Lake I turned onto my familiar course southwest bound for the thirty-six-minute flight. No sooner had I cleared the hill running by the airport road when that same debilitating agony shot through my lower back, on the other side this time. Knowing instantaneously what fate lay ahead I turned the seaplane and immediately landed, not even having time to call departure control. They must have wondered what happened with this blip on their screens that simply turned about face and disappeared off view? Back to the hospital, I managed to drive myself this time, where it took an overnight stay to rid myself of this scourge through an operation by a urinary specialist in Nassau. I awoke in the operating theatre with a very large Bahamian nurse holding my hand smiling while she whispered, 'Well, honey, there ain't no more secrets!' she smiled having helped explore my genitals with a probe! A calcium build-up had formed the stones up due to lack of fluid intake – affecting my Flight Medical having been reported, which would take five years to drop from my records. I carried a bottle of water with me from that day onward, never having to repeat that ordeal. Being the proverbial camel and not needing liquids during the course of a day was a qualification I do not recommend holding to anyone! My holistic aviation doctor had one word advise besides the water, 'magnesium' Paul, it will precipitate the calcium build-up inside your body.

There are always incidents in any commercial aviation business. Some we had to work through, with our own seaplanes failing mechanically more often somewhere way out of the way, sometimes we would hear of others we knew well and their misfortunes. One could hardly escape this career without witnessing first-hand crashes, breakages and fatalities. I had seen a really awful squall line approaching from the southeast one day demonstrating how really violent weather that can speed through the islands and cays at ferocious rates, displaying an ominous purple dark line ahead of it. Seeing these weather systems, without hesitation, I would turn and flee to land in the quiet of some protected water. I had been on charter in the Berry Islands and mere minutes away from calling approach into Nassau. The line of weather far too intimidating to continue I called my house to explain a decision to about turn. My mother answered, 'Thank God you are not coming its blowing about sixty here and awful!' I told her with a client on board I would run back to be with John Davis, the caretaker of Alder Cay. There was a houseboat we could stay on and secure the seaplane onto the beach in the lee of the wind. My client looked relieved after speaking with John on the marine of my predicament.

'Come on home Paul, I have plenty space with some fresh crawfish salad and ice-cold beer for dinner!'

On return to Nassau the following morning we learned this same system had caught one of the Piper Aztec pilots down in the Exumas, pulling the fully loaded aircraft out of the sky. Another aircraft from the same company, or maybe just a friend trying to help, set off toward the scene of the distressed plane falling to the same fate as the first victim. After the weather had dissipated a third aircraft ventured out to the rescue only to bring five or six souls back to Nassau in an Igloo cooler, being all that was left to recover. Running from weather was a practice I was well versed in and far from shy in implementing!

Weather took the life of our friendly Customs Officer from Chub Cay, Mr. Whylly, who, having being an aircraft magazine enthusiast all those years, finally took himself to flight school in Florida and on passing his license bought a single engine Cessna. As a low-time pilot flying somewhere in the Berry Islands maybe en route to Nassau, he fatally ploughed into poor weather. He did not survive the ensuing crash. The news hit us hard for he truly was a nice person to know when clearing customs formalities in Chub Cay.

In the winter months our business was encroached with large competing seaplanes from New York, fronted by a Bahamian during their off-season up north. During the winter freeze the Cessna Caravan would fly to the Bahamas and take up commercial operation in our islands. There was little we could do and with phones still ringing for us to fly we left well alone, resentful that a situation reversed would not have allowed a Bahamian operator to arrive and fly in the States! I had witnessed these American pilots loading their passengers soaked with saltwater into the aircraft without requiring they dry their feet. They themselves would climb into the cockpit with soaking wet clothing onto the plush leather upholstery and start the turbine without a thought as to what damage all that salt was doing. It wasn't their plane, so what the hell? No wonder that at the end one season, after taking months of income back to the States, their undercarriage failed to deploy on the last stop before reaching home base. Damage estimated somewhere around $250,000 ensuring no profit that season.

In February of 2006 guests staying at Sampson Cay watched the same New York Company Caravan having picked up passengers and back-taxied for a take-off into the wind toward the marina. Several spectators commented, 'that looks too short a distance?' as the aircraft turned and gained speed for lift-off. Unfortunately, their observations proved correct as the million-dollar seaplane clipped the apex of the hill behind the marina peeling the $400,000 floats away like a banana skin, sending the remains careening down the bushes on the other side of the cay. Everyone luckily escaped the wreckage unharmed but badly shaken.

At the end of the year, our long-time friend Charlie, over on the west side of Andros, had a freak accident in his single de Havilland Otter. Low water and clinging clay-type mud held the aircraft down as it tried in vain to gain enough speed for take-off in the wide opening near his fishing lodge. Pulling the plane airborne proved too much as it stalled into the ground cartwheeling into pieces and catching fire. Fortunately Charles escaped in time to avoid certain injury. Aviation can be a most unforgiving venture at times. A year earlier we lost another acquaintance living at Norman's Cay becoming the second person we knew there to perish.

While flying toward the Exumas I heard a familiar voice on the radio. It was another Steve who lived down in Normans Cay with his children and parents who visited and owned the old wooden house on the East side. 'Comin' up behind you Paul,' he warned. Knowing his twin engine Baron was very much faster I looked both sides to see where he was coming from. Suddenly the twin roared overhead of my cockpit to complete a barrel roll acrobatic manoeuvre right off my nose. Fearing severe wake turbulence from his two propellers at that short distance I swerved to the left and downward with my passengers asking nervously 'what was *that*?'

'Nice piece of flying Steve but shit that was *way* too close!' I ordered sternly into my microphone. 'Sorry 'bout that!' came the quick reply. 'Couldn't resist!' Steve was a talented pilot but once inside that Baron he could be a mischievous hotshot with the controls. He knew his airplane well, but pulling an acrobatic manoeuvre right over Nassau International did not fare well with controllers in the tower. Down at the cay we all watched him several times doing loops and rolls in his twin sometimes with a guest on board coming precariously close to the water. There was comment about 'one day he will get into trouble and only hope that his children would not be flying with him'. Sure enough that day arrived with news of a crash off the end of Normans Cay runway. I was passing sometime later and saw the wreckage lying broken in about twelve feet of water. Landing close by I anchored my seaplane within a few yards of the submerged Baron and swam over to see what may have happened. There was no one on board but struck with the seat belt lying unfastened and the windshield having broken away. The pilot had to have been ejected through the front end of the aircraft? All the instrument gauges were frozen to the second of impact leaving evidence of a very high-speed contact with the ocean. There were reports of smoke coming from one of his engines and maybe a failed attempted at returning to the airstrip? Steve's body was found a day later along the shoreline, a family in shock with the loss of their son. He had been alone in the cockpit, a very sad time for all of us who knew him.

In earlier years, an aircraft disaster that had struck close to home was the loss of our good friend Jerry Hughes. He had retired after a long career owning Diesel Power in Palmdale, central Nassau. A well-qualified mechanic in his own right, Jerry had maintained his own single engine Cessna 172 that he kept down in one of the old hangars at Normans Cay having moved to his house located on the west side of the island. That fateful day showed broken rules coming back to bite him? An airworthiness directive, called an 'A.D.' in our business, had notified all Cessna owners about a required fix of the pilot-seat mounting rails that secured the seat to the floor. We heard that Jerry performed his own fix, proving fatal and giving new meaning to the phrase 'Jerry-rigging'. Loading his aircraft at General Aviation one beautiful Bahama morning, ground crews saw him fill the light airplane with hazardous materials such as cans of paint, propane cylinders and many provisions needed for his house. Taking off behind him minutes later was Dale Harshbarger in his single engine Beechcraft; owner of 'Mac Duff's' bar and grill located just to the West side of the runway at Normans. As Jerry approached the runway it is theorised that his dogs, always knowing the sound of his plane, had maybe rushed down to meet him as they often did. We guessed that on short final to the strip his dogs possibly ran out too close for comfort leading him to suddenly abort his landing? Pulling back quickly on the yoke to avoid them, his seat may have come lose from its mount throwing him backward shoving all his unsecured heavy cargo aft as well? The centre of gravity dramatically shifting dangerously too far back had the aircraft instantaneously climb vertically, where the pilot would have no chance of regaining control having fallen backward himself. The plane stalled dramatically straight down into the pine trees midway down the runway exploding in a ball of fire leaving an ominous plume of black smoke rising above the island. Dale could see this appear in front of him, as did the staff on Highbourne Cay knowing instinctively something awful had just happened.

Plane crashes are always a dreaded part of life in our world of aviation. The first question strangers often asked unashamed, 'Have you ever crashed'? Some of us just destined without choice to join the select few that have been involved. All of us on the lake had some near misses at sometime in our careers. Flying that amount of hours in all types of scenarios were bound to lead us near trouble once in awhile. We handle them to the best of our ability and all of us are still here. On hearing about my incident, Colin my mentor, tutor and close friend, glad to hear I had not hurt anyone, filled me in to a statistic about pilots chances of involvement in accidents being 90% happening within the first 500 hours of flying experience in a new type of aircraft? I had only acquired 200 hours in the Bush Hawk. Experience after twenty years proved that breaking the rules more often led to a poor outcome during a mishap. Acts of God being one thing where a familiar Twin Beechcraft, that we all new as a freighter between Nassau and Florida, suddenly disappeared off the radar just west of Goulding Cay on the final approach to Runway 09. The seasoned pilot being quite elderly could have well suffered heart failure with his passenger friend not having enough knowledge to keep the aircraft flying? They disappeared into thousands of feet of ocean. A DC3 aircraft dating back to the 1940s also used for freight between Florida and the Bahamas, losing an engine after take off from Runway 14 desperately tried to bank quickly for a hasty return to the airfield. Losing an engine has a necessary procedure to be carried out quickly in order to raise the chances of survival; the aircraft should be immediately set up into straight and level flight, banking slightly toward the powered engine with power adjustment and feathering of the failed propeller. The surviving engine of a twin aircraft at high power will try to raise that wing dangerously high if not controlled immediately resulting in a deadly roll over stall. It is essential to push the nose forward in that first instant of alarm, an entirely unnatural act for some to keep the airplane flying allowing a recovery to then change course once control is regained. If the aircraft won't fly any more means tackling the best approach possible for putting the machine down under some semblance of control; hence the successful landing in the Hudson River that fateful January morning in New York. I found that from flying a floatplane all those years offered many more options seemed available in an emergency than the dedicated land plane pilots are used to. Time and again I have heard of that tunnel-vision view of 'must get back to the runway;' instead of choosing a long flat piece of water where one could bid the aircraft goodbye and walk away to fly another day. The DC3 stalled into the pine trees by Carmichael Road in a ball of fire killing the pilot.

There are good endings to poor situations and some quite awful. A small commuter operated by a local charter company was inbound to Nassau apparently running low on fuel, a situation that should not have happened with calculation being correct. Loss of power just shy of the airport had the pilots make a good command decision to use the shallow calm waters of the south side of New Providence for a landing zone. Everyone got wet but lived to tell the tale. In contrast, a light twin charter service departed Nassau heading to San Salvador with much sadder result. Rules of flight were cast aside leaving the overweight and overloaded airplane struggling off Runway 14 in a strong northeasterly wind. It was blowing so hard I could not fly a seaplane that day. This is the longest runway at the airport with a distance of 10,000 feet. The seasoned well-liked pilot chanced to use the length and power in the hope of gaining enough speed to rotate. Racing with the wind more from his rear proved fatal. He managed eventually to get airborne where Nigel watched the ensuing crash while driving along the Coral Harbour Road next to the runway. There could well have been an engine failure and being so very close to the airfield convinced the pilot think he could make a safe return? Mistakes came in milliseconds. The crippled aircraft was turned quickly with full power remaining on one side and to complete the catastrophe the landing gear was suddenly lowered adding to the imbalance. Our friend watched helplessly as the plane so out of control roll over on its back for the short fatal plunge into Lake Killarney, killing all on board. Had the pilot immediately pulled back power on the surviving engine with controls taking the aircraft to straight and level, that shallow flat lake in front of him offered miles of safe landing? The choice *was* there, but the reaction was wrong. Crashing an airplane is not a club one wants to ever attend but a split second decision to 'do it by the book' as close as possible, in more ways than not, drastically raises the chances of survival?

Those of us who flew countless hours of 'bush flying' did, whether here in the islands or outback of Alaska, if we were honest and admit, push the rules beyond the threshold many times; but if things went wrong our margin for survival still remained. A Maule's performance figures are very conservative at best. Those who have spent any considerable time in these machines know they can be so very forgiving with load restrictions placarded in the conservative range, where rule of thumb and wink of the eye suggest 'if you can fit everything inside and close the door, it will fly'! Yet break the rules and even a Maule can fall out of the sky, as one fully loaded M-7 did, departing out of the tiny airstrip on Fowl Cay in the

Exumas. Demonstrating a short take-off would have proved successful if only the pilot had not thrown in an immediate dramatic steep climb. The fabric airplane stalled back into the island with terrible injuries to those on board; all saved again by the quick response of the Exuma Park Warden and local island managers.

Those who climb aboard our aircraft as passengers are no different from pilots themselves who fly on board a commercial airliner; we are in full trust of those up front in control. We know that the person flying that machine has spent countless hours developing the needed skills to handle almost everything thrown at him or her; reckless breaking the rules of safety keep showing us unsatisfactory endings to most aviation disaster stories.

With my charter service in full swing through the early years of the new millennium I began to feel my company at the Lake property not as appreciated as in the early years. Too many people accessing the private property and a sudden rise in my rent sent a clear message, it was time to move, and clear indeed I must get out of the water! I planned the purchase of a new Maule, one last seaplane on amphibious floats. Now at last we would own a seaplane that could be stored in a hangar at the airport adding years to the life of this new aircraft. The fresh water lake had given twice the life span of those planes that sat 24-hours-a-day in the saltwater. An amphibian may triple the lifespan of this new investment? The downside would be operating from Nassau International Airport where traffic delays both in the air and on the ground would cut my turn around time. There would be fewer flights each day bringing income down with the expense of operation going up; amphibious floats brought whole new maintenance issues themselves. There would be monthly fees at the FBO, landing fees and paying for fresh water to wash down with each day. The pros outweighed the cons and I made the last phone call to Brent Maule at the factory. 'One more time Brent!' I exclaimed, 'this time we do it right,' as I referred to the construction and special order I would need for another seaplane that would spend its life soaked in saltwater every day. This model would be their M-7 mounted on Baumann Amphibious floats with the 260HP engine and same three-blade McCauley propeller, instrumentation would be as complex as the Found Aircraft, fetching a cost of $350,000; quite a hop from the first Maule cost back in 1989. It was the year 2006 and I was approaching 10,000 hours of flying experience, a long haul from that solo with 9 hours to my name!

Our world was ever-changing. We heard news of the French high-speed trains breaking a world record traveling at over 350 MPH, NASA's Messenger spacecraft makes a fly-by of Venus on its way to Mercury. Space exploration is reaching much further goals than that of merely landing on the moon. Achievements of the extraordinary barely receive mention while newscasters are more fixated with the scandal of characters like Anna Nicole Smith, a model–actress, who has established herself in the Bahamas to create more chatter intimately involving local politicians and celebrities. She buys a house not far away from us in Coral Harbour, dying from drug overdosing in Florida at the age of thirty-nine, with a funeral service at Sandyport in Nassau and buried not far from my well-loved first business partner of the 70s, Rudy Campbell, laid to rest in the cemetery near Lake Cunningham. The world is indeed a small place. There seemed no boundaries for speed and exploration yet conversely mankind still manages on a daily basis to fight wars and kill each other *en masse*, somewhere on this blue planet that spins in the darkness of the universe. We are a species of unique contradiction lauding the creativity of some human beings and trying to rid ourselves of others. A young single mother who scribbled a story outline on a paper napkin in a local coffee shop now has completed the final book in her Harry Potter series, selling over eleven million copies in the first 24 hours. She will become richer than the Queen of England. Young men are still blowing themselves up in suicide bombings, killing over 500 people in Iraq this August. In November when my last seaplane is ready for pickup at the factory we read about a tropical cyclone killing over 10,000 people in Bangladesh. Tornadoes earlier in the year ripped towns apart in America. The year-ends with news of former president of Pakistan, Benazir Bhutto, being assassinated and twenty others killed in a bomb blast, while in Kenya rioting erupts after a presidential election. I look back on the early years of this writing and see little difference in human behaviour through the decades where my earlier thoughts continue to be reinforced, seemingly on the whole as a race, still totally unable to all get along with each other.

I am getting tired. Plans of slowing down are entering my psyche; in one more year I will turn sixty. How the hell did that happen? There is more to achieve but its time to maybe look ahead and enjoy the fruits of all this labour? With the ordering of a new plane based it at the airport it seemed natural to search for a property closer to work. Living in Montagu Heights and commuting every day across the island seemed a daunting task with the impossible traffic situations that had developed on New Providence even while still riding a classic old Honda 700 Shadow motorcycle. There were plans for a new road system but that would take years. The catamaran was moored in the Exumas but if we could find a house with water access that could change things drastically. When things are supposed to happen they often do without warning. Old acquaintance Stafford Morrison had recently died. I had known him from early history in the days of diving with Underwater Tours. Stafford when stubble-bearded had a resemblance to Ernest Hemingway and was good friends with Gardner and crew working out of the Nassau Yacht Haven while living next door to Nassau Harbour Club as a chef. He later branched out to the world of 'salvage' with his classic old wooden hulled boat *The Flying Swan* docked along his seawall in Coral Harbour. Stafford, a proverbial pirate in nature, had strayed into the world of smuggling finally handing himself in to the American authorities after the net finally closed in. He spent seven years as a guest of the United States in detention before returning to live out his life in the house on Devonshire Drive. New Providence could be so small a world: Stafford's sister lived in the house next door to me in Montagu with Suzanne coming home one afternoon declaring she had found a house in Coral Harbour for sale. How strange this quiet island community had re-entered my life once again. 'You will need to use your imagination,' she said cautiously knowing well my first reaction on seeing the property. 'Dear God, it's a wreck!' I declared walking inside the old dilapidated home. Stafford's daughter, holding her young son, named after her father, agreeing, 'it will be quite a project!' Looking outside at the small swimming pool and 130 feet of canal frontage sold me immediately; I had enough vision to transform this property. Now all I needed was to sell Montagu to pay for a severe renovation that stood ahead. We came to a financial agreement deciding, that come what may, the move would happen as soon as possible. In the agreement, the house would be checked for termite and pests first. The inspection went well and during conversation the young man who carried this out made mention of 'having to move and did we know anywhere in the East part of New Providence was for sale?' The rest is history. He saw the Montagu property and wanted the landscaped lot behind along with it as a total package. Something the real estate agents all said would never happen. With ample capital in hand the renovation of Stafford's old house began and the catamaran was sailed back to Nassau to be berthed at her new home. Work was only ten minutes away and gone were the traffic nightmares of Nassau town. The only hint of the city was the charming glow of the lights at night seen miles away while listening to the call of nightjars as they swooped through the moonlit trees.

A few years earlier while at anchor in Normans Cay Pond we boarded another Gemini catamaran called *Perigee* owned by friends Doug and Debbie Craig. During a conversation over a rum and coke Doug mentioned his love of flying. Having helped us with part of the escort of our own new boat I threw out a challenge to him. 'Get your pilot's license, a seaplane rating and enough hours to come on my insurance and come fly for us!' He could not believe I was serious but without much hesitation he secured all the qualifications one after the other over in Florida during the following months and years. Time had arrived when I could use a break from flying. The house renovation was a full-time occupation even with the skilled help of my faithful 'Rasta Man' from Cat Island who I met through a contractor employed for some carpentry on our previous home, a rough looking soul with a heart of gold and the ever-present joint tucked in the corner of his mouth. The only man I knew who could get pulled over by the cops, have his little stash taken and then he run after their car asking for it back! And they gave it to him!

'The name is Glen Campbell, Mr. Harding, but I can't sing a lick!' he introduced himself with firm handshake and warm smile. During the next three years Glen and I worked together on everything from laying tile to asphalt shingles on the roof. The original 1950s wood we found still in incredible condition but the task at hand needed more help. Friends Jim, Jo and son Scott who started as clients on the old day trip to Rose Island some thirty years ago arrived from Michigan to stay and complete our new roof that we discovered inside to have been ingeniously strapped for hurricanes even in those early decades. I have found these relationships do not rely on how much one sees of each other but a connection that remains well in tact when apart. Some we meet months later, sometimes years, and it's as if we were together yesterday. We constructed floating docks and knocked down walls with dinners every night on the outside patio being the only habitable spot on the property. Friends such as these we could count on only one hand. Months later Suzanne and I escape northward to visit Jim and Joanne with a road trip to the Upper Peninsular of Michigan. Magnificent forests with hidden waterfalls line our route camping in a fifth-wheel each night and a walk along the shore of Lake Michigan. 'There's no way that amount of water can be all fresh!' I jested with my hosts who beckoned I taste it to confirm. We traverse the magnificent Mackinaw suspension bridge than spans the Straights of Mackinaw, spanning 27,372 feet making it the sixteenth longest suspension bridge in the western hemisphere, opened in 1957, a concept envisioned since the 1880s with decades of struggle to begin the construction project. On June 25 1998, exactly forty years since its dedication the bridge counted it's 100 millionth crossing! We arrive on the other side to Mackinaw Island where time seems to have stood still on an island and resort area, covering 3.8 square miles in land area located in Michigan on Lake Huron, at the eastern end of the Straits of Mackinaw, between the state's Upper and Lower Peninsulas. The island was home to an Odawa settlement before European exploration began in the seventeenth century. It served a strategic position as a centre on the commerce of the Great Lakes fur trade leading to the establishment of Fort Mackinaw on the island by the British during the American Revolutionary War and site of two battles during the War of 1812. In the late nineteenth century the island became a popular tourist attraction and has received extensive preservation to now be listed as a National Historic Landmark. The four of us rode the horse-drawn carriages for a tour of the island and dined on fabulous local food.

A gentleman from central Florida and his lady came flying with me one day through the Exuma Cays. We dined in Staniel Cay and enjoyed the famous 'seagull flight' back down the islands at about ten feet in altitude at 120 mph. Tracy and Rae were thrilled at the ride promising to return shortly for another seaplane experience. Before happening however I received a phone call that started fairly abruptly.

'Damn you, Paul, you just cost me half a million dollars!' Tracy said in mock stern voice. 'What the hell have I done now, Mr Forrest?' I asked in return jest. He explained quickly that he had so loved the seaplane adventure and having previously acquired a seaplane rating at Browns Seaplane Base decided to make addition to his fleet. A successful search found one of the few custom-built Maule turbine models with the Allison 420HP engine as power plant. There were only about five of them out there in use and some owned by film stars and country-western artists ssuch as Tim McGraw. This particular model had been modified by Ed Caesar, a world champion hang glider pilot from Van Nuys, California, the only pilot to ever win a film Oscar for a hang gliding documentary he produced. He died of a brain aneurysm on the ramp of Van Nuys airport about 3 weeks after Tracy closed the deal on the airplane, having promised to teach him to fly the plane. With his friendship of amphibious expert Harry Shannon, the Maule on Aerocet amphibious floats was collected from California. 'Now I need to know the tricks of how you fly floats in short spaces!' Tracy asked. He came back to the Bahamas to fly my last straight float seaplane; piloting and training with me sitting in the right seat, the very place I had learned earlier under the tutelage of Marcus Mitchell. There is something very special about being able to pass on the knowledge and skills we acquire over all those hours spent in these machines. I had Tracy descending a few feet above the bushes at Normans Cay, getting to the water as quickly as he could manage, easing the seaplane into ground effect and settling gently on the water with over half the pond left in front of us. He was now a Maule pilot and ready for handling his very powerful seaplane, one that could dramatically climb off a runway in mere feet heading almost vertically skyward; the air traffic controllers inside Nassau Tower could not believe the outrageous performance of this red and white seaplane!

The next time I saw Tracy would be from his kind invitation to meet in British Columbia as his guest at King Pacific Lodge for a weeks fishing and adventure. I relished being back to the Canadian province I loved for its dramatic mountains, stunning forests, inland lakes and the blowing orcas seen in the waterways that thread some of Canada's most beautiful landscapes. Meeting in Bella Bella we arrived in his Maule turbine to the famous floating hotel owned by the CEO of Sony in the wilds of the Canadian northwest to enjoy experiences only seen in an elaborate travel show. We fished offshore and flew into the outer landscapes of British

Columbia to land in opaque turquoise glacial lakes where the surface so perfectly mirror like it took some skill to land safely. A Bell Ranger helicopter arrived one morning to take us into the mountains landing on a pebble bank next to a flowing river. From here we would drift downstream fishing for salmon all day in an inflatable that was carried on board the chopper along with our guide. Experiences such as these were surreal, repeated again later with our long-standing friendship. Tracy surprised me with a call some months later with news of yet another arrival in his private hangar over at Sanford Regional Airport, his new Citation jet. 'I am coming to pick you up in South Carolina while you are there to hop you over to the factory in Georgia and pick up your new Maule!' What he would do for any excuse to fly!

I called Doug Craig, living in the panhandle of Florida, asking if he were interested in some float flying. Before we could start working for us he would meet us for a check-ride in the new Maule awaiting pickup at the factory. As we landed the Lear at the abandoned military base at Spence Field, Doug was at the factory door waiting for us. Bidding goodbye to Tracy and watching him roar skyward again we walked through the hangar doors to see a gleaming white Maule sitting on amphibious floats. 'You are going to let me fly your brand-new plane!' Doug beamed in delight. My fifth airplane; something I could not guessed or fathomed would happen when I drove out of those boarding school gates that day with my grandfather so many years ago. I just stood there for a minute or two relishing the moment and feel of accomplishment coming this far in my career. Jorge would have been proud of his grandson and my father certainly missed out. We slog away in our daily lives trying desperately to make ends meet and then, every once in a while, surprisingly able to grab opportunities as they speed past us reaping wonderful reward. There are many who choose not to take that leap. I believe this is a life of chance and have never been able to resist the risk of at least taking that leap, for most often it proved the best thing I could have done. Mediocrity has never been an option – where that came from in my genetics God only knows? Maybe that old codger who sat at the far end of that dismal room in Yorkshire who had once paddle-wheeled across the Atlantic Ocean? Here I am some forty years later, standing on that factory floor staring at my *fifth* new airplane, I could now see clearly where so much effort, over so long a span in time, all actually went.

Before arrival in Florida I had called Rich Hench, owner of Florida Seaplanes also located in the centre of the state. He was the Florida agent for Maule using them in his school and I needed some amphib practice and training. He could not assist me this go around but did share a name and number of a friend living on a lake who had a M-7 on amphibious floats. I arranged to stay at a hotel nearby and he arrived the following morning for me to have flight time in his aircraft. I started in the right seat but after one landing on the grass strip he used we changed seats. 'I can see the 10,000 hours in the way you fly, Paul,' he remarked. 'Be my guest and have some fun!'

Later I am sitting with Ray Maule in the co-pilot seat of my new plane. He gives simple instruction about flying the amphibious airplane off a short grass strip behind the factory. The seaplane springs to life sounding smooth and inside the cockpit that welcome 'new smell' with its impressive leather interior. The last registration C6WET jumps off its runway eager to fly; we practise familiar manoeuvres with landings in the lake by B.D's house where the swans graciously give way routinely to a seaplane splashing down.. Their webbed feet pushing clean white bodies through the water with such grace sending a minute silent bow wave out in front. Showing their true amphibious ability, they lower their feet to waddle onto the grassy shore and flap their wings, proudly shedding clear fresh water droplets from their feathers. Ray is getting us familiar with raising and lowering an undercarriage while choosing landings on water or the land runway. All those years of straight floats one never has that need of such discipline. There is a gear warning system now mounted within my instrument panel and if one is late in dropping the landing gear an annoying voice repetitively reminds us to 'select landing!' Failure to raise the wheels on a water landing will result in an instantaneous head-over-heels with a seaplane lying hopelessly upside down in the water and pilots having to swim out to survive. Marcus' pilot friend and mechanic who had helped me years earlier while staying in the Exumas, disconnected 'that voice' in his cockpit being annoyed with it constantly blaring warning and while landing at Bell Island one day distracted by something. In an instant the Cessna 206 was submerged with himself strapped in the seat upside down! I never disconnected the voice but did turn down its volume some so as not to perturb my passengers.

Douglas flew the Maule after I had been checked out. I stood by the landing strip watching him practise touchdowns on the grass and then in the lake nearby. Seeing my own aircraft flying was real reward and my friend flew it well with finesse not often found in low-time pilots. This last part of my career was going to be fun all over again. Lessons to be learned about maintenance came as quite the shock during the next few months. As soon as saltwater came into play the game changed drastically. I called my friend Harry Shannon who owned and operated Amphibians Plus on the airfield in Bartow, Florida telling him I had finally made the move to amphibious floats and based at Odyssey Aviation in the hangar on Nassau International Airport. He agreed to become my new maintenance facility and if need be would fly over to the islands and help out with anything major that required repair. Warm saltwater was incredibly mean to the different metals found within the construction of the light Baumann Floats I now owned. I had improved the maintenance and lifespan of the seaplane as it sat in the fresh water lake but now a new gauntlet had been thrown at my feet. Getting rid of the effects of salt from an aircraft that sat on dry land required a wash-down system of some magnitude. Still based also at Odyssey was friend Glen Wales, a Canadian who had flown Sandy MacTaggart, my client who owned Soldier Cay, around the world in a Grumman Goose; now flying and maintaining the Cessna Caravan for Little Pipe Cay in Exuma; Glen had been at the FBO while first known as The Jet Centre before being owned later by the Odyssey Aviation franchise helmed by Steve Kelly and his amazing crew. Glen had constructed the reverse osmosis fresh water system that supplied the FBO with its fresh water and gave him the ability to hose down the large amphibian he flew with 80 psi of near pure fresh water after each day's flying. He watched me at the end of my first flying days washing off my new seaplane with 'stinky water' as he aptly called it coming out of the city water supply with a pressure that a thumb hold could stop!

'You need to do all you can to keep the salt from winning Paul. Use my water and we can settle up each month for the gallons you use?' He kindly offered. The difference when I turned on his system was incredible. I could blast the airframe and undersides of the floats and landing gear sure to rid the harm of our salty environment? So pure was the water I did not have to labour further with a chamois leather to remove water spotting. Glen maintained an office within the hangar and a workshop to be coveted by any aircraft owner. The times he saved the day with 'just the right tool', uncountable times during my years based there. With his dry wit, vast knowledge and always a joke on hand we shared some good times and an ice-cold Coors after hours with our seaplanes both sharing the friendship with Harry over in Florida.

Within a short period of time Doug came motoring up the canal in Coral Harbour aboard his Gemini catamaran to dock along the same sea wall, his commercial flying career about to begin for the next year or so. I would fly with him for about a month so he could experience all the many various landing sites the seaplane business had us visit each week. He got know the island managers and meet everyone living through the islands that may be calling on him to fly. He invested in a scooter and daily we watched him putter up toward Odyssey about ten minutes away, sandwiches packed and a secret beer or two that he shared each evening with Michelle, our fuel truck driver at Odyssey, before leaving for home at the end of a long day on the ramp. Doug flew really well and cared for the Maule as if his own. He played with the swimming pigs down on Big Majors Spot and navigated the narrow creeks of Andros with skill. One day we had an actual emergency on board. Departing off the main runway in Nassau we were headed southeastward when in a split second an awful sound came from the engine with a noticeable loss of power. There was no hesitation between the two of us. He was pilot in command; being in the left seat took control of the situation with a gentle turn back toward the island. No sooner had we made the turn when the noise took another ominous rougher tone. Looking at the EGT gauge, measuring exhaust gas temperatures of all the cylinders we saw immediately how 'cold' two of the cylinders had now become. We had four cylinders left out of six giving us enough power if coaxed gently to get us safely back to the field. Further failure and there was a good choice of water landings both in the calm ocean or the lake neighbouring the airfield. Both of us had been flying this new plane too lean in the fuel mixture causing the cylinders to run too hot burning the valves of two needing immediate repair. Calling the Tower controllers, we expressed a 'slight' problem on board and needed to return to the field. Walton asked if we were declaring an emergency to which we replied 'Not yet!' The lesson was an expensive one not to go strictly by the manual rather be conservative at first and get used to how each engine behaves for a while. Trying to save expensive fuel can cost a load more in the long run; the lessons never stop when flying airplanes.

I felt relieved when chance arose to escape work with someone else at the helm. We experienced the wilds of Alaska with friend and neighbour Paul Baker coming face to face with 800-pound coastal brown bears mere feet away under the guidance of Captain Lee Robbins who had bought a small slice of paradise in Lisbon Creek, Andros, to fly-fish when the chance arose. Lee had been an infamous bush pilot in Alaska pioneering his own property in the wild to build his own home. Flying over remote regions of the state allowed him to observe from above where many of the bear populations congregated for the salmon feeding season. Sketching rough maps in flight he was able years later to revisit these magical places with his charter boat and give guests the experience of a lifetime! He had become a close friend and asked us to join in exploring for a fortnight the interior of Alaska and along the coast of Kodiak Island where he lived. Stepping ashore on the shallow river beds where ice cold waters raced seaward we walked quietly toward the huge bears while they searched the shallows for speeding salmon swimming upstream to lay their eggs.

'Stay very quiet and little movement,' Lee would direct us to a place on the riverbed where he knew the bears by name. 'Stay right here and Lydia will walk right past us!' Sure enough, the monstrous golden-coloured bear would saunter slowly down the waters edge and pass us within less than twenty feet away. The sheer size of the animal would capture our attention being so very close out in the wild without any form of protection. Lee carried a canister of pepper spray but never had to use it during his years of guidance. The great bears head lay forward with dark brown eyes looking our way then totally disregard our presence. Her fur was thick and golden in the sunlight. As each foot stepped silently forward the huge dark claws became clearly visible leaving a heavy imprint in the mud, she was magnificent.

He placed us in some spots on the river where bears in couples would approach and walk past again with just a hint of a glance in our direction. Darker animals with more stern expressions as they passed by closely. Chasing the racing silver and red bodies of salmon their huge claws would scoop the big fish out of the water in a shower if silver droplets. Holding the struggling fish in their paws they would tear it in half within seconds their mouths smeared in fresh blood. Photography was amazing, material found within the pages of *National Geographic*, with unique opportunities as a mother escorting three very small cubs suddenly made her way across the riverbed and came directly toward us.

'This changes things!' Lee warned in a quiet whisper taking us back several paces to the edge of a bush line giving enough space for the large female and babies to pass. The mother bear suddenly changed her course again coming more toward us. Slowly we crouched low remaining motionless as she approached closer, our backs now against the bush line, within feet away to sniff the air in measure of any possible intrusion by the huddled group of humans. With an exhaled grunt, she continued on leaving her three cubs behind her to follow obediently while each small body stared up at us wondering what these brightly coloured creatures were that starred back at them. We were in a location called 'Geographic' well describing the stunning Alaskan wilderness we experienced for ten days. Vast mountain ranges surrounded us showing the remaining grey ash of volcanic eruptions from years past amongst huge patches of power white snow that remained in the higher peaks. The green meadows flowed gently downward with clumps of emerald trees that gave shelter to the bears at night. The flat lands below were sheathed with acres of waving golden grass and ferns where the racing rivers all flowed into the sea, gurgling with the constant strong flow of glacial water that danced with sparkling flashes of sunlight. There were places we played at anchor with no human for hundreds of miles save one day a lone yachtsman coming alongside in his dinghy asking for some provisions as he had run out of food some days earlier. Warm fresh made brownies and vegetables were more than welcome.

Paul had made arrangement with a girlfriend he knew from Anchorage in years past to fly out and meet us for part of the adventure. Out in the wide-open spaces of Alaska we could hear the approaching seaplane chartered from Andrew Air in Kodiak. With wide sweeping turns the Cessna 206 made its graceful approach and flawless splashdown near our charter yacht *Single Star.* The seaplane came to a stop and the propeller stationary as we approached in the inflatable tender. The pilot climbed out of the cockpit to escort his passenger safely aboard our boat. He looked at me with a startled voice, 'Paul is that *you?!*' How small can this world be with a pilot I knew from the seaplane base in Florida now here on the other side of the continent in the middle of nowhere! 'Scooter I can't believe we meet out here of all places, small world my friend!' He had moved to this beautiful country some time ago now flying full time as an Alaskan bush pilot.

The bears on Kodiak Island were quite different and could stand over ten feet high. After arriving along the shoreline Lee promised that Kodiak bears would be within a few feet away the next morning. Sailing the waters of Alaska huge black streamlined bodies of orca whales would run alongside. Their tall dorsal fins slicing the dark ocean waters like a submarine periscope. On occasion the long dark impressive body of a surfacing fin whale could be seen off our bow. Loners for the most part they could reach ninety feet long and weigh up to a 130 tons. Sea lions huddled in a mass of brown silky bodies dove off the rocks as we passed close by and bald eagles screamed as they erupted from tree line along the rich shores. The scene was something from those spellbinding nature shows we had all watched on television as youngsters, an experience well recommended for those who love the wild outdoors. As promised the bears were there. We could dinghy slowly within feet of where yearlings played in the clear cold water as the huge mother stood guard cautiously a few feet away. Her hair was longer and silky in appearance with white tufted ears tuned to every sound. Some locations close to the Kodiak shoreline we passed huge clusters of sea otter communities all bobbing in unison on the surface of the frigid ocean. Many lay on their backs with shellfish stored in the fur of their exposed furry bellies, they would calmly chose one to crack and consume as we slid by, they almost seemed to wave! We walked the thick forest carefully, choosing a path through the thick bracken adorned trails to find open cleared spaces under fallen tree limbs where the big Kodiak bears had slept the night before. Kodiak is one amazing wildlife adventure never to be forgotten.

Paul had driven the 34-foot camper from Anchorage down to Homer, the halibut capital of Alaska. We found my original seaplane instructor from Browns Seaplane Base, Billy Smith, who lived here working for Alaska Airlines recommending the local restaurants to feast on the legendary Alaskan King Crab dripping in butter and ice-cold beer to chase it down. There is no taste that can compare! Memories were certainly made here as we recounted tales of flying in the bush. Pilots share a very special camaraderie no matter where in the world we would meet, from here in the wild northwest to the open Mara Plains in Kenya or the lakeside in central Florida, it was always a special connection.

C6-WET became probably the most photographed aircraft in the western hemisphere. That famous little blue and white seaplane kept showing up on YouTube, television advertisements, promotional posters for the Bahamas and in many magazines. Film crews for movies or product advertising such as Ralph Lauren and Victoria Secrets often chartered me for the day. Many times I did not have to fly on set, merely have the plane positioned for the director to shoot pictures. Film shoots were long in hours often beginning at dawn finishing at dusk and very tedious work that I charged for accordingly. Film crews notoriously inefficient with a dozen people doing the work just three of us could have achieved. The exposure however was useful and our company name became a household name within the islands and beyond. This new world of high speed internet displayed our story around the planet in milliseconds. It was a strange phenomenon all through my life in the Bahamas having my close friend Nigel with Powerboat Adventures sharing that close exposure to the film industry. From the early days as a scuba instructor finding myself with Lloyd Bridges for a few days over on Paradise Island while watching a film set starring Jean Simmons and Shirley Jones to saying hello one morning to Sidney Poitier as he rode Cabbage Beach on horseback; flying on an Out-Island picnic in a Bell Ranger helicopter with Rod Taylor and his friends and then being underwater every day for a week under the direction of Lamar Boren, while doubling for pop-singer Mickey Dolenz of the Monkeys. The most bizarre filming day came with a charter request from a couple of visitors staying in Nassau. 'We travel all over the world where I can film my wife posing in the most beautiful places,' I was informed. 'Do you have anywhere in the outer islands where the colours are astounding and we have complete privacy?' The last part got my attention knowing well a landing in Shroud Cay Cut would fit the request perfectly.

Flying over the northern Exuma Cays both passengers were excited at the location choices but touching down in Shroud Cay sealed the day for them. The iridescent swirling mass of turquoise water and creamy sand bars brought amazed comments as we dropped anchor along the peaceful private shores of the cay. With his wife lying outstretched on the floats the husband clicked away frame after frame. 'Would you mind if she takes off her top?' he asked politely. 'No, not at all, this is the right place to be!' I added making it out to be something quite blasé. His lady was petite and good photographic material. They shared other pictures taken in the Grand Canyon, draped over motorcycles in Arizona to name a few. 'Would you mind if she is completely naked, Paul?' came the next question after a few minutes posing. 'Be my guest,' I replied trying to be as nonchalant as possible, 'Oh Lord if *only* my school mates could see me now hard at work trying to make a living here!' Draped naked over the seaplane with the waters of Exuma all around this set of photographs were beautiful for any man to appreciate. 'Captain would you take a seat next to my lady, a picture with the captain and his seaplane would make a great shot!' 'Why certainly' any man would not hesitate! A couple weeks later a CD arrived in the post as promised. The photos were amazing. How could one go wrong with a sexy seaplane at anchor with some naked beauty sprawled upon her deck? While at work one day my wife confiscated the evidence never to be found, a small bone of contention between pilot and spouse. Damn, they would have added some welcome spice to this publication!

Flying seaplanes took the meaning of 'work' to a new level where each flight into the islands gave no clue who we would meet; an early morning pickup to a huge mega yacht at anchor laying on a calm ocean, miles from anywhere to collect Robert DeNiro's son, his father came out in the tender to bid him farewell dressed in disguise even where there was no other soul seen for miles. I said boldly, 'Good Morning Mr D!' as he came alongside the aircraft while floating near the yacht. Some of the famous passengers I have to say were delightful. Montel Williams, the American television host was very special soul and we chatted on both his flights into the Exumas, as was Michael Keaton flying with me to fly-fish at Kamalame Cay in Andros. It took David Copperfield a while to warm up. On arrival at the seaplane he insisted his girlfriend sit with him, his father up front, asking frequent flyer and estate agent George Damianos to fold up like a pretzel in the small rear compartment. He was exploring the possibility of purchasing a gorgeous private island belonging to John Melk, part owner of Waste Management and Blockbuster Video, to name a couple of his many conglomerates. I had flown John when he first arrived in the Bahamas who was a pilot in his own right taking him with the same estate agent to explore Musha Cay with it in mind to purchase. We landed on the calm west side of the island to taxi up to the beach where they could simply step ashore. We counted seventeen-palm trees in all. By the time he had purchased and built several houses, docks and maintenance facilities and then landscaped with hundreds of coconut palms, the investment stood near $54 million. The island now resembled something from the pages of *Country Life*. He had asked if I thought a fully restored de Havilland Beaver on floats would fare well in the islands? I mentioned he might want to keep it in fresh water at home and charter a plane here? David did buy the island and made further improvements adding it to the rental market at about $250,000 a day. In later years I would meet some of the guests who stayed on the island as I pulled up to the gorgeous beach. The musicians always loved seeing the Maule arrive. Bono in those all familiar sunglasses would stroll down the beach to say hello and in Harbour Island one day, while waiting for guests, I felt someone standing alongside turning, to see the familiar much shorter figure said simply, 'Nice plane, would love to have a go in her!'

'Good morning, Mick!' I replied. 'You're welcome to come for ride,' I offered with him declining gracefully as he had a breakfast to attend in a few minutes. Mick Jagger often came through the Bahamas and his yacht adorned with two helicopters perched on the top deck, always a recognised welcome visitor to our country. David Copperfield every now and again needed transporting back to the mainland to and from his illusion shows in Las Vegas where, as time went on, he spoke once in while remaining quieter in the co-pilot seat than most. That vivacious personality we watched while on stage or in front of a camera being one of his illusions off stage I reflected. Joe Lewis was fun to fly; British businessman, Chairman and majority stockholder of the Tavistock Group which owns some 200 companies in 15 countries, now living in Lyford cay, owner of Tottenham Hotspurs football club, various famous restaurants and golf clubs including the recent Albany complex on New Providence with Tiger Woods and Ernie Eles. An avid art collector with a collection estimated at a billion dollars including works by Picasso, Matisse and Lucian Freud. Joe joking with me in flight that he had build a new super yacht that was so big she could not anchor close enough to the beach in our shallow waters so needed something smaller?

Near the end of my flying career I did meet a personality who I had high regard for with his talent in the industry of film, his productions and direction always fun to watch. Receiving a charter one afternoon to another renowned mega-yacht in the Exuma Cays with guests arriving in Nassau needing to meet their hosts already at anchor. Circling the impressive boat, I recognised the hull as one that usually catered to the more high-end clientele. I offered the passengers a view of their yacht and also to let the crew know of our approach to landing. Guests already on board always waved up enthusiastically at their fellow guests method of arrival out in the wilds while I fizzed quickly at low altitude over their yacht. I would talk to them a few minutes from arrival on the marine radio and suggest a place to meet. This day we were near the outer cays west of Staniel Cay, about half way down the island chain. I could see the inflatable tender racing to a small beach on one of the scrub cays where off-loading would be straightforward. Making my approach I banked impressively to flatten the seaplane out on its final approach allowing it to sit gracefully onto the surface of the ocean. I could see someone sitting in the bow of the tender shooting a video camera of my landing and taxied directly up to where he sat. I pulled the mixture allowing the propeller to stop and exited the plane to secure the floats on the beach. The cameraman finished filming his sequence and lowered the camera to say hello.

'Well, I know that sequence will come out perfectly!' I exclaimed recognising the familiar face of Stephen Spielberg. 'Nice landing!' he replied coming down to meet his guests. 'Well, thank you,' I replied adding, 'Enjoy your time in the Exumas!' 'Oh we will, it's so gorgeous here,' as he bid farewell.

I was flying regularly for Johnny Depp's island, now managed by long-time friend Tara Roberts, partner C.J., friend Steve, along with her great crew of Bahamian lads. Tara had moved from management of Cistern Cay owned by French billionaire Bernard Arnault, CEO of the world's largest luxury goods company with an estimated worth exceeding $37 billion making him the richest man in France. He is the Chairman of Christian Dior S.A. and major holdings of names such as Louis Vuitton, Netflix, Carrefour, Celine, Princess Yachts and Hennessy to name a few. He is also a noted art collector including pieces by Picasso, Yves Klein, Henry Moore and Andy Warhol. I had the pleasure of flying him to his island in the early days, touching down in the waters just off Cistern Cay and bumping the seaplane onto his beach. Mr. Arnault shares my birthday of March 5th a year after me. Now located at Little Halls Pond Cay, the phone would often ring with a request for a pickup down at the island for Tara to complete a days provisioning in Nassau and return her that afternoon. We would call the staff inbound on the marine radio, so that on landing with a full load, C.J. or Steve would have the all-terrain vehicle ready parked on the white power sands. We would all form a line and unload the groceries in minutes. When Johnny was arriving for a visit I often would meet his G5 as it taxied into Odyssey Aviation. The FBO crew always pulled out all the stops for his arrival, standing inline to meet him. Exiting the jet, I always received the first hug in greeting while he then took time to say hello to each of the staff.

'Good to see you brother!' he would say. 'Welcome home,' was always the reply. Of all my famous customers, I would definitely say that Johnny Depp was the most cordial and real human being in that profession that I have met. Always a gentleman and always interested in our wellbeing and that of his staff on the island. Johnny had become very relaxed flying in the Maule. We chatted through headsets on all of his flights catching up with progress and plans for his island and the love of the Bahamas where he and his family could walk the nearby settlements without the hassle of mainland press hounding them at every opportunity. The day arrived when weather conditions were as pristine as we could ask for. His yacht lay off its mooring on the west side of Little Halls Pond Cay and he waved from the deck as I made approach to land. I asked if I might give him a flying lesson as promised after first meeting. 'Gorgeous out there today, JD!' He smiled and agreed if he could bring a guest along. I had never met his favourite director, Tim Burton or sister Chisti who acted as part of his management team. Passengers loaded we taxied the seaplane into a take off position parallel to his island. I explained a few fundamentals and we flew off the water for a pleasure ride around the neighbouring cays. The view was stunning and they enjoyed the experience hesitating only with any steep turns I initiated for dramatic effect.

'Damn! I love this little machine!' Johnny would exclaim as we touched the water so smoothly without feeling the landing.

There were times when we would receive an invitation aboard his yacht for dinner while passing through Nassau on which he frequently travelled with his New Zealand captain, Graeme, at the helm. Dining on board in the islands some days we found ourselves the only guests invited to join him that afternoon. The classic yacht had been painstakingly restored in Turkey. Her interior décor brought back to life as it originally had been off the drawing board. Red velvet wallpapers and classic lighting only out done by the immaculate wood bright work throughout the ship. The atmosphere was always relaxed and he treated us always graciously as close friends. The crew were all part of the family and cared for his well-being magnificently. In time, we were just that, family. Johnny would not use anyone else for flying as long as I was in the country and available. He felt comfortable to have his family and small children at the time seated on the Maule for the forty-minute flight to his island. Needing absolute privacy for boarding a boat taking him to his island one day he used our seawall to moor at. Walking through our Coral Harbour house just completed, complimenting us on a lovely home, always considerate.

Sitting on the aft deck of his boat, sipping a fine French red wine, he and Graeme had a fun conversation smoking large cigars as one afternoon wore on.

'If the cards had not dealt us this way of life, Graeme, what would you like to be doing? Johnny asked. 'You first Boss!' the New Zealander asked as they reclined on the cushions of the classic restored yacht. As Johnny was considering his reply I was headed southbound for a landing at Bell Island to pickup Tom and Judy who were managing the larger neighbouring island belonging to the Aga Khan IV who had invested recently in the Bahamas. I could see the familiar classic line of Johnny's yacht *Vajoliroja* from miles away, the prominent funnel and Jolly Roger ensign flying from the mainstay. The Pirate was aboard so I thought appropriate to come down low to the water enabling me to fizz past him at 100 mph to say hello.

'I would love to be *that* guy!' Johnny exclaimed as the blue and white seaplane wagged its wings in recognition. A later get-together had the star recount that story to me while we sat together on the same aft cushions recommending that I 'get writing all these amazing stories down in a book'. I could only smile at the thought of the world's leading movie star wishing he could be me if things were different!

The irony that all these film characters fame comes at considerable cost. My bank account may be quite the opposite, but my lifestyle is still one to be coveted by many I have spoken with over the years. I often considered how good a card I had been dealt and ever grateful for everything these beautiful islands had offered me. With two amazing careers as the expression goes, 'I got to bite the cherry twice!'

In all professions there would be days not considered at all glorious yet filled with emotion. The stories of yachtsmen that got swept away in the strong tides of Ship Channel Cay and my frantic search of a father taken away from his frantic family one night by an unnecessary accident, the hours spent aloft in vain and having the memory of his body never being found. The flight made into the Land and Sea Park to try and rescue another yachtsman trying to secure his anchor only to pass out underwater. I arrived to the awful stillness of a lifeless body lying in the evening light and having to fly the distraught wife back to the mainland for preparation of her husband's flight home in a casket. I reached over the seat while flying to hold the ladies hand as she wept quietly behind me. Once in a while there would be light in the memory of lives saved.

One morning a group of locals from Blackpoint, Exuma, heard rumour of a drug shipment ditched from a small plane in the northern cays. Being reputed scallywags, all racing in their fast-open skiffs to see if there was any free 'booty' floating for them to retrieve in the open ocean, somewhere near Ship Channel Cay and Highbourne Cay. Not paying attention and trying to elude the authorities that were out there also giving chase, one boat screamed over a protruding coral reef tearing the bottom out of their boat sending the two unsuspecting souls into the water. Strong flowing tidal waters again trying to claim lives by sweeping the two men westward with the incoming tide. They had no life jackets managing to hold onto a floating plastic fuel canister and a piece of Styrofoam from one of the damaged seats. For hours they were taken away from civilisation headed toward Andros and the deep body of water called 'The Tongue of the Ocean'. To cross this, drifting afloat, would be the greatest hazard with large sharks and commercial shipping that traversed here, their chances of survival minimal should they survive this far a journey remembering well that day I swam with the whale in the open ocean. I received a call from Ray Darville at the Bahamas National Trust headquarters on Waderick Wells Cay asking if airborne that afternoon could I fly a search pattern? He and several boats had scoured the ocean for miles without success. We discussed quickly where they had gone overboard and what the tides were doing that time of day. If they were intact drifting out there alone the prevailing winds would have tremendous influence over their course. From all these years of spending my life on the ocean I could just 'feel' where these men might be? I did have a flight that afternoon returning from taking Kevin and Audrey back to Soldier Cay in the Central Exumas where they managed the island for Sandy MacTaggart. Taking on full fuel before leaving Odyssey would give me time in the air to donate toward the search during the return journey. The only factor against my success was the time of day. It was late in the afternoon and already the sun was painting the once blue water a much darker opaque as it began to set. I started my search where they had entered the water knowing this from the wreckage of their skiff. Estimating that wind and tide were headed in the same direction that afternoon I came to the conclusion while floating it would be the wind that held the dominant influence. I followed the wind lines clearly seen from above all the time communicating with Ray in the Park Patrol boat headed out toward the banks in the direction of Andros. Air traffic controllers also had me on their radar screens knowing I was in a search pattern toward the West. Two or three times I made this sweep down the wind lines to no avail. The sun was dipping fast toward the horizon as a dark orange orb in the sky with precious time running out. I thought there might be time for one more turn and as the seaplane banked around the warm orange light of the setting sun caught something floating a hundred yards away on the surface. It was momentary and a small object appearing light in colour.

'Got something!' I exclaimed into the marine radio microphone. Ray acknowledged saying he could actually see me circling miles ahead of him now. Flying south of New Providence I flew toward the small floating object catching the reflective orange tinge of the setting sun soon to suddenly see an arm waving frantically, a lone body of a man clinging for dear life to a scrap of Styrofoam. I purposely swooped down low almost to the surface of the sea telling Ray excitedly 'I have him!' He was speeding toward the seaplane clearly visible ahead. I contacted ATC at the airport saying I had found a survivor but needed extra minutes out here for the rescue boat to see him, that I would need an instrument clearance to make the approach into Nassau after official sunset. The marine radio came to life within my headset with Ray exclaiming that he has the survivor safely in sight. I turned the Maule northward to head home with one more extremely low pass over the waving man. Low enough to see his smile.

Ray had picked him up successfully to learn in disappointment how his companion had lost strength earlier in the day, letting go of his floatation and sinking silently below the waves. The young man was a father of two children and was returned safely to his family at Blackpoint. In appreciation toward Ray and myself the whole town had come together having a plaque manufactured to express their gratitude with a request that we attend a town meeting to be presented with their gift. We were all men of the sea and when it came time, come what may, pulled together as one.

Recent weeks have seen events take turns that were beyond my imagination a short time ago. My creation of a self-sustaining little company business back in 1976 actually sold within the last hours of residing full time in the Bahamas. I had finally reached that critical point in one's life where reality was to be faced head on. No shirking; 'You are tired and not enjoying this "work thing" any more' I would muse quietly to myself. 'Your performance is not honed to perfection and in aviation, which is inherently unforgiving, that matters a whole lot!' I owed my valuable clientele the honesty of knowing 'when to say when' and walk away from commercial flying; a very bittersweet moment for any pilot to face. A recent third divorce, something I had vowed vehemently would never happen again, demanded that I work full-time at the highest possible amperage to financially recuperate in vain some of my losses. Gone were the beautiful house, the boat, the car and most of the personal savings. At sixty-four-years old it took a shit load of courage to walk away from all 'that stuff' which had been acquired so painfully slowly, taking huge amount of effort, dedication and a whole career to accrue. In hindsight, thank God I did. It took equal or more courage to walk away from an eighteen-year relationship where I had told myself 'you have made your bed this time and will lie on it come what may'. I had watched in dismay a wonderful partner finally succumb to her family nemesis and kill everything lovely we once shared. I had watched alcohol take hold of my own father and was glad to be rid of him at age twenty-one, never to set eyes or hear from him again. Damned shame it came back to haunt us yet again in marriage. Work had become God and both of us fell victim. With personal family tragedy coming in repeated fashion, poor Suzanne fell victim to the disease. Coupled with our poor handling of the workload, the relationship with everything good corroded away and overpowered everything we had aimed for. The price we would pay for peace and survival would be exorbitant. I did not possess the fortitude to remain miserable within my own household. I have witnessed couples that 'stick it out for better or worse' and remember so very clearly during my last ceremony, making light of the phrase, voicing clearly 'no more worse!' The magic was gone. Sleep had become scant for weeks, walking the empty rooms of my house at night desperately trying to solve the problem facing us both. She begged me to quit working but I could see we were beyond that to help? My adrenal glands kept me tuned for my work as an aviator. The effect of my decision on this lady was going to be devastating. She had lost all the men in her life tragically. Her father in a corporate plane crash, a brother on the highway changing a tyre and then her twenty-one-year-old son to suicide. Now she was going to lose a husband. All the counselling in the world at this point was fruitless. We were both worn to the core. If she were to leave this island there might be a chance to recuperate from the ravages of the bottle. The Titanic was going down and there was no way this captain was going with it.

A Skype call on my computer from a mutual friend four years prior was the proverbial straw that was to break the camel's back. One more time personal history repeating its uncanny self, where very strangely in the height of crisis, someone of significance arrived within the very hour of need. I have thought about this long and hard. This fateful turn has happened to me not once but three times in succession. It is not mine to question any more. Julia was an English psychologist with work taking her to New York where for some strange reason chose that day to make the call. Both our screens came alive. On hers she saw the wreckage of a friend, visibly shaking her. On mine I saw a radiance that stirred something in me I thought was gone forever. She knew in a heartbeat what the problem was and offered to fly down immediately offering help to her two island friends. I had charter flights all the next day after she arrived and came home six hours later only to be taken to one side and told there was irreparable damage, not privy to their conversation. In two days our friend left for England leaving one offer that saved my sanity. 'All you need to do is call me'. Life is simply way too short; I made that call and within short weeks I bailed on my marriage with an uncontested divorce before the Chief Justice coming surprisingly swift.

I tried to talk myself into believing that good hard work at full tilt for the next two years would help me recuperate financially? I had maintained some income property as part of the legal agreement and now as a bachelor in a new long-distance relationship I felt that I could rebuild the scant funds left in my accounts. Julia was packed and on her way Bahama bound, however this lovely lady was no pushover. Tough-love presided in our household. She had reached into that dark hole and pulled me out of the muck to the safety of love and understanding and the 'repair job' was going to be rough going at times. I had to learn the hard lessons of relationship bereavement. No matter what the outcome, feelings that presided at the time between the two parties, the actual mourning of loss takes a long time to play its part. It would not take weeks but months and more. My new partner had left her home country and business to be with a man she knew had the potential to be a good match with. It was something I became bound and determined to prove to her that she was dead right! Age was now against me and I had taken a bold step into the future feeling deep down this would be the right thing for all parties concerned?

I truly felt that life gives back reward sooner or later in some way or other. I had survived a plane crash without hurting a soul and experienced really unusual encounters with some creatures in the sea that I probably should not have been that close to. One final incident in the seaplane had me thankful for good fortune and the skill needed to pull off something catastrophic. The maintenance of amphibious floats is one constant battle, finding early on why other Bahamian pilots would not touch this side of the profession. They witnessed the amount of time it would take to simply wash the aircraft down each day, seeing so very often the seaplane tilted over to one side on a jack with Wilfred and me lying prostrate on the concrete ramp trying to struggle with some part that needed replacing. They saw nothing but continuous maintenance, let alone while manoeuvring the machine along a shoreline having to get personally soaked at times; having to swim the seaplane to safety or pull it away from being stranded on a falling tide or that sudden change in wind direction pushing my very expensive machine toward certain destruction in some form or other. Seaplanes for most aviators are too much aggravation and far too expensive to keep in the air. It was far less hassle to look after a twin-engine aircraft that one could simply close the door, turn the key and drive home for the evening?

Chapter 32
End Game

On September 21 2005, a Jet Blue Airbus A-320 airliner made an emergency landing at Los Angeles. After take-off from Burbank, California, the pilots realised a failure to retract the undercarriage. Flying over Long Beach Municipal airport, controllers could see the nose gear rotated ninety degrees to the left, the wheels facing sideways to the fuselage. A decision was taken to land at LAX offering the longer and wider runways with all the needed emergency equipment in place. The pilots flew the 140 passengers and six crew in figure eight formations for two hours to burn off fuel as the A-320 did not possess capability to dump fuel. Jet Blue passengers were able in this day and age, with their DirecTV satellite sets on board, to actually watch live feeds of themselves in flight as being reported on live shows from Los Angeles. Before the performed landing the video was however cut off. Keeping the Airbus on its main gear for as long as possible the nose wheels finally made contact with the runway, quickly destroying the rubber tyres and metal rims sending a shower of sparks under the fuselage. Keeping the nose off the runway for as long as the pilots could they did not use any reverse thrust we often hear after touchdown. Seven minutes later the passengers all disembarked safely.

This flight came vividly to mind after taking off to collect passengers one morning from Kamalame Cay in Staniard Creek, Andros. The day was a glorious Bahama blue early morning light with barely any breeze. I had requested avgas the night before and would pre-flight on arrival at Odyssey Aviation. Monique, Erika and Athena were on duty greeting me with their usual warm smiles while pressing the button to open the sliding doors onto the ramp lest my stride be interrupted. Michele, our trusty fuel truck driver, was standing on a step ladder adding the few gallons to the main tanks I needed for the short fifteen-minute flight over.

'Good morning, Pablo,' he always greeted me. 'Bonjour, Michele,' I always replied in his native Creole. The pre-flight ritual in the cool morning air performed on our airplanes was a welcome one, a way of starting the relationship with the machine that was to work hard alongside us during the hot day ahead. I walked around the aircraft in a set pattern just as we all had done back in flight school over twenty-three years earlier. There were many things to check and a simple glance at the all to familiar machine would tell very quickly if anything was out of place. Climbing up on the diagonal strut steps I could easily reach the oil stick cover on the cowling. Levels in their place I would secure the cover carefully lest it pop open in flight. Draining each fuel sump to make sure there was no water in the fuel. Undercarriages of the two pontoons were carefully inspected and sprayed with lubricant at the beginning and end of each working day, each wheel assembly given a small squeeze of fresh grease to ward off the possible entry of corrosive saltwater. Climbing aboard I would perform another check of the instruments and interior before turning on the master switches to hear the gyros spooling up. Turning the ignition key the faithful Lycoming engine sprang to life. The much-used fun acronym F.A.R.T.S. came into play as a final check: Flaps, Area Clear, Radios On, Rudders up for land takeoff and inflight, Transponder on, Seat-belts fastened.

Thaddeus, our head of line staff, suddenly appeared in front of the Maule ready to wave me forward when he saw me ready to taxi. Kwame was on duty in the tower. 'Good morning, Mr Harding' he would always acknowledge politely to the small blue and white seaplane as it left the Odyssey ramp. 'Need a back taxi this morning or straight out from Lima?' he asked knowing well my pattern of departures. 'Just me, so Lima will be good' I replied as a small covey of quail ran across the taxiway. The distance was short to the end of Runway 14, but being so fast off the concrete I would need less than half that distance for a safe departure. I squeezed the throttle and the Maule raced down the concrete to rotate quickly as she always did so very well. A quick right climbing turn westward and I reached the gear lever to retract the undercarriage, one white indicator light, two whites, three whites, and no fourth white. Damn. The right front wheel was not indicating the up position. From the pilot seat I had no direct visual on the nose wheel but those magic wing mirrors Harry Shannon had designed showed clearly the wheel hanging downward and appearing stuck in that position. Tower control switched me over to Departure Control and Lorenzo's familiar growly voice said,

'Good morning, Paul.' 'Morning Mr. Carroll, all is good?' I asked. 'Very well, thank you.' The joy of flying in this island community was being 'family'. It was friendly for the most part and very efficient with exception during an American holiday weekend. An air traffic nightmare unfolding as the days progressed with a serious backlog of private jets assembling at both FBO's located at Nassau International. Our system overflowed with Miami airspace clogged to maximum creating local traffic and radio delays where frustrations soon boiled from the airliners down to small seaplanes held in line. It became so bad I eventually gave up operating after 11 am on such a holiday period where a pilot could be stuck in a cue on the ramp watching engine temperatures soar toward red line. The only time I sorely missed operating off Lake Cunningham where I could come in and out at my own pace.

Out over the ocean on this day it was evident that recycling the landing gear showed a failure to the right nose wheel. I informed my air traffic controller and then called Margaret over at Kamalame on my iPhone, now linked to my Bose headset by Bluetooth technology. How times had changed from that old hand microphone and crackling speaker above our heads aboard the little Cessna 150 at Rockledge. I explained the dilemma and asked she get my clients to Fresh Creek out on an Aztec charter plane I knew based over there. 'Good Luck!' she exclaimed as we hung up. I recycled the undercarriage back down for the last time where green indicator lights showed three of the gear locked down but not that fourth nose wheel. Not being able to rely on that wheel being locked meant a possible collapse on touchdown. The Jet Blue landing was mine to replicate on a small scale. I declared an emergency to my controller who cleared the approach and departures for me to land on Runway 09. Using this runway meant that the main Runway 14 would not be impeded should I experience a gear failure. I was very grateful to be alone and not have to subject passengers to this stunt however it turned out. Walton had taken over duty in the tower, 'low-low' I had nicknamed him always thrilled at a close pass after take off west bound from runway 32.

I could see the fire engines racing into place at the far end of Runway 09 near the taxiway intersections. The other 'Pablo', Paul Pyfrom, was parked on the taxiway after landing his Caravan on Runway 14. He said quickly over the radio 'Good luck, Pablo,' watching my approach. The

Maule could be flown at such low airspeeds down the runway I played a similar card to what happened with the Airbus that September day. I was able to keep the main gear on the tarmac and nose wheels just above for quite some time as the speed bled away after touchdown. The noise of metal scraping concrete and smell of burning rubber told me instantly the wheel was being destroyed but it did not fall forward as expected. I came to a standstill seeing the fire engines race toward me. Turning off the main fuel selector and master switches I exited the seaplane as she stood limp over to one side of the runway having left a fifty-foot dark scar on the surface.

'Nicely done, captain!' the fire chief said enthusiastically as he came to greet me. I was astonished that the small nose wheel assembly had completely worn the wheel and rim away scaring the concrete with the stump of steel that remained in place without folding under the weight of the airplane. It had been a soft touchdown but the strength of that steel gear assembly something to marvel at. Wilfred arrived within minutes after I had called from the air. We failed to find a fix and asked Odyssey to send out their tow machine that could support the destroyed wheel and take me back to the hangar. It was a $3000 repair with Harry having to fly in from Florida carrying a replacement gear assembly while future flights I lost while out of service adding to the loss. Seaplanes: they could break your heart and pocketbook all too often, all too quickly.

The last Maule I owned gave little troubles for the amount of reliable service it provided. Strange mechanical incidents started occurring as the aircraft became about five years old, a ritual with each I owned. A sudden shaking in the air while outbound again to Andros provided me with a split decision of whether to perform a quick about turn or just keep going. My two passengers were so engrossed with sightseeing they never gave hint of feeling something strange. Flying half way over the Tongue of the Ocean 'home' always becomes the preferred choice but not always the one taken. I had the wind behind me now and my destination attainable within a shorter time it would have taken to return to base and besides, I had been paid in full for the charter so preferred not to let my clients down if kept safe? Landing at Kamalame I beached the seaplane in a quiet, private place where I could remove the cowling to investigate without my guests seeing their pretty transport suddenly in pieces. From top to bottom I could not find anything to give hint where the vibration was coming from. I called Wilfred who could not offer further clues and tried the Maule factory with little result. I decided to chance a flight locally to see how it performed knowing a landing site within seconds away, having practised this once before in the Exumas years ago. The sound stayed calm after take-off and I ventured eastward for home. About five miles out from the airport the shuddering began again. Easing the throttle helped find a happy medium where the seaplane stayed in flight although noticeably slower. Passing over the threshold of Runway 09, a relief and the landing a smooth ending. After washing down we asked the plane be towed into the hangar where Wilfred and I began the search again. From the engine, we moved forward to the propeller discovering on the removing the nose cone the rubber support boot inside, invisible from the outside, had shattered into pieces rattling around inside the metal nose housing. Will had never seen anything like it with the factory admitting it was the first they had ever experienced.

There are times when human error takes its toll creating a situation that stays in memory. Check, double check becomes the lesson when finishing a simple oil change. That last hose clamp holding the oil cooler hose on to the engine cowling needs to be tightened sufficiently. If slid into place and not screwed down immediately the slightest distraction can leave one to forget. Twice while in the air seeing the engine temperature gauge soaring toward red line. The clamp had slid out of position and vibration removed the cooling hose away from the air intake on the cowl. The first time I was heading toward the Exumas and able to turn around immediately where Lake Cunningham offered the first available runway and alternatively the airport itself. A familiar distinctive voice of Jason with ATC gave me immediate clearance to land and pulling into Odyssey I shut down as soon as reaching the ramp. The engine was hot but not over done. The second time traveling the East coast of Andros heading toward Tiamo Resort in the South. This incident leaving no choice but to land in the calm shallows where at anchor I could de-cowl the engine and reach inside to secure the cooler hose once more. I had become so proficient at removing the cumbersome cowling alone even while floating in the open water I still arrived on time for my passenger pickup. The following oil changes I smiled at Wilfred with screwdriver in hand, 'I know Mr. Harding, check, double check!'

The little seaplane was getting tired, as was her owner. My last aircraft now five years in continuous service meets a familiar milestone in seaplane behaviour; parts of her are simply wearing out. As much as aircraft owners pay for higher engine part tolerances there comes time to rebuild, or better replace! Time has arrived yet again where my faithful machine begins to let me down. This aircraft was in fine condition with lots of life left in her but annual inspection was soon approaching, one that could be more extensive than usual? At this point in my life I felt it appropriate to maybe call it a day with this career, taking into account UK Civil Aviation rules demanding the mandatory retirement from commercial flying at age sixty. I explored the dilemma with our Flight Standards Department who were very forgiving but sceptical about treading into precedents not yet granted in their administration. I explained in Canada and Alaska, as examples, it was commonplace to see commercial float pilots well in to their seventies and even eighties still operating, rules mandating that they pass a more rigorous flight medical and flight check ride. FSI found room for 'exemption' to the retirement mandate and granted my permission to continue flying with first class medicals and satisfactory flight checks from Faron when he had flights from Marsh Harbour to Nassau scheduled.

As exhilarating as taking flight is there comes a time when the joy of what it takes to remain aloft starts to wane. Commercial flying is work, and more so when it's your own business compounded brutally owning a water plane. Once in the air all is so very magical for anyone who flies, but behind the scenes just getting there consumes vast amounts of hours in preparation, maintenance, paperwork and most of all, expense. A series of solenoid problems, one with the starter motor and the other for the battery began plaguing me with failure. I lost two days of charters in a row having met my passengers, loaded them and luggage on board to hear that all to familiar 'click click' of a failed solenoid as I turned the ignition key. Having to then admit a mechanical failure, unload the disappointed clients and find them an alternative inconvenient means of travel by land plane. With my spirit bruised repeatedly, while leaning against the float one evening I admitted to my machine out loud 'We're done here, time to part company my friend'. I pat the cowling affectionately saying quietly 'thank you for all you have done' and gave the black propeller blade a final slide of the hand and walked into the terminal building without looking back; no one knowing that was my last commercial day's work and a quiet exit seemed fitting.

In recent times the romantic tale of island life and the changing attitudes of younger Bahamians come to show a disappointing ugly side. As a visiting psychologist, my new partner became involved with volunteer services amongst local ladies crisis groups. She gave talks to local women facing abuse at home, a plague that was spreading through our lovely country. The police force had a crisis representative who invited her to talk. She had a purpose being in our islands and was here to offer valuable input, but the deteriorating behaviour of Bahamian men in public towards attractive women walking downtown Bay Street became too demoralising for my English partner, unaccustomed to the Caribbean street demeanour, we as local Bahamians know for the most part to be harmless banter. Times were becoming very insecure and menacing in our island nation. Gang culture had infected some of our local youth. Drugs infested our society having started years ago. I knew of personal friends whose wives suffered the awful degradation of rape. Illegal weapons became relatively easy to acquire contributing the murder rate about tenth worst per capita on the planet, we have 149 killings in 2015! As a society that tended to brush things aside situations only seem to change drastically when crime touches us personally. Our police force not able to keep up?

Ladies we were acquainted with in the western district of New Providence were rightfully becoming afraid to be out in public, spurred with a robbery at gunpoint in broad daylight in the parking lot of City Market food store, some now hide within the confines of their homes; constant sexual innuendo from passing black men as my new partner walked down the street or riding her bicycle, a phenomena that if not edified about this cultures 'island behaviour', can prove threatening and unsavoury. I wrote a scathing letter of disgust to our prime minister, the Honourable Perry Christie with copy to the editor. Nothing happened, as per usual in this little country of ours, a discourteous silence; a recent referendum to our constitution in 2016 offering equal rights for women even failed, our country yet again proving how 'third world' we choose at times to remain. The two of us finally had enough. The town was clean and colourful with gorgeous blue skies and horse drawn carriages but its soul was dark, menacing and seemingly to date, irreparable. My girlfriend left the island feeling it was time to be 'home' and close to ageing parents and a daughter living not so far away. With my loss of home, boat and life as I always knew it along with divorce and now retirement I felt time to leave this once beautiful place. Long gone were the days where we could swim unafraid off the public beaches on New Providence, leaving cars and homes unlocked we now lived with theft and violence published almost daily. I weighed the situation well deciding that fate had handed me this card of change for a reason, there were blue skies and exciting places to explore elsewhere than this archipelago. With business responsibilities concluded and my lady back in England where she could breathe again, buying that British Airways ticket was an easy choice.

I began to pack all our belongings. It took weeks or sorting and dumping all that we tend to hoard and hang on to through the years. A local professional broker came to help me out. One cardboard box turned in to forty. My island apartment took on a surreal empty look. One last time corruption would leave a foul taste in my mouth. After leaving the island the broker kept the money I had paid in full only to leave all my belongings sitting in bond at the airport. The taste of this place was becoming increasingly bitter by the day, now having to pay twice to have my freight shipped. Criticism comes easily when one is unhappy. I was tired of mozzies singin' in my ear and sugar ants invading my kitchen and that damned rat living inside my bar-b-q on the patio; I take offense when someone spits in street or performs that awful island habit of honking snot through their nose. After all these years I still cannot fathom the Caribbean culture phenomena; so fortunate to live in such glorious surroundings, yet still littering their beautiful islands, especially our glorious beaches over a public holiday. I talk myself into believing my story here was over. Airplanes flown, airplanes crashed, airplanes sold; close encounters with some magnificent beasts of the deep and some outrageous adventures to remember; Johnny's words coming to light. It was simply time to put these stories on paper?

The days counted down with my partner not quite believing that her 'island boy' would actually make this leap of faith. Within a day of leaving a phone call from young Paul Aranah Jr, son on Paul Sr who founded Trans Island Airways years ago having worked alongside my father in the days of Bahamas Airways, asking me to meet him at his office in Old Fort Bay. 'I want to buy your company,' the twenty-four-year-old entrepreneur exclaimed! Here was an interesting turn of events putting the two sons, of slight age difference, together after all this time to form a binding business deal. At twenty-four I could hardly find my way out of a paper bag yet here was this tall good-looking lad giving an incredible presentation and accounting of his accomplishments and dreams. He was going to build the largest, most diverse charter service within the country. To complete the picture needed a seaplane operation added to his fleet and what better than the twenty-three-year established business called 'Safari Seaplanes'? It took about ten minutes to seal the deal, to see my legacy continue in capable hands now worth everything to me. Paul was to acquire the company shares, the Maule seaplane and all the spare parts inventory I possessed along with my client list and contacts over the years to keep the operation flowing as I had to the last days. The logistics of his success lay in my finding him a crew that could manage and fly the seaplane. I knew immediately who would fit this bill. Several months prior I had nearly entered negotiations with a commercial seaplane company out of Florida. They had the expertise but not the cash flow for purchase in their early years. Now was the time for a new partnership to be offered that would work for us all.

A charismatic ex-US Navy Top Gun fighter pilot, Captain Rob Ceravolo and his partner Captain Nick Veltre had started Tropic Ocean Airways some year's prior over in Florida. Both men had met in the same seaplane base I was familiar with in Winter Haven. Nick had been Rob's flight instructor with the two men becoming friends and business partners in a new venture they called Tropic Ocean Airways. Their company flourished and grew to five amphibious aircraft of Cessna 206s and Caravans; to join up with my company and offer them the Bahamas territory was an incredible chance for both businesses to thrive. The introduction to young Paul was a natural turn of events that I hoped would work like a charm. My clientele would be offered the same service once again with the choice of larger seaplanes if needed all year round, linking to Paul's jets and larger fleet of land planes. We all shook hands and concluded the paperwork with my attorney. Before leaving for the UK I was to make one last flight with three Pauls in the aircraft! Paul Aranah Sr and his son joined me at Odyssey Aviation and we taxied out of the ramp for a take-off on Runway 14. I rotate the Maule off the runway telling young Paul 'your aircraft'. As I had been told so many years ago fizzing down the coastline of Eleuthera in a Piper Arrow with my first instructor Colin, I now passed on the compliment 'he has the touch', seeming Paul Jr having flown the Maule for years. We flew southeastward to Normans Cay completing some air work while landing in the pond. I taught the young pilot how to follow the tree line as close as possible to shorten his landing zone as I had done with my friend Tracy. The Maule touched the water and came to a stop with yards. There was a lot of smiling on board that seaplane as both seasoned pilots saw what that little plane could do. Paul's father enjoying the splashdowns watching his son fly like an expert in the small runways I created for him to practise in. We parted company back at Odyssey for young Paul to leave for Austria and ferry another Lear jet across the Atlantic. I would leave for England and return in about a month for a two-week training session with Nick who would be chief pilot on the seaplanes.

There were no fears or regrets about walking away. I had thought parting company from this lovely seaplane, that had given me so many incredible hours of her time, would have been a tough experience. The realisation that my name and service would be carried on here made it feel as if there were no absolute goodbyes. I had learned not to be greedy about my years of service. To fly is a privilege we pilots work hard for. The success that I reaped over those twenty-three years had only come with the utmost dedication and damned hard work and huge expense. Those who coveted what I had achieved had no idea what it actually entailed to produce. Only those who create their own enterprise and make it that successful know full well what each of us who flies for a living, has to generate. We admire each other without envy. There is a time however to draw that line in all walks of life. In relationships that must end and a business that has run its course. It was time. To actually implement the move takes copious amounts of fortitude. I was to remain a small part of the operation as a director of my company but the helm taken by young men who had the right stuff. It was a very satisfying feeling to know that my seaplane service would still be seen cruising down the Exuma Cays providing people with service and thrills that had be talked about for over twenty years. The month went by in the UK quickly finding us both back on British Airways' Speedbird headed southwest bound to the Bahamas. We were Paul's guests staying on Cable Beach for ten days and my teaching started almost immediately. Nick and I spent some pleasurable hours together going through aircraft systems and all the parts I had in stores. We then went flying. Nick is a seasoned seaplane pilot and familiar with flying the Maule at Browns Seaplane Base only to have him realise it had been my old seaplane on straight floats that Jon Brown had purchased years ago! The amphibian he was now flying showed him some experiences not imagined by most pilots. I took him through the Exumas first to repeat what Paul Jr had done. Then came Andros.

The resort of Kamalame Cay owned and operated by Brian and Jennifer Hew and their son David was my lead client. Kamalame is situated in Staniard Creek a short hop from Nassau, and at best a mere dribble of water tucked in the mangroves of North Andros Island. Brian's landscaping business in South Florida had been destroyed in hurricane Andrew. With insurance he was able to recoup creating the miracle of Kamalame Cay out of a small, flat, near barren scrub cay situated in Staniard Creek, Andros. It truly was the proverbial phoenix rising out of the ashes of destruction; now a 5-star, lush landscaped world-class destination having become my leading client. The Maule was about the only seaplane that could operate safely within the confines of that short a space. I had seen Charlie navigate in there with his Cessna 185 but a Caravan that tried one day fell foul, hitting a dock piling. I took the helm first to show Nick what that Maule could do. A fairly steep turn over the resort and line up for that creek headed in to the wind. One needs a fairly full tide to pull this off safely with the water going from three feet to three inches in a nano-second. Down to the bushes of mangroves and over the last of the foliage we take off the power smoothly, letting the seaplane sit gently on the water one float at a time not feeling her touch the surface. Friction takes hold and the aircraft settles. Nick gives a yelp of approval. We land in only half the small narrow creek leaving bags of room to play with. I back-taxi the seaplane and show my co-pilot what the aircraft can do with a normal load of two passengers and light luggage. Way up in the far corner of the creek again we initiate the turn with water rudders. The prevailing wind takes hold, turning the seaplane windward like a weathervane as the rudders are raised and the throttle squeezed in smoothly. This is the only aircraft that you dare to take off with a closed creek in front of you bordered at the end with fifty-foot pine trees and telegraph cables running across your path and almost dry sandbar just ahead! You need an airplane that you trust implicitly for this manoeuvre. The Maule speeds across the calm creek waters and within seconds telling it's time to fly. Amazingly only half the space is taken up as we rocket skyward to pass the end zone at over 200 feet in altitude. Nick gives another yell of approval, 'Holy shit, Paul, this airplane can fly!' We land again to switch seats giving Nick landing and take off a try. He pulls it off effortlessly exclaiming, 'you can keep that Caravan flying, this is the only way to go!' With all those thousands of hours under my belt I am repeatedly awed at the performance and welcome the adrenalin rush of flying in that machine; the feeling of accomplishment at seeing others share the joy is immense. Some things never leave us, thank God.

My new partner has worked feverishly to make a small cosy flat home in the seaside town of Eastbourne, nicknamed the 'Sunshine Capital of England'; East Sussex boasts the reputation of being the mildest county in England. It would be a new start for us both. Peaceful days and thoughts of new adventures were only capped by our awakening to the cry of seagulls each morning. I was near my ocean. Old manuscripts were unpacked; faded pages with old typewriter print asked to be written with new computer word processors. No more thickening 'white-out' correction fluid and blowing on the paper to make it dry, now automatic spellcheck takes over while we make sure it is set to 'British English'. There are stories to be told, lots of stories. Some fiction has buzzed around in the brain since the 1970s but an autobiography gave immediate chance of a book project; the life of a twelve-year-old schoolboy, being taken from his birth country of England to live in one of the colonies over the other side of the Atlantic Ocean, recounting the awful experiences of an English boarding school and on to a new life creating careers from scratch others only dreamt of doing seems a good tale to tell? The English winter gives way to a welcome spring. The wettest winter on record with devastating flooding has spared our part of the coastline. In the southwest regions of the UK storms bombarded the coastlines about every three to four days with hurricane force winds, a pattern lasting for weeks. In the Western World, such storms would be considered as a Category One hurricane with all the hype of modern television, yet here it was 'just another gale'! Floodwaters swell the River Thames, ravaging the valleys it traversed. Small boats cruise the streets. Magnificent estates and common suburbia suffer as one. Fields became shallow oceans with cold wind streaked inhospitable waters, roads impassable with car roofs just visible below the surface, bordered each side with leafless cold branches. Villages are isolated, yet here in East Sussex welcome sunshine returns every two or three days. The air slowly becomes warmer and the budding flowers respond generously, a carpet of yellow daffodils border the roadsides to dance in unison to the gentle breezes falling from The Downs. A carpet of magnificent bluebells in the old village churchyard gives chance of nature photography to stir the creative juices as a fulfilling pastime. By early March, I entered my sixty-sixth year. Impossible, I muse, recalling the adage, 'time flies when you are having fun'. I sit on the shore in the lee of a cool breeze to feel the heat of the sun burning my skin again, England in March! I compete with a neighbour upstairs for who has the most tan, the Bahamians would not believe. I talk to my new adopted dad, aged ninety years. 'You're young yet!' he says. Near thirty years more yet to come? The thought of such frailty impeding my old frame seeps a feel of dread.

My lady friend sees the light in me fading. She comments on my appearance of sadness. 'You don't laugh like you used to. You are so quiet.' I am just drifting through my days I explain. 'I am not really sad in its literal sense; some empty spaces at the moment.' She replies, 'You're not the star any more in your seaplane, just one of us now'. Ouch, that had a sting to it. It's a strange practice where some take chance, maybe relish, bringing one down off a well-deserved pedestal that had taken a life's work to achieve. Besides *I* was not the star, rather that beautiful floatplane receiving all the attention. I had always given credit where credit due, life is hard and personal achievement certainly worthy of admiration. Maybe that's a part of it that feels so strange. That daily thrill is gone leaving an emptiness; the exhilaration of that view down the length of runway stretched out before me, the welcome flow of adrenalin as I climb toward the heavens with the ground falling underneath. I am prompted again to fly at Shoreham Airport having explored early after arrival finding aviation, as Colin had so accurately pointed out, too cost prohibitive and restrictive in the UK. Add the recent loss of all my belongings, having worked faithfully hard for, now suddenly vanished to some strange destination thanks to the airlines loss taking over a year to retrieve it all, from Panama of all places! My surroundings are so foreign adding time for bereavement to fade. Retirement I am learning is a whole bereavement in itself. It is a loss even after letting go of a full career voluntarily with welcome timing and good circumstance. The new days here in England, mostly indoors, are hopelessly insufficient after having a career outdoors full of adventure, colour, mischief and excitement. As hard as one works, eventually worn into an emotional frazzle, stepping away gives way to an emptiness. Knowing one made the decision in good time and had 'a good run' at life with all its rewards, slowly, ever so slowly leaves this pilot feeling accomplished enough to move forward to different days ahead.

I love walking the shoreline and exploring the cliffs above Beachy Head, we enjoy the coffee shops and excursions to London on the train. I have always loved trains, my last memory a luxury trip through the Canadian Rockies. London is a magical city as were New York, San Francisco and Vancouver. Sitting aloft in the old theatres watching a Shakespearean play, riveting one's attention and appreciation of the arts. I am introduced to the London Opera House never having the appreciation of listening to it, yet watching a live performance added the necessary dimension to be utterly absorbed. Eating outside afterward in Covent Garden is magical; we meet Colin there one day while he is close by. The English towns however, even after a lifetime away appear foreign as they pass in the train; unattractive redbrick, everywhere faded with soot. I could never accept the thought of having to live in such places. Rows of countless houses all cloned in exactness appearing utterly drab in Edwardian repetition; depressing to this eye trained in blue and turquoise. The people are so different, accents so strange, the Queen's English noticeably absent as I walk uncomfortably through crowds of milky heavy white bodies milling Terminus Road in Eastbourne. We talk in the afternoon light about our feelings. A common experience shared with similar circumstance of both losing our homes. There is something so very grounding about owning your own home, bought and paid for. A man's home really is his castle. The cliché so apropos when house suddenly gone, a prevalent feeling of loss lingers like a nagging toothache, numbing one's senses one day then fading the next. It comes in waves, bringing an involuntary trickle of wetness down my cheek. We make mention of personal failure. Failing is to learn and life is about change. To travel this far in our journey, starting with so little and achieving so much feels perverse to end with a huge chunk of it quite simply gone. Our loss creates a space needing to be filled, but paradoxically brings slight relief having shed so much responsibility. Having a partner certainly alleviates the difficulty of healing alone. I feel an impatient need to fill the gaps and be rid of this retched ache once and for all.

'You are an Englishman, you are home,' my friend insists leaving me unconvinced. I may have been born here, but life as an 'island boy' almost all of my years leaves an indelible impression I never wish to fade away. I am a Bahamian in my heart and proud of it, as I am watching the Union Jack flying true in the breeze. I bathe in the luxury of having two countries to love. Sure enough, as the days flow into weeks and the season finally changes so does the weight start to lift off my shoulders. Nightfall brings an ease of mind now. Sleep comes easily with healing taking time and patience; one of my downfalls that needed to be honed is at last becoming quite refined. Letting go of a life well loved takes ages I learn, if ever perhaps? To savour it as one does a really fine wine or exquisite piece of music helps me realise how very fortunate I was even being a small part of that journey. On reflection and re-reading this publication I can freely admit good fortune; the pursuit of this unusual way of life paid handsomely, often at a high price but always with invaluable lessons.

The only real loss felt now and again as a slight twinge from within, not being aloft and the colours before me each day both on the ground and way up at altitude. Those of us who have shared the experience of being 'up there' while civilisation remains below in the chaos of traffic or bustling together in busy streets is a privilege pilots share when airborne. To float past those magical clouds, magnificent towers of white cotton wool while holding that beautiful machine in my hands navigating their canyons in sweet symphony of motion; I feel the lovely curse of creating a profession that cannot be replaced. Pilots who have to call it quits face a special dilemma as we walk each day with eyes cast 'up there' envious of that soaring gull or the airliners contrail. Flight stays a welcome guest while watching the many birds that frequent the feeders in our garden, short take-off and landing performed by sparrows. Their young perch precariously among the small branches, feathers trembling while waiting for food; noisy starlings behave as rambunctious teenagers crashing into the feeders without a shadow of grace, their landings need practise. They scatter in an instant as the heavy woodpigeon approaches on short final bending the branch precariously under his weight on touchdown. River estuaries display water birds performing my familiar approach to the surface. That graceful descending turn into left base; staying in ground effect they glide silently for yards while bleeding off airspeed to finally touch down into wind with a gracious splash. I am surrounded by magnificent English gardens with their rich colours of roses and lupins; artistic history is my neighbour with Virginia Woolf's house just down to road from us. Fifteen minutes away I photograph Charleston Estate through all the seasons, home of the Bloomsbury group who rebelled against their Victorian lifestyle; still my eye craves the hibiscus and bougainvillea. I allow this new place to feel like home from here on the ground that is so gentle in its form. Sussex is so very female. Her smooth curves apparent wherever we gaze; in my youth, I failed to notice this landscape displaying such perfect contours. Someone has let their pastel crayon drift gently in waves across the page; I am trading blues for greens. The curving perpetual motion of waves having given way to stationary rolling hills sculptured with gentle lines. This soft countryside may yet be my salvation spying the colourful wings of paragliders drifting gracefully off the peaks of rounded hills. They soar in the rising air, silently floating by me like drifting condors as I sit perched on the magnificent cliff above Beachy Head Lighthouse. This England is far more attractive than that of my schooldays.

Living by the coast the sky is still big and the ocean, even opaque; thank God the ocean, close by. The blue above is still beautiful and the gulls cry sounding the same. I feel a new confidence in being able to adapt, learning to be satisfied in making life be 'good enough'. This fish out of water in these early days has me quiet and reflective. Cool moist air has replaced warm ocean waters flowing over this ageing skin. It is a relief not to profusely sweat, with fabric clinging to one's skin while that trickle of water runs down the small of your back. I am not an out-going soul when off my aviation stage. This adaption may come slowly. 'Patience,' I whisper and accept the things I cannot change or maybe simply change the things I cannot accept. There are adventures planned to include a flight with the Aeroshell Acrobatic Team in Oshkosh, Wisconsin, and meet that remarkable Captain of the infamous USAir flight ditching into the Hudson River that cold January morning. I was flying in a formation of six T-6's, probably one of the most engineered aircraft ever manufactured. My pilot was a Delta commercial airline pilot who joined the Aeroshell Team as a side-line. He told me there had been over 17,000 of them produced by North American Aviation and so easily maintained not becoming obsolete for years after production, fondly quoted as being the '5000 lb. tail dragger with a mean streak!' We departed Oshkosh runway in formation and immediately went into a series of loops, no longer experiencing the inner-ear balance problems from back in flight school days flying a Cessna 150. Within minutes he called through our intercom saying, 'Your airplane!' To fly her was a dream and very exhilarating being surrounded by the team we were part of. Only Tracy could have arranged such a gift?

Africa comes calling with an offer to stand again on the Mara Plain. An adventure flying co-pilot in a new Citation jet with our friends Tracy and Rae, taking us first through Prague where history oozes from every wall. Grand stone-carvings adorn the most famous of seventeen bridges that cross the River Vltava; the Charles Bridge crosses the longest river in the Czech Republic, witnessing this fabulous city develop over the last 1000 years. A city one has to revisit in order to absorb a mere taste of its character. We walk the ancient streets feeling the presence of princes and kings. Imaginations leap back to the year 929AD where Prince Wenceslas was assassinated and buried in St. Vitus' Rotunda, the church he founded now where one gazes upon the stunning St. Vitus Cathedral. He became Bohemia's most beloved patron saint, giving us 'Good King Wenceslas' the Christmas carol. There are streets where one can so easily be haunted by the sound of Nazi Germany pounding through the occupied city, yet in an instant be overpowered by the fabulous aromas of Czech cuisine spilling from the hundreds of outdoor cafes.

We rotate off the runway in Tracy's Citation heading southward to approach hours later over the magnificent sprawling desert of Jordan landing in Aqaba. Flight following from air traffic controllers on this leg of the journey proved a challenge with both pilots in the Citation struggling to understand the local dialects as we are handed off from one service to the next, eventually instructed at 39000 feet to squawk '1200', an unheard-of practice, using the visual flight rule code at that high an altitude! The desert lay out in panorama through the Citation cockpit as we make a final approach talking at last to Aqaba approach. Here the infamous battle of

July 6 1917 was fought for the Jordanian port. The attacking forces of the Arab Revolt led by Auda ibu Tayi advised by T. E. Lawrence victorious over the Turkish defenders. I will hike through the ancient civilisation of Petra and walk in the shadow of Lawrence of Arabia, standing in the very cave he used as lodging during the campaign. At our hotel, my personal guide for the drive to Petra greets me the following morning. Petra is a famous archaeological site in Jordan's southwestern desert. Dating around 300BC it was the capital of the Nabatean Kingdom. As we approach the hidden city I am shown from the high cliffs above how well camouflaged the ancient city was from intruders; accessed only via a narrow canyon called Al Siq containing tombs and temples carved into pink sandstone cliffs, earning its nickname, the 'Rose City.' Perhaps its most famous structure is Al Khazneh, a temple with an ornate, Greek-style façade that I hike the six kilometres to stand in front of, and absorb the monumental task of construction in those early years from 312BC. I ask how it was possible to keep each structure so perfect alignment and parallel in their columns? Engineers would stand on high ground opposite each construction site and with a method of signals guide the masons to perfect their angles of stonework. Tombs and dwellings carved into the rock before the creation of iron tooling. Petra referred, as the 'centre of civilisation' was the crossroads of the Middle East where main trade routes gave its success from the most precious of commodities in that region, water. Excavations have demonstrated that it was the ability of the Nabataeans to control the water supply that led to the rise of the desert city, creating an artificial oasis. An area often visited by flash floods the archaeological evidence demonstrates the Nabataeans controlled these floods by the use of dams, cisterns and water conduits. These innovations stored water for prolonged periods of drought, enabling the city to prosper as huge camel caravans traversed this crossroad city numbering up to 10,000 animals at a time, their owners required to pay for water, shelter and goods needed for their on going journeys. The surrounding hills gave way to what once was the main avenue bordered each side with amphitheatres and the ancient equivalent of a modern financial district. I explore the tombs and caves all carved to linear perfection with stone hand tools. How could anyone cut so much rock absolutely straight with ceilings that high? I record the mesmerising structures on film to find a young Jordanian lad offering a camel for hire; riding such an animal for the first time within the crumbling walls destroyed by an earthquake in AD363 taking most of the buildings and crippling the vital water supply structures, a city to be finally abandoned after the next disastrous earthquake in AD551. Riding camel-back through the ancient city felt as if stepping back in time bringing vision of Peter O'Toole playing Lawrence, an experience quadrupled, never to be forgotten by this Bahamian seaplane pilot!

It is so very welcome to touch the soil of Kenya again. Tracy kindly allowed me to perform my first landing of the Citation into Nairobi Airport. After touchdown and custom's formalities, we transferred our belongings to awaiting vehicles for the overnight stay in the New Stanley Hotel, history repeating itself for me being here where Alastair and I swam in the pool after a safari in the African bush near forty years prior. The following morning after breakfast we climb aboard a waiting Cessna Caravan piloted by an acquaintance of Tracy's for a breath taking flight over the East African escarpment and into the Mara Plains. Losing altitude and approaching the level ground of a bush airstrip we see herds of scattering wildebeest, gazelle and zebra. The terminal building a lone small acacia tree where our two guides from Micato Safaris await our arrival. I step down and place my flat palm ceremoniously on the Mara grass; Africa draws you back forever, lodged within the crevasses of one's soul, requiring me to now touch the land once more whispering quietly, 'I have returned'. They drive us through the grasslands and scattered bush stopping now and again for us to absorb scenes of the Mara. Herds of grazing elephant, prides of lion and herd after glorious herd of African animals. The Land Rover pulls up to a thicket of acacia trees where a single rope and wooden bridge cross the small stream below. Huge crocodiles lie basking motionless on the mud bank below in the Kenyan sunshine. Our hosts graciously give a tour of the campsite. Tracy's luxurious tent is pitched alongside the small river below where several adult hippopotamus lie quietly in the cooler shallows. I am reminded of their enormous size and the huge two and a half ton male that submerged below our small boat on Lake Naivasha some forty years earlier. Accommodations are surreal. This is a style out of the *Rich and Famous* TV shows well beyond our dreams. Huge canvas tents fully furnished with king-size beds, all the trimmings and a large brass bathtub where we soaked in hot water watching the zebra graze just feet away! Nightfall brings the familiar sounds of an African bush not heard since leaving school while Maasai herdsman guard our tents from encroaching lion that wander into camp during the darkness to the sound of chattering hyena and braying zebra. We awaken in our tents to the call of guinea fowl and watch vultures circle the nights kill under a lone acacia tree balancing on the far hill while sipping fresh steaming coffee on the veranda.

The first safari of the day we come upon a pride of young adult lion and a pair of cheetah within mere feet from our vehicle. Magnificent elephants herds stride by without fear while crocodiles slide with eerie stealth into the muddy rivers well away from the wallowing hippos while gracious giraffe graze the canopy of thorny acacia trees. We find a pair of elephants in the afternoon where one carries the broken shaft of a poacher's spear embedded just behind its massive ear. Our guides call in to notify the rangers who organise a vet to come and save the gorgeous animal. The following day starts in the early darkness with a ride through the pitch-black bush toward an awaiting ride in a hot air balloon. As the first light of day etches the dawn sky the sound of roaring flame from propane canisters cause the massive balloon to slowly rise off the ground. When fully inflated while tethered to the ground we load into the passenger basket. The manhandled ropes are released allowing our pilot to guide the monstrous craft aloft to begin its graceful drift over the Kenyan plains below while a dark red orb of the rising sun casts our giant shadow over the grasslands causing animals below to scatter. After an hour, we begin the descent toward the tall grasses that wave in a light morning wind. The approach is cleverly piloted with our heavy basket bumping the rough ground below, finally coming to a complete stop where the fabric above us begins its collapse into the grass alongside. A full team of men await our landing and take control of the grounded balloon while we exit to find a long table displaying an amazing array of food and beverage for a breakfast on the open savannah. This safari far differing my first experience of sleeping in the open on the ground in the African bush! Another morning we hear our guide's radio come alive with news of a female giraffe having given birth that night, now facing a dilemma of survival on the Mara. We arrive at the scene with mother and baby its umbilical cord shining bright red in the morning sunlight huddled tightly between its mother's forelegs. Surrounding them a pride of eight young mature lions on a training exercise to kill. Nature's way allows us to witness the dance of death for over an hour where the mother giraffe displays absolute courage in the defence of her youngster with frontal kicks that if making their target would easily shatter a lions' skull. The pride fails this day, setting the pair free to run safe; the news from our guides the following morning however, not so good for the baby giraffe.

We leave Kenya with reluctance after an amazing experience; spotting an adult leopard in the late evening light of our last day on the Mara, followed with a huge campfire dinner laid out for us near the campsite under the stars. Our Maasai protectors standing elegantly in traditional dress reflecting their colours in the flickering firelight. We fly a relatively short hop in our private jet down to Tanzania, history repeating itself with me crossing the boarder at Arusha all those years ago after finishing school. This visit would be a far cry from back then finding us in the New Livingstone Hotel complete with grazing zebra on the hotel lawns by the swimming pool where mists of Victoria Falls visible some distance downstream. 'Keep your patio doors closed,' we are warned by the front desk staff, 'the monkeys will enter to steal your belongings!'

Victoria Falls are beyond description for the most part. We walk through the forest along narrow pathways toward the thunderous roar of falling water: donning raincoats to keep us dry while amazingly close to the boundaries of the cascading waters that cover us with a fine cool mist, reflecting rainbows against the thundering mass known locally as 'the smoke that thunders'; rightfully one of the seven wonders of the world lie exactly halfway down the Zambezi River taking its 2700-mile journey from source to the sea. Discovered by Dr. David Livingston in 1855 the sensitive Scotsman almost forgot to make record of his description, being overwhelmed at the sight from his canoe and named the falls after his Queen in England. The good missionary's heart is buried in Africa. Our second day there Tracy's generosity once again treats us to a heart stopping experience above the falls in a Bell Ranger helicopter.

The magnificence of Table Mountain in Cape Town came into view from our cockpit as we made approach into South Africa. Scenery of mountains and ocean that surround the beautiful city almost take your breath away. The town we explore down by the waterfront coming alive with South African male choirs singing in the market place everywhere displaying colour and life. We are escorted to a fine vineyard to lavishly dine and sample their famous wines and circle The Cape of Good Hope by helicopter. We part company sadly with our hosts and fly commercially home on British Airways, landing some twelve hours later at Heathrow on a damp English morning. Life resumes with nearly another year passing while we nestle in the South Downs of Sussex near the historical town of Lewes. We find a creative writing course offered by the Arvon Society staying on a retreat once the house and gardens of former playwright John Osborne, a nineteenth century building with modern renovations sitting on a beautiful twenty-six-acre estate in the hills of Shropshire near the Welsh border. During the week there, we meet seventeen other writing enthusiasts under the tutelage of authors Horatio Clare and Miranda France. Horatio and I found much common ground in that he was an accomplished nature and travel writer once working as a producer with the BBC. His two memoirs were fascinating and I recently finished his incredible journey around the oceans of the world aboard container ships written skilfully in *Down to the Sea in Ships*. Miranda also a well published writer, getting acclaim from the *New York Times* about her 1988 book *Bad Times in Buenos Aires*. With Horatio's encouragement and Miranda's guidance I come to the close of this effort, I did however tell Horatio in jest that I would place the title 'Dr' before his name as his handwriting was atrocious, far outweighed by his fabulous teaching ability! Our group would reunite the following year for a week in the coastal town of Loo in Cornwall. I was drawn to the atmosphere of this holiday town with its quaint narrow streets and hillside cottages overlooking fine beaches and ocean water displaying its clarity where the Gulf Stream, after passing our Bahamas, ends its long journey across the Atlantic. Walking the harbour side wharf in the clear blue mornings of Cornwall I am mesmerised being able to see all the way through the clear cold English ocean that runs this shore.

The Far East is presented to me for the first time with my partner having business in Singapore. Would I like to join her? With accumulated air miles, most certainly! I stroll through the Botanical Gardens built by the British in decades past and sense the throbbing commercial commerce along Orchard Road. With my last Nikon SLR sold in the UK I treat myself to the new D7200. There are photographic prospects in the future and having the right equipment a must. I could be in any major city here with huge chain stores glaring signs of capitalism in every direction.

Modern skyscrapers reach endlessly toward the sky clustered in the financial district. My taxi driver boasts of being able to walk the streets of the city alone any time of night in perfect safety with almost zero crime as its statistic. An old Singapore Street offers Alaskan king crab while exotic aromas of Chinese cuisine waft through the clambering markets on Bugis Street. The call to prayer from the temples sees the evening lights of ancient buildings shine bright against the modern city structures. With business complete, we take opportunity to discover the palm-laden grounds of a hotel in Bali lying southward with a two-hour flight. A deep blue ocean washes familiar palm tree strewn beaches, chaotic streets awash in a maze of motor scooters and traders beckoning us in. Bali is larger than I envisioned, more commercial and very busy in places. It reignites a familiar love of the islands from whence I came. I want to explore the tranquil inner tropical forest and wildlife but my guide never arrives citing he had a ceremony to attend that day. We soon learn that ceremonies take precedent and occurred with rabid frequency in this country! By day we eat the most wonderful crispy duck on a bamboo terrace above emerald rice paddies and sip ginger tea, nestled into the hillside of terraced plantations.

Later a visit to friends living in a fabulous old restored farmhouse in Correze, Limousin, France, treating us to graceful villages with ancient stone bridges spanning quiet rivers below. History standing still while few guests filter through the cobbled streets. We buy fresh artichokes in the local markets and sip steaming strong French coffee each morning with a warm croissant. My last visit to France being the only holiday father took me on abroad, visiting Nice on the south coast. I was twenty years old when he included an educational experience one evening saying, 'If I were to ever visit a strip club make sure it is high end!' so escorted mother and I to Maxime's. Rich red velvet interior and fabulous looking ladies adorned dining area, raising my appreciation for beautiful examples of the fairer sex! From here we flew over to the island of Corsica and sipped Ouzo on the Mediterranean coast.

Life changes when we least expect it. My partner is uncomfortable with my apparent unease of where we live, voicing more often the discomfort of watching a 'fish out of water' trying to adapt to life in England. I had reacquainted myself in Nassau to long time friends and distant family through social media where here in England the pictures of home shone brightly in the eyes of this 'island boy'! Added to the equation is the writing, for here I am looking out toward the South Downs shrouded in fog while describing all those fabulous tropical adventures that sparked a young English lad's imagination some fifty years ago. We are at an age where one can touch base with friends known since childhood, all discovering the magic of high speed internet. Our world has indeed become tiny, able to talk with my Australian dive partner through our computers for free, seeing each other clearly some fourteen hours in different time zones. Technology has us spoilt, with paper use disappearing from daily life and young students these days barely mastering the skill of handwriting, while able to text message on a smartphone with lightning speed. I marvel at photographs taken by my long-time artist friend Melissa, where I am able to share warm hellos not appreciated by my English partner. 'What is this thing with Melissa?' I am asked yet again by another girlfriend. 'Nothing' I sigh, 'we have not even held hands for goodness sake!' My English friend makes it known that her days of travel are coming to a close. Corporate globetrotting has worn thin and she desires to stay put on England's shores close to family and friends. She dislikes the heat and expresses the love of getting wet in the English rain, not believing my expressions of contentment in my new lifestyle. I have grown to love my adopted family always offering the warm hospitality of their home and traditional English Sunday lunches. It was nice to have a mum again and the father I never had. I was encouraged to travel on my own to maybe find 'a place in the sun' that we could escape to from time to time, the thought of having 'best of both worlds' instantly very appealing. A suggestion of Turkey from her friend was brought to my attention: admitting a country not ever stirring my spirit for some unexplained reason. With the ingenuity of Google, it was easy to discover a magical place aptly named The Turquoise Coast. Anything with that colour in its description would catch my attention in a heartbeat. Looking at real estate listings in that region I soon learned of the affordable possibilities in a villa investment. We had investigated buying a flat in Eastbourne that closely fit my profile belonging once to the famous explorer Ernest Shackleton who had led three expeditions to Antarctica. The blue historical plaque adored the outside of the property and it was within easy reach of the Sussex shore and the cliffs of Beachy Head. Circumstance delayed the transfer of my funds from Nassau and would have taken everything I had been able to save so we passed on the deal. Arriving in Turkey I discovered the glorious little town of Kalkan nestled beautifully inside a bay of the southwest Mediterranean, embraced by spectacular mountains. I could only describe it to friends as a familiar character 'ski-town in the summertime' with quaint cobbled streets, an amazing array of restaurants, shops and a fabulous fresh market every Thursday with a charming harbour; Bahama blues with mountains! What really caught my attention were the Turkish people, polite, friendly and the most hospitable a visitor could ever hope to meet. A flight from London Gatwick was barely three hours and the drive to Kalkan near two hours. My agents took me to a property I found in town but proved too close to neighbours for my taste. Living in resort towns one gets an eye for the more attractive areas and I pointed to the far end of the bay asking if anything was available. They noted my good taste and within minutes I was standing on the balcony of a three-bedroom villa with private swimming pool overlooking the gorgeous Mediterranean Sea sporting a price tag less than a two bedroom flat in Sussex. I phoned home for an opinion and immediately got a 'go for it' reply.

The fun ride lasted near a year when my girlfriend suddenly changed her mind, wanting nothing more to do with my investment asking me to sell and live full time in the UK. I had a taste of the 'the blue' again and found the idea of isolation from the outside world unattractive. We drifted rapidly apart with her recommending I spend the Christmas Holidays in Michigan with my friends, a message coming across loud and clear the UK commitment had sadly come to an end. A last-minute effort with a counsellor affirms from him that 'Paul is solar-powered' and needs exposure to surroundings he loved all his life. My friend is not enamoured with this description but one I hold on to as it being true. I miss the vibrant colours of my Bahamas; those of us fortunate enough to live abroad become very visual in nature, although mentioned earlier, I feel should be reinforced here. There is a conscious attraction on awakening to those glorious island days. Admit it or not, one withers in the grey. For those of us with island life in our blood we even distinguish between days of 'that dramatic light' and just another day in the sunshine. Days when everything is ultra crisp, the palms dark green fronds glisten in the dancing sunlight, the bougainvillea is iridescent, the sea almost jumps off the landscape, it is *that* blue! I miss my ocean and crave to be airborne once more, to feel alive. There was so much more living to do than caught within the confines of an English retirement way of life. With writing on the wall, we arranged I pack and leave while she was away on a work-related trip back to Singapore. With heavy heart, I watched my lady drive away on business knowing more likely to be the last we saw of each other. I left England to share the holidays with my close friends in Michigan. Here I was surrounded by the love of the amazing Schaafsma family that had shared so many days on my boat and plane; the grown grandchildren all musically talented beyond words gifted a Christmas to refresh the soul. Two weeks later I travelled back to Florida for updating my pilot's license with Harry in Bartow. He met me at Orlando International and we embraced emotionally. A true friend who knew well I was damaged goods at this point. We met several times for the man-to-man chats and his compassionate wisdom shone through pointing me in a good direction. 'You need to be airborne,' he said gently. 'Let's get you current again in a Lake Amphibian!' With a new Medical in hand he had me climb into the left seat of his water plane rotating off a Bartow runway once more proving the breath of fresh air I needed, we practice water landings in the large lake near the airport where with open canopy my hand pulled through the cool Florida fresh water, I was in a cockpit once more, I was close to home.

Visiting long-time friends Harvey and Diana in Naples at the time came with an invitation to stay with them in Nassau the following weeks. I was adrift having no clue where the tide of life would wash me ashore. I was however close to my homeland and tempted to board a Bahamasair flight home. I reconnected with my daughter and saw grandchildren that had grown. A dinner planned at the Green Parrot, once home base to my first seaplane, had me make a phone call so long awaited in my life. Without hesitation, instinctively I dialled Melissa. The evening was magic although she too recognised a damaged soul. Warm tropical air kept us comfortable with a light breeze off the harbour drifting through the moonlit palm trees made the company even more intimate while background island melodies from a band of familiar faces confirmed I was indeed back where I belonged and next to those I loved. I recounted the story of a discontented partner expressing dislike over Melissa's social media responses and quoted 'we had not even held hands'. Melissa laughed out loud 'sorry to say, you were fibbing with that one!' recalling a memorable innocent day sitting in the warm shallows of an Exuma Out-Island years ago. We shared family stories not surprisingly finding aviation threading its way through both our lives. As it had been with Suzanne with her stepfather a navigator flying 'The Hump' in Europe during the Second World War, Melissa's dad had worked for Mackey Airlines, BOAC and Chalks. Her mother's father, an Italian immigrant in NYC, Raimondo Quattrocchi was Amelia Earhart's personal tailor, custom making all of her flying Jodphurs; Amelia making it known publically she would only wear flying clothes that were made by him. Melissa's mother Maiola remembers well, going with her father to meet Amelia at the airport as an 11 year old, and Amelia offering to take her mother for a ride in her plane, this was in the 1920s and alas very shy, declined the offer, but knew the relevance of such an honour as she grew older. Maiola's rich Italian heritage is steeped in art and dress design. Her uncle Raimondo's brother Edmondo was a world famous sculptor who led a very jet-setting, social life in his heyday sculpturing the world's largest stone statue located in Meaux in France, designed by his colleague MacMonies; the statue a gift from the United States to France in gratitude for the Statue of Liberty. Maiola Quattrocchi was a well-known dress designer in NYC before Michael Maura swept her off her feet during a vacation to Nassau in 1954-55. Her brother Nino, created the nurses uniform for the US nurses in the Second World War. Listening to these stories I only wished my family had shared such intimate detail of their past, a lesson our children's generation hopefully learns appreciating the values of family history.

Two days later I was leaning once more over my balcony in Turkey, bright red hibiscus were in full bloom and the bougainvillea starting to blossom. The lemon trees were full of fruit and my new banana trees had taken root. The sun was setting displaying a vast array of colour to the west silhouetting the mountain ranges at the far end of Kalkan Bay, always a magical scene. It was still quite cool; we have 'winter' there! The deep indigo of the Mediterranean giving comfort as I allowed the next few weeks to heal my damaged soul, time alone to reflect on my life, to revisit all the twists and turns that circumstance bombards us with through the journey. Time to tap the computer keys and get this book project finished as promised by the end of summer. I had new direction once again with a thoughtful invitation to breakfast the day before leaving Nassau allowing my long time lovely friend listening patiently and affectionately to what life had thrown at me. Melissa offered valuable input knowing well the main issues that had affected my last few months, putting me back on track as to where I should be, that our lives had crossed back and forth through these last thirty-five years for a reason, that we were indeed birds of a feather loving our art, nature, animals, photography, the oceans, travel and a peaceful existence. We would stay in close contact from here on. 'Damn, we should have got together years ago,' we joked. 'You were always with some damned blonde!' she laughs back.

The islands seemed to have climbed out of that dark place since my departure two years ago? The new road system has been completed alleviating much of the traffic stress save business hours and school time. Not owning a motorcycle any longer brings thought of at least a scooter for ease of manoeuvre through the busy Nassau streets. Cable Beach appears immaculate in its environmental maintenance now pleasing to the eye. In fairness one has to award the improvements to our little island until once again the power failures return! There will always be disgruntled chatter about the politicians but it seems elevated upon my return, utter despair toward the extravagant Baha Mar hotel complex, way overdue yet near completed on Cable Beach entering bankruptcy and never opening. There prevails a real scorn over an unpopular VAT taxation imposed on Bahamians; the most successful recorded imposition of a VAT taxation taking in near one billion dollars in the first year from a population of just over 390,000. The populace fed up with their government's lack of transparency in explaining where on earth all those funds disappeared to. There are marches in protest; thousands taking peacefully to the streets about a city dump still burning uncontrollably from time to time polluting our fabulous island. We hear an outcry against the possibility of Chinese fishing fleets being allowed to fish our waters and irreplaceable natural resources being up for sale? Additional marches in months to follow with even more Bahamians from all walks of life voicing their displeasure about several government failings; a once passive society now becoming passionate about making things right in our country while calling for change. What the voting booths produce will be another matter. The killings seemed to have subsided somewhat and related to the still existing gang culture? Our little town had indeed grown to inherit the worst of cities' bad habits where comparisons odious we still deem ourselves more fortunate than most. One only had to watch the world news for that reinforcement.

I visit my aviation family at Odyssey Aviation received with warm embraces. We have missed each other but hints of searching for another aircraft brings smiles and affirmation – I should be in the air again soon having found a pretty little Cessna 172 in Ohio. I walk over to the large hangar seeing Glen's Caravan still gleaming from his maintenance perfection. Familiar aircraft are hiding from the sunshine with a very forlorn blue and white Maule tucked abandoned into the far corner. She is dirty and unkempt with tyres going flat. A sad ending to a glorious career as the Caribbean's most recognised seaplane. The partnership seemed to have failed and golden opportunity lost with my charter company in cold storage. In sadness, I walked around the once beautiful airplane patting her one more time on the cowling in recognition of a great partnership between man and machine.

An invitation arrives by email one day. Natalie is marrying Thomas in a garden ceremony a few weeks from now. She understands the distance from Turkey too far to make that journey but wanted me to know their plan. I knew in an instant this was the cue I was waiting for. I would arrive unannounced to be seated in that garden to watch her walk toward her new husband. Conspiracy began with Keith in Daytona at 'bike week' with his Harley Davidson friends sharing that he too would be seated there to surprise her and surprised she was as I sat proudly with Melissa at my side. 'I don't have a home here anymore,' I explained to my lovely friend about the possibility of living in the Bahamas again, 'Oh yes you do!' came instant response with a warm smile. Life back home in Nassau is tranquil once again. Surrounded by the familiar comforting blues and swaying palm trees that captivated my soul as a twelve-year-old, I am at peace; excited with new aviation adventures on the very near horizon. We are invited to care take a beautiful home on Elbow Cay in Abaco, falling deeper in love with Hope Town. There are dreams of moving close by and awake to chortle of Bahama parrots and walk the powder white beaches; maybe a cottage on Man-O-War Cay? Its time for out-island living away from the city chaos. With a Cessna parked at Marsh Harbour makes conveniences not far away offering the best of both worlds? Through conversation discovering my new partner's favourite country abroad to be Turkey of all places. She had visited further north up the coast to Marmaris while guest aboard a friends' private yacht. 'Well Muddo!' came the fun Bahamian expression of joy when I disclosed I had bought a villa on the Turquoise Coast; another of many boxes 'ticked' in our shared similarities. I never left the Bahamas again except both of us returning to Kalkan a few months later sharing endless bounties of the Turkish culture. We explored magnificence among the ancient ruins in Xanthos and further north to Tlos admiring visible streets of 5000 years ago to scrambling down treacherous goat paths to discover the famous Tomb of Pegasus. We walk the warm sands of Patara, Turkey's longest beach of 16 kilometers and sip Turkish tea in Kas, exchanging dreams of another airplane after return from a trek through Saklikent Gorge; a national park established in 1996 with a stunning gorge 980-feet deep and eleven miles long. Turkey is probably the most diversely beautiful country yet discovered. Its people the hidden gems from the outside world where vulgar western press draws inaccurate pictures leaving only those who visit able to rightfully contradict.

We fly home to our Bahamas where far out in the ocean the very devil himself is being born. Matthew will be his name and his fury soon felt throughout our gorgeous archipelago.

The thirteenth named storm of the 2016 hurricane season began as a tropical wave exiting the African coast on September 22, developing into a strong tropical storm as it approached the Leeward Islands. As the storm tracked westward across the Caribbean Sea it entered an unusual period of 'explosive intensification' becoming Hurricane Matthew on September 29, reaching Category 5 the following day! It weakened slightly with a predicted turn northward something we learned to fear here in the Bahamas. Storms that creep up behind or 'underneath' us approaching Cuba have bad reputations of hitting us hard, our last being Michelle some years earlier. On October 4, Matthew hit the Tiburon Peninsula of Haiti. It was as if this monster the size of Texas had intelligence knowing how to avoid the mountainous terrain of both Haiti and neighbouring Cuba to the west, navigating skilfully through the clear passage between the two countries in order to maintain ferocity with the Central Bahamas in its sights for a direct hit as a Category 4 hurricane. We all prepare for the worst securing our houses, moving our vehicles to safer ground, taking boats out of the water but the hit was harder than expected. The first half of the storm blew 120 mph with winds wailing over New Providence from the northeast shattering trees and smashing our small island with driving rains. As Matthew moved northwestward it again used its uncanny ability aiming its eye directly through the narrow gap between Nassau and Andros. The warm summer waters of the deep ocean fuelled this beast to lash us even harder with its larger more persistent south side, blowing ferociously for six hours at hurricane force from the southeast. Ancient trees arched under the screaming pressure of constant 140 mph wind where gusts of 165 mph finally forced them to succumb damaging walls, houses and blocking streets. Roofs peeled away from some buildings on both sides of the eye-wall. The wind was relentless and never-ending. Circulation blowing this hard for this long piled seawater onto the southern shores, creating storm surges than filled the shallow streets with feet of water. My old neighbourhood of Coral Harbour along with neighbouring Adelaide Village and Lyford Cay all decimated by wind and water. I learn my old home there one of the very few not to receive any roof damage, we had done well in that restoration. We were in the eastern part of the island, equally blown apart but not flooded as the west. The north shore of Andros is beyond recognition being the strongest hit by a hurricane since I moved here in 1960 and compared to the ferocious storm of 1929 that also decimated New Providence. Matthew in its agonising slowness of forward speed finally pulled away headed for the central Florida coastline pounding Grand Bahama into devastated submission, destroying Freeport with a gust that broke the airport wind gauge, stopping at 195 mph. Its persistent intelligence kept the monster traversing the shores of the southeast United States, finally dying in the mid-Atlantic Ocean. A storm for the record books that created untold homeless people in Haiti and Cuba, deaths there rising above a thousand as I write. The total estimate on damage almost uncountable at this point in time taking weeks to assess, to date close to $7.5 billion!

We awake to the whine of chainsaws. It takes three days to cut our way out of the neighbourhood. Our beautiful Royal Poinciana trees that were in exquisite bloom this year are lying on the ground like shattered dinosaurs. Their huge ageing trunks splintered and foliage scattered over yards of road. Magnificent silk cotton trees that have seen our generation and many previous are crippled and broken, trees blocking almost every road in Nassau. Buildings are a mess with roofs torn, while roads are impassable with severe flooding especially on the western side of New Providence. Many of us lucky not to receive such damage but in all every person in these islands have not escaped the onslaught in some way or other. We have no power, no communication for the most part waiting for crews to come to our rescue and return our island paradise so some sense of normality. We don't see the Jamaican electrical crews here to help us recover this year, the local power company struggles to repair the infrastructure. This will take years for Mother Nature to play her part and present our island as is was before this cruel bombardment she placed upon us. It's been four days now and the saws grow quieter, the power is restored and we can talk with the outside world. We still hear the hum of distant generators where not all are as fortunate, with their electricity still off. An electrical substation catches fire, adding woes to the power grid. Relief from far away is arriving by plane as the world responds to all of us affected. The milky warm ocean is calm again and slowly we see through to the corals below. The turquoise is returning, as we slowly, very slowly, resemble our familiar Bahamas once more. The price of living in paradise can indeed be high. It would take a lot more for islanders to be beaten into submission hence our survival since Columbus departed these fair shores.

It's near mid-October; hopefully near the end of hurricane season, trees are showing new growth, as if springtime has arrived four months early, properties being repaired and roads clear; we are green again. A weak weather system lies over the archipelago blowing cooler air from the northeast with welcome rain this morning as we soon say farewell to another Bahamian summer; not good today for flying or boating and after near forty years, it really doesn't matter anymore. The days click by as the year draws to a close. Our islands seem to breath new life as December enters the scene, there are stunning calm days before Christmas arrives. Traffic is its usual holiday nightmare tempting me rather slip into a flat calm, crystal clear ocean at the end of our road. It's below zero over most of North America, news pictures of snow-blocked highways with driving nightmares throughout the States in blizzard conditions while we bask in 80F tropical days. There are adventures ahead and the New Year holds promise, I will be aloft yet again to drift by those towering white magnificent clouds floating serenely above one of the most beautiful oceans in the world. We are very fortunate to be Bahamian.

I create a metaphor for myself, a large clay cauldron that I call 'my life as a whole', full of adventures, tragedies, experiences, and challenges. Of highs and lows and day-to-day living. Added to the pot is the liquid I can aptly name 'time'. My vessel seems to have sprung a leak recently. The once smooth clay has developed some insidious cracks allowing the liquid to find every possible avenue of escape. It seems to happen faster than before, seeping into the ground never to be slowed. Retrieval is futile; why scratch the soil after the fluid has disappeared? The level now so low the cauldron takes on a hollow sound. It is described as 'having character' but fact remains it has simply aged, with days becoming blinks of an eye. We eat breakfast and it is sunset again. Months blur into each other and before we realise another year has simply vanished. It is near 2017. Where on earth did Orwell's *1984* disappear to? This tall frame remembers clearly a young gangly twenty-year old driven, eons ago, by his grandfather through those forbidding wrought iron gates of that damned boarding school in Petworth; all of a sudden I am sixty-eight years old. A friend recently guessed I was in my late fifties; I wanted to stoop and touch her feet in respect! Maybe there is a-ways to go yet with retirement seeming a bittersweet pill to swallow?

I am again living in Nassau, the very country the young schoolboy was introduced to in July of 1960. My frame aches. Old tennis injuries send an occasional jolt of electricity from my hip causing a quick grasp of support lest my legs give way as they did that fateful day while playing golf at South Ocean. The smooth tanned skin of that young dive instructor at the Nassau Beach Hotel has taken a well-worn look of some old character from a Hemingway novel. The damaging tropical sunshine has taken its toll on the thinning hairline; the parenting of father time and Mother Nature has not proved so lenient. Every now and again I spy an old acquaintance not seen in years. Some look disastrous to my critical eye, their hair gone or greyed, who am I to talk, they appear quite thinner and frail or some opposite, rotund and over weight. Do I bare any resemblance to this description? My answer comes with humour while standing in the 'senior line' at the bank where I receive scowls and sarcastic comment from other patrons in that much longer line next to me about my eligibility to be standing here. 'Do the math,' I say with a scowl … '1948!'

Lightning Source UK Ltd.
Milton Keynes UK
UKOW07f1839261017
311565UK00009BA/179/P

9 781911 525233